A DICTIONARY OF LITE

ABC or *gradus ad Parnassum* [stairway to Parnassus, the seat of the Muses], for those who might like to learn. The book is not addressed to those who have arrived at full knowledge of the subject without knowing the facts.

Ezra Pound, *ABC of Reading*

Bernard Dupriez

A DICTIONARY
OF LITERARY
DEVICES

Translated and adapted by
Albert W. Halsall

HARVESTER
WHEATSHEAF

New York London Toronto Sydney Tokyo Singapore

© University of Toronto Press 1991

Originally published in French as
Gradus: Les procédés littéraires (Dictionnaire)
© Union générale d'éditions 1984

This edition first published 1991 by
Harvester Wheatsheaf
66 Wood Lane End, Hemel Hempstead
Hertfordshire HP2 4RG
A division of
Simon & Schuster International Group

Printed on acid-free paper

Printed in Canada

British Library Cataloguing in Publication Data

Dupriez, Bernard
   Dictionary of literary devices.
   1. Literature. Style
   I. Title II. Halsall, Albert W.
   803

   ISBN 0-7450-1055-5
   ISBN 0-7450-1056-3 (pbk)

For Mary, Alison, and Colin

Contents

Translator's Preface

Rhetoric is the greatest barrier between us and our ancestors. If the Middle Ages had erred in their devotion to that art, the *renascentia*, far from curing, confirmed the error. In rhetoric, more than in anything else, the continuity of the old European tradition was embodied ... Nearly all our older poetry was written and read by men to whom the distinction between poetry and rhetoric, in its modern form, would have been meaningless. The 'beauties' which they chiefly regarded in each composition were those which we either dislike or simply do not notice. This change of taste makes an invisible wall between us and them. Probably all our literary histories ... are vitiated by our lack of sympathy on this point. If ever the passion for formal rhetoric returns, the whole story will have to be rewritten and many judgements may be reversed.

C.S. Lewis, *Literature in the Sixteenth Century*

The remarkable resurgence of rhetoric in recent years and the current application, to texts of all kinds, of literary theories which derive their methodologies from many modern disciplines, both scientific and otherwise, mean that modern readers are likely to meet, in creative as well as in critical texts, terms specific to literature as a code demanding from its initiates a kind of specialized competence most apparent at the terminological level. The reading contract offered by many modern and postmodern texts no longer incorporates the old Romantic assumption that reading provides 'direct' communion with the author, a process affording privileged insight into the mind of a presiding genius. Many modern and postmodern texts call attention to their artifices, having then no need to create other artifices to conceal them. This fact, though it may imperil the illusion of 'reality' once held to be essential to critical pleasure, offers readers familiar with the theory of such devices a different kind of critical enjoyment.

In addition, readers who themselves aspire to become authors able to address questions more sophisticated than those treated in ideological or commercial criticism dealing with the evaluation of texts must express themselves in a modern idiom. (The discussion of such matters as the desirability of canonizing or purchasing, as opposed to the necessity of marginalizing or censuring, new texts occupies the evaluators, modern paradigms for whom might be, on the one hand, Leavis, and on the other, the reviewer of fiction in your local newspaper.) While it may still be possible to believe the old Romantic theory that all literature is no more than disguised autobiography (the work *is* the author, and vice versa), other approaches, both less existential and less gossipy, suggest themselves. Whether pursued with methods based upon criteria as different as semiotic rigour or rhetorical plausibility, the analysis of texts increasingly requires from its adepts the acquisition of a species-specific metalanguage at once referential and conventional.

The 'common-sense' application of so-called 'ordinary language' to the description of texts which prove themselves extraordinary in every degree, from the refinement of their lexicon and syntax to their assertion of 'contrary-to-the-fact' states of affairs existing in worlds possible but not actual, soon reveals its methodological inadequacy. The structuralists likened this adaptation of a linguistic tool designed for one specific purpose to another quite different and frequently altogether inapt, to 'bricolage,' or amateur 'do-it-yourselfship,' and exemplified it with the case of the amateur handyperson's use of a screwdriver to hammer nails. Such amateurism explains why some modern readers have been unable to make the necessary generic distinctions between the kinds of reference made by 'literary' texts, as opposed to those made by journalistic or historiographical texts, to 'reality' and 'non-reality,' to history and fiction. Notorious examples like the 'Hitler Diaries' show the folly of misapplying literary criteria like verisimilitude to narratives defined by quite different generic demands and expectations.

By drawing the attention of readers to the art or artificiality of literary texts, the specialized language of ancient, medieval, classical, and modern (but not Romantic) criticism exposes common sense as an inappropriate, because simple-minded, method of comprehending and interpreting verbal structures which are frequently non-commonsensical, anti-commonsensical, or even nonsensical. In recent years, the theory of textuality which held (1) that a non-problematic relationship exists between 'the' world and its representations in possible worlds and (2) that criticism of texts should employ the 'plain style' of discourse has yielded to a contrary theory. The belief that text and world are not concomitant, and that extratextual language and intratextual language do not necessarily display the same features, has brought with it the preference for a critical discourse as generically discrete, cryptic, and encoded as is its creative equivalent. These developments, which have become progressively apparent to me over a thirty-year exposure to literary criticism, also led me to translate and adapt Bernard Dupriez's *Gradus: les procédés littéraires*.

After hearing him speak at the annual meeting several years ago of the Canadian Society for the History of Rhetoric and after having used *Gradus* both in literary research and in teaching, I became convinced that its equal did not exist in English. No similar dictionary of literary terms that I have found provides in its definitions as much useful information deriving from as many fields. Linguistics, poetics, semiotics, socio-criticism, rhetoric, pragmatics, and so on combine in ways which enable readers quickly to comprehend many of the codes and conventions which together make up the concept of 'literarity.'

After I had decided to translate *Gradus*, the question became one of method. It was obvious from the outset that the examples illustrating the devices must themselves come in most cases from modern texts rather than from those produced in the ancient or medieval periods, or during the Renaissance. In the translation it would have been easy to repeat examples of techniques, devices, tropes, figures, and forms which appear in the more than fifty such dictionaries I have on my shelves. But not only is it depressing to see, as one follows the definition of a term from dictionary to handbook, or from literary companion to specialized critical work, that the same example (frequently borrowed from Quintilian or Shakespeare, from Boileau or Fontanier) reappears time and again, but also that it not infrequently reappears (sometimes even in the same dictionary) as an example illustrating different devices. Needless to say, I have included what seemed to me the most relevant among traditional examples in *Gradus*. Readers will quite readily supply their own modern equivalents and, should they feel so inclined, are requested to send them to the translator for inclusion, with my thanks, in any subsequent editions of this book.

The principal problem involved Professor Dupriez's preference throughout *Gradus* for examples deriving from difficult modern literary works by twentieth-century authors, most frequently French or French Canadian. By difficult I mean authors who, in the context of an adaptation into English of French literary devices, exhibit those for which no close equivalent exists in 'canonical' English texts. Such was the problem, for example, presented by his predilection for surrealist authors. Surrealism as a 'high-culture' movement produced few English writers. Yet I was reluctant to abandon a literary approach which offered so many strikingly paradoxical examples. I began by translating Dupriez's examples taken from Michaux, Breton, Queneau, Cendrars, and others, and indeed a considerable number of such translated examples remain in the text you hold in your hands. However, it soon became clear that not only was the poetry lost in translation, as Virginia Woolf warned, but so also was the humour. In fact, I found myself constantly constrained to 'explain the joke,' a process which usually killed it.

In casting around for equivalents, it was the humorous side of surrealistic polemic that pointed me in what seems the right direction. When I asked myself why there did not appear to be an equivalent in English, I realized that in fact the humour I sought has occurred constantly in English in such 'low culture' modern forms as post-1960s 'satire,' in radio and television popular comedy, and so on. The kind of outrage caused, for example, in 1920s France by the surrealist addition of a moustache to the Mona Lisa, or by Marcel Duchamps's exhibition of a urinal as a 'ready-made' art object, recurred in the Anglo-Saxon world in the 1960s, for instance, when the 'Beyond the Fringe' group parodied the English establishment's proprietary attitudes towards 'England's' victory in the Second World War, and again in the 1970s when the Monty Python group filmed the life of a mistaken messiah in a narrative set in the Middle East at the time of Christ. In addition, such sources quite deliberately exposed the frequently artificial nature of conventional behaviour – linguistic, logical, or empirical – in ways both defamiliarizing and ludic. However, such examples do not form an exclusive category, or produce an anti-canonical dictionary. A glance at the Index will reveal examples drawn also from the best-known modern authors.

It remains for me to express my appreciation to those who have contributed to what for me has proved an enormously enriching experience. Bernard Dupriez both saved me from committing egregious errors (the definitions of *syllepsis* and *zeugma* are a case in point) and indicated where he wished to change the original articles in *Gradus,* or to add to their number. My colleague at Carleton University, Genie Zimmerman, frequently discussed problems in the definition of rhetorical terms and provided me with a welter of examples from all sources. Among Carleton students in comparative literature who helped by their efforts as readers, researchers, checkers, and occasionally as guinea pigs in linguistic and rhetorical experiments, I would particularly like to thank Christine Seck. Diane Slimmon corrected (some of) my naïve presuppositions about the teaching of rhetoric, as opposed to grammar, in Canadian secondary schools, and I adapted (some of) the definitions accordingly. Greg Schmidt of the Carleton University School of Business provided the invaluable expertise necessary to the production of the first word-processed version.

I would also like to thank Prudence Tracy of University of Toronto Press for her belief that a dictionary of rhetorical and literary terms based on multilingual sources and drawing examples from both of Canada's official languages should be published in Canada. To Ken Lewis go my gratitude and admiration for his correction of the text's many inconsistencies. And to Gwen Peroni, who input the final version, I am also indebted. My belief that commonplaces still have a place in modern discourse permits me to add that none of the above should be taxed with any remaining errors or infelicities.

On a more practical level: terms marked with an asterisk are the titles of the main entries in the dictionary; examples have been quoted from modern editions whenever possible; and publishing information for quoted works (including critical works cited in the text by the author's name only) appears in the Bibliography.

Abbreviations

Ex	Example
Exx	Examples
neol.	neologism
OED	*The Oxford English Dictionary.* Compact edition. Oxford: Oxford University Press 1971, 1987. 3 vols.

OEDS	*Supplement to the Oxford English Dictionary.* Compact edition.
other def.	other definition(s)
R1, R2, ...	**Remark 1, Remark 2, ...**
syn.	synonym(s)

Extracts from the
Original Introduction

The following pages contain an alphabetical listing of traditional literary figures, defined on the basis of a sampling of modern texts ... Due consideration of their overall system ... has led me to propose some new definitions and also some novel concepts.
...

[*Gradus* aims to encourage the personal involvement that readers achieve with literary texts by increasing their understanding of rhetorical forms, and by helping them to produce their own readings.] Having learned to recognize the interplay of literary forms, readers will perhaps be no longer satisfied either to remain passively subject to the text's impregnating influence, or to practise mere classification of texts by attaching to them identifying labels. Readers may become capable of 'playing' the works over for themselves, and of making room for themselves within works. Analysis and classification of the figures may well help readers to engage in the creative extension of the self by and through their experience of literary texts.

Terminology

The two thousand-odd terms listed in the Index belong, neologisms apart, to four socio-historical strata. The most ancient group, composed of legal and logical terms going back to Corax and Aristotle, includes: *ab absurdo, abjuration, adjuration, antanaclasis*, antanagoge, antiparastasis*, apagoge, apodioxis*, etc. The most abundant source is classical philology, extending from the Middle Ages to modern times, taking its inspiration largely from antiquity. For example: *abruption, acronym*, acrostic*, adynaton*, allegory*, alliteration*, anacoluthon*, anadiplosis*, anagram*, anapest, anaphora*, anta-*

podosis, anticlimax*, etc. The most natural source is everyday language, which gives us, for example, *accent**, *address*, *allusion**, *ambiguity**, *anecdote*, *annotation*, *apology*, *apostrophe**, *archaism**, *argument**, *aside*, *paragraph**, *slang**, etc. Some of these terms have acquired a specifically rhetorical meaning, including, *abridgement**, *abstraction**, *adjunction**, *agreement*, *alternative**, *amplification**, *attenuation**, etc. The most recent contributions derive from modern science, especially from linguistics and psychology, some of whose concepts characterize literary devices. The corresponding terms include: *actualization*, *aggrammatism*, *allocentric discourse*, *amalgam*, *application*, *ataxism*, *autism**, *autonymy*, *paradigmatic/syntagmatic axis*, etc.

I have excluded all but a few terms from other languages, retaining only those that have been Gallicized [or Anglicized] (*kerygma*, *leitmotif*, *oxymoron**, etc.), or that have become current (*ad hominem**, *concetti*, *in petto**, *isocolon*, *hiatus**, etc.), or that quite simply are useful (*bathos**).

In the case of synonyms, I have used the most current term to designate the main entry, thus preferring, for example, *accumulation** to *athroism*, *congeries*, *synathroesmus*, or *conglobatio*; *threat** to *comminatio*; and *preterition** to *paralipsis* ... Just as psychoanalysts have replaced *hermaphroditism* with *intersexuality*, I propose to replace *polyptoton* with *isolexism**, and *synchisis* with *syntactic scrambling**. When concepts require new names, I have followed the practice of the ancient rhetors, who named figures by the current words designating their operation. For example: *alluvion*, *approximation**, *change*, *concretization**, *notation**, *permutation**, *syntactic recapitulation**, *recovery*, *restart**, *schematization**, and *typographical variation**. I have formed others by processes of composition, derivation, or analogy: *confusion*, *counter-interruption**, *deportmanteau word*, *pseudo-language**, and *situational** signs.

Ancient terminology retains other attractive features, including 'slightly exotic, odd or magical professional or craftsman's terms,' as Jean Paulhan writes in *Enigmes de Perse*. Because of phonetic and lexical evolution, such terms have been replaced in general use by synonyms, and the Greek and Latin learned words have, in the main, become restricted to rhetoric. *Litotes** used to mean any kind of attenuation*. In modern French usage, *litotes* has come to designate only the rhetorical device consisting in 'saying less in order to mean more.' *Apocope** and *aphaeresis** used to mean any kind of summary, just as *antiphrasis** meant ironical understatement; *prolepsis** meant anticipation; and *crasis** meant any contraction.

Semantic evolution has caused the loss of meanings that I have occasionally recalled: *aposiopesis**, *epithet, epitrochasmus**, *irony**, *metalepsis**, *metastasis**, or *recrimination**.

In most instances, the name of a figure merely emphasizes one of its characteristics, a fact that causes certain ambiguities. I have attempted to disambiguate the following terms: *adjunction**, *disjunction**, and *zeugma**; *antanaclasis** and *diaphora**; *antimetathesis**, *antimetabole**, and *antimetalepsis*; *allegory** and *personification**; *brachylogia** and *ellipsis**; *enallage**, *hyperbaton**, and *synchisis**; *epanalepsis**, *anadiplosis**, and *anaphora**; *epiphonema** and *epiphrasis**; *equivoque** and *approximation**; *incoherence** and *non sequitur*; *bombast*, *verbiage**, *psittacism**, and *verbigeration**; *pictogram** and *ideogram*; *prolepsis** and *flash-forward**. In all my decisions, general usage or the opinion of specialists furnished the predominant criteria. May I remind readers exasperated by such subtle distinctions that lexical oppositions may be nullified, every term may be used broadly, and also that the meaning of every text depends on the decisions made both by its author and by its readers.

Under the headings *actant**, *echo* effect*, *enunciation**, *intonation**, *line** (*of poetry or verse*), *narrative**, *rhythm**, *rhythmic* measures*, and *syntagm**, I have described analytical methods covering various devices, whole galaxies of terms too little known to merit more detailed treatment. Meanwhile theological terms like *blasphemy**, *apocalypse**, and *eucharist* have been retained for their utility in the study of religious texts.

...

The Rhetorical Phenomenon

When the definitions are compared to the rhetorical phenomena themselves, the natural complexity of the latter seems quite different from the terminological complexity of the former. Contrary to what one might think, the most-used figures are those least recognized by rhetoricians (*pauses**, *intonations**, *rhythms**, *types of sentence**, for instance). The very familiarity of such figures results in their being taken for granted. As soon as they become more complicated (*reticentia*, *exclamation**, *hypotaxis* or *period**, *rhythmic* or *metric verse*, *irony**, and so on), they begin to take shape, acquire properties, and so become less common. That process explains why figures are believed to be forms of special or 'refined' language.

Extracts from the Original Introduction

In reality, figures abound not only in literature but in everyday language, as modern advertising demonstrates abundantly. 'Figures' (in Latin, *schemata*; i.e., 'structures') accumulate through admixture or superimposition even in the shortest textual segments. The ability to recognize them from their definitions does not serve only literary analysis. In fact, they constitute a system immanent in all of culture (metonymy* and metaphor*, for instance, are essential to the semiology of objects); they occur in all problems of [human] communication, whether the participants use public or private languages or some other sign system; they provide the link between the individual unconscious mind, whose roots are physiological, sunk in the family and social environment, with its impulses, intentions, and memories, and the sentence expressed as 'surface-structure,' situated and concrete, a visible gesture leaving a [definite] trace. Figures should not, therefore, be defined as being different from, or 'modifications' of, 'ordinary language,' following the all too familiar criterion of stylistic deviation. Such a theory may be useful in stylistics, under certain conditions (see B. Dupriez, *L'Etude des styles*, pp. 181, 213), but the problem of establishing a zero variant, one, that is, without its own specific value, will always remain insoluble, because the rhetorical phenomenon will be present in the variant itself, since the former is subjacent to language. According to Saussure, the elements of style, like those of language, possess only differences, 'without a positive term.' Figures only modify language accidentally. The basic ones, which are not only those 'of thought' or those 'of passion,' as classical authors believed, exist at a level 'deeper' than the expressive one.

Figures give proper, albeit conventional, form to the often undiscriminated surge of the self into the world. It is impossible to speak without figures. When they occur in first- or second-level articulations (alliteration*, metaplasm*, etc.), the author is playing on words or meanings. This is rhetoric foregrounded, laid bare, and is thus of the most visible, but not the most common, kind. The same process occurs *a fortiori* in poetics.

Everything is rhetorical that relates to the speech act. Amplification* enlarges the text just as a microscope magnifies our view of muscular tissue. In order to specify the rhetorical phenomenon, one restricts its field of play to discourse*, as opposed to objective reality, or even to the subject (see below, subjectal meaning*). The rhetorical phenomenon occupies the interspace where subject and object are joined by language and which is itself forgotten, only becoming perceptible when displaced, or when functioning emptily, artificially, or when foregrounded as 'oratorical' (see below, false –*). The rhetorical phenomenon is neither the self, nor the world, nor language; but neither self nor world nor language can exist without it.

The result is that the rhetorical phenomenon is easily ignored. James Joyce, the greatest modern connoisseur in the theory and practice of rhetorical forms, seemingly had little more initially than a schoolboy's exposure to its theory (see 'The Study of Languages' in his *Critical Essays*). Uninformed critics reduce the writer's craft to a few tricks, to experience, or to 'genius.' However, as P.-M. Lapointe says: 'Like the musician, the poet must know his craft, in a very craftsmanlike way, before beginning to write. Craftsmanship is *the* prerequisite.' It is precisely the task of a scientific poetics to clarify the common and yet complex nature of the craft. How many ambiguities and, in the final instance, errors in public meetings and written declarations, in contracts and scientific papers, even in conversation, can be put down to mere forms of speech that no one seems aware of let alone able to avoid? For example, the character Satan: is he a real being, or an ancient and durable myth*, or a rhetorical personification* of the idea of evil?

'Rhetorical' does not then signify necessarily a peculiar or superficial linguistic trick. The rhetorical impulse has its roots deep in the unconscious. Only pure rhetoric is ridiculous and has a deservedly bad press. Yeats defined such rhetoric as 'the will struggling to do the work of the imagination.' Tropes may be abused, like anything else.

...

Classification

Alphabetical 'disorder' helps the user to establish the key word sought. But a reader examining a sample text or a set of related concepts needs some order of classification based on a clarifying theory ... No figure can occupy infinite space, limited as it is by each of its neighbours. Public opinion, usage, and tradition may all support or restore concepts that have become relevant in other socio-cultural groups. Groups and individuals simplify in their own ways.

...

Extracts from the Original Introduction

Readers choose their own meanings, or they try to discover how the text came into being. It may be the result of several complex, overdetermined creative acts and may embody several coinciding figures. As for shapelessness and confusion in discourse, they are figures too and may have been chosen as such. The text-producing act must have its own mode of expression which, whether the result of combination, amalgamation, or suppression, is specifiable because it happened and because its existence is guaranteed by rereading or rewriting. These existential co-ordinates establish its place with regard to other signifying systems.

And the definition of the 'figure' itself? Let me merely say that a figure is a syndrome, or set of characteristics – a fact which explains differences in the definitions* of figures, as well as the multiplicity of over-elaborate figures and the relative dearth of basic ones. Ignorance of the mechanics of definition has encouraged too much defining. Traditional rhetoric and poetics are old-fashioned and confused; they define less by reference to significant classifying units (classemes) and more by reference to properties, thus sowing confusion by multiplying perspectives. Neither the proximity between rhetorical devices nor the possibility of their multiple transformations ever becomes clear. It would be different if a figure were defined as belonging to a structured and operational set, the rules of which govern the changes possible in it at the different levels: narrative, linguistic, compositional, and so on. The sets themselves might be formalized, with symbols* suggesting abstractly the operations occurring in the matrices that are controlled intuitively by poets or indeed by any speaker.

The reason for such complexity is that a characteristic is never exclusive to the figure it defines. Chiasmus* has one feature in common with parallelism* (syntactically similar members), another with inversion* (the reversed order of terms). The same is true of antimetabole*, which is also a form of repetition*. The characteristics necessary to the definition of figures number about sixty; their possible combinations reach into the millions. Bernard Lamy was right in believing that 'the number of figures is infinite.'

...

A DICTIONARY OF LITERARY DEVICES

A

ABBREVIATION A graphic reduction (as in 'etc.' for 'et cetera'). See Marouzeau.

Exx: Engl. (English), F. (French), Amer. (America[n]), Can. (Canada)

Ex: The narrator of Dickens's *Mystery of Edwin Drood* remarks (in ch. 11) on the 'mysterious inscription: P.J.T. 1747' over the door of Mr Grewgious's chambers, and then proposes throughout the ensuing narrative a number of possible explanations: 'It might mean Perhaps John Thomas ... Pretty Jolly Too ... Possibly Jabbered Thus,' etc.

Ex: 'My identity as a poor F[rench] C[anadian] condemned me, as a result of two centuries of [linguistic] delirium, to speak badly, without taking any pleasure in language' (Hubert Aquin, *Trou de mémoire*, p. 95).

Analogous definition: a set (or sets) of initials, when the abbreviation has replaced a substantive. **Exx:** USA, AD, BC, MA, NJ

R1: Abbreviation is a metaplasm* and should be distinguished from abridgement*. Abbreviation is graphic reduction to a letter or letters; abridgement is the reduction in sounds to a syllable.

Allegorical readings of such groups of initials may have a comic effect. According to David Gersovitz, for instance, the abbreviated forms of the names of certain airlines give rise to the following satirical messages: 'L.I.A.T., the Carribean carrier based in Antigua, came to stand for *Leave Island Any Time* or *Luggage in Another Town*. P.A.L., as in Philippine Airlines, has been known to earn its unauthorized moniker of *Plane Always Late*. T.A.P. of Portugal naturally lends itself to *Try Another Plane* ...' (*Ottawa Citizen*, 21 March 1987).

The mark of abbreviation is the abbreviating period, which is not inserted in French if the word's final letter appears in the abbreviation itself (e.g., Dr, Mme). Fowler (under 'period in abbreviations') advocates the same procedure in English: 'Abbreviations are puzzling ... and everything that helps the reader to guess their meaning is a gain. One such help is to let him know when the first and last letters of the abbreviation are also those of the full word, which can be done by not using the period, but writing *wt* (not *wt.*) for weight, *Bp* (not *Bp.*) for bishop, *Mr* (not *Mr.*) for Mister ...' In fact, both usages frequently occur in English.

A series of initials may form a new word; see acronym*.

R2: Abbreviation serves a useful function in inscriptions; for example, R.I.P. on a gravestone, I.N.R.I. on a crucifix. It may also have a euphemistic function: 'That's B.S., and you know it.' Or in proper names: 'P ...

draws a face by joining a profile onto a semi-profile, and the result is twice as lifelike as the real face' (Henri Michaux, *Passages*, p. 70; P stands for Picasso). If complete anonymity is sought, asterisks may be used: 'la princesse ***' (i.e., 'la princesse trois étoiles' [three stars]). An equivalent in English is 'Lady Asterisk,' the (parodic) name of a character in Siegfried Sassoon's *The Complete Memoirs of George Sherston*. For formal abbreviations, see discourse*, R2.

R3: The *OED* defines *brachygraphy* as the 'art or practice of writing with abbreviations ... shorthand, stenography,' and a *brachygrapher* as a shorthand-writer. Ex: at the end of a letter, 'T.T.F.N.' for 'ta-ta for now.'

R4: Another type of abbreviation consists in suppressing vowels (as in the semitic languages, where they are optional). Exx: Vncvr, Mtl, Hmltn (Vancouver, Montreal, Hamilton). Pons proposes (p. 11) that the corresponding literary procedure be called 'devocalization.' Swift offers some examples – Pdfr (Podefar), Ppt (Puppet) – as does Joyce: 'Considerable amusement as caused by the favourite Dublin street-singers L-n-h-n and M-ll-g-n' (*Ulysses*, pp. 396–7).

R5: Certain abbreviations have been turned into words. One hears *aresveepee* for R.S.V.P. Abbreviations do not usually take the plural. See lexicalization* and oblique* stroke, R1.

R6: In some French 'New' novels, as in some of Kafka's novels and stories, the hero is designated by a simple initial. Exx: 'A' in Robbe-Grillet's *La Jalousie*, 'K' in Kafka's *The Castle*.

ABRIDGEMENT In the case of a word, the substitution of a reduced form for the full one, as in 'metro' for 'metropolitan,' or 'plane' for 'aeroplane.' See *OED* and Marouzeau.

The device is frequently used in slang and jargon, exemplifying what Martinet calls the 'law of the least linguistic effort' (*Eléments de linguistique générale*, sect. 6–5). Exx: 'just a sec.' for 'just wait a second,' or 'la prof.' for a female teacher in French school slang.

Literary examples include both cases of specialists' jargon and made-up forms. Ex:

If only you knew how boring it is
At the Manic
You'd write to me a lot more often
At the Mani ... couagan.

G. Dor, 'La Manic,' a popular song in Quebec. [The Manicouagan River in Quebec is the construction site of vast hydro-electric dams.]

Ex: 'I g into a bu full of passen' for 'I get into a bus full of passengers' (R. Queneau, *Exercises in Style*, p. 79, under 'apocope'). See apocope*.

4

R1: The absence of an abbreviating period will have been noted in the above examples; abridgement is an audible, rather than a graphic, device. This type of metaplasm* is much used in the formation of pet names; for instance, 'Col' for 'Colin,' 'Ali' for 'Alison,' 'Alex' for Alexander' or 'Alexandra,' etc.

R2: Abridgement may be achieved by curtailment of an initial syllable. **Exx:** 'Nadette' for 'Bernadette,' 'Tony' for 'Antony.' In the already cited case of Alexander, removal of prefix and suffix produces the abridgement 'Lex,' which a Hollywood press agent, presumably, appended to one of the screen Tarzans, Lex Barker.

R3: A syntagm* may be abridged by the suppression of several words (e.g., 'Phantom' for 'Phantom of the Opera') or by the creation of a new form composed of some of the original's surviving elements. **Exx:** 'Amex' for 'American Express'; 'Boul' Mich' for 'Boulevard Saint-Michel'; *Les Miz* for *Les Misérables*. See acronym*.

R4: Abridgement may be accompanied by gemination*, or doubling of the initial syllable. **Exx:** Jon Jon, Mimi, Zsa Zsa.

R5: Abridgement and abbreviation are often confused. Thus, the title of Thomas Pynchon's novel *V.* refers to an initial the hero finds in his dead father's notebook. *V.* is therefore an abbreviation (hence the period). Strictly speaking, then, both *V* and *V,* would be incorrect in the title of a novel by Marguerite Duras, *Le Ravissement de Lol V. Stein*.

R6: Abridgement is sometimes demanded for reasons of modesty, whether ironical or not. **Ex:** 'He saved the situa. Tight trou. Brilliant ide' (Joyce, *Ulysses*, p. 221). Asterisks, sometimes followed, or replaced, by initials (e.g., 'Lady L***'), are used to conceal proper names. See also swear-word*, R1; and ellipsis*, R1.

ABSTRACTION As a literary device, abstraction consists in replacing an adjective of quality by a substantive, or a verb of action by a circumlocution*, so as to isolate and draw attention to some abstract phenomenon.

Ex: 'Bend the binarity of your kneecaps towards the earth' (Lautréamont, *Les Chants de Maldoror*, 5.6).

Ex [concerning a collar and waistcoat/vest]: 'two articles of clothing superfluous in the costume of mature males and inelastic to alterations of mass by expansion' (Joyce, *Ulysses*, p. 583).

Other meaning(s): See riddle*, R2; amalgam*; lexematic inversion*, R2.

R1: Abstraction may be a form of verbal flamboyance. **Ex:** 'Conversation-aids' was the expression for armchairs in the parlance of French seventeenth-century 'précieuses,' or blue stockings. Maupassant speaks ironically about the type of metonymy* which substitutes one of the qualities possessed by an object for the object itself, a type which the Goncourt brothers employed frequently: 'Those who nowadays fabricate imagery without taking enough care concerning abstract terms, who have rain or hail falling on the *cleanliness* of windows' (*Pierre et Jean*, preface).

R2: Abstraction is frequently synecdochic. Exx: 'Her Majesty'; 'Canada beat Russia at hockey'; 'One might treat the linguistic structure of the declarative sentence as a *microcosm of power relations* in a capitalist society' (M. Davidson, L=A=N=G=U=A=G=E *Book*, p. 149); 'Belpo went straight to his favourite distillations [of grain; i.e., whiskies]' (U. Eco, *Foucault's Pendulum*, p. 79).

R3: In nominal syntagms*, abstraction is achieved by reversing the functions of adjective and substantive. The adjective becomes the first lexeme by taking the form of its corresponding abstract noun, and the substantive becomes the defining complement. Thus 'the binarity of your kneecaps' replaces 'your two knees,' and 'the cleanliness of windows,' 'the clean windows.'

R4: Abstraction achieved by substituting for an object one of its qualities is a kind of emphasis* (see emphasis, R1) and is fairly characteristic of so-called 'feminine' style. Ex: 'She was thin ... She had dressed this thinness in a black dress with a double sheath of tulle, also black, and very low-cut' (Marguerite Duras, *Le Ravissement de Lol V. Stein*, p. 14). But abstractions also abound in scholarly writing, particularly in the social sciences: 'The problem of order, and thus of the nature of the integration of stable systems of social interaction, that is, of social structure, thus focuses on the integration of the motivation of actors with the normative cultural standards which integrate the action system, in our context interpersonally' (Talcott Parsons, *The Social System*, quoted in Lanham, 1974, pp. 71–2).

R5: Mathematical language concretizes abstractions: the statement 'multiplication is commutative' is written 'a x b = b x a.' And in literature, 'scenic description' supplies concrete examples of abstract notions. The following extract demonstrates the reasons for 'neuroticism': 'Mafia his wife was in on the bed playing with Fang the cat. At the moment she was naked and dangling an inflatable brassière before the frustrated claws of Fang who was Siamese, gray and neurotic' (Thomas Pynchon, *V.*, p. 111).

R6: The ability to spot ideas or values underlying actions (or serving as pretexts for them) is another kind of abstraction: *ideology.* Ex: *'I'm ready to give my life for an ideal! –* Come on! Come on lads! Smash that youth's face in! – Gather round me, the young ones! Defend me! Hearing this appeal, several among them felt *Youth battling with Strength*. There followed an exchange of blows' (W. Gombrowicz, *Ferdydurke*, p. 39).

In *The Great War and Modern Memory* Paul Fussell lists a series of abstractions used by British propagandists to hide the existential horrors: 'The enemy is *the host* ... the draft-notice is *the summons* – to enlist is to *join the colours* ... the army as a whole is *the legion*' (p. 22).

R7: Abstraction invites personification*.

ACCENT A phoneme or group of phonemes is articulated with additional force (or is prolonged, or the timbre is changed). See K.L. Pike, *The Intonation of American English*; Z.S. Harris, *Structural Linguistics*, chapter 6; Crystal, 1971, pp. 33–5; Ducrot and Todorov; and Grammont, *Traité de phonétique*, pp. 15, 18.

One of the differences between the British and North American accents is the position of the stress in a syntagm*. In adjectival phrases having the form article + adjective + noun, British speakers still tend to stress the noun, North Americans the preceding adjective. Compare 'the Lost *Boys*' (Brit.) and 'the *Lost* Boys' (N. Amer.).

In French, the final, or tonic, accent is normally lengthened and placed on the last syllable pronounced (see Léon, p. 58). Other accents, known as 'emphasizing accents' (*accents d'insistance* in French) and characterized by increased resonance, may add stress to the end of a sentence (see exclamation*), or of a syntagm, and may be combined with the normal accent, or be extended over several syllables. Ex: 'JEANNE (in a clear, triumphant voice): Et quand *Jeanne* au mois de Mai monte sur son cheval de bataille, il faudrait qu'il soit bien malin celui qui empêcherait toute la France de partir' (P. Claudel, *Jeanne d'Arc au bûcher*, in *Théâtre*, 2:1238).

Clearly English metre, with its long and short syllables, permits the same phenomena more routinely (obliques [/] mark primary stresses; dots [•] secondary stresses; dashes [–] indicate unstressed syllables):

> / – – / – / – / – /
> Something there is that doesn't love a wall,
> – / – / – / – / – •
> That sends the frozen-ground-swell under it,
> – / – / – / – • – /
> And spills the upper boulders in the sun,
> – / / • / – / – /
> And makes gaps even two can pass abreast.
>
> Robert Frost, 'Mending Wall'

Affective accents* and antithetical accents*, which are optional, are peculiar because they stress the beginning of a word. Epitrochasmus* exploits the phonetic accent of a word.

Accent (Affective)

Other definitions: 1. A tone expressing feelings (a pathetic, oratorical, haughty, bitter, ironic, etc. accent). This definition is concerned with the rhythmic or melodic qualities of sentences, rather than simply with accent (see punctuation*).
2. Vocal inflexions peculiar to the inhabitants of a particular region (a standard English, American, or English-Canadian accent, a Parisian or a Québécois accent). This usage defines collective speech habits. See mistake*, R2, and phonemic lengthening*, R1.
3. A graphic sign which, in French, is placed over a vowel to indicate its quality (an acute accent, é; a grave accent, è) or its timbre and length (a circumflex accent, ê); a mute vowel, mute e, for instance, has no accent. The proposal made by a group of French schoolteachers in 1989 to suppress the circumflex accent drew this response from the *Manchester Guardian Weekly* (10 Sept. 1989, p. 12): '[Suppression of the circumflex accent] would be a severe blow for every schoolchild facing examinations. Generations of children in Britain, struggling with intractable texts to be rendered into English, have been rescued by the sudden glorious sighting of a circumflex and the remembrance that where it now stands there once stood the letter "s." Thus *hâter*, which might have suggested enmity, is suddenly revealed as "to hasten," *forêt* emerges as "forest," while for those who had harboured doubts there is no further mystery about the meaning of *bâtard*.'

ACCENT (AFFECTIVE) This is broadly synonymous with the emphasizing accent, or indeed even with the emotional, pathetic, or oratorical accent (see Marouzeau and Quillet). See accent*.

However, unlike the antithetical accent*, the term *affective accent* has acquired a more restricted meaning. It is an 'accent expressing intensity ... which emphasizes words indicating values ... Such words, pronounced in exasperation, acquire an extra accent on the first consonant' (Morier, under *affectif*). Morier gives the following example: 'C'est inconceivable.' In English, one might say, for instance, 'That's *too* much, no *way*,' etc.

R1: The affective accent, which is peculiar because it emphasizes a consonant, deserves a more distinctive name. Nor does it necessarily express exasperation. Ex: 'The rain in *Sp*ain stays mainly on the *pl*ain' (G.B. Shaw, A. Lerner, and F. Loewe, *My Fair Lady*). It may be asserted that, in all cases, such accentuation of consonants invigorates the words thus pronounced. Why not then be more specific and call it an 'energetic' accent? The expression 'affective accent' covers too many different kinds of stress, whose nuances are difficult to specify using an external criterion. The *pathetic* accent may refer to feigned sentiment; the *oratorical* accent to a 'sublime' tone of voice or delivery; the *emotional* accent to some confusion experienced by the speaker; the *expressive* accent to stylistic *colour*; the *over-emphatic* accent to an excess of stress, and so on.

ACCENT (ANTITHETICAL) Some accents stress the beginning of a word, both in French and in English. **Ex:** 'I go now from a corruptible to an *in*corruptible crown' (Alec Guinness as Charles I in the film *Cromwell*, 1970). Dauzat and Marouzeau ('Accent affectif et intellectuel,' in *Le Français moderne* [March–April 1934], pp. 123–6) discovered one placed on the first consonant (see affective accent*) and another on the first vowel. They claim the latter is an accent which gives 'intellectual emphasis.' Morier is more precise when he speaks of an *antithetical accent*: 'an accent stressing the first vowel of a word, which is emphasized in order to contrast it with its opposite, or to make an intellectual distinction ... e.g., "We preferred not to speak of his *a*ttentions, but rather of his *in*tentions towards us" ' (Morier, under *antithétique*). Compare the modern English '*un*believable' or '*in*credible.'

R1: Garde (*L'Accent*, p. 45) confirms the placing of the two accents in French and offers the following example: 'C'est *a*bominable! C'est *t*errible! [affective emphasis]. Ce n'est pas *a*bominable, ce n'est pas *t*errible, c'est *n*ormal [intellectual emphasis].' See also P. Lieberman, *Intonation, Perception and Language.*

R2: Logical emphasis necessarily stresses units of meaning, whether a morpheme or a word. **Ex** (suffixes):

SARA TURING: [He's working on] ... iodine.
ALAN TURING: Io*dates*.

> Hugh Whitemore, *Breaking the Code*, act 1

But the intermediate syllables do not carry the accent in 'I didn't say Mont*e*bello, but Mont*e*verdi' because the unit of meaning in this case is the whole word. Nor would we say, 'C*i*ncinnati' or 'V*a*ncouver.'

Marouzeau and Morier quite rightly state that the first term in an opposition (the one denied) may remain implicit. **Ex:** 'That's perfectly *a*moral.'

R3: In spoken language, the antithetical accent is the sign of the statement made in an assertion. **Ex:** 'This *is the way*, not that way.' It's also aesthetically important (see assonance*, R2).

ACCUMULATION (L. 'heaping up') A combination of terms or syntagms similar in nature or function, or of those having the same final sound.

Exx: 'and there is ever heard a trampling, cackling, roaring, lowing, bleating, bellowing, rumbling, grunting, champing, chewing, of sheep and pigs and heavyhooved kine' (Joyce, *Ulysses*, p. 242); 'I gained a real impression, too, of the vast organism that is an army: all those separate units which allow the whole to function – ordnance, transport, clothing, feeding, animals, signals, engineering, roadbuilding, policing,

Accumulation

communications, health and sanitation ...' (William Boyd, *The New Confessions*, p. 114).

Synonyms: *accumulatio*; amplification* (Lanham, Preminger); 'congeries' (Quinn); synathroesmus; systrophe; *conglobatio* (a 'heaping up of descriptions of a thing without defining it' [Lanham, p. 98]); *amas* ('a heap' [Paulhan, *Enigmes de Perse*, p. 74]); *athroisme* (Quillet, Lausberg); *synathroisme* (Littré, Lausberg); *conglobation* (Fontanier, p. 363). It should be noted, however, that Littré, Morier, and Quillet restrict the latter term's use to the piling up of proofs in forensic oratory.

R1: Accumulation may be used as a facile means of amplification:

Oh yes, I remember him well, the boy you are searching for:
he looked like most boys, no better, brighter, or more respectful:
he cribbed, mitched, spilt ink, rattled his desk and
garbled his lessons with the worst of them;
he could smudge, hedge, smirk, wriggle, wince,
whimper, blarney, badger, blush, deceive, be
devious, stammer, improvise, assume
offended dignity or righteous indignation as though to the manner
born.

Dylan Thomas, *Quite Early One Morning*, p. 50

R2: Accumulation and enumeration* are not always clearly distinguishable the one from the other. Both may be long, baroque (see baroquism*), disorderly (see verbigeration*, R3), or arranged so as to form a climax or anticlimax* (see *gradatio*). But accumulation may be the less logical of the two; it switches between different viewpoints and is able to continue seemingly *ad infinitum*, whereas enumeration does have a purpose in view, even if the enumerated elements are contradictory. Lanham quotes the following poem as an example of enumeration which divides the 'subject into adjuncts, cause into effects, antecedent into consequents':

How do I love thee? Let me count the ways.
I love thee to the depth and breadth and height
My soul can reach, when feeling out of sight
For the ends of Being and ideal Grace.
I love thee to the level of everyday's
Most quiet need, by sun and candlelight.
I love thee freely, as men strive for Right;
I love thee purely, as they turn from Praise.
I love thee with the passion put to use
In my old griefs, and with my childhood's faith.
I love thee with a love I seemed to lose
With my lost saint. I love thee with the breath,

Smiles, tears of all my life – and if God choose,
I shall love thee better after death.
              Elizabeth Barrett Browning, *Sonnets from the Portuguese*, no. 43

Once all possibilities are envisaged, the series enumerated ends. Some series, even seemingly complete ones, remain necessarily open and are therefore accumulations. Ex: 'Oh! but he was a tight-fisted hand at the grindstone, Scrooge! a squeezing, wrenching, grasping, scraping, clutching, covetous old sinner! Hard and sharp as flint, from which no steel ever struck out generous fire; secret, and self-contained as an oyster' (Dickens, *A Christmas Carol*, 'Stave one').

Ex (the following is an accumulation of paradoxes):

To dream the impossible dream,
To fight the unbeatable foe,
To bear with unbearable sorrow,
To run where the brave dare not go,
To right the unrightable wrong,
To love pure and chaste from afar,
To try when your arms are too weary,
To reach the unreachable star
              Dale Wasserman, 'The Quest,' in *Man of La Mancha* (1965),
                   a musical play based on Cervantes's *Don Quixote*

R3: When the terms heaped together are not of the same nature, the accumulation is confused. Spitzer calls it 'chaotic, close to verbiage*.' Ex: 'What syllabus of intellectual pursuits was simultaneously possible? Snapshot photography, comparative study of religions, folklore relative to various amatory and superstitious practices, contemplation of the celestial constellations ... ' (Joyce, *Ulysses*, p. 587). This may turn into verbigeration*.

R4: Accumulations of adjectives have been said to characterize 'epithetical style' (Lausberg). Ex: 'and red green yellow brown russet sweet big bitter ripe pomellated apples' (Joyce, *Ulysses*, pp. 379–80). If they are heaped together in disorder, they may be said to form a confused medley of qualifiers. See also epitheton*, and for examples of accumulations of lexemes, see synonymy*, R1.

R5: The accumulation of qualifiers slows the presentation of information (see suspension*, R3, and parastasis*). Conversely, the accumulation of proper names or short sentences seems to speed it up. Ex: 'We spent a week idling about Devon in weather that had suddenly turned chill. East Budleigh, Hayes Barton, over to Compton (the castle most picturesque), off to Plymouth, across to Exeter ... Small inns, roaring fires, cold coaches, long and colder walks, and the shire's justly famous cream. That to me made up our week' (L.B. Greenwood, *Sherlock Holmes and the Case of the Raleigh Legacy*, p. 131).

Ex:

Then shall our names,
Familiar in his mouth as household words,
Harry the King, Bedford and Exeter,
Warwick and Talbot, Salisbury and Gloucester,
Be in their flowing cups freshly remember'd.
Shakespeare, *Henry V*, 5.3.41–5

R6: See epitrochasmus* for the accumulation of short words; see title* (conferring of), R4, for accumulation of titles. For accumulation of personifying verbs, see personification*, R2; for accumulation of questions, see question*, R2.

ACCUSATION To represent someone as being guilty of a crime.

Ex: 'Henry Flower. No fixed abode. Unlawfully watching and besetting' (Joyce, *Ulysses*, p. 372).

R1: In an insinuation, the accusation is conveyed indirectly, or hinted at obliquely. For accusatory arguments, see antiparastasis*, R5. For disguised accusations, see question*, R3.

R2: An accusation of intent is one based, not on fact, but on a more or less gratuitous attribution of criminal, or evil, intentions to one's adversary. For instance, a simple request draws from an individual the reply that not only is she or he too busy to comply at the moment, but the aggressive retort 'You're determined not to allow me a moment's peace, aren't you.'

ACRONYM A group of abbreviatory initials, more or less lexicalized, or treated phonetically and semantically as a word. Lexicalization* is more pronounced if the acronym is written as a word (e.g., NATO). If its individual letters are separated by periods, it remains closer to simple abbreviation (e.g., N.A.T.O.).

Acronyms are pronounced as if they were new words, a process called 'integrated pronunciation' (e.g., 'Unesco,' 'flak' [from *Fliegerabwehrkanone*, 'anti-aircraft cannon']), or by considering each letter separately, in 'disjunctive pronunciation' (e.g., U.S.A.). In the second case, called 'alphabetism' by Crystal (1987, p. 90), it is possible to transcribe the pronunciation literally. Exx: 'TeeVeeOh' for TV Ontario; 'Ashellemm' for H[abitation] à L[oyer] M[odéré] ('subsidized housing, council house').

Another type of acronymic formation stems from the reduction of words to their first syllables. Exx: 'Benelux' for the group of countries formed by Belgium, the Netherlands, and Luxembourg; 'Telbec' for Compagnie de Télécommunication du Québec.

The invention of original acronyms may constitute a literary device. Ex: 'Le Syndicat des empêcheurs de rire en rond à l'Opéra,' referred to in a footnote to page 185 of Réjean Ducharme's *La Fille de Christophe Colomb* as SDEDRERALO (the 'union for the prevention of laughter at the idiocies of opera-plots'; i.e., UPLIOP in English).

Analogous term: siglum. The abuse of sigla is popularly called 'Alphabet Soup' and was parodied by Peter Cook and Dudley Moore:

COOK: R.B. was an M.O. in the R.N.V.R. ... I saw old T.D. in the Y.M.C.A.
MOORE: I thought he was with T.W.A. in L.A.
COOK: No, he's with B.E.A. in S.W.3. D.G. is a V.I.P. in the U.S.A. T.D. is a Q.C. with the D.T.'s. I'm with I.C.I. ... doing sweet F.A. Well, I'm off for a P. in the W.C.

'Initials,' in *Not Only But Also* [TV program, 1965]

R1: Acronyms provide one of the sources used to form proper names (see denomination*, R2). The newly formed lexeme may engender a lexical series (see J. Dubois, *Etude sur la dérivation suffixale en français moderne et contemporain*, p. 75). Original derivatives are then derived in their turn by the use of the same device. Exx: 'NDPers,' 'Péquistes,' members, respectively, of the New Democratic Party and of the P[arti] Q[uébécois].

R2: The use of acronyms may become a literary* game based on the possibility of readings texts in several ways. The game itself may also become a literary device. Ex: 'We call it [the house] D.B.C. because they have damn bad cakes' (Joyce, *Ulysses*, p. 204).

R3: False acronyms may be encountered that are in reality allographs* ('variants of a grapheme' [Crystal, 1987, p. 194]), in which the graphemes are read phonetically. Ex: FMRFIJ; that is, when read aloud, 'éphémère effigie' ('ephemeral effigy') (Robert Desnos, *Corps et biens*, p. 6).

R4: Graphic artists convert sigla into symbols*, in which case, since they evoke more directly the object referred to, they become *icons*. When, as in trademarks, they evoke certain qualities, they are *emblems*. The Jaguar emblem of the motor car presumably suggests, rather than frequent and expensive thirst, the qualities of speed and grace with which its makers would prefer that one associate it.

R5: For the typographical problem which arises when acronyms occur at the end of a line of typing or printing, see typographical caesura*.

Acrostic

ACROSTIC A poem whose subject, or the author's name, or that of the dedicatee may be read in the word formed by the initial letters of each line. As Brother William explains to Adso: 'The text of the verse doesn't count, it's the initial letters that count. Each room is marked by a letter of the alphabet, and all together they make up some text that we must discover!' (U. Eco, *The Name of the Rose*, p. 218).

Ex: 'Acrosticountry,' a poem by the contemporary Canadian poet Stephen Scobie, presents a 'panorama of the chief cities of Canada together with the associations evoked by these cities in the poet's mind' (my thanks to Professor Ludwig Deringer of the Catholic University of Eichstatt for pointing out this example):

Virgin In Character
Tries On Regal Insignia:
Admirable.

Vicarious Anxiety,
Neurotic Concern: Out
Under Vancouver's Endless Rain.

Sweet And Sexy Kisses.
And Truly Original
Olfactory Nuances.

Slagheaps' Ubiquitous Debris
Buried Under Rubble
Yecch.

Too Old? Right On,
Nichol. Too Old.

'My Own Nation' Trudeau.
'Reject Everything Anglais'
Lévesque.

The medieval French poet François Villon signs several of his ballads by placing the letters of his name at the beginning of the lines in the final verse, or 'envoi.' Ex:

Voulez-vous que verté vous dise?
Il n'est jouer qu'en maladie
Lettre vraye que tragedie
Lasche homme que chevalereux
Orrible son que melodie
Ne bien conseil qu'amoureux

(Very well, I'll speak truthfully.
In sickness alone is gaiety.
Look for truth in plays and tragedy.

Lordly knights will show cowardice.
O music gives discord, horribly –
Now only a lover gives good advice!)

> Villon, 'Ballade des contre vérités,' trans. Beram Saklatvala as
> 'A Ballad of Paradoxes,' in *Complete Poems of François Villon*, p. 161

Forms of double acrostic exist which make words by combining the initial letters (acrostic), or middle (mesostich), or final letters (telestich). Ex (quoted by Espy, *The Game of Words*, p. 27):

> *U*nite and untie are the same – so say yo*U*
> *N*ot in wedlock, I ween, has the unity bee*N*
> *I*n the drama of marriage, each wandering go*û*T
> *T*o a new face would fly – all except you and *I*
> *E*ach seeking to alter the *spell* in their scen*E*.

The unknown author has here combined an acrostic with a telestich. The opening letters of the lines form UNITE; the closing letters, UNTIE.

R1: Acrostics belong to the realm of cryptography*. See literary* games.

R2: As Eco demonstrates, acrostics may serve as plot-devices in mystery stories: 'The system of words was eccentric ... It was purely a mnemonic device to allow the librarian to find a given work. To say of a book that it was found in "quarta Acaciae" meant that it was in the fourth room counting from the one in which the initial *A* appeared, and then, to identify it, presumably the librarian knew by heart the route, circular or straight, that he would follow, as ACAIA was distributed over four rooms arranged in a square' (U. Eco, *The Name of the Rose*, p. 320).

ACTANT A function of plot-development sometimes or 'usually' played by a 'character,' depending on one's theoretical bias.

Etienne Souriau (in *Les Deux cent mille situations dramatiques*) designated six functions and described them as follows: the *force orientée* (Fo) or 'directed power,' the *bien souhaité* (Bs) or 'object of desire,' the *obtenteur souhaité* (Os) or 'desired obtainer,' the *opposant* (Op) or 'antagonist,' the *arbitre de la situation* (Ar), the 'arbiter' or 'referee,' and the *adjuvant* (Ad) or 'helper.' Vladimir Propp, who studied the 'morphology of the folk-tale' from the same point of view, differentiates seven types of characters: the hero, the princess or person desired, the aggressor or villain, the donor or provider of magical devices, the 'dispatcher' who sends the hero forth on his adventures, the helper, and the false hero. A.J. Greimas (*Sémantique structurale*, pp. 176–80) stretches these notions to cover more abstract entities and suggests the following concordance between his and the earlier systems, taking as his example the 'classical philosopher':

Ad Hominem (Argument)

ACTANTIAL PARADIGMS

SOURIAU	PROPP	GREIMAS	EXAMPLE
Fo	hero	subject	philosopher
Bs	princess	(desired) object	the world
Ar	dispatcher	dispatcher/donor	God
Os		receiver/beneficiary	humanity
Op	aggressor/false hero	opposer	matter
Ad	helper	helper	the Mind

These paradigms should be applied flexibly to specific works, and excessive claims should not be made for the system. A character may serve a function which distinguishes him or her from all others in the same text, or the same character may assume several functions. The paradigms need to be re-allocated at times. Thus, in Montherlant's theatre, for example, it is possible to reduce the number of characters to four; the reduction reveals dramatic constants evolving in a way which parallels the author's affective situation (see B. Dupriez, 'Les Structures et l'inconscient dans le théâtre de Montherlant,' *Protée*, no. 6, pp. 47–64). Actantial analysis needs to free itself from the complications of plot and will be clearer if it recognizes the relevance to plot-analysis of point of view or focalization. See narrative*.

R1: Actantial analysis may also be practised, not only in accordance with some general plot dialectic, but by means of a rigorous delineation of specific plots, as Claude Bremond proposed in *Logique du récit*. Such an analysis begins with characters who are considered in detail as they participate in each event in the action, and even in the three stages essential to the event itself: (1) potentiality; (2) realization; and (3) outcome. Characters are classified as either agents or victims; as either influencers, helpers, or protectors or those whose function is to degrade or frustrate; and as either acquiring merit or earning retribution. According to Philippe Hamon (*Le Personnel du roman*, 1983), even realistic descriptions transform actors into actants, and so constitute actantial indices. Many devices used by those who favour this approach remain undefined. See communication*, other def., 2.

R2: Actants may be reversed; see flip-flop*, R3, and antimetabole*, R3.

AD HOMINEM (Argument) An argument that is valid only against one's current adversary, either because it is founded on one of his logical errors, inconsequential arguments, or concessions, or because it is aimed at a particular detail of his individual nature or system of beliefs. See Lanham, *A Handlist of Rhetorical Terms*; and Lalande, *Vocabulaire technique et critique de la philosophie*.

Ex: Churchill's reputed denigration of Attlee: 'He was a modest man, with much to be modest about.'

16

Ex: 'Forever! ah my Lord, think *of yourself* / How terribly cruel that word is to someone in love' (Racine, *Bérénice*, 4.5).

Alternative definition: 'An argument which contrasts current opinion of a man with his prior actions or words' (Littré, in *Trésor de la langue française*). This is a very specific meaning which likens the device to retortion* or retaliation, and is frequently used in politics to contrast pre-election promises with post-election realities.

R1: The *ad hominem* argument is an attack. When it is used to hide the absence of valid arguments by impugning the person instead of seeking to refute that person's ideas, it is pure 'rhetoric' and, as such, fallacious. However, the combination of an attack on the morals, for instance, of a candidate for office, together with the casting of doubt on the candidate's trustworthiness produces the kind of *a fortiori* argument that, in 1987, ended the presidential aspirations of Gary Hart (if 'immoral,' then all the more politically 'untrustworthy'). *Ad personam* might be used to designate the corresponding positive or 'friendly' argument. Ex: 'You, as a lover of Chopin, should know that ...,' etc.

R2: In order to avoid a charge of sexism* in argumentation, one should logically envisage the necessity of adding a parallel term, the *ad feminam* argument, to describe one used against a female adversary.

ADJUNCTION A kind of ellipsis* by which a word used in one part of a sentence is not repeated in the contiguous one. The elliptical proposition is added to a sentence which is already syntactically complete; hence the name, 'adjunction.'

Ex: 'His eyes are brown, his hair blond.'

Ex: 'The pack will be going into a curve when suddenly two cars, three cars, four cars tangle ... Laurence Mendelsohn had a vision of an automobile sport that would be all crashes. Not two cars, not three cars, not four cars, but 100 cars would be out in an arena doing nothing but smashing each other into shrapnel' (Tom Wolfe, *The Kandy-Kolored Tangerine-Flake Streamline Baby*, p. 33). See also zeugma*.

R1: Fontanier contrasts adjunction and ellipsis*, in the latter of which the omitted words are not found in a contiguous clause. But he also contrasts it to zeugma* (see *Les Figures du discours*, p. 336), unlike Lanham, Preminger, Fabri (2:156), Littré, and Robert. The distinction he proposes is that adjunction must occur (as in the first sentence quoted from Wolfe) before the full proposition has been asserted, so that the whole sentence forms one and the same complex proposition.

This distinction seems unnecessary, given that, without the adjunction, the sentence would be complete anyway (see disjunction*, R3).

Adjunction may occur at the beginning (protozeugma), in the middle (mesozeugma), or at the end of a sentence (hypozeugma).

R2: Nowadays adjunction is a mode of syntactic development, especially in spoken language. Indeed, it's the simplest way to connect two adjacent assertions (see assertion*, R5). Ex: 'A shell ... Boom ... which hits the bridge. The principal arch buckles, disintegrates ... digs a hole in the roadway, an enormous pit ... a crater into which everything around topples ...' (L.-F. Céline, *Guignols Band*, p. 17). Adjunction is possible even when the sentence seems to be already complete. Ex: '[He] would build a house there. In the winter an igloo' (Yves Thériault, *Agaguk*, p. 10).

R3: If the adjunctive element does not serve the same function as the stated one, there is semi-adjunction, which is frequent in parataxis*. Ex: 'I arrived, I made inquiries, I left.' Any syntactic unit separated at the end of a sentence may be placed in semi-adjunction by means of specially reinforced punctuation. Ex: 'Brought by force into the intimacy of this barricaded house. In the middle of winter. At the side of the road, between Sainte-Anne and Kamouraska. On the night of January 31' (Anne Hébert, *Kamouraska*, p. 210). If the final separated syntagm is introduced by a conjunction, a comma will suffice. Ex: 'You will have a fine dowry, and a rich legacy' (Raymond Queneau, *Pierrot mon ami*, p. 95).

R4: Usage decides which elements are elided. In the following quotation, Gide creates an unusual example of adjunction by repeating *if*: 'Oh! if time could only turn back to its beginning! and if the past come back!' (*Les Nourritures terrestres*, in *Romans*, p. 245).

R5: Adjunction leads to hyperbaton* (see hyperbaton, R2) and parataxis* (see parataxis, R2).

ADYNATON Hyperbole involving magnification of an event by reference to the impossible. See Lanham, Lausberg, and Preminger.

Exx: 'I'd walk a million miles for one of your smiles' (Al Jolson, 'My Mammy'); '... Through caverns measureless to man' (Coleridge, 'Kubla Khan')

Ex (a publicist's example): 'This gravy makes bricks digestible.'

Analogous terms: *fatrasie* ('dealing with impossible or ridiculous accomplishments' [Preminger]); cock-and-bull story

R1: If it uses the fantastic to extend the possibilities of the real world, adynaton is pure rhetoric. Ex:

Had we but world enough, and time
...

> ... I would
> Love you ten years before the Flood:
> And you should if you choose refuse
> Till the conversion of the Jews.
>
> Andrew Marvell, 'To His Coy Mistress'

Ex: 'The air was so damp that fish could have come in through the doors and swum out the windows, floating through the atmosphere in the rooms' (G. Garcia Marquez, *One Hundred Years of Solitude*, p. 292).

In such comparisons, the second term may be anything provided it is sufficiently fantastic: 'Djeky is as elusive as the wind, as fire, or as space itself' (*Geste de Djeky* in Kesteloot, ed., *L'Epopée traditionnelle*, p. 45). The question of isotopic coherence becomes more acute when the same text claims that 'Djeky ... swallowed the ocean and spat it out again.' The question need not be settled in the same way as in the case of *fatrasie*, which seems nearer to verbigeration*. What Morier calls 'impossible' *fatrasie* were French medieval verse forms ('usually of eleven lines,' according to Cuddon) founded on incoherent or impossible statements. Ex: 'I saw an eel – Fixing her daughter's hair – On top of a steeple' (an old song, which the *Dictionnaire du surréalisme* classifies under 'possible'). Some trace of these forms survives in the *comptine* or French children's sing-song rhyme. One function of the *comptine* is to designate, by the *counting-out* of its syllables, who is either to leave the game or to be 'it' and chase after the other participants. Exx (in English): 'Eeny, meeny, miney, mo'; 'O U T spells *OUT*, and so are *you*,' etc.

Adynaton, when used by surrealist writers, combines the fantastic with the rhetorical. Ex: 'One day our friendship will have become so substantial that, simply by looking at me, it will be able, like a razor, to carve furrows in my flesh' (Réjean Ducharme, *L'Océantume*, p. 116). It thus retains one meaning, whereas surrealistic dissociation* serves rather to deconstruct the mental structures to which it refers.

Alan Bennett used adynaton in a parody* of the doctrine of numerical attrition which served as a criterion for the judgment of success and failure in the so-called 'Great' War: '[Teacher dictating to class]: "If the ten million dead of the 1914–18 War were to march in column of fours through the Gates of Death, it would take eighty days and eighty nights for the column to pass through ... In the light of this information, I want you to calculate (1) the width of the Gates of Death to the nearest centimetre, and (2) the speed in m.p.h. at which the column was marching"' (*Forty Years On*, 1968, act 1).

AGNOMINATIO (alt. sp. *adnominatio*) Remotivation* of a proper name through etymology*, metanalysis*, or translation*. In other words, a proper name, instead of retaining a purely conventional relationship with its referent, receives the meaning of the common noun it expresses (*Smith* becomes the smith who shoes horses), or of its constitutive elements (*Smithson* becomes 'the smith's son'), or of elements that can be read into it through simple homophony with words of the same language or other languages. See *OED*, Littré, and Ducrot and Todorov.

Exx: 'And I say unto thee, That thou art Peter, and upon this rock I will build my church' (Matt. 16:18); 'MEPHISTOPHELES: Ah how evil is the Evil One!' (P. Valéry, *Mon Faust*, in *Oeuvres*, 2:346).

Other definitions: 1. Scaliger, Marouzeau, and Lausberg make *agnominatio* a synonym of paronomasia*.
2. The *OED* points out the same relationship and to this partial identification adds that *agnominatio* is also a form of alliteration*. Lanham suggests that *agnominatio* may involve play on the sound of words while paronomasia involves play on their sense.
3. As a first meaning for *agnominatio*, Morier gives the 'evocation of a proper name (which is not pronounced) by means of other words similar in sound' (see allusion*, R5). In a poem from Henri de Régnier's *Vestigia Flammae* (p. 109) which begins 'O Roméo,' Morier claims that the expression 'eau muette' suggests 'Juliette' to an obsessed Romeo or to a reader whose mind is predisposed to complete the 'allusion' to the play.

R1: In his definition, Littré does not distinguish *agnominatio* clearly from proper denomination* when the former is motivated by a common noun. So he would include among examples of *agnominatio* 'Lieutenant Létourdi' ('Thoughtless') and 'Madame Vabontrain' ('Speedy') which indeed are very close to it because they play on two meanings of name and noun. (They do so, however, in a way opposite to the one we have defined: they go from common noun to proper name. Thus there is motivation, rather than remotivation*, of an existing proper name.)

R2: The context uses the second meaning in various ways, negatively for instance: 'DORINE: This Mr. Loyal seems very disloyal' (Molière, *Tartuffe*, 5.4).

R3: *Agnominatio* is a form of word-play* often used in familiar language. Ex: 'Madame Maura ne m'aura pas' ('will not get me'). However, Etienne Souriau reminds us (*Revue d'esthétique*, 1965, p. 28) that 'in French, jokes made by playing upon proper names are likely to be as ill received as are "personal remarks" in English.' Ex: 'Paul de Kock. Nice name he' (Joyce, *Ulysses*, p. 221). Joyce changes names and titles for reasons of irony*: 'The delegation, present in full force, consisted of Commendatore Bacibaci Beninobenone ... Monsieur Pierrepaul Petité-patant, the Grandjoker Vladinmire Pokethankertscheff ... Hiram Y. Bomboost ... Ali Baba Baksheesh' (ibid., p. 252). In this example equivoque* reinforces word-play*.

ALLEGORY A literary image in which the relationship between vehicle and tenor applies not globally, as in simile* or metaphor*, but element by element, with accompanying personification*. See Cuddon, Frye, Girard, Lanham, Littré, Morier, Preminger, Robert, and Lausberg.

Ex: 'Reverie ... a magical young girl, unpredictable, tender, enigmatic, provocative, from whom I never seek an explanation of her escapades' (André Breton, *Farouche à quatre feuilles*, p. 13).

In the following example, the narrator reveals the allegorical nature of his characters in a final scene of anagnorisis or recognition: 'After that it did not seem strange when next day the pigs who were supervising the work of the farm all carried whips in their trotters. It did not seem strange to learn that the pigs had bought themselves a wireless set [and] were arranging to install a telephone ... Napoleon himself appear[ed] in a black coat, ratcatcher breeches, and leather leggings' (George Orwell, *Animal Farm*, pp. 114–15).

Synonyms: 'extended metaphor,' 'métaphore filée.' See apocalypse*.

R1: Allegory differs from other imagery because of the number of elements compared. It embodies the distinction which separates, albeit in briefer form, simile and metaphor. There exist allegories in which the tenor is clearly separated from the vehicle by 'like' or some other sign of analogy (see comparison*, R2), and others in which the two commingle.

R2: As in metaphor* (see metaphor, R1), the tenor may be suppressed. That, for Fontanier, was indeed the precondition of allegory as such (see *Les Figures du discours*, p. 114). He claims that when tenor and vehicle mingle, the result is *allegorism*. This is not a trivial remark since allegorism would be defined, in that case, as partial, or semi-allegory. (We recommend the use, in French, of the term *métaphore filée* ['running metaphor'] to describe such cases.)

Does this mean that allegory should necessarily be enigmatic, or 'undecidable' in deconstructionist terms? Allegory may of course be so (see riddle*, R1), but normally the context indicates the tenor. Such is the case in all the examples cited by Fontanier. When, for instance, in his *Art poétique*, Boileau declares, 'I prefer a stream to a raging torrent,' he is speaking about authors, and therefore obviously about their style.

Fontanier gives greatest importance to the coherence possessed by terms forming the vehicle; any incoherencies lessen the impact of the allegory. Nowadays we seem to prefer a shift in meaning from tenor to vehicle. Ex: 'You have a clear conception of the people of God. A great flock – good sheep and bad sheep – kept in order by mastiffs – the warriors, or the temporal power – the Emperor, and the overlords, under the guidance of the shepherds, the clerics, the interpreters of the divine word' (U. Eco, *The Name of the Rose*, p. 200).

R3: Allegory is often defined as personification* (see Morier, first meaning; Lausberg, second meaning) since the latter figure usually involves several metaphors (see metaphor, R4). An image's anthropomorphic aspect is clearest in an allegory which, through personification, dramatizes and renders its tenor in visual terms. (See the last example quoted.) Personified allegory may be brief, but care must be taken to avoid figuration made inadvertently ridiculous by excess. Ex: 'Go, and may love serve as your mahout, sweet elephant of my thoughts' (Tristan Derême, *La Verdure dorée*, p. 1).

R4: Every trope involving detailed comparison is not an allegory. Ex: 'He really has a musical flair, thought Dancourt. He treats every meeting symphonically. The theme is announced, developed in major and minor, pulled about, teased, chased up and down dark alleys, and then, when we are getting tired of it, he whips us up into a lively finale and with a few crashing chords brings us to a vote' (Robertson Davies, *The Lyre of Orpheus*, p. 2). The substitution of 'dark alleys' and 'crashing chords,' concrete terms for abstract ones, seems simply to produce metonymy*.

One concrete term sometimes replaces another: 'the flock of tactile sensations grazes in the limitless fields of skin' (M. Leiris, *Aurora*, p. 20). In the following example, a concrete phenomenon is allegorized in abstract terms: 'NOTES ON THE DAWN OF DAY. Here is the most recent edition of day's oldest text: the verb SUN develops its conjugations of colours; it comments upon all the varied propositions of light and shade which make up the discourse of time and place' (P. Valéry, *Oeuvres*, 2:859).

Changes of point of view and of vocabulary also occur: 'The first operation in medical history, which had Adam for patient, was an intercostal incision. One post-operative complication took the form of a ravishing young woman' (L.-M. Tard, *Si vous saisissez l'astuce*, p. 11). In his *Exercises in Style*, Raymond Queneau tells the same story in ninety-nine different ways by borrowing the idioms specific to such widely differing disciplines as philosophy, botany, medicine, gastronomy, zoology, mathematics, and so on.

One might call detailed or 'allegory-like' metonymy 'application,' thus borrowing a name from Cartesian mathematics. One semantic set is in fact compared to another when one points to elements common to both. See Angus Fletcher, *Allegory: The Theory of a Symbolic Mode* (1964) and Philippe Dubois, 'La Métaphore filée,' in *Le Français moderne*, July 1975.

R5: As a form of allegory, application may be co-extensive with a whole work. Exx: J. Bunyan, *Pilgrim's Progress*; J. Swift, *Gulliver's*

Travels; G. Orwell, *Animal Farm*; R. de Obaldia, *Le Tamerlan des coeurs*; H. Aquin, *Prochain Episode*.

R6: For the differences between allegory and apologue*, see the latter, R1; see also diatyposis*, R1, and riddle*. Allegory is a feature of the 'sublime' or 'high style' of expression (see grandiloquence*, R1).

ALLITERATION Multiple repetitions of an identical sound. See Cuddon, Fontanier, Lanham, Lausberg, Marouzeau, and Preminger.

Exx (initial consonant): 'cool, calm and collected'; 'sing a song of sixpence'; 'villainous violinist.' Also alliterative is the title of Benjamin Britten's *Simple Symphony*, as are those of its four movements: boisterous *bourrée*, playful *pizzicato*, sentimental saraband, frolicsome finale.

Ex: 'Pour qui sont ces serpents qui sifflent sur vos têtes?' ('For whom do you bring those serpents hissing upon your heads?') (Jean Racine, *Andromaque*, 5.5, trans. George Dillon, in *Three Plays of Racine*, p. 58).

Ex (assonance, or alliterated vowels): 'Warm-laid *gra*ve of a womb-life *grey*; / *Ma*nger, *mai*den's knee ...' (G.M. Hopkins, 'The Wreck of the Deutschland,' 1.7).

Synonyms: paromoeon (Lanham); paragrammatism (Littré); parachresis (Fontanier); 'rebound' ('successive repetitions of the same vowel within a word' [Morier]; e.g., *lugu*brious, *ho*rror, *nepenthe*)

R1: Alliteration is not necessarily the reproduction of a sound for allusive purposes, as is the case in the famous Racinian example involving snakes. It may also make a text reverberant or narcotic, as in the following example: 'The moan of doves in immemorial elms / And murmuring of innumerable bees' (Tennyson, 'The Princess,' 11.202–3). Alliteration may also create a comic effect, as the following example involving initial consonants shows:

> To sit in solemn silence in a dull, dark dock,
> In a pestilential prison, with a life-long lock,
> Awaiting the sensation of a short, sharp shock,
> From a cheap and chippy chopper on a big, black block.
> W.S. Gilbert, *The Mikado* (1885), act 1

R2: The last example quoted exhibits the device called 'head-rhyme' by some critics, who name the repetition of vowels 'assonance.' Such consonantal repetition emphasizes the utterance's affective accent* and, as Morier remarks, extends the meaning of assonance at the expense of alliteration.

R3: Alliteration's notoriety means that it is used in a very broad way to designate all figures of sonority except rhyme (see musication*, R1;

echo* effect, R1; imitative harmony*, R1; paronomasia*, R2; tautogram*, R2). Both Valéry and Morier speak of *intrasonance* (to distinguish the device from *multisonance* or variety in the sounds used).

ALLOGRAPH (neol.) A text transcribed into another set of words. Homophones replace the original words; the process seems to change the meaning of the phrase or sentence.

Exx: 'Eureka! You doan smella so good yourself' (Chico Marx, quoted by Redfern, p 12); 'La rue meurt de la mer. Ile faite en corps noirs' [for 'La rumeur de la mer. Il fait encore noir'] (J. Cocteau, *Opéra*, p. 41).

The homophones involved may be taken from another language, a process which creates bilingual examples. See Luis d'Antin van Rooten's *Mots d'Heures: Gousses, Rames* (1967) and Ormonde de Kay's *N'Heures Souris Rames* (1980). Among their allographic English 'nursery rhymes' are such pastiches of early 'French' poems as: 'Georgie Port-régie, peu digne en paille, [Georgy Porgy, pudding and pie,] / Qui se dégeule sans mais. Dame craille. [Kissed the girls and made them cry.] / Où haine de bouées ce qu'aime à tout pilé [When the boys came out to play] / Georgie Port-régie règne. Ohé [Georgy Porgy ran away]' (O. de Kay, *N'Heures Souris Rames*, p. 1).

R1: To 'spot' the allograph, the receiver must submit the sound chain to metanalysis*, as in the case of a charade or rebus (a pictographic allograph):

HILL
JOHN = John Underhill, Andover, Mass
MASS

Grambs, p. 86

R2: Allographs are apt to be allusive. Ex: 'la des-mots-cratie' puns on free speech, a feature of the regime in question.

R3: Alphabetical allographs transcribe the original in an abridged form. Ex: 'Et LN? LR' (for 'Et Hélène? Elle erre [errs]') (Queneau). See acronym*.

ALLUSION A reference, by means of an evocative utterance, to something implied but not stated. See Abrams, Bélisle, Cuddon, Fontanier, Littré, Robert, Preminger, and Z. Ben-Porat, 'The Poetics of Literary Allusion,' *PTL* 1 (1976), pp. 105–28.

Ex: 'Sliding for home: a play in nine innings' (Frank Moore, 1987).

Ex: 'The same resonance of spirit has been caught so evocatively in Canada's unofficial national anthem, Quebec folksinger Gilles Vigneault's *Mon pays, c'est l'hiver*' (P.C. Newman, *Company of Adventurers*, p. 5).

Ex: In Quebec, the Canadian parlour game 'Trivial Pursuit' is called 'Quelques arpents de pièges' (literally 'a few acres of traps'). The allusion is, of course, to Voltaire's dismissive reference to Canada as being merely 'quelques arpents de neige' (*Candide*, ch. 23).

Ex: 'The mistress of the house had to lock everything up – the "tantalus" [security-frame for the decanters], the cellar, etc.' (Robert Hughes, *The Fatal Shore*, p. 347).

Analogous expressions: tacit, implicit, or indirect reference, usually brief in nature

R1: Allusion, like tropes, which it resembles in this respect, is a deviation of meaning, but one which involves a sentence or its equivalent (rather than a single word). Allusions may therefore be:
– *metaphorical*. Ex: 'To Carthage then I came / Burning' (T.S. Eliot, *The Waste Land*). The reference to Saint Augustine's *Confessions* echoes the opening of book 3, which recounts Augustine's unspiritual youth.
– *metonymic*. Ex: 'There it is [in the clandestine areas of human activity] that surge into view those great spiritual lighthouses, similar in shape to less innocent signs' (L. Aragon, *Le Paysan de Paris*, p. 143). The abstract expression 'less innocent' suggests the more concrete, phallic referent alluded to. See also metalepsis*.
– *synecdochic*. Ex: 'the sun's temperature being that of its disintegrating atoms' (M. Duras, *Hiroshima mon amour*, 1959).
– *allegorical*. Ex: 'Argive Helen, the wooden mare of Troy in whom a score of heroes slept' (Joyce, *Ulysses*, p. 165). Here the allusion is historical or mythological, in which there is agreement between original and secondary models on several points. In the following use of the same allusion taken from a computer manual, however, the reference is uni-functional: 'A Trojan horse is a program that claims to do some nifty task but instead pulls some nasty trick on you, like deleting every file on a disk, corrupting the file allocation table, or reformatting the disk' (Don Berliner, *Managing Your Hard Disk*, p. 541).
– *catachretic*. Ex: 'A mouth well made to hide / Another mouth' (P. Eluard, 'La Halte des heures,' in *Oeuvres complètes*, 1:731). 'To hide' for 'to kiss' because there are no other possible meanings.
    Allusion also has recourse occasionally to syllepsis*, in which two possible meanings exist at the same time. So the village story-teller laughs at Tartarin by speaking of his gun 'qui ne partait pas,' which means both that it didn't 'go off' and that its owner never left his village, despite his often reiterated boast that he would go hunting in Africa (A. Daudet, *Tartarin de Tarascon*, ch. 2).

R2: According to their content, allusions may be historical, mythological, literary, political, comminatory, erotic, or private. Ex (a literary allusion): 'I wore a baggy old woman's dress ... and a straggly grey wig. I must have looked like one of the witches in *Macbeth*' (Robertson Davies, *The Rebel Angels*, p. 287). The erotic allusion seems to be the easiest to decode since it can be achieved by mere lexical erasure*. Exx: 'He thinks of only *one thing*'; 'Everyone knows she likes *it* very much'; 'Are you getting *enough?*' See also euphemism*.

Other semantic contents remain available: all that is necessary for allusion is the presumption that the decoder will understand. Perception of the allusion remains fairly subjective, however. Some receivers see allusion everywhere, others nowhere. So allusion is a most useful device for the clandestine communication of ideas. Ex: Gilles Vigneault's song 'Mon pays, ce n'est pas un pays, c'est l'hiver' ('My country is not a country, it is winter'). Is this only an antithesis* emphasizing that meteorological conditions serve as the relevant definitional characteristic of Quebec? That was not the first view taken by the Canadian government, which began by banning the song for its subversive allusion to Quebec separatism.

So allusion may be hidden or transparent. Peter Hutchinson quotes, for example, an allusion made in Hardy's *Tess of the d'Urbervilles*: 'Alec d'Urberville whistles a line of "Take, O take these lips away," but, suggests the narrator, "the allusion was lost upon Tess." The narrator may be suggesting that Tess is simply ignorant of the source: the song sung by the Boy to Mariana in act IV of *Measure for Measure*' (*Games Authors Play*, p. 58).

R3: Allusion needs to be distinguished from implication*.

R4: Evocation, a narrative veiled by the discourse* (see discourse, R1) which includes it, is a kind of allusion, as is metalepsis*.

R5: Some allusions involve only sounds. See *agnominatio**, other def.; counter-pleonasm*, R4 and R5; alliteration*; echo* effect, R3; and tautogram*, R2. Others involve only graphic forms (see graphy*, R1, and allograph*, R2). If disseminated throughout a text, allusion becomes a kind of anagram*.

R6: Allusion favours periphrasis* and has a role in the definition of puns* (see pun, R1). It may increase concision (see epitheton*, R3). It may cause amusement (see wit*, R1), supply the vehicle for threats* (see threat, R1), serve to prolong sarcasm* (see sarcasm, R2), or make a silence more pregnant (see interruption*).

ALTERNATIVE The speaker asks the listener or reader to choose between two mutually exclusive possibilities.

Exx: 'Your money or your life'; 'It's one of two things, either *x*, or *y*.'

Ex:

Maid of Athens, ere we part,
Give, oh give me back my heart!
Or, since that has left my breast,
Keep it now, and take the rest!

Byron, 'Maid of Athens'

R1: The non-exclusiveness of the two terms produces the *false alternative* form (and/or), which means that the choice itself is of little importance. **Ex:** 'I will perform *x* and/or *y*.' This conjunctive disjunction brought the following blast from Fowler: 'The ugly device of writing *x* and/or *y* to save the trouble of writing *x or y or both of them* is common and convenient in some kinds of official, legal, and business documents, but should not be allowed outside them' (*Modern English Usage*, p. 29). Modern usage has not respected his preference. See also oxymoric* sentences, R1.

R2: Strictly speaking, the alternative is a kind of argument. The *OED* defines alternative as a 'proposition containing two statements, the acceptance of one of which involves the rejection of the other' and illustrates this definition with the following example: 'The brief, simple alternative of Mahomet, death or the Koran' (H. Rogers, *Ecl. Faith*, 1853, p. 422). The most rigorous form of alternative is the discursive *dilemma* in each of the inescapable hypotheses of which the consequences are identical. Miriam Joseph explains (p. 363) and illustrates the dilemma and its rebuttal as follows:

In its full form the dilemma consists of a compound hypothetical proposition as the major premise, a disjunctive proposition as the minor, and a simple or a disjunctive proposition as the conclusion ... E.g.: *Euathlus* gave some money in hand to his rhetorical doctor *Protagoras*, and promised to pay the rest when *Euathlus* should win the first cause he pleaded. *Protagoras*, when he later sued *Euathlus* for his money, said, if *Euathlus* overcomes me, then by his bargain and by its composition he must pay me the money; if he loses, then by course of law. Not so, responded *Euathlus*, if I lose, then according to the terms of my promise, you get nothing; if I win, then the judgement will discharge me from paying the debt.

Ex: 'JEAN VALJEAN: If I speak, I am condemned, / If I stay silent, I am damned' (V. Hugo, *Les Misérables*, musical version, lyrics by Herbert Kretzmer [1985]).

The dilemma is not always formally marked as such. **Ex:** 'We always die too soon, or too late' (J.-P. Sartre, *Huis-clos*, p. 89). Or, in other words, the absurd event has no 'right' moment. The dilemma's refutation consists in the demonstration of its inadequacy to cover all eventualities. When faced with it, we acknowledge its inevitability by refusing all other possibilities in favour of one of those posited.

R3: The alternative may be offered to the reader. In fact, Todorov (*The Fantastic: A Structural Approach to a Literary Genre*) sees the reader's hesitation between alternative interpretations as being the principal characteristic of fantastic narrative. Henry James's story 'The Turn of the Screw' offers an obvious example of the device: readers' hesitation cannot be resolved either by opting for a psychological explanation of 'supernatural' events or by accepting their supernatural nature (see Christine Brooke-Rose, *A Rhetoric of the Unreal*, pp. 128–229). See also double* reading and attenuation*, R1.

AMALGAM (SYNTAGMATIC) The expression of several syntagms*, or indeed several assertions*, in a single phonetic word. The transcription of this phenomenon depends on graphic elision and juxtaposition.

Ex: 'Abyssinia.' for 'I'll be seeing you.'

Ex: A conversation in French-Canadian *joual* between two (anonymous) fishermen: '– Lodjo. – Lopol. – Mansava? – Pommal. – Kostapri? – Coupparchaudes. – Sorddapa? – Ménépitoué?' This phonetic transcription becomes in a standard graphic representation: '– Hello, Joe. – Hello, Léopold. – Comment ça va? – Pas mal. – Qu'est-ce que tu as pris? – Un couple de perchaudes [Canadian perch]. – Quelle sorte d'appât [bait]? – Des menés [fry]. Et puis toi?'

In English, the word-game 'Knock, knock' invites the creation of syntagmatic amalgams:

Knock, knock.	Who's there?
Sarah.	Sarah who?
Sarah a doctor in the house.	

Knock, knock.	Who's there?
Howard.	Howard who?
Howard you like a punch on the nose?	

AMBIGUITY Only prior knowledge of the context saves many utterances from ambiguity. We can distinguish Empson's 'seven types' of *deliberate* ambiguity (see, for instance, diaphora*, antanaclasis*, approximation*, equivoque*, spoonerism*, syllepsis*) from *involuntary* types (see cacemphaton*, amphibol[og]y*); also those deriving from metanalysis* (see cacemphaton*, equivoque*, diaphora*, etc.); from ambiguities fostered by 'indefinite' grammatical morphemes or polyvalent constructions (see amphibol[og]y*, squint*, and negation*, R1 and R2); those exploiting polysemic words (e.g., diaphora* and antanaclasis*) or idiomatic syntagms; those deriving from what semioticians call 'double' isotopy* (i.e., from two coincident but colliding universes of discourse); and, finally, ambiguities present in the idea expressed.

1. **Ambiguities arising from polysemic words.** This type is more frequent than is generally believed, although it is most often perceived by someone who deliberately takes things the 'wrong' way or who pretends not to be familiar with the isotopy* or with the subject under discussion. Ex: In one of his conversations with Ophelia, Hamlet feigns madness by deliberately confusing the conventions regulating social intercourse with the sexual connotations which he virtually accuses her of reading into his first question:

HAMLET: Shall I lie in your lap?
OPHELIA: No, my lord.
HAM.: I mean, my head upon your lap?
OPH.: Aye, my lord.
HAM.: Do you think I meant country matters?
OPH.: I think nothing, my lord.
HAM.: That's a fair thought to lie between maids' legs.

Shakespeare, Hamlet, 3.2.119–26

Ambiguities which are unconscious or naïve connote the speaker. Malapropisms, for instance, such as 'He is the very pineapple of politeness' or 'as headstrong as an allegory on the banks of the Nile,' besides denoting a kind of solecism, remind the competent reader or listener of their first utterer, Mrs Malaprop in Sheridan's *The Rivals*. See also: 'I feel like Joan of Arc with the Dolphin' (G. Vidal, *Duluth*, p. 122).

Ambiguities may also be used as the basis for sarcastic remarks: 'Leurs poitrines reluiront des crachats que méritent leurs visages' ('On their chests will gleam gobs/gongs which should be on their faces') (L. Tailhade, *Imbéciles* ..., p. 222). By antiphrasis*, *crachat* (spit or saliva) has acquired the secondary meaning of 'medals'; the reference to the word's etymology makes for an easy pun*. See remotivation*, R1.

2. **Ambiguities deriving from polysemic syntagms.** Ex: 'No news is good news.' A syntagm is said to be *idiomatic* when it acquires a specific meaning which is more or less independent of that inhering in its constitutive elements. The latter may, in that case, promote a secondary meaning; hence the ambiguity. Exx: Both British and American English have several euphemistic idioms to refer to death: 'kick the bucket' (Brit.); 'cash in one's chips' (Amer.). A French example: 'Nos hommes d'Etat ont tout pour eux. (C'est pourquoi, d'ailleurs, il ne reste rien pour les autres)' (Henri Rochefort, *La Lanterne*, no. 1). Here, the syntagm's 'first' meaning, 'Our politicians have everything going for them,' is accompanied by a second, viz. that they hold all the available

advantages. This then makes possible the ironic consequence, which 'explains' why no one else has any advantages at all. See also antanaclasis*, R2.

Sometimes the idiomatic meaning is secondary. Ex (on a photographer's display window): 'Ici, on vous fera de beaux enfants' (Jean-Charles, *Les Perles du facteur*, p. 71). 'We'll make your children look handsome' replaces 'We'll help you to beget fine children.' This example borders on syllepsis*.

3. Ambiguities produced by inadequately defined lexemes. The ambiguity may arise from the utterance's global meaning: no answer is found to the questions posed by its main theme. So, in Paul Valéry's *Mon Faust*, for example, when Lust rereads what Faust dictated to her, she remains unsure about the meaning of the words 'What if my wife's conduct is normal' (P. Valéry, *Oeuvres*, 2:283). This is because Faust did not indicate the meaning attached in the specific context to the concept of 'normality' or 'custom.' The lexeme's meaning therefore remained *ill-defined*.

The *Proverbs of Solomon* skilfully exploit the possible ambiguity of the following verses: 'Answer a fool according to his folly, lest he be wise in his own conceit' (26.4–5). The phrase 'according to his folly' makes the two pieces of advice appear contrary to one another, whereas they are in fact identical: (1) 'Don't answer a fool foolishly, or you risk resembling him'; (2) 'Answer the fool by calling attention to his folly, so that he doesn't imagine that he is wise.' A receiver tries to complete such utterances by suggesting what their meaning 'might' be, and supporting these hypotheses with anything known about the speaker. **Ex:** 'Once again, doctor, I take the liberty of making a moral and a physical appeal to you' (Jean-Charles, *Les Perles du facteur*, p. 82). The lady expressing herself thus has no ulterior motive.

R1: Ambiguity caused by ignorance of the relevant isotopy* is rarer but remains possible for texts lacking a context. Ex: 'Conjunction is not adjunction.' Was this said by a grammarian, a logician, a mathematician, a biologist ...? In each case the syntagm would have a meaning specific to the discipline. Ex: 'Major purge strengthens Gorbachev.' Only knowledge of the context enables readers to decide whether the Soviet leader's physical or political 'health' is involved.

R2: Ambiguity is sometimes deliberately chosen as a rhetorical device, so as to promote 'agreement' by positing already existent unanimity among users of the code:

> In today's atmosphere of open records and ready lawsuits, a Lehigh University professor has come up with a system of doublespeak to pan job applicants without risk. Under the system, dubbed LIAR or Lexicon of Inconspicuously Ambiguous Recommendations by

economics professor Robert Thornton, managers and teachers can hide behind ambiguity when asked to write recommendation letters ... [For example]: To describe a lacklustre employee, he said, a manager would write: 'In my opinion, you will be very fortunate to get this person to work for you.' To describe a candidate who is woefully inept, he recommends saying: 'I most enthusiastically recommend this candidate with no qualifications whatsoever.' To describe a candidate who is so unproductive the position would be better left unfilled: 'I can assure you that no person would be better for the job.' To describe a candidate who is not worth further consideration: 'I would urge you to waste no time in making this candidate an offer of employment.'

Any of the statements might be taken as praise, Mr. Thornton said ... 'Whether perceived correctly or not by the candidate, the phrases are virtually litigation-proof,' he said, noting that court rulings have opened up employment records to workers. (Extract from a United Press release, 1987)

R3: *Semi-ambiguity* exists when the expression lacks clarity, not in meaning, but in syntactic point of view. The noun complement, with *of*, easily becomes ambiguous, for example, because the second noun may just as well be the subject as the object of the first noun's action. In the phrase 'the criticism of Frye,' the genitive is said to be *subjective* if Frye is doing the criticizing, *objective* if he is being criticized. In the expression 'Attila, the scourge of God,' 'scourge' may be understood as a natural cataclysm. The Romans, however, took the word in its literal sense as designating an implement for separating the wheat from the chaff, and thus as a means of punishing Christians who lived like pagans. See meaning*, 5.

AMPHIBOL(OG)Y (The figure is written both as 'amphiboly' and as 'amphibology.') Ambiguity deriving from grammar, morphology, or syntax. See Frye, Fowler, Lanham, Lausberg, and Littré.

Ex [a lady telegraphs her husband]: 'Missed the train. Will leave tomorrow, same time.' The husband's response: 'Well then, you'll miss it again' (Jean-Charles, *Les Perles du facteur*, p. 65).

Indefinite parts of speech can never be *too* precise. Ex: 'the French teachers' strike' – either the strike of French-speaking teachers or of teachers of French. Here's an extract from a letter addressed to Social Security: 'J'ai été malade au lit *avec* le docteur pendant une semaine' (Jean-Charles, *Les Perles du facteur*, p. 199). Equivalent ambiguity would result in English from the use of the preposition *under*. 'Dangling' participles produce syntactic ambiguity because they may apply to any mentioned referent. George Puttenham, the Renaissance poetician, discussed amphibol(og)y as follows: ' ''I sat by my lady soundly sleeping / My mistress lay by me bitterly weeping." No man can tell by this, whether the mistress or the man, slept or wept: these doubtful speeches were used much in the old times ... by the Oracles of Delphos ... and in effect all our old British and Saxon prophesies be of the same sort' (quoted by Joseph, p. 301). An obvious example, from *Macbeth*, concerns the prophecy affirming Macbeth's unique vulnerability to an adversary 'not of woman born' (5.5.42).

The syntactic arrangement of sentences may also create ambiguity. Ex [on a sign near a small village school]: 'Attention! School! Don't run over the children. Wait for the teacher' (Jean-Charles, *Les Perles du facteur*, p. 71).

R1: Amphibol(og)y is a defect, but like all types of ambiguity* it has its uses, either as a source of evocative effect (it demonstrates a character's verbal and mental incompetence) or of word-play*, which makes it similar to semantic syllepsis*. Ex: 'Posters mean business.' In *A Midsummer Night's Dream* (5.1.10), Quince, by his clumsy syntax, makes of his prologue a *captatio malevolentiae*, rather than the opposite which he intended:

> If we offend, it is with our good will,
>
> ...
> We do not come, as minding to content you,
> Our true intent is. All for your delight,
> We are not here. That you should here repent you,
> The actors are at hand: and by their show,
> You shall know all, that you are like to know.

R2: Usually, such errors are easily corrected, as Quince's auditors comment sarcastically: 'This fellow doth not stand upon points ... he knows not the stop ... a sound, but not in government ... His speech was like a tangled chain nothing impaired, but all disordered.' Correction consists here in syntactical rearrangement, as the comments imply.

R3: See also dissociation*, R9.

AMPLIFICATION The grandiloquent development of ideas so as to make them more richly ornamented, broader in scope, or more forceful.

Ex: 'To rejoice, to be joyful, to be filled with joy, to feel one's heart burst, spill over with joy. Oh how joyous, how tender to prefer such internal, undisciplined joy to a life ordered by an external, unchanging necessity ...' See accumulation*, R1. Roget's *Thesaurus of English Words and Phrases* clearly has particular value for the amplification of ideas.

Synonyms: expansion, extension

Antonyms: précis, contraction, summary

Other definitions: Classical rhetoricians applied the term to the treatment of the whole discourse. Amplification to them implied the art of finding the best arguments and of exploiting them in accordance with a logical and persuasive plan*, preferably based on their mounting intensity. Such a process of reasoning* demanded description, comparison, examples, a discussion of motives, pathetic elements, reminiscences, quotations elicited from prominent citizens or from poets, explanation, and justification. In short, discursive amplification would employ an accumulation* of arguments, of facts, or of sentences or synonyms. **Ex:** 'CICERO: It is a sin to bind a Roman citizen, a crime to scourge him, little short of the most unnatural murder to put him to death; what then shall I call his crucifixion?' (quoted by Quintilian, *Institutes of Oratory*, 8.4.4.). When such *oratorical amplification* is felt to go 'too' far, it is judged 'overstated,' 'pathetic,' 'superfluous,' 'verbose,' 'diffuse,' 'mere speechifying,' in short the 'empty rhetoric' of which we conventionally accuse those with whom we disagree. See verbiage* and grandiloquence*.

R1: Amplification may serve to emphasize; it may take the form of concretization* (see concretization, R1), of example (see reasoning*, R2), of enumeration*, *gradatio**, paraphrase*, apologue*, apostrophe*, or cliché*. See also rhythm* (of the action).

R2: The opposite of amplification is *condensation* (*OED*; Greimas, *Sémantique structurale*, p. 74), by means of which the speaker strives to say everything in a few words (see recapitulation*), or even in a single term (denomination*).

R3: Allied to amplification is the refusal, whether for reasons deriving from the constraints imposed by versification or for rhetorical effect, to use pronouns as a means of avoiding the repetition of a lexeme:

> Upon the king! let us our lives, our souls,
> Our debts, our careful wives,
> Our children and our sins lay on the king.
> Shakespeare, Henry V, 5.4.2–4

Occasionally, too, out of a taste for fine-sounding Christian names: 'Catherine tried at once to leave Michel so that no one should see them together. Michel tried to stop Catherine' (A. Hébert, *Les Chambres de bois*, p. 28).

ANACHRONISM A mistake* in dating.

The mistake may be read as either accidental (the clock in *Julius Caesar*) or deliberate as in the following example: 'As Napoleon and

Beryl flee the burning city in his carriage, two crazed Russian priests – could one of them be Rasputin? – attack the carriage with flaming torches' (Gore Vidal, *Duluth*, pp. 253–4). Cuddon contends (p. 35) that Shakespeare's clock is 'used deliberately to distance and to underline a universal verisimilitude and timelessness,' much as do versions of the plays in modern dress. Such hermeneutical decisions are best left to the individual reader. In Robertson Davies's *What's Bred in the Bone*, the anachronistic representation of a monkey in a 'medieval' painting serves as a plot-device enabling the hero to demonstrate his competence as authenticator and art historian.

R1: Genette has shown that in Proust's *A la recherche du temps perdu* spatial and thematic parallels contrary to the chronological order of events incline the narrative towards a-temporality or a-chrony (see *Narrative Discourse*, ch. 1).

This also happens in surrealistic rhetoric. Ex: 'My nose bleeds as much as did Holofernes' head when Napoleon cut it off' (Réjean Ducharme, *L'Océantume*, p. 146). In this example, we have a substitution* of Napoleon for Judith rather than an anachronism. We may therefore define *achrony* as one of the factors used to produce a perspective which ignores temporality. The *Dictionnaire des media* also proposes the term *uchrony* for temporality which goes beyond the usual chronological frame of reference (notably in science fiction).

R2: One literary genre which may seem somewhat obsolescent is the dialogue of the illustrious dead. This consists in a dramatization (see hypotyposis*) of conversations between personages from the past; such conversations are represented as taking place in our present and in that mythic place where all the dead 'meet' each other. Because of their structuring anachronistic device, such dialogues may bring together, for instance, the Holy Roman Emperor, Charles V, and Stalin. They may just as well be termed parachronic, or achronic, since by placing them outside time, their authors confer upon them a certain abstract quality. This enables them to use the dialogues as vehicles for the judgments they plan to make more or less explicitly on the characters introduced or upon their authors' own times. (The American TV interviewer Steve Allen recently hosted a version of such dramatized dialogues between the illustrious dead on American Public TV called 'Meeting of Minds,' and Patrick Watson 'interviewed' various Canadian historical personages on the CBC TV program 'For the Record.')

R3: See dissociation*, R2.

ANACOLUTHON A breakdown in the syntactic construction of a sentence. See Cuddon, Fowler, Marouzeau, Preminger, and Robert.

Exx: 'Leaving for the office, Smith's car would not start'; 'Or what man is there of you, whom if his son ask bread, will he give him a stone?' (Matt. 7:9).

Other definitions: 1. Fowler (p. 393) speaks of *nominativus pendens*, 'a form of anacoluthon in which a sentence is begun with what appears to be the subject, but before the verb is reached something else is substituted in word or in thought, and the supposed subject is left in the air ... Cf., in Shakespeare, "They who brought me in my master's hate, I live to look upon their tragedy" (*Richard III*, 3.2.57).'
2. Lausberg (p. 459) defines anacoluthon as imbalance or asymmetry, rather than as incoherence* or breakdown in sentence-structure. Viewed rhetorically, anacoluthon occurs in a period* or complete sentence when a single part of either protasis or apodosis is missing. (Strictly speaking, these latter terms, in English at least, designate respectively the clause expressing the condition and the main clause of a conditional sentence; see *OED*. However, modern linguists also use them in a more general way to designate subordinate and main clauses of sentences.)

R1: Lausberg's definition makes anacoluthon a figure of style rather than a (sometimes expressive) stylistic weakness. As an error in style it is not always obvious. Ex: 'He couldn't go, how could he?' Anacoluthon is only frequent in spoken language. A speaker begins a sentence in a way implying a certain logical resolution and then ends it differently. A writer would begin the sentence again, unless its function were to illustrate confusion of mind or spontaneity of reporting. Both functions are characteristic of interior monologue, and to the extent that Molly Bloom's monologue* consists of a single unpunctuated sentence, it contains hundreds of examples of anacoluthon, of which the following is taken at random: '... I suppose she was pious because no man would look at her twice I hope Ill never be like her a wonder she didnt want us to cover our faces but she was a welleducated woman certainly and her gabby talk ...' (Joyce, *Ulysses*, p. 608). See restart*, R1.

R2: When the sentence is recast as it proceeds, the result is *anapodoton*. This is a kind of anacoluthon, such as occurs when an antecedent sentence which remained in suspense is taken up again in a new, asymmetrical form to serve as the beginning of a consequent sentence. Ex: 'If you declare yourself incompetent to judge, as is your right, – *if that's your attitude*, I will act accordingly' (Marouzeau). See restart*, R1.

R3: When the sentence is abandoned before the end, the phenomenon is called *anantapodoton* or *particula pendens*. Exx: 'If you only knew ...'; 'That is *so* funny ...' Morier defines anantapodoton as a 'kind of anacoluthon in which, of two correlative elements presenting an alternative (*some ... others ...*, for example), only the first is expressed.' Ex:

'Sometimes he expressed his enthusiasm at the idea of the trip; *and then what did he stand to gain far from his homeland and family?*' (The parallel expression, 'sometimes he was despondent at ...,' or its equivalent, has been abandoned in favour of a rendering in free indirect style.)

R4: Certain examples of anacoluthon derive from the combination of two incompatible elements. The French translator of *War and Peace* produced the following example: 'Les hommes de l'Occident étaient en marche vers ceux de l'Orient afin de s'entretuer' (for 'et ceux de l'Orient étaient en marche les uns vers les autres'). This anacoluthon is 'corrected' by over-simplification in the English version as follows: 'The people of the West moved eastwards to slay their fellow men' (Tolstoy, *War and Peace*, trans. Rosemary Edmonds, 2:718).

ANADIPLOSIS Repetition* of the last word of one sentence, or line of poetry, as a means of (sometimes emphatic) liaison. See Lanham, Lausberg, Littré, Morier, and Preminger.

Ex:

For I have loved long, I crave reward.
Reward me not unkindly: think on kindness,
Kindness becometh those of high regard.
Regard with clemency a poor man's blindness.

Bartholomew Griffin, *Fidessa*, XVI

R1: Preminger distinguishes between *emphatic* and merely *linking* anadiplosis. Compare the following examples: 'Both princes and population groaned *in vain; in vain* did the King's brother, *in vain* did the King himself clasp Madame to his bosom' (Bossuet, *Oraison funèbre de la duchesse d'Orléans*); 'To me, it's *a tragedy. A tragedy*, everyone knows what that is. It leaves you defenceless' (A. Camus, *L'Etranger*, p. 136). See grandiloquence*, R1.

R2: In a conversation, anadiplosis serves (by lexical repetition*) to link the replies together. Ex: To Stephen, who has described the soul as a 'simple substance,' Bloom replies: 'Simple? I shouldn't think that is the proper word' (Joyce, *Ulysses*, p. 518).

R3: Anadiplosis slips imperceptibly into reduplication*. Ex: 'Universal suffrage rules like a tyrant and like a tyrant with dirty hands' (Stendhal, *Lucien Leuwen*, ch. 65).

R4: Anadiplosis is the natural device for linking together relatively extensive discursive units, such as paragraphs. Ex:

'Help yourselves from the Platter of Plenty.'
The Platter of Plenty was a joke ... (Robertson Davies, *The Lyre of Orpheus*, p. 5)

For examples formed by even larger textual units (chapters, for example), see epanalepsis*, R4.

R5: A series of anadiploses forms a concatenation*.

ANAGRAM A word or words obtained from the transposition of the letters forming another word or words. See Beckson and Ganz, Frye, and Robert.

Exx: violence / nice love; Evangelists / Evil's agents

Exx: *chien/niche; Carmen Tessier / être sans merci* (J. Lacroix, *L'Anagram-mite*). The following 'poem' uses the same nine-letter group (*aegimnrst*) in four different anagrammatic configurations to recount the preparations being made for the departure of the *Mayflower* in 1620:

> xxxxxxxxx and repainting and refitting ...
> They patched the little vessel with the notion
> Of xxxxxxxxx oppression, and the ocean.
> When she was shipshaped, holystoned and gleaming,
> Aboard the pilgrim xxxxxxxxx came xxxxxxxxx.

Willard R. Espy, The Game of Words, p. 41

Solution: Remasting, mastering, emigrants, streaming

Synonyms: A 'metagram' is 'a kind of puzzle turning on the alteration of a word by removing some of its letters and substituting others' (*OED*). Littré, however, in his *Dictionnaire de la langue française*, taking his inspiration from the Greek, gives the term a more general meaning, synonymous with metaplasm*.

R1: Anagrams serve above all to create pseudonyms. **Exx:** Alcofribas Nasier, for François Rabelais; Alcuinus, for Calvin(us). These are perfect anagrams, which use the same letters as are found in the original word. The first letter of *Alcofribas Nasier* is the 3rd of *François Rabelais*. Then come in order the 13th, 5th, 6th, 1st, 2nd, 7th, 11th, 10th, 8th, 4th, 14th, 16th, 15th, 12th, and 9th letters of the patronym.

If the anagram reverses, without scrambling, the order of letters, the result is a palindrome*, which may be either a word in common use or an invented word.

R2: The anagram may also combine with a paragram*. **Ex:** Ivirnig, the hero of *Les Oranges sont vertes*, is an (approximate) double of the author, his name being drawn from *Gauvreau* through consonantal anagram and vocalic paragram (the *o* sound becomes an *i*).

R3: Antimetathesis* is an anagram (often only a very partial one) spread out along the syntagmatic axis.

R4: According to Saussure, the anagram, by disseminating letters or sounds throughout the text 'outside of the temporal order of its elements' (J. Starobinski, *Les Anagrammes de F. de Saussure*, p. 255), causes words to be read 'into' the words printed and so allows for different, clandestine, 'hypogrammatic' readings. Certain critics like J. Kristeva and H. Meschonnic see in the anagrammatic view of literature a way of exposing the 'unconscious' content of a poetic work. In *Gulliver's Travels* (1726), however, Jonathan Swift indicated clearly the dangers to the producer and receiver of such arbitrary 'anagrammatic readings' (random censure and more or less implausible allegorical readings respectively):

> In the kingdom of Tribnia [an anagram of 'Britain'] ... plots were discovered by 'the anagrammatic method' – by transposing the letters of the alphabet in any suspected paper, they can lay open the deepest designs of a discontented party. So, for example, if I should say, in a letter to a friend, 'Our brother Tom has just got the piles,' a skilful decipherer would discover that the same letters which compose that sentence, may be analysed into the following words, 'Resist, – a plot is brought home, the tour.' ('A Voyage to Laputa,' ch. 6)

See paragram*, R4. If done intentionally, the device is a graphic allusion* (see allusion, R5) or a device of cryptography* (see cryptography, R2). Anagrams are a source of literary* games. Ex: Lewis Carroll devised the anagrams 'Flit on, cheering angel,' from 'Florence Nightingale,' and 'Wilt tear down all images?' from 'William Ewart Gladstone' (Augarde, pp. 75–6). The derivation of a seemingly apt semantic content from the rearranged elements forming proper names is a form of cryptography*.

ANAMNESIS Originally a form of Hebraic religious thought; if used rhetorically, reminiscences of actual events replace the expression of an idea or of a feeling.

Ex: 'To him who divided the Red Sea in sunder ... And made Israel pass through the midst of it ...' (Psalm 136: 13–14)

Synonym: remembrance

R1: Anamnesis belongs in the ancient literary genre of *eucharistia;* see celebration*, R4.

R2: Flashbacks* in narrative* present remembered events as re-experienced in the present by character and reader together. Such flashbacks frequently serve as a means of 'explaining' a character's subsequent actions. In Camus's *L'Etranger*, for instance, Meursault's narrative recapitulation of events leading to the death of his victim serves to discredit the too simple solution, namely his guilt. His account of the act itself reveals that he acted involuntarily, whereas his account of his trial indicts the legal system which condemned him to death.

ANAPHORA The repetition* of the same first word in successive phrases, clauses, or sentences. See Cuddon, Frye, Girard, Lanham, Morier, and Preminger.

Ex:

One passed in a fever,
One was burned in a mine,
One was killed in a brawl,
One died in jail,
One fell from a bridge

Edgar Lee Masters, 'The Hill'

Ex: 'Fog everywhere. Fog up the river, where it flows among green aits and meadows; fog down the river, where it rolls defiled among the tiers of shipping ... Fog on the Essex Marshes, fog on the Kentish heights' (Dickens, *Bleak House*, ch. 1).

Other definition: For *anaphoric extension* of the definite article, see explanation*, R4.

Synonym: epanaphora (Frye, Lanham, Morier, Preminger). See also epanalepsis*, other def., 2.

R1: Anaphora is a 'technique of coordination and replacement allowing for, and even emphasizing, juxtaposition' (G. Antoine, *La Coordination*, p. 1291). It is a natural means, therefore, of creating accumulations* of analogical, antithetical, or heterogeneous elements. The following example combined anaphora with epiphora* to produce symploce*:

Where the city of the faithfullest friends stands,
Where the city of the cleanliness of the sexes stands,
Where the city of the healthiest fathers stands,
Where the city of the best-bodied mothers stands

W. Whitman, 'Song of the Broad Axe'

The following is a combination of anaphora with antithesis*:

For everything there is a season, and a time for every matter under heaven
a time to be born and a time to die;
a time to plant, and a time to pluck up what is planted;
a time to kill, and a time to heal;
a time to break down, and a time to build up;
a time to weep, and a time to laugh;
a time to mourn, and a time to dance;

...
a time to seek, and a time to lose;
a time to keep, and a time to cast away;
...
a time to love, and a time to hate;
a time for war, and a time for peace.

Eccles. 3:1–9

These kinds of anaphora, which vary the lexemes within each repeated unit, are examples of reprise*, and so produce substitutive collages*.

R2: As a figure, anaphora, like epiphora* and symploce*, belongs to the 'sublime' style (see grandiloquence*, R1). Anaphoric lexemes form motifs*. Anaphora itself contributes to the production of parallelisms* (see parallelism, R3) and refrains* (see refrain, R2).

ANASTROPHE Reversal of the usual order of terms in the same group. See Frye, Lanham, Lausberg, and Preminger.

Exx: *muros intra* instead of *intra muros*; 'at speed incredible.' Such reversals may bring a change in meaning: 'the person responsible' as opposed to, for example, 'a responsible person.'

Ex:

Time present and time past
Are both perhaps present in time future,
And time future contained in time past.

T.S. Eliot, 'Burnt Norton,' in Four Quartets

Synonym: hyperbaton* (see hyperbaton, R1)

R1: Anastrophe as a variety of inversion* is distinguished, strictly speaking, by the fact that the latter affects complete syntagms*. Anastrophe merely reverses the order of words within a syntagm. **Exx:** 'Backward run the sentences, till reels the mind' (from a parody of *Time* magazine); 'Day one midday towards' [i.e., 'one day towards midday'] (R. Queneau, *Exercises in Style*, p. 133); 'Yet I'll not shed her blood; / Nor scar that whiter skin of hers than snow' (Shakespeare, *Othello*, 5.2.3–4).

R2: Anastrophe in English seems less strictly controlled than in French. Anastrophe is only possible in French in certain fixed expressions or with qualifiers (adjectives or adverbs). **Exx:** 'sans lien aucun'; 'Qui plus est ...'; 'plus encore/encore plus'; 'pas même/même pas.' Usage limits even more strictly the possibilities of anastrophe of noun and adjective (see A. Blinkenberg, *L'Ordre des mots en français moderne*).
  In English, on the other hand, the upsetting for rhetorical effect of such normal word order as preposition before noun, adjective before

noun, or object after verb occurs without the perpetrator of such prose passages being immediately accused of 'poetic' tendencies. The relative frequency of such anastrophes as 'Came the dawn' or 'to the manner born' is one of the traits distinguishing anglophone from francophone syntax. In the following example, taken from Valéry Larbaud's French translation of Joyce's *Ulysses*, we can see that the translator omitted the English anastrophe: 'Notre âme blessée de la honte du péché se cramponne à nous toujours plus, *femme cramponnée à son amant*, plus, toujours' (p. 48). The original has: 'Our souls, shamewounded by our sins, cling to us yet more, *a woman to her lover clinging*, the more the more' (p. 40).

ANGLICISM A peregrinism* taken from English.

Ex: 'J'ai commencé d'un petit air *matter of fact* et naturel pour ne pas les effaroucher [startle]' (N. Sarraute, *Portrait d'un inconnu*, p. 17).

Anglicisms include French words deriving from English (like *redingote*, from *riding-coat*), those which have only recently become part of current French usage (like *bifteck*, from *beefsteak*), and all those which, because of pressures placed on modern living by technology ('Micro Channel,' 'IBM') and the media ('le *Look*'), seek to penetrate the French language. See Etiemble, *Parlez-vous franglais?*; G. Colpron, *Les Anglicismes au Québec*. M. Kington's *Let's Parler Franglais* and *Let's Parler Franglais Again* (1981, 1982) parody naïve or ignorant combinations of bilingual 'faux-amis' (see gallicism*) or false cognates. Pierre Daninos, in *Les Carnets du Major Thompson*, tells the story of a cultural schizophrenic who strives to find exact equivalents for English phenomena in French and vice versa. His failure to do so and the compensations he discovers in his passage between two sets of equally ethnocentric presuppositions supply the novel's peripeteia.

R1: Foreign elements penetrate more or less completely. *Pipeline*, pronounced in French 'peep leen,' has merely lost its English sound, and the official translation (*oléoduc*) has little currency. Some anglicisms only involve syntax (l'actuel [present] gouvernement' for 'le gouvernement actuel'). Lexically, a *borrowing* – 'living-room,' for instance – differs from a *calque*, like *salle de séjour*, which is more insidious. (See Martinet, *La Linguistique: guide alphabétique*, p. 309). A complete translation of an English term into French needs a root and a French suffix (as in *vivoir*; i.e., *vivre* [to live, living] + *oir*, a regular French ending as in *parloir* [parlour], and so *vivoir*, 'living-room'). However, special meanings given to already existing French words may also replace anglicisms: 'convivial' has thus replaced 'user friendly.'

When a word exists in both languages but with different meanings, the result is a semantic anglicism. Ex: 'Les architectes ont leur *convention* annuelle' (for their 'congrès annuel'); 'convention' in French means

Announcement

'agreement' or 'treaty.' Graphic anglicisms: *réalizer*, *abbr*éviation.

R2: All that is necessary to turn an anglicism into a literary device is that it be expressive. Ex: *La Guerre, yes Sir!* (R. Carrier). The expression *yes Sir*, which denotes submission, recalls that French Canadians fought the last war under constraint from English Canada. An anglicism's characteristic connotation is not necessarily evocative, but may simply be part of the word itself. Ex: *'Boys* du sévère.' These are the first words of André Breton's *L'Amour fou*: they avoid both the religious connotations of the words *ange* (angel) and those associated with the too commonplace *garçon* or *serveur* (waiter). The term refers, because of its colonial connotation, to young male domestic servants and, translated, the expression becomes: '(The) servants of strictness.'

R3: Anglicisms, like gallicisms*, are sometimes a matter of pure (or parodic) snobbery. Ex: 'Les membres de ce *bar* ... passent leur temps à boire du *stout*, du *porter* et de l'*Old Tom gin*, en mangeant des *mutton-chops* avec des *pickles*' (A. Jarry, *La Chandelle verte*, p. 374). The following example parodies 'franglais'/'Frenglish':

> *Bonjour. Hrumph. OK, stand facile. Bon. Vous savez chaque jour 6,000,000 dolphins sont exterminés. Moi, je trouve cela un très mauvais show. Mais au Fund de la Wildlife du Monde il y a un effort tremendeux pour combattre ce mayhem. Donc, envoyez vos cheques marqués 'Sauvez le Dauphin.' Immédiatement. A propos, savez-vous que le mot dauphin signifie 1) un dolphin 2) le fils de la monarque? Donc, Charles, Prince de Wales, est un dolphin ...* (M. Kington, *Let's Parler Franglais Again*, p. 5)

ANNOUNCEMENT Prior (private or public) communication of a subsequent event.

Ex: 'To the Red-Headed League: "On account of the bequest of the late Ezekiah Hopkins, of Lebanon, Pennsylvania, U.S.A., there is now another vacancy open which entitles a member of the League to a salary of 4 pounds a week for purely nominal services. All red-headed men who are sound in body and mind, and above the age of twenty-one years, are eligible"' (Conan Doyle, *The Complete Sherlock Holmes*, 1:178).

Analogous terms: declaration, notice, message, proclamation (see discourse*). The Annunciation is the term specific to the announcement made to Mary that the son conceived 'in [her] womb ... shall be called the Son of the Highest' (Luke 1:31–2).

R1: In a narrative*, an announcement serves as an anticipation (see flash-forward*, R3), that is, as a device of proleptic repetition* (see repetition, R5). In a discourse, it is called a *division* (into kinds or classes; see plan*) and marks a transition* (see transition, R1). On the radio, it may take the form of a station identification ('This is CFCF'; see notation*, R1). The announcement of government policy is often made implicitly. Ex: see Roosevelt's declaration of devaluation quoted under implication*.

R2: Classified advertisements (newspaper ads, items on notice boards, etc.) are announcements offering specific individual transactions. Ex: see ellipsis*, R1.

R3: An announcement may fulfil a performative function by concretizing an event which is already generally expected or is a matter of common knowledge. See prophecy*, R1.

R4: In the evangelical announcement, or kerygma, the sender of the message is unknown because (He?) is transcendent and invisible. See prophecy*, R3.

ANTANACLASIS A diaphora* which occurs in a dialogue*, or indeed in an advocate's speech (see Lausberg). The speaker takes up the words of the interlocutor, or of the adversary, and changes their meaning to the speaker's own advantage. See Frye and Joseph.

Exx: 'Proculeius reproached his son with *waiting for* [i.e., 'anticipating'] his death, and the latter replied that he was not *waiting for* it. Well then, replied the father, in any case, please *wait*' (Quintilian, *Institutes of Oratory*, 9.3.68–73); 'I [i.e., Jim Hacker] smiled sympathetically. "So that's agreed. A quiet word. Reach a gentleman's agreement." Humphrey scowled. "But she's not a gentleman. She's not even a lady!"' (J. Lynn and A. Jay, *Yes Prime Minister*, 2:136).

Lanham calls antanaclasis a 'homonymic pun*.' Verest and Vuillaume (p. 16) compare the term to the logical fallacy called *ignoratio elenchi* ('irrelevant conclusion' [Lanham]), which shows that they see it as a device used in dialogue*. Ex: ' "Valentulya, you're always clicking your spoon on your glass after taps and I'm sick of it." "How do you expect me to dissolve the sugar?" "Silently" ' (A. Solzhenitsyn, *The First Circle*, pp. 72–3). Compare the old riddle*: 'How do porcupines make love? Carefully.'

Other definitions: 1. diaphora* (Dumarsais, p. 243; Fontanier, pp. 347–9; Morier, Elkhadem, *The York Dictionary of Literary Terms*). Antanaclasis is a specific form of diaphora.
2. Preminger, in the entries on anadiplosis* and pun*, describes antanaclasis as a form of punning repetition*.

Analogous terms: 1. Anaclasis (repetition of a word spoken by someone else 'to stress its meaning or importance' [Elkhadem, p. 8]). Ex:

Antanaclasis

HAMLET: How came he mad?
FIRST CLOWN: Very strangely, they say.
HAMLET: How 'strangely'?

Shakespeare, *Hamlet*, 5.1.171–3

Ex: '[Maimas]: "Don't expect me to make an omelette without breaking eggs." [Zadkiel]: "I was thinking about breaking hearts" ' (Robertson Davies, *What's Bred in the Bone*, p. 123).
2. For Fontanier (pp. 347–8), antanaclasis is a form of paronomasia* 'in which the form and sounds are exactly the same in words whose meaning is different and which are brought together.' The poet Guillaume Colletet (1598–1659), having received a gratuity from Cardinal Richelieu in thanks for an obsequious short poem, expressed his gratitude in these terms: 'Armand, qui pour six vers m'as donné six cents livres / Que ne puis-je à ce prix te vendre tous mes livres' ('Armand, who for six verses gave me six hundred francs, why can't I sell you all my books at the same rate?'). As the example shows ('livres' means both 'francs' and 'books'), we have homonymy* but not repetition of the same meaning.

R1: When, in replying, one takes up another's words, even in the absence of diaphora*, there occurs what Lausberg (p. 939) calls *reflexio*, 'the act of a reflecting mind.' Antanaclasis, then, is a devious form of such reflection, which plays on ambiguity*, and usually has recourse to puns*. There is therefore a kind of *coq-à-l'âne** (see *coq-à-l'âne*, R2) and also of false retortion*.

R2: The dialogue* may only be implied. **Ex:** 'Je l'sais qu'tu veux mon bien, mais tu l'auras pas, mon sacripant' ('I know you desire my *bien*, but you won't get it, you scoundrel'). In this monologue*, which by implication* is 'addressed to' a politician, a farmer takes up the word *bien* used by the politician to mean the 'welfare' of the constituents, and turns it back against him by declaring that he won't get the farmer's 'wealth' (second meaning*). The reflection obviously concerns the difference existing, in the speaker's opinion, between the politician's spoken and unspoken motivation.

R3: If based only on homophony, antanaclasis becomes a game. **Ex:** 'PROTÉE: "Ah, je voudrais *la voir* [la belle Hélène]." BRINDOSIER: "Vous voudriez *l'avoir*?" ' (P. Claudel, *Protée*, in *Théâtre*, 2:240). The play is on 'seeing' and 'possessing.' An English equivalent occurs in a Monty Python sketch: 'FIRST SPEAKER: "x knew his mother." SECOND SPEAKER: "And knew her bloody well." '

R4: The modalizing terms of antanaclasis include: just(ly), particularly, (e)specially, principally (see enunciation*, R3, and counter-litotes*, R2).

R5: Antanaclasis of the referent is an argumentative evasion or 'cop-out' (see argument*, R2). Ex: " 'Do you still like books?" he asked ... I said that books burned more quickly than coal, but that for want of any other fuel, I still used them' (G. Bessette, *Le Libraire*, p. 23).

ANTEPIPHORA The repetition* of the same expression or of the same line at the beginning and end of a period* or stanza*. See Morier.

Ex:

> To-day we have naming of parts. Yesterday,
> We had daily cleaning. And to-morrow morning,
> We shall have what to do after firing. But to-day,
> To-day we have naming of parts. Japonica
> Glistens like coral in all of the neighbouring gardens,
> And to-day we have naming of parts.
> Henry Reed, 'Naming of Parts,' in *A Map of Verona and Other Poems*

Ex:

> Adorable witch, do you love the damned?
> Say, do you know the unforgivable sin?
> Do you know poisonous remorse,
> Which makes our hearts its target?
> Adorable witch, do you love the damned?
> Ch. Baudelaire, 'L'Irréparable,' in *Les Fleurs du mal*

R1: Antepiphora is an intermediate form of symploce* and of inclusion* since it defines the limits of a paragraph or stanza, rather than of a phrase or a whole work.

ANTICLIMAX A device consisting of a magnificent announcement* which leads to almost nothing. The text takes a sharp about-turn and fizzles out.

Exx: 'MRS. MARTIN: "Oh well, today I witnessed something extraordinary. Something really incredible ... In the street, near a café, I saw a man, properly dressed, about fifty years old, or not even that, who ... you'll say that I'm making it up ... He was tying his shoelace which had come undone" ' (E. Ionesco, *The Bald Soprano*, in *Four Plays*, pp. 21– 2); 'The evening of the surrender of Breda, Roger de la Tour de Babel took his stick and went out' (R. Ducharme, *Le Nez qui voque*, p. 9).

R1: Anticlimax is a kind of *surprise* which consists in preparing the reader for something other than what happens.

R2: The device plays on the linear nature of language (i.e., on its syntagmatic axis), which prevents the reader from knowing in advance what will 'happen next.' The text contrives to make one expect marvels and then becomes all the more astonishing when it deflates expectation. Bringing together opposite extremes is one type of surrealist image* (see image, R1).

R3: Various figures, notably *gradatio**, combine with anticlimax to create disappointment and so become 'deceptive' (see bathos*; punch* line, R2; extravagant* comparison, R4). Anticlimactic conundrums (see riddle*) are easily composed. Ex: 'Know what they do with banana skins in China? They throw them away.' The truism* used as an emphatic comparison* also produces surrealistic anticlimax. Ex: 'Two pillars ... were to be seen in the valley, taller than two pins. Indeed, they were two enormous towers' (Lautréamont, *Les Chants de Maldoror*, 4).

R4: Anticlimax has its own intonation*.

ANTILOGY A contradiction in terms or ideas. See *OED* and Robert.

Exx: 'A twosided triangle, a virtuous tyrant' (*OED*); 'squaring the circle'; 'almost quite ready'; 'Even if it's true, it's false' (H. Michaux, *Tranches de savoir*, in *L'Espace du dedans*, p. 339); 'On the stroke of five thirty six o'clock' (R. Queneau, *Pierrot mon ami*, p. 32)

Antonym: tautology*

R1: Antilogy, which is related to sophistry* and to paralogism*, is in fact a defect in reasoning* (see reasoning, R1). The defect is pushed so far that not only do the ideas involved seem mutually contradictory, but the meaning of the words themselves also prevents any possibility of conciliation.

R2: Antilogy should not be confused with oxymoric* sentences in which the two extremes, when placed in parallel, remain compatible each in its separate sphere. Antilogy resembles oxymoron*, in which a single meaning may emerge, as, for example, in expressions such as 'jumbo shrimp,' 'open secret,' etc.

R3: Antilogy belongs in the realm of paradox*, since the incompatibility existing between its terms cannot but offend against common sense. If no intelligibility remains, antilogy constitutes a nonsense*.

R4: A quite frequent figure used by modern theorists is *false antilogy*, a formal opposition resolved by some deeper meaning. Ex: 'the signifier demands another place ... in order that the word which it supports may lie, that is, present itself as the Truth' (J. Lacan, *Ecrits*, p. 807).

ANTIMETABOLE A mutual exchange between two sentences or clauses of their constituent words in such a way that each word occurs in the place and with the relationships possessed by the other. See Morier, Preminger, and *OED*: 'A figure in which the same words or ideas are repeated in inverse order.'

Exx: 'Love's fire heats water, water cools not love' (Shakespeare, sonnet 154); 'Ask not what your country can do for you, ask what you can do for your country' (J.F. Kennedy, inaugural address); 'Women are changing the universities and the universities are changing women' (Germaine Greer, *TLS*, 3–8 June 1988, p. 629); 'The gambling known as business looks with austere disfavor on the business known as gambling' (A. Bierce, quoted in Frank S. Pepper, *Twentieth-Century Quotations*, p. 158).

Synonyms: antimetalepsis (Lausberg); antimetathesis* ('inversion of the members of an antithesis*' [*OED*, Littré]); *reversio* (Fontanier, pp. 381–2, Lanham); *commutatio*. When the propositions have opposite meanings, Lanham's definition, given below, like that of Group MU (*A General Rhetoric*, p. 125), indicates some of the taxonomical problems involved in the definition of this figure which is close to so many others:

> Antimetabole; chiasmus*; *commutatio*; *permutatio*; counterchange. In English inverting the order of repeated words to sharpen their sense or to contrast the ideas they convey or both (AB:BA); chiasmus and *commutatio* sometimes imply a more precise balance and reversal, antimetabole a looser, but they are virtual synonyms: 'I pretty and my saying apt? or I apt, and my saying pretty?' (*Love's Labour's Lost*, 1.2.21). (Lanham, p. 10)

Other meaning: See antimetathesis*.

R1: A metabole* is a figure which uses different words to say the same thing, whereas an antimetabole uses the same words to say something else. Quintilian's famous example is apposite: 'Non ut edam vivo, sed ut vivam, edo' ('I eat to live, I do not live to eat') (*Institutes of Oratory*, 9.3.85).

R2: Antimetabole is useful for challenging causal relationships. **Ex:** Do we study the Classics because they are classic, or are they Classics because we study them?

The figure's air of originality makes it a favourite with writers of all historical periods. **Exx:** 'He was a rake among scholars, and a scholar among rakes' (Macaulay, speaking of Richard Steele in his July 1843 review of Aikin's *Life of Addison*); 'And what do they know of England, who only England know' (R. Kipling, *The English Flag*). A company of saints carved on a typanum is described as: 'united in their variety and varied in their unity, unique in their diversity, and diverse in their apt assembly ... beyond reduction to vicissitudes and to vicissitudes reduced' (U. Eco, *The Name of the Rose*, pp. 42–3).

R3: An antimetabole which differs somewhat in form from those already discussed is the one which inverts actants* around a lexeme. **Exx:**

'It's not the men in my life that count, it's the life in my men' (Mae West); 'This is not the end. It is not even the beginning of the end. But it is, perhaps, the end of the beginning' (W. Churchill, 'Speech,' 10 Nov. 1942).

R4: Unless one term is made subordinate to the other, there is only false antimetabole. **Ex:** 'Emptiness and love, love and emptiness' (Y. Thériault, *Cul-de-sac*, p. 83).

R5: See paronomasia*, R7; chiasmus*, R2; epiphora*; and *reversio**, R1.

ANTIMETATHESIS Placing together two words which differ in the order of succession of some of their letters and therefore in their meaning. See Lausberg.

Exx: *navo an vano* (Lausberg, p. 887); vain Ivan; vole love; time, emit, item, mite, etc.

Exx: 'S'il se pouvait un choeur de *violes voilées*' (L. Aragon, *Les Yeux d'Elsa*, p. 67); 'Le *fiat* et le *fait*' (P. Claudel, *Journal*, 2:873).

Other definitions: 'Inversion* of the members of an antithesis*' (*OED*). See also antimetabole*.

Synonyms: antimetabole*, antimetalepsis (Lausberg, Littré, Morier), retortion*, antistrophe (Littré)

R1: Antimetathesis is a variety of paronomasia* and more generally of repetition*; the two words must follow one another or occupy corresponding (syntactic) positions.

R2: Another type of antimetathesis is acoustic chiasmus*, which may occur inside a single word. Thus 'metamathematic' presents the vowels *e–a*, and then *a–e*. In *l'artiste attristé*, we have (partial) acoustic chiasmus between consonants accompanied by acoustic parallelism* of vowels.

R3: A perfect antimetathesis would be an anagram* if there were graphic replacement without rapprochement along the syntagmatic axis. **Exx:** 'misanthrope: spare him not; presbyterian: best in prayer' (T. Augarde, *The Oxford Guide to Word Games*, p. 77).

R4: If composed of elements which read the same forwards as backwards, antimetathesis becomes palindrome*. **Ex:** 'Madam I'm Adam. And Able I was ere I saw Elba' (Joyce, *Ulysses*, p. 113).

R5: See also equivoque*, R2.

ANTIPARASTASIS A refutation which consists in showing that the object of complaint or condemnation is on the contrary commendable.

See Littré and Morier (the term remains uncollected in anglophone rhetorics).

Ex: ' "You abuse quotation [by giving too many]" ... "There are not as many as you think, their quality, aptness, rareness, and vividness deceive you about their frequency" ' (Valéry Larbaud, *Sous l'invocation de Saint Jérôme*, p. 215).

R1: Antiparastasis without proof or explanation is less trustworthy. Ex: ' "But don't you think," asked the teacher, "that instilling naiveté into one's pupils is a bit archaic, anachronistic as a device?" "Exactly, anachronistic devices are the best" ' (W. Gombrowicz, *Ferdydurke*, p. 28). Striking out blindly against an adversary's strongest argument* with the expression 'That's all the more reason why I'm right!' is a common trick surprising only to the over-serious debater.

R2: Antiparastasis sometimes is present only in one's tone of voice (see intonation*).

R3: The opposite case, which consists in proving that the object praised is, on the contrary, to be condemned, is also an example of antiparastasis. The same subject is repeated (parastasis*) but from the opposite point of view. Ex [Gillou has announced that he wants to enter the Resistance]: 'GEORGES: In short, he would like to take up courage as a summer hobby. Idleness produces many things' (H. de Montherlant, *Théâtre*, p. 704).

R4: The corresponding literary genre is the *apology*, which combines praise with defence or justification. *Personal apology* takes its author as subject.

R5: The person accused may refute the condemnation without making an admission of guilt. Ex: 'He should rather be praised than blamed, *if it were indeed true* that he had done what he is accused of' (*Encyclopédie*, 1751).

ANTIPHRASIS 'A word used in a manner contrary to the natural one' (Fontanier, p. 266). See also Cuddon, Lausberg, Littré, and Robert.

Exx: A mother calls her child a 'little monster,' or a speaker uses the common antiphrastic imperative: 'Take your time, we've got all day!' Other common examples: 'Tell me about it!' (i.e., 'Don't bother, I know all about it already.'); 'I could care less about ...' (i.e., 'I couldn't ...'). See also threat*, R1; asteismus*, R2; euphemism*, R6; and persiflage*, R1.

Other definitions: Morier, following Quintilian, describes antiphrasis as being synonymous with irony*, as does Frye, who merely cross-refers the two terms. Lausberg distinguishes between them. For him, irony exists in the tone of an utterance, whereas antiphrasis is rendered obvious by context and situation. For the distinction between irony of utterance and irony of situation, studied by Muecke, Booth, and others, see irony*. Irony may exist without antiphrasis; it is simpler, then, to see irony as subsuming antiphrasis among its many varieties. Ex: 'Come into my parlour, said the spider to the fly.' Even without explanation, the invitation is seen to be a veiled threat*, and as such is antiphrastic.

Synonym: an untruth, or 'counter-factual' (*contre-vérité*), reduced to a single word, according to Littré and Lausberg. In our opinion at least, antiphrasis communicates clearly enough the opposite content of the term it uses that there is no untruth, fraud, or lie perpetrated. Ex: 'It has ... an excellent engine [spoken over the sound of one clearly failing]' (E. Ionesco, *Le Salon de l'automobile*, in *Théâtre*, 4:198). This is a counterfactual statement, not antiphrasis, since the salesman has no intention of conveying anything else but what he says.

R1: The strength of antiphrasis derives from an implicit assertion* (see implication*) such as 'What is meant is so true that we can even *affirm the contrary* without creating obscurity.' Ex: 'She came to know ... the world, that cavern full of *honorable people*' (Montherlant, *Romans*, p. 766). So antiphrasis is context-dependent (see litotes*, R2, and sweet* talk, R2).

R2: When the receiver fails to recognize antiphrasis, the speaker exaggerates it to emphasize its improbability. Ex: ' "Is he intelligent?" "Very, a genius, in fact." ' Appeals to the judgment of the person addressed are also possible: 'No one is unaware ... / As everyone knows ... / It is well known that ...' A special kind of intonation* is also available for such statements.

R3: French lexicographers, while not taking the device into account, nonetheless attribute contradictory values (scorn and affection, for example) to a single term: the Robert dictionary, under 'ça' (indef. pron. 'that'), quotes Brunot's example of a mother saying as she points to her child, 'You see how attached one gets to *that*!' (*La Pensée et la langue*).

ANTITHESIS The contrasting of two ideas: the negative presentation of its opposite makes the principal idea more striking.

Exx: 'Neither the one hurt her, nor the other help her; just without partiality, mighty without contradiction, liberal without losing, wise without curiosity' (Sir Philip Sidney, *The Arcadia*); 'Canada is the businessman's paradise, the man of letters' hell' (J. Fournier, *Mon Encrier*, p. 48); 'It's not the pale moon that excites me ... Oh no, it's just the nearness of you' (Hoagy Carmichael).

Raymond Queneau ridicules the device's artificiality in his *Exercises in Style*: 'It was neither the day before nor the day after, but the same day. It was neither the Gare du Nord nor the Gare de Lyon, but the Gare Saint-Lazare' (p. 44). See redundancy*, R3.

R1: Antithesis is a popular form of emphasis. Ex: 'That and nothing else.' (See also allusion*, R2.)

R2: Sometimes the thesis, or principal idea, remains implicit. Ex: 'Soap cannot tolerate dirt' (H. Michaux, *Face aux verrous*, p. 54).

R3: Antithesis, particularly implicit antithesis, is a natural device which has its own auditive marker. See antithetical accent*.

R4: Gorgias advised joining antithesis to homoioteleuton* to form isocolon members in a sentence (see sentence*). Cicero, Quintilian, and Saint Augustine all transmitted and followed this advice, combining the three devices under the heading 'Gorgianic figures' (M. Comeau, *La Rhétorique de Saint Augustin*, p. 51; E.P.J. Corbett, *Classical Rhetoric for the Modern Student*, pp. 437–8, 459, 464–5). Antithesis is a characteristic feature of Petrarchism (see imitation*, R3). Both English and French neo-classical authors used and abused antithesis: it made the construction of periods easier (see period*, R2). Ex:

> Be not the first by whom the new are tried,
> Nor yet the last to lay the old aside.
> A. Pope, 'An Essay on Criticism,' 2.335–6

Albalat, who gives it two chapters in *La Formation du style*, boldly asserts that antithesis is 'the key, the explanation, the generating principle of half of French literature, from Montaigne to Victor Hugo' (pp. 192–3).

R5: Rhetorical antithesis is generally confused with enantiosis, which stresses essential (rather than accidental) oppositions. The followers of Pythagoras considered good and evil, odd and even, single and multiple, etc., as the source of everything logical. It is antithesis, taken to mean enantiosis, that deserves G. Durand's criticism: 'Its implicit manicheism haunts the greater part of Western thought' (*Les Structures anthropologiques de l'imaginaire*, p. 453).

R6: Again English and French usage of rhetorical terms may differ, for Redfern puts enantiosis closer to irony*: 'An enantiomorph is a mirror-image, and enantiosis means saying (ironically) the reverse of what you mean. "Enantiodromia" is a term from Heraclitus, and denotes the process ... whereby things meet their opposites. It means "clashing together" ' (W. Redfern, *Puns*, p. 103).

R7: Antithesis can take the form of a distinction* (see distinction, R2); it produces surprise (see negation*, R1); allows for the alignment of hypotheses (see supposition*, R4); and depends upon synonymy* (see synonymy, R6).

ANTONOMASIA The substitution* of a proper name for a common noun or vice versa. See Fontanier (p. 95), Frye, Lanham, Lausberg, and Preminger.

Exx: a 'Daniel' for a judge (*Merchant of Venice*, 4.1.334); the 'Corsican Monster' for Bonaparte

Ex: '... each of us carries his Mexico and United States within him, a dark and bloody frontier we dare cross only at night' (C. Fuentes, *Old Gringo*, p. 187).

Other name: synecdoche* (Fontanier). Quintilian points out the same similarity.

R1: Antonomasia is a stylistic embellishment: the Augustan Age, the Age of Pericles, the Sun King, the Virgin Queen, the Diva. It corresponds, according to Barthes, to the mythic 'incarnation of a virtue in a figure' (see *L'Aventure sémiologique*, p. 129): Cato for courage; Job for patience; in our own day, Churchill for courage, Pope John XXIII for goodness.

It may derive simply from the fact that individuals who are considered great are well known (their proper names become common names). **Ex:**

Some village Hampden that with dauntless breast
The little tyrant of his fields withstood;
Some mute, inglorious Milton here
Some Cromwell guiltless of his blood.
                    Th. Gray, 'Elegy Written in a Country Churchyard'

Ex: 'My mathematics teacher predicted I would become a Vauban' (Ph. Aubert de Gaspé, *Les Anciens Canadiens*, p. 35).

They become common nouns, in the grammatical sense, when used without a capital letter, since their origin as proper names has been lost, as in *pander*, or *jeroboam*.

R2: The Greeks named the years after the principal magistrate, the eponymous archon, their towns after the gods (e.g., Athens): they thus substituted one proper name for another. A modern eponymy is the 'Oedipus complex.' See metonymy*, R6.

R3: Antonomasia occurs spontaneously: 'London is deciding ...' ('London' stands for the British government); 'The Quay d'Orsay refuses to comment'; 'Is Quebec Corsica?' (for 'Has the central government abandoned you?'). See concretization*, R3.

R4: See also denomination*, R3; metonymy*, R4; personification*, R1; meaning*, 4; synecdoche*, R1 and R7; and title* (conferring of), R5.

APHAERESIS Dropping a syllable or a letter from the beginning of a word. See Frye, Lanham, Lausberg, Marouzeau, and Preminger.

Exx: 'neath, 'mid, 'fore, 'though, 'cause, etc.

Ex: 'Ot us sengers' (for 'Got on bus, passengers') (R. Queneau, *Exercises in Style*, p. 78).

Other definition: suppression at the beginning *or end* of a word (Quillet)

R1: Aphaeresis is a metaplasm*.

R2: Children learning to speak first tend to retain only the final syllable of words (-*nette* for *marionnette*, -*range* for *orange*), then two syllables (-*anna* for *nanna*, -*octor* for *doctor*). Loose pronunciation ('*xactly* for *exactly*) has thus something childish about it. But in '*tention!* (for *Attention!*) economy of effort and efficiency come into play.

R3: Like apocope*, aphaeresis most commonly involves the slack use of an expression rather than a literary device. Cases in French such as Breton's writing of *Humour* as '*Umour* (*Dictionnaire abrégé du surréalisme*, under 'Vaché'), although seeming to be covered by the definition, are rather in our view exceptional graphs chosen to represent a special meaning*. See graphy*.

APOCALYPSE A phantasmagorical allegory* (see fantastic*) whose theme is the revelation of coming events or of present, though hidden, realities.

Ex:

> Things fall apart; the centre cannot hold;
> Mere anarchy is loosed upon the world,
> The blood-dimmed tide is loosed, and everywhere
> The ceremony of innocence is drowned.
> W.B. Yeats, 'Second Coming'

R1: Apocalyptic extravagance refers, not to the fiction itself, but to some transcendental, religious, or surreal aspect of it. **Ex:** 'And the times of the end will have come, and the end of time ... On the first day at the third hour in the firmament a great and powerful voice will be raised, a purple cloud will advance from the north, thunder and lightning will follow it, and on the earth a rain of blood will fall. On the second day ...' (U. Eco, *The Name of the Rose*, p. 404).

Allegory* and the type of narrative* which develops an explicit process of enunciation* (sometimes becoming a dialogue* with the reader) aim to confer on the phantasmagorical content itself the status of reality or truth. Apocalypse attempts to unite two contrary effects; hence the surrealists' admiration for Lautréamont.

R2: An ancient literary genre, apocalypse flourished in the Bible (in the book of Daniel), in the Kabbala, and in the Koran. Difficult to decode, it slips easily into hermeticism. **Ex:** 'It's *him* ["The Interloper!"] that will come as the Antichrist, to lead men into the flaming bowels of perdition, to the bloody end of wickedness, as Star Wormwood hangs blazing in the sky ...' (Stephen King, *The Dark Tower (1): The Gunslinger*, p. 50). Cuddon remarks (p. 50) that 'sermon literature abounds in apocalyptic visions.' But the hermetic nature of apocalyptic utterances is often counterbalanced by trivial observations, pat answers to fundamental questions, colloquial language, and by a kind of simplicity intended to be reassuring.

R3: Apocalypse includes *apotheosis*, the hero's triumph, when he, in public view, is raised to the skies. **Ex:** 'And they beheld Him in the chariot, clothed in the glory of the brightness, having raiment as of the sun, fair as the moon and terrible that for awe they durst not look upon Him. And there came a voice out of heaven, calling: *Elijah! Elijah!* And he answered with a main cry: *Abba! Adonai!* And they beheld Him, even Him, ben Bloom Elijah, amid clouds of angels ascend to the glory of the brightness at an angle of fortyfive degrees over Donohoe's in Little Green street like a shot off a shovel' (Joyce, *Ulysses*, p. 283).

R4: See also prophecy*, R2.

APOCOPE Omission of a letter or syllable at the end of a word. See Frye, Lanham, Marouzeau, Morier, Preminger, and Robert.

Exx: 'oft' for 'often'; *encor* for *encore*; Hallowe'en

Synonym: ecthlipse (Lausberg, p. 493)

Antonym: paragoge* (see paragoge, R1)

R1: According to Lausberg (sect. 490), apocope is a variety of abridgement* (suppression of a letter); according to Marouzeau, it is a showy means of rounding off a sentence*, of turning it into a type of punch* line (see punch line, R1). See also metaplasm*, R1.

R2: In English, elision* is the omission of a vowel or syllable in the pronunciation of a word or syntagm* (e.g., 'I'm' or 'let's') (*Concise Oxford Dictionary*); in French, it is apocope of a final letter before a word beginning with a vowel: l'art, de l'or, etc.

R3: The progressive disappearance, in French, of the mute *e* has produced various difficulties in verse because feet are syllabic. By the sixteenth century, Ronsard had already opted for apocope. Instead of writing 'Rolland avait deux épé-es en main,' he insists on 'deux épé's en la main.' 'Don't you feel,' he argues, 'that these two *épé-es en main* offend a delicate ear?' (quoted by Grammont, *Le Vers français*, p. 464). The advice was taken, notably by Ronsard's rival, Philippe Desportes (who wrote 'des charbons inutils,' rather than the more grammatically correct form, 'inutiles'). As Boileau remarked (*L'Art poétique*, 1:131), however, 'Malherbe intervened ...' Thanks to his rigorous defence of the mute *e* in verse, classical French writers of tragedy composed in alexandrines (twelve-syllable lines), which modern actors can only plausibly pronounce as having eleven, ten, or even nine syllables, a manner not always compatible with rhythm. On this problem, see line* (of poetry).

The principal apocope authorized by French classicism is that of the *s* following an elided mute *e*. Ex: 'Tu l'emporte, il est vrai' (Lamartine; i.e., six syllables, rather than seven if the *s* remains: *emportes*).

One elegant way of avoiding the problem is to elide a final *e* by following it with words with an initial vowel (e.g., mar*bre* onyx). This is what Théophile Gautier frequently does, for example. Morier calls this type of line *vers plein*, and he calls *vers ajouré* (i.e., 'pierced') the line containing one (or several) pronounced mute *e*'s.

R4: If clear pronunciation of a 'mute' *e* is desired, the spelling *eu* has become necessary in modern French. Ex: 'Tout de même l*eu* temps, c'est l*eu* temps. L'passé, c'est l'passé' (R. Queneau, *Le Chiendent*, p. 295).

R5: The problem of the mute *e* apart, apocope particularly attacks final liquid consonants in French (e.g., *table*, *propre*, *quatre*, in which the final groups tend to disappear in spoken language). Exx: Le minis(tre); 'C'est pas croyab' (Queneau, *Zazie dans le métro*, p. 31).

R6: In (verbal) delivery of the alexandrine, it is the unaccented final vowel of a word which tends to disappear. Ex: Ta chevlur' d'oranges (see Parent, ed., *Le Vers français au XXe siècle*, p. 34).

APOLOGUE A narrative* illustrating some 'truth.'

Ex: 'It is said that an Oriental caliph one day set fire to the library of a famous and glorious and proud city, and that, as those thousands of volumes were burning, he said that they could and should disappear: either they were repeating what the Koran already said, and therefore they were useless, or else they contradicted that book sacred to the infidels, and therefore they were harmful' (U. Eco, *The Name of the Rose*, p. 399). Parodic examples abound in modern literature:

Apologue

One afternoon a big wolf waited in a dark forest for a little girl to come along carrying a basket of food to her grandmother. Finally a little girl did come along and she was carrying a basket of food. 'Are you carrying that basket to your grandmother?' asked the wolf. The little girl said yes, she was. So the wolf asked her where her grandmother lived and the little girl told him and he disappeared into the wood.

When the little girl opened the door of her grandmother's house she saw there was somebody in bed with a nightcap and nightgown on. She had approached no nearer than twenty-five feet from the bed when she saw that it was not her grandmother but the wolf, for even in a nightcap a wolf does not look any more like your grandmother than the Metro-Goldwyn lion looks like Calvin Coolidge. So the little girl took an automatic out of her basket and shot the wolf dead.

Moral: It is not so easy to fool little girls nowadays as it used to be. (James Thurber, *The Thurber Carnival*, p. 283)

R1: Originally apologue belonged to oral literature. It is close to myth* (see myth, R1), as is parable (see below). Later, apologue became a way of amplifying ideas, one which differed from hypotyposis* because of its purely imaginary nature and especially because of its implicit or explicit 'moral.' Thus the *fables* of Aesop or of La Fontaine are frequently apologues.

When the underlying truth (the theme; the 'noema' according to Morier; the 'moral' in the case of a fable) is clearly expressed, the apologue is related to simile*; when the truth is implicit, it is linked to symbol*.

If the theme is some truth of a religious nature, one speaks of *parable*. Exx: the evangelical parables of the ten virgins, the marriage feast, the sower, etc.

The apologue is interpreted globally rather than by establishing a term-for-term equivalence. Indeed, without such a stipulation, the apologue would be an allegory* or extended comparison*.

R2: The expression of an idea by means of an *anecdote* employs the same device (a more or less detailed narrative* containing relevant speeches made by the characters). However, strictly speaking anecdotes deal with imaginary events (hence the meaning of *anecdotal*, and the related *anecdotage*: 'that which does not treat of the essential question'). Therefore they actually constitute forms of the *exemplum*. Thus: 'MONICA: Now I would have the housework to occupy me, so I would feel better. But with the maid we have, how could I? ... Look. By hiding it from her I had kept myself a bit of dust, in a corner, for me on Sunday ... Just enough for a little dusting. Well, this morning, my dust had flown, cleaned up' (J. Audiberti, *L'Effet Glapion*, p. 142). See also simulation*, R4.

R3: The apologue is an excellent argument* for an author who wishes to convey certain shades of meaning*, more of a sentimental than of a legal nature. Ex: '[The English governor of French Canada] behaved like a stranger who, in the home of a family gathered together to commemorate one of its beloved deceased, would turn up uninvited at the feast, sit down at the table, drink and sing, on the pretext that he was the owner of the house' (J. Fournier, *Mon Encrier*, p. 62). It may replace a line of argument (see reasoning*, R3).

APOSIOPESIS A sudden interruption, betraying an emotion, a threat*, or hesitation. See Frye, Lausberg, Morier, Preminger, and Lanham.

Exx: 'You remember Elizabeth, sort of statuesque-looking; she's the one who ...' (Margaret Atwood, *Life before Man*, p. 38); [Marcelle is pregnant and believes that her lover has kept her condition secret; but, as a result of the allegations made by a friend, she guesses that the latter has been informed] 'She grows pale: '*He ... Oh! the ...* He swore that he would tell you nothing' (J.-P. Sartre, *L'Age de raison*, p. 226).

Lanham (p. 15) adds that the 'idea, although unexpressed, is clearly perceived.' Ex: 'You can go to H—!' Turco (p. 71) distinguishes a form of 'implied aposiopesis [which] substitutes another letter, syllable, word or passage for the dropped material.' Ex: 'You dear friend, who talk so well, / You can go to H–ertford, Hereford and Hampshire' (G.B. Shaw, A.J. Lerner, and F. Loew, *My Fair Lady*).

Synonyms: reticence, reserve

R1: Aposiopesis is a type of interruption* (see interruption, R1) characterized by the fact that its causes are personal and of an emotional order (see Lausberg, Morier). Frequently (as in the above example from Sartre), its cause is indignation, but it might also be an excess of pleasure, simulated or otherwise.

R2: Unlike Preminger (p. 42), who separates aposiopesis from preterition*, Dumarsais (5:285) and Fontanier (pp. 135–6) place aposiopesis among the different types of preterition, emphasizing the device's oratorical nature. (See false –*.) This is classic aposiopesis, which consists in 'suddenly stopping in the course of a sentence, to convey by the little that one says, and with the aid of the utterance's contextual circumstances, what is supposedly suppressed, and frequently much more' (Fontanier, p. 135). As such, it is a trick of discursive *pathos* (see argument*). Ex (expressing a threat*):

LEAR: No, you unnatural hags,
I will have such revenges on you both,
That all the world shall – I will do such things –

What they are, yet I know not; but they shall be
The terrors of the earth.

Shakespeare, *King Lear*, 2.4.281–5

Ex: ' "The Government's position is not a particularly healthy one just at the moment," said the Dean. "It only needs a nudge ..." ' (Tom Sharpe, *Porterhouse Blue*, p. 212).

Ex (expressing fear): ' "I said I'm hurt. For God's sake come ..." ' (ibid., p. 209).

R3: According to Lamy, the flow of the discourse* is not necessarily held back, but simply chopped up by the hasty insertion. This is certainly the case when it expresses hesitation. In the following example, the hero is searching for a word: 'In an api ... tho ... in a sad and solitary apotheosis' (Marie-Claire Blais, *Une Saison dans la vie d'Emmanuel*, p. 60). Aposiopesis also may express distractedness [McCoy asks Bloom the time of the funeral, but Bloom's thoughts are elsewhere, on Martha's letter]: 'Eeleven' (Joyce, *Ulysses*, p. 60).

These are examples of spontaneous, natural aposiopesis. They are frequent in interior monologue*, where one does not trouble to finish one's sentences. Ex: 'All quiet on Howth now. The distant hills seem. Where we. The rhododendrons. I am a fool perhaps ... Where I come in. All that old hill has seen. Names change: that's all. Lovers: yum, yum' (Joyce, *Ulysses*, p. 308). (The interior monologue contains an imagined dialogue*.)

R4: *Reticentia*, the rhetorical figure, resembles the word's current meaning (an attitude of reserve) when it consists of a refusal to complete a sentence. Ex: 'The laugh is in my ... / A tear is in my ...' (H. Michaux, 'Glu et gli'). The speaker may also stop upon seeing that the person addressed has already understood an utterance's meaning. This is reticence based on, or producing, complicity (Marchais).

R5: Aposiopesis has its own intonation* (see intonation, R3) and its own expressive punctuation*.

APOSTROPHE The orator suddenly breaks off to address someone or something. See Cuddon, Fontanier (p. 371), Frye, Morier, Preminger, and Robert.

Ex: Milton's narrator interrupts *Paradise Lost* to apostrophize Light: 'Hail holy Light, offspring of Heaven first-born, / Or of the Eternal coeternal beam / May I express thee unblamed?' (3.1–3).

Exx: 'Ring out, wild bells' (Tennyson, *In Memoriam*, 2); 'O Beer! O Hodgson, Guiness, Allsop, Bass!' (Charles S. Calverley, 'Ballad')

Other meaning: a graphic sign of elision*

R1: Nothing is more natural than the address made to another speaker (see dialogue*; discourse*, R2). Apostrophe is rhetorical when one of its elements is unexpected, either because, in a narrative*, the process of enunciation* is made explicit by means of a second-person pronoun designating the reader (see below, R2); or because, in a discourse*, some general truth is addressed specially to the attention of the listeners; or because the author pretends to address absent persons, ideas, or objects.

One, rather lofty, mark of apostrophe is the initial vocative, *O* or *Oh!*, which differs from the call *Ho!* (as in 'What ho, within'); there exists also an exclamative *O*, different from *oh*. Compare: 'O nuit désastreuse!' (Bossuet); 'O gull! O dolt! / As ignorant as dirt!' (*Othello*, 5.2.163); 'O rare Ben Jonson' (John Berryman, 'A Thurn,' from *His Toy, His Dream, His Rest,* p. 126). See also prosopopoeia* and false –*, R1.

R2: One might call an *address* a passage in a literary work in which the author names and describes the reader, as for instance in one of the final stanzas of Pushkin's *Evgeny Onegin*, or in the first chapter of the final book of Fielding's *Tom Jones*. The address may also be placed at the beginning of a work (e.g., Baudelaire's 'Au lecteur,' the prefatory poem to *Les Fleurs du mal*).

The address differs from the *dedication*, a handwritten or printed formula accompanying the gift to a private individual of a work or copy of a work. Ex: 'To that impeccable poet, to that perfect magician of French Literature, to my dear and much venerated master and friend Théophile Gautier ... I dedicate these sickly flowers' (Ch. Baudelaire, *Les Fleurs du mal*).

In the world of publicity, the device – rendered quasi-automatic by the advent of word-processed messages – of including in the message the name of the addressee ('Dear John Smith ...') is called *personalization*. See prayer*, R1.

R3: Apostrophe may combine the referential and phatic functions of communication* which a simple greeting would achieve in the real world (see exclamation*, R2, and injunction*, R3).

Apostrophe, however, may be addressed to no real person, but rather to some imaginary collectivity, made witness by the device to the truth of what is advanced. Such addresses to no one in particular have as their function the raising of the discourse's tone. It also happens that addresses are made to a second person in the hope that they will be overheard by a third party, as when a mother asks her two-year-old child to look for the scissors, knowing that her husband is not far away. This produces a double actualization of the receiver. The device is not as rare as it may appear. Thus Sganarelle, at the beginning of Molière's *Don Juan*, boldly scolds his own master, while pretending to be addressing another: 'I'm not speaking to you ... I'm speaking to the master I mentioned before.'

Apostrophe

The search for the 'right' addressee can produce *dubitatio**. Ex: 'Storms, sisters of hurricane; blueish firmament whose beauty I admit not; hypocrite sea, mirror of my heart; land with a mysterious heart; inhabitants of the spheres; God responsible for such magnificent creation, I call upon you; show me a good man' (Lautréamont, *Les Chants de Maldoror*, 5).

To *apostrophize* someone is to establish a surprising, often disagreeable, contact with that person. Ex: ' "Cock o' the walk," he screeched, "you stink, you gorilla." Gabriel sighed' (R. Queneau, *Zazie dans le métro*, p. 12). See also sarcasm*, R2; title* (conferring of), R1; and sweet* talk, R3.

R4: Apostrophe is a means of filling out a speech. See amplification*. Ex: 'Amen. So be it. Welcome, O life! I go to encounter for the millionth time the reality of experience and to forge in the smithy of my soul the uncreated conscience of my race' (Joyce, *A Portrait of the Artist as a Young Man*, p. 253). It is also a way of effecting a transition* (see transition, R1).

R5: For the tone of apostrophe, see celebration*, R1; intonation*, R3; and supplication*, R2. As for its construction, see apposition*, R5; and notation*, R6.

R6: Apostrophe may involve a metaphor*. Ex: 'Black sand, sand of nights which make you run so much more quickly than white sand, I could not stop trembling when I was given the mysterious power of having you slip through my fingers' (A. Breton, *L'Amour fou*, p. 81).

When the object apostrophized is a thing or idea, personification* is necessarily involved, but one must question the latter's degree of reality. Ex:

> O wild West Wind, thou breath of Autumn's being
> Thou from whose unseen presence the leaves dead
> Are driven, like ghosts from an enchanter fleeing
> ...
> Wild spirit, thou art moving everywhere;
> Destroyer and preserver, hear, oh, hear.
> P.B. Shelley, 'Ode to the West Wind'

Metaphorically, the object has become a person.

R7: Apostrophe may be diegetic (narrated indirectly rather than expressed by direct discourse*). Ex: 'Dr Upper, assuming a whining voice and a cringing demeanour, spoke to a mother – whom he called Mommy – in a monologue in which worship and obedience were mingled ... He had worked up his great Apostrophe to Mommy over many years, and of its kind it was a masterpiece' (Robertson Davies, *What's Bred in the Bone*, p. 115).

APPOSITION Characterization of one substantive or pronoun by another which follows it (see Fontanier, p. 297). A following noun that further describes or specifies (see Grambs, p. 144).

Exx: 'The holy bread, the food unpriced, / Thy everlasting mercy, Christ' (John Masefield, 'The Everlasting Mercy'); 'Night, my foliage and my glebe' (René Char, *Neuf Merci* ..., in *Oeuvres complètes*, p. 386).

Other names: epergesis (Lanham); epexegesis [archaic] (Lanham, Littré, Marouzeau)

R1: Apposition placed between commas and suppressible without loss to the rest of the sentence is simply explanatory ('accidental' as Fontanier emphasizes). In the absence of commas, identification of contiguous terms occurs within the assertion* itself. **Ex:** 'From *casual lakefront* sex to warm meaningful relationships ...' (G. Vidal, *Duluth*, p. 5). The apposition's integration can be made even stronger by the addition of a hyphen*. **Ex:** 'the rationalized power-ritual that will be the coming peace' (Thomas Pynchon, *Gravity's Rainbow*, p. 177). Apposition in this case is turning into lexical juxtaposition*.

Lanham, Frye, and Grambs, as well as the francophone grammarians and rhetoricians Dumarsais, Beauzée, Fontanier, Littré, and Quillet, only identify explanatory apposition, a grammatical device (e.g., 'Homer, the prince of poets'). They consider as apposition any characterization (even an adjective) placed between commas. **Ex:** 'A plain without a feature, bare and brown' (W.H. Auden, 'The Shield of Achilles').

R2: The pause* which precedes an apposition replaces the copula of an adjacent assertion* (it is the equivalent of *which is/are*), except in elliptical style (see ellipsis*), where it may replace the main verb (the understood copula *is/are*). **Ex:** 'under the crosses, the dead man's garden' (Tennyson, 'Merlin and the Gleam'). Similarly, in cases of enumeration* preceded by a colon, there is inverted apposition, the initial element being the predicate. The construction of asyndeton* (see asyndeton, R2) is quite different, since the implicit term (*and*) is one of co-ordination.

Even in normal apposition (adjacent assertion*), inversion* occurs. **Ex:** 'The son of a Hebridean tenant farmer, related through his mother to the Highland laird Maclaine of Lochbay ... was to become the laird of New South Wales' (R. Hughes, *The Fatal Shore*, p. 293).

The added substantive's role as predicate explains the absence of an article. The pause*'s importance derives from the absence of a taxeme (see parataxis*, R1); hence the name, 'apposition.' Without a pause, there would merely be an adjective or qualifier.

R3: Apposition may introduce metaphor*, metonymy*, or synecdoche*. (See simile*, R1.) Apposition also allows the removal of equivoque*

Approximation

deriving, for example, from the use of pronouns. Ex: 'Jim and Jack were brothers. When he, Jim that is ...'

R4: Appositional construction is the same as that of apostrophe*; hence the possibility of confusion. Ex: 'I remember thy name in the night, O Lord' (Psalm 119), for *'thy* name, O Lord' or 'thy name which is *The Lord.'* (See also successive approximations*, R3.)

R5: See also sentence*, 4; and title* (conferring of), R1.

APPROXIMATION   A double meaning* obtained by a single slight displacement of one or two phonemes in a sentence* or syntagm*. The device may only be inserted into a well-known expression or one of fixed meaning.

Ex: 'She used to say Ben Dollard had a base barreltone voice. He has legs like barrels and you'd think he was singing into a barrel. Now, isn't that wit' (Joyce, *Ulysses*, p. 126).

Other name: quasi-homonym (Dubois et al., *Dictionnaire de linguistique*)

R1: Approximation is one way of producing equivoque*. It may combine with allographs* (see allograph, R2); it is close to lexical scrambling*. The spoonerism* (see spoonerism, R1) is a more refined form of approximation which employs double displacement.

R2: In the broad sense, approximation is the slightly incorrect use of a word, or a slightly gauche turn of phrase (see Le Hir, p. 122). But in such a case, a transfer of meaning occurs, rather than lexicalization*: the meaning* becomes an approximate one. See also ellipsis*, R3.

APPROXIMATIONS (SUCCESSIVE)   Several non-synonymous terms given as having the same function: lacking something better, they present themselves as aiming at some signified concept situated on vocabulary's margins.

Ex: 'And that guilty, touching, childlike smile' (N. Sarraute, *Portrait d'un inconnu*, p. 109).

R1: The device occurs frequently in spoken language when speakers are unable to find the right words to describe their impressions. Equal units of suspensive intonation* serve to indicate the syntagms' identical function. See also squint*, R2.

R2: Approximations which spread over quite extensive segments sometimes occur: for example, over whole paragraphs. Exx: the Upanishads; and Charles du Bos's collection of critical essays *Approximations*.

R3: In apposition*, semes are added one to another; in successive approximation, they replace each other.

ARCHAISM A word no longer in use, or obsolete; a previous meaning which has yielded to a new one; an ancient construction lacking currency. See Cuddon, Grambs, Littré, Marouzeau, *OED*, and Robert. La Fontaine, for example, liked archaisms, and his works are full of them. Ex: 'Tel *cuide engeigner* autrui qui souvent s'engeigne lui-même' ('He who thinks he's deceiving others frequently deceives himself'). *Engeigner* (i.e., *tromper*) is a lexical archaism. Scott and Tennyson, in using them to give colour to conversation in historical romance, rendered themselves guilty of what Robert Louis Stevenson called 'tushery.' Ex: 'Knight / Slay me not: my three brothers bad me do it' (Tennyson, 'Gareth and Lynette,' in *Idylls of the King*). Meanwhile Fowler, who found *anent* at home only in a Scottish courtroom, quotes the following, which he considered both grammatically incorrect and imprecise: 'Dear Sir, Your remarks today on the result of the Canadian election anent the paragraph in the *Philadelphia Record* is, I am glad to see, the first sign of real appreciation of ...' (*Modern English Usage*, p. 29).

Ex (of archaic meaning): 'Verily,' which in the Gospels, or in historical novels, means 'in very truth,' was in Fowler's day (1906) 'perhaps confined to a single phrase ... *I verily believe*, which has the special meaning, "It is almost incredible, yet facts surprise me into the belief" ' (*Modern English Usage*, p. 677). See also etymology*.

Ex (of a morphological archaism): the use of subjunctives in modern English. Expressions like 'It *were* futile to attempt ...' or 'Do not ring unless an answer *be* required' merely confirm the following remark made by Porter Perrin: 'Today the subjunctive is a trait of style rather than of grammar and is used by writers chiefly to set their language a little apart from everyday usage' (*Harper Dictionary of Contemporary Usage*, p. 569).

Ex (of a graphic archaism in French): '[Une pensée] d'une singularité espovantable' ('A thought of *feerful* singularity') (Montherlant, *Essais*, p. 896). The English form 'betwixt,' sometimes shortened to "twixt,' is a near equivalent: 'Now is steel '*twixt* gut and bladder interposed' (A. Bennett, P. Cook, J. Miller, and D. Moore, *Beyond the Fringe*, Capitol Records W–1792, 1961).

For archaic pronunciation, see diaeresis*, R1. Modern producers like John Barton or actors like Ian McKellen, who delight in showing how Shakespeare's words were pronounced by the Elizabethans, rely on phonetic forms considered archaic in 'standard received' English. Exx: 'Now – pronounced "n-oew" as in our genteel "now"; time – pronounced "tay-eme"; murmur – pronounced "oo" as in Yorkshire and Lancashire; dark – pronounced with a short "a" as in "cat" ' (John Barton, *Playing Shakespeare*, pp. 52–3).

R1: In the French neo-classical period (seventeenth and eighteenth centuries), allowable archaisms were imitations of Marot; hence the term *marotisme* (see imitation*), a synonym at that time of archaism (Fontanier, p. 288).

R2: Legal language is full of archaisms. Terms prescribed in France by Colbert in 1667, for example, were only reformed in 1908. Similarly, anyone with experience of English or North American legalese will be familiar with expressions such as 'whereof,' 'thereof,' 'tort, tortious,' and so on.

R3: Imitation of archaic language may go to some lengths to achieve (parodic) authenticity. Ex: 'The nursingwoman answered him and said that that woman was in throes now full three days and that it would be a hard birth unneth to bear and that now in a little it would be' (Joyce, *Ulysses*, p. 316).

R4: Uncommon Latinisms (like *arcanum arcanorum*, for instance) are archaisms (see peregrinism*).

ARGUMENT An assertion* made in a process of reasoning* or speech; its function is to justify or explain another assertion. See *OED* and *Trésor de la langue française*.

Ex: 'JULIEN: "How could you allow this creature to call you his little wolf? I had forbidden you to speak to him." COLOMBE: "But *he's the author of the play*"' (J. Anouilh, *Colombe*, in *Pièces brillantes*, p. 270).

In literature, either assertion may be metaphorical, so increasing the ambiguity*. Ex: 'The past is a foreign country. They do things differently there' (L.P. Hartley, *The Go-Between*, p. 7).

Synonyms: proof, reason

Analogous term: allegation; that is, an assertion relied upon to justify one's position

Other definitions: synopsis (of a play, novel, etc.; see recapitulation*, R2); reasoning*

R1: The demands and abuses of oratory brought the creation and categorization of a thousand and one ways of discovering arguments. These are the *commonplaces* in the original meaning* of that term, otherwise called *topics*. 'Common' has degenerated, coming to mean 'banal, lacking novelty'; hence the current usage (see cliché*). But for Aristotle, commonplaces are opposed to specific places, which are the axioms of the various sciences, techniques, and disciplines. In book 1 of the *Rhetoric*, he examines the arguments specific to the three kinds of oratory: judicial (concerning the past), epideictic (concerning the present), and deliberative (concerning the future).

In the *Rhetoric*, Aristotle divides the topics according to *ethos* (the character of the author), *pathos* (that which moves the public), and *logos* (reasoning that is logical or illustrated by examples). Book 2 is entirely devoted to the explanation of these three kinds of topics: orators must present themselves in a favourable light, and thus display their ethical qualities; they must arouse in their audience certain passions – anger, affection, hatred, fear or confidence, indignation or pity – according to the persons alluded to. Among the methods used, Miriam Joseph reminds us, were 'figures of vehemence, mocks, taunts, chiding, reprehension, accusation, abhorrence, etc.' (*Shakespeare's Use of the Arts of Language*, pp. 391–2). There are almost forty 'logical' topics, notably: non-contradiction or the excluded middle, so called because it refers to cases in which the possibility of a compromise solution or 'happy medium' does not exist (a door must be either open or closed; one cannot be 'a little' pregnant); the link between an act and the person committing it (one who kills is a killer); the link between antecedent and consequent; that between the whole and its parts, or between the individual and the group; inseparables (you can't make an omelette without breaking eggs), and so on. These places or topics give rise to conclusions having plausibility rather than truth value. Hence the value of rhetoric relative to the 'exact' sciences: the field of rhetoric is human affairs, where nothing is clear-cut, or able to be categorized in binary oppositions of the 'black/white' kind. Angenot adds the following topics: the indifference shown by interested parties (There's no need to be more Catholic than the pope); the topic of waste (We must carry this through, or lose our investment); that of inflexible discipline (If you give in once, you'll have to give in all the time), etc.

Despite what has just been said, the 'logical' topics do aim to establish a *certain* truth value, of the kind necessary in human affairs. One of the most important is therefore the *rule of justice*, which consists in treating like things in a like manner. Ex: 'Is the burning of brick houses to be called a crime whereas that of bamboo huts only a peccadillo?' (M. Bardèche, *Le Procès de Nuremberg*, p. 174). To transgress this rule is to make unfair exceptions, or as the French proverb concerning weights and measures has it, 'faire deux poids, deux mesures' (to have a double standard).

The same rule is found in stronger form in the *a fortiori* argument (if *p*, then all the more *q*). Exx: 'If to die for one's prince were a glorious death / What would it be to die for one's God?' (P. Corneille, *Polyeucte*, 4.3); 'History is written by the winners, all the more so military history'; 'Even a European atheist will be offended by Hindu references to Jesus' (H. Michaux, *Un Barbare en Asie*, p. 119). This kind of argument must however avoid hyperbole*. Ex: 'Paintings of a lubricity to make a

Argument

captain of dragoons blush (the virginity of a captain of dragoons is, after the discovery of America, one of the finest made in a long time)' (Théophile Gautier, *Mlle de Maupin*, preface).

From Cicero on down, logical commonplaces have been replaced by more empirical topics. This change was due less to considerations of truth value than to growing forensic skill: cases came to be scrutinized from every imaginable angle. For example, *exhaustion* is the method that uses up all possible arguments (Robert); *diallage* (Lanham; Lausberg; Scaliger, *Poetices libri septem*, 3:64) is the discourse* deriving from this method in which argument follows argument, all tending to the same conclusion. Since Cicero, therefore, the manuals have taught, not the discovery of logical relationships, but rather the viewpoints one should adopt in order to discover arguments. The commonplaces have become those relating (1) to the person (race, nationality, origins, sex, age, education, way of life, wealth, class, character, tastes, etc.); (2) to the case itself (its sum and parts, its beginning, progression and end, the words used to describe it, its precedents, etc.); (3) to causes, manner, means, definition, comparison, hypotheses, circumstances (see Lausberg, sect. 373–99). Vuillaume (pp. 25–6) gives a mnemonic summary of topics in the form of the Latin verse: *quis, cui, pro quo, de quo, quando, ubi, quidque loquatur*. The dactylic hexameter thus formed gathers together the essential 'oratorical proprieties' which refer respectively to the orator himself, to the listener, to the person whose case one is pleading, or about whom one is speaking, and to the time, place, and subject in question.

Roland Barthes lists other topics including those of the ludicrous, the theological, the imaginary; see 'L'Ancienne Rhétorique: aide-mémoire,' in Barthes, *L'Aventure sémiologique*, pp. 85–165. In French, the word *topique* is masculine in linguistic usage, feminine in rhetorical.

Coveted by the ignorant, endlessly repeated in courses for future orators, the topics became even less flexible, being reduced to mere extracts to be imitated, 'ready made pieces, re-usable after only a little touching up in any speech at all' (Aristotle, *Rhetoric*, Budé edition, analysis of book 2, p. 32). Act 3 of Racine's *Les Plaideurs* contains an amusing example of topics used in this way, whereas act 2, scene 2, of Shakespeare's *Measure for Measure* provides a more serious example, since Isabel is pleading for her brother Claudio's life. A similar modern example is Reginald Rose's play *Twelve Angry Men*, virtually all of which consists of the conflicting arguments produced by the members of a jury debating the guilt or innocence of a prisoner charged with murder. Rose also wrote the screenplay for Sidney Lumet's memorable film (1957).

R2: In order to be valid, arguments must not only be correct in themselves, they must be relevant to the matter in hand. See *ad hominem**; alternative*; aposiopesis*, R2; refutation*; apologue*; quotation*, R3;

*communicatio**; and hyperbole*, R2. For admonition, see threat*, R2; and *praemunitio**.

Different kinds of argumentative tricks have been identified and taught (not always with a view to exposing them as such). Angenot draws attention to the following:
- the *a contrario* argument or *enantiosis*, in which proof is replaced by refutation of a contrary assertion. Ex: It's better to laugh than cry about something.
- the *corax* (from the name of the Sicilian believed by some to have invented argumentative rhetoric), by means of which a probable truth is overturned by saying that it's *too* probable. Ex: In mystery stories, the character at whom all the clues point must never turn out to be the real criminal.
- the *amalgam* or argument by assimilation, in which notions, phenomena, or different objects are considered as belonging in the same category. Recourse to the amalgam forms the natural approach of an abstract thinker who takes a given perspective; it is used constantly in mathematics. But it can give rise to confusions detrimental to one's case, which critical analysis would reveal. Ex: 'These helmeted, red-cheeked thugs accomplish the same task as the pure, venerable thinkers on whose works we were nurtured' (P. Nizan, *Les Chiens de garde*, p. 94). The antithetical physical appearances are irrelevant, strictly speaking, to the contrasting actions performed by the two groups.
- the argument of the *invented witness*, in which the help of an anonymous authority, an imaginary, distant, 'objective' arbitrator, is called in. Ex: 'I sometimes dream about what *future historians* will say about us. A sentence will be enough to describe modern man: he fornicated and read newspapers' (A. Camus, *La Chute*, p. 10).

Ex:

In a thousand years or so, when the first archaeologists from beyond the date-line unload their boats on the sands of Southern California, they will find much the same scene as confronted the Franciscan Missionaries. A dry landscape will extend from the ocean to the mountains. Bel Air and Beverly Hills will lie naked save for scrub and cactus, all their flimsy multitude of architectural types turned long ago to dust, while the horned toad and turkey buzzard leave their faint imprint on the dunes that will drift on Sunset Boulevard. (Evelyn Waugh, *The Essays, Articles and Reviews*, p. 331)

The more ordinary (i.e., representative) the witness, the stronger the argument. Ex: 'If a thousand years hence someone reads this text [by Lévi-Strauss], he will deduce from it that in the 11th century there existed in the south of France a religion whose god was wine' (J.-Fr. Revel, *Pourquoi des philosophes*, p. 145).

– the *ad ignorantiam* argument, by which one imposes on an adversary the burden of proving the contrary (Lalande). Ex: 'Prove to us that we are swimming against the current of our nature and of our history, and we will change course' (P. Nizan, *Les Chiens de garde*, p. 88).

– the pretext*

– the *loophole* (an evasive answer, prevarication, *ignoratio elenchi*, or fallacy of the irrelevant conclusion), in which the remarks made have no bearing on the question discussed. The *OED* defines the device thus: 'A logical fallacy which consists in apparently refuting an opponent, while actually disproving some statement different from that advanced by him; also extended to any argument which is irrelevant to its professed purpose.'

Evasive answers may sometimes be funny. Ex: On a poster proclaiming, 'Alcohol kills slowly,' an imbiber had written, 'Who the hell cares. We're in no hurry.' On another poster (displayed in a British city) which asked, 'What would you do if Jesus came to Liverpool?' an ardent soccer fan had written, 'Play Saint-John on the left wing.' (Ian Saint-John was at that time the Liverpool centre-forward.) *Ignoratio elenchi* (Joseph, pp. 197, 370; Vuillaume, p. 16; Verest, sect. 422) is an argumentative ploy by which, as though 'unaware' of the point of the debate, a speaker proves something else, thus imperceptibly (it is hoped) shifting the subject under discussion. Boris Vian exposes the device by foregrounding it: 'Gentlemen of the jury, we'll leave aside the motive for murder, the circumstances in which it took place, and also the murder itself. Under these conditions, what blame do you attach to my client?' (B. Vian, 'Le Brouillard,' in *Les Fourmis*, p. 155). See also antanaclasis*.

– the argument *ad populum*, which attempts by 'appealing to popular sentimental weaknesses rather than to facts or reasons' (Grambs, p. 7) to influence an easily persuaded audience

– the *apodioxis* (Morier), which rejects an argument without discussion, declaring it childish. Fabri (2:113) called it *contennement* (i.e., 'contempt' in eighteenth-century French) 'when we say that our opponent's speech is a small thing, less than nothing, or that it's irrelevant, distasteful, or incredible, or that it would be boring or ridiculous to speak of it.'

One useful variety peculiar to learned papers is the dismissal of a point on the grounds that it would take too long to discuss it. Ex (ironical): 'Is milk nutritious? The discussion of such a question would exceed the limits set upon this article' (A. Jarry, *La Chandelle verte*, p. 489). Or one can reject points by declaring them to be of secondary interest: 'obviously certain details of your paper might be discussed [a list of them is then given very rapidly], but we'll examine instead ...' If the point is too tricky to be put aside like this, it is avoided with the 'promise that, at the right time and place, we will discuss it fully, so that we do not seem to be evading it.' (Fabri [2:112] calls this an *intermission*.)

Angenot defines *disqualification* as another kind of argumentative dispensation one allows oneself by declaring that the baseness, triviality, or undue violence of an attack is enough to discredit its author. André Breton, the surrealist leader, uses the argument in *Légitime Défense* (p. 21) against one of the movement's critics: 'According to Marcel Martinet (*Europe*, May 15, 1926), the Surrealists became disenchanted with Surrealism only after the war *because there was no money in it* ... The responsibility for which assertion we leave to him, since its unfairness dispenses me from taking up his article point by point.' See also counter-litotes*; definition*, R1; etymology*; paralogism*; prosopopoeia*, R4; and sophistry*. For the *ad verecundiam* argument, see threat*, R3.

R3: Any argument used, even implicitly, in a process of reasoning* is open to the possibility of refutation*, unless one has recourse to the argument from authority (see quotation*, R3). The discussion of an argument's value is one of the techniques of amplification*, in the broad sense of that term (see also deliberation* and letter*).

R4: A good many arguments always remain implicit. These are the culture-specific presumptions and prejudgments which form the underlying presuppositions of argumentation.

ASSERTION A speech act giving the position of a speaker on a given subject. The assertion has two parts: the *topic* (Fr., *le thème*) or psychological subject, that is, what is spoken about or more exactly that about which something is said; and the *comment* (Fr., *le propos*) or psychological predicate, that is what is said (about the topic).

Although not always distinguishable, topic and predicate together represent the source of the sentence's syntactic constitution as a nominal syntagm followed by a verbal one. Ex: 'Shock *is indispensable*. Magicians *like darkness*.' The topic may figure in an initial phrase followed by a comma. Ex: 'In this house, Voltaire was born.' In this sentence taken from a tourist guide, the house is identified; the topic is thus in the adverbial complement, while the rest forms the predicate. Obviously, then, grammatical and psychological subjects do not necessarily coincide.

The verb which has an apparent subject allows for a clearer distinction of topic from predicate. Ex: 'There has been a watch lost.' This assertion serves to inform. The topic would be '(this is) what is happening.' If 'watch,' the real subject, were the grammatical subject ('A watch has been lost'), it would be less clearly evident that the topic is not the watch.

Logically, the predicate is distinguished by the fact that it may be said to be either true or false. Psychologically, it may be questioned or denied. Although not offering a perfect criterion, the French *emphatic* transformation 'c'est ... qui' (also called *pseudo-clivage* in French) draws attention to the predicate. **Exx:** *'C'est elle qui* est arrivée en retard hier' (*'She* arrived late yesterday'); *'C'est en retard qu'*elle est arrivée hier' ('She arrived *late* yesterday'); *'C'est hier qu'*elle est arrivée en retard' (*'Yesterday* she arrived late'). In all of these cases, the verb and its adjuncts are forced back into the topic. In the first instance, 'C'est elle qui est arrivée hier' implies that *'someone* arrived late yesterday.' To which is added that *in this regard* (on this topic, therefore) it must be said (this announces the predicate) it was *she* (who arrived late yesterday). In such cases, English achieves oral emphasis* through intonation*, whereas the sign of graphic emphasis is italics, as in the translations above.

In spoken language, the antithetical accent* plays an identical part in the emphatic formula, which is the principal reason for the apparent superiority in intelligibility enjoyed by the spoken over the written form.

The topic does not always appear explicitly. If sufficiently implied in the context or situation, it is elided. **Exx:** 'Very nice!'; 'Fameux!'; 'I never speak about it, but I think about it all the time' (A. Allais, *La Barbe et autres contes*, p. 64). P. Guiraud (p. 73) calls ellipsis* of the predicate (a rarer phenomenon) *locutive*: such elision* works by reference to situation, by tone, or through recourse to interjections*. **Ex:** 'At the present time, distances, pooh!' [i.e., they may be discounted] (J. Audiberti, *L'Effet Glapion*, p. 145).

Analogous expressions: predication (logic), affirmation

Analogous definitions: See Ducrot and Todorov (p. 314), Marouzeau (under 'phrase'), *OED*, and Robert.

R1: Assertion may take the form of a question*. In this case, it is the person addressed who is invited to take a position. On the other hand, assertions may be affirmative, negative (see negation*), or dubitative (see *dubitatio**). Sentences may express all the degrees, from assurance to doubt, in the appropriate forms: affirmative, negative, declarative, interrogative, exclamative, or injunctive.

R2: In generative grammar, assertion is a sentence modality, characteristic of its referential function (see enunciation*). J. Kristeva, in *La Révolution du langage poétique*, pp. 42–50, points out a relationship between syntactic constituents (see syntagm*) and 'the thetic phase of significance' composed of an enunciation* which concerns a *denotatum*. The creation, which may be called 'true' or 'false,' of a relationship between two elements is the 'logical property' of assertive utterances. Aristotle called such propositions *apophantic*, a term derived from the Greek αποφασις, which means both declaration and negation; hence, in the *OED*, *apophasis*, and in Littré *apophase*, 'denial, refutation,' as opposed to *cataphase*, 'affirmation.'

R3: There are various means of joining to the constituent assertion of the assertive sentence supplementary assertions, called *adjacent* (or second, third, etc.) assertions (or predications). These are adjunctions* (see adjunction, R2), interpolated clauses, parentheses*, appositions*, self-corrections*, and examples of hyperbaton*. Ex: 'We have here an example of what Gödel demonstrates – laboriously – in his system' (A. Badiou, 'Marque et manque,' *Cahiers pour l'analyse*, no. 10 [1969], p. 169). The adverb placed between two pauses is the equivalent of another assertion, which would state: 'but his demonstration is (very) laborious.' Ex: 'The propositions which define reality present as true something which is not (immediately) true' (H. Marcuse, *L'Homme unidimensionnel*, pp. 171–2). The parenthesis* is the equivalent of a concession* which would follow on from the paradox*: 'something not true, or at least not immediately so.' Ex: 'It is, I say, when eyes opened that truths and lies surfaced, and that illusion submerged mankind' (R. Ducharme, *L'Avalée des avalés*, p. 102). A simple comma may suffice: 'John Paul Vann was born, illegitimate, in 1924 in Norfolk, Virginia, of poor immigrant stock' (*Independent Magazine*, 15 April 1989, p. 21). That is: 'Vann was born in Norfolk, and he was born illegitimate' (see caesura*, R4).

R4: Oswald Ducrot, examining the implicit context of the assertion, proposes a stricter operating definition. He contrasts what is *posed* to what is *presupposed*. The posed is the element which the assertion presents as new, so that any negative or interrogative transformation erases it. The presupposition, which survives such transformations, is presented to the receiver as being implicitly self-evident, already accepted, beyond discussion. It thus has an illocutionary value, which is founded on social convention. (See finesse* and *coq-à-l'âne*, R5.)

Conversely, if what is posed contains no more than the relevant presuppositions, then the result is mere empty assertion, talking for talking's sake. Ex: 'Since Picasso devoted his life to art, the latter occupies an important place in his paintings.' As established by the science of discursive pragmatics, it is a law of the text that every assertion must contain an element that may be added to what has already been said or presupposed. (Discursive pragmatics, a discipline of recent origin, is a branch of linguistics; it studies utterances and enunciation*.)

R5: Assertion is the normal form of argument*. It has various degrees (see enunciation*, R1), as well as its own intonation*. Nominalization* resolves it. In more developed form, it becomes a period*. It appears in different kinds of sentences* and is articulated in diverse ways according to the position of the antithetical or expressive accent* (see expressive punctuation*, R2). In disguised form, it becomes a question* often implying a response* (see response, R1). Reduced to a single word it is emphatic (see emphasis*, R1).

ASSONANCE A mark of the poetic line. Miller Williams (*Patterns of Poetry*, p. 14) defines assonance as the 'relationship between words with different consonants immediately preceding and following the last accented vowels, which vowels have identical sounds (hit/will, disturb/bird, go/know, undoing/construing).' See also Littré.

In French, assonance is 'a verse-marker: the repetition* of the last accented syllable' (J. Pesot, conversation with the author). Ex:

> Il dormiront sous la pluie ou les étoiles
> Ils galoperont avec moi portant en croupe des victoires.
> > G. Apollinaire, *Poèmes à Lou*, in *Oeuvres poétiques*, p. 382

Other definition: Frye defines assonance in anglophone poetry as 'repetition* of middle vowel sounds' wherever in the line they appear. See alliteration*, R2.

R1: Rhyme* and assonance are varieties, in regular poetry, of the more general device homoioteleuton*, but frequently assonance is used as a synonym of homoioteleuton. Ex: 'We cannot dedic*ate*, we cannot consec*rate*, we cannot hallow this ground' (Abraham Lincoln, 'Gettysburg Address').

R2: In the case of homoioteleuton, accented vowels are identical, but no account is taken of consonants. Paronomasia* is a more general case employing similarities between several phonemes.

R3: One also finds cases in which only the post-tonic consonants are identical. The *Leys d'amors* (the most important treatise on the language and poetic practices of the troubadours of medieval Provence) calls the latter 'consonantal rhymes' [*rims consonans*]. P. Guiraud (*Essais de stylistique*) both points this out and quotes a recent example:

> Je sors! si un rayon me b*l*esse
> Je succomberai sur *l*a mousse.
> > A. Rimbaud, *Les Illuminations*

On the same subject, J. Mazaleyrat (*Eléments de métrique française*, p. 196) speaks of *counter-assonance*, a term which seems more relevant than *apophonic rhyme* (Morier; see paronomasia*, R3).

R4: Assonanced lines may be grouped to form *laisses* (see stanza*, R2).

ASTEISMUS 1. 'Refined, witty talk ... Facetious or mocking answer that plays on a word' (Lanham). See also Grambs, Jacobs, and Joseph.

Ex:

> BLAIR: Your letter mentioned some unsavoury business with choirboys.

PURVIS: _Savoury_ business, not unsavoury business.
BLAIR: Savoury business?
PURVIS: Yes. You know what a savoury is. Mushrooms on toast ... sardines ... or, in this case, Welsh rarebit.

Tom Stoppard, _The Dog It Was That Died_, scene 3

2. Delicate, clever banter or badinage which praises or flatters while appearing to blame or reproach. See Fontanier, p. 150; Genette (_Figures II_, p. 251); and Morier.

Ex: 'What! another chef d'oeuvre! Weren't those you had already published enough? Do you want [to drive] your rivals to utter despair?' (V. Voiture, quoted by Fontanier).

Other names: 'Civill Jest; Merry Scoffe; _Urbanitas_' (Lanham)

R1: Asteismus is a form of social irony*. French rhetoricians therefore unite it with its opposite: 'disguise blame under the veil of praise' (Le Clerc, p. 298; Verest, p. 106). Cyrano's famous 'nose speech' piles up example on example ('What a sign board for a perfumer!' etc.) which are also examples of chleuasmos*. The device is eminently rhetorical (see false –*, R1). It has its own intonation*.

R2: Since asteismus presupposes a certain connivance between the speakers, it is used mostly between friends. **Ex** [Brunet is proposing that Mathieu join the Communist Party. He thinks that involvement will be good for him]: 'Mathieu went up to Brunet and shook him by the shoulders (he was very fond of him). – You dirty bloody talent-spotter. It does me good to hear you talk like that' (J.-P. Sartre, _L'Age de raison_, p. 172). As the example shows, asteismus may include swear-words*. It is close to antiphrasis*.

ASYNDETON A kind of ellipsis* which omits the merely copulative conjunctions supposed to unite the different parts of a sentence. See Littré, Girard, Lanham, Lausberg (sect. 709–11), Le Clerc (p. 268), Paul (p. 141), Preminger, Quillet, and Robert.

Exx: 'I came, I saw, I conquered' (Caesar); 'That government of the people, by the people, for the people, shall not perish from the earth' (A. Lincoln, 'Gettysburg Address'); 'Rain, wind, clover, leaves became parts of my life. _Real parts of my body_' (Anne Hébert, _Le Torrent_, p. 37).

Ex:

For poetry makes nothing happen: it survives
In the valley of its making where executives
Would never want to tamper, flows on south
From ranches of desolation and the busy griefs,

Raw towns that we believe and die in; it survives,
A way of happening, a mouth.

W.H. Auden, 'In Memory of W.B. Yeats'

Other names: disjunction (Fontanier [p. 340], Girard, Lausberg [sect. 711], Littré, Paul, Quillet); dissolution (Le Clerc, p. 269); asynateton (Quillet); articulo, brachylogia*, dialyton, loose language, dialelumenon (all in Lanham, who uses a larger definition: 'omission of conjunctions between words, phrases or clauses')

Antonym: polysyndeton*

R1: Asyndeton expresses disorder (Spitzer, p. 283). Ex: 'There had been so many funerals since grandmother Antoinette reigned over her household, little black deaths, in winter, disappearances of children, of babies, who had only lived a few months, mysterious disappearances of adolescents in autumn, in spring' (Marie-Claire Blais, *Une Saison dans la vie d'Emmanuel*, p. 28).

R2: Since asyndeton is characterized by the absence of conjunctions and commas, it may happen that nothing, except the meaning, allows one to distinguish whether the second element is added to the first with the same function or whether it stands in apposition*. Ex: 'sadly and tenderly the woman stared at the children, the babies' (ibid., p. 53). Are we to understand two associated or dissociated groups?

This formal relationship is not unconnected with the effect of vague conjunction provided by asyndeton, whose assembled elements form a badly outlined concept. Ex: 'my mother confused names, events' (ibid.).

R3: When discussing asyndeton, it is better to avoid speaking of juxtaposition*, since the latter term has a specific, quite distinct meaning.

ATTENUATION We may group under this title the figures of extenuation*, euphemism*, and their ironic form, litotes*. These are figures of enunciation* whose function is to diminish, for reasons of propriety or otherwise, the real intensity of things.

Exx: oaths (see interjection*, R5); preterition* (see preterition, R1); certain negative constructions (see negation*, R3); certain kinds of questions* and tautologies* (see tautology, R2)

Analogous expressions in French: *écriture blanche* ('blank writing'); *degré zéro de l'écriture* ('zero-degree writing') (Barthes). See litotes*, R2.

Antonym: hyperbole*

R1: The attitude implied by such devices presents an alternative* to the reader, who may consider the attenuation as natural (if, for example, things are well known and 'speak for themselves') or as ironical (if, for example, it is a matter of controversial or repressed truths). If interpreted as ironic, attenuation provokes a vigorous reaction (see litotes*).

R2: Attenuation may be distinguished from reduction (see generalization*, R3), which belongs to the utterance and not to an attitude.

R3: Narrative* is attenuated by discourse*. Exx: See discourse*, R1, and truism*, R2.

AUTHORISM (*Mot d'auteur*) A word or remark which a reader recognizes as coming from the author rather than from a character.

Ex: 'AUDUBON. – "It's all the same to me. Besides, in this age of deep thinkers, talking nonsense is the only way to prove that one's own thoughts are free and independent"' (B. Vian, *Théâtre*, 1:233). The idea expressed is too deep to have come from the character, a child who has never grown up, but it is typical of Vian's attitude towards existentialism.

R1: The utterance may have maximum relevance to the character's situation: for a reader to recognize it as an authorism, it need only reflect exactly the author's ideas. See reactualization*, 1. Ex: 'DORA. – "If the only solution is death, we are not on the right path. The right path is the one that leads to life, to the sun"' (A. Camus, *Les Justes*, p. 165).

R2: Authorisms should be distinguished from parabasis*: authorial intrusions, comments, and digressions made in the present tense.

AUTISM 'A condition in which a person is morbidly self-absorbed and out of touch with reality' (*OEDS*). An attitude which consists in envisaging everything from a single strictly personal, 'subjective' point of view. See Marchais.

Ex: 'This happened in one of those unspeakably foul omnibi which fill up with hoi poloi precisely at those times when I have to consent to use them' (R. Queneau, *Exercises in Style*, p. 24).

R1: Autism has a basis in private experience. Ex: 'All of mankind's shaky science is in no way superior to the immediate knowledge I can have of my own being. I am the only judge of what there is in me' (A. Artaud, *L'Ombilic des limbes*, p. 72).

Solipsism gave Schopenhauer a base for his theories, to which, in *Aurora*, Michel Leiris has given literary form: 'The word *I* summarizes for me the structure of the world. It is only as a function of myself and because I deign to give some attention to their existence that things exist ... It is only as a function of myself that I exist and if I say that *it is raining* or that *the sea is evil*, these are only periphrases which express the fact that a part of myself has resolved itself into fine droplets or that another part is full of dangerous cross-currents' (p. 86). Such interiorization provides one mode for the formation of images* (see image, R5).

R2: We may distinguish autism from the naïve kind of egoism displayed by those who constantly call attention to themselves. Ex: 'I tell you, personally, I think there are some odd things in this life, it's only mountains that never meet' (R. Queneau, *Exercises in Style*, p. 82).

The egoism displayed by a Stendhal, a Barrès, a Wilde, a Burgess, or a Vidal, on the other hand, is a kind of autism, just as is the *apologia pro vita sua*. Ex: 'I know how to use a pen, but ever since I took my last written examination, the pen has always been for me a musical instrument: I still write orchestral scores with it but, associating it as I do with the shaping of notes and dynamic signals, I find it difficult to put it in the service of any written statement longer than *allegro ma non troppo*. Still, I do not have to make excuses for not being a literary penman ...' (A. Burgess, *But Do Blondes Prefer Gentlemen?*, p. xii).

R3: Autism may possess oral markers: a kind of fruity intonation* and a preference for the higher registers.

B

BALLAD or BALLADE A group of stanzas* in simple rhythm* (*baller* in French means to dance). In its strict form, the ballad has three and a half stanzas, each ending with the same line (see refrain*). The final half-stanza (or *envoy*) begins with an apostrophe* dedicating the poem to the beloved or to some other eponymous person.

Exx: 'La ballade des dames du temps jadis' (Villon; see acrostic*); 'Ballade of Dead Actors' (W.E. Henley)

R1: The ballad is a 'poem of fixed form' (see poem*): three octaves and a quatrain (see stanza*). The *grande ballade* has ten-lined stanzas. Ex: A.C. Swinburne's 'A Ballad of François Villon.' The *chant royal* has five and a half stanzas of eleven lines. Exx: H.C. Bunner, 'Behold the Deeds'; Wesli Court, 'Requiem for the Old Professor,' collected in Miller Williams, *Patterns of Poetry*, pp. 102–5.

BARBARISM A mistake* in vocabulary; a use of words or forms which do not belong to the language (as opposed to solecism*). See Fowler, Marouzeau, and Robert (who insists: 'a gross error').

Exx: 'youse'; 'ashphalt'

Fowler, who described the barbarism as 'an illiterate expression ... some word that, like its name, is likely to wound feelings' (pp. 48–9), cited 'Thou asketh' as a barbarism. The rarity of his example is an indication, perhaps, of the tolerance by anglophones of linguistic phenomena which francophones would condemn as barbarisms.

Other definition: Littré gives a wider meaning to barbarism: any expression which violates the rules of language. Barbarisms would thus include solecisms* and even examples of cacology*.

R1: Barbarisms are alterations, obtained by composition, derivation, or linguistic 'patching'; they always result from ignorance or confusion. This does not prevent them finding a place in literary works. **Ex:**

'Awright,' she said contemptuously. 'Awright, cover 'im up if ya want ta. Whatta I care? You bindle bums think you're so damn good. Whatta ya think I am, a kid? I tell ya I could of went with shows. Not jus' one, neither. An' a guy tol' me he could put me in pitchers.' (J. Steinbeck, *Of Mice and Men*, p. 86).

Each mispronunciation by the character makes possible movement towards other meanings. As may be seen here, barbarisms may produce effects directly, as well as through indirect evocation. In such cases, however, they resemble incorrect use of words (see incorrect* word, R3).

R2: The mistake* may be due to a borrowing from a foreign language. See peregrinism* and sarcasm*, R1.

BAROQUISM The search for the rarest, the most surprising, and most curious ideas, figures, and words.

Ex:

Anon out of the earth a fabric huge
Rose like an exhalation, with the sound
Of dulcet symphonies and voices sweet,
Built like a temple, where pilasters round
Were set, and Doric pillars overlaid
With golden architrave; nor did there want
Cornice or frieze with bossy sculptures graven;
The roof was fretted gold. Not Babylon,
Nor great Alcairo such magnificence
Equalled in all their glories, to enshrine
Belus or Serapis their gods or seat
Their kings, when Egypt with Assyria strove
In wealth and luxury.

J. Milton, Paradise Lost, 1.710–22

Baroquism

Ex:

> It was as if all the guests of the symposium were now in the crypt, each mummified in its own residue, each the diaphanous synecdoche of itself, Rachel as a bone, Daniel as a tooth, Sampson as a jaw, Jesus as a shred of purple garment ... From every corner of the crypt, now I was grinned at, whispered to, bidden to death by this macrobody divided among glass cases and reliquaries and yet reconstructed in its vast and irrational whole, and it was the same body that at the supper had eaten and tumbled obscenely but here, instead, appeared to me fixed in the intangibility of its deaf and blind ruin. (U. Eco, *The Name of the Rose*, p. 433)

Analogous terms: mannerism, preciosity, Marinism (see imitation*), Asianism. Littré proposes 'cataglottism' ('the use of well-chosen words'). Closer examination reveals cataglottism to be a 'false friend,' which the *OED*, citing Cotgrave, defines as a ' "kisse or kissing with the tongue." ' The *Supplement* to the *OED* recommends the deletion of the observation, but still retains in a modern example the English meaning of 'kissing.'

R1: The opposite of Asianism was 'Atticism' (see period*, R4), with Greek clarity and the democratic aim of persuasion being opposed to the fascination with the kind of beauty to be found in profuse detail. Atticism, however, was too *recherché* for some: one of its avatars, Ciceronianism (Erasmus), aroused in some humanists (Dolet, Justus Lipsius) a reaction, which became the 'anti-Ciceronian movement' and which rejected anything not going tersely and directly to the heart of the matter. The 'anti-Ciceronians' favoured concision, laconicism, and brevity, as did Orwell in his influential essay 'Politics and the English Language' (*Inside the Whale and Other Essays*, pp. 143–57).

R2: During the seventeenth century, French *précieuses* or blue stockings abused metonymical periphrasis*. **Exx:** 'We shall take the meridional necessities' for 'We are going to have lunch'; 'My good commoner, go and seek my zephyr in my precious' for 'Maid, go and get my fan from the cupboard' (A. Somaize, *Le Grand Dictionnaire des précieuses*, 1661).

But even today, baroquism triumphs in some comparisons*. **Ex:** 'Her amber comb divided the silky mass [her hair] into long orange threads similar to the furrows which the happy ploughman makes with a fork in apricot jam' (B. Vian, *L'Ecume des jours*, p. 7). Other figures used (and abused) in precious style: abstraction*, accumulation* (see accumulation, R2), oxymoron*, diaphora*, conceit*, enumeration* (see enumeration, R5), litotes*, periphrasis*, point*, homonymy*, wordplay*, semantic syllepsis*, and synecdoche* (see synecdoche, R3).

R3: If the ornamentation obscures meaning* completely, the result is phoebus*, the undecipherable text, the acme of baroque. A skilful author may prepare the reader for such obscurities, however, by first introducing simple prefigurations, before combining them later into formulas or points*.

R4: Asianisms, embroideries on gratuitous hypotheses or on the shape of letters, appear in Arabic literature up to the present day. Ex: 'Which is better: the upper or the lower lip? Would you like to know? What does it matter if both are velvet to my kisses, to my love' (G. Ghaneur, in Norin, ed., *Anthologie de la littérature arabe contemporaine*, 3:158). This is almost an example of a conceit*.

French neo-classical writers scorned this type of irrational development, but modern writers have returned to it. Ex: 'The sky was full [of stars], the sparkling *y* and the *i* of myriad' (C. Simon, *Histoire*, p. 355).

R5: Positivism classified all baroque or surrealist devices under the pejorative label of *procédisme*, or device-mania: 'Procédisme consists in saving oneself the trouble of thinking or more especially of observing, in favour of reliance on made-up terms or well-defined formulas ... In the XVIth century, the Gongorists and Euphuists, and in the XVIIth century, the Précieuses were all *Procédistes*' (*Annales médico-psychologiques*, quoted by André Breton in *Manifestes du surréalisme*, p. 74). What would these learned alienists, for whom scientific observation was the only type of thinking, have said about modern and postmodern 'potential' or 'disseminated' forms of French literature?

R6: If it lacks distinction, baroquism slips into burlesque*; lack of isotopy* produces device-mania. See false –*, R4, and extravagant* comparison, R3.

BATHOS A sudden fall in a climactic development. See Preminger.

Ex: 'A. de Musset, charming, likeable, subtle, graceful, delicate, exquisite, small' (Victor Hugo, quoted by P. Clarac in *La Classe de français, le XIXe siècle*, p. 202). The effect may be ironical or sometimes simply comical. Ex: 'A hundred petitioners go seeking jam, cigarettes, dollars and kicks in the behind' (R. Ducharme, *L'Avalée des avalés*, p. 96).

Other definitions: Longinus used the word as an antonym of *sublime*, whereas Pope in *Peri Bathous; or, Martinus Scriblerus His Treatise on the Art of Sinking in Poetry* (1728) used it to designate something at once pathetic and ridiculous. Preminger offers two definitions: 'an unintentionally ludicrous because ill-managed attempt at elevated expression' and 'deliberate anticlimax*.' This type of ridicule of some sublime aspiration through a final opposition aptly describes Claire's mockery of her own enthusiasm: 'CLAIRE: In his perfumed arms, the devil bears me away. He raises me up, I take off, depart ... (she stamps her heel on the ground) ... and I remain here' (J. Genet, *Les Bonnes*, p. 21). It also expresses Churchill's irony* at his post-war treatment by the British electorate: 'On the night of the tenth of May [1940], at the outset of this mighty battle, I acquired the chief power in the State, which henceforth I wielded in ever-growing measure for five years and three months of world war, at the end of which time, all our enemies having surrendered unconditionally or being about to do so, I was immediately dismissed by the British electorate from all further conduct of their affairs' (W. Churchill, *The Gathering Storm*, pp. 666–7).

R1: In its modern meaning, bathos combines *gradatio** (see *gradatio*, R5) with anticlimax* (see anticlimax, R3).

BATTOLOGY Unnecessary, tedious repetition* of the same thoughts in the same terms in similar clauses. See Littré and *OED*.

Ex: 'He wants me to answer that phenol is an oxydized derivative of benzene extracted from oil found in tar and coal, but I will not answer him that phenol is an oxydized derivative of benzene extracted from oil found in tar and coal!!' (R. Ducharme, *L'Avalée des avalés*, p. 196).

Ex ['East Village hippie describing the sexual customs of that scene (in *The Hippie Trip*, pp. 121–2)']: 'Now here, like Mary got screwed last night and she went and did it, well, gee whiz, good enough – wow, I mean what's it to me? I mean, wow, that's the way it is here' (Lanham [1974], pp. 89–90).

R1: Battology is a particular form of verbiage*. To distinguish it from redundancy*, perissology*, and pleonasm* (see pleonasm, R1), Marouzeau compares it to stammering*, probably for reasons of etymology* (Battos was a king who stammered; see Herodotus, 4:155). Justified repetition* is epanalepsis* (see epanalepsis, R2); if the speaker uses other terms, it is a metabole* or a paraphrase*.

BLASPHEMY Words deliberately outrageous to the deity.

Ex:' "If I believed in a God I would curse him," he said. "I would spit in his face. I would send him to his own hell" ' (Katherine Ann Porter, *Ship of Fools*, p. 321).

R1: *Profanities*, or familiar exclamations*, vaguely blasphemous in origin, are similar to interjections* (see interjection, R5). They liberate affectivity at the expense of the super-ego. Ex:

O God! O Montreal!

Preferrest thou the gospel of Montreal to the gospel of Hellas,
The gospel of thy connexion with Mr. Spurgeon's haberdasher to the gospel of Discobolus?

Yet none the less blasphemed he beauty saying, 'The Discobolus
hath no gospel,
But my brother-in-law is haberdasher to Mr. Spurgeon.'
O God! O Montreal!

Samuel Butler, 'Psalm of Montreal'

In any case, the profanity in question should be distinguished from
an exclamation* which invokes the deity without seeking to outrage it.
Convent-dwellers used to call this type the *ejaculation*. A current example: 'Jesus! Sweet Jesus! My God, Jesus Mary and Joseph!' This sort
of exclamation has become a banal kind of interjection. It resembles any
supplication* addressed to the super-ego. Ex: 'Mother! Holy Toledo!'

BLUNDER A mistake* arising from simple-mindedness or carelessness.

The French terms *nigauderie* and *niaiserie* frequently apply to mistakes due to simple-mindedness, whereas *sottise* designates a careless
mistake. In literary texts, both types of 'mistakes' are often deliberate.
Ex: 'Every life is many days, day after day' (Joyce, *Ulysses*, p. 175).

Analogous terms: howler, boner, bloomer, nonsensical or stupid
remark, nonsense*, blather (familiar), [to talk] cock (coarse), gaffe, *faux
pas*, blooper

R1: There are errors in pronunciation (e.g., *ash*phalt'), in vocabulary
(e.g., 'He is disinterested in the truth'), as well as in thought (e.g., 'Our
dog has gone missing. It is a portent of doom' [Sue Townsend, *The
Secret Diary of Adrian Mole, Aged 13 3/4*, p. 130]).

R2: Sometimes blunders are mimological. Ex:

LITERARRY CORNER.
A book for the hols. *'Rob Roy' by Charles Dickens.* (Grabber &
Grabber, 6s.)
To judge from the first page which i happned to see by mistake this
is something about a small boy who had to climb chimneys. Ak-
tually i would have thort this was quite super as you get black but
this one seemed to be rather sorry for himself. On page 5 there is a
pressed leaf and on page 77 some orange juice i spilt while the book
was acting as part of a fort. There seemed to be something about
some water babies or something soppy but i dont really kno. i
supose he must hav climbed the chimney to rob roy but this is only
a guess. (G. Willians and R. Searle, *Down with Skool*, p. 45)

Ex:

If you really want to hear about it, the first thing you'll probably
want to know is where I was born, and what my lousy childhood

was like, and how my parents were occupied and all before they had me, and all that David Copperfield kind of crap, but I don't feel like going into it, if you want to know the truth. In the first place, that stuff bores me and in the second place, my parents would have two hemmorrhages apiece if I told anything pretty personal about them. They're *nice* and all – I'm not saying that – but they're also touchy as hell. Besides I'm not going to tell you my whole godamm autobiography or anything. (J.D. Salinger, *The Catcher in the Rye*, p. 5)

Both these texts (as does *Adrian Mole*) 'reproduce' the voices of juvenile or adolescent narrators, attributing to them graphic blunders or ideas consonant with their age and view of the world. Blunders made by old people are put down to senility and form part of *anecdotage*.

R3: Simulation* (and pseudo-simulation*) of blunders is a principal source of comedy, as the number of synonyms* for the word *clown* attests: blunderer, buffoon, bungler, charlatan, clod, *farceur*, fool, harlequin, mountebank, punch, rustic, stooge, tumbler, etc.

BOUSTROPHEDON   Graphic transcription from right to left.

Exx: 'mangiD kcirtaP' (Joyce, *Ulysses*, p. 101); 'Llareggub Hill' (Dylan Thomas, *Under Milk Wood*); 'The input hadn't been IAHVEH, but HEVHAI' (Eco, *Foucault's Pendulum*, p. 40); 'elbaré'd elliuef al ed enneivuos em ej euq li-tuaf?' [i.e., 'fael elpam eht rebmemer I tsum?'] (R. Duguay, *Lapokalipsô*, p. 147).

R1: The order of the letters is reversed but not the letters themselves. It's not enough, therefore, simply to look at them on a transparency or in a mirror to decipher them, unlike in the following example: 'And in the medicine cabinet mirror, the word REDRUM flashing on and off. Suddenly a huge clock in a glass bowl materialized in front of it ... he saw the word REDRUM reflecting dimly from the glass dome, now reflected twice. And he saw that it spelled MURDER' (Stephen King, *The Shining*, p. 306).
    In the case of boustrophedon, suppression of separating marks like capital letters and apostrophes, and even of the divisions between words, produces graphic scrambling*.

R2: Boustrophedon, in its literal sense, means '(written) alternately from right to left and from left to right, like the course of the plough in successive furrows; as in various ancient inscriptions in Greek and other languages' (*OED*).

R3: See also palindrome* and allograph*, R3.

BRACHYLOGIA   A vice of elocution consisting of excessive brevity, pushed to the point of stylistic obscurity. See Littré.

'Elocution' is here used in Fontanier's sense of the term (Latin *elocutio*, 'the choice, the matching of words') or in the broader sense of 'the way of expressing oneself' (Littré, Larousse, *OED*), but not in its restricted, more recent sense (since 1850 in French) of '*the* "correct" way of articulating sounds in speaking' (Larousse). The *OED* gives this latter meaning as existing in English only since the seventeenth century. In the *Concise Oxford Dictionary* (1976 ed.), however, it is the only meaning listed for the term.

Ex: 'He sang his didn't he danced his did' (e.e. cummings). The missing elements (punctuation, signifieds) of this minimal sentence would be supplied: 'He sang his (part, songs?), (his friend? girl-friend?) didn't he, he danced his (measures, steps?), (he?) did.' See also anastrophe*, R3.

Analogous term: contraction

Other definitions: See Marouzeau; and Grévisse (*Le Bon Usage*, sect. 228, no. 1): 'a kind of ellipsis* consisting in not repeating an element previously expressed.' This is zeugma*. See also ellipsis*. Lanham: 'Brevity of diction; abbreviated construction; word or words omitted. A modern theorist differentiated this use from ellipsis*, in that the elements missing are more subtly, less artificially, omitted in ellipsis: "The corps goeth before, we follow after, we come to the grave, she is put into the fire, a lamentation is made" (Peacham).'

R1: Brachylogia is not always a vice. Sometimes its obscurity is the price paid for convenient brevity, or signals euphemism* or irony*. Exx: coffee-break (a break in which to have coffee); a social disease (one contracted through close [social] contact). Brachylogia is of great help to the novelist in avoiding repetition* of the declarative verbs (to say, etc.). Exx: ' "Sir," he accosted me [he said on accosting me]'; ' "What!" started my visitor [said my visitor, with a start].' Grévisse, in collecting these examples (sect. 559, rem. 6, no. 1), allows in good French usage only verbs containing the idea of *saying* something (to sigh, to express astonishment, to insist, etc.). Similarly Grambs (pp. 402–5), who offers over one hundred 'acceptable' English dialogue-verbs, castigates the use of what he calls 'facial verbs' and 'physiognomy-speak.' Exx: ' "Absolutely not," she frowned'; ' "Gladly," he chuckled'; ' "Let's do it!" they beamed.'

Brevity can play an expressive role: 'Je t'aimais inconstant, qu'eussé-je fait fidèle' ('I loved you faithless, what would I have done, [had you been] true?') (Racine, *Andromaque*, 4.5). Spitzer comments (p. 269): 'So concentrated a sentence can only express a soul's oppression.' (This example often falls under the rubric of ellipsis*. Some examples of brachylogia are no more than particularly strong ellipses.)

Brachylogia's very obscurity may have aesthetic importance, as in Valéry's expression 'terre osseuse' ('Cimetière marin,' v. 53), in which it functions as litotes*: the bones filling the ground in question are those of the poet's ancestors.

R2: Syntactic juxtaposition* is one of the forms of brachylogia. See also portmanteau* word, R1.

BURLESQUE Low, extravagant comedy.

Ex:

> If you're anxious for to shine in the high aesthetic line, as a man of culture rare ...
> Then a sentimenal passion of a vegetable fashion must excite your languid spleen,
> An attachment à la Plato for a bashful young potato, or a not-too-French French bean.
> Though the Philistines may jostle, you will rank as an apostle in the high aesthetic band,
> If you walk down Piccadilly with a poppy or a lily in your mediaeval hand.
>
> W.S. Gilbert, Patience

Ex:

> A poor mendicant friar and Grand Admiral of the slave hulks
> arrives at top speed by sea
> and after having made the usual demands
> This is my expeditionary corps
> This is your blood
> sermonizes Haiphong with shots of canonical law
> exterminating angels accomplish their mission and decimate the population
>
> J. Prévert, 'Entendez-vous, gens du Viet-Nam ...'
in La Pluie et le beau temps

R1: Both Littré and Hutchinson (*Games Authors Play*, pp. 94–5) distinguish between burlesque, parody*, and the *mock-heroic* poem. These are the three species of the *farcical* (or 'bouffon') genre. Burlesque treats a noble, heroic subject using vulgar characters and a low style (e.g., J. Gay, *The Beggar's Opera*, and B. Vian, *Le Goûter des généraux*). The mockheroic, on the other hand, is an epic form which gives lower-class characters *recherché* manners (e.g., Marivaux, *Le Télémaque travesti*). According to Littré, parody* too 'changes the class of the characters in the works travestied.' Hutchinson gives the following account of the burlesque elements found in Gay's *The Beggar's Opera*:

> Italian opera was in vogue in the early part of the eighteenth century, but its excesses were regretted by many of the leading English writers of the day ... Gay accordingly turned the traditional Italian

formula upside down. He used the title 'opera' but nevertheless chose a setting, characters and language which were completely at odds with audience expectations. Instead of courtly or mythological figures, he chose beggars, thieves, and prostitutes; instead of a dignified language, he employed the slang of the underworld; instead of great deeds, he portrayed crime on a grand scale, double-crossing and murder. Yet all this was contained within the operatic structure, constant references by characters to 'Honour' and 'Love,' the designation of the leading highwayman as 'Captain,' of the prostitutes as 'Ladies,' and so on, all of which link the present piece with dominant traits of its sources. (*Games Authors Play*, pp. 94–5)

R2: Burlesque came from Italy along with baroquism* and flowered in France in the seventeenth century with d'Assoucy and Scarron, while suffering Boileau's sarcastic sallies. In any case, 'burlesque' is now used in a less specific meaning*: see interjection*, R5, and celebration*, R2.

R3: *Mazarinades* are examples of burlesque persiflage* with a political angle. The term derives from lampoons in couplets circulated during the civil wars in France between 1648 and 1653 called the *Fronde*. Satirists directed their attacks against Cardinal Mazarin. Nowadays, the genre survives in France in caricatural drawings.

C

CACEMPHATON A combination of sounds producing an unpleasant utterance.

Lanham (p. 20) gives both the older meaning, 'scurrilous jest; lewd allusion*' or 'double entendre,' and the more modern meaning, 'sounds combined for harsh effect,' citing Peacham: 'when there come many syllables of one sound together in one sentence, like a continual jarring upon one string, thus, neither honour nor nobility could move a naughty niggardly noddy.' Augarde (p. 161) cites the following parody by Swinburne of his own abuse of alliteration*: 'From the depth of the dreamy decline of the dawn through a notable nimbus of notable moonshine, / Pallid and pink as the palm of the flag-flower that flickers with fear of the flies as they float' (A. Swinburne, 'Nephelidia').

R1: Cacemphaton may produce an equivoque*, but an undesirable one. Its remedy sometimes involves a departure from common usage.

CACOLOGY A defective expression which, although not grammatically incorrect, does violence to usage and logic (Marouzeau; see also Lausberg, sect. 1070); unacceptable pronunciation or use of language

(Crystal, 1987); bad pronunciation; impropriety of wording or unacceptable diction (Grambs).

In English, cacology emphasizes 'good,' received pronunciation, rather than grammatical correctness: elocution rather than logic. Ex: 'THE FLOWER GIRL: Ah-ow-ooh! Aaah-ow-ooh! Aaaaaaaaaaa-ow-ooh!!!' (G.B. Shaw, *Pygmalion*, act 1). The following French example emphasizes faulty logic: 'Les intentions des gardes ne se résument qu'à assurer leur confort' ('The guards' intentions extend only to assuring their own comfort'), a contamination of *se résument à* and *ne consistent qu'à* (Marouzeau).

Other definition: synonym of cacemphaton* (Marouzeau)

R1: Cacology is a generic term in French for a mistake*, specified so as to cover any error in language other than barbarism* and solecism*. It involves the misunderstanding of certain privileged associations (said to be 'logical,' but often merely imposed by usage) such as 'remplir une mission' ('to fulfil a mission') and 'atteindre un but' ('to reach a goal'); hence Marouzeau's criticism of 'remplir un but' ('to achieve a goal'), which nonetheless has become current in French.

The expression verges upon semantic incompatibility. As soon as it is motivated as an error, cacology becomes a device (see dissociation*), a means, for example, of reviving dead metaphor*. Ex: 'The hand that rocked the cradle has kicked the bucket.'

CACOPHONY An elocutionary vice, consisting of a disagreeable or harsh sound, produced by the collision of two letters or syllables, or by the too frequent repetition* of the same letters or syllables. See Cuddon, Frye, Lausberg, Marouzeau, Preminger, and Quillet.

Exx: 'The Leith police dismisseth us'; 'En l'en entendant parler.'

Poets combine harsh sounds for effect. Ex:

> Dry clashed his harness in the icy caves
> And barren chasms, and all to left and right
> The bare black cliff clanged round him, as he based
> His feet on juts of slippery crag that rang
> Sharp-smitten with the dint of armed heels.
> > Tennyson, 'The Passing of Arthur,' in *Idylls of the King*

Other name: dissonance*

Antonym: euphony

R1: Repetition of a syllable produces parechema*.

R2: *Tautophony* is cacophony due to excessive alliteration*. The Greeks, who were interested in the phenomenon, called tautophony involving *l* lambdacism; that involving *m*, mytacism; *i*, iotacism; *r*, rhotacism; and *s*, sigmatism. They distinguished between consonantal and vocalic tautophony. Ex: 'Progress is not a proclamation nor palaver. It is not pretense nor play on prejudice. It is not the perturbation of a people passion-wrought nor a promise proposed' (Warren D. Harding nominating W. Howard Taft in 1912). Corbett (p. 471) quotes this as an example of alliteration*, adding that such a 'scheme of construction' may also be deliberately used for comic effect, as in: 'He was a preposterously pompous proponent of precious pedantry.' Obviously decisions on what constitutes 'excessive' alliteration belong to the reader. See tautogram*, R2, and paronomasia*, R5.

R3: Hiatus* is not necessarily cacophonic.

R4: Imitative cacophony consists in reproducing unpleasant sounds, as in the above example from Tennyson. See imitative harmony*, R1.

CADENCE Harmony* resulting from the arrangement of words in a sentence or line* of poetry (see Robert); 'the natural rhythm* of language, its "inner tune," depending on the arrangement of stressed and unstressed syllables' (Cuddon).

Ex:

> Side by side, their faces blurred,
> The earl and countess lie in stone,
> Their proper habits vaguely shown
> As jointed armour, stiffened pleat,
> And that faint hint of the absurd –
> The little dogs under their feet.

Philip Larkin, 'An Arundel Tomb'

Ex: 'If a man were called to fix the period in the history of the world during which the condition of the human race was the most happy and prosperous, he would, without hesitation, name that which elapsed from the death of Domitian to the accession of Commodus' (Edward Gibbon, *Decline and Fall of the Roman Empire*, ch. 3). The longer periodic groups also feature *gradatio**.

Other definitions: 'Cadence' can also designate speed of oral delivery (see tempo*), or the 'melodic pattern preceding the end of a sentence' (Cuddon). See punch* line, R1.

R1: Morier defines cadence as 'rhythm entirely formed of repeated or symmetrical quantities,' a sort of renewed, rhythmic echo*. These are perfect cadences, frequent in poetical prose and in the prose poem (e.g., in Gibbon's *Decline and Fall*; Macaulay's *History of England*; Fénelon's *Télémaque*; or Chateaubriand's *Les Martyrs*). Such works incorporate 'prose cadencée,' or 'rhythmical prose.'

R2: In French, even prose which is only slightly rhythmical is said to be 'nombreuse,' that is, 'well-balanced.'

CAESURA The limit of a syntagm*. The caesura cuts off sets of one or more phonetic words, constituting what, from the viewpoint of syntactic function, makes a single clause or assertion*. It is thus a constant phenomenon in prose (see punctuation*), as it is in poetry. But it is usually studied only in rhythmic verse, where its role is essential. In Greek and Latin verse the break in the movement generally occurred in the middle of the third or fourth foot. In English verse, if the aim is to mark the hemistich, the pause comes near the middle of the line. (The hemistich designates half-lines cut off by the caesura. The first half-line is frequently called 'the' hemistich, as is the point of division itself.) In French verse, a caesura may be strong or weak (see R4 below) and should produce rhetorical effects by calling attention to the meaning of a line or lines. Traditionally, the caesura has been very free in English, falling either near the middle or end of a line, thus adding variety or music to lines or whole poems. Cuddon (p. 96) finds that the caesura may either 'emphasize formality and stylize' or 'slacken the stiffness and tension of formal metrical patterns.' Ex (of the latter):

> People are putting up storm windows now,
> Or were, // this morning, / until the heavy rain
> Drove them indoors. // So, / coming home at noon,
> I saw storm windows lying on the ground
> Frame-full of rain; // through the water and glass I saw
> The crushed grass, // how it seemed to stream
> Away in lines / like seaweed on the tide
> Or blades of wheat / leaning under the wind.
>
> Howard Nemerov, 'Storm Windows,'
> in *Collected Poems of Howard Nemerov*

In neo-classical French (and English) poetry the alexandrine, with its obligatory caesura after the sixth syllable, is an example of strongly rhythmic poetry. To test this assertion, let's take a twelve-syllable line with the caesura after the seventh syllable. 'Les capitaines vainqueurs // ont une odeur forte' ('The conquering captains give off a strong smell') (A. Gide, *Romans*, p. 142). Is this a poetic rhythm*? *Quot homines, tot sententiae*.

The importance of the placing of the principal caesura in French verse is still demonstrated by the fact that the decasyllable divided 5//5 is quite different from that divided 4//6.

Same definition: Boileau, *Art poétique*: 'Be sure that always in your verses the sense, interrupting the flow of words, suspends the half-line and marks the caesura.'

Other definition: French typographers call the division of a word at the end of a line a 'caesura' (Bernard Vié and Jean Chaumely, *La Composition automatique des textes*).

R1: Grammatical divisions are as various as syntagms*. The more clearly defined divisions – those surrounding an 'excluded' syntagm or those separating elements having the same function (see syntagm*, R2) – are usually marked at beginning and end by commas. Principal or secondary caesuras are therefore always equivalent to commas (and, *a fortiori*, to semicolons and periods). See monologue*.

In addition, expressive punctuation* may give rise to 'rhythmic' commas, in prose as well as in poetry. Ex: 'I became aware of a distinct, hollow, metallic, and clangorous, yet apparently muffled reverberation ...' (E.A. Poe, 'The Fall of the House of Usher').

R2: In metric verse, the most harmonious rhythm* is obtained by separating the rhythmic divisions from the caesuras. Ex:

An aged man is but a paltry thing,
A tattered coat upon a stick, unless
Soul clap its hands and sing, and louder sing
For every tatter in its mortal dress.

W.B. Yeats, 'Sailing to Byzantium'

R3: Normally there is no graphic mark of the caesura, but it may be indicated by a thin vertical wavy line, or by an oblique* stroke (here two obliques are used). Commas, which mark off assertions, coincide with caesuras, but caesuras occur without commas. Concerning the caesura's acoustic mark, Morier has established that in poetry it consists of a fall in intensity, sometimes accompanied by a pause*.

R4: In French, the presence of a 'mute' e which one can sound to greater or lesser degree at the caesura makes for hesitation.
(a) *French neo-classical syllabic verse* rejects the problem by not allowing a syllable ending in e to fall at the caesura except where elision is possible. Ex: 'Mais il me faut tout per//dr' et toujours par vos coups' (Racine, *Andromaque*). Thus the caesura does not necessarily entail a pause.
(b) The *epic caesura* consists in dropping an e (syncope*). Ex: 'Ci fait la gest(e)//que Turoldus declin(et)' (*Chanson de Roland*, last line). So the same difficulty may arise at the end of a line; in addition, everything said here about the caesura at the hemistich is true, *mutatis mutandis*, of its articulation at the end of a line: we will see this again when dealing with enjamb(e)ment*.
(c) Use of the *lyric caesura* consists, on the other hand, in giving the e the greatest possible value. Ex: 'La verrai-je // jamais récompensée?' (Charles d'Orléans, quoted by Deloffre, p. 37). In lyric poetry (i.e., poetry accompanied by a lyre) the 'mute' e supported a note which

was sung, making the pause quite natural, as in modern French popular songs. Ex: 'Ne me quitte pas' (six syllables; J. Brel).
(d) It is still possible to defer the mute syllable until the second hemistich, but the aesthetic effect is dubious. This is the *'overflow' caesura* (*césure enjambante*). Ex: 'Que la victoi // re venait avec moi' (Eustache Deschamps, quoted by Deloffre).

R5: It sometimes happens that the principal utterance occurs before, or after, the obligatory caesura, wherever there is only secondary articulation: this produces end* positioning. See enjamb(e)ment*, R2 and R3.

R6: The alexandrine without a caesura after the sixth syllable is romantic (4/4/4), or liberated (2//6/4, 4/6/2, etc.). See Morier. For *caesura for the eye*, see enjamb(e)ment*, R4. For *strophic (or stanzaic) caesura*, see stanza* and period*, R1.

CALLIGRAMME A word invented by Guillaume Apollinaire (1880–1918) to designate what he originally called lyrical ideograms (see *Oeuvres poétiques*, p. 1075); he arranged the poetic text so as to produce an approximate design of some corresponding subject.

Ex:

Cet	This
Arbrisseau	Little Tree
Qui se prépare	Which is preparing
A fructifier	to bear fruit
te	is
res	li
sem	ke
ble	you

Apollinaire, *Oeuvres poétiques*, p. 170

'The principle is to try to reflect the content of the poem by the graphics, as in George Herbert's "Easter Wings," Stéphane Mallarmé's "Un Coup de Dés," or John Hollander's "A State of Nature" ' (Group MU, *A General Rhetoric*, p. 239, n. 43).

Synonyms: concrete poetry; figurative poetry (see Robert, who gives as an example the song of the divine bottle in Rabelais's *Cinquième Livre*, in which the text is arranged in the form of a bottle). Morier gives 'vers rhopaliques' ('rhopalic lines'; i.e., lines of unequal lengths [OED]) and 'poème-dessin' ('poem-drawing').

R1: See imitative harmony*, R1; pictogram*; graphic line* of poetry.

CAPITAL A typographical character so called in opposition to lowercase characters (minuscules). The distinction made between small and large capitals (majuscules) allows the latter to stand as the initial letter in proper names composed in the former.

Ex: THE ILIAD; DON QUIXOTE OF LA MANCHA. See situational* signs, 1; emphasis*, R2; and graphism*, R1.

R1: Although an initial capital letter is the graphic sign of the proper name, capitalization of a whole word or words signals the title* of a work (see paragraph*, R1), or the word intended to stand out (the *vedette* or 'keyword': a term printed so as to make it as 'visible' as possible; the term derives from the Italian, *vedere*, to see). A word or phrase printed in red is a *rubric*. In a dictionary, the head word is also called an *entry* or *lemma*. See also discourse*, R2.

R2: Linguists put in SMALL CAPITALS the segment taken to designate the referent. See situational* signs, R7.

R3: In manuscript, the mark of capitalization is triple underlining (see emphasis*, R1).

CARICATURE The presentation of an object, of an idea, or of a person in an excessively unfavourable light, with overdrawn, exaggerated features. See Cuddon, Frye, Lausberg, and Robert.

Ex: 'Just arrived, at Mr. Bull's Menagerie, in British Lane, the most renowned and sagacious Man Tiger, or Ourang Outang called NAPOLEON BUONAPARTE ... He imitates all sounds; bleats like a Lamb; roars like a Tiger; cries like a Crocodile; and brays most inimitably like an Ass' (quoted by John Ashton, *English Caricature and Satire of Napoleon I*, pp. 200–1).

Dramatic caricatures in English include: Sir Epicure Mammon (Jonson, *The Alchemist*); Lady Bracknell (Wilde, *The Importance of Being Ernest*); and the generals, major-generals, marshals, and field-marshals leading the British expeditionary force in France (Joan Littlewood, *Oh What a Lovely War!*).

Antonym: euphemism* (see also celebration*, R3)

Other names: skit (Fr. *charge*); dysphemism (in opposition to euphemism); 'cacophemism' (Redfern, pp. 91–2)

Other definition: parody* (Littré, Robert)

Other meaning: a cartoon as in *Punch* (see burlesque*, R3)

R1: Like hyperbole* (see hyperbole, R2), caricature turns as much on the choice of terms as on that of the aspects of reality. Ex: 'this piece of meat in a uniform' (A. Solzhenitsyn, *The First Circle*, p. 83). Language abounds in marks, sometimes tenuous, of pejorative connotation, from contemptuous intonation* to insults* in flowery jargon* or low slang*. Ex: 'Near ate the tin and all, hungry bloody mongrel' (Joyce, *Ulysses*, p. 251). Such marks include certain suffixes in French (*-eux, -ard, -astre*: luxuri*ant*/luxuri*eux* [i.e., luxuriant v. lecherous]; chauf*feur*/chauf*fard* [chauffeur v. road-hog]; méde*cin*/médic*astre* [doctor v. quack]), as well as qualifying adjectives and syntagms ('lower class,' 'down-market,' 'puppet-like,' 'small-scale,' 'shady,' 'cheap,' etc.).

The marks of caricature need not proliferate in the sentence; they facilitate comprehension and signal enunciation*. A speaker has only to string together, for instance, words ending in *-ism*, a suffix which is in itself neutral, for the whole utterance to become pejorative.

R2: When the object caricatured is the person addressed, the result is an insult* (if it involves merely a flash of bad temper as manifested in a qualifier); it becomes sarcasm* or persiflage* if the criticism is more substantial, or made in front of witnesses.

R3: See also description*, R1, and portrait*.

CATACHRESIS Sometimes language appears not to offer a normal or proper term; a speaker may in such a case have recourse to tropological denominations, which sometimes enter the lexicon. (Quintilian called catachresis a 'necessary misuse,' for example.) See also Bénac, Dumarsais (p. 46), Lausberg, Le Clerc, Littré, Marouzeau, Preminger, and Robert.

Ex: The crossing-point of several highways may thus be called in Britain 'spaghetti junction'; whereas North American English rejects the British catachresis for the more literal word 'interchange.'

Exx: 'Spalding, the *longest* ball' [advertisement for golf balls allegedly with the longest carry]; 'Molson's dry beer' [presumably by analogy with 'dry' wine]; 'I will speak daggers to her' (Shakespeare, *Hamlet*, 3.2); ''Tis deepest winter in Lord Timon's purse' (*Timon*, 3.4); 'streaker'; 'Latin [or maths, physics, etc.] is Greek to me'; '[military] escalation, de-escalation'

Other definitions emphasize the misuse of a trope with no ornamental function and show the possibility of ridiculous consequences resulting from such misapplications. **Ex:** 'à cheval sur un âne' ('on a horse on a donkey' [literally]; i.e., 'sitting on, astride, a donkey'). See Cuddon, Espy (1983), Fontanier (pp. 213–19), Grambs, Gray, Lanham, Paul (pp. 137–8), Preminger, and Puttenham.

R1: Catachresis may be synecdochic (e.g., 'crash-helmet' for 'goggles,' or vice versa), metonymical, or metaphorical (e.g., 'source-language,' 'target-language'; see translation*), but it always produces denotation, not connotation. (Compare 'a streaker' and 'a filthy temper.' Only

'streaker' is catachretic since a 'foul' temper is also possible. See semantic neologism*.) Catachresis responds to the need to name, with a
single word, some new reality or one considered new. Thus when J.F.
Dulles upheld that if Vietnam went communist, all Asian countries
would follow suit one after another, someone created the expression
'the domino theory.' If there is a proper term, the image is not catachretic. See incorrect* word, R1.

R2: Many terms considered proper are catachretic in origin: a leaf (of
paper), the foot (of a mountain), balkanization (see antonomasia*), etc.
See also discourse*.

CELEBRATION Rhetorically speaking, celebration consists of
expressing one's joy by means of some stereotyped formula, or in some
more extended form (a line* of poetry, or verset*; a stanza* or paragraph*).

Ex:

'Let us now praise famous men' –
Men of little showing –
For their work continueth ...
Greater than their knowing.
R. Kipling, 'A School Song,' in Stalky & Co.

Other names: *benedictio* (Lanham); macarism or beatitude (formulas
beginning: 'Blessed is/are ...'); *epinicion* ('a triumphal ode commemorat-
ing a victory' [Cuddon]); panegyric (a speech praising an institution, a
person, a work); *blazon* (short verses in rhyming couplets, in praise,
frequently ironical, of a person); *tombeau* (prose and verse collection in
honour of the deceased); *encomium* (originally, praise sung in a street
procession, according to the *Grande Encyclopédie*; encomiological metre
alternates rapid and slow measures); paean ('a solemn song, in many
voices, sung in Greece on important occasions' [Littré])

Antonym: lamentation*

R1: Usual celebratory formulas include: long live, blessed be, happy
she/he/they, praised be, how fortunate that, Oh! happy (it is) that,
honour to, marvellous to, what luck that, let us rejoice because, let's
congratulate ourselves that, congratulations to, bravo for, hurrah for.
   Celebration, usually a collective act, has explicit, even institutional
marks, but it also can have subtler ones, intonations* only, so that its
sentiment of grateful joy may easily colour exclamations*, apostrophes*, or enumerations*. Ex:

All things counter, original, spare, strange;
Whatever is fickle, freckled (who knows how?)

With swift, slow; sweet, sour; adazzle, dim
Gerard Manley Hopkins, 'Pied Beauty'

Intimate celebration may reduce to a simple gesture*. 'With a single caress, I make you shine in all your splendour' (P. Eluard, *Oeuvres complètes*, 1:731).

R2: The word *praise*, more usual than *celebration*, will designate in what follows the literary genre which corresponds to the device, the *epideictic* genre. See discourse*. **Exx:** some prefaces; most presentations of lecturers; parts of the throne speech (the inaugural discourse). Burlesque praise exists too. **Exx:** Erasmus's *Praise of Folly*; the 'Celebration' collection edited by A. Morel (celebration of the pipe, of love, of silence, of the artichoke, etc.). See short* circuit, R3.

Praise addressed to the one celebrated, pronounced in his/her presence, is *laudation*, the opposite of sarcasm*; if self-interested, or excessive, it becomes flattery; if deceitful and base, fawning. A literary genre constructed on hyperbolic laudation is the *dithyramb*. The medieval equivalent was the *panegyric* (see extravagant* comparison, R1). See also antiparastasis*, R4.

R3: Celebration and lamentation* are opposed to euphemism* and caricature* respectively. The latter two constitute respectively meliorative and pejorative means of representation, whereas celebration and lamentation expose the sentiments experienced. Simulation* always remains possible, however.

R4: In Judeo-Christianity, there used to be a literary genre called the *eucharistia*, which expressed not adoration or even gratitude but rather collective admiration before what manifests the existence and presence of God. For the first Christian communities, this was principally Jesus' resurrection. (See Joseph, pp. 274, 397; J.-P. Audet, 'Esquisse historique du genre littéraire de la "Bénédiction" juive et de l' "Eucharistie" chrétienne,' *Revue biblique* 65 [1958], pp. 369–99.) One can distinguish three parts in texts which fall within the genre. (1) An exclamation* ('Blessed be Yahweh'), which is the Hebraic formula of benediction or *berrakhah*. This exclamatory form returns at greater length in the *Sanctus*. (2) A remembrance or anamnesis*, which states the motive for the preceding cry. Most often it involves a succession of concrete events. In the canon of the mass, there remain traces of these – not the *mementos* belonging to the supplication* – but the narrative* of the Last Supper and the text immediately following it (*Unde et memores*, 'We remember'). (3) An *acclamation* or *doxology* like 'Allelujah' (a word signifying 'Praise you Yahweh,' which is formed of three words: *hallel, u, Jah*), or a Christian form like 'Glory be to the Father, the Son, and the Holy Spirit.' The acclamation still exists at the end of the canon (*Per ipsum* ...). The final psalms of David, songs of triumph, are doxologies, as is the expression 'world without end.' (See Mahood, *Shakespeare's Word-play*, p. 110.)

The expression 'thanksgiving' is a translation of *eucharistia*. 'Thanks' represents a shift in meaning.

R5: *Epitaphs*, reduced perhaps to a simple inscription (name, dates and places of birth and death), often contain at least one sentence of celebration (e.g., 'a good husband, a good father'). Ex: 'Born of the sun, they travelled a short while towards the sun, / And left the vivid air signed with their honour' (Stephen Spender, 'I Think Continually of Those'). For another example, see distinction*.

CHIASMUS The placing in inverse order of the segments formed by two syntactically identical groups of words. See Lanham, Marouzeau, Morier, and Preminger.

Ex: Northrop Frye used chiasmatic arrangement to create the structure of *The Great Code*, the titles of whose eight chapters are repeated in inverse order in that book's two 'parts': part 1: 'The Order of Words'; ch. 1: 'Language I'; ch. 2: 'Myth I'; ch. 3: 'Metaphor I'; ch. 4; 'Typology I'; part 2: 'The Order of Types'; ch. 5: 'Typology II'; ch. 6: 'Metaphor II'; ch. 7: 'Myth II'; ch. 8: 'Language II.' As he explains (p. 79), the chiasmatic arrangement enables him to respect the 'typological' reading of the Old and New Testaments: 'Everything that happens in the Old Testament is a "type" or adumbration of something that happens in the New Testament, and the whole subject is therefore called typology, though ... in a special sense ... What happens in the New Testament constitutes an "antitype," a realized form, of something foreshadowed in the Old Testament.'

R1: Corbett (pp. 478, 573), Quillet (sect. 1244), Quinn (p. 93), Lausberg, and Robert compare chiasmus to antithesis*, which indeed does sometimes take chiastic form. Ex: 'I no; no I: for I must nothing be: / Therefore, no, no, for I resign to thee' (Shakespeare, *Richard II*, 4.1.201–2).

R2: Preminger compares chiasmus to antimetabole*. However, he introduces the following distinction: 'It would seem convenient to use the term *chiasmus* for the criss-cross order and correspondence in meaning or syntax of two pairs of words, whether or not involving word repetition, and restrict *antimetabole* to the narrower meaning of a pair of words repeated (usually with some morphological change) in reverse order.' Quinn (p. 95) calls chiasmus 'a large epanados.' Many collectors of tropes and figures continue to confuse the two terms.

R3: Littré does not mention the word. Lausberg (p. 361, no. 1) observes that although the word itself is an old one, its present meaning is recent.

R4: The inversion occurs almost always in the second group. **Exx:** 'I have changed in many things: in this, I have not' (J.H. Newman, *Apologia pro vita sua*, 1864); 'Taylor and Burton, Burton and Taylor became the licentious royalty of the sexy Sixties' (M. Bragg, *Rich: The Life of Richard Burton*, p. 162).

R5: Acoustic chiasmus exists (see antimetathesis*, R2).

CHLEUASMOS Irony* turned against oneself. Mockery, persiflage*, or sarcasm* at one's own expense, but performed with the expectation that others present will protest if only by a gesture. See Lausberg and Morier.

Exx: 'Stupid me!'; 'Well! aren't I clumsy!'

Ex: 'A fortnight ago I prepared a Ghost Story to read to you on this occasion. It was a lame affair, because I had to manufacture the whole thing ... Perhaps I had better be quite frank and admit that I stole the whole thing out of an old volume of *Chums*, and adapted it clumsily to a College setting' (Robertson Davies, *High Spirits*, p. 33).

Other definition: 'a sarcastic reply that mocks an opponent and leaves him no answer' (Lanham)

R1: Chleuasmos, a form of simulation*, does not practise to deceive; that is, use of the device does not necessarily indicate an attempt to provoke a categorical denial (of the speaker's 'worthlessness' by the person to whom the self-criticism is addressed). And yet that is what happens in a frequently quoted example: 'TARTUFFE: Yes, my brother, I am evil, guilty. A miserable sinner full of iniquity' (Molière, *Tartuffe*, 3.6). The hypocrite is manoeuvring to persuade Orgon that, for reasons of humility, he is accepting responsibility for evil doings, and that he is not guilty, whereas, in fact, he is. This is hyperchleuasmos.

R2: Another type of chleuasmos: 'Telling the truth ... but secretly wagering that its enormity – and the unusual character of such an avowal – will mean that it is taken as *"humorous"* and so will not be believed. *"I am Mephisto,"* Mephisto announces, and everyone falls about laughing. Including him, even more so, but not for the same reason' (D. Noguez, 'L'Humour ou la dernière des tristesses,' in *Etudes françaises*, May 1969, p. 159). The trick demands an actor's skill, because of the intonation which identifies chleuasmos as such.

R3: Chleuasmos is natural when one is led into speaking about oneself, because it allows for *compensatio** (see *compensatio*, R2). **Ex:** 'I sit writing every day under the bougainvillea and pay the inevitable price of having shown my face on British television. "I say," an elderly English-man comes trotting up. "We know who you are. But who *are* you?"'

(John Mortimer, *Manchester Guardian Weekly*, 12 March 1989, p. 21). In this case, there is also a kind of asteismus*.

CHRONOGRAPHY A type of description* which characterizes the time of an event by its attendant circumstances. See Fontanier, p. 424.

Ex: In Michel Butor's novel *La Modification*, the countryside seen through the train windows, small events, even the succession of reflections, mark the passing of time.

Exx: '[They have ordered beer]: "How do you pass your time?" she asked, *several bottles later*' (R. Queneau, *Le Chiendent*, p. 292); 'Two hours after compline, at the end of the sixth day, in the heart of the night that was giving birth to the seventh day, we entered the *finis Africae*' (U. Eco, *The Name of the Rose*, p. 460).

R1: The distinction between chronography and *chronology* is clear: the latter is a simple indication of the moment, in terms of the era, century, year, month, day, hour, minute, second, nanosecond, etc. Chronology may be ludic. Michel Butor takes pleasure in making it complicated in *L'Emploi du temps*, where precision leads to confusion. The well-known mistakes in chronology in Flaubert's *Madame Bovary* and in the sixty stories making up the Sherlock Holmes canon have been variously interpreted as deliberate or as the result of oversight.

R2: A *chronogram* is a Latin phrase in which the *I, V, X, C, D*, and *M*, when their numerical values (1, 5, 10, 50, 100, 500, 1000) are added up, provide the indication of a date. Ex: 'Paul Hallweg ... commemorates 1969, the year of the first landing on the moon, with: "*M*en *C*an *M*ake *L*unar e*X*cursions *I*n e*X*travagance' (Augarde, p. 96).

CIRCUMLOCUTION 1. The embarrassment felt at having to say something causes a roundabout verbal approach to the subject in hand. See Lausberg (sect. 1244), Littré, and Morier.
2. The 'use of many words where a few would do' (*Concise Oxford Dictionary*). See also *OED* and Fowler.

Ex:

JACK: Charming day it has been, Miss Fairfax.
GWENDOLEN: Pray don't talk to me about the weather, Mr. Worthing. Whenever people talk to me about the weather, I always feel quite certain that they mean something else. And that makes me so nervous.
JACK: I do mean something else.
GWENDOLEN: I thought so. I am never wrong.
JACK: I would like to be allowed to take advantage of Lady Bracknell's temporary absence ...

GWENDOLEN: I would certainly advise you to do so ...
JACK (nervously): Miss Fairfax, ever since I met you I have admired
you more than any girl ... I have ever met since ... I met you.
O. Wilde, *The Importance of Being Ernest*, act 1

In *Little Dorrit*, Dickens parodies techniques of verbal evasion practised by the bureaucrats in the 'Circumlocution Office,' a government department. More recently, Sir Humphrey Appleby, the civil servant represented in the television series *Yes Minister* and *Yes Prime Minister*, frequently uses circumlocution to flummox his 'master,' the politician Jim Hacker: 'I see. What you are suggesting is that, within the framework of the guidelines about Open Government which you have laid down, we should adopt a more flexible posture' (J. Lynn and A. Jay, *The Complete 'Yes Minister,'* p. 29).

Other name (in French): *ambages* (but only in the expression 'parler sans ambages,' 'to get straight to the point')

Other definition: Quillet, Robert, and Lanham compare circumlocution to periphrasis* (a comparison which is particularly valid etymologically).

R1: Circumlocution is to the sentence* what periphrasis* is to the word: it fills out a text (so a sentence may become a paragraph) but only indirectly addresses the subject in question.

CLICHÉ An over-used, trite, or commonplace idea or expression (see Cuddon and Robert). See also Bénac, Fowler, Frye, and Quillet.

Exx: 'golden hair'; 'ruby lips'

See James Rogers, *Dictionary of Clichés*; see also image*, 4. Fowler's examples include 'filthy lucre,' 'tender mercies,' 'suffer a sea change,' and 'leave no stone unturned.' N. Bagnall's *A Defence of Clichés* (1985) presents an opposing view.

Analogous terms: stereotype; ready-made syntagm* (not necessarily a pejorative designation)

R1: The above definition, by Cuddon and Robert, gives equal stress to trite expressions and banal ideas. Although they are not always clearly distinguishable, strictly speaking in French the word refers only to expressions, according to Rémy de Gourmont (*Esthétique de la langue française*, p. 189) and Marouzeau.

Banal ideas are often called *commonplaces*, which, incidentally, is an extended meaning of the synonym *topic* (derived from the Greek *topos*; see argument*). In certain cases, French uses the more accurate term *poncif*: 'a literary or artistic theme, a mode of expression, which, because of imitation, has lost all originality' (Robert). See also truism*, R1, and imitation*, R7.

R2: Since it is a stylistic defect, the conscious use of cliché connotes pretentiousness and an absence of sincerity. Ex:

Some answers are absolutely standard. No matter who is being interviewed, you can be sure that: (1) Everyone sharing the dais with the speaker is an absolutely marvelous and talented human being; (2) The film has been a pet project for years; (3) It doesn't matter if it wins a prize, because being here at Cannes is honor enough; (4) Nobody has the slightest idea what the message of the film is, or indeed if it has one; (5) All interpretations of the film by the journalists are quite plausible; and (6) It is just a shame the filming had to end, and everybody is looking forward to working together again as soon as possible. (R. Ebert, *Two Weeks in the Midday Sun*, pp. 128–9)

Cliché may be used ironically, or parodically:

The arrival of the worldrenowned headsman was greeted by a roar of acclamation from the huge concourse, the viceregal ladies waving their handkerchiefs in their excitement while the even more excitable foreign delegates cheered vociferously in a medley of cries ... amid which the ringing *evviva* of the delegate of the land of song ... was easily distinguishable. (Joyce, *Ulysses*, p. 253)

Charles Bally (*Traité*, sect. 99) emphasizes that clichés have 'evocative effects.' But, he adds, they may 'in certain cases, pass for original creations.' They do possess, or may appear to possess, the advantage of elegance and that of facilitating the amplification* of an idea, which explains their frequency in public speaking. Such 'originality' is, of course, open to parody*:

I have discovered that only last month the previous government signed a contract to import ten million pounds worth of office equipment from America ... Well, if the Americans are going to take us for a ride, at least the British people have a right to know about it. And we will fight them on the beaches, we will fight them ... (J. Lynn and A. Jay, *The Complete 'Yes Minister,'* p. 25)

R3: The problem posed by the cliché is that of a writer's originality. Does a writer have the right, as Proust believed for instance, to abuse 'ordinary' syntax? '[Writers] only begin to write well if they are original, if they themselves create their language. Correctness and stylistic perfection exist, but on the far, not the near, side of originality' (Proust, *Correspondance générale*, 6:94). When the desire for correctness takes precedence, he adds, the result may be expressions like 'discreet emotion,' 'smiling friendship,' etc.

R4: Certain clichés originate in metaphors* (see metaphor, R2). Others are comparisons* which have become trite forms of emphasis*. See simile*, R3. Extended clichés exist (see slogan* and proverb*, R1), which may acquire a very specific or 'extended' sense. See meaning*, 4. Foregrounding* occurs when their literal meaning contradicts them.

R5: Clichés are revived by the substitution* (see substitution, R2) of terms, by the deliberate introduction of (apparent) incoherence*. Ex: 'People in this country from coast to coast to coast ...' (Audrey McLaughlin, Yukon M.P., inaugural speech on becoming leader of the NDP party, 2 Dec. 1989). Irony* (see irony, R5) makes use of them as does well-wishing* (see well-wishing, R2).

CLICK Voiceless articulation independent of breathing produced by '[muscular] sucking movements made with the tongue or lips' (G. Straka, *Les Sons et les mots*, p. 30).

Exx: the sound of a kiss (rendered very approximately by 'smack'); the lateral explosion in the gums by which one calls an animal

R1: Clicks are noises* made by human beings outside the phonological and the graphic systems; hence the difficulty of their transcription. In Hottentot, where clicks form part of the linguistic structure, such transcriptions do exist. Certain clicks have a coded meaning in English or French. For instance, smacking the lips expresses relish; explosive lateral clicks are an invitation by French prostitutes to possible clients; central dental explosive inhaling signifies reproval ('tsk, tsk'). Then there are whistles of admiration; the aspirated s expressing pain; the *f* which accompanies a shoulder-shrug. All these expirated or aspirated consonants are quasi-interjections*.

COINAGE A neologism* originating neither from a noise* nor from existing lexical roots (see derivation* and compound* word); in other words, a word apparently coined out of nothing. See Lausberg.

Ex: 'The Korova Milkbar was a milk-plus *mesto* ... [which] had no license for selling liquor, but there was no law yet against prodding some of the new *vesches* which they used to put in the old moloko, so you could peet it with velocet or synthemesc or drencrom or one or two other vesches which would give you a nice quiet horrorshow fifteen minutes admiring Bog And All His Holy Angels and Saints in your left shoe with lights bursting all over your *mozg*' (Anthony Burgess, *A Clockwork Orange*, p. 5).

Other names: neologism*; artificial word (e.g., nylon, Kodak); esoteric word (G. Deleuze); blends (V. Adams, L. Bauer); *mot forgé; forgerie*

R1: Almost all coinages can be interpreted as portmanteau* words, according to G. Deleuze (*Logique du sens*, pp. 59–60), who proposes a distinction based on meaning*. A portmanteau word would be one in which the amalgamated terms refer to two or more distinct semantic series. **Exx:** *ballute* (< balloon + parachute); *chunnel* (< channel + tunnel); *dawk* (< dove + hawk, i.e., neither pro- nor anti-war).

R2: Coinages strictly refer to newly invented objects or to non-existent objects like the Jabberwock. **Ex:**

'Twas brillig, and the slithy toves
Did gyre and gimble in the wabe;
All mimsy were the borogoves,
And the mome raths outgrabe.

Lewis Carroll, 'Jabberwocky'

R3: Words may be coined from other existing words (see anagram* and palindrome*, R3) or from pure sounds.

R4: See substitution*, R1.

COLLAGE A process invented by the surrealist painters, who glued to their canvases bits of paper, fabric, etc., and which certain poets have imitated, creating 'preposterous combinations of disparate objects' (R. Caillois, quoted by Robert [*Supplément*, under 'collage']).

Ex:

They wash their feet in soda water
Et O ces voix d'enfants, chantant dans la coupole.
Twit twit twit
Jug jug jug jug jug jug
So rudely forc'd
Tereu.

T.S. Eliot, *The Waste Land*

Ex: 'A doll's arm, the chitterlings of a clock, a saucepan full of hatbands' (Dylan Thomas, *Quite Early One Morning*, p. 41).

Synonyms: incongruous combination, coincidental harmony. Frye adds (p. 109) that 'a *pastiche* is an unsuccessful collage, for some critics.'

Other definition: a text composed of fragments from previous texts. **Ex:** W. Lewino, *L'Eclat et la blancheur*. Pound's *Cantos* contain many examples of textual collage.

R1: Collage is a kind of dissociation* characterized by the bringing together of two objects with incompatible semes. It may be obtained artificially (see reprise*, R3), but to be truly poetic in the surrealist sense at least, it must spring from the unconscious (see dissociation*, R5). **Ex:** 'seins ô mon coeur' ('Breasts O my heart') (P. Eluard, *Oeuvres complètes*, 1:366).

R2: In surrealist poetry, it is sometimes difficult (and the difficulty is not always the fault of the reader) to decide which is dissociation proper (caused by the presence of two distinct isotopies*) and which *false dissociation* or incoherence* (*a single* possible isotopy is involved because at least one of the referents is understood figuratively). Ex: 'There are muffled drums even in light dresses' (P. Eluard, *Oeuvres complètes*, 1:353). This is not a collage, not, at least, if we are correct in taking 'in light dresses' as a metonymy* for the female body and 'muffled drums' as a metaphor* for mourning.

R3: Collage may take the form of a juxtaposition*, of anaphora* (see anaphora, R1), of reprise*, of a portmanteau* word, a maxim*, even of a simple assertion*. Ex: 'Aeroplanes fear gardens, justifiably' (J. Levy, in Aragon et al., *Dictionnaire abrégé du surréalisme*, under 'avion'). The creator of this curious collage is a painter, Max Ernst, who in an engraving with the peculiar title 'The plane-gulping garden' represented an aeroplane crashing into a garden (photographed in Breton's *L'Amour fou*, p. 112).

COLON A sign of punctuation* marking an articulation of meaning.
Whereas the period and semicolon define the limits of segments which may be written as separate sentences, and the comma indicates breaks in the syntagmatic flow, the colon marks the existence of a relationship between the segments which it separates. This, at any rate, is its specific role in French. In English, according to Fowler, it has acquired a special relational function also, which he limits to 'that of delivering the goods that have been invoiced in the preceding words ... [it is] a substitute for such verbal harbingers as *viz., scil., that is to say, i.e.,* etc.'
The relationship between segments exists because, for example, one part of the text involved enunciation*, the other presents the corresponding utterance. Ex [Persse McGarrigle speaking]: 'Remember how the poem ends: "And they are gone: ay, ages long ago / Those lovers fled away into the storm" ' (David Lodge, *Small World*, p. 40). (See enumeration*, R1.) On the other hand, the return to the level of the enunciating text requires only a comma. Ex: ' "I am tired," she said.'
The colon often marks the passage from a fact to its attributed cause: 'The more experience I acquire in art, the more art becomes torture for me: imagination remains stationary while taste grows sharper' (G. Flaubert, *Correspondence*, 4 Nov. 1857). Sometimes there is only a vague relationship between the two segments: 'In reality, there is neither beautiful style, beautiful drawing, nor beautiful colour: there is only a single beauty, that of the truth revealed' (A. Rodin, in *Le Nouveau Dictionnaire de citations françaises*, no. 12088).
When the segments separated by the colon are not clauses but syntagms*, the result is an assertion* in which the colon replaces the

copula (the verb *to be* or a verb of similar function). **Exx:** 'Total: six canteens'; 'a single boss, a single capitalist: Everyone' (J. Guesde, in ibid., no. 12414). See apposition*, R2.

Normally the subject under discussion precedes the colon, and what is said about it follows. **Ex:** 'POETIC LICENCE: there is no such thing' (Théodore de Banville, *Petit Traité de poésie française*). If the sentence already contains an assertion*, the colon introduces an adjacent assertion and replaces *i.e.*, etc., as Fowler pointed out. **Ex:** 'That was his pride: to startle people with such fine work' (A. Munro, *Who Do You Think You Are?*, p. 2).

COMMUNICATIO 'In order the better to persuade those to whom, or against whom, one is speaking ... one appears to consult them ... and to rely on what they decide' (Fontanier, p. 414). See also Dumarsais, Girard, Littré, Quillet, and Morier.

Ex [Cicero, to his client's opponent]: 'I ask you, what would you have done in such delicate circumstances?' (quoted by Fontanier). Anglophone compilers of figures (see Lanham and Joseph, for example) refer to this debating trick as anacoenosis.

Other definitions: 1. The basic sense of *communication* is: 'contact between speakers.' See enunciation*.
2. In French, a *communication* is a learned paper on a specific subject and presented at a conference.
3. Scaliger, Dumarsais, and Littré speak of a 'communication in words,' a figure by which one makes common to many what one says only for a few, as when, in Molière's *Tartuffe*, Orgon says to his son: 'Now then, *someone* can leave my house right now.' Fontanier prefers to call this figure 'association'; Morier, 'communion.'
4. 'Drawing from the principles of those addressed the admission of the truths one is trying to establish against them' (Amar du Rivier, *Rhétorique*, p. 102). This is a type of argument *ad hominem**.

R1: *Communicatio* belongs to the group of figures whose function is 'to gain the listener's goodwill either by offering praise (without ever flattering him), or by speaking about what he knows and likes' (J. Folliet, *Tu seras orateur*, p. 59). It seems to us essential to the definition of the device, therefore, that the public or someone really present be taken as judge of the case. See deliberation*; *dubitatio**; question*; R3; and simulation*, R2.

The anonymous author of the *Ad Herennium* emphasizes the necessity of creating sympathy in one's listeners. He recommends, in difficult cases, a device called *commiseration*, which consists in the listeners being invited to put themselves in the speaker's place. This attitude, a well-known example of which is the lecturer who tells of feeling perplexed when approached to speak, is dangerous when it usurps the place of the relevant arguments, in which case it becomes an argument *ad populum* (see argument*).

R2: *Semi-communicatio* consists in taking as judge some qualified, though absent, person. Ex: 'I defy any sane man to read the contending Parties' posters and proclamations, whichever they may be, without losing his appetite for a week' (G. Poulet, *Aveux spontanés*, p. 151). We are close here to the argument of the invented witness (see argument*, R2), unless the judge appealed to is some real third person. Ex: 'If we had wanted to adopt the normal style of the popular press, we could have compared this new professor to Sainte-Beuve or Taine. But what would he himself have thought of such flattery? ... He would either have smiled or lost his temper at it, and in either case, he would have been right' (J. Fournier, *Mon Encrier*, p. 103).

R3: One quite exceptional form of *communicatio*, and one which is the opposite of commiseration, consists in putting oneself as author (despite the risks attached) in the place of the addressee. So an application for work might take this form: 'Maybe you need an extra secretary' (Thierrin, *Toute la correspondance* ['Here I am' is understood]). Ex: 'O Man, my friend, why have I never yet spoken to you about the symphonic delights of listening to you listening to me? Because I do hear you hear me. You hear me and it's as if *you* were speaking. You don't hear me quietly, you hear me loudly. Each word that I say to you reverberates in you as in some golden grotto' (R. Ducharme, *Le Nez qui voque*, p. 254).

We might call the device *altruization*. It may also be used in respect of a character in a novel. Thus Butor's famous second-person narration (*'voussoiement'*) in *La Modification* marks the hero's otherness, which does not prevent the author from constantly adopting the latter's point of view (see focalization under narrative*, R3).

R4: The device has its appropriate intonation* suggestive of (simulated) deference.

COMPARISON The expression of a similarity (or of several similarities) between two entities of the same order, or quality, etc. In more developed form, comparison becomes parallel*; limited to its expressive role, it is simile* (see simile, R1); see also image*. Comparisons may have a polemical function (see reasoning*, R3).

R1: Simile is distinguished from simple comparison because the former introduces a qualifier (an adjective or adverb) whereas the latter brings in a supplementary grammatical actant* (a noun). Only the simile is a literary image*. Compare: 'sly as a fox' (simile) and 'sly as his father' (comparison).

True comparison allows the development of the predicate's expressed similarity between like objects (e.g. 'as sly as his father, but more obstinate, less quiet'), whereas false, pure, or rhetorical comparison necessarily introduces a subjective viewpoint and allows the development of the comparing elements. **Exx:** 'as sly as a fox'; 'My love is like a red, red rose'; 'A computer virus is a program, or set of instructions, that can enter surreptitiously through telephone lines or exchanged memory disks, hidden among legitimate information. It is called a virus because it also makes multiple copies of itself and sends those copies from computer to computer *as a biological virus may move from person to person*' (Philip J. Hilts, *Manchester Guardian Weekly*, 13 Nov. 1988, p. 18).

Vian plays skilfully on the possible confusion: 'A piece of bread as fresh as an eye, and like an eye, fringed with long lashes' (*Le Loup-Garou*, p. 183).

R2: 'Superlative depreciation' (Angenot) begins with a comparison in order to emphasize hyperbolically some defect. The speaker chooses some particularly feeble analogue and asserts that in comparison with the subject discussed, the analogue appears to have considerable value. **Ex:** 'I refuse to review *X*, a program so poor that it makes *Y*, by contrast, a model of modesty and thoughtful dignity.' The following extract from a review of the film *Love Story* (1970) makes the comparison implicitly: '*Camille* with bullshit' (Alexander Walker, *Halliwell's Film Guide*, 4th ed., p. 500). The same device operates in reverse: 'Vatel [Louis XIV's brilliant chef] is only a tyro compared to our *cordon bleu* cuisine' (J. Audiberti, *L'Effet Glapion*, p. 240). This is comparative hyperbole*.

R3: Comparison belongs among the commonplaces (see argument*, R1) and encourages expressivity (see discourse* and hypotyposis*, R1) in a sober style (see grandiloquence*, R1). It permits the extension of an argument (see reasoning*, R3) and provides a method for component analysis (see meaning*, 1). Comparison serves to establish correspondences*, emphasis* (see anticlimax*, R3), amplification* (see amplification, other def.), hyperbole* (see hyperbole, R3), and extravagant* comparison. It may slip into baroquism* (see baroquism, R2).

COMPENSATIO The neutralization of a lexeme's pejorative (or meliorative) connotations by joining to it a word or syntagm* of contrary effect.

Ex:

Though much is taken, much abides; and though
We are not now that strength which in old days
Moved earth and heaven; that which we are, we are;
One equal temper of heroic hearts,

Made weak by time and fate, but strong in will
To strive, to seek, to find, and not to yield.

Tennyson, 'Ulysses'

Other definitions: 'showing the resemblances and differences between two persons or objects' (Quillet). See parallel*. In the English rhetorical tradition, the term *compensatio* covers two figures of balance produced by contrasting evaluations, *antanagoge* and *antisagoge* (see Lanham, pp. 9, 11).

R1: Apparently, *compensatio* is a blending that relates neither to the denotative semes nor to the sentiments expressed (see oxymoric* sentiments, R2). It therefore rarely produces a literary effect (see below, however, the example from Vigneault). *Compensatio*'s most frequent task is to eliminate the undesirable connotations of terms one would like to render denotative. So, for instance, Empson comments upon the use made by some critics of *compensatio* to treat sympathetically Yeats's belief in fairies (see W. Empson, *Using Biography*, pp. 163–86). Or if one wishes to defend Gérard de Nerval's Illuminism, one says that he had 'a *sincere* bent towards illuminism' (L. Cellier, *De Sylvie à Aurélia*, p. 15). In the event that the appropriate lexeme is lacking, speakers may have recourse to some periphrasis* like 'in the best sense of the word.' Ex: 'Resistance poetry consisted, in the noblest sense of the word, of occasional works' (Bersani, ed., *La Littérature en France depuis 1945*, p. 13).

R2: *Compensatio*, the combination of a pejorative and a meliorative lexeme, protects a speaker against the risk attached to expressions of undue self-esteem or self-respect. Exx: 'O *little* fame, *poor* fortune, here I come to conquer you' (G. Vigneault, 'Petite gloire, pauvre chanson,' a Québécois song); 'Often, I have felt *threatened* by inspiration ...' (P. Perrault, *En désespoir de cause*, p. 15). See also chleuasmos*.

R3: If incorporated in an implication*, *compensatio* may invert connotation. Ex: 'In favour of a better kind of arrogance' (Eluard, *Oeuvres complètes*, 1:831). This implies that the arrogance in question is good: the lexeme becomes marked as meliorative.

COMPLAINT A popular sung poem* on a sad historical subject.

Ex: the complaint of the wandering Jew. Much of American country music, when sung, expresses complaints about the singer's life and times.

R1: The medieval complaint characteristically alternates only two rhymes, one of which 'is made to express repeated groans of anguish' (Morier).

COMPOUND WORD A word made up of distinct parts: the root and prefix. See Crystal; Leech; L. Bauer, *English Word-Formation*, p. 11; Marouzeau (under *composition*); *OED*; and Robert.

Exx: lifeboat; frostbite; polytone (quoted by Lausberg), a word invented by Voltaire on the model of *monotone*

Exx: 'My wishes raced through the *house-high* hay' (Dylan Thomas, 'Fern Hill'); 'Babies in upper bedrooms of *salt-white* houses dangling over water, or of *bow-windowed* villas squatting prim in neatly treed but unsteady *hill-streets*, worried the light with their *half-in-sleep* cries' (Dylan Thomas, *Quite Early One Morning*, p. 9).

Other definition: In *An Introduction to Modern English Word-Formation* Valerie Adams stipulates that a compound word 'is usually understood to be the result of the (fixed) combination of two free forms, or words that have an otherwise independent existence, as in *frostbite, tape-measure, grass-green*' (p. 30). Both Bauer and Marouzeau (under *mot*) add this distinction between words and affixes.

Analogous term: paralexeme

R1: English and French possess many compound words ('telegram,' 'seaworthy,' 'free-trader,' etc.). For the different types of compounds (copulative, attributive, subordinative, asyntactic, etc.), see Adams, Bauer, and Marouzeau (under *composition*). Neological compounds particularly interest the rhetorician. Some conform to already existing structures, as in the examples already quoted and in Dylan Thomas's common compounding procedure (e.g., 'fishing-boat-bobbing sea' in the Prologue of *Under Milk Wood*). Others are more eccentric, even bizarre. **Ex:** 'I was plat-bus-forming co-massitudinarily in a lutetio-meridional space-time and I was neighbouring a longisthmusical plaitroundthehatted greenhorn' (R. Queneau, 'Word-composition,' in *Exercises in Style*, p. 45). These are foregrounded forms of artificially compounded or made-up words (see neologism*) or even barbarisms*.

R2: Compound words, although frequently combining with derivations, differ from them, as the example from Queneau amply demonstrates.

R3: The device is quite popular: 'un-novels, counter-novels, antinovels, infra-novels, so many possible variables on the interminable new novel' (H. Aquin, *Trou de mémoire*, p. 74). See euphemism*, R2 (f).

R4: Should a word be called *decompounded* if it is withdrawn from a compound through, for example, amputation of a negative prefix? **Ex:** couth (from uncouth). Valerie Adams sets up the concept of the 'zero prefix' to cover examples like the verb *to cage* (= 'to put someone or something into a cage'), since the verb *to encage* already exists. The parts of a compound word may be separated from one another (see tmesis*).

CONCATENATION A word proposed by Beauzée to describe the kind of climax in which a word is repeated from one clause to another, thus serving to connect them together. See Littré, Lausberg, and Morier.

Ex: 'There is a sound like the knocking of railway trucks in a siding. That is the happy concatenation of one event following another in our lives. Knock, knock. Must, must, must. Must go, must sleep, must wake, must get up – sober, merciful word which we pretend to revile, which we press light to our hearts, without which we should be undone' (V. Woolf, *The Waves*, p. 339).

Ex:

> I read one poem. One poem is enough.
> O western wind ...
> O western wind, you are at enmity with my mahogony table.
> (V. Woolf, *The Waves*, p. 315)

Concatenation might appear to be anadiplosis*; but, according to Beauzée, at least two successive anadiploses are necessary to form concatenation.

Other definitions: G. Antoine gives concatenation as a synonym of polysyndeton* (*Les Cinq Grandes Odes de Claudel*, p. 36). Anglophone rhetoricians tend not to make this numerical distinction between anadiplosis and concatenation. Ex (listed by Lanham under 'anadiplosis'):

> For I have lived long, I crave reward
> Reward me not unkindly: think on kindness,
> Kindness becommeth those of high regard
> Regard with clemency a poor man's blindness.
> Bartholomew Griffin, *Fidessa*, 16

Other name: linked anadiploses

R1: A type of concatenation, typical of Indian poetry, is the *karanamala* or 'chain of causes.' Exx: 'Without satisfaction, how would there be appeasement; without appeasement, happiness; without happiness, pleasure; without pleasure, bliss?' (Asvaghosa, quoted by H.R. Diwekar, p. 69); 'Melancholy and sadness are already the beginning of doubt; doubt is the beginning of despair; despair is the cruel beginning of the different degrees of viciousness' (Lautréamont, *Poésies*).

This form must go back to the primitive concrete mode, the genealogy. Ex: 'Abraham begat Isaac, Isaac begat Jacob, Jacob begat Judah and his brothers ...' It requires very little to produce a link. Ex: 'grief, sadness, sadness and misery, misery and torment' (W. Gombrowicz, *Ferdydurke*, p. 156).

CONCEIT *Concetti* were expressions borrowed from Italian poetry prior to the Renaissance striking for their subtlety of meaning and mannered style (antitheses*, curious images*, mythological allusions*, etc.); both in France and in England the word finally came to designate all kinds of precious points*. See Bénac and *OED*.

Ex [on a flea which has sucked the blood of two lovers and which is to die at the hand of the lady]:

> Oh stay, three lives in one flea spare,
> Where we almost, yea, more than married are.
> This flea is you and I and this
> Our marriage bed, and marriage temple is.
>
> J. Donne, 'The Flea'

See also K.K. Ruthven, *The Conceit*.

Analogous definitions: See Cuddon, Frye, Lausberg, and Quillet. Some authors emphasize the pejorative aspects of the conceit. Grambs writes, for instance: '[a] cleverly evocative turn of expression, sometimes one that is affected or strained; intellectual whimsy; stylistic artifice.' Montherlant apologizes before committing one [after he has just denounced the *hollow verbiage* prevalent in 1939]: 'Allow me one *concetto*: in this hole, the nation is engulfed' (Montherlant, *Essais*, p. 906).

Preminger's definition is more specific: 'An intricate or far-fetched metaphor, which functions by arousing feelings of surprise, shock, or amusement ... The poet compares elements which seem to have little or nothing in common.' His example –

> When the evening is spread out against the sky
> Like a patient etherised upon a table.
>
> T.S. Eliot, 'The Love-Song of J. Alfred Prufrock'

– indicates that examples of conceit include simile* as well as metaphor*. The above examples of conceit are similar to the surrealistic image* (see image, R1).

Analogous terms: marinism; conceptism (a Spanish type represented in Herrera's works and which Bénac calls 'erudite allusion*'); Clevelandism (see Cuddon); shafts of wit*. R. Escarpit (*L'Humour*, p. 40) opposes conceptism to 'cultism' (see imitation*, 4). According to Escarpit, the former is ingenuity of thought, the latter of expression.

R1: Their preciosity makes conceits forms of baroquism*. Less precious, they would be witticisms, or *bons mots*. Ex: 'I have no foreign lan-

Concession

guages, except the French language, which is not a foreign language, except, curiously enough, for foreigners' (J. Audiberti, *L'Effet Glapion*, p. 142). For other types of witticism, see wit*; nonsense*, R1; simulation*, R3 and R4; and pseudo-simulation*, R4. Witticisms frequently employ periphrasis* (see periphrasis, R1) and have their own intonation*.

R2: The point* is a type of perennially topical conceit, which serves to produce persiflage* (see persiflage, R1).

CONCESSION Allowing one's adversary a point which might be disputed. See Littré. Fontanier adds (p. 415) 'in order to get a greater advantage later.' See also Lanham, Lausberg, Morier, *OED*, Quillet, and Robert.

Ex: '*I like disorder*, but not a mess.'

Analogous terms: epitrope (Frye, Lanham, Morier, Quillet, Scaliger); *paromologie* (Morier, Robert); *permissio* (Lanham). Epitrope is a foregrounded (see foregrounding*) concession which emphasizes the contentiousness of the point accorded. Thiebault, cited by Le Hir, calls a purely hypothetical concession *synchoresis*. Ex: 'Supposing that we were to admit ...' [the speaker then demonstrates the resultant improbabilities]. Lanham, however, defines synchoresis as the permission to be personally judged which a speaker gives to a questioner, and cites Falstaff: 'And here I stand: judge my masters' (Shakespeare, *Henry IV*, Pt 1, 2.4).

R1: Rhetorical concessions, or oratorical withdrawals, are acts of pseudo-generosity aimed only at convincing the jury of the extent and force of one's principal entitlement. The opposite is the *cession* or real relinquishment of a past claim. Ex: 'I am, alas! nonetheless obliged to recognize that Rodin was an artist of genius' (P. Claudel, *Oeuvres en prose*, p. 274). A cession made under coercion readily becomes aggressive. Ex: 'Yes, I dare say, I am only a traveller, a pilgrim on this earth. Are you anything more?' (Goethe, *The Sorrows of Young Werther*, trans. E. Mayer and L. Bogan, p. 99). However, a cession relating to actions under censure may also become a *confession* or avowal, followed in that case by an excuse*. Ex: 'I am aware that I am doing what I shouldn't; I know that I indulge in mad love affairs; but what [would you have me do]?' (Ronsard, quoted by Le Hir, p. 111). The avowal frees one of the fault.

R2: The briefest of concessions is 'yes, but ...' Other marks are 'I dare say ...' and 'To be sure ...'

R3: Pure concessions form the pretext for all the more scathing refutations*. Ex: '*It is understood that M. Barbusse is fair game for us*. Yet, here is a man who enjoys, on the same plane of action as our own, a reputation unjustified by any consideration of merit: who is not a man of action, nor a leading light intellectually, who represents nothing of positive value' (A. Breton, *Légitime Défense*, p. 39).

R4: Close to concession is *insinuation* described by Mestre as follows: 'The orator at first appears to interpret the listener's thoughts, before skilfully diverting them again to another subject.' **Ex:**

'Now all those who knew anything of the library's secrets are dead. Only one person remains: yourself.'
  'Do you wish to insinuate ...' the abbot said.
  'Do not misunderstand me ... I say there is someone who knows.'
(U. Eco, *The Name of the Rose*, p. 446)

R5: See also *ad hominem**; intonation*; and transition*, R1.

CONCRETIZATION A concrete example replaces the expression of an idea.

Exx: 'It's raining cats and dogs'; 'Mêle-toi de tes oignons' ('Mind your own business'); 'In the past, I had only liberty in my mouth. In the morning I spread it on my toast, I chewed it all day long. I carried with me into the world my breath which was deliciously perfumed by liberty' (A. Camus, *La Chute*, p. 153). See also abstraction*, R5.

R1: An idea may be expressed in terms more abstract than concrete or vice versa. **Ex:** 'You will always encounter difficulties in your work. The end of your difficulties will be the end of your work.' The *exemplum* is a characteristic device of concrete expression. But, when considered as a set of devices, concretization, just like abstraction* and generalization*, has effects which reach further afield. It distorts the given in order to create an effect.

R2: The effect in question frequently has something comical about it, because the idea in question is reduced to one of its more limited aspects. **Ex:** 'Indeed, reading, after all, consists merely of moving your nose from left to right and from right to left' (P. Valéry, *Oeuvres complètes*, 2:355). The gain in expressivity risks a loss of credibility. **Ex:** popular rhetoric concerning the punishments of hell.

R3: Similes*, metaphors*, metonymies*, and synecdoches* are sometimes concretizations reduced to a single word. The following example foregrounds the device: 'Many a man in love with a *dimple* makes the mistake of marrying the whole girl' (Stephen Leacock, quoted by F.S. Pepper, *Twentieth-Century Quotations*, p. 231). The same is true of antonomasia*: 'Some Cromwell guiltless of his country's blood' (Th. Gray, 'Elegy Written in a Country Churchyard') for 'some military leader.'

R4: Merely using an abstract word in the plural is enough to concretize it. Compare: Margaret's kindness / Margaret's kindnesses.

R5: The inversion* of lexemes may result in concretization. See also amplification*, R1; riddle*, R2; reasoning*, R2; and lexematic inversion*, R2.

CONTAMINATION The amalgamation into a single work of the material of two or several. See Bénac.

Exx: Stendhal's first two publications, *Vies de Haydn* and *Mozart et Métastase*, as well his *Histoire de la peinture italienne*, are in part plagiarized compilations of previous works.

Cuddon points out (p. 150) that contamination 'usually refers to the Roman practice of adapting and combining Greek New Comedy.'

Analogous terms: compilation, plagiarism

Other definitions: See portmanteau* word, R3. M. Pei and F. Gaynor define linguistic contamination as the 'effect exercised by one element of speech upon another with which it is customarily or accidentally associated, resulting in a *portmanteau* or *telescope word*' (*Dictionary of Linguistics*, p. 47).

CONTINUATION A rise in tone at the end of a syntagm*, so as to indicate simply that the sentence will continue. P. Delattre defines this very common melodic mark as a rise in the voice from medium to sharp pitch for a minor continuation (see expressive punctuation*, R1), and a rise to a pitch above the normal range in the case of a major continuation. (Cf. P.R. Léon, pp. 51–3.) The rise is at first rapid, then diminishes progressively, whereas in a question*, the pitch at first rises slowly then more and more rapidly, to reach the same maximum level of sharpness. (See, however, expressive punctuation*, R1 and R2.)

Delattre also distinguishes between a major continuation and an implication*, for which the downward curve is slightly prolonged after its rise.

Comparable to continuations are two straightforward melodies, called by Delattre *echo* and *parenthesis*, the first rising in character, the second descending. They accompany, without directly participating in it, an utterance inserted in a sentence.

Other fundamental kinds of intonation*, according to Delattre, include one which expresses finality, in which pitch descends from medium to low; exclamations* reverse the intonation of questions, passing quickly first from very high to low and then increasing in rapidity; and in commands, the same fall is an abrupt one. (See injunction*.)

COQ-À-L'ÂNE A form which skips between two unrelated ideas. See
J. Cohen, *Structure du langage poétique*, p. 167.

Ex:

MONIQUE: I would like to count the blonde pirates among my ancestors ... Aboard my sailing ship, I would demonstrate the energy they
have left me. I would disregard fogs.
BLAISE: How many masts?
MONIQUE: Eh?

J. Audiberti, L'Effet Glapion, p. 171

Synonym: to ramble on (in conversation); *parler à bâtons rompus*

Analogous definition: 'an incoherent manner of speaking or writing'
(Preminger)

Other definition: 'a discourse without coherence, linkages and ...
sometimes without meaning' (Bénac). He is referring to *coq-à-l'âne* the
ancient literary genre, the content of which Preminger defines as 'the
satiric treatment of the vices, faults and foibles of individuals, social
groups, and even institutions.' See verbigeration*, R2.

R1: *Coq-à-l'âne* is not synonymous with the English 'cock-and-bull
story,' an 'idle invention, incredible tale' (*Concise Oxford Dictionary*).
Coq-à-l'âne differs from a digression* because the latter departs, or
appears to depart, from the subject without breaking the discursive
thread*. For an example, see verbiage*, R5.

R2: Usually, *coq-à-l'âne* occurs in dialogue* and may produce word-
play*. It may be simulated: a speaker's reply misses the point in a
way that implies the speaker does not understand (see antanaclasis*).
Ex:

ALFRED: Turn on the box – hang on, where's the *Radio Times*? – ah –
is this this week's?
CONSTANCE: Forty-two-and-a-half, and all I've got is a headache.
ALFRED: Is this the new one? ... what's today?
CONSTANCE: Sunday.
ALFRED: No-no-no – what's – oh never mind ...

Tom Stoppard M is for Moon among Other Things,
in The Dog It Was That Died and Other Plays, p. 63

In a monologue*, *coq-à-l'âne* combines with inconsequence* and dissociation* to form the ancient literary genre already mentioned.
Preminger adds: 'Clément Marot, who created the form in 1530, was
the author of four *coq-à-l'âne*, all of them in the form of (generally)
octosyllabic verse epistles of varying length.'

R3: *Coq-à-l'âne* may be more than a device. Henri Michaux considered it to be a phenomenon in the stream of consciousness, heightened by hashish:

> Shovels fly
> then screams
> I get free
> the next moment, Naples

Each moment ... appears clearly, without flow or linkage either with the one before or after. Absolutely raw. Verses made up of *coq-à-l'âne* will be the style. (Michaux, *Connaissance par les gouffres*, p. 121)

R4: *Coq-à-l'âne* is most frequent when a conversation is not a dialogue* but a clash of two monologues*. **Ex:**

> TEACHER: How do you say 'Italy' in French?
> PUPIL: I've got a toothache.
>
> E. Ionesco, *The Lesson*, in *Four Plays*, p. 69

In the absence of a transition*, some general-purpose expression replaces it, like *à propos*, 'by the way,' etc. **Ex:**

> MRS. MARTIN: Thanks to you, we've spent a really Cartesian half-hour.
> FIREMAN: Speaking of that, the bald Soprano?
>
> E. Ionesco, *The Bald Soprano*, in ibid., p. 37

R5: Normal discourse* proceeds by avoiding both redundancy* and *coq-à-l'âne*. Ducrot (*Dire et ne pas dire*, p. 8) shows that two laws, the 'law of progression' and the 'law of coherence,' govern the linking of sentences. His distinction of statement from presupposition clears up the apparent contradiction between them. 'It is considered normal to repeat a semantic element already present in the preceding discourse, provided that it is repeated as a presupposition ... Progress should occur at the level of what is stated.'

Broadly stated, therefore, *coq-à-l'âne* would seem to occur when a sentence's presuppositions contradict either its own statements or previous presuppositions, whereas the descent into redundancy occurs when the statement made in a sentence merely reproduces statements or presuppositions in preceding sentences. Compare: 'She is not polite. You know that' (consequence); 'You know that she is not polite. She is so' (*coq-à-l'âne*); and 'You know that she is not polite. She is not' (redundancy).

CORRESPONDENCES The correlative use of two symbolic images* whose vehicle belongs to two different kinds of sensation, but whose tenor is identical. See Bénac and Preminger (under 'synaesthesia').

Ex: 'The summer airs, like Weber waltzes, fall' (Edith Sitwell, 'The Innocent Spring').

Ex:

> While singing in the minor key
> Their song mingles with the moonlight
> The calm, sad, beautiful moonlight.
>
> P. Verlaine, 'Clair de lune,' in *Les Fêtes galantes*

'Song' and 'moonlight' may replace one another because each represents, in its own sphere, the same intimate sentiment (as suggested by 'the minor key' and 'sad and beautiful').

Both the device's theory (synaesthesia) and its name come from Baudelaire's poem 'Correspondances':

> Perfumes, colours, and sounds recall one another.
> There are perfumes as fresh as baby skin.
> As sweet as an oboe, as green as fields.

By means of similes*, Sitwell and Baudelaire are trying to establish a relationship underlying distinct sensations.

R1: A correspondence is established between two images*, or more accurately, between two vehicles: it risks the confusion with analogy which unites tenor and vehicle. Occasionally, the two vehicles cause the tenor to blur, especially when an analogy, a more abstract kind of utterance, replaces it. Ex: 'She has the voice of her thighs. Slender. Elegant. Radiant' (J. Audiberti, *L'Effet Glapion*, p. 216).

R2: Morier (pp. 323–31), following Rimbaud's lead, sought to found correspondences upon values drawn from the sonority of the terms used. Open *a* (as in 'ate') would thus be bright red; closed *a* (as in 'cart') would be dark red, etc.

COUNTER-INTERRUPTION The suppression, not of the end of a text, but of the beginning.

Ex: 'Sir only I havnt known which way to turn since the funeral' (Peter Reading, *Ukelele Music*, p. 14). This beginning of a letter* from the speaker's cleaning lady suggests a conversation presumably interrupted at some previous moment.

Ex:

PORTRAIT OF THE MEIDOSEMS:
Besides, like all Meidosem women, she dreamed only of entering Confetti Palace. (H. Michaux, *La Vie des plis*, p. 125)

This 'single' characteristic (introduced by 'besides,' which implies that it is not the first) gives enough information about the young girl, which is why her 'other' traits, those which 'preceded' the one noted, are not considered worthy of mention.

Counter-Litotes

R1: The three spaced, or unspaced, periods at the beginning of a text are the graphic mark of the counter-interruption. Ex: '... after my fifth glass of kirsch, warmer blood began to circulate in my brain' (A. Gide, *Les Nourritures terrestres,* in *Romans,* p. 208). When omitting the beginning of a quotation*, one may place the three periods in parentheses or in square brackets.

R2: The meaning* of a counter-interruption depends in each case on the context, which permits the supposition that some of the text is not mentioned. Eluard gives the device a particular importance when he begins *Poésie ininterrompue* with a line of periods (see situational* signs, 6). According to Raymond Jean, by that Eluard means that the poet's voice is 'the prolongation and echo of a kind of voice more ... universal ... both that of the poet in his preceding works and that of all the people who preceded him' (R. Jean, *Eluard,* p. 104).

COUNTER-LITOTES Hyperbole* which tends to deflate an idea.

Exx: 'No smoking, remember the fire at the Charity Bazaar. [Written in pencil underneath:] No spitting, remember the flooding of the Seine' (Jean-Charles, *Les Perles du facteur,* p. 68); '[Writers of stories serialized in newspapers] kindly let it be understood that they were murderers and vampires, that they had contracted the vicious habit of killing their fathers and mothers, that they drank blood out of skulls, used tibias as forks and cut their bread with a guillotine' (Théophile Gautier, *Mlle de Maupin,* preface).

Counter-litotes may be unintended: **Ex:** 'That's the most unheard of thing I ever heard of' (Senator Joseph McCarthy, quoted by Corbett in *Classical Rhetoric for the Modern Student,* p. 487).

R1: Litotes* understates in order to emphasize. Overstatement whose function is to de-emphasize is thus counter-litotes.

R2: The device contains, implicitly at least, an ironic type of refutation*, which apparently answers the contrary argument* by colouring it differently; counter-litotes is, therefore, a type of antanaclasis*.

COUNTER-PLEONASM Instead of comparing different signifiers which have the same signified, a characteristic of the pleonasm* (see pleonasm, R1), a speaker uses different signifiers whose meanings are identical, at least functionally.

Exx: '[instruction in a computer program:] Type *type* to display the document'; 'You cannot *not* see it'; 'How do you calculate the *number* of numbers in a given *number* of *numbers*?'; 'Only take into account the *effects* which are *effectively* in place.'

R1: Counter-pleonasms represent an opposite type of mistake* to the pleonasm*; hence their name.

R2: When they relate to lexemes, they differ in meaning, a fact which distinguishes them from isolexism*. In addition, counter-pleonasms do not arise out of a desire for enhanced expressivity, but from a lack of vocabulary that confuses the idea expressed. The usual remedy is synonymy*. **Exx:** *'Enter "type" '*; 'effects *really* in place.' Syntactic changes and the substitution of grammatical tool-words also help. **Ex:** 'Calculate *how many* numbers there are in *n digits*.'

R3: The avoidance of counter-pleonasms accords with the use of language postulated in Saussurean structuralism: 'The linguistic fact can therefore be pictured in its totality – i.e. language – as a series of contiguous subdivisions marked off on both the indefinite plane of jumbled ideas and the equally vague plane of sounds ... Each linguistic term is a member, an *articulus* in which an idea is fixed in a sound and the sound becomes the sign of an idea' (Ferdinand de Saussure, *Cours de linguistique générale*, trans. W. Baskin, pp. 112–13).

It may well be possible to express different ideas by the same sets of sounds: polysemia and polymorphia are frequent phenomena. But the hypothesis concerning the system's clarity suffers from them as much as does communication itself. And so the surrealists amused themselves by denouncing faults in language. **Ex:** 'Il était une fois un rein et une reine' ('Once upon a time there was a kidney and a queen') (R. Desnos, *Domaine*, p. 211). *Reine* ('queen') is not the feminine form of *rein*, which means 'kidney' in French; the male equivalent of *reine* is, of course, *roi*.

R4: Deliberate counter-pleonasm, or *epizeuxis* (Foclin, cited by Le Hir; Lanham), is useful because it recalls, by acoustic allusion*, the principal lexeme in the assertion*. **Ex:** 'O horror, horror, horror.' Epizeuxis tends to become isolexism*.

R5: Reduced in scope, counter-pleonasm becomes allusion* and word-play*. See foregrounding*, R4.

COUNTERPOINT The alternation of several distinct isotopies*.

Ex: In *The Antiphonary*, Hubert Aquin tells two stories, one about the fifteenth century, the other about the twentieth. The two isotopies, or universes of discourse, sometimes coincide, and yet remain perceptibly separate:

> Strangely, Jules-César Beausang seems to have had no high regard for the great reformer, Zwingli. Beausang, an ardent Gomarist, remained so all his life which ... ended abruptly in Chivasso. When I went through Chivasso (with Jean-William ... We were on our way

to Turin) I did not recognize the Via Santa Clara, nor the inn where Jules-César Beausang suffered his death-agony. In Turin, however, I do remember seeing the church of San Fernando sopra San Tomaso (a modern church built on the ancient foundation of the parish church of San Tomaso) as well as the quarter ... where the fair must have been held at which poor Renata one day met her friend Rosalita ... But Jean-William at that moment had only one thing in mind: following the Sesia upstream to Modena. (Hubert Aquin, *The Antiphonary*, pp. 129–30)

On the other hand, isotopic limits may not be indicated, and the narrator risks giving the reader the impression of a kind of semantic scrambling* (a cryptographic device which consists in the substitution of lexemes from a different isotopy for the same number of lexemes in the first). A rapid reading of Sartre's *Les Chemins de la liberté* may produce the same effect. Sartre commingles episodes occurring simultaneously, although they are spatially distant from and independent of each other. Thus, at the beginning of volume 2, three separate threads unwind: (1) the Czechs are suffering persecution at the hands of the Germans (hero: Milan); (2) Daniel, a pederast, has just married Marcelle out of masochism; (3) Charles, a casualty, is being evacuated from the threat of war. Milan can scarcely prevent himself reacting to provocation, when his wife reminds him of his responsibility to his family:

He stuffed his hands in his pockets and repeated: 'I am not alone. I am not alone.' Daniel thought: '*I am alone*' ... Tears of rage filled Milan's eyes, and Daniel turned to Marcelle ... Caught like a rat! He had raised himself onto his forearms and was watching the shops go by. (J.-P. Sartre, *Le Sursis*, pp. 56–7)

The final two sentences refer to Charles, without naming him or signalling the transition*.

Counterpoint is possible in the theatre. Michel Tremblay, in *A toi pour toujours, ta Marie-Lou*, undercuts a couple's conversation with those that their daughters had several years later. The effect is remarkable, as much from the communicative as from the aesthetic perspective. In A. Brassard's production, for example, which separated the two pairs of antagonists, with the parents remaining in semi-darkness, there was little possibility of confusion.

R1: Counterpoint is sometimes reversed, or implicit. Ex: Jean Valjean, in the town of Digne, goes to City Hall, to the inn, then to the printer's. In inverse order, these were the three places in the same town visited by Napoleon six months earlier, 'as if there were some kind of interaction between the rise of Napoleon and the fall of Valjean' (A. Brochu, *Amour, crime, révolution: essai sur 'Les Misérables,'* p. 80).

R2: Involuntary confusion of isotopies produces disorder or surrealistic counterpoint. **Ex:** In *The Antiphonary* (1969), Hubert Aquin draws up a confused list of European and Quebec towns, and explains the lack of order in *Point de fuite* (1971, p. 101) by saying that it was 'as if his own memory of the trip was getting out of order.'

CRASIS The contraction of two syllables into one. See Elkhadem, Littré, Preminger, and Quillet.

Ex: 'The evil-hearted Grocer / Would call his mother *"Ma'am"*' (G.K. Chesterton, 'Song against Grocers').

Synonym: contraction

Antonym: diphthongization

R1: Synaeresis (see diaeresis*, R3) is, like elision*, a phonetic phenomenon affecting the coming together of two vowels. Crasis may also involve the intermediate consonant. See metaplasm*. In English, a kind of crasis occurs in expressions like *miniskirt, minigolf*, etc., in which a substantive and an adjective 'miniature' are contracted to form a single element (see Group MU, *A General Rhetoric*, p. 69).

R2: Elkhadem notes that the fusion of two separate vowels into one 'usually takes place in order to adhere to the metrical pattern.' **Ex:** *o'er* and *e'er* for 'over' and 'ever': 'And o'er and o'er the sand' (C. Kingsley, 'The Three Fishers').

R3: *Countercrasis*, marked in French by an *h* between the two vowels, occurs in order to make a clear separation between them. The *h* in 'lugu*h*ubre' also conforms to etymology*. **Ex:** 'J'adore l'alco*h*ol' (A. Jarry, *Oeuvres*, 1:152).

CRYPTOGRAPHY Encoded writing or numbers which may be decoded or deciphered if one has the key.
   We can distinguish two kinds of cryptography. In the first, the encoded message has an apparent meaning. **Ex:** 'Une bicyclette à deux roues est étendue dans la cave' ('A two-wheeled bicycle is spread out in the cellar'). This was the text of a BBC radio message sent to France in 1940 and quoted in the film *Le Matin d'Albert Camus*. In the second type, the message has no apparent meaning. **Ex:** 'Ed on to ay rd wa id sm yo da he nt ar re at pl rm ...' (R. Queneau, *Exercises in Style*, p. 129). These are two-letter permutations of the order of the signs used. The original sentence appears after a simple transposition of the first and second, third and fourth groups, etc.: 'One day towards midday on the rear platform ...' The decoding process is called *cryptanalysis*.

Cryptography

R1: For the formation of cryptograms in French slang*, see G. Esnault, *Dictionnaire historique des argots français*, under *largonji*. **Ex:** 'Un lourjingue vers lidimège sure la lateformeplic arrière d'un lobustotem ...' (R. Queneau, *Exercises de style*, p. 122). In her translation of Queneau, Barbara Wright (p. 158) converts this into 'rhyming slang' as follows: 'I see a chap in the bus with a huge bushel and peck and a ridiculous titfer on his loaf.'

For 'Cryptarithms or Alphametics,' puzzles in which letters are substituted for numbers to form an arithmetical sum, see T. Augarde, *The Oxford Book of Word Games*, p. 124. See also Esnault, under *javanais* ('double Dutch') – **Ex** (from Queneau): 'Unvin jovur vevers mividin suvur unvin vautobobuvus' [*vin, vur, ve, vu*, etc., added to each syllable] – or under *vers-l'en* (syllabic inversion*): **Exx:** brelica (calibre); Sequinzouil (Louis Quinze). This is backslang which, according to Cuddon (p. 68), 'can still be heard occasionally in London markets.' Barbara Wright (p. 159) renders the last quoted example from Queneau ('Unvin jour ...') as follows: 'Unway ayday aboutyay iddaymay onyay anyay essyay usbay.'

R2: Literary 'encoding' might be called an attenuated form of cryptography. It involves replacing certain key lexemes so as to disguise only the isotopy*. Eluard gives an example from Péret along with the key: 'Ah! quelle douceur, mon pope (ami). C'était comme une mince (danse) nouvelle et tout minçait (dansait) en moi. Jamais je n'aurais douillé (imaginé) cela. Et je t'assure que c'est bien fini avec les culottes (femmes) ... Après cela le brûleur (soleil) disparut dans un poussant (arbre)' (P. Eluard, *Oeuvres complètes*, 1:1169). Some of these terms are tropological, others are slang* terms, but with a different meaning. One message may also be concealed in another by means of acrostics*, anagrams*, and allographs*, or by means of paragrams*, or by the different types of scrambling*.

R3: Steganography is a type of cryptography which uses numbers and drawings as well as letters. See E. Souriau, 'Esthétique et cryptographie,' *La Revue d'esthétique* (1953), pp. 32–53. Incidentally, Eco's cryptogram and its solution (*The Name of the Rose*, pp. 155, 208) involving the substitution of signs of the zodiac for letters of the alphabet recall Souriau's use of the zodiac in *Les Deux cent mille situations dramatiques* (1950) to represent the different functions within a dramatic work. See also counterpoint*.

D

DÉCOUPAGE Graphic texts are divided into letters*, which are graphic units, and into words, which are theoretical combinatorial units. (We propose to add the following definition of the term to those already existing: a *word* is a group of phonemes which is endowed with meaning* and which cannot be divided into separate parts by other inserted 'words.') *Découpage* may affect syllables (see typographical caesura*, R1); or phonetic words, which are rhythmic units; syntagms*, which are functional units; assertions*, which are units of enunciation*; or sentences, paragraphs, or chapters.

Exx: 'Drinka Pinta Milka Day'; *'Ive* a right to sell flowers' (G.B. Shaw, *Pygmalion*, act 1); 'deux *tu l'as eu*' [the character pronounces this as *tulazu*] (J. Audiberti, *L'Effet Glapion*, p. 166). See logatom*.

The spoken text, especially when there are liaisons, invites metanalysis*. Cutting up *a naddre* or *a napron* gives respectively *an adder* and *an apron* as Jespersen noted. Grambs (p. 9) refers to these as examples of 'affix-clipping.' (See metanalysis*.) Similarly in French, *découpage* of *tropeureu* produces *trop heureux* ('too happy') and *trop peureux* ('too timorous'): usually the expression is only a single phonetic word.

Analogous term: delimitation

DEFINITION An assertion* whose subject is a thing or a word and whose predicate is an explanatory periphrasis* which designates the generic semes (classification), the specific semes (stipulative definition), or the virtual semes (example).

Ex: ' "Blitzer," said Thomas Gradgrind. "Your definition of a horse." "Quadruped. Graminivorous. Forty teeth, namely, twenty-four grinders, four eye-teeth, and twelve incisive. Sheds coat in the spring; in marshy countries, sheds hoofs, too. Hoofs hard but requiring to be shod with iron. Age known by marks in mouth" ' (Dickens, *Hard Times*, ch. 1).

Ex: 'Iris. 1. The name of a goddess in Greek mythology, who was the messenger of the Gods. By unfurling her scarf, she produced the rainbow' (R. Char, *Les Matinaux*, p. 97).

The *lexical* definition of a word belongs to the metalinguistic function of communication (see enunciation*, 6). Definition regroups various possible meanings*, since polysemy increases with frequency of use (Zipf's law). In literature, concretizing definitions and stipulative definitions, both of which give an idea precision, predominate. Exx:

'Genius (if at any rate one can speak thus of the great man's indefinable germ) must ...' (Baudelaire, *Oeuvres*, p. 1133); 'The body is a machine for living, no more. And since he [Napoleon] had embarked upon one of his pleasures, the search for definitions, he unexpectedly invented a new one: "Rapp, do you know what the art of war is? It is being stronger than the enemy at a given moment" ' (L. Tolstoy, *War and Peace*, trans. R. Edmonds, 2:235).

Merely exceeding the quite narrow limits of definition produces humorous effects. Ex: In francophone computerese, *carte blanche* means any non-perforated card, even a red one. Ex: ' "CANOE. A long hollow [tube] which keeps out the water," said the explorer' (H. Michaux, *Ecuador*, p. 180).

R1: Mestre (pp. 13–15) and Puttenham (*The Arte of English Poesie*, p. 231) distinguish the 'philosophical' or 'logical' definition as being 'dry and short' from the 'oratorical definition' (see also Le Clerc, p. 214; Lausberg, sect. 78). Other varieties include: 'descriptive' definition (see description*), which lists the parts and properties of the object described, matches causes with effects and circumstances, and even makes comparisons*. Pseudo-definition occurs when the predicate does not explain the semes of the subject but attaches new connotations to it, by means of metaphor* or synecdoche*. Thus definition may become a disguised argument*, all the more peremptory since it assumes the aspect of linguistic or logical definition. **Exx:** 'This pack of dogs called an army' (L. Tailhade, *Imbéciles et gredins*, p. 219); 'The frightful passage from the uterus to the grave we agree to call life' (L. Bloy, *Belluaires et porchers*, p. 29). Elliptical pseudo-definitions give an idea the force of a maxim*. Ex: 'Hell is other people' (J.-P. Sartre, *Huis-clos*, p. 92). *Operational* definitions offer a useful method for differentiating concrete examples; for an example, see assertion*, R4.

R2: Definition may become *identification*. Writing to a friend, 'I saw your wife,' Apollinaire might have added: she is both ugly and beautiful; a simple assertion. Replacing the adjectives by substantives produces: 'She is at once a horror and a beauty'; definition by classification. He in fact chose to write: 'She is ugliness and beauty,' conferring on the woman, by the simple syntactic device which turns definition into identification, the nobility belonging to a type.

Identification with concrete objects is possible and all the more striking. Ex: 'For I have spent my life waiting for you / And my heartbeats were but your footsteps'(P. Valéry, *Charmes*, in *Oeuvres*, 1:121).

R3: Victor Hugo's definitions often take question-answer form. Ex: 'What is an octopus? It is a sucker' (*Les Travailleurs de la mer*, 2.4.2).

R4: Essays of the scientific type make great use of definitions, which permit the avoidance of neology while rendering thought extremely specific. Thus G. Genette (*Narrative Discourse*, p. 157), studying repetition* in narrative*, calls the diachronic limits of a series of events their *determination*; 'the rhythm of recurrence' of the events, their *specification*; and the duration of each one, its *extension*.

R5: The use of abstract terms often broadens definitions to the point of imprecision. Ex: see ambiguity*, R2. But the definition of the terms of a problem is a means of finding good arguments* (see argument, R1). Definitions found in crossword puzzles are often no more than conundrums.

DELIBERATIO The pretence that one is weighing the arguments* with respect to a decision which has already been taken. See Fontanier, p. 412.

Ex: 'The Revolution had failed elsewhere, so what could the Bolsheviks do? Wait? Commit "hari-kiri" before the task's enormity? Or construct the socialist state in a single country? The latter is the route they chose' (Elleinstein, in *Le Monde*, 2 Aug. 1973).

R1: The speaker imitates for rhetorical reasons the discussions of a deliberating assembly. Each option is summarized in the form of a question*. The device resembles *communicatio**, the rhetorical question* (see question, R3), and *dubitatio**.

DENOMINATION Proper names are those attributed to individuals, places, organizations, or objects in order to designate them exclusively, by a word belonging to them 'in their own right,' because their 'common' names would not distinguish them from other identical individuals.

Analogous terms: The study of proper names has proceeded taxonomically by dividing referents into classes. *Reonymy* studies objects: names of boats, of restaurants, etc. *Hydronymy* studies names of rivers; *ethnonymy*, names of peoples; *phytonymy*, names of plants; *oronymy*, names of mountains; *hodonymy*, names of roads and streets; *zoonymy*, names of animals (*Encyclopaedia Britannica*, 1974 ed., 'Macropedia' under 'Names').

R1: The mark of the proper name is the capital letter. Ex: the Earth. In French, once a lexeme is turned into a proper name, or appropriated, determinants (articles, for instance, except in rare cases) are no longer necessary. In the same way, plural markings are only useful if appropriation is very weak. English usage is different. Compare: *les Smith* / the Smiths; *des Matisse* / several Matisses; *des Fords* / several Fords; *les 'Amphitryon' de Molière et de Giraudoux* / the Othellos of Shakespeare and Verdi; *ils se prennent pour des dons Juans* / they think they are Don Juan. As may be seen, in French, unlike in English, the *s* of the plural appears only when the proper name is used as a common noun. *Ford* no longer refers to the car's inventor, but to the title of numerous series of virtually identical objects; hence also, by contrast, in both French and English, the article: *une Ford* / a Ford. 'Dons Juans' refers to individuals having in common the hero's character. The same goes for nouns expressing nationality: *Un Suisse* / a Swiss.

When the capital letter disappears, it is because the name has become a common noun, and so appropriation no longer exists. Articles and the plural *s* are then regular. Ex: 'I saw a smith / several smiths at the forge,' as opposed to 'I saw (Bill) Smith yesterday.'

R2: In both French and English, names of individuals are formed of a first or given (baptismal or Christian) name, plus a middle name or names, and a surname or family name, or *patronymic* (i.e., a name derived from the given name of the father, following the common model in antiquity, and one still current in Russia and Acadia, the 'son of N'), later replaced by the name of a place of origin or ancient surname (e.g., Manchester, Dupont), and sometimes by a nickname (called ironically a *sobriquet*, which originally meant a 'tap under the chin') based on some individual trait. Exx: 'Richard Crookback' for Richard III; 'Tricky Dicky' for Richard Nixon.

In certain closed groups, the members of the invented society are 'rebaptised,' using nicknames or even titles* (heraldic names; boy scout, Ku Klux Klan, or religious titles, etc.). The conferring of titles* is a common expressive process.

Pseudonyms replace proper names with fanciful names. Exx: Ringuet and John Le Carré, pen-names of Philippe Panneton and David Cornwell respectively. *Cryptonyms* are false names used by detectives or spies. A family name which comes from the mother is called a *matronymic*.

Just as personal names may have ancient origins, place names also go back to antique linguistic substrata. Some appellations are referential. Ex: 'Charles the Bald.' If names of professions become family names in French, they retain the article. Ex: Lécuyer/Squire.

Names of institutions or organizations come from common nouns (Faculty of Medicine, The Old Spaghetti Factory, Electricité de France) or from acronyms*. Names of objects, industrial terms, and makes of products are frequently either compound* words (hovercraft, jetset), derivations* (Compuserve) or coinages* which resort to onomatopoeia* (popcorn), etymology* (Clairol, brand-name of a shampoo), metanalysis* (Sanka, a coffee 'sans caféine'; 'Nylon,' a fabric invented concurrently in New York and London), and portmanteau* words (Yoplait, the 'yogourt *qui plaît* / which pleases').

The conferring of proper names is constantly used in data processing; each 'program,' 'sub-routine,' and 'file' down to the smallest variable gets some more or less significant title*. Proper names sometimes play an important part in literature, since characters' names may have various connotations. Thus, in *Les Chambres de bois*, Anne Hébert constantly uses 'fine-sounding' given names, *Catherine, Michel, Lia*. Eugène Labiche, the nineteenth-century Parisian writer of bourgeois comedies, in order to find names which are comical but not too unlikely, combined anthroponymy with toponymy, combing the railway timetable in the process (according to E. Souriau, in *La Revue d'esthétique* [1965], p. 27). Some authors choose animal names: *Lebeuf* (ox) (Bessette, in *La Bagarre*); Bantam Lyons, the horse-racing fanatic in Joyce's *Ulysses*. Others take advantage of the liberty conferred by the use of nicknames. **Exx**: 'We'll keep the *Little one* here. Safe and sound with her children' (A. Hébert, *Kamouraska*, p. 99; to the speaker, one of her aunts, Catherine will always remain the 'Little one'); Hugh 'Blazes' Boylan, 'the worst man in Dublin' (Joyce, *Ulysses*). See sarcasm*.

In principle, proper names may appropriate any segment of the text: lexemes*, syntagms*, even morphemes. **Exx**: (1) 'My name is Neurasthenic' (R. Ducharme, *Le Nez qui voque*); Trollope's Mr Quiverful, who has fourteen children in *Barchester Towers*; (2) Gide, perhaps drawing his inspiration from the name of the architect of the Marseilles Basilica, Espèrendieu, invents for one of the families in *Les Faux-Monnayeurs* the evocative name of Profitendieu; Dickens produced Gradgrind in *Hard Times*, 'Dotheboys Hall' in *Nicholas Nickleby*, 'Eatanswill' in *Pickwick Papers*, and so on; (3) Victor Hugo gave us 'Je suis Tous, l'ennemi mystérieux de Tout' ('I am Everyone, the mysterious enemy of Everything'); this involves an appropriation of grammatical morphemes. Even puns* serve to create proper names: in Réjean Ducharme's works, we find *Ines Pérée* (unhoped for) and *Inat Tendu* (unexpected), and 'Dunrovin' is a name found on many gateposts both in and out of Scotland.

R3: Unlike personification*, proper denomination only affects the signifier. The general tendency is to create 'motivated' proper names, indeed to remotivate proper names (see *agnominatio**).

In the case of antonomasia*, the common noun functions as a proper name without losing its character, and so keeps the article. **Exx**: the Iron Duke, the Sun King.

Nicknames may have the marker '*dit* / alias, a.k.a. (also known as).' **Exx**: Blaise Cendrars, '*dit* Sans-bras,' because he had lost an arm in the First World War; 'Peter a.k.a. the Cruel'; former President Reagan, nicknamed the 'Gipper' (from a movie role).

DERIVATION A new lexeme formed by affixation. See Lauri Bauer, *English Word-Formation*; Valerie Adams, *An Introduction to Modern English Word-Formation*; Marouzeau; and Robert.

Ex: thinker; the suffix *–er* is added to *think–*.

Description

The set of words derived from the same *lexia* [neol.], or root, stem, or base (for distinctions between these terms, see Bauer, *English Word-Formation*, pp. 20–2), forms a *word-family*. The appropriate grammatical categories for lexemes are usually represented: noun, verb, adverb, adjective. Ex: clean, to clean, cleaner (noun), cleanliness, cleanly. But each word may take on a specialized meaning* and so become restricted to it.

In such cases, the possibility of syntactic construction is restricted. The needs of the sentence, or the necessity to avoid specific meanings* or supplementary connotations, force writers to create unusual derivations. Ex: '[This American professor] seems to be taking the line that English writers, from 1870 to 1914, were over-keen on preparing the nation for war. They suffered from "invasiophobia" and "isleophilia" ' (*Manchester Guardian Weekly*, 27 Mar. 1988, p. 28). If the derived word is useful, it may enter the language, where its effect is sometimes comical. Ex: 'And skeweyed Walter *sirring* his father, no less! Sir. Yes sir. No, sir' (Joyce, *Ulysses*, p. 32). Joyce conjugates *sir*, as if it were a verb (see transference*).

Other name: *Provignement*, the process of 'enriching vocabulary [with derivatives of existing words]' (*Harrap's New Standard French and English Dictionary*), was the term used to refer to neological derivatives introduced by the sixteenth-century French poets of the *Pléiade*. Zero derivation, or zero suffix, is frequently called *conversion*: 'the change in form class of a form without any corresponding change in form' (Bauer, p. 32). Ex: 'napalm' (noun) becomes 'to napalm' (verb).

R1: Suppression of a suffix may produce derivations which are 'regressive.' Exx: 'ad'; 'gent'

R2: Diminutives (or hypocoristic forms) are created either by abridgement* and gemination*, or by the addition of suffixes like *–ie* and *–ey*. Exx: Tom, Mimi, Charley, Laurie

R3: See also acronym*, R1; nominalization*, R4; neologism*, R1; isolexism*; and transference*.

DESCRIPTION External representation of a place, an object, an action (see hypotyposis* and diatyposis*), or a person (see portrait*).

Ex: 'A calculated, cast up, balanced, and proved house. Six windows on this side of the door, six on that side; a total of twelve in this wing, a total of twelve in the other wing; four and twenty carried over to the back wing. A lawn and garden and an infant avenue, all ruled straight like a botanical account-book' (Dickens, *Hard Times*, ch. 3).

Ex: 'Brother William's physical appearance was at that time such as to attract the attention of the most inattentive observer. His height surpassed that of a normal man and he was so thin that he seemed still taller. His eyes were sharp and penetrating; his thin and slightly beaky nose gave his countenance the expression of a man on the lookout ...' (U. Eco, *The Name of the Rose*, p. 15).

R1: In classical rhetoric, *topographia* is the description of a place (Fontanier, p. 422; Lanham, p. 100); *prosopographia*, that of a person. There were also names for descriptions of time: *chronographia*; of the earth: *geographia*; of water: *hydrographia*; of trees: *dendographia*; of the wind: *anemographia*.

A completely descriptive work of literature is not impossible, as Poe demonstrated in 'Landor's Cottage' and 'The Domain of Arnheim.' But excessive description has never been recommended, and it's possible to believe that descriptions in the *nouveau roman* sometimes caricature the obsession with objectivity. Ex:

> The two other chairs have been placed on the other side of the table, even further to the right, so as not to block the view between the two first ones and the balustrade of the veranda. Again because of the 'view,' these other two chairs have not been turned towards the rest of the group: they have been put at an angle, sideways to the openwork balustrade and the upper end of the valley ...
>
> The third one, which is a folding chair made of canvas stretched over a metal frame is set decidedly further back, between the fourth one and the table ... (A. Robbe-Grillet, *La Jalousie*, pp. 19–20; trans. A. Jefferson, in *The Nouveau Roman and the Poetics of Fiction*, pp. 136–7)

R2: As in the sciences, a diagram is worth several pages of text, and a photograph obviously 'says' more than a description, as, among others, Breton and Hemingway showed in *Nadja* and in *Death in the Afternoon* respectively. But photographs may also tell too much or fail to spotlight essentials.

R3: In descriptions, the roles played by verbs easily become artificial: 'a partly eaten rice pudding *was crumbling*; eggs *filled* a flowery salad bowl; a rabbit's liver *displayed* its purple viscosity; a towering pile of saucers *rose* [above the rest]' (J.K. Huysmans, *En ménage*, p. 51). As a result, certain authors prefer to use noun phrases: 'The table with the computer, printer, and boxes of discs. A few pictures in the space not occupied by shelves' (Eco, *Foucault's Pendulum*, p. 23). Notations*, particularly those specifying details of theatrical sets, regularly take this form. Ex: 'An entrance hall before a council chamber in the palace of Whitehall' (Maxwell Anderson, *Elizabeth the Queen*, 1.1).

For the importance of the signifier, see also parallelism*, R3, and reactualization*, 6.

Description

R4: Description, which plays a major part in Naturalist narrative*, risks appearing conventional (see epitheton*, R2); hence the following advice from Maupassant, the burden of which has since infiltrated the pedagogy of 'creative writing': 'The slightest object contains some unknown quality. Find it. To describe a blazing fire and a tree in a plain, stay in front of the fire and the tree until they no longer look to you like any other tree, any other fire' (*Pierre et Jean*, preface). The technique thus recommended is *observation*, which, when combined with focalization and narrative* produces the values connoted by the whole text. Ex: 'He climbed at the crest of the sandhill and gazed about him. Evening had fallen. A rim of the young moon cleft the pale waste of skyline, the rim of a silver hoop embedded in grey sand; and the tide was flowing in fast to the land with a low whisper of her waves, islanding a few last figures in distant pools' (J. Joyce, *A Portrait of the Artist as a Young Man*, pp. 172–3).

Description sometimes functions more modestly as a framing device placed around the action. The term *framing* (by analogy with cinematic framing) will be used here. 'By the framing device, the director forces the spectator to share his field of vision' (Fage and Pagano, eds., *Dictionnaire des media*). Narrowing the field 'leads the spectator's eye from a general view towards a single character or object' (ibid.).

Description may also be subjective, characters or objects being presented as seen by other characters, with whom a reader may gradually come to identify. This is what J. Pouillon (*Temps et roman*, p. 65) called 'vision avec'; Genette, *focalization*; Booth, 'limited point of view,' etc. Ex: 'To be a man, watched by women. It must be entirely strange. To have them watching him all the time. To have them wondering. What's he going to do next? To have them flinch when he moves, even if it's a harmless enough move, to reach for an ashtray perhaps. To have them sizing him up' (Margaret Atwood, *The Handmaid's Tale*, p. 83).

R5: In the absence of a correct term, a speaker has recourse to periphrasis* which may be merely descriptive ('a little green can,' for instance, when the product itself escapes the memory). B. Pingaud, in the 'Avis au lisant' (i.e., 'Foreword') to G. Perec's *La Disparition*, a novel written without the letter *e*, describes the latter periphrastically: 'Mum's the word then on the unknown core that's missing – *a not quite complete circle ending in a horizontal stroke.*' See lipogram*. Description is also one of the modes of amplification* and of definition* (see definition, R1).

R6: Butor's handy name for description which transposes a 'view' through memories (real or imagined) is *inner cinema* (*Intervalle*, p. 71). Compare: 'Darcourt was sitting in his dressing-gown gazing at his interior movie-show' (R. Davies, *The Lyre of Orpheus*, p. 110).

When description's function is to guarantee the authenticity of the narrative universe, we have Barthes's *reality effect*. Description which 'shows' may disguise its own process. If showing is foregrounded, on the other hand, we have description as pretext, as in the *nouveau roman*.

DIAERESIS The pronunciation as two separate vowels of a syllable formed of one vowel and a semi-consonant, so as to obtain an extra foot in the line. See Lanham, Lausberg (sect. 486), Marouzeau, Morier, *OED*, and Quillet.

Ex:

Miniver cursed the commonplace
And eyed a khaki suit with loathing;
He missed the medieval grace
Of iron clothing.
E.A. Robinson, quoted by the translators of Group MU's *General Rhetoric*

The translators of *General Rhetoric* add: 'Scansion forces us to pronounce *medieval* in four syllables' (p. 52).

Ex: 'Patience, patience'[i.e., four syllables in French, which helps to produce a seven-syllable line] (P. Valéry, 'Palme,' in *Charmes*). Morier uses the accentual mark called *diaeresis* ['] as a graphic mark of the phenomenon. Ex: 'Les sanglots longs / Des viölons ...'

Synonym: division (Lausberg)

R1: In French verse, the pronunciation of a mute *e*, which in everyday conversation would disappear, increases the number of feet in a line Ex: Patience. Like diaeresis, the phenomenon is archaic and both may be explained by the prestige possessed by syllabism in French versification. See line* of poetry.

R2: Diaeresis is a metaplasm* which may become a type of emphasis* in casual French speech. Ex: 'J'demande à vôhar [voir], interrompit Saturnin' (R. Queneau, *Le Chiendent*, p. 293).

R3: Synaeresis, the opposite phenomenon to diaeresis, contracts two syllables into one (see Cuddon, Lanham, Lausberg, Marouzeau, *OED*, and Quillet). Ex: the word *extraordinary*. In ordinary speech, both in French and English, the group *ao* reduces to a single sound. However, as is the case in careful English, the *a* is pronounced in careful French. For English usage, see Fowler; for French usage consult P. Fouché *Traité de prononciation française*, p. 38.

DIALOGUE An exchange of remarks between two persons or groups with each assuming alternately the role of speaker (I, we) and interlocutor (you).

Dialogue

Ex:

'I don't know why you do it,' my mother said. 'They're never grateful.'
'Do what?' I said, bulgy-eyed, breaking my vow of silence in my eagerness to know. (Margaret Atwood, *Lady Oracle*, p. 70)

Analogous terms: conversation; verbal exchange (Dubois et al., *Dictionnaire de linguistique*). An *antiphony* is a (religious) chant executed alternately by two choirs.

R1: The oral signs marking the reversal of roles are external to language (the change of speaker and tone); the graphic mark is a colon or dash (see situational* signs, 3). Reference to the speakers is sometimes implicit. **Ex:**

'His brother's rich
A somebody – a director in the bank.'
'He never told us that.'
'We know it though.'
'I think his brother ought to help, of course.'
                    Robert Frost, 'The Death of the Hired Man'

R2: Dialogue is the most natural mode for speech when it becomes verbal exchange. Most literary dialogues attempt to reproduce real or supposedly real conversations. They are thus examples of *mimesis*. Dramatic works are most often mimetic, with actors imitating fairly common types (the juvenile lead, a lady, an employee, etc.). Despite the possibility of individuation conferred upon them by actors skilled in their craft, such types may become stylized. Some actors specialize in certain roles which suit their physical and moral characters; such specialization leads inevitably to *type-casting*.

R3: Discourse* may include embedded dialogue which replaces indirect or reported speech. In this case, a character's *I* replaces the initial *I* of the implied author; a different character's *you* replaces the initial second-person address to an implied addressee. Double actualization thus takes place (see reactualization*). Dialogue becomes a means of diversifying and adding life to the exposition of a subject. This is second-degree, or second-level, dialogue, which is not without artifice, even when tending towards realism. Consequently, it is a figure, *dialogism*, discussed by Fontanier (p. 375), Lausberg, Joseph, and Lanham, and defined in the *OED*. Ex [a narrator / implied author engages in dialogue with his invented characters]: 'What do you expect, my friend? You're a victim of war' (M. Barrès, *Les Déracinés*, p. 356). Ex [Alceste invents a poet to whom he 'confides' the criticisms which he thus makes indirectly to his rival Oronte]: 'But, one day, on seeing some of his verse, I said to someone whose name I won't mention, that a gentleman needs to exercise iron control over the itch driving us all to write ... and that the desire to show off one's works exposes one to play a very poor part ... I showed him how, in our age, that desire has spoiled some very decent people' (Molière, *Le Misanthrope*, 1.2).

The mark of the passage from one level of dialogue to another (from an *I* attributable to the author to one attributable to a character, for example) is the introduction of a declarative verb (to say, announce, etc.), and the graphic signs are quotation marks. In familiar conversation in French, the expressions *kidi* and *kèdi* (i.e., *qu'il dit* and *qu'elle dit*, equivalents to English *he sez* and *sez she*) serve as opening quotation marks. Ex:

I went into a public-'ouse to get a pint o' beer,
The publican 'e up an sez, 'we serve no red-coats 'ere.'
The girls be'ind the bar they laughed an' giggled fit to die,
I outs into the street again an' to myself sez I ...
R. Kipling, 'Tommy,' in *Barrack-Room Ballads*

Ex: 'Là-d'sus, è [elle] lui dit: Vous avez eu des trucs à régler ensemble, et elle cligna de l'oeil [winked]. L'aut', i' [il] dit qu'i' n'comprenait pas. – Et Théo, qu'elle dit. J'l'connais pas, qu'il répondit d'un air furieux' (R. Queneau, *Le Chiendent*, p. 115).

A character may introduce other speakers into his speech; dialogism enters into his remarks in the same way as one narrative* may include another. Ex [Lenehan is speaking about Mrs Bloom]: 'At last she spotted a weeny weeshy one miles away. *And what star is that, Poldy?* says she. By God, she had Bloom cornered. *That one, is it?* says Chris Callinan, *sure, that's only what you might call a pinprick.* By God, he wasn't far wide of the mark' (Joyce, *Ulysses*, p. 193).

R4: Since dialogue consists formally of the replacement of third-person pronouns by pronouns of the first or second person, it is hardly surprising that the dialogic capacity may be extended, along with personification* (see personification, R1) of an artificial kind, to things or ideas (see prosopopoeia*; and *cheretema* in R8 below).

R5: The double actualization characteristic of dialogism occurs also without dialogue (without responses from the character addressed) and even in monologues* (speeches without addressees). Ex: 'The former addressed himself to the latter in these terms: I say, you, anyone might think you were treading on my toes on purpose' (R. Queneau, *Exercises in Style*, p. 87). Even dialogism tends toward mimesis, the principal device – along with simile* – of what is called Homeric style.

R6: The two speakers in a dialogue may be two aspects of the Self: this is *interior dialogue*, which used to be called *sermocinatio* (Lanham; Lausberg; Scaliger, 3:48), a form frequent in meditations on decisions

131

which depend on the morality of actions. **Ex:** W.B. Yeats's 'Dialogue of Self and Soul.' **Ex:**

> THOMAS: Peace, and be at peace with your thoughts and visions.
> These things had to come to you and you accept them.
> This is your share of the eternal burden,
> The perpetual glory.
>
> T.S. Eliot, *Murder in the Cathedral*, part 2

R7: Another kind of dialogue which remains pure form, the *dialogue de sourds* or 'dialogue of the deaf,' involves the criss-crossing of two monologues*, with both speakers pursuing their own trains of thought. **Ex:**

> PENELOPE: (OV distant) Dahling!
> (Bone takes no notice.)
> Dahling ...
> (He has heard but won't respond.)
> Help! Fire! Murder!
> BONE: (Murmurs) Wolf ...
> PENELOPE: Wolves! Look out! Rape! Rape! Rape!
> BONE: Not the most logical of misfortunes.
>
> Tom Stoppard, *Another Moon Called Earth*, scene 1,
> in *The Dog It Was That Died and Other Plays*

R8: Fabri (2:166) calls oratorical dialogue which presents a subject in question/answer form *cheretema* to be distinguished from *subjectio*, whose addressee is not a fiction. After counsels' speeches, the Greeks had a question and counter-question period called an *altercation*, from which tragic authors drew the inspiration for their writings, particularly for their *amoebean verses*, spoken alternately by two speakers (Bénac, Cuddon, Preminger, Robert). The second speaker was expected to 'cap' the remarks made by the first. **Ex:**

> PYLADE: You were deceiving me, my lord.
> ORESTE: I was deceiving myself.
>
> J. Racine, *Andromaque*, 1.1

R9: We can distinguish three types of dialogue following their different functions: *expositional* dialogue intended to inform the first addressee, that is, the public (see explanation*); *tonal* dialogue intended to present character; and *scenic* dialogue, in which the principal characters confront one another. For dialogue in the form of *interrogation*, see question*, R4.

R10: Dialogue may take monological form, as in a telephone conversation in which the speech of one of the parties allows the reconstruction of the other's. Cocteau constructed a playlet, *Le Bel indifférent*, in this way; Camus wrote a narrative, *La Chute*, in which the main character,

Clamence, both addresses himself directly to the reader and 'quotes' the latter's reactions; 'Fine city, no? Fascinating? That's an adjective I've not heard in a long time ...' (p. 8).

Conversely, dialogue becomes general conversation when there are several speakers. *Brainstorming*, for example, 'a technique intended to allow a group to produce the greatest possible number of ideas in the shortest time' (Fage and Pagano, eds., *Dictionnaire des media*), has a literary counterpart, given the necessity for dramatic concision.

R11: See also enunciation*, R3; antanaclasis*; apocalypse*, R1; apostrophe*; *coq-à-l'âne*, R4; prayer*, R1; prolepsis*, R1; repetition*, R2; response*, R2; emphasis*, R1; verbigeration*, R4; portrait*, R3; and rhythm* of the action, R1.

DIAPHORA Using a common term, in contrast to a proper one, a second time, but with a different meaning. See *Encyclopaedia Britannica*. See also Lanham, Lausberg, and Morier.

Exx: 'The heart has reasons unknown to reason' (Blaise Pascal, *Pensées*, 4:277); 'My advocation is not now in tune. / My lord is not my lord' (Shakespeare, *Othello*, 3.4.123–4); 'We must all hang together, or most assuredly we shall all hang separately' (Benjamin Franklin); 'In the view of numerous academicians, the anonymous authors of the four Gospels ... were working from second- and third-hand materials ... Consequently, *the Gospels cannot be taken as gospel*; that is, they cannot in every instance be considered as describing actual events' (*Time*, 15 Aug. 1988, pp. 35–6); 'When I was in New York last month, I was in one of those crazy cabs and the driver was a maniac. I told him, listen, I'd rather be the late Mr. Berle than the late Mr. Berle' (Milton Berle, *The Ottawa Citizen*, 14 Oct. 1989, p. H11).

Other names: antanaclasis*; *traductio* ('the transference of the meaning of one word to another' [Quintilian, 9.3.71]). Fabri derives his definition* from Quintilian's: 'repetition*, except that the word must remain equivocal and is repeated at the beginning of successive clauses.' **Ex:** 'Cures are achieved by doctors, cures are [ad]ministered by priests' (Fabri, *Pleine Rhétorique*, 2:161).

R1: Like antanaclasis*, which Empson discusses in *Seven Types* (ch. 3), diaphora is a kind of ambiguity* related to baroquism*. The two meanings* of the term repeated appear different because of their immediate context, as in the Milton Berle joke quoted above.

R2: Diaphora differs from homonymy* (see homonymy, R1), often becoming word-play* which may extend over several words. **Ex:** 'We don't take sides, we just take pictures' (motto of *Visnews*, a photographic department of Reuter's, quoted in *Sight and Sound*, Winter 1986–7, p. 27).

R3: Stiff or formal syntagms* may become false diaphoras. **Ex:** 'Let him at least try to see her. Then he will see' (J.-P. Sartre, *L'Age de raison*, p. 314).

R4: Strictly speaking, diaphora may play on homonyms without necessarily becoming word-play*. **Exx:** 'RICHARD: Base court, where kings grow base ... / That lie shall lie so heavy on my sword' (Shakespeare, *Richard II*, 3.3., 4.1); 'He said, "I suppose we are cousins more or less," but in his mind I suppose that in my case the word must for him rather have meant mosquito or gnat, and again I blushed angrily' [the French homonym, *cousin*, means both 'cousin' and 'gnat'] (Cl. Simon, *La Route des Flandres*, p. 8).

R5: Diaphora may also play upon *antonyms*. **Ex:** 'When I'm big [grown up], will I still be little [small in size]?'

R6: Some examples of diaphora result not from a change in meaning*, but in actualization. **Ex:** 'The king is dead. Long live the king [the new king].' Or from a change in the type of sentence*. **Ex:**

DE VALVERT: Villain, cad, stupid flat-footed clod.
CYRANO: Ah? ... And I am Cyrano-Savinian-Hercule de Bergerac.
E. Rostand, *Cyrano de Bergerac*, 1.4

R7: Most cases of tautology* (see tautology, R2) are redundant because they contain diaphora. See also distinction*, R2.

DIATYPOSIS Hypotyposis* (vivid, energetic description*) reduced to few words. See Lausberg, Littré, and *OED*.

Ex: 'A blonde who resembled Marilyn Monroe was kneading him with suntan oil' (Truman Capote, *In Cold Blood*, p. 229).

Other definition: In the anglophone rhetorical tradition (see Lanham, Peacham, etc.), diatyposis is also a figure 'whereby one recommends to another certain profitable rules and precepts. Polonius' advice to Laertes (*Ham.*, I.3, 58–80) is an outstanding example' (Joseph, p. 101).

R1: The same (quantitative) difference separates diatyposis from hypotyposis as distinguishes metaphor* from allegory*: fewer words, and therefore fewer things made visual; the scene is barely evoked, and comparisons* remain allusive.

Moreover, as is true for hypotyposis, some diatyposes are more visual than rhetorical whereas others are more rhetorical than visual. A current example of the latter in French: 'Avoir un oeil qui dit zut à l'autre' (i.e., to squint).

R2: The following examples of diatyposis describe by using negation*: 'Last scene of all / That ends this strange eventful history, / Is second childishness, and mere oblivion, / Sans teeth, sans eyes, sans taste, sans everything' (Shakespeare, *As You Like It*, 2.7.163–6); 'Oh worms! dark companions without ears or eyes' (Ch. Baudelaire, 'Le Mort joyeux.'

DIGRESSION A part in a work which treats matters apparently extraneous to the principal subject, but which nonetheless are essential to the author's goal. See Cuddon, Frye, Lanham, Lausberg, Littré, Morier, *OED*, Quillet, and Robert.

Ex:

> What business Stevinus had in this affair – is the greatest problem of all; – it shall be solved, – but not in the next chapter.
>
> CHAPTER XI
> Writing, when properly managed (as you may be sure I think mine is), is but a different name for conversation ... (L. Sterne, *Tristram Shandy*, vol. 2, chs. 10, 11)

Synonyms: *egressio* (Lanham, Lausberg); episode (Girard); excursus (Lanham). For Quillet, however, the excursus is a digression 'on a point of archaeology or philology, concerning a text by an ancient author.'

R1: Even a long digression may be placed in parentheses*. Ex [a drunkard, claiming to be an explorer, has just given a bizarre account of the customs of savages; this is how Bloom reacts to the tale]:

> Though not an implicit believer in the story narrated (or the egg-sniping transaction for that matter despite William Tell and the Lazarillo-Don Cesar de Bazan incident depicted in *Maritana* on which occasion the former's ball passed through the latter's hat) having detected a discrepancy between his name (assuming he was the person he represented himself to be and not sailing under false colours after having boxed the compass on the strict q.t. somewhere) and the fictitious addressee of the missive which made him nourish some suspicions of our friend's *bona fides*, nevertheless it reminded him in a way of a longcherished plan ... of travelling to London *via* long sea. (Joyce, *Ulysses*, p. 512)

Obviously, the device does not particularly make for clarity. It verges on *coq-à-l'âne** (see *coq-à-l'âne*, R1) and easily becomes verbiage* (see verbiage, R5).

R2: Morier emphasizes that digressions act as a kind of suspension*, aimed at keeping the receiver on tenterhooks. Ex: In Rostand's *Cyrano de Bergerac* (3.13), Cyrano recounts to Christian's rival, de Guiche, the story of his arrival from the moon so as to make possible Roxane's marriage to Christian.

DISCOURSE In the broad sense, a discourse is a set of syntagms*, oral or written, which in the view of the speaker or writer, constitutes a coherent whole. This broad sense, frequent in linguistics, is not a new one: the *OED* first records use of the expression 'parts of speech' to designate grammatical categories in 1509; the expression merely translates the Latin *partes orationis*.

However, it is only by catachresis* that 'discourse' may mean 'sentence.' A discourse is an organized collection of sentences. Thus sentences really form the *parts of (a) speech*, as Benveniste has shown. It will be objected, however, that the parts of a speech are themselves sentences organized into subsets which function as preamble, peroration, etc.

In rhetoric, there is every reason to consider that there exist as many kinds of discourse (in the broad sense) as there exist *genres*, that is *types* of works, or of linguistic functions (see enunciation*).

In the strict sense, *discourse* is a form which tends to influence others through the communication of ideas, emotions, or a desire for action; it strives to control concrete, actual situations. This function, which may be called *injunctive* (see enunciation*, R3), entails the following characteristics:
- a certain length (compare discourse and maxims*)
- a requirement for sustained internal coherence (see plan*)
- convincing argumentation (see argument*, *communicatio*, etc.)
- expressive figures (see repetition*, comparison*, etc.)
- clear, easily understood language
- oral delivery (speeches are normally spoken, although written out beforehand or transcribed after the event; an unprepared speech is an improvisation)
- numerous listeners (imaginary ones at least)
- a tendency towards elevation of tone

Since the sublime always risks appearing (and being) artificial (see grandiloquence*), it needs to be combined with simplicity. Ex:

> We shall not flag or fail. We shall fight in France, we shall fight on the seas and oceans, we shall fight with growing confidence and growing strength in the air, we shall defend our island, whatever the cost may be, we shall fight on the beaches, we shall fight on the landing grounds, we shall fight in the fields and in the streets, we shall fight in the hills; we shall never surrender.' (W. Churchill, speech, House of Commons, 4 June 1940)

Analogous terms: address; allocution (for a relatively short discourse).

For the statement of a speaker's position: manifesto, declaration, position-paper. For public announcements: notice, message, proclamation. For an accusation*: charge, indictment, diatribe, philippic oration. For the defence or praise of someone: plea, petition, apology, vindication, eulogy, panegyric, encomium, speech of congratulation, funeral oration. For the encouragement of certain dispositions: harangue, exhortation*, advice, *paraenesis* (moral exhortation), admonition or reprimand, objurgation or chiding, order of the day, briefing (definition and distribution of the tasks at hand). For religious subjects: sermon, homily, prayer*. For didactic subjects: lesson, lecture, *causerie*, report. Pejoratives: patter, puff, spiel.

R1: Narratives* introduced into discourse represent, according to Lanham (p. 68), examples of *narratio*, 'the second part of the seven-part classical oration. It tells how the problem at hand has come up, gives the audience, as it were, the history of the problem.' Because it takes on the elevation of tone characteristic of the surrounding discourse, narrative risks the loss of precise detail. Ex:

> Anne [of Austria] ... at an already advanced age, and Marie-Thérèse [of Austria] in the vigour of her age ... have been unexpectedly taken from us, the former after a long illness, the latter at one unforeseeable stroke. Anne, warned long in advance by a disease as cruel as it is incurable, saw death approach slowly, and in the guise which she had always found most terrible. (Bossuet, 'Oraision funèbre de M.-Th. d'Autriche')

What Bossuet might have said in narrative, rather than discursive, form was that Anne died of breast cancer, 'the disease so frightful even to the imagination,' as she herself wrote to Mme de Motteville (quoted by J. Truchet, in the Garnier edition of Bossuet's *Oraisons funèbres*, p. 235). *Attenuated evocation* replaces the proper term. (See allusion*, R4.)

Conversely, discourse may enter into narrative or dialogue* in the form of tirades, long passages of declamation. The works of Calderon, Shakespeare, and Corneille afford many examples; not forgetting the 'nose tirade' in act 1 of Rostand's *Cyrano de Bergerac*, or the vehement, abusive anti-establishment harangues of Jimmy Porter in John Osborne's *Look Back in Anger* (1957).

R2: One characteristic of discourse is the application of noble-sounding forms of address to listeners at principal points of articulation. Ex: 'Yet I cannot hide from you, Gentlemen and Philosophers (indeed there is not much that one could hide from you), that this view ... Do not think, Gentlemen, my view is very distant from that of our own Descartes' (P. Valéry, *Oeuvres*, 1:798, 799).

Oratorical discourse lends itself to frequent parody*. Ex:

'Gentlemen,' said the mayor, at as loud a pitch as he could possibly force his voice to, 'Gentlemen. Brother electors of the Borough of Eatanswill. We are met together here today for the purpose of choosing a representative in the room of our late –' Here the mayor was interrupted by a voice in the crowd. 'Success to the mayor,' cried the voice, 'and may he never desert the nail and sarspan business, as he got his money by.' This allusion ... rendered the remainder of his speech inaudible, with the exception of the concluding sentence, in which he thanked the meeting for the patient attention with which they had heard him throughout, – an expression of gratitude which elicited another burst of mirth, of about a quarter of an hour's duration. (Ch. Dickens, *The Pickwick Papers*, ch. 13)

Protocol determines the order of precedence of the listeners whom it is desirable to thank for their presence by addressing them by name at the beginning of a speech: 'Mister/Madame President/Prime Minister, Mr Minister, Ladies, Gentlemen,' etc.

R3: See also aposiopesis*; apostrophe*, R1; argument*, R1; attenuation*, R3; celebration*; quotation*, R3 and R5; *coq-à-l'âne*; dialogue*, R3; *gradatio*, R1; hyperbole*, R6; monologue*, R4; level* of language, R2; plan*; question*, R6; recapitulation*, R3; narrative*, R5; and meaning*, 8.

DISJUNCTION A syntactic construction in which elements common to several parallel clauses are separated, 'resolved into factors,' as it were, so as not to need repetition*.

Exx: 'Either I'm late or you're early'; 'The true relationship with God is, in contemplation, love, in action, slavery' (S. Weil, *La Pesanteur et la grâce*, p. 57).

Other definitions: See asyndeton*. Crystal (1987, p. 419) defines semantic disjunction as 'an alternative or contrasting relationship between elements in a sentence (*Either we're early or the bus is late*).' See alternative*.

R1: Disjunction is an elaborate form of zeugma*. See also enumeration*, R4; and seriation*, R1.

R2: English allows interruption* after a preposition. Ex: '[The Irish protestant church] abjured by him in favour of a Roman Catholicism *at the epoch of* and *with a view to* his matrimony in 1888' (Joyce, *Ulysses*, p. 588). The influence of English has produced the factorization in French of an actualized lexeme after two prepositions, conjunctions, or phrases, as the French translation shows: '[L'église protestante irlandaise] qu'il avait abandonnée plus tard en faveur du catholicisme à *l'époque de, et pour faciliter,* son mariage en 1888' (Joyce, *Ulysse,* p. 636, trans. Valéry Larbaud).

R3: Adjunction* and disjunction, far from opposing one another (as the prefixes *ad-* and *dis-* might lead one to expect) may sometimes appear to have the same structure: $y(x^1s^1/x^2s^2)$. See Lausberg (sections 739 and 743). But in the case of adjunction, the parallel member (x^2s^2) is not required by syntax, being added to an already balanced syntactic structure. Compare the example from Weil above with the one from Queneau under adjunction*. See also regrouped* members, R2.

DISLOCATION A device for emphasizing any part of a sentence by means of agents (personal or demonstrative pronouns) authorizing either anticipation or reprise*.

Exx: 'They are so proud, *Corsicans'; 'The other car,* where does *it* come from?'; 'And he added that besides, it deserved it, let it be closed, my place, why? because it was immoral. They took their time realizing that it was immoral, my place. In any case, it is closed, my place, very closed' (R. Queneau, *Pierrot mon ami,* p. 116).

Other name: 'segmented sentence' (J.-C. Chevalier et al., *Grammaire Larousse du français contemporain,* p. 100)

Other definition: Bally (*Traité,* p. 285) employs dislocation in a broader sense. For him, it is a case of parataxis*, or rather of *hyperparataxis,* in which not only the dependent relations between propositions remain implicit, but the propositions themselves are split up into several word-sentences, which remain grammatically quite separate. Ex: 'You can't seriously be thinking of such a thing' becomes 'Such a thing. Come now. Are you seriously thinking of it?' For a literary example from Beckett, see monologue*.

R1: Dislocation separates elements (most often using pronouns) whereas adjunction* joins other elliptical elements onto autonomous segments.

R2: Dislocation apparently serves to implement the desire to isolate the predicate from the subject by the use of some syntactic device. Ex: 'She took it from her, that is, Jane took the ribbon from Anne.' See also emphasis*, R1; theme*, R3; and isolexism*, R4.

DISSOCIATION 'The systematic rupture of articulation ... at sentence-level, through semantic dissociation of its subject and predicate, by choosing them among different series of terms having incompatible classemes' (P. Zumthor, *Essai de poétique médiévale,* p. 141).

   The definition must be extended to cover any syntactic combination which, although 'conforming to the code,' imposes association on terms semantically unassociable (see Angenot, pp. 127, 176). **Exx** (cited by

Dissociation

Angenot, pp. 185–206): 'soluble fish'; 'a morganatic avalanche' (non-pertinent adjective); 'the revolver with white hair' (Breton, collage*); 'My sister / divine like me / who am her brother *from time to time*' (B. Péret, non-pertinence of the adverb); 'A bell-clapper umbrella' (Tzara, noun phrase, collage*).

Synonyms: discordance (Angenot); contrast (Porter, *La Fatrasie et le fatras*); discontinuity (Richard, *Onze Etudes sur la poésie moderne*)

Other definition: distinction*

R1: Dissociation is apparently a fairly new concept whose predecessors include *fatrasie* or nonsense verse, *coq-à-l'âne**, etc. (See verbigeration*, R1.) However, in the older forms, the semantic rupture did not occur systematically at the level of the elements of meaning* possessed by the words of the language. Thus, Voltaire's nonsense verses, for example, merely confuse place names and multiply anachronisms* and bizarre combinations of sounds. **Ex:**

In Japan
Artemis's petticoat
Serves the Persian Ruler
When to Rome he goes without
A shirt.

Compare:

He has many friends, laymen and clerical;
Old Foss is the name of his cat;
His body is perfectly spherical,
He weareth a runcible hat.

Edward Lear, 'Self Portrait'

The novelty of the concept explains the multiplicity of terms proposed. We have kept 'dissociation' rather than 'discordance' because the former exhibits more clearly the fundamental separation occurring concomitantly with syntactic association.

R2: Dissociation needs to be distinguished from oxymoron* (see oxymoron, R1), and from dissonance*, both of which involve ruptures in tone (or in stylistic level).

R3: The terms of some dissociations are objects and so the latter form collages*. Other dissociations result from combinations of phrases and as such constitute examples of telescoping*.

R4: In order to be able to understand, or translate, Breton and certain other writers, it is important to know that their 'images*' must not, except in exceptional cases, be decoded as metaphors*, but as dissociations; that is, as expressions which possess dual isotopies*, with each incompatible term of a comparison* being taken literally. See image*, R1.

R5: Dissociation is not as gratuitous as one might think from reading certain theoretical texts. There are two isotopies*, as distant from one another as possible, but they have their psychological foundation in the creative subject. Michaux recounts the following exemplary experience. Having written, when under the influence of hashish, 'Paolo! Paolo! / crié d'une voix bordée de rouge' (*Connaissances par les gouffres*, p. 94), he comments later:

'A Voice edged in red.' A purely literary expression? No, not at all, but a precise phenomenon, well known to the hashish smoker, which says exactly what it should and which – I'm thinking about it now – would justify perfectly a certain literary device, which is not so artificial as all that.

When two sensations, two such hyper-sensations appear, equally strong, extravagant and importunate, having *ipso facto* put to shade concomitant sensations, one wants to express them in conjunction, as they appear, violently and precipitately, *ex aequo*. (Ibid., pp. 127–8)

R6: If one of the terms is taken to be figurative, the dissociation between the two terms taken literally is abolished by the underlying isotopy*, which becomes the only one in question. The only remaining rupture is at the figural level, and we speak in that case of *false dissociation*. (See incoherence*; for an example, see collage*, R2.)

R7: Dissociations exist in everyday language due to negligence. Ex: 'Children, from 14 to 65, can work.' See cacology*.

R8: Instead of dissociating lexemes from one another, an author may break the link which the audience establishes spontaneously between a discourse* and a supposed reality, so that the discourse's meaning* loses referential specificity. Ex:

MRS. SMITH: And Bobby Watson's aunt, old Bobby Watson might very well, in her turn, pay for the education of Bobby Watson, Bobby Watson's daughter. That way, Bobby, Bobby Watson's mother could remarry. Has she anyone in mind?
MR. SMITH: Yes, a cousin of Bobby Watson's.
MRS. SMITH: Who, Bobby Watson?
MR. SMITH: Which Bobby Watson do you mean?
E. Ionesco, *The Bald Soprano*, in *Four Plays*, p. 13

R9: Dissociation represents a higher degree of dissolution than adynaton*, equivoque*, syllepsis*, amphibol(og)y*, approximation*, etc. It not only strains meaning* but does violence to the global isotopy*, which as a result shifts towards nonsense*.

DISSONANCE The mixing of several tones. See Littré (sense 2) and Lausberg. Voltaire speaks of the mixture of styles. Preminger offers a restricted definition: 'poetic elements other than sound that are discordant with their immediate context.'

Ex: 'Them that asks no questions isn't told a lie. / Watch the wall, my darling, while the Gentlemen go by' (R. Kipling, 'A Smuggler's Song'). The first member, with its agrammatism, belongs to spoken language; the second, with its ironic use of lexical archaism*, is in the 'noble' style sometimes used in conversation intended to hide realities from children. For forty pages in *Ulysses* (pp. 240–83), Joyce alternated paragraphs in sustained style with those in slang*. Ex:

> In Inisfail the fair there lies a land, the land of holy Michan. There rises a watchtower beheld of men afar ...
> *I dare him*, says he, *and I doubledare him.* Come out here Geraghty, you notorious bloody hill and dale robber!
> And by that way wend the herds innumerable of bellwethers and flushed ewes and shearing rams and lambs ...
> So we turned into Barney Kiernan's and there, sure enough, was the citizen up in the corner having a great confab with himself and that bloody mangy mongrel, Garryowen, and he waiting for what the sky would drop in the way of drink ... (Joyce, *Ulysses*, pp. 241–2)

Other definitions: 'the meeting of discordant sounds' (Littré, sense 1; see cacophony*); 'a break in metre which parallels a sudden change of mood' (Morier)

R1: The use of noble speech for trivial subjects is a form of dissonance. Ex: 'Sir, what do you wish? Get lost, you weary me' (A. Jarry, *Ubu roi*, p. 43). In *L'Ironie*, Jankélévich shows that this kind of dissonance, which society finds objectionable, may result from sincerity.

DISTANCING A term proposed by Spitzer (*Etudes de style*, p. 209 et seq.) to designate an actualization which introduces 'a certain remoteness.'

First-person pronouns or possessive adjectives are replaced by proper names, common nouns, third-person pronouns, or articles. Exx: 'CAESAR: Caesar shall forth. The things that threatened me / Ne'er looked but on my back. When they shall see / The face of Caesar, they are vanishèd' (Shakespeare, *Julius Caesar*, 2.2.10–12); 'JOAS: Joas will never cease loving you' (Racine, *Athalie*, 4.4).

Demonstratives or neuter pronouns like 'one' may replace names and third-person pronouns. Ex [Brutus]: 'Friends, I owe more tears / To *this* dead man than you will see me pay' (Shakespeare, *Julius Caesar*, 5.3. 98–9). Ex [Lily Briscoe's interior monologue]: '... But *one* got nothing by soliciting urgently. One got only a glare in the eye ... For there were moments when one can neither think nor feel. And if one can neither think nor feel, she thought, where is one?' (V. Woolf, *To the Lighthouse*, p. 224).

R1: In these two categories of examples, the distancing effect is obtained by generalization*. Replacement of the singular by the plural, also pointed out by Spitzer, is more ambiguous. The so-called 'royal' plural (Queen Victoria: 'We are not amused' [*Notebooks of a Spinster Lady*, 2 Jan. 1900]) intensifies the effect made by the speaker rather than distancing her. Spitzer also draws attention to the use of abstract expressions in this regard. Ex [Brutus to the conspirators]: 'O Conspiracy / Shamest thou to show thy dangerous brow by night, / When evils are most free?' (Shakespeare, *Julius Caesar*, 2.1. 77–9). Finally, Spitzer mentions 'royal countries' in which monarchs receive the name of their fiefdom:

KING HENRY: Peace ... unto our brother France ...
FRENCH KING: Most worthy brother England ...

Shakespeare, *Henry, v*, 5.2

These are metonymies* used instead of 'you' or 'I.'

DISTINCTION   The splitting into two opposite terms of a notion generally held to be homogeneous. See Angenot and Perelman.

Exx: '[A cynic is] a man who knows the price of everything and the value of nothing' (O. Wilde, *Lady Windermere's Fan*, act 3); 'The profoundest egoism is not egoism' (M. Pages, *La Vie affective des groupes*, p. 336).

Synonyms: *distinguo*, paradiastole (Quillet, Lanham); dissociation* (Lalande; see also Perelman, pp. 550–5)

R1: Distinctions differ from dissimilitudes, in which the notions opposed to one another belong respectively to two things compared. In distinctions, the speaker simply discards one of the notions. Ex: 'In an S bus (not to be confused with a trespass), I saw (not an eyesore) a chap (not a Bath one) wearing a dark soft hat (and not a hot daft sack) ...' (R. Queneau, *Exercises in Style*, p. 51).

R2: The most elementary kind of distinction is the co-ordination which results from a repeated lexeme, an implicit form of diaphora*. Ex: 'There are lies and lies, statistics and statistics.' A facile form of distinction is self-correction* (see self-correction, R4).

R3: A speaker employing *oratorical* or *false distinction* claims to be opposing two notions whereas, in fact, two principles, two attitudes not on the same plane, are being opposed in a kind of antithesis*. Ex: 'I am not defending Germany. I am defending truth' (M. Bardèche, *Le Procès de Nuremberg*, p. 9).

R4: Isolexism* reinforces the device. **Ex:** 'Some day I shall tell the story of my descent into hell; and you'll see that it was not totally irrational, although it always did lack reason' (G. de Nerval, *Les Filles du feu*). So does paronomasia*. **Ex:**

> FAUST: Understand what I *say* to you, don't bother trying to understand what I *dictate* to you.
>
> ...
>
> LUST: I don't have my *answer*. Master ... I only have *remarks*.
>
> P. Valéry, *Oeuvres*, 2:280, 289

DOUBLE READING A (typo)graphical device permitting the reader to choose among several simultaneous readings, most frequently by means of parentheses excluding (even very short) segments; such exclusions produce quite different meanings.

Exx: '(typo)graphical'; '(s)he'; 'Paludes e(s)t [i.e., *is* or *and*] son double' (the title of an article by D. Viart in *Communications*, no. 19).

The oblique* stroke is also used. **Ex:** 'Sexual imagery is both covered and uncovered by writing which restores to it the sexual/textual secrecy of its lived totality' (R. Jean, 'Les Signes de l'Eros,' quoted by Cl. Simon in *Entretiens*, no. 31 [1972]). The device is also used in the case of words spelled in two different ways. **Exx:** amphibol(og)y*, enjamb(e)ment*.

DUBITATIO True or feigned *deliberatio** about an issue. The speaker hesitates, appearing not to know which word or line of argument to take, or which meaning to attach to an action. See Littré, Lausberg, Morier, and Quillet.

Ex [Cicero]: 'whether he took them from his fellows more impudently, gave them to a harlot more lasciviously, removed them from the Roman people more wickedly, or altered them more presumptuously, I cannot well declare' (quoted by Lanham [1968, p. 15], under *aporia*).

Ex: 'GUILDENSTERN: If it is, and the sun is over *there (his right as he faces the audience)* for instance, *that (front)* would be northerly. On the other hand, if it is not morning and the sun is over *there (his left)* ... *that* ... *(lamely)* would *still* be northerly' (Tom Stoppard, *Rosencrantz and Guildenstern Are Dead*, act 2).

Analogous definition: Fontanier (pp. 444–7) restricts the meaning to the impassioned hesitation 'of a soul which ... now desires one thing, now another, or better, neither knows what it does or does not want.'

Exx: Hamlet's anguished debates concerning the action he should (or should not) take with regard to Claudius; Hermione's anguish after sending Orestes to kill Pyrrhus, while time yet remains to save him (Racine, *Andromaque*, beginning of act 5). Unlike Hamlet, Hermione is closer to frenzy than indecisiveness.

Another definition: 'Simulated suspicion, resulting from anger, also simulated, with a view to prevent objection' (J. Suberville, pp. 202–3). **Ex:** In Racine's *Iphigénie* (4.6), Achilles knows that Agamemnon is going to sacrifice his daughter. He interrogates the former, pretending not to believe such a crime possible. This definition would make the device a kind of simulation*.

Analogous terms: *aporia*, hesitation, doubt, indecision, irresolution

R1: Limited doubt is a kind of *anacoenosis* or *communicatio*. As Chaignet emphasizes (p. 506); 'It [the device] confers on the orator the presumption of sincerity and good faith; he throws himself on the conscience, the intelligence, the judgment ... of his audience.' Thus, in a novel, the author/narrator appears to withdraw behind the facts when he hesitates to explain them precisely. **Exx:** 'For Sarah has remained in the studio, staring down at the garden below, at a child and a young woman, the child's mother perhaps ... There are tears in her eyes? She is too far away for me to tell' (John Fowles, *The French Lieutenant's Woman*, p. 398); 'She stared straight in front of her, towards the bare wall on which a blackish stain marks the place where the centipede was crushed last week, at the beginning of the month, the previous month, perhaps, or later' (A. Robbe-Grillet, *La Jalousie*, p. 27). *Dubitatio* serves also to forestall objections (see question*, R3).

R2: *Dubitatio* is not always an oratorical device (see assertion*, R1). The speaker's intonation* always conveys a high or low degree of assurance. Doubt is quite natural in interior monologue*. **Ex:** 'Although this – *must I say experience?* may be recaptured by many people ...' (H. Michaux, *Mouvements*, postface). *Dubitatio* divides or doubles back on itself as a thought develops. **Ex:** 'Yet he looked so desolate; yet she would feel relieved when he went; yet she would see that he was better treated tomorrow; yet he was admirable with her husband; yet his manners certainly wanted improving ...' (V. Woolf, *To the Lighthouse*, p. 135).

R3: If pushed too far, doubt acquires a surrealistic or ridiculous character. **Ex** [a highwayman holds his victims at pistol-point]: '... it certainly wouldn't be worth your while trying to escape because I'm a very good shot. I practise every day, well, not absolutely every day, but most days in the week ... I expect I must practise four or five times a week at least ... at least four or five, only some weekends ... like last weekend, there really wasn't much time, so that moved the average down a bit ... but I should say it's definitely a solid four days' practice every week ... at least. I mean ...' (Chapman et al., *Monty Python's Flying Circus: Just the Words*, 2:195).

R4: The interrogatory form is not the only marker of *dubitatio*. Grammatical markers include the conditional and the conjunction 'or'; syntagmatic forms: 'might it be possible that,' 'I wonder,' etc. For other forms, see preterition*, R4, and variation*, R2.

R5: *Dubitatio* may relate to the choice of addressee (see apostrophe*, R3). It may also reduce a subject to nothing (see negation*, R3).

E

ECHO (RHYTHMIC) The rhythm* of a succession of syllables or words repeats in the following group or groups. The recurrence of groups of identical length and/or stress.

Ex: 'Listen. *Rattarattarattaratta*. And then – shhh – over there. *Fattafattafattafatta*. And again. *Rattarattarattaratta – fattafattafattafatta*' (Julian Barnes, *Flaubert's Parrot*, p. 82). The group is: 4/4/4/4. The echo is simply due to the return of the phonetic groups. See also triplication*, R1.

Synonyms: rhythmic parallelism; 'equality' (Fabri); cadence* (see cadence, R1)

R1: This kind of echo occurs in regular alexandrines, if they are rhythmic. Rhythmic echo explains the relative frequency of alexandrines in French prose or free verse.

R2: When it affects phrases or whole sentences, rhythmic echo may create parallelisms*. Ex: 'She is drowning. Agenbite. Save her. Agenbite. All against us. She will drown me with her, eyes and hair. Lank coils of seaweed hair around me, my heart, my soul. Salt green death. We. Agenbite of inwit. Inwit's agenbite. Misery. Misery' (Joyce, *Ulysses*, p. 200).

ECHO EFFECT The return of identical phonemes associates two or several syntagms*, hemistiches, or poetic lines*.

Ex: 'And on a sudden, lo! the level lake / And the long glories of the winter moon' (Tennyson, 'The Passing of Arthur,' in *Idylls of the King*). The echo may derive principally from the consonants, as in the example from Tennyson, or from the vowels. Ex:

O let me try a triolet.
O let me try. O let me try
A triolet to win my pet.
O let me try a triolet

W.R. Espy, *The Game of Words*, p. 94

The probability of the purely fortuitous repetition* of phonemes increases with the length of the verse. The echo effect only obtains if the system of repetitions possesses a certain structure, which need not take into account every example. A reader retains those which, by their position and grouping, associate certain segments. Thus Mallarmé associates the following two hemistiches through their vowels, and the two-word groups by their consonants: 'Aboli bibelot \\ d'inanité sonore' and '\ Aboli bibelot \ d' \ inanité sonore \.'

R1: Echo effects differ from harmony* (see harmony, R1) and from imitative harmony*. The latter recalls some natural sound, as does onomatopoeia*. On the other hand, critics have long classed echo effects under alliteration*, a less polished device in which one or two sounds stand out by their frequency.

If the phonemes return together in the same order, the echo effect is similar to paronomasia*, or it combines to form leonine, or disyllabic, rhyme*, in which the word before the caesura* rhymes with the last word of the line of verse. Exx: 'the splendour falls on castle walls'; 'And the stately Spanish men to their flagship bore him then, / Where they laid him by the mast, old sir Richard caught at last' (Tennyson, 'The Splendour Falls' and 'The Revenge').

R2: Although nothing, in theory, prevents the combination of the echo effect with end rhyme* (see rhyme, R4), the former seems destined to replace the latter in free verse. Japanese poetry prefers it, excluding rhyme, whose music is considered too martial. (See Preminger under 'Japanese poetry.')

R3: Echo effects may extend from line to line until they fill a whole poem. Morier has shown that, very often, they may help the essential metaphors* or theme* to reverberate thanks to a kind of sonorous allusion* (see Morier, under *thème* 2, and *harmoniques*). In 'Dans la nuit,' H. Michaux offers a striking example. The vowels [a], nasal [ã], and [wi] constantly repeat:

Nuit de naissance
Qui m'emplis de mon cri ...
Toi qui m'envahis

The complete poem contains eight repetitions of [a], thirty of the nasal [ã], and thirty-two of [i], of which fifteen are preceded by the labio-palatal semi-vowel [w]. So, out of a total of 117 vowels in the poem, 70 repeat those in the title.

ECHOLALIA 1. 'Habitual or pathological repetition* of others' words or remarks' (Grambs).
2. The repetition of the final syllable of a word to achieve an echo* effect.

Ex (of def. 2):

> Gold on her head, and gold on her feet,
> And gold where the hems of her kirtle meet,
> And a golden girdle round my sweet; –
> *Ah! qu'elle est belle La Marguerite.*
>
> ...
>
> Of Margaret sitting glorious there,
> In glory of gold and glory of hair
> And glory of glorious face most fair; –
> *Ah! qu'elle est belle La Marguerite.*

William Morris, 'The Eve of Crecy'

Ex: 'These examples may seem sill*illy* [*bébêtes*]' (Group MU, *A General Rhetoric*, trans. Burrell and Slotkin, p. 53).

Synonyms: *rime couronnée* ('crowned rhyme') or *rhétorique à double queue* ('two-tailed rhetoric'). See Morier, under *queue*.

Other definition: a kind of palilalia or palimphrasia (see repetition*) consisting in the repetition of a speaker's final word or sentence (see Crystal, 1987, p. 271). Ordinary language calls the device 'parroting.'

R1: Echolalia is a kind of paragoge*.

R2: Palilalia is a feature of interior monologue, serving perhaps to hide short memory blanks. Ex: 'taken from us so young so brutally and now – taken taken – these two children that you're going to have to because certainly as long as he remains unmarried – unmarried unmarried – it will at least be a consolation – consolation consolation – now all your grandchildren here nearby ...' (Cl. Simon, *Histoire*, p. 27). The device might be recommended to an orator momentarily at a loss for words, but it would make such a lapse of memory too obvious. The orator might be better to employ such expletive bromides as 'in the final analysis' or 'at this moment in time.'

ELISION Dropping a vowel to avoid hiatus*; an apostrophe* (') generally marks such omissions.

In English, the rules of apostrophe often create problems because of confusion with the possessive. Fowler lists seven 'possessive puzzles,' six of which involve the apostrophe:

1. *Septimus's* [now standard] versus *Achilles'* [archaic, still used in verse]

2. 'Mr Smith (nor Lord London)'s intervention ...' ['the reasonable solution but has no chance against the British horror of fussy correctness'; avoid using the apostrophe in such cases]
3. *Somebody* / *everybody else's* [preferable to the 'pedantic though correct' *everybody's else*]
4. 'In "The Times" 's opinion [to be avoided in favour of 'In the opinion of "The Times" ']
5.'Five years' holiday' ['perhaps better' than 'five years holiday'; i.e., possessive v. adjectival noun]
6. The non-possessive *'s* ['may occasionally be used before a plural *s* as a device for avoiding confusion ... We may reasonably write *dot your i's and cross your t's*, but there is no need for an apostrophe in *but me no buts* or *one million whys*, or for the one we sometimes see in such plurals as M.P.s, A.D.C.s, N.C.O.s, the 1920s, etc.'] (*Dictionary of Modern English Usage*, pp. 466–7)

In French, elision is regular in certain cases (mainly mute final *e* followed by a word beginning with a vowel), but it is only marked by an apostrophe* in the few cases determined by graphic usage. Only the following are elided in French: *de, ne, le* and *la* (articles or unstressed pronouns), *je, me, te, se, que*, and *jusque* ('as far as, up to') before a vowel and *h*, except before aspirate *h* (as in *huit, onze, oui, un* [digit or number]), letters of the alphabet, quoted words, and certain words beginning with *y*. Add to these *ce* before *en* or an auxiliary verb; *lorsque* ('when'), *puisque* ('since'), and *quoique* ('although') before *il, elle, on, un, une*, and *ainsi* ('thus'); *quelqu'un* ('someone') and *presqu'île* ('peninsula'); and some compounds of *entre* and *si* before *il(s)*. Ex: 'J'm'en fous. J'les ai volés' (H. de Montherlant, *Romans*, p. 832). To these literary examples, whose function is to suggest spoken usage, compare similar usages in anglophone literary texts: 'D'you know what I'm goin' to tell yuh?' (R. Davies, *What's Bred in the Bone*, p. 112). See also apocope*, R4.

R1: Elision is a metaplasm*. When a letter is omitted before a word beginning with a consonant, the result is apocope*. See crasis*, R2.

R2: See caesura*, R5, for the specific problems of elision relating to caesura in French.

R3: *Counter-elision* in English speech consists in adding an unnecessary *h*: 'I 'ope *h*as 'ow you *h*are well'; in French speech it consists in emphasizing *e*: 'Un*eu* lettr*eu*.'

ELLIPSIS The suppression of words necessary to the full form of a construction, but which those expressed cause to be understood, without obscurity or uncertainty. (See Fontanier, p. 305.) 'Omission of a

Ellipsis

word easily understood' (Lanham). See Corbett, Marouzeau, Morier, Preminger, Quillet, and Robert. The more general definition given by Littré and Cuddon, 'the omission of a word or words from a sentence,' covers zeugma*, parataxis*, and brachylogia*.

Ex: 'Knew her eyes at once from the father' (Joyce, *Ulysses*, p. 124). A reader supplies without difficulty 'I' and 'she has,' actualizers whose function is to express the relationship between the lexeme and its environment. (In spoken language, when the environment is obvious, ellipses are common.) A reader may also supply the causal link ('because') between the two (completed) clauses, which shows that suppression of actualizers occurs after that of taxemes. (See parataxis*.)

Other definitions: 1. An elliptical narrative* strictly observes unity of action while avoiding any unnecessary episode and collecting the essentials into a few scenes.
2. C. Bureau (*Linguistique fonctionnelle et stylistique objective*) makes a distinction between ellipsis and non-repetition. In 'He recognizes us, comes to meet us, asks us ...,' *He*, according to Bureau, actualizes the three verbal syntagms*. We propose to make a similar distinction between 'performative' ellipsis, which is made possible by the context and avoids a repetition (e.g., 'Paul is four years old and Peter ten'); and ellipsis deriving from 'competence,' which is a feature of the language itself. **Exx:** a 'documentary' (film); 'un steak aux pommes' ('de terre' is understood).

R1: Ellipsis characterizes telegraphic style. **Ex:** 'Mother deceased. Burial tomorrow. Sincerely yours' (A. Camus, *L'Etranger*, p. 9). Or hastily written notes (i.e., 'notebook style'). **Ex:** 'Wait three days for next truck, ask advice of driver, certainly mechanic' (J. Hébert, *Blablabla du bout du monde*, p. 61). It may also signal a text dictated into a tape recorder, rather than written down. **Ex:** 'Once you have played it [*Hamlet*], it will devour you and obsess you for the rest of your life. *It has me*' (L. Olivier, *On Acting*, p. 77). Combined with abridgement*, ellipsis appears for practical reasons in short advertisements (want ads, etc.). **Ex:** 'Resp. girl (R.C.) wishes to hear of post in fruit or pork shop' (Joyce, *Ulysses*, p. 131).

R2: Brusque, authoritarian, or domineering style also cultivates the brevity offered by parataxis* and ellipsis. **Ex:** 'Thank you for your frankness. Carry on' (G. Bernanos, *Oeuvres romanesques*, p. 771).

R3: The most elliptical texts arise out of a kind of aphasia called agrammatism. Sentences are reduced to lexemes but retain their meaning thanks to intonation*. **Ex:** 'ambulance ... Gentlemen ... good! operate ... but where? full ... full ... full' (ibid.). Faulty knowledge of a language's grammatical tool-words also produces discourse* in which lexemes predominate and which might be called 'morphological erasure.' Ex: 'Bald deaf Pat brought quite flat pad ink. Pat set with ink pen quite flat pad. Pat took plate dish knife fork. Pat went' (Joyce, *Ulysses*, p. 229). Baby-talk also works in this way (see Crystal, 1987, pp. 235, 244; H. Hörmann, *Introduction à la psycholinguistique*, p. 256). Writers derive certain effects from it. Ex:

Baobabs many baobabs
baobabs near, far, round about
Baobabs, Baobabs.

H. Michaux, 'Télégramme de Dakar,' in *Plume*, p. 94

Written Chinese, which does without actualizers, possesses thousands of signs (one per concept), which restricted its use to the learned. In the same way, modern mathematics possesses its jargon* of nominal lexemes corresponding to symbols*: 'A union B. A inter B.' This too is a form of morphological erasure.

R4: Ellipsis often occurs in interior monologue*. Ex: 'Come. I thirst. Clouding over. No black clouds anywhere, are there? Thunderstorm. Allbright he falls, proud lightning of the intellect, *Lucifer, dico, qui nescit occasum*. No. My cockle hat and staff and his my sandal shoon. Where? To evening lands. Evening will find itself' (Joyce, *Ulysses*, p. 42).

R5: Fontanier (pp. 342–4) names *abruption* the ellipsis of the declarative verb in the passage from narrative* to discourse*, that is, from indirect to direct speech. He quotes Voltaire's *Henriade*: 'a woman distraught and dripping with blood: "Yes, it is my own son,"' adding: '[If you] write: "[a woman] who tells them furiously" ... you will no longer have the original's magical effect.'

The phenomenon produces focalization (see narrative*, R3). The suppressed segment would have introduced the narrator's perspective. On the other hand, direct discourse* gives the reader a kind of externalized or internalized contact with the character.

R6: For ellipsis of subject or predicate, see assertion* and notation*, R6. For ellipsis of the copula, see colon*, and apposition*, R2. Note also that numerous cases of metonymy* (see metonymy, R2) disappear if one develops the implications in the lexemes involved. We can therefore say that the semantic device of metonymy is frequently created by the grammatical device of ellipsis. The same holds for enallage* (see enallage, other def.). For diegetic ellipsis, see rhythm* of the action, R1.

R7: Ellipsis is a device of denomination* when it reduces a definition to its first term. Ex: 'Conjunction' for 'conjunction of contradictory words' (see oxymoron*). See also permutation*, R1. Ellipsis is one possible

Embedding

form of euphemism* (see euphemism, R2) and of emphasis* (see emphasis, R1). See also phoebus*, R4.

EMBEDDING The insertion of one sentence or syntagm* into another.

Exx: 'touching their still ears with words, still hearts of their each his remembered lives' (Joyce, *Ulysses*, p. 225); ' "I walk," she said, "did I forget to tell you? a long way each day" ' (Marguerite Duras, *Le Ravissement de Lol V. Stein*, p. 150).

Other definition: second-degree narrative* (Ducrot and Todorov, *Encyclopedic Dictionary of the Sciences of Language*, p. 298). See mirror*, R5, and staircase*.

EMPHASIS The use of various means to call attention to certain parts of a text.

Ex: 'It was the 1950s, for God's sake. Jane Russell. Cashmere sweaters. Couldn't my mother see that? *I am too old to wear an undershirt* ... I want to buy a bra." "What for?" ' (Nora Ephron, in Richler, ed., *The Best of Modern Humor*, p. 468; the italics appear in the original).

Synonymous: underlining, italic type, small capitals, boldface

R1: Forms of emphasis: In texts, the use of bold type corresponds to a raised voice in speech. (In a manuscript or typescript, underlining used to serve, but most word processors have a bolding capacity.) Italics often replace bold type (see situational* signs). To avoid confusion, single underlining marks a particular tone to be printed in italics; double underlining indicates small capitals; triple underlining signals capitals; a wavy line marks intensity, and a passage so underlined is to be printed in bold type. Various additional ways of indicating emphasis:
– syllabification or pronunciation of a word as a succession of separate syllables. Ex: 'men-da-ci-ty' (Tennessee Williams, *Cat on a Hot Tin Roof*, act 1).
– phonetic pause. Ex: 'A // frightful noise.' See situational* signs.
– repetition*. Ex: 'He said nothing. Nothing.' (See reduplication*.) In this case, the repeated word forms a complete assertion*, hence its power. Isolated as it is, its meaning is nonetheless clear because of the sentence which precedes it. Only the part containing the assertion is repeated.
– repetition* strengthened by some other means. Ex: 'I wanted to tell him that I was like everyone else, absolutely like everyone else' (A. Camus, *L'Etranger*, p. 95).
– repetition* in dialogue* form. Ex:

JOHN: In April!
MARC: April!
Georges F. Kaufman, in Richler, ed., *The Best of Modern Humor*, p. 83

– abnormal word order; that is, drawing attention to the beginning of a segment by dislocation*. Ex (ethnic humour indicated by inversion): 'The food! In my mouth to ashes the food is turning!' (Joseph Heller, in Richler, ed., *The Best of Modern Humor*, p. 241).
– situational* signs used for emphasis. Ex (dashes): 'If I owned all those telephones, oh boy – no business would run without me' (J. Heller, ibid., p. 241).
– segmentation of the sentence (hyperparataxis). Ex: 'Politics, I, you know ...'
– the use of 'it is ... he/she/it ... who/that ...' to present the subject of the sentence. Ex: 'It is for him to show the way.'
– ellipsis* (see aposiopesis*). Exx: 'He has such charm ...'; 'That's *so* funny [that ...?].'
– the seemingly pointless use of expletives (see Crystal, 1987, p. 61; for *expletion*, see Fontanier, p. 303). Ex: 'Free, my foot, ...' Analogous: the ethic dative, the dative of person indirectly interested: 'Answer *me* the telephone.'
– certain graphisms* (see gemination*)
– amplification*. Ex: 'No question of anything but the fullest support' (J. Lynn and A. Jay, *The Complete 'Yes Minister,'* p. 123).
– the use of abstractions*. Compare the following: 'anything that his peculiar mind had invented'; 'anything that a mind of that peculiarity might have invented.'

R2: The normal function of capitals is not emphasis: 'Capitals must ... be used for the initial letters of sentences and for the names of places, persons, months, days, and nationalities' (M[odern] H[umanities] R[esearch] A[ssociation] *Style Book*, p. 16). However, capitals, both small and large, may take on the function of bold type. Ex: 'Whether he wrote DOWN WITH BIG BROTHER or whether he refrained from writing it, made no difference' (George Orwell, *Nineteen Eighty-Four*, p. 19).

R3: The addition of devices for purposes of emphasis may be foregrounded: 'And it is only because I have in mind all those thousands of persons, not unlike myself, who ... are not always sure whether a sentence is Literature or whether it is just sheer flapdoodle, that I have adopted the method perfected by the late Herr Baedeker, and firmly marked what I consider the finer passages with one, two or three stars' (Stella Gibbons, *Cold Comfort Farm*, introduction).

R4: Various devices may create emphasis. See cliché*, R1; simile*, R3; counter-litotes*, R3; diaeresis*, R2; riddle*, R3; enumeration*, R5; epanadiplosis*, R1; lengthening*, R2; etymology*, other def.; euphemism*, R5; generalization*, R2; interjection*, R5; isolexism*, R3 and R4; metanalysis*, R1; pleonasm*, R1; rewriting*, R1; truism*, R2; litotes*, R3; anticlimax*, R3; exclamation*; distancing*, R1; and hyperbaton*. For emphasis in quotations, see quotation*, R7.

ENALLAGE Substitution of one tense, number, or person for another tense, number, or person. See Fontanier, p. 293. Lanham (p. 40) adds case, gender, mood, and part of speech as possible substitutions. See also Académie française, *Dictionnaire* (8th ed. 1932); *Dictionnaire de Trévoux* (1704); Joseph; Morier (sense 1); Lausberg (sect. 515); Peacham; and Quinn.

Ex: 'One move and you're dead.' Here are three further examples illustrating respectively substitution of the tense of the verb, of person, and of singular for plural: 'I was dying this morning worthy to be mourned; / I took your advice: I die dishonored' (J. Racine, *Phèdre*, 3.3); 'We would like to give you our version of ...' (popular singer introducing a solo effort); 'Whiles I threat, he lives; / *Words* to the heat of deeds too cold breath *gives*' (Shakespeare, *Macbeth*, 2.1.60–1). As may be seen, enallage is related to solecism*, which Joseph (p. 300) calls the '*ignorant* misuse of cases, genders, tenses.'

Other definitions: 1. Littré, citing as his example La Fontaine – 'So said the fox and the flatterers *to applaud*' – sees the infinitive, not as the form exchanged ('and the flatterers *applauded*'), but as the complement of a finite verb which is understood (i.e., 'and the flatterers *began* to applaud'). Consequently, influenced apparently by a note in the *Dictionnaire de Trévoux*, he defines enallage as a form of ellipsis*.
2. Marouzeau, Quillet, and Robert include under enallage the substitution of constructions which more accurately form examples of hypallage*.
3. Morier (sense 2), inspired by Virgil's line *Ibant obscuri sola sub nocte* ('They moved along in the gloom of the solitary night' [*Aeneid*, 6:268]), speaks of substitutions of adjectives. It is true that Lausberg has shown (sect. 685, 2) that in Latin, hypallage* of adjectives might be considered equivalent to enallage of adjectives (e.g., *obscuri* instead of *obscura*, *sola* instead of *soli*, with interchange of adjectives and their referents), but the same does not hold for English (or French), in which substitution of adjectives, a purely syntactic device, can only form a *double hypallage*.
Ex: 'Neiger de blancs bouquets d'étoiles parfumées' ('Snowing white bouquets of perfumed stars' [for 'perfumed bouquets of white stars']) (Mallarmé, 'Apparition'). This type of hypallage facilitates the creation of isocolons (see period*) and eliminates a 'natural' (i.e., banal) epithet.

R1: Enallage of propositions also exists, when the main clause in the sentence's meaning takes the grammatical form of a subordinate clause. Wagner and Pinchon (sect. 595) call this phenomenon *converse subordination*. Ex: 'For many years, everything about Combray except the place and drama of my going to bed had no meaning for me, when, one winter day, as I was going back to the house, my mother, seeing that I was cold, proposed that I should take, although it was not my custom, a little tea' (Proust, *A la recherche du temps perdu*, first sentence). The whole construction turns on the conjunction *when*, but the subordinate temporal clause following it, from the point of view of meaning*, is the main clause, because the 'real' main clause preceding *when* merely introduces a temporal circumstance, or rather, serves simply to situate the event in time.

In any case, if one considers the whole narrative*, the sentence appears to be situating what will follow, the taste of the *madeleine* and the memories it will revive. From that perspective, the clause is a temporal one, it is true, but the main clause, 'For many years ...,' is a sub-temporal. It would therefore be better to view things from the perspective of the sub-temporal promoted to the rank of main clause, as does Marouzeau, who calls it a superordinate clause, defining it as follows: 'the main clause is taken to be secondary in meaning' (*Lexique de la terminologie linguistique*).

END POSITIONING Transferring to the end of a clause or sentence an important or significant element, with normal word order being abandoned in favour of expressiveness. See Robert.

Ex: 'But wherein any man is bold – I am speaking foolishly – I also am bold ... Are they ministers of Christ? I – to speak as a fool – am more' (Paul, 2 Cor. 11:21, 23).

Other names: syntactic transfer; *trajectio* (Morier uses the term to refer to the transfer of adverbs in French)

Other definitions: 1. Transfer in prosody (*rejet* in French): at the end of a line or at the hemistich; see enjamb(e)ment*, R2; caesura*, R6.
2. Transfer of enunciation*. When a speaker takes no responsibility for certain expressions, he uses such transferring markers as quotation marks, indications of sources, and expressions like 'so called,' 'alleged,' 'what is called,' 'it says here,' etc. See situational* signs, 5.
3. The *traiectio in alium* (Lanham) is a shifting of the responsibility for an act onto someone else. See apodioxis (argument*, R2).

R1: The transfer of a syntagm* over an extended time in a long periodic sentence produces an effect of suspension* or, in a dramatic context, of suspense*. If the syntagm is transferred outside the sentence, we have hyperbaton*.

ENJAMB(E)MENT The sentence runs on from one line* (of poetry) to the next without there being a marked stop. See Frye, Marouzeau, Cuddon, Martinon, and Preminger.

Ex:

> The lighting rooms perfect a chequerboard
> Across apartment boxes. Through the popcorn
> Reek, hotdogs and chips, the air lets fall
> A rain of quiet coolness on the flesh.
>
> Earle Birney, 'Dusk on English Bay'
> in Charlesworth and Lee, eds., *An Anthology of Verse*, p. 73

Analogous definition: See Morier.

R1: Theorists of French classical poetry proscribed enjambment. The outcry provoked in 1830 by the first two lines of Victor Hugo's *Hernani* is well known: 'Serait-ce déjà lui? C'est bien à l'escalier / Dérobé ...' ('Is that already he? It [the noise] is on the secret / Staircase'). When 'the meaning does not permit a stop at the end of the line' (Ph. Martinon, *Dictionnaire des rimes françaises*, p. 34), the rhythm* instrumental in defining the poetic line* is jeopardized.

Enjambment may occur at the hemistich: 'the first syntactic group spills over into the second hemistich' without the possibility of a caesura* (Grammont, 1950, p. 43).

R2: The *rejet* is enjambment with a rhythmic pause* or caesura* maintained despite the fact that the sentence continues. Ex [recited with a pause after 'suddenly']: '... for the oyster suddenly / Snaps shut' (La Fontaine, quoted by Ph. Martinon, *Dictionnaire des rimes françaises*, p. 35). The *rejet* calls a syntagm* to the reader's attention by putting at odds rhythm and grammatical articulation. Placed thus, 'Snaps shut [*se referme*]' expresses suddenness. In English verse, the pause* is less marked:

> The world is too much with us: late and soon
> Getting and spending, we lay waste our powers.
>
> W. Wordsworth, 'The World'

R3: As the name indicates, *contre-rejet* is the opposite of *rejet*. The principal caesura* appears before the end of the first hemistich or line. The syntagm isolated between the two caesuras (the one semantic, the other rhythmic) is thus foregrounded.

The following double example displays *contre-rejet* at both the hemistich and the end of the line:

> Ils atteindront / le fond de l'Asturie, // avant
> Que la nuit ait couvert // la sierra de ses ombres.

(They will reach the depths of Asturia, before / Night covers the sierra with shadow.)

V. Hugo, quoted by Grammont,
in *Essai de psychologie linguistique*, p. 129

Fond and *avant* are foregrounded, in accordance with Hugo's expressive intent: the passage refers to the character's need to find a safe place to escape from pursuit.

R4: If the end of a line is not orally marked, there is enjambment, but the line's rhythm will not be perceived. If one pauses, the expression is cut in half. Such an artificial *rejet* is false. The French 'visual caesura' or *caesura 'for the eye'* is an enjambment at the hemistich which transforms the classical alexandrine into a romantic line. Ex (V. Hugo, quoted by Morier): 'L'ombre des tours faisait / la nuit dans les campagnes' ('The towers' shadow turned day into night in the countryside'). The rhythm*, of course, is: 'L'ombre des tours / faisait la nuit / dans les campagnes.'

R5: The appearance of rhythmic articulation in the middle of a syntagm* transforms enjambment into a case of 'forced' *rejet*, which Morier has called 'expected rhyme'; he gives the following example from Verlaine:

De ça, de là,
Pareil à la
Feuille morte.
([Blown] here and there, like a dead leaf.)

P. Verlaine, 'Chanson d'automne';
quoted by Morier, in Parent, ed., *Le Vers français au XXe siècle*, p. 98

The rhyme invites an unexpected pause after the definite article, *la*, thus expressing hesitation, abandonment.

R6: The French surrealist poet Louis Aragon, in particular, attempted to renovate French rhyme* (see rhyme, R3) by ending a line in the middle of a syntagm*, even in the middle of a graphic word. Ex:

Je vais te dire un grand secret
Le temps c'est *toi*
Le temps est femme Il *a*
Besoin qu'on le courtise.
(I'm going to tell you a great secret / Time is you / Time is a woman It *nee* / *Ds* to be courted.)

Aragon, beginning of *Les Yeux d'Elsa*

He calls the above 'complex rhyme,' 'made up of several words which break up the rhyming sound between them' (ibid.). Ex:

Ne parlez plus d'amour. J'écoute mon coeur *battre*
... Ne parlez plus d'amour. Que fait-elle là-*bas*
Trop proche et trop lointaine ô temps martyrisé
(Speak no more of love. I listen to my heart beating / ... Speak no
more of love. What is she doing over there / At once too near and
too far O martyred time)

Aragon, Le Crève-coeur, p. 78

The latter he calls 'modern enjambment ... in which the sound, the
rhyme straddling the end of one line and the beginning of the next,
splits up' (ibid., p. 77). The translation inadequately expresses the
rhythmic effect.

ENUMERATION A list which counts out, specifies, mentions items
one by one.

Ex: '[An executive] will pass, as is well known, the following stages in
his successful career: 1. Age of Qualification. 2. Age of Discretion.
3. Age of Promotion. 4. Age of Responsibility. 5. Age of Authority.
6. Age of Achievement. 7. Age of Distinction. 8. Age of Dignity. 9. Age
of Wisdom. 10. Age of Obstruction' (C.N. Parkinson, *The Law Complete*,
p. 126).

Analogous definitions: See Lausberg, *OED*, and Robert.

R1: Unlike accumulation*, enumeration constitutes a kind of definition*
characteristic of collective entities, and is therefore frequently preceded
by a colon or introduced by some inclusive term such as 'viz.' or
'namely.' Ex (colon):

They call it easing the Spring: it is perfectly easy
If you have any strength in your thumb: like the bolt
And the breech, and the cocking-piece, and the point of balance.

Henry Reed, 'Naming of Parts,' in A Map of Verona

R2: Enumeration is a type of amplification* particularly useful because
it translates the abstract into concrete terms, the general into the
particular. Jakobson sees it as the exposure of the paradigm, which is
not part of the poetic function of communication. Enumeration serves
chiefly to display something, in a small space.

R3: An enumeration which aspires to exhaustivity is an inventory. Ex:
'Eeltraps, lobsterpots, fishingrods, hatchet, steelyard, grindstone,
clodcrusher, swatheturner, carriagesack, telescope ladder, 10 tooth rake,
washing clogs, haytedder, tumbling rake, billhook, paintpot, brush, hoe
and so on' (Joyce, *Ulysses*, p. 586). A partial enumeration is like an
exemplum. Alternatively, only the extremes may be listed, leaving the
rest implied. Ex: 'Women, monks, old people, all came down' (La
Fontaine): *a fortiori* the men and children.

R4: The listing of individuals when they each refer to other elements – as in disjunction* – produces distribution or merismus (Lanham, Lausberg). **Ex:** 'Maybe the Chapdelaines thought about it, each in his own way; the father with the invincible optimism of a man who knows he is strong and thinks he is wise; the mother with sorrow and resignation; the others, the youngsters, in less precise terms and without bitterness' (Louis Hémon, *Maria Chapdelaine*, p. 40). See also seriation* and apposition*, R2.

R5: Superfluous enumeration is a form of baroquism*. **Ex:** 'Not to inherit by right of primogeniture, gavelkind or borough English, or possess in perpetuity an extensive demesne of a sufficient number of acres, rods and perches' (Joyce, *Ulysses*, p. 585).

False enumeration is a kind of emphasis*. **Exx:** 'Three reasons for buying [a condominium] downtown: location, location, location' (advertisement in the *Ottawa Citizen*); '... the first three essentials of the literary art are imagination, imagination and imagination' (Ambrose Bierce, *The Devil's Dictionary*, in *The Devil's Advocate: An Ambrose Bierce Reader*, p. 289). In such cases the elements are arranged to form a climax* (see climax, R2).

For chaotic enumeration, see accumulation*, R3, and verbigeration*, R3. The Orient has a tradition of non-systematic enumeration. **Ex:** 'There are seven ways of getting rich through trade: frauds relating to the goods, sale on commission, sales in partnership, sales to devoted customers, price-fixing, the use of false weights and measures, foreign trade' (R. Daumal, *Bharata*, p. 163). Borges foregrounds the practice: 'Animals are divided into those a) belonging to the Emperor, b) stuffed, c) tamed, d) suckling pigs, e) mermaids, f) fabulous, g) unleashed dogs' ('Otras inquisiciones,' quoted by Michel Foucault, in *Les Mots et les choses*, p. 7).

R6: Points enumerated may be numbered without each one constituting a paragraph, unless indentation is used (in which case the segment begins with a capital letter).

R7: For other uses of enumeration, see *gradatio**, R2; homoioteleuton*, R3; celebration*, R1; recapitulation*, R2; synonymy*, R3; and telescoping*, R2.

ENUNCIATION The act of enunciating, of producing a self-sufficient unit of spoken language or set of linguistic signs. Every enunciation occurs only once. Even when several enunciative acts produce the same utterance (e.g., 'Hello!'), they do not coincide, since each occurs at a distinct point, which may be defined as the intersection of time, place, and person.

Enunciation includes seven orienting characteristics. These are the seven elements in the communication model: (1) speaker, (2) contact,

Enunciation

(3) addressee, (4) situation, (5) content of the message or utterance, (6) the language used, and (7) the aesthetic form of the message. These characteristics define what Jakobson called the linguistic functions of communication (we have added situation to Jakobson's six functions; see notation*), to which correspond seven quite distinct types or 'modalities' of sentences, as well as seven genres.

1. When enunciation centres on the speaker, the text's function is emotive (or *expressive*); the sentence takes the form of an exclamation* (an interjection* or more or less complete sentence); the genre is the monologue*.

2. When enunciation centres on the contact between the interlocutors, the text has a 'phatic' or *contact* function; the sentence is a greeting, call, or address (see apostrophe*); the work is a dialogue* or conversation between several speakers. Phatic expressions include: 'Isn't that so?'; 'Eh?.' See also pseudo-language*.

3. When enunciation centres on the addressee or receiver, the function is said to be 'conative' or *injunctive*; the sentence modality is injunctive since it involves the speaker obtaining something from the receiver; the work is a discourse* in the narrow or rhetorical sense of the word.

4. If enunciation centres on its real, frequently implicit, surrounding framework, it has a *situational* function which states the relevant temporal and spatial co-ordinates; the sentence is a simple notation*. Works belonging in this genre include bibliographies, almanacs, telephone directories, indexes, tables of contents, etc., which situate things or persons at a particular point.

5. Enunciation centred on the content of the message has a denotative or *referential* function; the modality is assertion*; the genre is narrative* (action situated outside the receiver's present) or explanation*. (Note that the referent is the real object denoted in the message and often remains implicit. Considered thus, it always belongs to the situational function, which does not, however, prevent our speaking of the referential function in connection with the denotative function, since it is the referent which gives rise to the utterance.)

6. Enunciation centred on language as a set of structures or of expressive usages has a *metalinguistic* function; the modality is lexical definition* (in which the theme* is itself the autonymical focus of attention); the genre: dictionary, glossary, catalogue, thesaurus, grammar.

7. Enunciation centred on aesthetic form has a *poetic* function; modalities: all kinds of artistic transformations; genre: any literary work.

Analogous term: *narration* (as opposed to what is narrated; see narrative*)

R1: Besides these 'functions' possessed by sets of signs, the *Dictionnaire de linguistique* lists various ways of approaching the relationship between author and reader established by texts. These include the relative position of the speakers (equality, superiority, inferiority); their respective degree of involvement (expectation, intention, promise); the degree of assertion* (predictions, statements); the way in which what is stated relates to the expected or permissible attitudes (warnings, information); the distance from the text taken by the subject and the possibility of the receiver reading it as though he or she were its author (e.g., as in manuals); modalities of agreement (possibility, necessity); the receiver's inclusion in or exclusion from the group addressed (connivance, simulation* or 'masking' of appearances); and, finally, the types of argument* (objection, refutation*, etc.) As may be seen from this list, a whole barrage of discursive devices exists, not only in literature, but in social and political life and in psychology.

R2: The utterance sometimes coincides with its enunciation. Austin called *performative* those verbs which may accomplish, at the time and place of the utterance and between the two persons communicating, the concept evoked (*How to Do Things with Words*, 1962). Exx: I say; I swear; I promise; Excuse me; etc. So there exists a 'meaning effect' which adds to the meaning and is engendered by the enunciation rather than by the utterance itself. It concerns the persons alluded to by the shifters (morphemes whose referents are context-related). A promise exists because a speaker, at a particular time and place, said 'I promise.' This is an *illocutionary* act whose value derives from the fact that it is addressed to a particular person in particular circumstances. See implication* and litotes*.

In *Dire et ne pas dire*, Ducrot showed that illocution has legalistic overtones. The social customs of the group confer on a particular formula a certain degree of obligation which transfers to the speaker. The *oath*, for instance (see Fontanier, p. 442), commits one to sincerity. The fact of swearing on some sacred object (the Bible, 'on my mother's life,' etc.) or of adding hypothetical maledictions ('may I die if I have not told the truth') simply emphasizes the definitive nature of the commitment.

Locutionary acts (mere productions of an utterance) differ from *perlocutionary* acts, which concern the speaker's unavowed intentions and which remain a subject of conjecture and interpretation (Ducrot and Todorov, p. 343). For example, the function of questions* may be to help someone, to embarrass someone, or to make that person feel we value his or her opinion.

R3: **Marks of enunciation within the utterance:** In speeches, spontaneous dialogues*, and even soliloquies, enunciation is very close to utterance: both refer to the same present universe (e.g., 'Do you think ...'; 'It seems to me ...'). The 'shifters' (Jespersen, Jakobson) used establish the poles of the enunciation.

Intonation* is the principal illocutionary and perlocutionary marker.

Enunciation

A main clause, or an adverb, makes the function of intonation explicit (e.g., 'It's *already* eleven o'clock'). Connotation often draws its excessive importance from intonation by defining the speaker's attitude and also by creating obligations of propriety (responses* to questions*, acceptance of implication*). The markers within the utterance permitting examination of the speaker's point of view have been studied under the heading *modalizing terms* (Ducrot and Todorov, p. 325). Ex: 'Exactly, that's ...' introduces a change in point of view because of the implicit affirmation that one sees things more clearly than one's opponent. This expression is often found, therefore, in antanaclasis*.

Once the subject under discussion becomes less immediate, enunciation becomes distinct from the utterance, entering another world. From then on, it is either deleted, or there is double actualization. (See monologue*, R2.) In that case, enunciative markers include:
– the use of past tenses, a characteristic of narrative*
– adjectives like 'so-called' or 'alleged,' or quotation marks drawing attention to a term's relevance, in the narrator's opinion
– mention of the author or public (see parabasis*). Ex: 'Some years ago, when I was the Editor of a Correspondence Column, I used to receive heart-broken letters from young men asking for advice and sympathy' (Stephen Leacock, 'How to Avoid Getting Married,' in *Literary Lapses*, p. 48).
– mention of the text as a narrative*, or literary work of some kind. Ex: 'Having reached the end of my poor sinner's life ... I prepare to leave on this parchment my testimony as to the wondrous and terrible happenings that I happened to observe in my youth, now repeating verbatim all I saw and heard, without venturing to seek a design ...' (U. Eco, *The Name of the Rose*, p. 11).
– mention of the text as a text (the metalinguistic function). Ex: 'Nor, for that matter, could I call Salvatore's speech a language, because in every human language there are rules and every term signifies ad placitum a thing, according to a law that does not change, for man cannot call the dog once dog and once cat, or utter sounds to which a consensus of people has not assigned a definite meaning, as would happen if someone said the word "blitiri" ' (ibid., p. 47).

R4: Utterances may, without losing their correlative enunciation, engender other utterances in respect to which the former play an enunciative role. There are then three levels of actualization, as is the case, for example, in second-degree narrative* (see narrative*, R4).

R5: When utterance and enunciation are actualized on two distinct planes, pretended confusions between them may result from more or less deliberate blunders*, irony*, or exaggerated 'elegance.' Thus Jacques Ferron allows himself to be contradicted by one of his own characters (*La Barbe de Fr. Hertel*, p. 105) or alternates between figurative and literal meanings, which produces unexpected twists in the plot. In *Amélanchier*, for example, a rabbit called Mr Northrop becomes a character who expatiates on the British Navy and lampoons British humour, all the while nibbling on a carrot. See also Woody Allen's story 'The Kugelmass Episode,' in *Side Effects*, and his film *Purple Rose of Cairo* for the passage of a character from one diegetic (i.e., narrative*) universe to another. For other enunciative games, see preterition*, R1.

R6: For more information concerning enunciation, see: apocalypse*, R1; situational* signs, 5; colon*; excuse*, R1; nominalization*, R1; parenthesis*, R4; personification*, R1; prophecy*, R1; prosopopoeia*, R2 and R3; and reminder*, R2.

EPANADIPLOSIS The ending of the second of two correlative clauses with the word or words that began the first. See Dumarsais, (4:139), Scaliger (4:30), Lausberg, and Morier.

Ex: 'You bleed when the white man says bleed. You bite when the white man says bite, and you bark when the white man says bark' (speech by Malcolm X).

Other names: epanastrophe (Littré, Lausberg, Morier); inclusion* (Marouzeau; Quinn, p. 88); epanalepsis* (Lanham, Morier, Preminger)

R1: The effect sought by epanadiplosis is emphasis*, even hackneyed or hyperbolic repetition*. Ex:

Possessing what we still are possessed by
Possessed by what we now no more possessed.
Robert Frost, 'The Gift Outright'

Some examples seem to occur simply by chance. Ex: 'A donkey immobile on a terrace, like a statue of a donkey' (G. Cesbron, *Journal sans date*, p. 166).

EPANALEPSIS 1. The repetition* of a single word or words, or of a complete phrase. See Littré, Lausberg, Morier, and Preminger.
2. The repetition of a word or words after an intervening word or words, whether for emphasis* or clarity, as to resume a construction after a lengthy parenthesis*. See Preminger.

Exx: 'Tomorrow, and tomorrow, and tomorrow ...' (Shakespeare, *Macbeth*, 5.5.19); 'She's just a shadow of her former self! a shadow of her former self! The poor thing had aged a hundred years! a hundred years!' (Colette, *Chéri*, p. 72).

Epanalepsis differs from other types of repetition* in that it involves an asseverative fragment of an autonomous text. If reduced in scope, the repeated segment still contains the essential assertion* or statement. Ex: '... a hundred years! a hundred!'

Other definitions: 1. Morier and Preminger add a second meaning: 'by modern authorities, most often and most usefully defined as the ending of a clause or sentence with its own opening word or words.' In our view, this definition is that of epanadiplosis* or inclusion*.
2. Marouzeau: repetition of a term or expression either at the beginning or end of successive groups, or at the end of the first and beginning of the second (e.g., 'but I *saw, saw* with my own eyes, *saw* it as I see you'). This is a combined definition of anaphora*, epiphora*, and anadiplosis*.

R1: Epanalepsis involving only a single word approaches reduplication*. According to Lausberg (sect. 618), *reduplicatio* becomes epanalepsis when a single word separates the two identical terms (e.g., 'Think, Master, think ...'), which is corroborated by the fact that in such a case the repeated word is the equivalent of a syntagm* containing the one to which emphasis attaches.

R2: Pointless epanalepsis is battology*. Ex: 'But they are not where I am when I have closed my eyes. Where I am when I have closed my eyes, there is no one, there's only me' (R. Ducharme, *L'Avalée des avalés*, pp. 8–9).

R3: Repetition of a title at the beginning of a chapter or poem also constitutes epanalepsis. In many poems the first line serves as title in the absence of an assigned one. **Ex:** 'And death shall have no dominion' (Dylan Thomas, 'And Death Shall Have No Dominion').

R4: When used to join together extensive textual segments (paragraphs, chapters, etc.), epanalepsis may act as a liaison in the same way as anadiplosis* does between sentences and paragraphs. **Ex:**

> If the fine weather continues, said old Mrs. Chapdelaine, the blueberries will be ripe for St. Anne's Day.
> The fine weather did continue and, in the first few days of July, the blueberries ripened ... (Louis Hémon, *Maria Chapdelaine*, pp. 67–8)

See also restart*, R1.

R5: Epanalepsis may occur at more or less regular intervals, like a refrain*. **Ex:**

> Here is the efflux of the soul,
> The efflux of the soul comes from within ...
> ...
> The efflux of the soul is happiness ...
>   Walt Whitman, 'Song of the Open Road,' 7–8

R6: Semi-epanalepsis, which introduces variation into the repetitions, may become anaphora*, epiphora*, and symploce*. **Ex:**

Speeding through space, speeding through heaven and the stars,
Speeding amid the seven satellites and the broad ring, and the
  diameter of eighty thousand miles,
Speeding with tail'd meteors, throwing fire-balls like the rest
                              Walt Whitman, 'Song of Myself,' 33

EPANORTHOSIS A return to something already said, either to
reinforce or soften it, or to retract it completely (see Fontanier, p. 408).
Having 'second thoughts.' See also Cuddon, Lamy, Peacham, and
Quillet.

Ex: 'He in a few minutes ravished this fair creature, or at least would
have ravished her if she had not, by a timely compliance, prevented
him' (H. Fielding, *Jonathan Wild*, book 3, ch. 7).

Synonyms: *correctio* (Lanham), *expolitio* (Morier), retroaction (Fontanier)

R1: Epanorthosis is a parastasis* embellished with one of the marks of
self-correction*, although the latter is briefer. Ex: ' "Arrest you!" said
Holmes. "This is really most grati – most interesting" ' (Conan Doyle,
'The Norwood Builder'). Fontanier contrasts epanorthosis, a figure of
thought, to correction, a figure of style.

R2: A *retraction* is but one of the possible forms of epanorthosis. Ex:
'Old Marley was as dead as a doornail. Mind! I don't mean to say that
I know, of my own knowledge, what there is particularly dead about a
doornail' (Dickens, *A Christmas Carol*, stave 1). The device may extend
throughout a whole work of self-criticism: this is called a *palinode* after
the poem by Stesichorus in which he recanted his earlier harsh words
about Helen of Troy. Chaucer also used the palinode as a device in *The
Legend of Good Women,* presented as an apology for his *Troilus and
Criseyde*. In his *Errata*, Raymond Queneau criticizes his own theory
concerning the growing importance of spoken over written language.
  A solemn retraction, whose solemnity is emphasized by reference to
some sacred object, is an *abjuration*.

R3: The device may be a matter of pure form, as in the already quoted
Dickensian pseudo-retraction which continues: 'I might have been
inclined, myself, to regard a coffin-nail as the deadest piece of iron-
mongery in the trade. But the wisdom of our ancestors is in the simile;
and my unhallowed hands shall not disturb it, or the Country's done
for' (ibid.).

R4: It frequently happens that a poem's first line contains the essential
idea which the subsequent lines develop. Ex: 'The hand that signed the
paper felled a city' (Dylan Thomas, 'The Hand That Signed the Paper').
This seems to be a kind of epanorthosis or regression*; hence the
importance of the incipit (the punch* line is the opposite device).

EPENTHESIS Insertion of a letter or sound within a word. See Group MU, Joseph, Lanham, Lausberg (sect. 483), Marouzeau, and Quillet.

Exx: the *b* in *thimble* (*Concise Oxford Dictionary*); the first *h* in 'as*h*phalt'

Analogous definitions: 'insertion of a letter, phoneme, or syllable into the middle of a word: e.g.: "visitating" for "visiting" ' (Oulipo, *A Primer of Potential Literature*, p. 198); 'the appearance within a word of a non-etymological phoneme. E.g.: *chanvre* (hemp) which comes from *cannabis*' (Robert); 'a parasitic sound' (Dubois et al., *Dictionnaire de linguistique*); 'a phoneme which arises to aid the mechanics of articulation' (Morier)

Analogous terms: paremptosis ('the addition of a word in a sentence complete in itself' [Lanham]); the addition of a letter (not a syllable), according to Lausberg and Littré

R1: A term of ancient grammar which corresponds to a modern device. **Exx:** 'steadyfast, Goldylocks'; 'Merdre' (Jarry, *Ubu roi*); 'Urlysse' (R. Ducharme, *L'Avalée des avalés*, p. 265); 'Proemes' (Fr. Ponge).
    Emile Pons (p. 10) calls multiple epenthesis *saupoudrage* or 'sprinkling.' He thinks that Swift fabricated his term 'Hounyhnhnms' from the French word *hom(me)* pronounced (naturally) by horses. The following is an example of *saupoudrage* in Joyce: 'My eppripfftaph. Be pfrwritt' (Joyce, *Ulysses*, p. 211).
    The device resembles the phenomenon psychiatrists call *embololalia*: 'the use of virtually meaningless filler words, phrases, or stammerings* (or so-called hesitation-forms) in speech, whether as unconscious utterings while arranging one's thoughts or as a vacuous, inexpressive mannerism, e.g., "you know," "well," "like," "I mean," "uh" ' (D. Grambs, *Literary Companion Dictionary*, p. 112).

R2: Epenthesis is a metaplasm*. See also euphemism*, R2.

EPIGRAM A short poem which often ends with a satirical dig. See Bénac.

Exx:

Macaulay tells us Byron's rules of life
Were: Hate your neighbour; love your neighbour's wife.
                 W.R. Espy, *The Game of Words*, pp. 96–7

'On an Ageing Prude'

She who, when young and fair,
Would wink men up the stair,
Now, old and ugly, locks
The door where no man knocks.
                 Ibid.

Analogous terms: blazon (see celebration*); pasquinade ('a lampoon hung up in some public place' [Cuddon, p. 475])

R1: In his *Traitté de l'épigramme*, Guillaume Colletet gives 'madrigal' as a Spanish or Italian equivalent of the epigram. The *madrigal* which aims, in the main, to entertain, frequently does end with an ingenious punch* line.

R2: From the fifteenth to the nineteenth century, the epigram first rose to the dignity of a literary genre, then fell into disuse. Its function was the skilful criticism of holders of high office. Then, as more democratic government gradually replaced royal favouritism, such criticisms became more theoretical (less often directed *ad hominem*) and quit the salons for more public arenas. If it is remembered that epigram simply means *inscription*, then the contemporary form of the genre appears in inscriptions like those so highly esteemed during the 'events' of 1968 in France. Such inscriptions are not mere *graffiti*, like those found on school desks or in public lavatories, but consist of slogan*-like forms having political aims and repercussions. Ex: 'I like Ike.'

R3: See also negation*, R7; literary* games; and sarcasm*, R3.

EPIGRAPH A quotation* placed, as a clue to the sense, at the beginning of a work or chapter.

Ex: 'Does there not pass over man a space of time when his life is a blank? THE KORAN sura 76' (epigraph in John Updike's *The Coup*).

Ex:

> The very day we landed upon the Fatal Shore,
> The planters stood around us, full twenty score or more;
> They ranked us up like horses and sold us out of hand,
> They chained us up to pull the plough, upon Van Diemen's Land.
> – Convict ballad, ca. 1825–30
>
> Epigraph in Robert Hughes's
> *The Fatal Shore: The Epic of Australia's Founding*

R1: The author's general intention may be clarified by an epigraph, or epigraphs may be used ironically. Part of the pleasure a reader gains from epigraphs derives from the decision to take them 'seriously' or not. Ex: 'But as to myself, having been wearied out for many years with offering vain, idle, visionary thoughts, and at length utterly despairing of success, I fortunately fell upon this proposal ... – Jonathan Swift, *A Modest Proposal*' (quoted at the beginning of Margaret Atwood's *The Handmaid's Tale*).

R2: See also imitation* and lexical erasure*, R2.

Epiphany

EPIPHANY For Joyce, a moment of profound, spiritual revelation when an observer perceives the 'real' significance of an act or object: a 'sudden spiritual manifestation' (J. Joyce, *Stephen Hero*, p. 216). As Eco writes: '... a thing becomes the living symbol of something else, and creates a continuous web of references. Any person or event is a cypher which refers to another part of the book. This generates the grid of allusions in *Ulysses* and the system of puns in *Finnegans Wake*' (U. Eco, *The Aesthetics of Chaosmos: The Middle Ages of James Joyce*, p. 7).

Ex: 'The instant flashed forth like a point of light and now from cloud on cloud of vague circumstance confused form was veiling softly its afterglow. O! In the virgin womb of the imagination the word was made flesh' (Joyce, *Portrait of the Artist as a Young Man*, p. 217).

Joyce's epiphany is not unlike the moments of intense pleasure deriving from personal revelation achieved by Marcel, the narrator of Proust's *A la recherche du temps perdu*. David Nokes describes Joyce's epiphanies as 'acts of verbal magic that give old words a rub and make them new, offering not a jingle of words, but a jangle of ideas' (D. Nokes, ' "Hack at Tom Poley's": Swift's Use of Puns,' in Probyn, ed., *The Art of Jonathan Swift*, p. 46).

R1: See mistake*, R4.

EPIPHONEMA An exclamation*, frequently sententious, used to end a narrative*. See Bary, Le Hir, Girard (p. 299), Lausberg (sect. 879), and Robert.

Ex: 'I forced the last stone into its position; I plastered it up. Against the old masonry I re-erected the old rampart of bones. For the half of a century no mortal has disturbed them. *In pace requiscat!*' (E.A. Poe, 'The Cask of Amontillado,' in *Selected Writings*, p. 366).

Modern narrative tends to avoid epiphonema or to employ it ironically. **Ex:** 'And now they [the ghosts of Saint Patrick and Cleodolinda] are in [the narrator's guest room in Massey College], how shall I ever get them out? Beware of compassion!' (Robertson Davies, 'Refuge of Insulted Saints,' in *High Spirits*, p. 72).

Other definitions: 1. Neither Joseph nor Lanham includes exclamation as a characteristic of epiphonema, although both see it as a sententious utterance used to conclude a passage, poem, or speech. Fontanier (p. 386f.) finds the classical definition too narrow and adds: 'a short and vivid afterthought ... about a narrative ... but whose general nature makes it absolutely distinct from it ... and which precedes, accompanies, or follows it.' This would produce 'initial, terminating or interjectional' epiphonemas. Their vivid or sententious turn of phrase accompanied by a change of tone implying generalization* and a 'moral lesson' would distinguish them from ordinary parenthetical remarks. Ex: the morals of fables.

2. Marouzeau: 'an utterance added to explain a previous utterance (I said nothing to him, since he was so preoccupied).' This is rather epiphrasis* or rationalization.

R1: Epiphonema is a partial parabasis*. However, if the 'short and vivid afterthought' is not detached, if its 'general nature [does not] make it absolutely distinct,' or if it remains attached to a character, the device is no longer partial parabasis, but is closer to epiphrasis*.

EPIPHORA   Placing the same word or words at the end of two or more clauses or sentences. See Lanham, Littré, and Lausberg.

Ex:

Breast that presses against other breasts it shall be you!
...
Root of wash'd sweet-flag! timorous pond-snipe! nest of guarded duplicate eggs! it shall be you!
...
You sweaty brooks and dews it shall be you!
...
Broad muscular fields, branches of live oak, loving lounger in my winding paths, it shall be you!

W. Whitman, 'Song of Myself,' 24

Other terms: epistrophe (Joseph, Lanham, Lausberg, Littré, Morier); antistrophe (Lanham, Littré, Quillet); *conversion* (Fontanier, p. 330). According to Fabri (2:161), however, *conversion* consists in repeating the same sentence three times at regular intervals, whereas according to Girard (p. 281) *conversion* consists of symmetrical repetition*. Ex: 'He has done me too much harm for me to speak any good of him; he has done me too much good for me to speak ill of him.' (See antimetabole*.)

R1: We have preferred the term *epiphora* over *epistrophe* because the former better reveals the link with anaphora*. See epanalepsis*, R6.

R2: Epiphora is a feature of periodic style (see period*) but appears also in poetry, as the example from Whitman shows.

EPIPHRASIS   A sentence or part of a sentence specially added seemingly to indicate the author's feelings or those of a character.

Ex: 'It's Monday tomorrow, I will hear the old people's confessions. *That's nothing.* Tuesday the children's. *I'll soon be finished*' (Alphonse Daudet, 'Le Curé de Cucugnan,' in *Lettres de mon moulin*).

Ex [newsreader]: 'Events in Lebanon took a new turn today ("it says here" [or] "I'm sorry, I'll read that again") ...'

Other definitions: Fontanier (p. 399), Littré, and Morier speak of the addition of secondary ideas. Such a definition, which is less accurate, would make epiphrasis comparable to hyperbaton* of a parenthetical or interpolated clause (Fontanier also mentions this, p. 318). The term does not appear in the *OED* or in Webster's *New World Dictionary*. Lists of literary or rhetorical terms in English give examples of epiphrasis under hyperbaton*.

R1: A partial parabasis*, epiphrasis frequently takes the form of a parenthetical or interpolated clause, or indeed of an interpolation within a parenthesis*: 'There is no sculptor who does not make you think of death (although many sculptors, *so much the worse for them*, have never thought about it at all)' (A. Pieyre de Mandiargues in Oster, et al., *Nouveau Dictionnaire de citations françaises*, no. 15836). With the appropriate intonation*, the parenthesis may become a kind of reduplication*. **Ex:** 'The expression on Mr. Octave's face when he saw the [cigarette] smoke in his bedroom (*his bedroom!* ...), and the ash on his carpet (*his carpet!* ...), was worthy of the theatre' (H. de Montherlant, *Les Célibataires*, in *Romans*, p. 861).

R2: Epiphrasis is close to epiphonema*. Morier observes that it frequently expresses a restriction. See the example under allusion*, R2.

R3: In Greek poetry, the group formed by strophe and antistrophe also contains the *epode*, made up of two lyrical lines of unequal length. The epode is not unrelated to epiphrasis.

R4: The abbreviation N.B. [*nota bene*], when placed in the margin or at the foot of the page, signals in modern texts an extra-textual remark directed to aid the reader's better understanding.

EPITHETON The use, above all for rhetorical purposes, of conventional epithets, helpful to expressivity but virtually meaningless. See Joseph, Lanham, Littré, and Puttenham.

Ex: 'Hacker: "You know Godfrey, there's a lot of nonsense talked about the Civil Service. It is actually a marvellous, *efficient, professional* organisation capable of tremendous effort and speed. It is full of *talented, dedicated* people who do all they can to make Government policies become law"' (J. Lynn and A. Jay, *The Complete 'Yes Minister,'* p. 99).

In the past, grammarians contrasted *epithet* with *adjective* rather than with *predicative* adjective; in so doing, they designated rhetorical quality not function. Despite Lausberg's apparent belief that epithetical style is one which uses many epithets, it is not the accumulation of adjectives but their use as pure ornament which characterizes epitheton, according to Littré, Puttenham, etc. Accumulations of adjectives produce a different figure: accumulation*, not epitheton.

Other definition: Fontanier distinguishes *epithet* (p. 324) from *epithetism* (pp. 354–7). For him, as for Puttenham and Littré, an epithet is an adjective 'serving only to adorn a discourse or make it more vivid,' suppressible without changing the meaning. The following is a parody* of the 'Homeric' epithet: 'a broadshouldered deepchested stronglimbed frankeyed redhaired (etc.) hero' (Joyce, *Ulysses*, p. 243).

R1: Epitheton is a device of 'sublime' style (see grandiloquence*, R1). Le Clerc, however, views it rather as a defect of style. 'Every time [the epithet] fails to characterize or modify the substantive ... ban it as pleonastic.' His example is: '[Crevier] quite rightly ridiculed Chapelain for praising the fair Agnes's *doigts inégaux* [fingers of different lengths].' For epithets used as padding in the period*, see sentence*, 5.

R2: The ancient rhetorical distinction between adjectives and epithets has resurfaced in another form in more recent critical terminology. Lausberg (sect. 680, 1) opposes characteristic epithets and *unnecessary* epithets. Marouzeau distinguishes between *natural* epithets (e.g., 'the big sky') and *circumstantial* epithets (e.g., 'a pretty face'). Natural epithets are those which apply independently of circumstance. Exx: 'It's the war, the whole bloody war' (Nicholas Monsarrat, *The Cruel Sea*, p. 213); 'The sea, the vast sea' (Baudelaire, 'Moesta et errabunda'). Natural epithets tend to 'depict' or 'display' the object represented.

The qualifying syntagm* is also natural or circumstantial, whether referring to a noun or verb. This is the case with the Homeric epithet (e.g., 'swift-footed Achilles'). Ex: 'An incoming train clanked heavily above his head, *coach after coach*' (Joyce, *Ulysses*, p. 65).

R3: Epitheton reduces what Morier calls a text's *density*, that is, the 'proportion of concepts ... relative to the number of words.' 'Concise writing seeks high conceptual density by means of ellipses, allusions ... Prolixity on the other hand ... prefers ... pleonasm* and periphrasis*.'

EPITROCHASMUS An accumulation* of short, expressive words; frequent in invective: 'Traitor! coward!' A rhythmical figure.

Ex: 'The world is a fine place and worth fighting for' (E. Hemingway, *For Whom the Bell Tolls*, p. 55).

Other definitions: '(Gr. run lightly over, treat briefly) ... a swift movement from one statement to the other; rapid touching on many different points. (*Coacervatio* is the opposite figure)' (Lanham, p. 45). His example:

All Kings and all their favorites,
All glory of honours, beauties, wits,
The sun itself, which makes times, as they pass,

Is elder by a year, now, than it was
When thou and I first one another saw:
All other things to their desctruction draw,
Only our love hath no decay.

John Donne, 'The Anniversary'

The *OED* proposes 'a hurried accumulation of several points,' and the *Larousse du XXe siècle* offers: 'the accumulation of strong ideas in a concise form.'

R1: This figure is not collected by Fontanier, Joseph, Lausberg, Littré, Marouzeau, or Preminger.

R2: Recognizable in the word *epitrochasmus* is *trochee*, a rapid metrical foot containing one stressed syllable followed by one unstressed, the latter of which may be dropped in the 'tailless trochee.' Care must be taken lest the *monosyllabic line* be identified necessarily with epitrochasmus. Ex: 'Til noon? Till night, my lord, and all night too!' (Shakespeare, *King Lear*, 2.2.140).

EQUIVOQUE The introduction, by means of a graphic or other modification, into a sentence already complete in meaning, of a second, quite distinct and complete (or almost complete) meaning.

Augarde (p. 145) quotes the following example of 'equivocal verses,' in which ambiguous loyalties are expressed: 'patriotic as it stands but revolutionary if the lines are read in the numbered order':

1. I love my country – but the King
3. Above all men his praise I sing,
2. Destruction to his odious reign
4. That plague of princes, Thomas Paine;
5. The royal banners are displayed
7. And may success the standard aid
6. Defeat and ruin seize the cause
8. Of France, her liberty, and laws.

C.C. Bombaugh, *Gleanings for the Curious*, 1890

Redfern (*Puns*, pp. 120, 171) gives as examples of equivoques: intentional (pun*: 'an eavesdropper is an icicle') and unintentional (howler, lapsus: 'Population of US broken down by age and sex'; 'Incest more common than thought in British Isles').

Synonym: double meaning

Analogous term: pun* (see pun, other def.)

R1: Equivoque is a kind of extended ambiguity* going from allograph*, with or without meaning, to semantic syllepsis* in which a sentence has no need of modification to evoke a second meaning. Equivoque can result from pronunciation or from the choice of a pronoun (see apposition*, R4).

R2: Approximation* is an equivoque which only affects one word; a spoonerism* is an equivoque resulting from antimetathesis*; cacemphaton*, sometimes because of scrambling* (see syntactic scrambling, R1), is parasitic equivoque. See also dissociation*, R9.

R3: Holorhymes are phonetic (but not rhythmic) equivoques, decodable thanks to their two written forms. Ex (quoted by Redfern, p. 100):

Gal, amant de la reine, à la tour Magne, à Nîmes
Galamment de l'arène alla, tour magnanime.

If the holorhyme occurs only at the end of a line, one has rhyming equivoque. Ex (quoted by Redfern, p. 100):

There's not a sea the passenger e'er pukes in,
Turns up more dangerous breakers than the Euxine.

Lord Byron, *Don Juan*, 5.5.7–8

When holorhymes occur in prose, they are called homophones (words different in meaning but alike in sound). Ex: 'When the Flood had subsided and the animals were leaving the ark, Noah blessed them saying, "Increase and multiply." To which two snakes replied sadly, "We can't, we're adders" ' (quoted by L.G. Kelly in 'Punning and the Linguistic Sign,' *Linguistics*, no. 66 [1971], pp. 5–11).

R4: The Grands Rhétoriqueurs cultivated equivoque in their poems at the end of the fifteenth century. Among the forms listed by Paul Zumthor (*Anthologie des grands rhétoriqueurs*) were bilingual, double, and triple equivoque as well as *retrograde equivoque* or chain rhymes, in which the beginning of the second of two successive lines repeats the last word or words of the first but with a different meaning: 'Trop durement mon coeur souspire; / Pire mal sent que desconfort' ('Too strongly does my heart sigh, / Worse evil it feels than mere discomfort' [p. 273]). See also spelling* out, R2, and metanalysis*, R2.

R5: The popular BBC panel game 'My Word!' in which Frank Muir and Denis Norden concocted narratives containing spoof explanations of well-known sayings or quotations relied heavily on equivoque. Exx: 'You can't have your cake and eat it' became 'You can't have your kayak and heat it'; 'And so to bed' (Pepys) became 'And saw Tibet.' 'So he passed over, and all the trumpets sounded for him on the other side' (John Bunyan, *Pilgrim's Progress*) became 'So he passed Dover, and all the strumpets undid for him on the other side' (F. Muir and D. Norden, *The 'My Word!' Stories*, pp. 11, 30, 23).

R6: In daily life, unconscious equivoque may form a revealing lapsus*.

Erasure (Lexical)

R7: See also *agnominatio**, R3; meaning*, 9; and phoebus*, R4.

ERASURE (LEXICAL) Instead of using proper names, specific common nouns, or even propositions, the speaker uses demonstratives or indefinite, almost meaningless grammatical and lexical forms (e.g., 'thingamujig,' 'what-d'you-call-it').

Exx: 'I'll never forget Whatshisname' [title of film, directed by M. Winner, 1967); 'The Life, Death, Miracles of Saint Somebody'; 'Saint Somebody Else, his Miracles, Death and Life' (R. Browning, *The Ring and the Book*, book 1, 80–1); 'Bonnie wee thing, cannie wee thing, / Lovely wee thing ...' (R. Burns, 'The Bonnie Wee Thing'); 'His thoughts flew like flaming arrows: he must not forget to mention this; he must remember to speak of that, about this, and about that, too' (A. Solzhenitsyn, *The First Circle*, p. 181).

R1: We owe the theory of this device to a mathematician turned fiction writer: 'It was Lewis Carroll who advised the timid to leave blank some of the words in their letters ... Or to put completely indefinite nouns: *aliquid*, it, that, thing, thingamy or thingum(a)bob' (G. Deleuze, *Logique du sens*, p. 59).

R2: 'The use of numbers without specifying what they determine' (H.-R. Diwekar, *Les Fleurs de rhétorique de l'Inde*, p. 63), sometimes found in hermetic texts, is also a kind of lexical erasure. Exx: 'He kept the five, obtained the triad, took in the triad, conquered the pair, and then discarded the pair' (Ramayana); 'The one becomes the two, the two becomes the three, and the three rediscovers unity in the four. Axiom of Mary the Copt' (epigraph* in Hubert Aquin's novel *The Antiphonary*).

R3: In everyday language, a kind of lexical erasure exists whose effect is to broaden the scope of an assertion*. Ex: 'It [the air] will do you good, Bloom said, meaning also the walk, in a moment' (Joyce, *Ulysses*, p. 539). See also parataxis*, R2.

R4: Lexical erasure is a kind of allusion* (see allusion, R2), also of euphemism* (see euphemism, R2). The device is involuntary in amnesic aphasia, or simply when one cannot find the right word.

ERASURE (OF SUBJECT) The German diarist and aphorist Georg Christoph Lichtenberg (1742–99) seems to have invented this device, which consists in defining out of existence the subject of a discourse*. He is considered a humorist with his 'knife without a blade and lacking a handle,' but the device may correspond to some deeper concern, as examples like 'I died before my birth' suggest. See J.P. Stern's *Lichtenberg*. The surrealists imitated him. Exx: 'For the moment an absence of eggs on the plate, no plate' (S. Dali, quoted by Eluard in

Oeuvres, 1:1173); 'A sentence without words, sounds or meaning' (H. Michaux, *Connaissance par les gouffres*, p. 142). See also extravagant* comparison.

R1: The device is a kind of nonsense*.

EROSION A kind of repetition* in which a part of the text disappears each time it is repeated.

Ex: In Stanley Kubrick's film *2001: A Space Odyssey* (1968), Hal the homicidal computer 'lobotomized' by the pilot whose life is threatened, reverts to a first memory, a nursery-song: 'Daisy, Daisy give me your answer do, / I'm half-crazy, all for the love of you ... Daisy, Daisy give me your answer do, / I'm half-crazy ... Daisy, Daisy give me your answer do ... Daisy, Daisy ... Dai ...' Erosion and the ensuing silence signal the computer's 'death.' (See G.D. Phillips, *Stanley Kubrick: A Film Odyssey*, p. 192.)

R1: Rhetorical erosion seems intended as a kind of emphasis, or as an echoing device, or even as a way of pointing to new meanings in the successive syntagms*. Ex: 'In this restaurant, if you don't eat meat, then you don't eat.' Ex: '... during those long journeys which we made separated from one another, I now know that we were really together, we were really, we were, we' (P. Eluard, *Oeuvres complètes*, 1:373).

R2: Joyce employs the opposite device which, naturally enough, we shall call *alluvion*. Ex: '... outriders leaping, leaping in their, in their saddles' (Joyce, *Ulysses*, p. 198). An example from modern publicity: 'Dubo, Dubon, Dubonnet.' An example combining both erosion and alluvion:

Because I do not hope to turn again
Because I do not hope
Because I do not hope to turn

T.S. Eliot, 'Ash Wednesday'

ETYMOLOGY In its 'learned' or strict meaning, etymology consists of a return to a word's origin (or *etymon*) so as to comment upon or modify its meaning*.

Exx: 'Computerists often use the term *booting* DOS, which comes from the phrase "pulling yourself up by the bootstraps" ' (D. Berliner, *Managing Your Hard Disk*, p. 26); ' "Obscenity" is one of the rare words which have to be referred to their etymology in order to be granted at least the spectre of a meaning. *Obscenus* means inauspicious and it is perhaps related to *caenum*, signifying filth' (Anthony Burgess, *TLS*, 12–18 Feb. 1988, p. 159).

Etymology

This relatively rare use of etymology confuses its meaning with that of the archaism*. But etymology may also be used as an argument*. Ex: '... the line between poison and medicine is very fine; the Greeks used the word "pharmacon" for both' (U. Eco, *The Name of the Rose*, p. 108). This is linguistic or formal proof if ever one existed. Plato, and even Aristotle, considered it legitimate and for centuries philosophers imagined they could discern the essence of things from the composition or sound of words (see Isidore of Seville's *Etymologiae* and, as late as the seventeenth century, comparisons made between English or French and Hebrew).

The graphic variants used by modern existentialist writers represent a recent phase of the method. Following Heidegger's example, they insert new ideas into well-worn words. Ex: 'We thus come to see the subject as *ek-static* and an actively transcendental relationship between the subject and the world' (Maurice Merleau-Ponty, *Phénoménologie de la perception*, p. 491).

Jean Paulhan's short treatise *La Preuve par l'étymologie* ('Proof by Etymology') seeks to undermine a reader's naïve confidence in this type of proof, which is so close, as he says, to punning. Such proofs almost always involve unscientific or 'popular' etymology, cases of *paronymic attraction*. As Redfern remarks, 'this kind of creative etymology is sometimes called *ethymologia*' (*Puns*, p. 86) and leads to humorous absurdities both intended and involuntary. Exx: '... there were doctors who refused to accept Freud's clinical proof that men could have hysteria on the grounds that the word was derived from ὑστέρα and could only therefore apply to women' (Molly Mahood, *Shakespeare's Wordplay*, p. 170); 'And is not the cat the animal beloved by the Catharists, who according to Alanus de Insulis are so called from "catus," because of this beast whose posterior they kiss, considering it the incarnation of Lucifer' (U. Eco, *The Name of the Rose*, p. 328).

In rhetoric, etymology is almost always false but, even in the form of an argument* which proves nothing, remains eloquent. Children realize this as they explore the lexicon by means of irrefutable rhetorical etymology. Ex: 'If Mars is the god of war, then a "Mars" bar must be a deadly weapon.' In the process they discover both language and the world, that is, the (in)capacity of the one to explain the other. Texts like *Down with Skool* by Geoffrey Willans and Ronald Searle, *1066 and All That* by W.G. Sellar and R.J. Yeatman, and Sue Townsend's *The Secret Diary of Adrian Mole* attempt to reconstruct a world (still latent in adults) where a child learns even through the whimsical use of words and their motivation.

Other definition: Marouzeau gives: the combination in the same construction of words related by etymology (e.g., 'to live one's life') or meaning (e.g., 'sleep the big sleep'). Grammarians more often call the device an *internal complement*, which is a form of lexematic emphasis*, pleonasm* but not perissology*.

R1: When (false) etymology attacks proper names, it becomes a kind of compliment or persiflage*. Ex:

Thou, Leonatus, art the lion's whelp.
The fit and apt construction of thy name,
Being Leo-natus, doth impart so much.

Shakespeare, *Cymbeline*, 5.5.443-5

See *agnominatio**.

R2: Etymology is the principal means of remotivating a word (see remotivation*, R1). Ex: Derrida's use of the word 'dissemination' to mean 'the splitting up of semes.' See also battology*, R1, and homonymy*, R2.

EUPHEMISM The disguising of disagreeable, odious, or painful ideas by the use of expressions which do not express such ideas literally (see Dumarsais, *Des Tropes*, 2:5). See also Cuddon, Elkhadem, Frye, Lausberg, Marouzeau, Quillet, Morier, and Robert.

Exx: a growth (cancer); to waste (kill); tickle the ribs (flog); massage parlour (brothel). See J.S. Neaman and C.G. Silver, *Kind Words: A Thesaurus of Euphemisms* (1983).

Ex: 'FIGARO [who has just been insulted by the Count]: Those are the familiar kindnesses with which you have always honoured me' (P. de Beaumarchais, beginning of *Le Barbier de Séville*).

Ex:

... everybody gathered to look in the entryway of the Boys' Toilet when the word went round: Shortie McGill is fucking Franny McGill!
Brother and sister.
Relations performing.
That was Flo's word for it: *perform*. (Alice Munro, 'Privilege,' in *Who Do You Think You Are?*, p. 28)

Synonym: transumption (Fabri, 2:157). See also irony*.

R1: Euphemism is a kind of attenuation*. Antonym: dysphemism; see caricature*. It differs from extenuation* (see extenuation, R1; also celebration*, R3). It belongs to sublime style. See also grandiloquence*, R1.

R2: Euphemistic forms:

Euphemism

(a) Metonymy* and metaphor*. Frequent in current expressions. Exx: 'rear end'; 'to go to bed with someone'; 'blossom' (pimple); 'cherry' (hymen). See also metalepsis*.

(b) Double negation* or negation of the contrary. Ex: 'Republics, the last, and not the least pernicious form, of authoritarian government' (G.-A. Lefrançais).

(c) Allusions*. Ex: 'Electronic countermeasures or reconnaissance' (spying).

(d) Implication*. Ex: 'His studies? Well, he works very hard ...' (i.e., 'that's the most that can be said').

(e) Metaplasm*. Exx: 'vamp' (vampire, seductive woman); 'cripes' (Christ); 'pee' (piss).

(f) Compound* words. Ex: 'an under-achiever (Pleasant-sounding expressions exist nowadays to refer to stupidity)' (G. Bessette, Le Libraire, p. 152).

(g) Ellipsis* or lexical erasure*. Ex: 'Ladies' for 'Ladies' Room,' that is, lavatory or toilet (both euphemisms, of course).

Euphemism sometimes takes the form of metalepsis* (see metalepsis, R1). Implication* or italics make it easier to spot.

R3: Euphemism may cause misinterpretation. Ex: 'Mary and Joseph never knew one another before their marriage. It's in the Bible, Dad.' And so euphemism, to avoid misunderstandings of this sort, sometimes needs to be foregrounded. Ex [in the British Saturday Review in 1861]: 'we encounter ... the miserable Dr. Blandling in what is called ... a blue funk' (quoted by Neaman and Silver, Kind Words, p. 125).

R4: Euphemism is a factor in semantic deterioration. If we say, so as to avoid worrying anyone, rather than a disturbing situation, only a serious situation, we cause serious to lose its meaning (intermediate between tragic and comic), and it becomes a synonym of grave. Similarly, gay used to mean 'happy' and was the adjectival form of the noun gaiety. Homosexual appropriation of the term has compromised the linguistic structure linking the two forms. When a euphemism is no longer recognized as such, pejoration results.

R5: On the other hand, if euphemisms are too clearly evident, their effect, instead of being one of attenuation*, is reversed: this phenomenon is meiosis*. Ex: 'It isn't very serious. I have this tiny little tumour on the brain' (J.D. Salinger, The Catcher in the Rye, p. 55). Metaphors* and double negation* do not prevent euphemism from acting as a kind of emphasis*. It may also be foregrounded by the use of preterition* (see preterition, R1).

R6: Counter-euphemism exists as a kind of antiphrasis* which uses a pejorative form to avert the supposed ill luck attached to a meliorative

178

term. A current example in French: 'Les cinq lettres!' (i.e., 'merde') in place of 'Good luck,' which is believed to be unlucky. Contrast among English-speaking actors the wishing of ill luck in order to pre-empt disaster: 'Break a leg!'

EXCLAMATION A form of assertion* characterized graphically by an exclamation mark (see expressive punctuation*), and orally by a rise in the voice which is clear but less marked than in a question*. (The rise in pitch affects the first enunciated vowel and so is usually followed by a rapid descent to a lower or concluding pitch. Delattre [see continuation*] saw the fall as the characteristic feature of exclamation, which, indeed, allows it to be distinguished from questions*, in which the rise affects the tonic vowel.) The exclamation principally serves the emotive (or expressive) function of langue; that is, in the word's strict sense, the function centred upon the speaker; see enunciation*, 1.

Exclamations are frequently elliptical, use interjections*, and replace certain lexemes with adjectives, pronouns, or adverbs of interrogative form. Ex: 'Bless my heart, how very odd! Why, surely there's a brace of moons! See! the stars! how bright they twinkle ...' (Sir Theodore Martin, 'The Lay of the Lovelorn [In Imitation of Tennyson],' in Michael Roberts, ed., *The Faber Book of Comic Verse*, p. 152).

Ex:

How doth the little crocodile
Improve his shining tail,
And pour the waters of the Nile
On every golden scale!
     Lewis Carroll, 'How doth the little crocodile,' in ibid., p. 187

As the above example shows, the limits between questions and exclamations are not always clear: it is sometimes possible to substitute one for the other without harming the overall meaning.

Analogous definitions: Dumarsais, Fontanier (p. 370), Joseph (p. 389), Lanham, Lausberg (sect. 809), Littré, and Robert define exclamations as expressions of emotion; this meaning is a more restricted one. Marouzeau's definition is more formal: an interjectory word (e.g., 'Hi!') or simple sentence in which added intonation* makes up for grammatical insufficiency.

R1: Any sentence with an exclamation mark added or with an oral intensive accent* becomes an exclamation: injunctions*, threats*, supplications*, sarcasm*, caricatures*, well-wishing*, celebrations*, insults*, excuses*, and curses (see blasphemy*, R1). Even pure exclamations, empty of explicit content, are possible: applause, whistling of various kinds, ovations.

Excuse

R2: Apostrophes* are followed by exclamations whose principal function is conative. Compare 'Jane!' as a greeting with 'Jane!' as an expression of surprise at an unexpected meeting.

R3: Exclamations persist in free indirect style. Negative exclamations may have positive meanings. Exclamations may serve to emphasize (see emphasis*, R3); they have their own intonation*.

EXCUSE An argument* touching on the speaker's good faith or goodwill, and offered to avoid possible reproach.

Ex:

> I know there are readers in the world ... who find themselves ill at ease, unless they are let into the whole secret from first to last, of every thing that concerns you.
>   It is in pure compliance with this humour of theirs, and from a backwardness in my nature to disappoint any one soul living, that I have been so very particular already. (Laurence Sterne, *Tristram Shandy*, vol. 1, ch. 4).

R1: In literary texts, excuses may be addresses to the reader; they are devices of enunciation* and frequently take the form of parabasis*. But they may also be purely rhetorical. Ex: 'In the beginning of the last chapter, I informed you exactly *when* I was born; – but I did not inform you *how*. No; that particular was reserved entirely for a chapter by itself; – besides, Sir, as you and I are in a manner perfect strangers to each other, it would not have been proper to have let you into too many circumstances relating to myself all at once' (L. Sterne, *Tristram Shandy*, vol. 1, ch. 6).

The expression 'Excuse me' implies sorrow which may also produce, however, recriminations* or refutations*, as may be seen in the expression 'Excuse *me!*' meaning '(Please) get out of my way!' An expression of *regret* is an unjustified excuse. Ex: 'Philosophy – put my remark down to my ignorance – seems to me to be in a state of crisis' (Valéry, *Oeuvres*, 1:799). Some *justifications* come without an excuse. Ex: ' "Then why do you want to know?" "Because learning does not consist only of knowing what we must or we can do, but also of knowing what we could do and perhaps should not do" ' (U. Eco, *The Name of the Rose*, p. 97). *False (or rhetorical) regret* accompanies a refusal and adopts a tone of ironic pleasure. Ex: 'I'm sorry to have to say this, but you seem to be confusing *objective* with *subjective*.'

Pseudo-justification exists, consisting of excusing oneself without offering a reason. Ex: 'And it's not my fault if the word immediately recalls Rimbaud' (Claudel, *Oeuvres en prose*, p. 258). Pseudo-justification is natural precisely because speakers feel that they ought to be able simply to report a criticism without necessarily accepting it. Or they may excuse self-reference by an ironic gesture or smile, or by the use of

180

an exclamation mark in parentheses. Ex: 'A friend has called me to ask for some information on my written work (!)' (Michaux, *Connaissance par les gouffres*, p. 60, n. 1).

R2: One may excuse the choice of a word by the use of an expression placed after it. Ex: 'Well, I'll be buggered. Excuse my French' (A. La Bern, *Goodbye Piccadilly*, p. 220). Common expressions: 'if I may say'; 'if I may venture to say'; 'forgive me for saying'; etc.

Rhetorical hesitation may be used to introduce and excuse too learned a word. Ex: 'One sees living coral, ... what do you call them? – madrepores' (Gide, *Romans*, p. 969).

R3: In the past, excuses were placed at the end of a work, disguised as farewells: 'Excuse the author's mistakes'; and, in works of piety, 'Brothers, pray for the copyist.' Or they may occupy a place of honour in the prologue, as they do, albeit in ironic form, in *Don Quixote*. They may follow a confession (see concession*, R1). They have their own intonation*. They quite properly precede a re-examination of presuppositions (see finesse*, R1).

R4: Semi-excuses exist (see preterition*, R1, and licence*, R1 [*correctio*]); as do anticipated excuses (see prolepsis*, R1).

EXHORTATION A discourse* by means of which a speaker urges a listener to undertake an action represented as being worthy of merit.

Ex: 'Once more unto the breach, dear friends, once more, / Or close the wall up with our English dead ... / On, on you noblest English ... / Be copy now to men of grosser blood ...' (Shakespeare, *Henry V*, 3.1.1–23).

Ex: 'Of course, if by any chance you think there is a reasonable doubt in this case you will follow Mr Rumpole's advice and acquit the defendant Glassworth of this serious charge ... But if you think the prosecution case is unanswerable ... then it is your plain duty, in accordance with your oath, to find the defendant guilty as charged' (John Mortimer, *The Trials of Rumpole*, p. 172). The use of 'if ...' is here an attempt to disguise exhortation under a cloak of 'objectivity.'

Analogous terms: conjuration (a solemn appeal in the name of something sacred); adjuration (a summons or earnest request; the person making the request may even invoke the divinity. See also well-wishing*, R2)

R1: Speakers may exhort themselves to greater efforts (even ironically, as in the following example):

Be still, be still my soul; it is but for a season;
Let us endure an hour and see injustice done.
A.E. Housman, *A Shropshire Lad*, no. 48

EXORCISM A formula or gesture capable of long-range action.

Ex: Abracadabra

Ex: 'He [Salvatore] made a deep bow, muttered through half-closed lips a "vade retro," devoutly blessed himself, and fled ...' (U. Eco, *The Name of the Rose*, p. 48).

Analogous terms: magic spell, incantation, mantra, sorcery, sortilege

Other definitions: a conjuration (see exhortation*); invocation or use of the holy name to expel evil spirits

EXPLANATION A (frequently brief) discourse* added to certain assertions* in order to clarify a word or action, etc.

Ex: ' "Do you know, Rapp, what military art is?" he [Napoleon] asked. "It is the art of being stronger than the enemy at a given moment. *Voilà tout!* [That's all there is to it!]" ' (Leo Tolstoy, *War and Peace*, 2:935).

Ex: 'He kissed her hand and called her *you* and *Sonya*. But their eyes met and said *thou*, and exchanged tender kisses. Her eyes asked his forgiveness for having dared, through Natasha, to remind him of his promise, and thanked him for his love. His were thanking her for offering him his freedom, and telling her that one way or another he would never cease to love her' (ibid., 2:352).

Analogous term: scholium (see paraphrase*), a marginal note or explanatory comment, especially one by an ancient grammarian on a passage in a classical author (*Concise Oxford Dictionary*)

R1: Explanation is one of the mainsprings of the traditional novel. In the modern novel, since existence precedes essence, the hero acts first and asks why later, sometimes in vain. An absurd universe provides no explanations.

When explanations come in the guise of speeches attributed to characters, they are called *expositional dialogue.* Ex: 'AGNES: I was brushing my teeth after dinner. It's only the two middle ones that come out – the rest's my own, what there is, but of course, it's the *gap*, isn't it?' (Tom Stoppard, *Teeth*, in *The Dog It Was That Died and Other Plays*, p. 72). See also response*, R2; epiphonema*, other def.; and rhythm* (of the action), R1.

R2: Explanations may fill whole chapters or treatises, or may be reduced to a single parenthetical lexeme. Ex: 'He must, however, have known other [women] in London' (G. Bessette, *L'Incubation*, p. 10).

R3: Presuppositions call for explanation. Ex: 'Zola was Zola, *i.e.*, rather gross as an artist, but with hearty lungs and big fists' (J.-K. Huysmans, *A Rebours*, preface). See tautology*, R2. A request for an explanation is formulated as a request for meaning: 'What does that mean?'

R4: See also interjection*; prophecy*, R1; reasoning*, R5; response*, R2; and translation*, R3.

EXTENUATION The substitution, for the real idea under discussion, of an idea of the same kind but weaker. See Lausberg, Scaliger (3:81), Le Clerc (p. 300), and Littré.

Ex: 'Disputes ... express nostalgia or aspiration, hope or regret, *a malaise at any rate*' (R. Aron, *La Révolution introuvable*, p. 93).

Synonyms: underrating (*OED*); diminution (Littré, Quillet); tapinosis (Paul, p. 172; Preminger)

Antonym: hyperbole*. (*Hypobole*, which might appear etymologically to be the opposite of *hyperbole* and therefore synonymous with *extenuation*, is in ancient rhetoric a synonym for *subjectio*, a strategy by which one advances one's own case by supplying an answer to one's own question [see Lanham, Lausberg].)

R1: Extenuation is a form of attenuation* but differs from euphemism*, which attenuates pejorative connotation rather than force.

R2: Extenuation may be reduced to intonation*, as in some modern plays, notably those of Beckett.

R3: By repressing expressivity, one surpasses zero-degree banality and sinks below the level of truism*. Ex: 'Language recoils from only one thing, that is, being reduced to silence' (Francis Ponge, *Le Parti pris des choses*, p. 136). The device offers the speaker's critics the smallest target to aim at. When used in evidence, it is a refuge from attack.

R4: Extenuation is standard when one speaks about oneself. Ex: 'With regard to my moods, I believe I have a right to complain of those who accuse me of misanthropy and reserve: it seems that not a single one of them has considered me to be worthy of closer examination' (Jean-Jacques Rousseau, *Correspondance*, ed. Dufour, 1:378).

EXTRAVAGANT COMPARISON The qualification or presentation of an object, idea, argument*, or person as more powerful and more extraordinary than all others. See Curtius, p. 200.

Exx: '[S.J.] Perelman is, like Groucho himself, at his best when he takes the figurative literally ... He is at his better than best when he writes dialogue' (Anthony Burgess, *But Do Blondes Prefer Gentlemen?*, p. 469); 'Thomas Jefferson is, despite his slaves, a transplanted Englishman of large culture, to whom John Kennedy, honouring forty-nine Nobel prizemen in 1962, paid the best tribute: "The most extraordinary collection of human talent ... that has ever been gathered at the White

House – with the possible exception of when Thomas Jefferson dined alone" ' (ibid., p. 228).

R1: Frequently, the point of comparison* is perfection itself, in which case we may justly speak of *paroxysmal* comparison. **Exx:** 'ALVARO: I tolerate only perfection' (H. de Montherlant, *Le Maître de Santiago*, in *Théâtre*, p. 627); 'At the least crossing out, the principle of total inspiration is ruined' (P. Eluard, *Oeuvres complètes*, 1:478).

The medieval literary genre panegyric made paroxysmal comparison the first of its 'commonplaces,' as Curtius shows: 'A favorite piece of flattery is to the effect that the person celebrated surpasses the gods ... Walafrid Strabo praises a certain Probus for writing better poetry than Virgil, Horace [and so on]' (E.R. Curtius, *European Literature and the Latin Middle Ages*, pp. 162–3).

A modern (parodic) form combines the medieval *gab* ('an idle vaunt, a piece of brag or bravado' [*OED*]) or 'boast' with a comparison of an idyllic past, productive of a 'superior' brand of individual, to an inferior present, responsible for the 'effeteness' of modern youth. The parody* involves turning the idyll into a narrative* incorporating grotesque claims to a past period of extreme, 'heroic' poverty:

> FIRST YORKSHIREMAN: In them days we wuz glad to 'ave the price of a cuppa tea.
> SECOND: A cuppa cold tea.
> THIRD: Without milk or sugar.
> FOURTH: Or tea.
> FIRST: In a cracked cup, an' all.
> SECOND: Oh, we never 'ad a cup. We used to 'ave to drink out of a rolled up newspaper.
> THIRD: The best we could manage was to suck on a piece of damp cloth.
>
> G. Chapman, J. Cleese, T. Gilliam, E. Idle, T. Jones, and M. Palin, 'Four Yorkshiremen' in *Monty Python Live at the Theatre Royal, Drury Lane*, Polygram, Charisma Records CA-1–1502

See erasure* of subject.

R2: What distinguishes extravagant from ordinary comparisons is that the former imply that, by going 'further,' the speaker gets the better of real or possible addressees (hence the paroxysmal or irrefutable form of the device).

R3: The principal marks of extravagant comparisons are the comparative and superlative forms; adverbs of liaison like 'not only ... but more'; expressions such as 'it would be better to say' or 'I would go so far as to say'; and proverbs like 'Diamond cut diamond' (i.e., wit or cunning is met by its like). See lexical mirror*, R1.

We may well judge that the whole of the French preciosity movement in the seventeenth century, which was itself the heir of mannerism, neo-Platonism, and Platonism, offers an example of generalized extravagance, both in its content and form, adopted by an aristocratic group. On the other hand, classical writers considered such excessive attention to detail an affectation and so a lack of naturalness. See baroquism* and Lausberg, p. 523.

R4: Like *gradatio**, which ascends to a climax or descends to an anticlimax*, extravagant comparisons may also produce diminutions. Ex: 'But he had only been in Prussia – and then only on the front' (A.I. Solzhenitsyn, *The First Circle*, p. 11). Another kind of extravagant comparison is the *hypercorrection*, as a result of which, by striving to speak more correctly than others, one falls into error. Ex: ' "Ah, my dear *vicomte*," put in Anna Pavlovna, "Urope" (for some reason she pronounced it *Urope* as if it were a special refinement of French which she could allow herself in conversing with a Frenchman), "Urope will never be a sincere ally of ours" ' (Tolstoy, *War and Peace*, 1:429). Extravagant comparisons may also take the form of corrections. See self-correction*, R1.

If it ends tautologically, an extravagant comparison is anticlimactic. Ex: 'A strange business ... I could say more: this business is really ... er ... strange.'

One may also present in a comparison* the weaker term as the stronger, which produces ironic implications*. Ex: 'It is worse than a crime, it is a blunder' (Boulay de la Meurthe, on hearing of the execution of the Duc d'Enghien in 1804).

R5: Irony*, triplication*, and foregrounding* combine in the deflation of extravagant comparisons in the following anecdote:

In the late seventeenth century, the finest instruments originated from three rival families whose workshops were side by side in the Italian village of Cremona.

First were the Amatis, and outside their shop hung a sign: 'The best violins in all Italy.' Not to be outdone, their next-door neighbours, the family Guarnarius, hung a bolder sign proclaiming: 'The best violins in all the world.'

At the end of the street was the workshop of Anton Stradivarius, and on its front door was a simple notice which read: 'The best violins on the block.' (Freda Bright, *Decisions*, p. 121)

F

FALSE – Since most devices have both a form and a meaning, it is possible to separate the former from the latter. Thus a familiar form may have a new meaning: this is artifice. Ex: the kind of question known as *rhetorical* (or false) because it hides an assertion. The kind of etymology* by means of which one changes the meaning* of a word while pretending to be simply going back over its semantic evolution is false or vulgar etymology to the linguist. Quotations* may be invented according to need. Personification* is always false because it presents inanimate objects or ideas as people. *Permissio** is a false permission, as the latter term is usually understood. The *open letter* is only formally a letter addressed to a single receiver since in reality it is a public text.

Synonyms: mere (as in expressions like 'mere sophistry'; see concession*, R3); rhetorical (in the term's pejorative sense); figurative (see comparison*, R1); oratorical

R1: Some false figures have been specifically named. Preterition* is false reticence; prosopopoeia*, false apostrophe*; *subjectio*, false dialogismus; ; litotes*, false attenuation*; licence*, false encouragement given to oneself; asteismus*, false insult* or false sarcasm*; parody*, false imitation*; adynaton*, pure hyperbole*; pretext*, a false reason.

R2: The discovery of numerous cases of sham figures may have caused critics to declare all rhetoric false and to add that, as such, it is a form of composition capable only of producing deviation from 'normal' language, a fact which deprives the text of the truth conferred by natural forms. Thus, Valéry quotes the following remarks from Mallarmé's table-talk: 'Art is false! and he explains how an artist is one only when at his best and when making an effort of will' (P. Valéry, *Oeuvres*, 2:1226).

From there to a condemnation of both art and poetics there is but one step, which has often been taken throughout history. But it is a fact that such so-called falseness is itself most often false: it only seems to simulate. Artifice which fools no one is honest: simulation* becomes pseudo-simulation*.

Truly false devices do exist nevertheless, such as sophisms*, which are intended to trick. And to specious arguments* correspond apparent refutations*, which simulate falseness. 'It is unwise and naïve to refute seriously an argument that is not serious' (Chaignet, *La Rhétorique et son histoire*, p. 152).

There also exist true devices necessary to meaning that therefore are the opposite of pure figures. True prosopopoeia* (see prosopopoeia, R2) is a form of delirious exaltation. Hypotyposis* becomes 'evocation' (see prosopopoeia, R3). Is not any means a good one which achieves its objective (since no utterance is entirely aimless)?

R3: When falseness becomes a value in itself and is turned into an art-object, it is *kitsch*. The deliberate display of art's artifice is known as foregrounding* the illusion.

R4: The parading of devices (see baroquism*, R5) and, more recently, forms like surrealistic substitution*, 'potential' literature, and dissemination systematize formal transformation. Computers may well produce curious new developments in this area.

FANTASTIC (THE) The representation as real of an episode incompatible with reality.

Ex: 'As Gregor Samsa awoke one morning from uneasy dreams he found himself transformed in his bed into a gigantic insect' (Franz Kafka, 'The Metamorphosis,' in *The Complete Stories*, ed. N. Glatzer, p. 75).

The presence of any supernatural being serves to define the fantastic. Ex: 'And suddenly, to my intense dismay, there was – right before me in the Chapel – a red dragon, having seven heads and seven horns, and seven crowns upon his heads ... "O the Devil!" I exclaimed ... "Great Lord, what is your will?" ' (Robertson Davies, 'When Satan Goes Home for Christmas,' in *High Spirits*, p. 55).

When overdone, the fantastic degenerates into mere phantasmagorical hyperbole*. The evanescent variety of fantastic narrative* presents ghosts, hallucinations, apparitions, and so on, as in the following parody*. Ex: 'But Malachias' tale began to freeze them with horror. He conjured up the scene before them. The secret panel beside the chimney slid back and in the recess appeared – Haines! Which of us did not feel his flesh creep! He had a portfolio of Celtic literature in one hand, in the other a phial marked *Poison*' (Joyce, *Ulysses*, p. 336).

R1: We need to distinguish between the fantastic proper and the purely fictional which does not pretend to be faithful to reality but rather foregrounds the fictional illusion itself. Ex: Alphonse Allais has a Swedish narrator who tells the story of drownings caused by the overflow from a water-colour representing the sea, which was painted, it should be pointed out, by an artist who used seawater in his water-colours (*La Barbe et autres contes*, p. 112).

R2: Fairy stories, which used to be 'dramatic works founded on marvels' (Bénac), have turned from the fantastic into mere fiction and have nowadays come to mean 'irrational and poetic worlds' (Cocteau) where surrealists like Cocteau are quite at home. Ex: 'Now there is no longer anyone in Paris except an old dead grocer's wife whose face is soaking in a fruit-dish full of cream smiles' (R. Desnos, *Pénalités de l'enfer*, quoted in P. Berger, *Robert Desnos*, p. 115). So mirages and illusions, analogical or simulated, link up with dreams which, because they represent themselves as such, are not really fantastic. Ex: 'I have been turned into a number. I am falling down a well which is also a piece of paper, passing in and out of equations' (R. Desnos, 'Rêves,' quoted in Berger, *Robert Desnos*, p. 114).

R3: The English *gothic* novel is a species of the fantastic with witches, dark forests, twisted trees, spider webs, and haunted houses, which Jane Austen parodied in *Northanger Abbey*.

R4: See also image*, R1, and prosopopoeia*, R3.

FINAL WORD A work's last word, phrase, or sentence, which leaves the reader with a certain impression (see plan*) and which forms a sign of completion.

Ex: the words 'The End' or 'Curtain'

Common forms: 'that's it, finished'; 'that's all (there is)'; 'one more thing and that's all'; 'that's all folks!' (the sign-off to the 'Loony Tunes' series of cartoons). In fairy stories: 'They all lived happily ever afterwards and had lots of children.'

Exx: 'It is cold in the scriptorium, my thumb aches. I leave this manuscript, I do not know for whom; I no longer know what it is about: *stat rosa pristina nomine, nomina nuda tenemus*' (U. Eco, *The Name of the Rose*, p. 502); 'Moral: there exist obsessive ideas, they are never personal; books talk among themselves, and any true detection should prove that we are the guilty party' (U. Eco, *Postscript to 'The Name of the Rose,'* p. 81). See also punch* line, R2.

R1: There frequently exists between a work's *title* and its *final word* a connection which displays the text's closed nature. Sartre's *Age of Reason* ends with the hero reflecting: 'I have attained the age of reason.' In oral literature, the work's first sentence is often repeated. See inclusion*.

Ionesco has shown the pure contingency of endings by repeating the first scene at the end of *The Lesson* and *The Bald Soprano*. Calvino, on the other hand, draws from the work's own logic the necessity of making an end. On the final page of his novel, he puts the following words into the mouth of his 'Reader,' who has married Ludmilla, one of the characters:

Ludmilla closes her book, turns off her light, puts her head back against the pillow, and says, 'Turn off your light, too. Aren't you tired of reading?'

And you say, 'Just a moment, I've almost finished *If on a Winter's Night a Traveller* by Italo Calvino.'

R2: The text's *final word* is not the *last word*: that belongs to the reader.

R3: See point*, R1.

FINESSE (Fr. *impasse*) The analytic distinction between affirmation and presupposition (see assertion*, R4) explains various devices, particularly the finesse. Finesse consists in treating as basic presuppositions ideas known to be contrary to those of one's opponent, whom one thus seeks to oblige to accept them implicitly, or to take up once again points of violent disagreement, a procedure which may appear tactless or aggressive. (See Ducrot, *Dire et ne pas dire*, pp. 95–7.)

Ex [to a friend just eighteen]: 'So? Did they let you in last night?' (to find out whether he went to see an 'adult' film).

Analogous terms: 'trick' questions*; hidden presupposition

R1: The device is called a 'finesse' by analogy with the stratagem or ploy used in bridge.

R2: An excuse* is often used before an answer which returns to what has been presupposed. Tom says to Dick, who suspects that Harry will be coming: '*I'm sorry*, Harry won't be coming.' (See Ducrot, *Dire et ne pas dire*, p. 92.)

R3: The finesse is a trap or pitfall set in order to cause an opponent to lose face. Ex: In a French classroom, a boy asks his lady teacher to translate the English sentence 'I have the five roses' ('J'ai les cinq roses'), a syntagm* which in French can be treated as being homonymous with 'I have pink breasts.'

FLASHBACK (Fr. *déchronologie*) A narrative reversion to previous events.

Ex: 'Even now, bereft in what might not be for much longer her own kitchen, Helen had to hold back a little yelp of laughter as she remembered the mild way in which he had said, "There's no hurry, is there?" and the incredulity she must have shown as he continued' (Dennis Potter, *Ticket to Ride*, p. 157).

Analogous terms: analepsis (Genette); retro-narrative. See also reminder*.

Antonyms: flash-forward*, anticipation, prolepsis*

R1: Flashbacks differ from simple references to a past event, in which case the narrative present, or allocentric anchorage (see narrative*), does not change. (See, for example, anamnesis*.) In Potter's text, quoted above, 'she remembered' produces a different anchoring, which serves to situate the other tenses used (particularly 'he had said'), placed at the moment when Helen's husband, John, speaks, not at the moment when Helen 'had to hold back' her laughter, and so when she remembers having (probably) had the thought. Which is to say that a flashback supposes that the narrative presents the previous episode as a relived scene. See reactualization*, 7.

The scene is often presented as a short reminiscence, or 'flash,' inserted between two actions and attributed to a character. Thus, by a sort of dreamlike hallucination, Elisabeth, stretched on her servant Léontine's bed, slips back to the time of her childhood and imagines herself back in the house where her aunts raised her:

> It's very strange. Léontine's things are slowly changing ... The paraphernalia of the rich and saintly old spinsters is now spread out on Léontine's dresser ... The treasures of my aunts, the three little Lanouette sisters, are laid out on the white-veined black marble. (A. Hébert, *Kamouraska*, pp. 41–2)

If the retrospective movement is not attributed to a character, then the author must assume responsibility for it, and thus be revealed more or less explicitly, as in folk-tales where the story-teller's interventions are essential.

In *A la recherche du temps perdu*, the author presents himself as a character and forms a kind of *intermediate narrator*. In adventure novels for children, the narrative* sometimes personifies its young readers, allowing them, as it were, to take up a position inside a character who asks questions to which flashbacks and flash-forwards offer answers. One might therefore say that there exists also an *intermediate reader*.

In the detective novel, on the other hand, in which suspense* must be maintained, it is common practice to hide the hero's correct guesses from the reader. Thus, when Lemmy Caution, the intermediate narrator of P. Cheyney's *Poison Ivy*, goes alone into the house occupied by Rudy's gang, he already knows that he can count on Carlotta, Rudy's mistress, a fact about which he carefully omits to inform the reader (see *Poison Ivy*, ch. 8). Genette has named such an omission in a narrated episode *paralipsis*. (For a different meaning of the term, see preterition*.)

R2: A flashback to an already narrated episode is repetitive and constitutes a reminder*.

R3: Flashbacks are rarely disorderly; they substitute logical or psychological order for chronology. Ex: 'By that time, Florentine had begun to watch for the arrival of the young man who, the night before, among many teasing remarks, had led her to understand that he found her pretty' (G. Roy, *Bonheur d'occasion*, p. 11). The scene of the previous evening is recalled just as Florentine 'surprises herself' and then discovers the cause of her surprise.

FLASH-FORWARD The insertion in the story-telling process of a scene which happened after the event currently being related.

Ex: 'The daughter [Mlle de Saint-Loup] whose name and fortune permitted her mother the hope that she would marry a prince of the blood ... *later chose as husband* an obscure man of letters, and thus dragged the family down to a lower rank than that from which she had started' (Proust, *A la recherche du temps perdu*, 3:1028).

Synonyms: *anticipation* (Fr.); prolepsis* (Genette)

Antonyms: flashback*; analepsis (Genette)

Other definitions: See prolepsis*.

R1: The flash-forward skips forward in 'story-time' without affecting the time of narration. It does so by conserving the one while at the same time remodelling (through the use of the adverb 'later') the latter's allocentric anchorage. Its temporality distinguishes it from expectations, forecasts, declarations of intent, and promises (see prophecy*, R1), which, because they are centred in the narrator's deictic 'here and now' and because they are expressed by a future tense, the reader cannot accept as certain. Such expected events may not in fact come to pass. Ex: 'The day will come when the dancer in me will escape by shedding its hard skin, and my real legs will leave on the bed the withered scales rendering them immobile' (A. Hébert, 'L'Ange de Dominique,' in *Le Torrent*, p. 112). Such is the conviction held by a young invalid obsessed by her desire to be a dancer. Dickens foregrounds the difference between flash-forward and forecast in *A Christmas Carol* through the device of the 'Ghost of Christmas yet to come,' who 'shows' Scrooge what will happen if he does not change his ways. In a story told in the past tense, the future becomes the conditional (or 'future in the past') retaining the same temporal value. Delexicalized, or 'prospective' (Benveniste), forms like those which say an event 'was to' or 'was going' to happen are also found. Ex: 'The commercial struggle in the Mediterranean Basin *was not to cease* before the fall of Carthage.'

These two future modes may be conferred on the author, who will then play the prophet within the story. We might call this effect 'pseudo-prophecy,' a novelistic trick whose main advantage is that it leaves unchanged the story-time's allocentric anchorage. Ex [Renata has gone into a convent]: 'She still thought about Mauricio Babilonia, about his oily perfume and the butterflies which fluttered around him, and she *would continue* to think about him every day of her life until that autumn dawn still far off when she *would die* of old age, with an identity different from her own and without having said a word, in some dismal hospital in Cracow' (García Marquez, *One Hundred Years of Solitude*, p. 275).

The use of the flash-forward does not necessarily risk leading the reader astray because of the changes of temporal coherence it introduces into a narrative*. Historians too indulge in prolepsis*, as in the following account of the rivalry between two early explorers of the Canadian North: 'Neither man *would realise* his goal. [James] Knight *was to die* on one of Hudson Bay's bleakest outcroppings; [Henry] Kelsey *would be recalled* to England under a cloud of unsubstantiated suspicion and vanish from the Company's books with no official mention of his thirty-eight year loyal service' (Peter C. Newman, *Company of Adventurers*, p. 293).

R2: The science-fiction novel is anchored in a real present. It would be logical in the genre to use the future tense, the time both of its 'science' and of its 'fiction.' But such is not the common convention. Futurists hold fast to past tenses (the 'past historic' in English, the *passé simple* in French, for example), which are narrative tenses probably because such tenses imply a greater degree of 'reality' than does the future.

Considered carefully, however, such past tenses anchor readers at a point so hypothetical, so far from the future, that they must begin to feel blasé, accustomed as they soon become to the strangest inventions, which seem already dated. The author must therefore present as quite natural inventions which need detailed description*, since such descriptions form essential characteristics of the genre. The use of the future tense would cancel the dilemma; even the present tense might be enough. **Ex:** 'This is a new camera. The picture develops automatically. There's no need to do anything' (P. Claudel, *Protée*, in *Théâtre*, 2:406). Temporal displacement* is scarcely perceptible here. It might even be possible to claim that there is in fact no temporal displacement, given that the camera in question has in fact been invented by the Polaroid Company since Protée spoke these words.

R3: The announcement*, which reduces a flash-forward to a summary, is a declaration of authorial intent; hence the introductory formula: 'It will be seen later that ...' The offer of a curiosity-provoking glimpse of future events is a kind of *bait*, also called a 'hook,' when used as an introductory trailer to films or television dramas. The device is also used constantly in the final picture(s) of weekly cartoon serials, in illustrated story magazines, and at the end of chapters in detective fiction. **Ex:** 'Somehow I gotta hunch that I'm goin' to get some place with this job soon' (P. Cheyney, *Poison Ivy*, end of ch. 6). The bait in this case is only a false lure since there are nine subsequent chapters.

FLIP-FLOP In two syntactically identical verbal sequences, two elements having the same function are exchanged.

Ex:

Yes I have a glass leg
and I have a wooden eye.

J. Prévert, *La Pluie et le beau temps*, p. 9

The device tends to produce a brand-new meaning. **Ex:** 'In the poet's case / The ear speaks, / The mouth listens' (P. Valéry, *Oeuvres*, 2:547). But the most common effect is humorous. **Exx:** 'I have ears to speak and you have a mouth to hear me' (A. Jarry, *Ubu roi*, p. 103); 'Cross the *i*'s and dot the *t*'s.'

Another definition: The displacement of lexemes (e.g., that of the verb by its extension and conversely) during translation; 'blown away,' from 'emporté par le vent' (literally, 'carried off by the wind'). See Vinay and Darbelnet, sect. 88.

R1: The term *chassé-croisé* ('set to partners') comes from the *Larousse du XXe siècle* , where it designates a traditional dance figure: 'two couples placed face to face ... the gentlemen go off right, behind the ladies, while the ladies pass in front of them on their left.'

R2: The flip-flop resembles hypallage*, syntactic scrambling*, and the mistake*. Ex: 'Could a swim duck' (Joyce, *Ulysses*, p. 257). See also permutation*.

R3: The device is possible in narrative*. O. Henry has a marvellous example, as André Breton reports: the meeting of a young servant girl pretending to be a millionairess with an extremely rich heir pretending to be a waiter (*Anthologie de l'humour noir*, p. 247). Equally familiar is the situation of the eponymous heroes in the operetta *Cox and Box*, which Sir Francis Cowley adapted from a farce by J.M. Morton and to which Sullivan contributed the music. Actants* may thus exchange functions, as P. Maranda has shown (in Chabrol, ed., *Sémiotique narrative et textuelle*, p. 133). He proposed the term *flip-flop*, which comes from data-processing, for the figure.

FOREGROUNDING For a device to be *foregrounded* (B. Tomachevsky, in Todorov, ed., *Théorie de la littérature*, p. 300), it must first be false in the rhetorical sense of the term (see false –*); then the author must display with satisfaction the artifice, emphasizing that it forms a trick of the trade.

Ex [in the middle of a description of the hero's mother]: 'Description of physical appearances and mannerisms is one of several standard methods of characterization used by writers of fiction' (John Barth, *Lost in the Funhouse*, pp. 73–4).

Foregrounding

Ex: 'Corollary to the relative fictive law of absolute uniqueness is the *simultaneity effect*, which is to fiction what Miriam Heisenberg's law is to physics. It means that any character can appear simultaneously, in as many fictions as the random may require. This corollary is unsettling and need not concern us other than to note, in passing, that each reader, like each writer, is, from different angles and at different times, in a finite number of different narratives where he is always the same but always different. We call this *après* post-structuralism' (Gore Vidal, *Duluth*, p. 20).

R1: The device is common in contemporary literature. **Ex:** 'At this rate our hero, at this rate our protagonist will remain in the funhouse forever. Narrative ordinarily consists of alternating dramatization and summarization' (J. Barth, *Lost in the Funhouse*, p. 78).

R2: Even mistakes* may be foregrounded. **Ex:** 'Henry was his father's son and it were time for him to go into his father's business of Brummer Striving. It wert a farst dying trade which was fast dying' (John Lennon, *In His Own Write*, p. 66).

R3: Tomachevsky (p. 301) describes as follows the foregrounding of other writers' devices: 'An author seeks to ridicule the opposing literary school, to unveil and destroy its creative system.' This is *pastiche*. See parody*.
   Or else one pours irony* on facile journalistic hyperbole*. **Ex:** 'The highest tide this century (That's the fifteenth I've seen) ... Each highest tide of the century breaks my poor heart' (A. Allais, *La Barbe et autres contes*, pp. 111–12).

R4: Foregrounding a cliché* (see cliché, R4) is a common form of word-play*. **Ex:** 'It's a step forward for the human spirit, always supposing that the human spirit is two-footed like the human body and like it capable of taking steps' (R. Queneau, *Saint-Glinglin*, p. 25). The simplest way to compose a conundrum is to foreground a figurative expression: 'the foot of the mountain ... becomes a conundrum if I ask: "What has a foot and can't walk?"' (A. Jolles, *Formes simples*, pp. 115–16).

R5: Were it intended, involuntary foregrounding would produce wit*. **Ex:** 'Cannabis grows wild on many Himalayan hillsides: it will be difficult to eradicate the evil [the growing of the weed] *at its root*.' (True enough!) See tautology* and counter-pleonasm*.
   A speaker has only to indicate he is conscious of a mistake* for it to be taken as deliberate. **Ex:** 'A boy with such a fine future before him. Before him, naturally, not behind' (R. Queneau, *Saint-Glinglin*, p. 55). *Before him* is redundant. Queneau is here treating a current expression ironically. Foregrounding of quotations* also occurs. See substitution*, R2.

G

GALLICISM A peregrinism* taken from French.

Exx: 'For a moment the gunslinger felt mixed feelings of nostalgia and fear, stitched in with an eerie feeling of *deja vu*' (Stephen King, *The Dark Tower (I): The Gunslinger*, p. 48). Some authors retain the accents* from the French original: '*Déjà vu* haunted me beside the silent, gleaming pipelines' (Douglas B. Lee, 'An Arctic Dilemma,' *National Geographic*, Dec. 1988, p. 864).

Gallicisms include English words deriving from French (like *debonair*, from the Old French *de bon aire*, 'of good disposition'), as well as those which have only recently become part of current English usage (like *couturier, haute couture*) and those for which no exact English equivalent exists: *blasé, naif, ballet, coupon, bistro, café*, etc. M. Kington's *Let's Parler Franglais* and *Let's Parler Franglais Again* (1981, 1982) parody naïve or ignorant combinations of bilingual '*faux-amis*' (see anglicism*), syntactic infelicities, or false cognates. Agatha Christie constructed her stereotypical detective, Hercule Poirot, on gallicisms. As well as possessing several comic characteristics (vanity, fastidiousness) which her narrator believed to be typically Gallic, Poirot has frequent recourse both to French words and to gallicisms in his conversation without, of course, allowing them to impede the reader's desire to know 'whodunnit':

> 'I thank you, no,' said Poirot, rising. 'All my excuses for having deranged you.' ...
> 'The word derange,' I remarked ... 'is applicable to mental disorder only.'
> 'Ah!' cried Poirot, 'never will my English be quite perfect. A curious language. I should then have said disarranged, *n'est-ce pas?*'
> 'Disturbed is the word you had in mind.'
> 'I thank you my friend. The word exact, you are zealous for it.'
> (Agatha Christie, *The Murder of Roger Ackroyd*, p. 180)

R1: Foreign elements penetrate more or less completely. *Café*, in which the French accent* is commonly pronounced in English as a *y*, has thus lost its French sound, and familiar usage sometimes reduces it further, especially in the U.K., to 'caff.' Some gallicisms only involve syntax (e.g., 'the word exact').

When a word exists in both languages but with different meanings the result is a semantic gallicism. **Ex:** 'The *ascension* of Everest' (for 'ascent'). Graphic gallicisms include extraordin*aire*, id*é*al, r*ô*le.

R2: All that is necessary to turn a gallicism into a literary device is that it be expressive. Ex: 'But the Ambassador was unperturbed. "I think otherwise our President will be very hurt. Not personally, but as a *snurb* to France." I *think* he meant snub. It sounded like "snurb," but I don't know what a snurb is' (J. Lynn and A. Jay, *Yes Prime Minister*, 2:90). A gallicism's characteristic connotation is frequently evocative. Ex: *bonne bouche*, a tidbit reserved for last, suggests the delights of French cuisine.

R3: Gallicisms, like anglicisms*, are sometimes a matter of pure (or parodic) snobbery. Ex: 'Sergeant Bird, so wittily nicknamed Oiseau' (Dylan Thomas, *Quite Early One Morning*, p. 50). Fowler (p. 219) gave the following examples which involve the literal translation of French words or idioms: '(to) *jump* or *leap to the eyes, to the foot of the letter, give furiously to think, knight of industry, daughter of joy, gilded youth, the half-world, do one's possible, to return to our muttons, suspicion* (= *soupçon*), and *success of esteem*.' Although some of his examples are no longer current (if indeed they ever were), one sees what he means.

GAULOISERIE 'Joviality in the excess of realism concerning the physical aspect of love' (Sebeok, ed., *Encyclopedic Dictionary of Semiotics*, p. 825); amusing anecdotes of a Gallic nature; that is, frank, free, and 'spicy' (*Harrap's New Standard French and English Dictionary*).

Ex: 'And I have a heart as big / As a Damascene lady's ass' (G. Apollinaire, *Oeuvres poétiques*, p. 53).

Other names: risqué stories, smut

R1: See slang*, R1; spoonerism*; intonation*; and vulgarism*, R1.

GEMINATION Doubling of the first syllable in formations like *geegee, bêbête*, and *fifille* (Marouzeau, second meaning). See also Robert.

Ex: 'The jejune jesuit' (Joyce, *Ulysses*, p. 4).

Other definitions: '*Rhet*. The immediate repetition of a word or phrase, or the using of a pair of synonymous expressions, for the purpose of rhetorical effect [e.g., "My God, my God"]. *Gram*. a. The doubling of an originally single consonant sound. b. The doubling of a letter in the orthography of a word' (*OED*). Marouzeau proposes the terms *dittology* and *dittography* to cover the two forms within the grammatical concept. Double consonants belong among the many graphic forms of emphasis*.

R1: Gemination, like aphaeresis*, is a characteristic of childish language. Exx: 'beddybyes'; 'geegee'; 'Jacob Two-Two and the dinosaur' (Mordecai Richler). It therefore is a common way of forming diminutives. Exx: Jon-Jon, Lulu, Fifi.

R2: Gemination easily takes on pejorative overtones, as in the example quoted from Joyce.

GENERALIZATION A generalization, in the term's current meaning, extends over a large number of cases an observation which has only been verified in a few, sometimes only in a single one. (*Ab uno disce omnes.*)

Ex: 'All the swans I've seen are white. All swans are white.'

R1: Skilful generalization is related to scientific induction and moves fiction towards applied psychology. Ex: 'A classical understanding sees the world primarily as underlying form itself. A romantic understanding sees it primarily in terms of immediate appearance' (Robert Pirsig, *Zen and the Art of Motorcycle Maintenance*, p. 61). But in rhetoric as in everyday conversation, the abuse of generalization is the rule because speakers argue emotionally. Exx: 'The best students always *are* flunking. *Every* good teacher knows that' (ibid., p. 124); '... in fact *any* two frames of reference can be made to yield a comic effect of sorts by hooking them together and infusing a drop of malice. The frames may even be defined by such abstract concepts as "time" and "weather": the absent-minded professor who tries to read the temperature from his watch or to tell the time from a thermometer is comic' (Arthur Koestler, 'Humour and Wit,' *Encyclopaedia Britannica* [1974], 20:741).

R2: When pushed to absurd limits, generalization becomes a rhetorical trick, a device for securing emphasis*: this is the pseudo-generalization. Ex (a current example incorporating antimetabole*): 'When the going gets tough, the tough get going.' Ex: 'There is, in fact, no formal difference between inability to define and stupidity' (R. Pirsig, *Zen and the Art of Motorcycle Maintenance*, p. 185).

R3: It is generalization of a personal subject which produces distancing*. See also epiphonema*, other def., and monologue*, R1.

R4: Generalizations are obtained by combining actualizing terms (e.g., *the, all, each, every*) with abstract lexemes. Ex: 'Yet each man kills the thing he loves ...' (O. Wilde, 'The Ballad of Reading Gaol'). Concrete images* also produce them. Ex: 'There are few moments in a man's existence when he experiences so much ludicrous distress, or meets with so little charitable commiseration, as when he is in pursuit of his own hat' (Dickens, *Pickwick Papers*, ch. 4). Conversely, *particularizations* come from sentences which begin with concrete terms and often with actualizing forms like *a, some, my, your, I think, It seems to me*, or *In my opinion*. However, the proposition which follows such a form may remain general in scope.

R5: Generalizations tend towards reductionism. Ex: 'The whole of

Hegel's *Phenomenology of Mind* is nothing more than the description and history of the various figures of unfortunate consciousness' (J.-M. Palmier, *Sur Marcuse*, pp. 122–3). This is no mere attenuation*, as occurs in the case of concretization* (see concretization, R1); the generalization here distorts the datum.

R6: Diegetic generalizations consist in narrating only once something which happened several times. G. Genette showed the frequency of what he calls 'iterative narrative*' in Proust. Ex: 'For a long time, I used to go to bed early.' *Iterative* or *frequentative* aspects of narrative* are marked in English and in French by adverbs which define the overall duration, rhythm of occurrence, and extension of repeated units (e.g., 'last year,' 'every other day,' 'each summer'). The 'repetitive' imperfect tense, if used with sufficient frequency, marks the change from indirect to direct speech (see narrative*), within which framework the verb becomes a general past tense.

GESTURE A signifying movement, capable of announcing, illustrating, or replacing a sentence, or of serving to describe or interpret something.

Ex:

INT. TRAIN. DAY
The compartment is full, six passengers. Four of them are 'LOCALS,' including one pretty GIRL. The fifth is COMISKY, an American salesman ... COMISKY concentrates on the GIRL, who is wearing a fur hat ... COMISKY takes her hat and puts it on his head. He prevents her from snatching it back.
COMISKY: I will take you home to America. I love you. Mrs Comisky will learn to love you, give her time.
(He brushes aside interruptions and defends the hat.)
I love you. Is this man your husband? Forget him.
(He kisses her hand gallantly. She snatches her hat back. He takes a swig from a proffered bottle.)

Tom Stoppard, *Neutral Ground, a Screenplay*,
in *The Dog It Was That Died and Other Plays*, p. 111

Ex: 'Casting my eyes along the street at a certain point of my progress, I beheld Trabb's boy approaching, lashing himself with an empty blue bag ... suddenly the knees of Trabb's boy smote together, his hair uprose, his cap fell off, he trembled violently in every limb, staggered out into the road, and crying to the populace, "Hold me! I'm so frightened!" feigned to be in a proxysm of terror and contrition, occasioned by the dignity of my appearance. As I passed him, his teeth loudly chattered in his head, and with every mark of extreme humiliation, he prostrated himself in the dust' (Dickens, *Great Expectations*, ch. 30).

R1: There are 'gestures' which only involve the face: these involve mimicry or *dumb show*. Others are too far removed from the subject described to have any meaning except in the mind of an observer. Ex: 'A person who watched the interview between the dead and the living, scrupled not to affirm, that, at the instant when the clergyman's features were disclosed, the corpse had slightly shuddered, rustling the shroud and muslin cap, though the countenance retained the composure of death' (N. Hawthorne, 'The Minister's Black Veil').

R2: *Mime* is theatre without words. When the action is comic (as in the Italian theatre), it is pantomime, in that term's extended meaning. Interjections* partake of both gestures and words. See also monologue*, R1; parataxis*, R2; and symbol*, 2.

R3: Some codification of gestures seems to have established a more or less international language, particularly in the case of 'pre-linguistic' gestures, which signify attitudes underlying sentences: see monologue*, R1. Thus a reader of Stoppard's screenplay may decode without great difficulty movements indicated simply by the generic expression (gesture) and which remain undescribed. R.L. Birdwhistell (*Introduction to Kinesics* [1952]) and Desmond Morris (*Manwatching: A Field Guide to Human Behaviour* [1980]) offer explanations of a large corpus of international gestures.

R4: All gestures, even the smallest, such as moving closer or further away and staring or averting the eyes, modify the respective situations of the speakers. Exx: see celebration*, R1; euphemism*, R2; excuse*, R1; exorcism*; and reactualization*, 2.

GIBBERISH (Fr. *baragouin*) Phonetic or lexical deformation, which aims at creating the impression that one is speaking a foreign language, whereas in reality the text is decodable by reference to one's native language.

Ex: ' "You zee," said he, "it iz te bess vor zit still; and now" you shall know who I pe. Look at me! zee! I am te Angel ov te Odd!" ' (E.A. Poe, 'The Angel of the Odd'). See also reactualization*, 5.

Other definition: Incorrect and unintelligible language (*Concise Oxford Dictionary*; *Petit Robert*). This broader sense is current (see phoebus*).

Synonyms: counterfeit language; hybridization (see peregrinism*, R3); jargon* (in the broad sense)

R1: The simplest form of gibberish occurs as a device of peregrinated pronunciation. Ex: 'Wurn dayee abaout meeddayee Ahee got eentoo a buss ...' (R. Queneau, 'For ze Frrensh,' in *Exercises in Style*, p. 169). Inspector Clouseau, the character created by Peter Sellars in the series of films involving the 'Pink Panther,' also spoke in this way ('I haave a buuuhmp on my 'ead,' etc.).

R2: There exists a *counter-gibberish* that consists in conferring the appearance of a particular language on a text which in reality is only decodable by reference to some other language or set of procedures. In chapter 6 of Rabelais's *Pantagruel*, for instance, a student of 'l'alme, incylt et célèbre académie que l'on vocite Lutèce' speaks a Latinized form of French.

More subtle is the 'langage paralloïdre' invented by A. Martel (reviewed by E. Souriau, in the *Revue d'esthétique* [1965], pp. 38–9). Ex: 'Le Mirivis des naturgies' means 'le Miroir Merveilleux du Visage des Surgies de la Nature' ('the marvellous mirror of the Face of Nature's Surges'). This is glossolalia*.

R3: Texts produced by automatic writing, from which the intention to communicate almost disappears, allow expression of an instance of the Self (or Not-Self) analogous perhaps to the instance which surfaces in glossolalia*.

GLOSSOLALIA Verbigeration* of a religious nature. It occurs in a situation and before a public which confer on it a function of prophecy* or prayer*. Although unintelligible and structureless, the unintelligibility is made intelligible at the level of the enunciation*, both from the point of view of production and reception. The perception of meaning* in such a discourse* signals membership of the charismatic movement.

Expression: 'the gift of tongues' (Paul of Tarsus, *Epistles*)

R1: Literary examples include Lucky's speech in act 2 of Beckett's *Waiting for Godot*. Some poetic texts may come close to glossolalia. Ex:

> In the world which He has created according to his will Blessed
> Praised
> Magnified Lauded Exalted the Name of the Holy One Blessed is He!
> Allen Ginsberg, 'Hymmnn,' in
> Ellmann, ed., *The Oxford Book of American Verse*, p. 928

R2: See also gibberish*, R2, and pseudo-language*, R3.

GRADATIO 'The presentation of a succession of ideas or feelings in such an order that what follows always expresses a little more or a little less than what precedes, in accordance with either a mounting or descending progression' (Fontanier, p. 333). See also Littré, Marouzeau, Morier, Preminger, and Robert.

Exx: 'To strive, to seek, to find, and not to yield' (Tennyson, 'Ulysses');

'Let's face it. Let's talk sense to the American people. Let's tell them that there are no gains without pains' (Adlai Stevenson, speech).

Synonyms: For mounting *gradatio*: the marching figure; ascendus; methalemsis (Lanham); the climbing figure; climax (Joseph, Lanham, Lausberg, Preminger); progression; snowball (Bergson, *Le Rire*, p. 61). For descending *gradatio*: anticlimax* (Dr Johnson, Preminger, Quillet); bathos* (Pope, Preminger).

Other definition: See cadence* (rhythmic *gradatio*).

R1: *Gradatio* is a device fundamental to amplification* in periodic discourse*. It belongs to the sublime style (see grandiloquence*, R1, and period*, R4). Ex (using *gradatio* with *sorites* [see reasoning*, R1], Rosalind foregrounds the figure by virtually defining it to Orlando): 'For your brother and my sister no sooner met but they looked; no sooner look'd but they lov'd; no sooner lov'd but they sigh'd; no sooner sigh'd but they ask'd one another the reason; no sooner knew the reason but they sought the remedy: and in these degrees have they made a pair of stairs to marriage' (Shakespeare, *As You Like It*, 5.2.35).

R2: *Gradatio* is also a way of ordering items in an enumeration* or accumulation*. Ex: 'It is a sin to *bind* a Roman citizen, a crime to *scourge* him, little short of the most unnatural murder to *put him to death*; what then shall I call his *crucifixion*?' (Cicero, quoted by Quintilian, *Institutes of Oratory*, 8.4.4.).

R3: Despite its apparent usefulness, the distinction between mounting and descending *gradatio* is often ill-founded because it applies also to the signifier which sometimes descends when the signified mounts in intensity, as Spitzer shows (*Etudes de style*, p. 282) with regard to Racine's line 'I saw him, I blushed, I paled at the sight' (*Phèdre*, 1.3). The stylistic crescendo serves to represent a decrescendo in Phèdre's emotional mood. In the case of intensity of expression, practically the only examples found are climaxes.

R4: Morier distinguishes various types of *gradatio*, notably: *rhythmic gradatio* (e.g., the rhopalic period whose clauses get longer and longer); *numerical* (e.g., groups of two, three, ten, etc., syllables or feet); *intensive* (e.g., *love, cherish, adore*); and *referential*, by means of which the reader is predisposed to accept terms that otherwise might be found 'too' original.

R5: *Gradatio* leads to extravagant* comparisons. If, however, the final term's value opposes those expressed in the rest of the series, the result is an anticlimax*, or, in other words, bathos*. A transition* (see transition, R1) may be disguised by a *gradatio*. See also variation*, R2.

GRANDILOQUENCE Lofty, grandiose speech or language.

Ex: '... Mr. Micawber rising. "I have no scruple in saying, in the presence of our friends here, that I am a man who has, for some years, contended against the pressure of pecuniary difficulties ... Sometimes I have risen superior to my difficulties. Sometimes my difficulties have – in short, have floored me. There have been times when I have administered a succession of facers to them; there have been times when they have been too many for me, and I have given in, and said to Mrs. Micawber in the words of Cato, 'Plato, thou reasonest well. It's all up now. I can show fight no more.' But at no time in my life," said Mr. Micawber, "have I enjoyed a higher degree of satisfaction than in pouring my griefs (if I describe difficulties, chiefly arising out of warrants of attorney and promissary notes at two and four months, by that word) into the bosom of my friend Copperfield" ' (Dickens, *David Copperfield*, ch. 17).

Analogous terms: bombast; pompous, turgid, or flatulent style; highfalutin, declamatory, or affected language. Pathos is overblown emotion, the 'pornography of emotion,' according to the *Los Angeles Times* (16 Mar. 1988, p. 1). See also amplification*.

Antonyms: concinnity; anti-Ciceronian style. *Concinitas* was a Latin ideal proposed by Cicero against rhetorical embellishment. Anti-Ciceronian style was a movement begun by the sixteenth-century humanists Justus Lipsius and Etienne Dolet, in reaction against the sometimes gratuitous imitation of Cicero practised by other humanists. As a tautegorical ideal, anti-Ciceronian style refused everything non-functional, but without becoming terse to the point of laconicism. (The *OED* calls 'tautegorical' a nonce-word attributed to Coleridge [*Aids to Reflection in the Formation of a Manly Character*], 199): 'The base of symbols and symbolic expressions: the nature of which as always tautegorical [i.e., expressing the same subject but with a difference] in contra-distinction from metaphors and similtudes that are always allegorical [i.e., expressing a different subject but with a resemblance].')

R1: The ancients recognized three types of discourse*: the *grand, middle,* and *low* or *plain* styles (as well as the coarse or vulgar styles, which were mentioned but dismissed as unworthy of examination). Rhetors taught, as means of attaining the grand style: anaphora*, allegory*, prosopopoiea*, epitheton*, euphemism*, *gradatio*, and hyperbole*. (In *On Style*, the Greek critic Demetrius offered in addition an *elegant* variety, somewhere between the grand and middle types. Modern linguistics has only retained three levels* of language, having eliminated the grand style in favour of the *sustained*.) Ex: 'A tenured professor could commit the Sin against the Holy Ghost and get away with it, if he could find the right lawyer' (R. Davies, *The Lyre of Orpheus*, p. 116).

Those wishing to acquire the middle style were content with anadiplosis*, comparison*, and apostrophe* since they aimed neither at embellishment nor idealization.

For a long time, bombast was merely excessively grand style. The question remains, however, as to where 'excess' begins. From the seventeenth to the nineteenth century, extraordinary elevation of tone was considered normal in moments of great importance. As an example, here is a period* proposed in 1783 as a model of a harmonious sentence (Sir William Temple is addressing Lady Essex on the death of her child):

> I was once in hope, that what was so violent could not be long: but, when I observed your grief to grow stronger with age, and to increase, like a stream the farther it ran; when I saw it draw out to such unhappy consequences, and to threaten, no less than your child, your health and your life, I could no longer forbear this endeavour, nor end it without begging of you, for God's sake and for your own, for your children and your friends, your country and your family, that you would no longer abandon yourself to a disconsolate passion; but that you would at length awaken your piety, give way to your prudence, or, at least, rouse the invincible spirit of the Percys, that never yet shrunk at any disaster. (Quoted by Hugh Blair, in *Lectures on Rhetoric and Belles Lettres*, lecture 13, note).

The disappearance, begun in the past and still proceeding, of classical oratorical style means that nowadays any attempt at grand style will be dismissed as grandiloquent. Already, in 1783, Blair discussing what he thought two forms of dramatic bombast, 'fustian and rant,' declared: 'Shakespeare, a great but incorrect genius is not unexceptionable here. Dryden and Lee, in their tragedies, abound with it' (ibid., p. 49).

R2: Grandiloquence is the simplest means of producing macrology, that is, redundancy* without repetition*. See the example from Joyce under verbiage*, R2.

R3: Grandiloquence which cannot be sustained becomes ridiculous, as Mr Micawber's speeches reveal. See incoherence*, R3, and persiflage*, R1.

GRAPHISM (neol. in English) A feature peculiar to an individual's writing. See Robert.

Exx: the different ways of crossing the *t*; the slope of letters

Ex [Bloom is thinking about disguising his handwriting]: 'Remember write Greek ees' (Joyce, *Ulysses*, p. 229).

Analogous terms: handwriting, idiographeme, idiography (a set of idiographemes). An *autograph* is a text entirely in the author's hand.

R1: The shape of the letters of the alphabet has evolved over the centuries and may well have derived from pictograms*. Ex: the letter *A*, which lay on its side in Phoenician, was inverted in Cretan and so had the same shape as the head of an ox; now, an 'ox' was called *alf* (cf. *alef* in Hebrew) and began with the sound *a*. It seems that the alphabet may have been formed in much the same way as it is taught nowadays to children: '*p* is for pipe,' and so on.

The shapes of the characters became stylized, first in the copyists' shops; then, thanks to the printing press, they became more precise and subsequently more varied. There are models for about 1500 different sets in the *Encyclopedia of Type Faces* by Jaspert, Berry, and Johnson. Within each set, different fonts (the various sizes of characters measured in points), small (lowercase) letters, capital (uppercase) letters, and characters in roman or italic and normal or bold-faced type may be chosen.

There thus exists a graphism for printing. The Letraset Company sells transparencies by means of which different characters and symbols* may easily be traced. Computers with 'enhanced' keyboards and character-composing functions make possible, in combination with laser or dot-matrix printers, various sets of graphisms. Lumitype, which can imitate characters of any shape, allows for the composition of whole volumes based on a specimen page of an author's handwriting. See J. Peignot, *De l'écriture à la typographie*, p. 147.

R2: A signature is *the* graphism, *par excellence*. Certain artists reduce it to initials or to a *monogram*; that is, to one, two, or three letters, usually the initial letters of their first name(s) and surname. In a monogram, however, the same stem or curve serves two or three different letters, or the letters of a proper name may be interwoven into a single character-group. Here are samples of initials and monograms taken from Fr. Goldstein, *Monogram Lexicon*:

W. W.   W. W.   W W   W   WW   WW

Many institutions, printing houses, magazines, and commercial firms have their own monogram or initials (in the past their coat of arms and seal). **Exx:**

These stylized designs become emblematic of the institution. They are denotative in their own right and possess very high iconicity. Analogous term: logo or logotype, a '(single piece of type bearing) non-heraldic device chosen as badge of organisation and used in advertisements, on notepaper, etc.' (*Concise Oxford Dictionary*). See Fr.-M. Ricci and Ferrari, *Top Symbols and Trade Marks of the World* (1973), 7 vols. Others are more gratuitous or contingent, as may be seen from present-day avant-garde typography or from the illuminated capital letters in medieval manuscripts.

R3: The use of idiography need not exclude aesthetic considerations, as Chiang Yee showed for Chinese characters (*L'Ecriture et la psychologie des peuples*, fig. 4). Graphisms may also bring about remotivations*. Ex: Croe$u$.

R4: Handwriting in which individual strokes are shapeless and illegible is said to be spidery.

R5: See gemination*, other def.; graphic juxtaposition*, R1; onomatopoeia*, R2; and pictogram*.

GRAPHY A way of representing words through writing; an element of such representation.

Graphy: a writing-system. There is *phonetic graphy*, which is adapted as closely as possible to pronunciation; *customary* or *traditional graphy*, which no longer reflects pronunciation (compare *–ough* in 'rough,' 'through,' 'though,' etc.); and *etymological graphy* (as in 'doubt,' in which the *b* is intended as a reminder of the Latin *dubitare*). Exx: see equivoque*, R3; onomatopoeia*, R1; and interjection*.

Analogous terms: *spelling*, with a normative connotation; *grapheme*, 'an element of a graphic system' (*qu*, for example; see Crystal); *literary graphy*, an expressive modification of customary spelling (e.g., the replacement of *yes* by *yeah* and *you* by *yuh* or *y'* to draw attention to the reduction of *yes* and *you* in current spoken language)

R1: Graphy permits distinctions between homonyms (see homonymy*). Literary graphy makes possible allusion* and is related to approximation*. Ex: ' "That's the pint, sir," interposed Sam; "out with it, as the father said to the child, wen he swallowed a farden" ' (Ch. Dickens, *Pickwick Papers*, ch. 12).

R2: Certain graphic forms attempt to turn peregrinisms* into English, sometimes by deriding them. Ex: 'Mademoiselle from Armenteers, / Hasn't been kissed in forty years, / Hinky dinky, parley-voo' ('Red Rowley,' Song of the Great War, 1914–18). The same is true in French. Exx: 'bisness' (Montherlant, *Romans*, p. 908); 'piqueupe' (Queneau, *Pierrot mon ami*, p. 77). See anglicism*, R1; and gallicism*.

R3: Some dadaists, in their attacks on words, inserted in their poems what they called 'motscollésensemble' or 'wordstucktogether.' See graphic juxtaposition*.

R4: Hyphens are graphic signs sometimes used independently of oral usage, which shows that writing-systems have a certain autonomy with respect to speech. **Ex:** 'A *little used* car is not necessarily the same as a *little-used* car or a *hard working* man as a *hard-working* man or *extra judicial duties* as *extra-judicial duties*' (Fowler, under 'hyphens' in *A Dictionary of Modern English Usage*). The semiotic functions of some graphic arrangements were studied by J. Bertin in *Sémiologie graphique*. See also 'graphic prosody' (under line* of poetry or verse).

R5: Certain typographical devices allow attention to be focused on the value of particular words. **Ex:** 'The poodle grew *grew* **grew** GREW' (cited by Angenot, p. 510). See typographical variation*; pictogram*; and situational* signs, 1.

R6: For polygraphy, see paragram*, R4. Cases of graphic remotivation* sometimes occur.

H

HAPLOGRAPHY A mistake* consisting in writing once what should have been written twice. A copyist skips a segment of the text (several letters or lines), deceived by the identical nature of the first and last elements in two passages.

Exx: What I owe your solitude [solicitude]; he prefers classism [classicism].

Analogous terms: homoioteleuton* (see homoioteleuton, other def.); a *desideratum* is a lacuna, something lacking but needed or desirable in a copy of a manuscript.

R1: Haplography is similar to haplology* (see haplology, R1).

R2: *Dittography* (OED) consists in writing an element within a segment twice. **Ex:** statististically [statistically].

HAPLOLOGY Uttering once what should be uttered twice.

Ex: *Febr'y* for *February*

R1: Some cases of haplology are purely graphic and cannot be sus-

tained in prunciation [pronunciation]. These are example of haplography*.

R2: Haplology is close to crasis* insofar as syllables brought together
by the omission are alike in some way. Ex: 'The authority of interpre-
tive [i.e., interpretative] communities' (subtitle of *Is There a Text in This
Class?* by Stanley Fish).

R3: See parechesis*, R4.

HARMONY The effect produced on the ear by certain correspondences between groups of sounds. If the corresponding groups follow
one another closely or are arranged symmetrically, a delicate ear, with
a little training, discerns and finds satisfaction in the correspondence.
See M. Grammont, *Le Vers français*, p. 386.

Ex:

> Then the camel men cursing and grumbling
> And running away, and wanting their liquor and women,
> And the night fires going out, and the lack of shelters,
> And the cities hostile and the towns unfriendly
> And the villages dirty and charging high prices
> T.S. Eliot, 'Journey of the Magi', 11–15

R1: In the case of the echo* effect, comparisons are made on the basis
of identical sounds; in that of harmony, all vocalic sounds come into
play combining the harmonics ('sounds whose frequencies are mul-
tiples of the same base frequency' [*Lexis*]) of the elements which form
them. They constitute 'dyads' (two vowels) or 'triads' (three vowels) of
partly different sounds.

R2: Harmony may also be due to rhythm*. In the example from Eliot
quoted above, it is the anaphoric function of *and* followed by the
parallel set of present participles which partly creates a harmonious
effect. In addition, anaphora* combines with polysyndeton* in the
metrical form of the verse. Group MU envisage such figures of rhythmical repetition* as the basis of harmony in poetry: '... harmony and
metrics are systematic groups of practices and rules, two vast syntactic
figures that proceed by addition and repetition' (*A General Rhetoric*,
p. 75). See cadence* and period*, R2 and R4. If harmony prevails over
meaning, the result is musication* (neol.).

HARMONY (IMITATIVE) Arrangements of words into a sound
which seeks to imitate some natural noise*. See Fontanier (p. 392), Le
Clerc (p. 186), Marouzeau, Quillet, Morier, and Robert.

Ex: 'The moan of doves in immemorial elms, / And murmuring of innumerable bees' (Tennyson, 'The Princess,' 202–3).

Synonyms: harmonism (Fontanier); phonometaphor (Guiraud)

R1: This figure may be achieved by the use of alliteration*, onomatopoeia*, (rhythmic) division, sentence-construction, cacophony*, etc. Graphics may reinforce it as in *calligrammes** or the different effects seen in the speech-bubbles in cartoon strips. Exx: 'The crooked skirt swinging, whack by whack by whack' (Joyce, *Ulysses*, p. 48); 'Howl, howl, howl, howl' (Shakespeare, *King Lear*, 5.3.257).

R2: When tempo is imitated, the more exact term is *imitative rhythm*. Ex: 'Half a league, half a league, / Half a league onward' (Tennyson, 'The Charge of the Light Brigade'). The gallop is in the verse.

HEAD-TO-TAIL A principal lexeme receives a secondary lexeme's function and vice versa, thanks to the necessary transferences.

Ex: 'It's his lost wallet that makes him mad' (instead of 'the loss of his wallet').

Analogous terms: hypallage*, transferred epithet, *sicilia amissa* (Deloffre), lexematic inversion*

R1: We have taken the expression 'head-to-tail' from the analysis of syntagms* into their immediate constituent parts. In such analysis, the 'head' is the part of the syntagm having the same function as the whole syntagm itself (Dubois et al., *Dictionnaire de linguistique*); thus, for example, the noun is the 'head' in such groups as noun + adjective, noun + noun-complement, or noun + relative clause. The other part, or modifier, is here considered to be the 'tail' of the group into which inversion* introduces a 'head-to-tail' transfer.

This type of inversion is common in metaphor*. Ex: 'the pebbles of noise' (Eluard, *Oeuvres complètes*, 1:230).

R2: If the secondary lexeme is more abstract than the principal one (which remains the syntagmatic node from a psychological, if not from the syntactic, point of view), the effect is an abstraction* (see abstraction, R3); if it is more concrete, a concretization results.

HENDIADYS One by means of two; 'twinning'; 'Siamese twins' (Fowler); 'a combination of addition, substitution, and (usually) arrangement; the addition of a conjunction between a word (noun, adjective, verb) and its modifier (adjective, adverb, infinitive), the substitution of this word's grammatical form for that of its modifier, and usually rearrangement so that the modifier follows the word:

"furious sound" becomes "sound and fury" ' (Quinn, p. 102). See also Cuddon, Frye, Marouzeau, Morier, and Preminger.

Exx: 'try and go' for 'try to go'; 'She and her lips were recounting ...' (Eluard, in Aragon et al., *Dictionnaire abrégé du surréalisme*, under *lèvres*). Even when each of the elements clearly implies the other, the device calls attention to them separately.

R1: The reformulation does not always produce a single syntagm*, but the co-ordinated 'twins' may seem slightly gratuitous or caused by the formal constraints of verse. **Ex:** 'Summertime and the livin' is easy' (Gershwin, *Porgy and Bess*), rather than 'living in summertime.'

R2: Possible also is the opposite of hendiadys: the formulation, by means of subordination, into a single syntagm* of two elements which might be co-ordinated. **Ex:** 'the thick starchiness of [Antoinette's] petticoats' (M.-C. Blais, *Une Saison dans la vie d'Emmanuel*, p. 80) instead of 'the thickness and starchiness ...'

HIATUS The break between two vowels coming together not in the same syllable; the clash is heightened if the two are close or similar.

Exx: 'And grew on China imperceptibly / Rococo images of Saint and Saviour' (W.H. Auden, 'Macao'); ' ' "And arter all, my lord," says he, "it's a amable weakness" ' (Dickens, *Pickwick Papers*, ch. 23). Clearly, the shock produced by *a-a* is greater than that of *a-i* or *o-i*.

Other definitions: 'a gap which destroys the completeness of a sentence or verse' (Preminger); 'discontinuity, a rupture in narrative continuity' (Fage and Pagano, eds., *Dictionnaire des media*). These usages are figurative.

R1: Although the prohibition forbidding hiatus in classical poetry remains well known, that hiatus has little exercised either English or French grammarians indicates that the two languages tolerate the phenomenon. However, in English, the indefinite article, for instance, is usually altered to avoid hiatus: 'an apple.'

R2: Isocrates seems to have been the first to denounce hiatus as cacophonous (see cacophony*, R3) in the fourth century B.C., followed by the Romans and later by the French Academy from the seventeenth to the twentieth century. When it is regarded as dissonance*, it may be eliminated by means of aphaeresis*, crasis*, elision*, or synaloephe (Elkhadem).

R3: See caesura*, R1, and line* of poetry, 2.

HOMOIOTELEUTON Placing at the end of sentences, clauses, or phrases words having the same final syllable or syllables.

Homoioteleuton

Ex: 'The best actors in the world, either for tragedy, comedy, history, pastoral, pastoral-comical, historical-pastoral, tragical-historical, tragical-comical-historical-pastoral ...' (Shakespeare, *Hamlet*, 2.2.414).

Synonyms: rhymed prose (Morier); 'an early form of end rhyme' (Elkhadem)

R1: Homoioteleuton is nothing more than 'prose-rhyme' (Brian Vickers, *In Defence of Rhetoric*, p. 263) or assonance* (see assonance, R2) in prose. **Ex:** 'All books are divisible into two classes, the books of the hour, and the books of all time ... There are good books for the hour and good ones for all time; bad books for the hour, and bad ones for all time' (John Ruskin, *Sesame and Lilies* [1865], 'Lecture 1').

R2: Most modern rhetorical theorists (Dumarsais, Fontanier, Joseph, Lanham, Lausberg, etc.) make the ancient distinction between homoioteleuton and homoioptoton. Homoioptoton consists in placing words with similar case-endings near one another. However, both Joseph and Lanham point out that the distinction 'practically disappears' (Joseph) in English 'since the question of inflections is not crucial' (Lanham). Leech (pp. 82–3) modernizes this distinction in his definition: 'the repetition of the same derivational or inflectional ending on different words.' He gives the following as an example:

– Not for these I raise
The song of thanks and praise;
But for these obstinate question*ings*
Of sense and outward things,
Fall*ings* from us, vanish*ings*,
Blank misgiv*ings* of a creature
Moving about in worlds not realized.
Wordsworth, 'Ode: Intimations of Immortality'

R3: Homoioteleuton points up antitheses* (see antithesis, R4) and enumerations*, as in the example from Shakespeare already quoted.

R4: The French neo-classical critic Jean-François Marmontel (1723–99) advised against 'inopportune' homoioteleuton (i.e., at the middle and end of a line): 'In our poetry, we make it a law to avoid consonance in two hemistiches; the same rule should be observed at the rests in a period' (*Oeuvres*, 8:31). However, such internal/external homoioteleuton delights English-speaking audiences when it occurs in the patter-songs of Gilbert and Sullivan:

A very delectable, highly respectable,
Threepenny bus young man!
Patience [1881], libretto by W.S. Gilbert

HOMONYMY In the *Game of Words*, Willard Espy lists (pp. 126–32) a 'homonym lexicon' of some six hundred items in English. In French, about a thousand words have two, three, four, or more homonyms (other words with the same pronunciation). Writing usually permits distinctions between them.

Ex: 'Blest be that beast who, though he preys on others, / Gives praise to God, and prays all beasts be brothers' (Espy, p. 125).

W. Redfern, in his study of word-play* in English and French, makes the following relevant distinctions between words similar in form and different in sense: 'Some distinctions are unavoidable, for instance that between polysemy (one word used in different senses like "doublet") and "homophony" (several words distinct in meaning but sounding alike); or between homonyms, single words for different things, and their opposite synonyms, different words for single things ... Further distinctions include heteronyms, words identical in spelling, but different in both sound and meaning (tear = weeping, tear = rip) ... and homographs, words identical in spelling and pronunciation, but having different origins and meanings (as in race = rush and nation)' (Redfern, *Puns*, pp. 17–18). Such coincidences produce various devices:
– counting-out rhymes. Ex: ' "Fire, fire" said Mrs. McGuire, "Where, where?" said Mrs. Ware' (Hesbois, p. 29).
– echo-effects. Ex: see the one in the example from Espy quoted above.
– surrealistic similarities like those quoted by Redfern from Laforgue: ' "*violouptés à vif*" – "rapeture on edge"; "*sangsuel*" – which translates as "leecherous" ' (Redfern, *Puns*, p. 90).
– comic comparisons. Ex: 'I met a wise antelope, born in a zoo; / And I wish that I knew what that new gnu knew' (Espy, p. 125).

R1: Homonyms differ from diaphora*, in which the passage is not from one word to another but from one meaning* to another possessed by the same word. However, see diaphora*, R4.

R2: If two syntagms* are pronounced identically, homonymy becomes homophony in the broad sense. (The restricted sense is defined as follows: 'Two signs are said to be homophones when they are used to represent the same sound. E.g. *s* and *t* in *torsion* and *portion*' [Marouzeau]. Etymologically, *homophone* means 'having the same sound'; homonyms are also homophones.) Ex: First man: 'My wife's gone to the West Indies.' Second man: 'Oh! Jamaica?' First man: 'No – she went of her own accord.'

R3: Proper names do not escape homonymy. Ex: The various individuals named Henry Ford have to be distinguished by their place in the dynastic line (I, II, III, etc.). If someone else possesses your features rather than your name, you have a double or *look-alike*. Sentences may also be homophonous. See 'holorhymes,' under equivoque*, R3. For partial homonymy, see approximation* and paronomasia*, R2.

R4: Homophony and homonymy also occur in snatches of overheard foreign speech. **Ex:** 'In fractured French, "*de rigueur*" can be nothing but a two-masted schooner, "*au contraire*," "away [in the country] for the weekend," and "*à la carte*," "on the wagon" ' (Espy, p. 112).

R5: Word-play* based on homonymy is characteristic of preciosity (see baroquism*, R2).

HUMOUR The reason for the difficulty often felt by those attempting to define humour is that the device or set of devices in question expresses one's feeling concerning the mind's limitations and the banality of objects. Humour may be defined as the conscious acceptance of the difference between an ideal state of affairs and reality, a difference unhesitatingly emphasized as a means of extricating oneself from it.

Ex: 'I remember sharing the last of my moist buns with a boy and a lion. Tawny and savage, with cruel nails and capacious mouth, the little boy tore and devoured. Wild as seedcake, ferocious as a hearth-rug, the depressed and verminous lion nibbled like a mouse at his half a bun and hiccupped in the sad dusk of his cage' (Dylan Thomas, 'Holiday Memory,' in *Quite Early One Morning*, p. 22).

See also flip-flop*, R3; hyperbole*, R4; portrait*, R2; substitution*; and truism*, R2.

R1: Humour and wit* belong together. Humour may be exercised against any set of ideals, fine sentiments, or high thoughts (see the poetry of Jules Laforgue, Lewis Carrroll, or Edward Lear). **Ex:** 'Samuel Johnson, the story goes, ran into a college friend he had not seen for forty years, and in the course of their conversation they got to comparing their lives. "You are a philosopher," the man said to Dr. Johnson. "I have tried in my time, too, to be a philosopher, but I don't know how; cheerfulness was always breaking through" ' (*The Philosophy of Laughter and Humour*, ed. John Morreal, p. 1).

Humorous allusions* to famous texts employ substitutions*. **Ex:** 'A jug of rain, a loofah, bread – and thou' (Frank Muir and Denis Norden, *The 'My Word!' Stories*, p. 147). Humour may also be applied to language itself or to various languages (see macaronicism*).

R2: Humour and irony* are not incompatible, and humour also uses pseudo-simulation*. **Ex:** 'Sir, I would like to ask for your daughter's hand.' 'Why not? You've already had the rest of her.' See also chleuasmos*, R2.

R3: Humour works well when foregrounding naïveté or obvious blunders*. Ex [After a long and suggestive conversation concerning a wife's sexual preferences, the apparently suave questioner asks desperately]:

'You've, er, er, done it?'
'Done what?'
'Slept ... with a lady?'
'Yes.'
'What's it like?'

> G. Chapman et al., *Monty Python's Flying Circus:*
> *Just the Words*, 1:40

R4: *Black, sick,* and *gallows humour* are three forms which laugh at tragic or macabre themes. **Exx:** 'One of the advantages of nuclear war is that all men are cremated equal' (J. Crosbie, *Crosbie's Dictionary of Puns,* p. 58); ' "Mummy, mummy where's daddy?" "Be quiet and eat what you're given" '; ' "What is your last word, accused?" "I beg you to send me wherever you please, just as long as it is under the Soviet government and the sun is there!" ' (A.I. Solzhenitsyn, *The Gulag Archipelago,* pp. 269–70).

HYPALLAGE Transposition of the natural relationship between two elements in a proposition. See Joseph, Lanham, Lausberg, Marouzeau, Preminger, Quillet, and Quinn.

Exx: 'Melissa shook her doubtful curls'; *'apply the wound to water* for *apply water to the wound'* (*Concise Oxford Dictionary*); 'Winter kept us warm, covering / Earth in *forgetful snow'* (T.S. Eliot, *The Waste Land,* part 1); 'The razor-scarred back-street café bar' (Dylan Thomas, *Quite Early One Morning,* p. 40).

Other name: 'transferred epithet' (Cuddon, Joseph). This is only one species of hypallage.

R1: The following passage, concerning a British author crossing the U.S. on a lecture tour, contains hypallage involving a change of mood (i.e., passive for active): 'There one goes, unsullied as yet, in his Pullman pride, toying – oh boy! – with a blunderbuss bourbon, *being smoked by a large cigar,* riding out to the wide-open spaces of the faces of his waiting audience' (Dylan Thomas, *Quite Early One Morning,* p. 149). See enallage*, other def., 3.

R2: Like enallage*, hypallage is an apparent mistake*. All changes of grammatical function are not valid cases of hypallage. Puttenham, who calls hypallage the *changeling,* points out that the user of this figure perverts meaning by shifting the application of words: '... as he should say, for ... *come dine with me and stay not, come stay with me and dine not'* (cited by Joseph, p. 295).

The mistake* becomes a figure by expressing a meaning*, albeit an unexpected one. According to Guiraud (p. 197), 'The device is related to the aesthetics of vagueness; by suppressing the relationship of necessity between determined and determinant, it tends to liberate the latter.'

R3: The surrealists used the device to create discordance. **Ex:** 'The bed was sleeping soundly' (Jean Arp, *Jours effeuillés*, p. 192). Compare: 'Cast off the continents. Hoist the horizons' (R. Ducharme, *L'Avalée des avalés*, p. 13).

R4: See flip-flop*, R2; metaphor*, R3; sweet* talk, R2; and hendiadys*, R2.

HYPERBATON The addition to an apparently already complete sentence of a word or syntagm* which is thus strongly emphasized. See Quintilian, 9.4.26; and Morier.

Exx: 'About suffering they were never wrong, / The Old masters' (W.H. Auden, 'Musée des Beaux Arts'); 'Run like a billygoat over the grass you should keep off of' (D. Thomas, *Quite Early One Morning*, p. 54); '[Man's] chief occupation is extermination of other animals and his own species, which, however, multiplies with such insistent rapidity as to infest the whole habitable earth and Canada' (Ambrose Bierce, *The Devil's Dictionary*, under 'Man').

Other definitions: 'the name given to any intended deviation from ordinary word order' (Quinn, p. 40); 'schemes of unusual or inverted word order' (Corbett, p. 466); '1. A generic figure of various forms of departure from ordinary word order including *anastrophe, transgressio, hysteron proton, hypallage, hysterology*, *parenthesis*, *epergesis*. 2. Separation of words generally belonging together' (Lanham, p. 56)

R1: In antiquity, the word *hyperbaton* had a very broad meaning. Forcellini, in his *Lexicon*, includes synchisis* and tmesis* in the list of figures under hyperbaton. Lanham excludes them. Most theorists, including those already mentioned, plus Marouzeau, Quillet, Lausberg (sect. 716–19), and Preminger, have been content to return to the definition of hyperbaton as an inversion* which expresses 'a violent movement of the soul' (Littré).

Hyperbaton may well be considered to result from inversion* because it is possible to recast the sentence so as to integrate the added segment. But the effect characteristic of hyperbaton derives rather from the kind of spontaneity which imposes the *addition* of some truth, obvious or private, to a syntactic construction apparently already closed. Hyperbaton always consists in an adjacent assertion* (see assertion, R3). This appears all the more clearly when the grammatical link seems loosest, as in the case of *and* preceded by a comma. **Ex:** 'The arms of the morning are beautiful, and the sea' (Saint-Jean Perse, quoted by Daniel Delas, *Poétique-pratique*, p. 44).

R2: Most cases of hyperbaton – those whose function in the sentence is already represented by another word – are, from a syntactic standpoint, adjunctions*. However, nothing prevents the repetition by means of such an adjunction of some already expressed segment for reasons of emphasis*. Ex: 'This happened once and only once.'

R3: See also epiphrasis* and emphasis*, R3.

HYPERBOLE An exaggerated or extravagant statement, used to express strong feeling or produce a strong impression, and not intended to be understood literally (see *OED*). See also Abrams, Corbett, Frye, Grambs, Ducrot and Todorov, Joseph, Lanham, Lausberg, Marouzeau, Preminger, and Robert.

Exx: 'To make enough noise to wake the dead'; 'And yet here was Quality; a tiny, almost unnoticeable fault line; a line of illogic in our concept of the universe; and you tapped it, and the whole universe came apart, so neatly it was almost unbelievable' (R. Pirsig, *Zen and the Art of Motorcycle Maintenance*, p. 196); ' "Corniche! I want you to go to the Netherlands and kill a man." "At your service, Meister. Shall I take my dagger or rely on the poisoned chalice?" "You will rely on the poisoned word. Only that will do the job" ' (R. Davies, *What's Bred in the Bone*, p. 408).

Other definition: the 'figure [used] for lying' (Fabri)

Other names: emphasis* (Bénac); exaggeration (Robert); *superlatio* (Lanham; Fabri, 2:158); auxesis (Quinn; Barthes, p. 200); the 'Loud Lyer,' the 'Overreacher' (Puttenham)

R1: Counter-litotes* deflates through ironic hyperbole.

R2: It is not always possible to tell whether it is the content or the form which is hyperbolic. Ex: 'Leo had to take on the running of the household ... The President of the Cabinet does not feel so overworked' (Montherlant, *Romans*, p. 767). Is it purely rhetorical to compare a bachelor's household chores with the duties of a statesman?

   Grand guignol is semantic hyperbole, more precisely a kind of exaggeration which makes an appeal to the basic instincts. Ex: the story of M. Delout, his face covered in blood because of a fall from his window, who comes to ask the concierge for the number of his room (Breton, *Nadja*, pp. 147–8).

R3: Hyperbolic markers include such augmentative affixes as the prefixes *hyper-*, *extra-*, and *maxi-*; or the suffix *-issimus*; periphrastic comparisons like 'the kind of rancid, wretched terror compared with which a murderer's palpable fear is trifling' (Witold Gombrowicz, *Ferdydurke*, p. 190); and accumulations* of superlatives or of such excluding expressions as 'only' or 'the only.' Ex:

The dearest idol I have known,
Whate'er that idol be;
Help me to tear it from Thy throne,
And worship only thee.

W. Cowper, Onley Hymns, 1

The ultimate expedient is to denounce the inadequacy of language. Ex: 'Through a species of unutterable horror and awe, for which the language of mortality has no sufficiently energetic expression, I felt my heart cease to beat, my limbs go rigid where I sat' (E.A. Poe, 'Ligeia').

R4: Strained or excessive hyperbole may represent thought artificially stimulated, as Michaux showed in the case of poetry written under the influence of mescalin (*Connaissances par les gouffres*, pp. 15, 92, etc.), or may simply be humorous in intent. Exx: comic definitions* like 'noise: skeletons dancing on a tin roof' and 'slime: jellyfish copulating in Brylcream.'

R5: Hyperbole of a more or less 'dormant' nature abounds in current speech. Exx: 'hair-splitting'; 'I'm very attached to him' [i.e., not literally 'fastened' or 'tied,' but metaphorically 'fond of']; 'He somehow contrived to misunderstand' [i.e., he 'carefully planned'?].

R6: Hyperbole is obligatory in public speeches addressed to the great, even more so in pre-Revolutionary Europe or in certain oriental courts. One must still know how to avoid excesses which soon become subject to parody*. Ex: 'Her Majesty's civil servants spend their lives working for a modest wage and at the end they retire into obscurity. Honours are a small recompense for a lifetime of loyal, self-effacing discretion and devoted service to Her Majesty, and to the nation' (J. Lynn and A. Jay, *The Complete 'Yes Minister'*, p. 232). Hyperbole intended as mere flattery belongs under grandiloquence*.

HYPERHYPOTAXIS The insertion of too many subordinate phrases and clauses.

Ex: 'But the truth was that Phutatorius knew not one word or one syllable of what was passing – but his whole thoughts and attention were taken up with a transaction which was going onwards at that very instant within the precincts of his own Galligaskins, and in a part of them where of all others he stood most interested to watch accidents: So that notwithstanding he looked with all the attention in the world, and had gradually screwed up every nerve and muscle in his face to the utmost pitch the instrument would bear, in order, as it was

thought, to give a sharp reply to Yorick, who sat over against him –
Yet, I say, was Yorick never once in any one domicile of Phutatorius's
brain – but the true cause of his exclamation lay at least a yard below'
(L. Sterne, *Tristram Shandy*, vol. 4, ch. 27).

R1: According to Thérive (quoted by Spitzer, *Etudes de style*, p. 468, n.
3), hyperhypotaxis is a period* intended to be read silently rather than
aloud. Its development reflects the diverseness and multiplicity of
effect discernible in leisurely reading, whereas classical periods take on
the rhythm* of sustained oratory.

R2: A clumsily constructed hyperhypotaxis is a synchisis* (see also
syntactic scrambling*).

R3: Classification of sentences in decreasing order of complexity
produces: hyperhypotaxis, hypotaxis (see period*), the average sentence*, parataxis*, and hyperparataxis (see dislocation* and monologue*).

R4: Spitzer (*Etudes de style*, p. 407) identifies three types of hyper-
hypotactic periods: 'exploded,' 'superimposed,' and 'arched.' In Spitzer's scheme, the example from Sterne quoted above would fall into
the 'superimposed' category.

HYPHEN Used in spelling certain expressions (composite nouns or
adjectives, etc.), intentional hyphenation* becomes a literary device in
some cases. Two possibilities exist:
1. Lexicalization of a syntagm*. Ex: '... you women's-cultural-lunch-
club-organizing *Saturday Review of Literature*-reading-substantial-
inheritance-from-soft-drink-corporation-awaiting old-New-Hampshire-
family-invoking Kennedy-loving-just-wunnerful-labelling Yank bag'
(Kingsley Amis, *One Fat Englishman*, p. 24). See compound* word, other
def.; and graphy*, R4.
2. Syllabification. Exx: 'Pho-to-graph ... he stammered' (G. Bernanos,
Oeuvres romanesques, p. 847); 'She repeats un-com-pro-mi-sing, separating each syllable ostentatiously' (A. Hébert, *Kamouraska*, p. 96).

R1: Both cases involve a single word made up of disjoined elements,
which are either words or syllables. Without the hyphen, the syllables
would be even more disjoined because of the spaces between them. Ex:
'Ah! yes, I want ... to banish *i dle ness* forever from my life (Marie-
Claire Blais, *Une Saison dans la vie d'Emmanuel*, p. 46). This is disarticulation of a word for ironic reasons. However, see typographic
caesura*, R1.

R2: By lexicalizing syntagms*, some philosophers create translations*
which replace and improve upon obscure neologisms*. Ex: the existentialist expression 'Being-in the-world' (*l'être-au-monde*). The device

Hyphenation

seems to come from German, a language which has numerous words composed by juxtaposition*. See etymology*.

R3: See situational* signs, 3(a); caesura* (typographical), R3; punctuation*, R1; asyndeton*, R2; oblique* stroke, R3; apposition*; compound* word; tmesis*; translation*; and approximation*, R3.

HYPHENATION Division of a word too long for right-hand justification. The division occurs between syllables and is marked by a hyphen*. The rules differ in French and English.

Synonym: typographical caesura* (French)

R1: In English, manuals of style devoted to the presentation of typescripts discourage the use of the typographic caesura in compound* words. The MLA Style Sheet (2d ed., 1970, p. 8), a standard for academic publishing in North America, is quite clear: 'Never end a typed line with a hyphen which is to be printed, for the compositor may drop the hyphen and join the two parts in one. Instead, sacrifice appearance and put the entire compound on the next line.' And the MHRA Style Book (1978, p. 4), in its 'Notes for Authors, Editors, and Writers of Dissertations' in Britain, also advises against leaving the problem to the compositor: 'If a line ends with a hyphen it may not be clear to the printer, particularly if the passage is in a foreign language, whether he is to set the word as a hyphenated compound or as one word. When a broken word is not to be hyphenated this should be indicated by curved lines ⊃ to show that the parts of the word are to be joined. For words not so marked the printer will normally follow copy and print the hyphen. This problem may be avoided if the typist is instructed never to allow a break in a foreign word at the end of a line but to carry over the whole word to the next line.' Both texts pre-date the current wide use made by authors of word processors capable of encoding instructions to be read by automatic printers concerning right-side justification or ragged edges. Many problems of incompatibility between systems remain.

Graphic and sonic divisions sometimes converge, sometimes diverge. For instance, ch, gn, ph, and th only transcribe a single sound in French and are therefore not separated. On the other hand, consecutive vowels in hiatus* (e.g., 'thé/â/tre') constitute syllables not separated, unless they involve prefixes (e.g., 'pre-arrange'). Needless to say, such complications inevitably provoke confusion.

R2: Ease of reading precludes division before mute syllables in French (e.g., es-[pèrent], but not espè-[rent]) and also, in both English and French, hyphenation at the foot of a page. Common sense precludes the isolation of a single letter at the end of a line or the displacement of fewer than three: absolu and obéi are therefore not divided. The aesthetic sense demands that, at the end of a paragraph, there be a segment longer than the indented space marking the beginning of the next paragraph.

R3: Compound* words divide at the hyphen. Not subject to the typographical caesura* are: acronyms* (e.g. UNESCO), numbers or dates expressed in figures (e.g., 1, 520, 300; 1991); and administrative numbers (e.g., 7869432).

HYPOTYPOSIS Hypotyposis paints things so vividly and with such energy that they become in some way visible; it also turns a narrative* or description* into an image*, a picture, or even a living scene (see Fontanier, p. 390). See also Quintilian, Dumarsais (2:9), Joseph, Lanham, Lausberg (sect. 400), Littré, OED, Quillet, and Robert.

Ex: 'Here is now such swarms of a small sand flyes that wee can hardly see the sun through them and where they light is just as if a spark of fire fell and raises a little bump which smarts and burns so that we cannot forbear rubbing of them as causes such scabbs that our hands and faces is nothing but scabbs. They fly into our ears nose eyes mouth and down our throats as we be most sorely plagued with them' (James Knight, Journal, 11 Aug. 1717, quoted by P.C. Newman, Company of Adventurers, p. 194).

Ex: 'Here, over the bridge, come three Javanese, winged, breastplated, helmeted, carrying gongs and steel bubbles. Kilted, sporraned, tartan'd, daggered Scotsmen reel and strathspey up a side-street, piping hot. Burgundian girls, wearing, on their heads, bird cages made of velvet, suddenly whisk on the pavement into a coloured dance. A Viking goes into a pub. In black felt feathered hats and short leather trousers, enormous Austrians, with thighs big as Welshmen's bodies, but much browner, yodel to fiddles and split the rain with their smiles. Frilled, ribboned, sashed, fezzed and white-turbaned, in baggy-blue sharavari and squashed red boots, Ukrainians with Manchester accents gopak up the hill' (D. Thomas, Quite Early One Morning, p. 142).

Synonyms: enargia, energia (Peacham, Du Bellay, Joseph, Lanham); image* (Boileau)

R1: Descriptive hypotyposis may be distinguished from its rhetorical counterpart in which action is an artificial representation of an idea. The power of such artifice is made graphically clear in the comparison* made by the Indian scholar H.-R. Diwekar (Fleurs de rhétorique de l'Inde, p. 36) between a verse from the Ramayana (1.63.20) ('The eldest son is generally the father's favourite, Oh king, and the youngest the mother's') and a verse from the Aitareya Brahmana (7:3) 'Seizing the eldest son, he said: "Not this one!" – "Nor this one!" said the mother [seizing] the youngest one').

Hypotyposis is therefore a development of the image* in both meanings of the term: a visual image and a rhetorical image (metonymy* or metaphor*). Ex: 'Life, you know, is rather like opening a tin of sardines. We are all of us looking for the key. Others think they've found the key, don't they? They roll back the lid of the sardine can of life, they reveal the sardines, the riches of life, therein, and they get them out, they enjoy them. But, you know, there's always a little bit in the corner you can't get out. I wonder – I wonder, is there a little bit in the corner of your life, I know there is in mine' (Alan Bennett et al., *The Complete Beyond the Fringe*, p. 104). Similes*, allegories*, and applications (see allegory*) are all examples of hypotyposis when they 'paint a picture.'

R2: The opposite of hypotyposis is schematization*.

R3: Is the essential function of hypotyposis to 'embellish' or 'depict,' as classical theorists thought? Does the figure only exist for the reader? Michaux's experiments at the limits of perception confer on hypotyposis a different origin, one found in hallucinations. Situations, characters, and actions may spring from a consciousness out of control, one which offers pictures felt to be real-life experiences. Ex: 'Enough ... *"No more writing!"* ... And then in the darkness behind his closed eyelids, he sees, suddenly, violent men rise up, who make fierce negative gestures, then a whole troop, then a procession of discontented people with placards, a line of people protesting and threatening. *"No more"* had turned into a group of strikers!' (H. Michaux, *Les Grandes Epreuves de l'esprit*, pp. 98–9).

R4: If the scene described calls to mind a scene in a painting or film because each character assumes a characteristic pose, the result is a *tableau*. Ex: 'Mollie and Josie Powell. Till Mr Right comes along, then meet once in a blue moon. *Tableau!* O, look who it is for the love of God! How are you all? What have you been doing with yourself? Kiss and delighted to, kiss, to see you. Picking holes in each other's appearance. You're looking splendid. Sister souls. Showing their teeth at one another. How many have you left? Wouldn't lend each other a pinch of salt' (Joyce, *Ulysses*, p. 302).

R5: Diatyposis* is a short form of hypotyposis.

HYSTEROLOGY In a narrative*, circumstances or details which should follow are situated chronologically before. See Littré, Lausberg, and Quillet.

Exx: 'He arranges the spices in alphabetical order, on a special shelf in the kitchen. He builds the shelf' (M. Atwood, *Cat's Eye*, p. 404); 'UBU. – I'm going to light a fire while I'm waiting for him to bring the wood' (A. Jarry, *Ubu roi*, 4.6).

Other definitions: Lanham (p. 58): 'A phrase is interposed between a preposition and its object: "I ran after with as much speed as I could, the thief that had undone me" (Peacham).' See also Joseph, p. 295.

Synonym: hysteron-proteron (Marouzeau). Lanham adds: '[Richard] Sherry [*A Treatise of Schemes and Tropes*, 1550] makes the term mean *Hysteron Proteron* ... He gives *Prepostera Locutio* as the Latin equivalent.'

R1: When the inversion of segments responds to some hidden cause, the device is similar to flashback* or flash-forward*. The classical example – 'Let us die and rush into battle' (Virgil, *Aeneid*, 2.353) – expresses a psychological truth, since in order to throw oneself against enemy forces, one must have already decided to die. Cocteau's aphorism is similar: 'Find first, then seek.'

On the other hand, since it is a mistake*, hysterology connotes stupidity, naïvety, or at any rate absent-mindedness. Exx: 'During one of his fits, he committed suicide and set fire to the house'; 'I'm going to kill that magician. I'll dismember him and then I'll sue him' (Woody Allen, 'Oedipus Wrecks,' in *New York Stories* [film, 1989]).

I

IMAGE (collective noun: imagery) **1.** Since the image lies at the heart of poetry, all poetic schools have quarrelled over it. But the confusion surrounding it arises not only because of the differences among the various logical systems to which it is made subject. Above all, confusion derives from the elusive quality of some poetic texts. Any attempt to limit their meaning* would be merely tendentious. The true image says many things at once in what is frequently the only possible way. Perception of what imagery proposes will be aided by a few fundamental distinctions.

2. Image and trope. Ex:

Wait for a while, then slip downstairs
And bring us up some chilled white wine,
And some blue cheese, and crackers, and some fine
Ruddy-skinned pears.
                    Richard Wilbur, 'A Late Aubade,' in *Walking to Sleep*

This is a *visual image* (syn.: mental image), which should be distinguished in poetry from the real images, either drawn or painted, found for instance in *posters*: '(illustrated) texts exhibited in a public place.' Details about visual images will be found under description*, hypotyposis*, diatyposis*, portrait*, and prosopopoeia*. Visual images are not always without symbolic significance. The same poem contains the lines 'You could be sitting now in a carrel / Turning some liver-spotted page.' This visual image, unless interpreted figuratively as referring to the writer of the page and to the swift passage of youth into age, rather than to the page itself, could not serve within the poem's overall economy as indicated in it, viz. as an element in its 'Gather ye rosebuds' theme*.

Literary images are so called because they introduce into a well-defined and relatively short portion of the text a second meaning* (see meaning, 8) which is no longer literal, but analogical, symbolic, or 'metaphorical': either in the form of a single word (see metaphor*) or syntagm* (see comparison*), or of a succession of words or syntagms (see allegory*).

Strictly speaking, the literary image is therefore a device which consists in the replacement or prolongation of one term (called the 'tenor' or subject compared), which indicates what is 'literally' designated, by the use of a second term, which maintains a merely analogical relationship with the first: the author relies on the reader's sensitivity to supply the link. The analogue is called the 'vehicle' or 'object' and is used to designate reality by figurative means: the vehicle is to be taken 'figuratively.'

The existence of some literal term, expressed or not, seems essential to the formation of traditional literary images, but the relationship between the two must also be one of analogy. Indeed, if the relationship between the two terms is close enough to form a single isotopy*, the result is metonymy* or synecdoche*.

Tropes are devices which function by replacing the literal term with another in some way related to it (see meaning*, 4).

3. Tenor and vehicle. The literary image is sometimes said to be *abstract* or *concrete* according to whether the vehicle is more abstract or more concrete than the tenor. Abstract images are rare. Exx: 'The Cambridge ladies who live in furnished souls' (e.e. cummings); 'Streets that follow like a tedious argument / Of insidious intent / To lead you to an overwhelming question' (T.S. Eliot, 'The Love Song of J. Alfred Prufrock,' 7–9). Concrete images are more natural. Ex: 'Bent double, like old beggars under sacks, / Knock-kneed, coughing like hags, we cursed through sludge' (W. Owen, 'Dulce et Decorum Est'). See also generalization*, R2.

The symbolist image is a concrete image whose tenor is an intuition or feeling difficult to transmit in non-figurative form. Ex:

Tyger! Tyger! burning bright
In the forests of the night,
What immortal hand or eye

Could frame thy fearful symmetry?

W. Blake, 'The Tyger'

4. Usage. From the point of view of usage, a distinction is made between 'dead' or worn-out images, or clichés*, and 'revived' or 'new' images. Clichés are images so worn-out by overuse that the vehicle, having lost all its original connotational power, immediately evokes the tenor; its figurative function is no longer perceptible. Such images are dead or, at any rate, moribund. **Exx:** 'Are you a man or a mouse?'; 'to raise oneself by the bootstraps'; 'Many are called but few are chosen.'

A *revived image* (or rejuvenated cliché*) appears when the context or some morphological change breathes new life into the tenor's original, latent meaning. **Ex:** Groucho Marx is said to have answered the above inquiry – 'Are you a man or a mouse? – with 'Throw me a piece of cheese and you'll find out.' To 'boot' a computer, or literally to turn it on, revives the dead image of self-improvement thanks to bootstraps. And Noah Jacobs records a new twist to the evangelical cliché* regarding the disparity between those called and chosen: 'Many are called but few get the right number' (*Naming Day in Eden*, p. 132).

If rejuvenation of the cliché is achieved by restoration of a word's literal meaning, the result is frequently humorous: 'Familiarity breeds children' (Mark Twain). When two clichés with incompatible vehicles are combined, the resultant 'incoherence' may revive the image (see incoherence*).

New or *original* images avoid such mishaps by their refusal of the commonplace.

5. A.J. Greimas proposed a functional concept regarding imagery (see *Structural Semantics: An Attempt at a Method*, trans R. Scleifer and A. Velie, p. 100): the isotopy*. A text's isotopy is the field of reality to which its different parts refer. In the case of literary images, the isotopy is complex. Blake's 'tyger' refers at once to an animal and to the theory of the Divine Creation of the world. Usually, however, in the case of a complex isotopy, one of the terms is favoured over the other: a greater degree of reality is attributed to it. The description of the *bateau ivre* or 'drunken boat' provided by the French symbolist poet Arthur Rimbaud (the example cited by Greimas) relates rather to Rimbaud (the tenor or subject compared) than to a boat (the vehicle or comparing object). In such a case, Greimas speaks of a 'positive' complex isotopy. Since it is the tenor which normally provides the image's focus, he considers it to be the 'positive' isotopy; the vehicle, because it is to be taken in a 'figurative' sense, he considers the 'negative' isotopy.

These distinctions become essential in the (admittedly exceptional) case of images referring to a 'negative' complex isotopy, or to one in which positive and negative are 'in equilibrium.' Apparently, an absence of isotopy, or *ectopy*, may also be envisaged.

Image

According to Greimas, there is a negative complex isotopy when the vehicle, although it must be understood figuratively, nonetheless receives from the author, and so also from the potential reader, a degree of reality or truth superior to that possessed by the tenor (which nonetheless remains the positive term). Ex (provided by Greimas): Mr Dupont thinks he is a star. A literary example:

> I'm a riddle in nine syllables,
> An elephant, a ponderous house,
> A melon strolling on two tendrils.
> O red fruit, ivory, fine timbers!
> This loaf's big with its yeasty rising.
> Money's new-minted in this fat purse.
> I'm a means, a stage, a cow in calf.
> I've eaten a bag of green apples,
> Boarded the train there's no getting off.
>
> Sylvia Plath, 'Metaphors,' in *Crossing the Water*

The vehicle (an elephant, a melon, etc.) is assumed by the author to be totally real; the tenor is only partially real.

To the negative complex isotopy belong hallucinations, which the surrealists class as a kind of image (see below, R1), and dreams which are mistaken for reality (cf. 'I am dreaming that I am not asleep' [Eluard, *Oeuvres*, 1:933]).

As for the balanced complex isotopy, it is achieved by images whose complex isotopy is both positive and negative; that is, when the reality of the tenor is assumed to be equally as true as that of the vehicle (but no more so). As an example, Greimas gives the Simba (or Lion) warriors, who feel themselves to be both fully lion and fully men. The poetry of Pierre Reverdy (1889–1960) tends towards this type of isotopy. Thus in 'Le Coeur soudain' ('Suddenly the Heart') (*Ferraille*, 1937), 'the appetite of the breakers' refers both to a seascape and to swirling instincts, as is indicated by a similar but opposite line*: 'Emotion capsizes on the rocks.' Images which refer to a balanced complex isotopy, that is, to one 'in equilibrium,' are not dissociations*, the usual type of surrealistic image. Such balanced expressions remain images since, although the two terms have the same degree of reality, they retain a figurative relationship one to the other. This is what gives Reverdy's poetry its particular flavour. Understanding poetry held to be hermetic may simply be a matter of discovering the theory under whose auspices it was conceived.

Finally, a word about the absence of isotopy. Purely metaphorical uses of images seem possible: in such cases, terms would only be vehicles, having as their sole function the representation of 'something else,' although what this something else might be remains a mystery. Several texts by Michaux appear to fall into this category; for example,

'La Nuit des embarras' and 'La Ralentie.' **Ex:** 'It was at the arrival, between centre and absence, at Eurêka, in the nest of bubbles ...' ('Entre centre et absence,' in *Lointain intérieur* [1938]). Such a theory of poetry would be covered by Michaux's guiding principle (a principle which itself needs to be 'understood'): 'In darkness we will see clearly, brothers. In the labyrinth we will find the straight way' ('Contre!' in *La Nuit remue* [1935]). This is a poetics of total interiorization. See autism*.

The question of isotopy* arises whenever two signifieds belonging to two distinct 'universes of discourse' are brought together. See pun*, metonymy*, and oratorical syllepsis*.

R1: Since the surrealists, the word *image* has taken on very wide significance. As far as Breton was concerned (see Aragon et al., *Dictionnaire abrégé du surréalisme,* under *image*), a *surreal image* occurs when an expression 'conceals an enormous dose of apparent contradiction' (see dissociation*); when 'one of the terms [is] curiously concealed' (see metaphor*); when, 'after a sensational beginning, it seems a weak disappointment of aroused expectation' (see anticlimax*); when 'it draws upon itself for a ridiculous *formal* justification' (see musication* and verbigeration*, R3); when it is 'hallucinatory' (see fantastic*); when it 'lends quite naturally to abstractions a concrete mask, or vice versa' (see above); when it implies the negation of some elementary physical property (a kind of paradox*); or when, more generally, 'it provokes laughter' (see humour*). As may be seen, the word *image* designates to Breton all kinds of devices, provided it be surrealist, that is, that it 'present the arbitrary to the highest degree' and that it take a long time to 'translate it into practical language' (ibid.).

It is not hermeticism which assures the quality of surrealistic 'images,' nor is it their originality. 'The further apart and more exact the relationship between the two realities compared, the greater the power of the image,' wrote Reverdy (quoted by Breton, *Manifestes du surréalisme,* p. 31). Semantic separation may also impose itself by its exactitude. Gratuity and contradiction act as *a fortiori* proofs, possessing the beauty of a kind of truth. Breton also said: 'Beauty will be convulsive or it will not *exist.*' And: 'It is from the somehow fortuitous comparison of the two terms that a particular light bursts forth, *the light of the image* to which we are infinitely sensitive. The image's value depends on the beauty of the spark produced ...' (Breton, *Manifestes du surréalisme,* p. 51). The poet is less the author than the *place* where there occurs a phenomenon whose composite parts exist less within the poet than in the world and in language. (See dissociation*, R5.) This explains the poet's nature, which is often obsessive, distressing, ironic, vengeful, and so on.

R2: See also hypotyposis* (an image which paints a picture).

IMITATION Although the only limits to imitation placed on art by Aristotle include the whole of nature (such a theory of imitation includes the foregrounding of aesthetic devices, as Souriau points out), some authors have not hesitated to produce sincere, non-parodic imitations of culture, or at any rate of their predecessors' works (see parody*).

Such imitations become 'isms,' nouns formed from the admired author's surname with the added suffix -*ism*. Modelled on Pindarism, Petrarchism, etc., modern French speaks of: Apollinarism, Balzacism, Malrucism [from Malraux], Mauriacism, Proustism, Valérism, Verlainism, and so on. Although such neologisms* are possible in English, only Clevelandism and Pinterism immediately spring to mind as current examples. Ex: Pope's *Imitations of Horace* belong in this intertextual tradition.

Other definition: Fontanier (p. 288) employs *imitation* when speaking not of other authors but of other languages. This we call peregrinism*.

R1: *Marotism* (Clément Marot [1496–1544] wrote poems in a witty, epigrammatic style dubbed 'élégant badinage' by Boileau [*Art poétique*, 1674]), which has been in use for centuries, has taken on a broader meaning in French (see archaism*, R2).

R2: *Pindarism* (Pindar was a Greek poet in the fourth century B.C.): 'praise of the gods and of heroes, moral commonplaces ... eloquence, learned mythological imagery' (Bénac). Ex: *Amers*, by Saint-Jean Perse.

R3: *Petrarchism* (Petrarch was a fourteenth-century Italian poet): 'verse which is characterized by artificial diction, puns*, conceits*, complex prosody, casuistical argument, and, in general, hermetic abstruseness' (Cuddon).

R4: *Gongorism* or cultism (Gongora was a poet of the Spanish Golden Age): 'Latinistic vocabulary, and syntax, intricate metaphors*, excessive hyperbole*, rich colour images*, mythological allusions* and a general strangeness of diction' (Cuddon).

R5: *Euphuism* (*Euphues: The Anatomy of Wyt* [1578] and *Euphues and His England* [1580], works by John Lyly): 'an ornately florid, precious and mazy style of writing (often alliterative, antithetical and embellished with elaborate figures of speech)' (Cuddon).

R6: *Marinism* (Marino was an Italian poet of the sixteenth and seventeenth centuries): 'extravagant imagery*, excessive ornamentation and verbal conceits*' (Drabble).

R7: Clichés* are imitations of the speech or thought of 'the-man-in-the-street'; psittacisms* are parrotings, or repetitions* by an uncomprehending speaker.

R8: Pressed too far, imitation turns into *plagiarism* or literary theft. Jarry enjoyed pointing out how Georges d'Esparbès (1864–1944), in a short story entitled 'Petit-Louis,' had plagiarized Kipling's story 'Toomai of the Elephants' in *The Jungle Book* (see A. Jarry, *La Chandelle verte*, p. 262). Such unacknowledged use of another's text risks the accusation of dishonesty.

But where does plagiarism begin? In his *Discours de Suède* (*Essais*, p. 1071), Camus wrote: 'Personally, I cannot live without my art.' He had quoted van Gogh on the same subject in *L'Homme révolté* (ibid., p. 661): 'In my life and also in my painting, I am quite capable of doing without God. But, in my suffering, I cannot do without something greater than msyelf, the power to create, which is my life.' Camus had made his own this 'admirable [albeit familiar] groan of anguish,' adapting it to his own situation, expressing it in his own terms.

It must also be said that some so-called examples of plagiarism far surpass their models. Thus P.-A. Lebrun (1785–1873) is the author of a poem called 'Cimetière au bord de la mer,' in which the plan, the order of imagery, and even the text of ten of the lines are very similar to Valéry's poem 'Le Cimetière marin' (see R. Sabatier, in the *Revue des deux mondes*, Dec. 1972, pp. 535–40). In such a case, one speaks of intertextuality to avoid the pejorative connotations that would be out of place.

Cases of ironic plagiarism occur. In *Les Faux-Monnayeurs*, Gide indicates daybreak thus: 'La paupière de l'horizon rougissant déjà se soulève' ('The reddening horizon's eyelid is raised') (*Romans*, p. 275). The sentence is taken *verbatim* from Mauriac. The absence of quotation marks is obviously not a matter of cheating but rather, in our view, a teasing challenge to the reader.

IMPLICATION A form of words whose semantic content leads the reader to understand, in addition to their primary meaning*, something else which is not immediately apparent but which follows from what has been said, once one thinks about it.

Ex:

COMMANDING OFFICER [to a World War II British pilot who has agreed to 'lay down his life' to improve morale]: Get up in a crate, Perkins, pop over to Bremen, take a shufti, don't come back ... Goodbye, Perkins ...
PERKINS: Goodbye, sir – or is it – *au revoir*?
COMMANDING OFFICER: *No.*

(Bennett, Cook, Miller, and Moore, 'Aftermyth of War,'
in *The Complete Beyond the Fringe*, p. 74

Ex: 'In 1979, however, a defector from [the Masonic Lodge] P2 – a journalist named Mino Pecorelli – accused the CIA. Two months after

Implication

this accusation, Pecorelli was murdered' (M. Baigent, R. Leigh, and H. Lincoln, *The Messianic Legacy*, p. 426).

By virtue of the law of *exhaustivity* (Ducrot), implication, even in the parodical first example quoted above, plays on what is not being said. The conversational convention presupposes that speakers say what they know about the matter under discussion. If they say nothing about the finality of the decision taken, it is because they think it better to talk of other things. Another recent example is the definition given by an African leader: 'A specialist is someone who does not work in his own country.' For another example, see euphemism*, R1.

Implication may also come into play as a result of what is said (rather than left unsaid). Ex: 'Even friar Giroflée showed himself useful; he became a very good carpenter, and even something of a gentleman' (Voltaire, *Candide*, ch. 30). If he became so, he could not have been one previously, and since he had been a monk at that time, Voltaire is ultimately loosing his apparently innocent barb against the religious orders.

Implication may function by denying something else; this would be a form of litotes*. Ex: 'It was not Esdras and Da'Bé that she first thought of' (L. Hémon, *Maria Chapdelaine*, p. 114). It was François with whom she is in love, as the reader guesses.

Implication may even work by means of antiphrasis*; that is, by affirming the contrary. This is how many *declarations* need to be interpreted, particularly those intended to reassure the public at moments of crisis. Ex: Roosevelt in July 1933: 'The United States is seeking a dollar which will have the same purchasing power and value for repaying debts in a generation as the one we want to ensure now for the immediate future.' One must read 'between the lines' to see that what the president is in fact announcing in this way is a devaluation of the dollar. A literary example:

Two roads diverged in a wood, and I –
I took the one less traveled by,
And that has made all the difference.

R. Frost, 'The Road Not Taken'

The roads implicitly refer to choices of possible careers or lovers.

Analogous: hint; a look or word which speaks volumes; in conversation: 'I see what you mean'; insight (Le Clerc, p. 216: 'To give someone an insight consists in allowing someone to guess something of what one is thinking; this technique, when used tactfully, is most agreeable because it allows others to exercise and display their intelligence.')

R1: Implication is not unlike allusion*, which, however, evokes a fact, person, or object rather than an assertion*. Allusion refers to something known which is introduced into the text from outside, whereas implication follows from the text itself. Ex: 'He jests at scars who never felt a wound' (Shakespeare, *Romeo and Juliet*, 2.21). The ultimately tragic consequences of Romeo's inexperience are implied.

R2: Rhetorical implication, which aims at communicating what is not said, is therefore linked to irony*. It differs from logical implication, which belongs to philosophy and which demands enunciation*. Ex: 'When two statements are combined by placing the word "if" before the first and inserting the word "then" between them, the resulting compound statement is a *hypothetical* (also called a *conditional*, an *implication*, or an *implicative statement*)' (Irving M. Copi, *Introduction to Logic*, p. 245).

R3: Ducrot makes a distinction between implication and *presupposition*. See theme*, R1, and assertion*.

R4: Implication in advertising is as artful as it is tempting. Ex: 'Large, elegant, sunny, available right now' [an advertisement for apartments].

R5: It needs only the addition to an assertion* of a superfluous detail for the latter's restrictive function to become apparent. Ex: 'What a nice breakfast this morning!' risks the rejoinder: 'You didn't like yesterday's?' A literary example: 'After my wife had pronounced, foolishly saying that *St. Urbain's Horseman* was the best novel I'd written so far (making me resentful, because this obviously meant she hadn't enjoyed my earlier work as much as she should have done) I submitted the manuscript to my editors' (Mordecai Richler, *Shovelling Trouble*, p. 12).

INCLUSION A device consisting of beginning and ending a poem, story, or play with the same word. See Quinn.

Ex: 'It may be that universal history is the history of a handful of metaphors ... It may be that universal history is the history of the different intonations given a handful of metaphors' (J.L. Borges, 'The Fearful Sphere of Pascal,' in *Labyrinths*, pp. 189, 192).

Ex:

Ask me no more: the moon may draw the sea

...

Ask me no more.

Tennyson, 'Ask Me No More'

Other definitions: 1. Following several authors like Bary (see Le Hir, p. 129), Marouzeau restricts the meaning of inclusion to epanadiplosis*. However, his definition – 'Beginning and ending a sentence or verse with the same word' – lacks precision. We prefer to keep *epanadiplosis* for examples of the type he specifies and to use *inclusion* for those

involving whole works (however minimal), since the aesthetic effect is quite different.
2. In logic, inclusion is a characteristic of the relationship between two classes. The species is included in the *genus*. This definition is important for the analysis of synecdoche*.

INCOHERENCE Mixed metaphor*, that is, one combining two incompatible images*. See Lausberg, meaning 2.

Ex (quoted by Lausberg, on the subject of an orator): 'He is a torrent that becomes inflamed.' Fowler quoted (p. 361) the following oratorical salad: 'No society, no community can place its house in such a condition that it is always *on a rock, oscillating* between solvency and insolvency. What I have to do is to see that our house is *built upon a solid foundation*, never allowing the possibility of the Society's *lifeblood being sapped* ...'

Analogous terms: false dissociation* (see dissociation, R6); 'tasteless word selection' (Fowler)

Other definition: [Ideas, words, sentences] which do not follow, which do not form a single well-articulated whole' (Lausberg, meaning 1). This is an extended meaning* which includes dissociated words, inconsequential ideas, and *coq-à-l'âne** at sentence-level. Incoherencies occur also between narrative episodes. Ex: Protos's arrest in Gide's *Les Caves du Vatican*: a moment earlier he had been declared above suspicion.

R1: Incoherence could be restricted to mixed metaphor*, not only when incompatibility arises between irrelevant classemes of the vehicle (e.g., the ship of state sailing on a volcano), but also when marginal semes of the tenor clash with equally marginal semes in the vehicle (or vice versa). An example taken from an official record and collected by Jean-Charles: 'An Habitué of brawls, he had long since kept a revolver as his bedside book.'

R2: When one of the terms of a surrealistic image* lends itself to a metaphorical meaning, the distance necessary for the 'spark' to travel creates incoherence between tenor and vehicle. Ex: 'This downpour is a flash in the pan' (Eluard, *Oeuvres*, 1:725). This represents a comic revival of the cliché* 'a flash in the pan': as may be seen, mixed metaphor is not always a defect. Traditional and surrealistic definitions of the image* (as dissociation) come together here in quite a curious way.

R3: Deliberate incoherence remains the best way of ridiculing grandiloquence*. Ex: 'And when all was said and done the lies a fellow told about himself couldn't probably hold a proverbial candle to the wholesale whoppers other fellows coined about him' (Joyce, *Ulysses*, p. 520).

R4: Incoherence results from semes misplaced in the context (more accurately from classemes ruled out by the isotopy* and yet still included). This does not prevent there being in that context relevant semes which seem to justify the kind of clumsiness that goes unpunished in everyday conversation. Ex: 'The horse made superhuman efforts to free itself.'

INCONSEQUENCE A flight of fancy by which two ideas with no apparent logical link are co-ordinated.

Ex: 'I'd sooner have been a judge than a miner ... It's safer work judging than mining. You're not troubled by falling coal, for one thing. You don't get that down your Guild-halls. It's a feature of your Guild-hall life, the absence of falling coal ...' (Bennett, Cook, Miller, and Moore, 'Sitting on a Bench,' in *Beyond the Fringe*, Capitol Records W-1792, 1961).

Other name: *non sequitur*

R1: Inconsequence, which resembles the combination of oxymoric ideas, differs from *coq-à-l'âne**, in which widely divergent ideas are not co-ordinated.

R2: The invention of amusing examples of inconsequence produces the literary game 'Cross Questions and Crooked Answers' (see Augarde, pp. 166–7).

R3: Despite its obscurity, inconsequence may be full of meaning*. Ex: A recent documentary televised by the American Public Broadcasting Company ('Frontline: The Earthquake Is Coming,' 23 March 1988) reported that a Californian geologist claimed to be able to predict, with 83 per cent accuracy, future earthquakes based on the number of advertisements in his local paper for lost dogs and cats.

INCORRECT WORD Giving a word a meaning* different from the one in common usage; that is, using a word to refer to something other than what is meant. Incorrect words can only occasionally be pinpointed by reference to context.

Exx: 'I trudged, wincing at the toothache in my calf ...' (Anthony Burgess, *But Do Blondes Prefer Gentlemen?*, p. 91); 'The American bases have superimposed an encirclement complex on the older interventionist trauma' (Fowler, p. 461). Fowler included the latter example of the incorrect use of Freudian terminology among his 'popularized technicalities.'

Antonyms: proper word; *mot juste*; appropriate expression

Other definition: According to Lausberg (sect. 533), among words considered incorrect are imprecise synonyms*, words not in current usage, invented words, and those belonging to a particular region, technological field, trade, or occupation. This definition, which reflects ancient ideas on the sustained style, gives a broader meaning to the term.

R1: Incorrect words differ from catachresis*, in which there is no corresponding correct word. It may happen, however, that the correct term exists but is not known to the speaker. Ex: 'It's not far from that pole ... That metal pole ... The pylon? Yes, that's it.' Such spontaneous examples of the use of incorrect words are semi-catachretic, resulting, as they do, from a momentary loss of words.

R2: Attenuations* are incorrect in part since they bear only upon connotation (see euphemism*).

R3: Just as semantic and lexical neologisms* differ, so do incorrect words contrast with barbarisms*. The latter involve the lexical nature of words, the former only the desired meaning*.

R4: Purisms and hypercorrections also produce incorrect words. Ex: 'When James the footman says *chicking* for "chicken," he is being hypercorrect, leaning over backwards to be correct' (*OEDS*).

INJUNCTION A type of sentence which expresses the conative function (see enunciation*) of language (urging the addressee to behave in a certain way).

Ex (current): 'Make my day!'

Ex (literary): 'LADY CAROLINE: John! If you would allow your nephew to look after Lady Stutfield's cloak, you might help me with my work-basket' (O. Wilde, *A Woman of No Importance*, act 1).

Ex (negative injunctions to a young actor): 'Never underestimate the audience, never patronize them ... Never cheapen yourself or your profession ... Remember the court jester: he didn't dare perform badly' (L. Olivier, *On Acting*, p. 370).

As the first literary example shows, the imperative is not the only grammatical form of injunction. Other forms include the future tense, as in the following parody* of 'biblical' language: 'You shall wear shined shoes at Speech Day and enjoy the delights of strawberries and cream and salmon may-on-naise! You shall wear your shined shoes in the Classical Fifth and in the Classical Sixth also shall you wear them' (John Mortimer, *Clinging to the Wreckage*, p. 49).

Injunctions also take the form of noun phrases (e.g., 'Attention!'; 'Silence!'), gestures*, and noises* (e.g., the judge's hammering with the gavel to request silence in court). Lexicalized forms appear in such main-clause verbs as 'I order you to ...' and 'I want you to ...'; sometimes they are understood (e.g., 'Let no one go out'). As a mental attitude, injunction has expanded into a literary genre (see discourse*), but its purest form remains the imperative, characterized by the absence of pronouns designating the subject of the action (an absence implying all the more strongly the subject's immediate presence, however).

Analogous terms: mandate, command

R1: For various types of sentences and their corresponding functions, see enunciation*. Injunctions also take either positive or negative form (orders and prohibitions). They are analogous to questions* in that they presuppose from the receiver an answer, not of the assertive kind, but one which constitutes an attitude (acceptance or refusal).

R2: Although the word *injunction* implies the superiority of the speaker, the injunctive function is still exercised by a speaker whose inferiority may be real, mandatory, or simulated. In such cases, the same type of imperative is found, as in supplication*, for instance.

Other injunctive formulas – submissive, polite, or attenuated – occur under different forms: requests, propositions, suggestions, advice, etc. A *motion* is a formal proposal in a deliberative assembly.

R3: A *(vocal) summons* (and its rhetorical form, an apostrophe*) is preliminary to an injunction, aiming to establish the contact necessary for a possible injunction. It belongs therefore to the phatic rather than to the conative function of language. Ex: 'Friends, Romans, countrymen ...' (Shakespeare, *Julius Caesar*, 3.2.78).

R4: Injunctions do not have their own graphic marker: they employ both exclamation and question marks without being able to render the quite different real intonations* they involve. Ex:

> PLAYER: Go! Having mudered his brother and wooed the widow –
> the poisoner mounts the throne! ...
> ROSENCRANTZ: Oh, I say – here – really! You can't do that!
> PLAYER: Why not?
> ROSENCRANTZ: Well, really – I mean, people want to be entertained ...
>   Tom Stoppard, *Rosencrantz and Guildenstern Are Dead*, act 2

R5: Insults* and threats* may take injunctive forms. Ex: 'Get stuffed! ... We'll see about thee in a minute, impudent young pup!' (Keith Waterhouse, *Billy Liar*, pp. 40, 42).

IN PETTO (Ital. 'in the breast') Part of an utterance which the speaker keeps private by not speaking aloud. See *Concise Oxford Dictionary*, Robert, and Dubois et al., *Lexis*.

Insult

Ex: 'Paris pointed out the width of the bull's shoulders, the breadth of its flank. "And his coat is smooth without scars or imperfections; fit for a God," he said, and inwardly thought: *He is too good for sacrifice; he should be saved for breeding. Any old bull will do to strike off its head and bleed on an altar*' (Marion Zimmer Bradley, *The Firebrand*, p. 144).

The text may use the device to indicate self-censorship exercised by a character or narrator: 'I was beginning to say, "You know, darling, I think you have feelings, too, deep down," but the Witch had already resumed the formal attitude she assumed for public appearances. I let the matter drop' (K. Waterhouse, *Billy Liar*, p. 63).

R1: *In petto* remarks differ from *asides*. In the latter, the utterance is heard by someone, by the spectators, for example, when it is made in a dramatic work (see monologue*, R3). In a public meeting, asides have very few hearers, frequently only one (synonym: undertone).

R2: The use of *in petto* as a noun is not current in either English or French.

R3: *In petto* remarks interrupt the discursive thread*. For an example of an *in petto* remark accompanied by double parenthesis*, see situational* signs, 4.

INSULT The use of one or more pejorative lexemes which, by means of an apostrophe*, form the predicate of an implicit assertion* concerning the person addressed.

Exx: 'I felt myself all of a fever and like drowning in redhot blood, slooshying and viddying Dim's vulgarity, and I said: "Bastard. Filthy drooling mannerless bastaard" ' (A. Burgess, *A Clockwork Orange*, p. 25); 'TZARA: By God, you supercilious streak of Irish puke! You four-eyed, bog-ignorant, potato-eating ponce!' (Tom Stoppard, *Travesties*, act 1).

The subject may be designated specifically, as in the following example, in which a change of tone makes the insult all the more gross (see swear-word*):

'Outraged of Telford' has written to
tell the Editor how, last
Saturday, she and her spouse
went to the precinct to shop.

There was 'a group of young teenagers
lounging round in a doorway'
sprawling and picking their spots.
One, a girl aged about 12,
...

said to him [the spouse] 'What do you think of the
youth of Telford, eh, sexy?'
'Not very much,' he replied,
shaking her free of his arm.

Whereupon she became violent,
spat phlegm into the man's face,
screamed, 'Well, I'll tell you what, cunt,
we think *you're* old fucking shits!'

Peter Reading, *Ukelele Music*, p. 75

Other term: invective

Antonyms: compliment, flattery

R1: Insults differ from caricature*, in which some third party is the
subject of the assertion*. In the case of persiflage* and sarcasm*, the
pejorative lexemes are not applied to the person addressed, at least not
directly.

R2: R. Edouard, in the introduction to his *Dictionnaire des injures*,
distinguishes insults from *reproaches* (which are well-founded criticisms), threats* (which are future-oriented), and *outrageous attacks*
(which are cruelly wounding). He reduces the power of insults by
attributing them merely to 'illogical and momentary fits of irritation' or
to the 'need to attract attention,' that is, to the expressive and phatic
functions of communication. The injunctive function of insults forces
others to see themselves in a new and unflattering light; in extreme
cases, if they are assumed to be true, they may have a referential
function.

R3: Institutionalized insults accompanied by parodic ceremoniousness
in the form of 'roasts' of celebrities or well-known comedians confer
litanies of back-handed compliments on their recipients. Valéry has the
demons of hell recite such a litany to their master, for whom it constitutes praise, of course: 'Prince of Evil, hear us; Heart of the Abyss,
spare us! ... Arch of Hatred! Pit of Lies! Shadow of the truth!' (P.
Valéry, *Oeuvres*, 2:340).

R4: Insults may take various forms. See injunction*, R5, and false –*, R1
(the case of asteismus* or pretended insult).

INTERJECTION Interjections exist at the limits of language understood as a code, somewhere between gestures* and word-sentences. As
human noises* uttered by speakers, their meaning* differs in accordance with context and form, but nonetheless remains codifiable.

Ex: 'Huuuh! the drover's voice cried, his switch sounding on their

Interjection

flanks. Huuuh!' (Joyce, *Ulysses*, p. 81). The written forms *Huuuh*, *Huuuh*, although they refer to known interjections, deviate from dictionary forms like *whoa*. In thus rendering vocal acts in a specific way, they may modify their meaning. One can distinguish, then, between different meanings attributed to the same or to similar interjections. J. Tardieu (*Un Mot pour un autre*, pp. 16, 85) distinguished in this way between: *Ah?*: a sign of astonishment, demanding an explanation* or expressing incredulity; *Ah!*: the satisfaction at seeing the materialization of some event long awaited with hope and concern; *Ah! Ah!*: said with rising intonation, and confirming what was suspected to be fact. Some purely French exclamations collected and interpreted by Tardieu: *Ah! Bah!*: a polite answer, but one of disbelief and, basically, of indifference; *Ah! la-la, la-la-la-la!*: an expression of a person's reaction to disaster.

As may be seen, although dictionaries provide lists of interjections, their codification exists only in part and their meaning depends on melodic factors like tone, pitch, and so on. Deserving also of consideration is the Canadian interjection *Eh!*, as in 'Canadian Eh!'

A (far from complete) list of interjections: Ah! (A)hem! Ahoy! Alas! Bravo! Blast! Boo! Brrr! Damn! Eh! Eh? Eureka! Fie! Fore! Gee up! Ha! ha! ha! H[a/e/u]llo! Hallelujah! Hear hear! Hey! Hi! H'm! Hold on! Hurrah! Hush! Jeez! No go! Now then! Ooof! Oops! Ow! Oh! Ouch! Out! Pah! Pffft! Poof! Pooh! Pstt! Right! Swoosh! Ugh! Uh! Uh! Well then! What! Whew! Whoa! Yuk! See also click*.

R1: The ancients scarcely considered interjections, or cries 'thrown between' two sentences, to be part of (the) language. Indeed, from the viewpoint of syntax, only sentences merit consideration (see Crystal, 1987, p. 91; Wagner and Pinchon, p. 494; J. Dubois, p. 17f). But viewed as a phenomenon of syntagmatic flow, interjections are segments isolated by rhythm* and melody which nonetheless retain, despite their isolation, the same meaning they possess in their own context: this might make of them the shortest kinds of sentences (compare 'Yes' and 'No') with various possible functions. See enunciation*. Interjections with an expressive function: *Ouch!*, *Eeek!* (terror), *Tee-hee!* (a literary form of laughter), *Ugh!*, *Blast!* Interjections having a phatic function: *Hi!*, *Hey there!*, *Ickle! Tickle!* (or the like, said to get a baby's attention), and, best-known of all, the famous *Er ... Er ...* of a speaker lost for words. Some interjections have an injunctive function: *Hush!*, *Ahem! ahem!* (an invitation to discretion in a conversation), *Gee up!* Or a referential function: *Go on!* (an ironic form of agreement), *Ss! ... Ss!* (of admiration). See J. Tardieu, *Un Mot pour un autre*, pp. 85–113; and L. Tesnière, ch. 45

When its function is referential, the interjection (and its intonation*) is the equivalent of a predicate whose subject exists in the specific context. Thus *Oh!* indicates a response* to an objection (an exclamation* used to interrupt the person objecting). Ex: 'Oh! I'm far from being a fatalist.' In a narrative*, interjections signal the passage to direct utterances (either at the level of what is narrated or at that of the narration). Ex: 'All right, let him worry about that all he wants. As for me, I'm on a higher plane. I do not stoop to him. He's less than the dust beneath my chariot wheel. Yah, yah, ya-ah! Less than the du-ust!' (Dorothy Parker, 'But the One on the Right,' *New Yorker*, 19 Oct. 1929, p. 25).

R2: Some interjections elude codification; they are mere human noises* whose transcription remains approximate: we will call them *quasi-interjections*. Ex: 'Aham! ... Aham!' (Joyce, *Ulysses*, p. 197; the passage describes the warming powers of gin).

The quasi-interjection is a mimology* and may have a very precise meaning. Ex: 'Me. de Coetquidan said simply: "Hrrr ..." His uncle had said: "*Hrrr*," which meant: "Now, my boy, you're beginning to meddle with what doesn't concern you" ' (H. de Montherlant, *Romans*, pp. 747–8).

R3: Interjections differ from non-human noises* and from onomatopoeia*, the codification of sounds. Such noises are introduced into sentences either as nouns or as a kind of adverb of manner. They could not form a direct human utterance, complete in itself, as do interjections and quasi-interjections.

R4: Pseudo-language* appears to be very similar to interjections both because it also possesses a clear-cut form within a system of sounds, graphemes, and rhythmic units, and because it seems to be made of words, although the latter have neither meaning* nor syntactic specificity. But pseudo-language does not reproduce the interjection's spontaneous linguistic act; on the contrary, its origins must be sought in language, duly constituted as such, of which its prolonged sentences and expressive or melodic rhythms* are no more than a distant imitation.

R5: Fairly close to interjections are *oaths*, also often codified, and having a principally expressive function. (See Courault, 2:127.) Ex: 'One of the Crokes made a woeful wipe at him one time with his caman and I declare to God he was within an aim's ace of getting it at the side of his temple. Oh, honest to God, if the crook of it caught him that time he was done for' (Joyce, *Portrait of the Artist as a Young Man*, p. 182).

In order to desecrate, oaths must exceed the limits of what is generally considered permissible. Québécois profanity involves repetition of the names of the sacred altar vessels, chalice and ciborium, as well as of the host and tabernacle (see blasphemy*, R1). Ex: 'By the tripes of all the popes, past, present and future, no! two-hundred thousand times no!' (Théophile Gautier, *Mademoiselle de Maupin*, preface).

Interruption

Oaths are often distorted (see attenuation*). **Exx:** *Gee whiz!, Crumbs!, Jeepers creepers!, Holy Toledo!, Gad!, G–dammit!* Québécois distortions include: *'stie* (i.e., *Hostie!* [host!]), *tabarnouche, chriss, cibole, ciboaque* (i.e., *ciboire* [ciborium]).

Whereas interjections are often well received (as familiarities helpful to communication), oaths, because they have something in common with swear-words*, risk giving offence. They would simply be means of conferring emphasis*, except that in some circles they are considered blasphemous. **Ex:** ' "Talk bloody sense, man!" he roared. "By Christ, if this is what they learned him at technical school, I'm glad I'm bloody ignorant!" ' (K. Waterhouse, *Billy Liar*, p. 79).

In Quebec, *Chriss* is introduced into sentences as an emphatic lexeme. **Exx:** 'un chriss de fou' (equivalent to 'a bloody fool'); 'mon chriss de tabarnak d'hostie de câliss'!'

R6: Violent or savage sentences or human noises* tend to become screams.

INTERRUPTION A voluntary action or utterance that prevents the discourse* from proceeding continuously.

Ex: ' "I am inclined to think –" said I [Dr Watson]. "I should do so," Sherlock Holmes remarked, impatiently' (Conan Doyle, *The Valley of Fear*, ch. 1).

Ex: ' "I agree with you, Minister," came the reply, much to my surprise. "There is indeed scope for economy ..." "Then ..." I interrupted, "... where, for God's sake?" ' (J. Lynn and A. Jay, *The Complete 'Yes Minister,'* p. 68).

Other definitions: Fontanier (p. 372) and Puttenham (see Lanham, p. 60) give to interruption the meaning of aposiopesis*. Fontanier distinguishes it from *reticence*, whose silences are, in his view, charged with allusions* all the more pernicious for being silent.

R1: Strictly speaking, interruptions are caused by external events; for example, someone's arrival or a telephone ringing: 'ALMA (to John): And I always say that life is such a mysteriously complicated thing that no one should really presume to judge and condemn the behavior of anyone else!' (*There is a faraway "puff" and a burst of golden light over their heads. Both look up. There is a long-drawn "Ahhhh ..." from the invisible crowd. This is an effect which will be repeated at intervals during the scene.*) There goes the first skyrocket! Oh, look at it burst into a million stars!' (Tennessee Williams, *Summer and Smoke*, part 1, scene 1). When the cause is a psychological event, either expressive or impressive, the interruption is called aposiopesis*.

R2: In a narrative*, interruptions are signs of mimesis*. **Ex:**

– I was just round at the courthouse, says he, looking for you. I hope I'm not ...
– No, says Martin, we're ready. (Joyce, *Ulysses*, p. 279)

Suppression of the beginning, rather than the end, of the text produces counter-interruption*.

R3: The reason for some interruptions lies in the obviousness of what is to follow: judged unnecessary, its enunciation is dispensed with so as not to fatigue the reader. In such cases, *etc.* is used. Ex: 'And, to his credit, he handled it superbly. At once out came all the appropriate phrases: "But I'm sure ... whatever made you think? ... no question of anything but the fullest support ..."' etc.' (J. Lynn and A. Jay, *The Complete 'Yes Minister,'* p. 123). If repeated, *etc.* becomes (even more) ironic. Ex: 'STUPID WAGERS: A certain Pascal etc., etc.' (J. Prévert, *Paroles*, p. 182). Ex: In the musical comedy *The King and I*, Oscar Hammerstein II wrote a song called 'Etc. etc.' to allow the King of Siam to display his domineering nature.

R4: Interruptions do not always entail suppressions. In the following curious example, by means of a device reminiscent of the process of dictation, the recovery of control involves the repetition* of part of the interrupted discourse:

The end of the rigid index finger approaches the circle formed by the dial of the watch fastened on ...
the circle formed by the dial of the watch fastened on his wrist and called ... (A. Robbe-Grillet, *Le Voyeur*, p. 253)

INTONATION Whereas rhythm* involves the duration of segments (measured in centiseconds) and emphasis* concerns principally their intensity (measured in decibels), intonation modulates *pitch* (measured in Hertz) in relation to a basic or medium tone which differs from one individual to another. Variations in pitch, characterized by their deviation and contour, produce *the melody of sentences*.

Any spontaneous utterance is accompanied by various melodies whose changing nuances are difficult to transpose onto the musical scale because, unlike the well-tempered clavier, they do not conform to octaves divided into five tones and two semitones, but bring into play intermediate tones. Prose melody is the opposite of *recto tono*, which is both musical and fixed. In this context, the natural is inimitable. For an actor, it consists in constant intuitive reinvention of noteless melodies more expressive of a character's feelings than the text itself.

Electronic instruments (spectographs, for instance) nowadays allow for the fairly accurate recording of intonation. But despite frequent attempts (see the bibliographies in D.B. Bollinger's *Intonation and Its*

Parts or P.R. Léon's *Essais de phonostylistique*), their interpretation remains uncertain.

At least three functions may be assigned to such recordings.

(a) The relevant part of the phenomenon may be localized, since intonation plays a part in marking the boundaries of textual articulations.

(b) Consequently, for the same succession of sounds, intonation may assign different contents. Ex: In 'He would have died but for his dog,' uttered with steeply rising intonation (level 4; or 5 if said with emotion), *died* implies that he is still alive thanks to his dog.

(c) Intonation reveals the speaker's private thoughts. Thus, 'That's cunning!' with a rising or falling melody becomes respectively meliorative or pejorative. By the use of musical notes, Morier transcribes (under *mélodie*) different intonations of the sentence-ending 'Le savais-tu?' ('Did you know?') and others like it, which are able to convey, as the case may be, a request for information, suspicion, aggressive astonishment, justified distrust, friendly *dubitatio**, incredulity mixed with astonishment, ironic incredulity, antiphrasis*, hesitation, and so on.

Such tones, used constantly in oral language, are immediately restored by readers, which is why by reading a text aloud, one reveals, down to the smallest detail, one's understanding or interpretation of it. But at present there exist only rudimentary means of transcribing such understanding and attributed meaning. See expressive punctuation*. See Crystal, 1987, pp. 169–73.

R1: Which are the significant indications we should transcribe? P.R. Léon (*Essais de phonostylistique*) identified several.

1. The most important is the *contour* of the melodic curve, which may be written down in musical notation (see Morier, *Dictionnaire de poétique et de rhétorique*, pp. 616–33). A less onerous kind of transcription consists in placing under the vowels one or more black dots according as the melody sinks slightly or markedly, and in putting one or more circles above the vowels in the case of a rising melody. Two black dots correspond to level 1, three to level 5. Exx:

(1) You didn't know? (friendly doubt)

(2) You didn't know that? (astonished disbelief)

(3) You didn't know that? (surprise and suspicion)

(4) You didn't know? (ironic doubt)

A mingogram is 'a graphic recording which includes several simultaneous and complementary graphs. The term is a gallicized form of "Mingograf," [the product-name] of a Swedish apparatus for studying heartbeats which has been adapted to the needs of research in phonetics' (Morier, p. 770, under *mingogramme*). The graphs produced by the mingogram can be projected onto a five-level scale (see Léon, pp. 20–39), or expressed in a diagram like the one below, or coloured and turned into dots which traverse the line in the text, considered to be the base line which represents the medium level, no. 2.

LEVELS	RANGE
5 high-pitched	_____
4 high	_____
3 infra-high	_____
2 medium	_____
1 low	_____

See continuation*.

2. We must also take into account the *separation* between the peaks and troughs in the melodic contour. The deviation is all the greater as feelings mount. Any exclamation*, any true or even simulated emotion, causes the voice to rise to level 5, at the end of either a syntagm* or a sentence (see Léon, p. 52).

3. *Intensity* (weak, medium, or high) denotes, for example, timidity (i<) or sadness (i<), or, on the contrary, anger (i>), indignation (i>), or advertising 'hype' (i>). Medium intensity denotes neutrality of tone or only slight feeling such as surprise (i=) or wariness (i=). Morier uses one, two, or three (in the case of extreme force) acute accents (´, ´´, ´´´) written above the letter for an intensity accent affecting a single vowel, consonant, or short segment.

4. *Duration.* Another characteristic of advertising hype is its rapidity. Intonation in expressions of anger, indignation, and fear is also rapid, but slows down in those denoting surprise, timidity, and sadness, and is much slower still in expressions of cheerfulness. These changes in speed may be represented by v<<, v<, v>, and v>>.

5. *Register* (sound quality). The average register of the human voice varies with the individual since it is his or her *medium* of expression. However, an individual's register may undergo variation as his/her feelings change from moment to moment. Sadness is denoted by lowering the bass register (as an average of the unaccented syllables). A powerful rise in register accompanies fear, surprise, or hype; the rise is very powerful in the case of anger. This might be represented as m<,

241

m>, and m>>. Léon speaks of a register's 'symbolic' value, and Crystal (1987, pp. 174–5) of 'sound symbolism.'

R2: The description, possibly even the transcription, of different types of intonation would facilitate the identification, in something more than a merely intuitive fashion, of a great number of literary devices whose tone makes them 'sing.' The following is a list of those which appear in the present dictionary, and which seem to possess a melody – or melodies – of their own:

anticlimax* – antiparastasis* – apology – aposiopesis* – apostrophe* – approximation* – assertion* – asteismus* – autism* – chleuasmos* – *communicatio** – concession* – disapproval – *dubitatio** – epiphonema* – euphemism* – exclamation* – excuse* – gauloiserie* – howler – imitation* – insult* – interjection* – irony* – licence* – metastasis* – mimology* – mockery – monologue* – *optatio* – palinode – parabasis* – paradox* – parody* – parroting – *permissio** – persiflage* – preterition* – prolepsis* – prosopopoeia* – pseudo-tautology – psittacism* – question* – quibble* – quotation* – rhetorical question – recrimination* – refutation* – riddle* – sarcasm* – self-correction* – slogan* – soliloquy – supplication* – surprise – suspense* – threat* – wish – witticism.

The following is an example of intonation which changes the meaning of an assertion*: '– "So things seem better like this?" "Better! Better! I take them as they are" ' (Jules Romains, *Monsieur Le Trouhadec*, in *Théâtre*, 2:133).

INVERSION A reversal of what is considered the normal or usual order of the constituent parts (words or word groups) of a sentence (see Marouzeau). See also Fontanier (p. 284), Lausberg, Morier, *OED*, and Preminger.

Exx: 'Fifteen children he had' (Joyce, *Ulysses*, p. 124); '*The House Beautiful* is the play lousy!' (Dorothy Parker, in *Life*, quoted by Pepper, *Twentieth-Century Quotations*, p. 358).

Other definitions: In rhetoric, inversion means 'turning an opponent's argument* against him; also called the figure of retort' (*OED*, Preminger). Ex: 'I did dislike the cut of a certain courtier's beard. He sent me word if I said his beard was not cut well, he was in mind it was. This is called the Retort Courteous' (Shakespeare, *As You Like It*, 5.4.72).

In prosody, inversion means the turning of feet by substituting stressed for unstressed syllables, or vice versa. Ex (using a trochee for an iamb in iambic verse):

Cátcht | bý Cóntá | gion, like | in pun | ishment

Milton, *Paradise Lost*, 10.544

Robert O. Evans, who quotes the above example (see Preminger, pp. 402–3), comments: 'In traditional English verse, inversion of stress is a common device for securing variation, occurring most frequently in the initial foot and often immediately following the caesura, only very rarely in the final foot.'

R1: Inversion only has figurative value if not demanded syntactically, and its effect is stronger for being unexpected.

R2: Frequently, inversion's role is to call attention to either subject or predicate. **Ex:** 'Morning sex she'd had enough of in her time' (Julian Barnes, *Before She Met Me*, p. 124). See apposition*, R2.

R3: Aesthetric inversion may aim to make a sentence's movement reflect that of the object or behaviour described. **Ex:** In a recent film, inversion is the characteristic device identifying the speech of the Jedi master-teacher, Yoda: 'Harm I mean you not. Away put your weapon' (George Lucas, *The Empire Strikes Back*, 1980).

IRONY 1. Expressing in the form of a joke, intended seriously or not, the opposite of what one thinks or wants others to think (see Fontanier, p. 145). See also Corbett, Scaliger (3:140), Littré, Quillet, Lausberg (sect. 583), Morier, and Preminger.

Exx: 'What a fine day!' [said on a day of obviously inclement weather]; ' "Truly this is the sweetest of theologies," William said, with perfect humility, and I thought he was using that insidious figure of speech that rhetors call irony, which must always be prefaced by the pronunciatio, representing its signal and justification – something William never did' (U. Eco, *The Name of the Rose*, p. 145).

2. Anglo-Saxon writers on rhetoric (see, for instance, D.C. Muecke, *The Compass of Irony*, and W.C. Booth, *A Rhetoric of Irony*) distinguish the kind of ironic statement described by Fontanier from the kind of ironic situation in which a speaker through 'self-ignorance' commits the 'irony of self-betrayal.' (See also Abrams, Cuddon, Morier ['immanent irony'], Preminger, and Woodson). Such is the case in the following instance where the fictional medieval speaker, Bernard Gui, papal inquisitor and opponent of the doctrine prescribing clerical poverty, is represented as supporting the pope for reasons of self-interest: 'And I know for certain that not long ago, in Avignon itself, with necromancies of this sort philters and ointments were prepared to make attempts on the life of our lord Pope himself, poisoning his foods. The Pope was able to defend himself and identify the toxin only because he was supplied with prodigious jewels in the form of serpents' tongues, fortified by wondrous emeralds and rubies that through divine power

were able to reveal the presence of poison in foods' (U. Eco, *The Name of the Rose*, p. 329).

Analogous terms: 'Drie Mock' (Puttenham); *dissimulatio*; enantiosis; *illusio* (Lanham); antitrope (Littré groups irony, sarcasm*, and euphemism* under this term)

R1: Preminger places under the rubric *irony*: litotes*, hyperbole*, antiphrasis*, asteismus*, chleuasmos*, mockery (see persiflage*), imitation* (pastiche), puns*, parody*, and false naïvety. His criterion is that, in the case of irony, only the author is sure of the true meaning of what is said. If the meaning* is too clear, irony turns into sarcasm*, insults*, threats*, etc. This conforms to the Greek meaning of the term ειρωνεια ('interrogation'): the reader must ask what may have been meant. This is irony in the strict sense. However, Morier also includes a large number of figures in his entry on irony (as well as some of those in Preminger's list, he includes preterition*, *permissio**, and *gradatio**, before partially identifying humour* as the 'irony of reconciliation'). Such compilations of figures under the rubric *irony* lend plausibility to the contention of Group MU and others that irony is a 'superordinate' figure capable of marshalling numbers of ordinate tropes in the interest of global textual strategies.

R2: Irony may be reduced to no more than a speaker's tone of voice, which may force a novelist to specify what a character really means. **Ex:** 'She added without the slightest discernible irony in her voice: *"I feel safe with you, I never have to fear the unexpected"* ' (J.-P. Sartre, *L'Age de raison*, p. 114). Graphic signs available are parentheses surrounding either exclamation or question marks. **Ex:** 'The present Dean (!)' The suggestion, made by Alcanter de Brahm (see *L'Ostensoir des ironies* [1899]) that a reversed question mark be used as the sign of irony failed to gain currency. Muecke comments (p. 56): 'The only proper comment on his suggested *point d'ironie* is *point d'ironie: plus d'ironie.*' As well as revealing de Brahm's real name, Marcel Bernhardt, Booth adds (p. 206, n. 9) that the proposed symbol would have been inadequate, requiring in addition 'a set of evaluative sub-symbols: * = average; † = superior; ‡ = not so good; § = marvellous; ‖ = perhaps expunge.'

R3: Irony is not always playful. Fontanier points to *contrefision* or painful irony. Bénac specifies that the ironist may wish to convey that 'those who claim the proposition is true, are either stupid, which provokes his mockery, or dishonest, which arouses his indignation.' This definition is similar to the Anglo-Saxon view of irony mentioned earlier. Irony in this extended sense has become a form of mockery (see persiflage*).

R4: Irony employs allusion*, implication*, and cliché*, as well as the figures already mentioned.

ISOLEXISM (neol.) The return, within a sentence, of a lexeme already uttered, but in different conditions.

Isolexism comes in four distinct forms:

Isolexism by derivation: The same lexical element returns in different words. Ex:

Mock mockers after that
That would not lift a hand maybe
To help good, wise or great
To bar that foul storm out, for we
Traffic in mockery

W.B. Yeats, 'Nineteen Hundred and Nineteen'

Morphological isolexism: Repetition of the same word in different actualizations; that is, within the nominal syntagm, only number, article, and possessive, demonstrative, or indefinite adjectives change. Exx: 'It is true that you may fool all of the people some of the time; you can even fool some of the people all of the time; but you can't fool all of the people all of the time' (A. Lincoln, quoted in Alexander McClure, *Lincoln's Yarns and Stories*, p. 81); 'Work in the service of man, for every man, for everything in man' (Pope Paul VI, 10 June 1969); 'Cursed be Canaan; a servant of servants shall he be unto his brethren' (Genesis 9:25).

Syntactic isolexism: Actualization of the same word with different grammatical functions; that is, prepositions may be modified in noun phrases, and conjunctions in verb clauses, as may the equivalents of either. Ex: '... government of the people, by the people, for the people ...' (A. Lincoln, 'The Gettysburg Address,' 1863).

Syntagmatic isolexism (or reiteration): The same word, with the same actualization and function, is added on to another syntagm in the same sentence. Ex: 'Over then, come over, for the bee has quit the clover' (R. Kipling, 'The Long Trail').

It will be better to group these four types of isolexism under the same name, not only so as to avoid the proliferation of terminology, but also because they frequently are combined. Exx: 'Please please me' [title of a song by the Beatles]; 'Nothing is enough to the man for whom enough is too little' (Epicurus). The essential feature of the device is the lexeme's return, which imprints the formula on the memory. Ex: 'Let me assert my firm belief that the only thing we have to fear is fear itself' (F.D. Roosevelt, First Inaugural Address, March 1933).

Isolexism may, however, result merely from negligence (e.g., 'Skiers were skiing') or may be an easy way of inventing a tautophony: 'a hunter hunting hunted with other hunters.' Compare this with the isolexic rigour of: 'How much wood would a woodchuck chuck if a woodchuck could chuck wood?'

Other names: conjugates (for isolexism by derivation: Aristotle, *Topics*, 2.23.1397a 20; Thomas Wilson, *The Rule of Reason*; Abraham Fraunce, *The Lawier's Logike*, [see Joseph, pp. 338–9]); *dérivation* (Le Clerc, p. 269; Fontanier, p. 351); declension (for morphological isolexism: Le Clerc); *traductio* (also for morphological isolexism: Lanham; Fontanier, p. 352 ['traduction']; Morier); *polyptoton* (for morphological and syntactic isolexism: Fontanier, p. 352; Lanham; Lausberg, sect. 640–8; Quinn). In Greek and Latin, the latter term applied to the repetition of words in different cases (Gr. *polyptoton*: 'various cases'). In the same way, *homoioptoton* (Gr. 'in a like case with a similar inflexion'; see Lanham, Lausberg, sect. 729) applied to repetition of endings in the same case, similar in sound. Such figures are no longer possible in modern analytic languages, and, as Lanham says (p. 54) of homoioptoton, 'English uses the term loosely, often making it synonymous with *Homoioteleuthon*, often making it mean simply rhyme*.' We have followed this assimilation; see homoioteleuton*.

R1: Isolexism is the opposite of grammatical reprise*.

R2: Polysemic isolexisms turn into word-play*. Ex: 'Vats of porter wonderful. Rats get in too ... Rats: vats' (Joyce, *Ulysses*, p. 125).

R3: Morphological or syntactic isolexism is a way of emphasizing a noun or even of emphasizing a proper name by refusing to use a pronoun. Ex: 'Long may'st thou live in Richard's seat to sit, / And soon lie Richard in an earthy pit!' (Shakespeare, *Richard II*, 4.1.218–19).

R4: Dislocation* and the refusal to use pronouns permit emphasis of any lexeme forming the focal points of a predicate. Ex: 'Unbelievable! That must seem to you unbelievable!' This is false isolexism, closer to reduplication*.

R5: Some isolexisms have become part of the language. See etymology*, other def. Ex: 'To live one's life, sleep the sleep of the just ...'

R6: Lexical mirroring (see mirror*) consists in subordinating the different lexical parts of an isolexism one to another.

ISOTOPY A term proposed by Greimas, composed of *topos*, 'a place,' and *isos*, 'equal, same.' Isotopy is not a device, but a concept necessary to the definition of devices. Consider the case of a lexical word; once inserted into a text, it refers not only to a meaning but also to a referent (see enunciation*, 5); that is, it designates something which is part of the world outside language. The type of reality evoked by the set of elements making up the text forms its *universe of discourse* or isotopy. An isotopy exists when the words used refer to the 'same place.' An isotopy is situated in a *cosmological, noological, historical,* or *anthropological dimension* according to whether it involves objects, ideas, actions, or persons. For example, in the case of the expression 'Small is beautiful,' the context imposes one among several possible isotopies. *Small* may belong to the universe of objects: this will give 'the small hat,' 'the small bouquet,' etc. It may designate a child. It may also enter the noological dimension and the sentence then means: 'Smallness is more beautiful [than largeness].'

R1: Greimas analysed *complex isotopies* (see image*, 5). *Multiple isotopies* have been studied since antiquity (see meaning*, 6 and 7). A *double isotopy* creates ambiguity* (see ambiguity, 1). Conversely, a *single isotopy* reduces dissociations* (see dissociation, R5) to images*.

J

JARGON Language which is inaccessible to non-specialists.

Ex: David Monaghan describes as follows the fictional language of espionage invented by John Le Carré [David Cornwell]: 'Le Carré offers nearly two hundred words and phrases ... Thus, amongst his forty or so terms used to describe types of spies are such felicitous titles as "little ships," "secret whisperers," "burrowers," "coat trailers," "Golden Oldies," "ju ju men," "lamplighters," "pavement artists," "shoemakers," "vicars." Elsewhere, to be cleared of suspicion is to be "graded Persil" and to threaten and bribe simultaneously is to carry out a "stick-and-carrot job" ' (*Smiley's Circus: A Guide to the Secret World of John Le Carré*, p. 11).

Other definitions: gibberish* (*Concise Oxford Dictionary, Petit Robert*); 'artificial language used by the members of a group desirous of remaining uncomprehended by outsiders or of distinguishing themselves from the common: criminal, schoolboy jargon' (Marouzeau). The latter definition gives a restricted meaning which includes much that is better defined as slang* (see slang, R1). In his *Style: An Anti-Textbook*, Richard Lanham devotes a whole chapter (pp. 69–93) to American jargon: 'No one can deny that America in our time has produced the finest flowering of specialist gobbledegook the planet has seen. Witness the bureaucratic mumblespeak ... American jargon is such fun to contemplate, so full of pompous self-satisfaction on the one hand, and cynical, knowing, ritual mystification on the other that description hardly knows where to begin' (p. 69).

R1: What remain reserved for members of the group are more often special meanings than lexical words themselves. **Ex:** 'Derivatives of constant functions are zero. Is the reciprocal case true? *i.e.,* is a function whose derivative is zero a constant?' (Fr. Roure and A. Buttery, *Mathématiques pour les sciences sociales,* 1: 155).

R2: Scientific jargon has invaded the novel. **Ex:** 'Inside their brains they shared an old, old electro-decor – variable capacitors of glass, kerosene for a dielectric, brass plates and ebonite covers, Zeiss galvanometers with thousands of fine threaded adjusting screws, Siemens milliammeters set on plate surfaces, terminals designated by Roman numerals, Standard Ohms of manganese wire in oil, the old Gulcher Thermosaule that operated on heated gas, put out 4 volts, nickel and antimony, asbestos funnels on top, mica tubing ...' (Thomas Pynchon, *Gravity's Rainbow,* p. 518). Compare Alain Robbe-Grillet and Hubert Aquin. See also nominalization*, R4.

R3: The languages invented by computer programmers (Basic, Fortran, Cobol, Pascal, etc.) are jargons formed in some instances from English prefixes, roots, or suffixes. Similarly, the names given to newly invented substances: nylon, orlon, lycra, corfam, etc. In some sectors, such newly coined denominations have so proliferated as to make necessary the publication of glossaries.

JUXTAPOSITION (GRAPHIC) A graphism* which eliminates the spaces between words.

Exx: 'Wotalotigot' [i.e., 'what a lot ...,' an ad for chocolates]; 'Nationalgymnasiummuseumsanatoriumandsuspensoriumsordinaryprivatdocentgeneralhistoryspecialprofessordoctor' (Joyce, *Ulysses,* p. 252).

Analogous term: Run on (typography)

R1: In Raymond Queneau's work, analogous graphisms are syntagmatic amalgams* like 'Keskya?' ['Worizit?'] (*Le Chiendent,* p. 238). Joyce prefers to juxtapose two lexemes (lexical roots) to form a new sememe (global signified). **Ex:** 'He smellsipped the cordial juice' (*Ulysses,* p. 142). See lexical juxtaposition*.

JUXTAPOSITION (LEXICAL) Whether words are joined together by hyphens or by graphic juxtaposition*, the result is the same: such devices amalgamate syntagms* or lexemes, thus inventing new words whose global meaning is the sum of the individual meanings possessed by the segments. **Ex:** 'Davy Byrne smiledyawnednodded all in one' (Joyce, *Ulysses,* p. 145). Davy makes only one movement, but there is no single word to describe it; hence the juxtaposition of the three constituent actions into a single attitude.

R1: In the case of apposition*, there is a principal lexeme to which the others are related; in that of juxtaposition, all lexemes exist on the same footing, amalgamated into a whole which unites all their semes into a new sememe. Ex: 'par une totale dissipation-dérision-purgation' (H. Michaux, 'Clown,' in *L'Espace du dedans*, p. 249).

R2: By juxtaposing contrary lexemes we present the whole semantic field covered by an idea, however paradoxical. The surrealists did not miss this opportunity. Ex: 'La beauté sera érotique-voilée, explosante-fixe, magique-circonstancielle ou ne sera pas' ('Beauty will be both erotic and hidden, exploding and settled, magic and circumstantial or there will be no Beauty') (Breton, quoted by P. Eluard, *Oeuvres*, 1: 727).

JUXTAPOSITION (SYNTACTIC) Two or more terms are brought together, a process resulting in a combination which presumes some unexpressed relationship between the words united.

Ex: 'cash down, home free.' See also Marouzeau.

Ex: *L'Amour la poésie* ('Love Poetry') [the title of a collection of love poems by Eluard; instead of the more usual noun phrase 'poèmes d'amour']

Other definitions: In general, theorists reduce syntactic juxtaposition to asyndeton*: see Corbett, Georgin, Lanham, Quinn, and Robert. Group MU (*A General Rhetoric*, pp. 70-1), discussing metataxes or figures which by 'acting on the form of sentences ... focus attention on syntax' (ibid., p. 63), see syntactic juxtaposition as an example of 'nominal sentences' or parataxis*, the suppression of syntactic links between signifiers. Fowler discussed the suppression of such links both within and between sentences under 'Verbless sentences.'

R1: Syntactic juxtaposition is a type of brachylogia*. Corbett (p. 470) quotes the following example from a speech by John F. Kennedy: 'that we shall pay any price, bear any burden, meet any hardship, support any friend, oppose any foe to assure the survival and the success of liberty.' Another example: 'The children run, the pigeons fly off. Races, white flashes, minor rout' (Sartre, quoted by Group MU, p. 71).

L

LAMENTATION Rhetorically, lamentation consists in the expression, in some conventional form of words or phrases, of a feeling of sorrow.

Exx: Alas! What a tragedy! What a pity! Hell! Oh no!

Lapsus

Exx:

> The elders of the daughter of Zion
>   sit on the ground in silence;
> they have cast dust on their heads
>   and put on sackcloth.
>
> Lamentations 2:10

> What passing bells for these who die as cattle?
>   – Only the monstrous anger of the guns.
>   Only the stuttering rifles' rapid rattle
> Can patter out their hasty orisons.
> No mockeries now for them; no prayers nor bells;
>   Nor any voice of mourning save the choirs, –
> The shrill, demented choirs of wailing shells;
>   And bugles calling them from sad shires.
>
> W. Owen, 'Anthem for Doomed Youth'

Other names: In antiquity, several literary genres served as vehicles for lamentation. Threnody (Gr. 'wailing song') was a song of lamentation or dirge: 'originally a choral ode, it changed to a monody which was strophic in form' (Cuddon). *Neniae* were 'funeral poems sung in primitive times at Rome by the female relatives of the deceased, or by hired singers' (Harvey, in *Oxford Companion to Classical Literature*). The *consolatio*, or condolence, also had its own theme, viz. 'everyone must die' (see Curtius, p. 100). Nowadays, funeral orations are less common, but letters and telegrams of condolence remain. Corsica still has the *vocero* or funeral chant sung by the *vocératrices* or female mourners.

LAPSUS An inadvertent slip, either of the tongue (*lapsus linguae*) or in writing (*lapsus calami*). See *OED* and Robert.

Ex: 'Population of U.S. broken down by age and sex' (quoted by E. Tempel, *Humor in the Headlines*, p. 149).

Other names: parapraxis (Redfern, *Puns*, pp. 117–23); *lapsus loquendi*, *lubricum linguae*, *lapsus pennae* (Grambs, p. 207)

R1: Freud showed that several kinds of mistakes*, even mere slips of the tongue, have their origin in the unconscious. There is the example of the wife explaining that her ailing husband does not need a special diet: 'He can eat and drink what I want' (*The Psychopathology of Everyday Life*, in *The Basic Writings of Sigmund Freud*, ed. A.A. Brill, p. 77). On what have come to be called 'Freudian slips,' Helen McNeil comments: 'A sub-group of sexual puns, [they] endanger the speaker because they communicate more about his secret associations than he wants others to know' (quoted by Redfern, p. 118). **Ex:** 'A lady once expressed herself in society – the very words show they were uttered with fervor and under the pressure of a great many secret emotions: "Yes, a woman must be pretty if she is to please the men. A man is much better off. As long as he has *five* straight limbs, he needs no more!" ' (Freud, *The Psychopathology of Everyday Life*, p. 77; Freud's emphasis).

R2: A particular kind of slip, called *attraction* (*Concise Oxford Dictionary*), is false agreement caused by syntactic proximity. Ex: 'The wages of sin *is* death.' Other slips result simply from confusions between terms similar in sound. Ex: 'There is a French widow in every bedroom affording delightful prospects' (G. Hoffnung, quoted by Augarde, p. 178).

R3: Self-correction* (see self-correction, R2) usually follows a lapsus.

LENGTHENING   The inordinate drawing out of a phoneme with a view to rendering an object or movement more perceptible.

Exx: 'My Lor-or-ords, Ladie-ie-ies, and Gen'leme-e-e-en'; 'The-e-e-y-y-y're off'; ' "But it's true, isn't it?" said Lucy. Annie said: "Ye-e-es, it's true ... but well, he's in politics" ' (J. Lynn and A. Jay, *The Complete 'Yes Minister,'* p. 140); 'Eileeeeeeeeeeeeeeen! Yoooou arree my Queeeeennnn ...' (Spike Milligan, *Puckoon*, p. 40); 'Jazz jazz jazzzzz' (R. Duguay, *Ruts*, p. 19).

R1: The figure is essentially one of sound and has various transcriptions. Accompanying it are melodies and inflections which are impossible to write down and which actors rediscover or re-create according to their talent. Ex: 'PENELOPE: Oooooh ... Aaaaah ... I can't fight you any more – It's too lovely – oh – don't stop – ah – I don't care if he comes in –' (Tom Stoppard, *Another Moon Called Earth*, scene 1, in *The Dog It Was That Died and Other Plays*).

R2: Some cases of phonemic lengthening have an emphasizing or comic function: Ex: 'Good-bye-ee, good-bye-ee, wipe a tear, baby dear, from your eye-ee ...' (song in Joan Littlewood's *Oh What a Lovely War!*, act 1).

R3: Gregorian chant is often recitative on a single note (plainchant) followed by a melody sung on the final accented syllable. The term *melismatic* describes a song 'in which one syllable flowers out into a passage of several notes. It [melisma] means much the same thing, then, as *Coloratura, Fioratura,* or *Divisions'* (P.A. Scholes, in *The Oxford Companion to Music*, p. 618). The troubadours of medieval Provence had a conventional graphic sign (*melisma*) indicating which melody to sing on a particular syllable in their songs (see Th. Gérold, *La Musique au Moyen Age*). Ex: Many of Handel's oratorios, including *The Messiah*, lengthen syllables by repeating or varying notes sung on them.

R4: One kind of phonemic lengthening is the tremolo. Ex: Dame Edith Evans, as Lady Bracknell in act 1 of Wilde's *The Importance of Being Ernest*, produced a tremolo-effect when she pronounced the words 'ha-a-a-and-ba-a-ag' in the lines:

Letter

LADY BR.: Where did the charitable gentleman who had a first-class ticket for this seaside resort find you?
JACK (gravely): In a hand-bag.
LADY BR.: A hand-bag?

LETTER A written monologue* in which the signatory assumes a dialogical relationship with the addressee. The genre is a mixture of global enunciation* and included utterance. It begins with a notation* of time and place and an apostrophe*, possibly marked affectively (e.g., 'Dear ...,' 'My Dear ...'). In official letters, the addressee's official title constitutes the *form of address* and appears on a line by itself above the first line of text.

The plan* of a letter, other than one which merely 'rambles naïvely on,' follows that of a formal conversation. Remarks about the weather, and health matters, or requests for news, for instance, are means of establishing contact (the phatic function of communication). An outline of one's intentions, reasons, and arguments to justify steps taken or to be taken may follow. A request to be remembered to one's relatives, the offering of one's best wishes, and expressions of affection or courtesy (i.e., some polite formula), all of these both announce and defer the ending of the communication. For the different rhetorical flourishes, both formal and informal, used to close letters in French, see, for example, J. Serres, *Le Protocole et les usages*, p. 56, or C. Grégoire de Blois, *Nouveau Dictionnaire de la correspondance*, pp. 59–78. The final word in a personal letter may express the writer's relationship to the addressee. Ex: 'Your affectionate daughter.'

Analogous terms: missive (an official letter); epistle (archaic); cover, envelope; note, a few lines, a short word; *billet doux* (a 'love letter'). Formal letters frequently differ from informal ones in that they are typed rather than handwritten.

Other meaning: a unit in writing theoretically corresponding to a phoneme. For the 'letters' which form the alphabet, see graphism*, R1, and symbol*, 3, R1. A triliteral word has three letters, a tetragram has four (*OED*).

R1: The epistolary genre has had an impact on literature. The epistolary novel flourished in the eighteenth century, and letters still appear frequently with documentary value in novels today. Newspapers publish 'Letters' from correspondents in Moscow, Washington, London, etc., as well as 'letters to the editor.' Poems appear in the form of letters or even as telegrams. The 'private' correspondences of both the famous and the unknown continue to be published.

R2: *Open* letters are published when sent and constitute political acts.

LEVEL (OF LANGUAGE) Three distinct levels are usually asserted by stylisticians like Bally or Vinay: popular language, everyday (or current) speech, and sustained (or polished) language. Socio-linguists like Peter Trudgill prefer a continuum running from formal to informal language (marked 1 and 3 below). By combining elements from examples of each it is possible to posit an interface of 'neutral' language (2):

1. I require your attendance to be punctual.
2. I want you to be punctual.
3. I want you to come on time.

P. Trudgill, *Sociolinguistics: An Introduction*, p. 110

The only real differences are a few phonetic, lexical, or grammatical markers scattered throughout an utterance which form parts of the subsets existing within the general system of language. They no longer reflect a fixed socio-linguistic stratification of speakers but indicate different situations or circumstances: trivial or solemn in nature, for example. Naturally, speakers who are able to perform at all levels exploit their talent. In literature, word-play* based on the levels is possible; see dissonance*. Ex (of popular language): ' "Over my dead body," said the Chef. "Over my bloody dead body" ' (Tom Sharpe, *Porterhouse Blue*, p. 88). Ex (of popular pronunciation): ' "Gawd," said Skullion irreverently' (ibid.). For an example of sustained language, see grandiloquence*.

Analogous terms: low, middle, or elevated tone; familiar, plain, or sublime style; low or noble words, terms, or expressions

R1: When popular language abandons ordinary linguistic structures and slips into the esoteric mode, it turns into slang* or argot.

LEXICALIZATION A previously non-lexical segment (a letter of the alphabet, digit, noise*, abbreviation*, grammatical word, or syntagm*) is treated as a lexical unit (actualized or used in a derived sense or compound noun).

Exx: 'to the nth'; (i.e., 'to any extent, to the utmost'): 'For the nth time, sit down!'; 'He's a nobody'; 'an overall'; a 'gopher' or 'gofer' (i.e., 'go for,' an employee sent on errands); 'But me no buts' (John Bartlett's *Familiar Quotations* contains under 'but' more than twenty examples of lexicalized or transferred expressions). See also noise*, abbreviation*, R5, and hyphen*.

Ex: 'Thank me no thankings, nor proud me no prouds' (Shakespeare, *Romeo and Juliet*, 3.5.153).

Ex: 'Sandwiched between San Francisco and Berkeley both physically

Licence

and psychologically, Oakland has been hard put to establish a singular identity. Gertrude Stein did not help when she immortalized her native city with the line "There's no there there." Although Oakland is still primarily an industrial city and not a centre of tourism, there is *some* there there' (B. Thompson, *The American Express Pocket Guide to California*, p. 136).

Ex: 'Should the morpheme *flation* become widely accepted ..., it would be lexicalized and Webster's new edition would list it' (A. Makkai, quoted in the *OEDS*, under 'lexicalize').

R1: Lexicalization differs from transference*, which operates on lexemes already formed. The *ego* and *id* as well as such existentialist terms as the *For-Itself* and the *For-Others* are examples combining the lexicalization of pronouns and syntagms* with transference (in this case, with substantivation). Ex: 'They really prefer the *We are* to the *We will be*' (Camus, *Essais*, p. 686). Hyphens* may reinforce the cohesion of the extended groups.

LICENCE Freedom of expression ... by means of which one says more than is permitted or appropriate (see Fontanier, p. 477). See also Lanham (*licentia*) and Quillet.

Ex: 'So that I would have hesitated to exclaim, with my finger up my arse-hole for example, Jesus-Christ, it's much worse than yesterday, I can hardly believe it's the same hole. I apologise for having to revert to this lewd orifice, 'tis my muse will have it so' (S. Beckett, *Molloy*, p. 101).

Synonym: parrhesia (Fontanier, Joseph, and Lanham [also *parrosia*])

Other definition: poetic, grammatical, or prosodic licence: the liberty enjoyed by the poet to escape from the rules (Cuddon, Frye, and Preminger). See solecism*, R1, and mistake*, R5.

R1: Lanham makes a distinction between parrhesia ('Gr[eek], free-spokenness, frankness, candid speech' [p. 73]) and *Correctio*: '*Diorthosis; Prodiorthosis: Praecedens Correctio*. Preparing the way for saying something the speaker knows will be unpleasant to his auditors: "Although I realize how offensive this will sound, it is something that must be said" ' (p. 28). In the example above from Beckett's *Molloy*, the request for permission to speak candidly about unpleasant things takes the form of an apology coming after the fact.

R2: Fontanier, in discussing licence, observes that it can hardly be classed among figures of thought and banishes it from his system, which does not include attitudinal figures.

R3: It is considered good form either to avoid licence or to precede it with an excuse*. **Exx:** 'May I say that [in polite company]?'; 'May I say that word?'; 'It must be said.'

LINE (OF POETRY OR VERSE)

A 'poetic' disposition of textual elements. In the case of oral verse, whether sung, read aloud, or merely printed, the choice of a particular type of line is above all a matter which concerns the rhythmic elements used. In the case of written verse, the choice concerns graphic elements. The role of images* and sounds, however important it may sometimes be, is of less importance when we need to define the line of poetry.

There are three ways to appreciate and study rhythm* in English and French poetry. We will therefore examine syllabic, rhythmic, and metrical verse. We will begin at the renaissance of the poetic line: free verse, which possesses a visual form, namely, the graphic line, a form discussed under (5) below.

See also: acrostic*; antepiphora*; celebration*; dialogue*, R8; diaeresis*; emphasis*; epitrochasmus*; harmony*; homoioteleuton*, R1; homonymy*, R3; maxim*; paragraph*, R1; parechesis*, R3; poem*; refrain*; rhyme*; rhythmic echo*, R1; situational* signs, 5; stanza*; tautogram*; tempo*, R3; *verset*.

1. Free verse / vers libre. Its rhythm resembles that of prose poetry; that is, it is characterized by a certain regularity of accent* (see below, 'rhythmic verse'). It differs from prose, however, by its use of pauses*, which are more frequent and more significant. It is often possible to make the pauses count in the rhythmic structure of free verse. **Ex:**

White as an almond are thy shoulders; /
As new almonds stripped from the husk. /
They guard thee not with eunuchs; /
Not with bars of copper. /
Gilt turquoise and silver are in the place of thy rest.
A brown robe, with threads of gold woven in patterns, hast thou
gathered about thee,
O Nathat-Ikanaie, 'Tree-at-the-river.'

Ezra Pound, 'Dance Figure'

R1: We have here borrowed from the theory of stress regularity (see below, 'rhythmic verse') the system for marking accents* by a dot over the vowel. Pauses* are marked by commas, semi-colons, or periods.

R2: Rhythm is so essential to free verse that the lack of a widely accepted system of notation must be regretted. If poets were to place markers above or below rhythmically accented vowels, and to indicate pauses with oblique* strokes, that might suffice to give back to poetry the originality and lively rhythms it shares with music and song.

R3: Given the lack of such markers, as is almost always the case, nothing prevents a reader from applying to the study of the rhythms of free verse a variety of principles, those of graphic or syllabic poetry, of stress regularity, or even those of ancient prosody. We thus achieve quite new poetic maxims, better thought out, and more expressive, than those in prose. See also noise*, R4; interjection*, R2; and echo* effect.

R4: Free verse is frequently printed in spatial arrangements that facilitate its semantic and rhythmical interpretation and that, in so doing, present it as graphic verse.

2. Syllabic verse. The measure of lines by syllable count establishes their rhythm*. This is the theory governing the classical French poetic line, which also conforms to the rules governing rhyme* and caesura*. From the fifteenth to the seventeenth century, other rules were imposed, at least in the principal genres like tragedy, the epic, religious poetry, and ceremonial lyric poetry. For instance, rhymes, to be accompanied by a 'supporting consonant,' were to appear rarely, and words could not rhyme with composite forms of themselves (e.g., *view* might not rhyme with *interview*); hiatus* was forbidden; as were enjamb(e)ment* and end* positioning, etc. (See F. Deloffre, *Le Vers français*, pp. 46–7, 53, 109, 115, 120–1.)

Although the twelve-syllable alexandrine, the decasyllabic epic line, and the octosyllable were the most-used forms, all lengths were (and remain) possible, and Victor Hugo, in his poem 'Les Djinns' ('The Genies' or 'Jinnees,' sprites or goblins of Arabian tales) employs them one after another. Poets writing in English have also used monosyllabic, disyllabic, trisyllabic, and tetrasyllabic lines; lines of five, six, seven, nine, and eleven syllables; as well as alexandrines, decasyllables, and octosyllables. Martinon points out lines of thirteen, fourteen, 'and even' sixteen syllables (p. 18) in French poetry, and Miller Williams (pp. 146–7) includes a fourteen-syllable poem written in English. Such lines are probably rhythmic rather than syllabic.

In traditional or fixed-form poems, lines are isometric (i.e., they have the same number of syllables) or occasionally heterometric. (See also stanza*.) As a curiosity, we may point to rhopalic verse (from the Greek 'club-like,' thicker towards the end), which may go from one to *n* syllables (see Preminger).

R1: French phoneticians, following Grammont's example, questioned the phonetic reality to which syllabic lines respond. Of course, it is possible to assign to each syllable in French approximately the same value or length, but syllabification in itself is not inherently poetic. *Syllabic verse* becomes harmonious when it is also *rhythmic* verse (see below).

R2: French eighteenth-century actors recited Racine's verse tragedies as if they were in prose (see apocope*, R3). Later, the Romantics, by authorizing pauses* which ruin the regular rhythm* of classical verse, intended to 'break up the line's unity.' By so doing, they wished to superimpose the rhythm of spoken language upon poetry (see Deloffre, pp. 129–30), thus making possible Romantic or ternary alexandrines (i.e., twelve-syllable lines with three accents*).

R3: Musset continued the same 'revolutionary' movement, which consisted simply in suppressing rhyme* (and also some excessive rhythmic uniformity). Thus French prosody moved towards *blank verse*, which though neither originally nor exclusively English, has become 'the distinctive poetic form of our language' (John Thompson, in Preminger). It consists of any number of lines of unrhymed iambic pentameter (lines of five metrical feet going [x /]). Ex:

> A Book of Verses underneath the Bough,
> A Jug of Wine, a Loaf of Bread – and Thou
> Beside me singing in the Wilderness –
> Oh, Wilderness were Paradise enow!

> Edward Fitzgerald, *Rubáiyát of Omar Khayyám*, quoted in Frances Stillman, *The Poet's Manual and Rhyming Dictionary*, p. 16

3. Rhythmic verse. Here, rhythm is determined by the regular repetition of rhythmical accents, irrespective of the number of intervening unaccented syllables, all of the same length. It thus becomes possible to beat time, and lines acquire a rhythm* in the musical meaning of that term. The length of pauses* also counts, of course, and, as in music, stress may fall upon a silence. Normally, however, the stress falls upon accented syllables (see accent*), although it sometimes falls on the pretonic syllable.

This kind of line is the norm in poetry written in English and other Germanic languages. Turco (pp. 19–20) quotes (and marks the stress of) the following example of Hopkins's 'sprung rhythm' (note that the dots here indicate secondary stresses):

> The world is charged with the grandeur of God
> It will flame out, like shining from shook foil
> It gathers to a greatness, like the ooze of oil
> Crushed. Why do men then now not reck his rod?

> Gerard Manley Hopkins, 'God's Grandeur'

Line (of Poetry or Verse)

R1: Since mingogram recordings (see intonation*) produce no trace of rhythmical accents*, Henri Morier had recourse to a trick analogous to one used by conductors when beating time: tapping the microphone stand with a stick, which leaves an immediate, precise, and easily identifiable aural record of the *ictus*, or accent mark [/]. This very simple device produces several discoveries or rediscoveries: the presence of an *ictus* before and after a line, the caesura* which comes between two such accent marks, etc. (see Turco; Williams; and Parent, ed., *Le Vers français au XXe siècle*, pp. 85–122).

4. Metrical verse. The rhythm of metrical verse, more flexible and varied than that of Western music, derives from a relatively arbitrary division into bars or feet (but one which respects the tonic accents). Any duration counts (not forgetting silences) – long or short syllables, even consonants (particularly the liquids). The whole forms an 'arabesque,' in Souriau's words. The melody of the sentence completes the aesthetic effect.

This is the prosody of antiquity, both in the Orient and the Occident. We no longer count syllables or accents, but feet, which may be catalectic (the final foot lacks a syllable). The most harmonious metrical groups have been codified: thus the dactylic hexameter, the line Virgil used, is a six-measure line whose ante-penultimate foot is a dactyl. (See rhythmic* measure for a list of possible measures according to Greek and Latin metricians.) In the case of French prosody, our mingographic records of various types of delivery, in particular those made by Etienne Souriau, indicate syllabic durations difficult to classify into short/long categories. There would need to be at least four classes: very short (up to 20 centiseconds); short (from 20 to 40 centiseconds); long (40 to 60); very long (more than 60).

Sixteenth-century French poets of the 'school' called the Pléiade, most notably Jean de Baïf, produced imitations of Latin prosody in French. But what exactly does French prosody consist of, from the viewpoint of metre? A recording made by Apollinaire and kept in the Phonothèque Nationale (the French national library of sound recordings) shows that he favoured, when reading his poems, a precise metrical prosody, one with exceptional incantatory powers. And Souriau, an expert in aesthetics, also attempted to rethink classical prosody from the metrical angle. He showed that the best way to read alexandrines was probably to divide them into rhythmic measures. In such a case, the alexandrine may be redefined as 'a pentameter with a caesura* on the fifth semi-measure whose first foot is either pyrrhic, or iambic, or trochaic ... The second is a dactyl, amphibrach or tribrach. The third, which includes the caesura, is a trochee ... The fourth contains the same feet as the second; and the fifth and last is always an amphibrach, either complete (ending with a feminine rhyme [i.e., a word ending with a mute *e*]), or catalectic ([ending with] a masculine

258

rhyme)' (Etienne Souriau, *Musique et poésie*, in *Correspondance des arts*, p. 204).

R1: If we place a rhythmical accent* on the final tonic syllables of phonetic words, we obtain, in French only, combinations of iambics, anapaests, and paeon fourths: (˘˘˘¯; i.e., 3 shorts and a long). But this rhythmical notation is only good for French prose and for some syllabic and free verse.

R2: Souriau showed (p. 192) that, for French verse, the bar line should in general be placed 'at the beginning, not at the end of the stressed syllable.' Morier's observations confirm this: 'The *ictus* [or accent mark] indicates the *attack* made on the vowel.' Under these conditions, it is clear that the final tonic syllable of a phonetic word most frequently begins a new foot. In addition, the caesura* arrives within the foot causing it to stretch. Indispensable to the unity of the line, this was a familiar requirement of French neo-classical prosody.

R3: Readings by poets (e.g., the recordings made by Paul Valéry, Louis Aragon, and Emile Verhaeren at the Phonothèque Nationale) show that in French it is possible, by means of an intensifying or purely rhythmical accent*, to lengthen most unaccented vowels, just as it is equally possible to shorten some tonic vowels by placing them inside a longer phonetic word. Consequently, nothing prevents a return to metrical verse, nor metrical scansion of most French verse which is said to be *syllabic*. The actual rhythmic structure of such poetic readings presents a practically virgin territory for study. By superimposing rhythmical markers onto recordings made by some fairly typical authors (e.g., the recording made by René Char of his poem *La Sorgue*) we noted: (1) that isochrony of measures is demonstrable; (2) that the bar lines marking measures within a line of poetry may be moved towards pauses and away from long vowels; (3) that such displacements, followed by replacements, occur every two lines, in a kind of alternation breaking the monotony of a too rhythmical reading. The regular rhythm of a line is therefore a phenomenon largely independent of spontaneous phonetic data (the different accents* of prose).

5. **Graphic prosody.** Graphic lines are cut off by blank spaces at each end, or broken up and scattered across pages, as in Mallarmé's *Un Coup de dés jamais n'abolira le hasard* (1897), or even transformed into iconic, ornamental, or abstract diagrams. (See *calligramme** and typographical variation*.)

Both traditional poetry and *vers libres* already possess a graphic 'spatial ... or shaped' dimension (Miller Williams, p. 141), which, although elementary (a matter simply of their division into lines and stanzas), forms their essential characteristic. In addition, positioning of the text within limits less wide than the justified margins (see situa-

Lipogram

tional* signs, 5) suffices: (1) to assign to them 'markers of poeticity
whose perception as a prerequisite orients the way they are read' (D.
Delas and J. Filliolet, *Linguistique et poétique*, p. 182); (2) to encourage
vertical or diagonal connections supplementary to the syntagmatic
(horizontal and linear) layout of the poem; (3) to suggest a perception
of the poetic fact, at once 'globalizing and integrative,' and of the type
of integration which 'selects the relevant units as a function of the
relevant forms' (ibid.).

Graphic artists who work in publicity realize the possibilities offered
by the multi-dimensionality of the text on the page. But poets in the
Eastern Bloc and also those in Germany, Italy, France, and Latin
America have maintained their distance both from the movement
which compares texts either to *musique concrète* (lettrism), and from
abstract painting (spatialism). The spatialist poem may be reduced to a
simple ornamental pattern, or to one which reproduces the energy
expended during its creation. Ex: Ian Hamilton Finlay's 'Au Pair Girl,'
in which the three-word title supplies both the body of the poem and,
when arranged in the shape of a pear, provides the oratorical syllepsis*
linking the poem's visual and linguistic elements.

Spatialist poetry may also conjugate the relationship between a text
and a pattern, as in Emmett Williams's 'Like attracts Like,' for instance,
or between text and linotype (see the review *Aspects*) or in some more
complex form.

R1: Since antiquity, writing, or calligraphy, has been in some traditions
a graphic art: one thinks of Persian manuscripts, Japanese woodcuts,
and so on. Moslem civilization, in particular, since it condemned
human representations of the Divinity, decorated its architectural constructions with stylized patterns in which may be deciphered *versets**
from the Koran, unsurpassable examples of visual lines of poetry.

R2: In order to read graphic verse, segments of the same kind may be
linked together (as in Mallarmé's *Un Coup de dés*, for example).

LIPOGRAM A text in verse or prose from which the author banishes
a particular letter of the alphabet.

Exx: In 1939 Ernest V. Wright, a Californian musician, published
Gadsby [Los Angeles, Wetzel], a fifty-thousand-word novel which does
without the letter *e*, the commonest letter in English. In 1969 Georges
Perec published *La Disparition*, in which no word contains the letter *e*,
the commonest letter also in French. (In direct contrast, Perec published
three years later a *univocalic* novel, *Les Revenentes*, which uses a single
vowel, again *e*.) See the quotation under description*, R5; and for a
historical survey of lipograms and univocalics in world literature, see
Augarde, pp. 109–13, and Espy, 1971, p. 157.

R1: 'The whole difficulty resides in the choice of the letter suppressed and in the length of the text,' notes P. Fournel (*Clefs pour la littérature potentielle*, p. 126). He points out ironically that (in French) his own statement is a lipogram of the letter *w*.

R2: Perec proposed that the device which consists in writing without the use of certain words be called *liponomy*. Ex: A British TV game in the 1950s, 'Take Your Pick,' included a 'yes-no' section in which contestants were rewarded if they were able to answer questions without using 'yes' or 'no.' In French, see Henry de Chenevières, *Contes sans 'qui' ni 'que'* (i.e., stories without *who, whom*, or *which*).

LITERARY GAMES Some literary games use devices of composition. They may be defined as forms into which participants are invited to insert contents, as skilfully as possible.

Acronyms*: Each contestant proposes for solution an acronym* of his or her own making. Exx: *Arbaonwsas*: 'A rose by any other name would smell as sweet'; *Nitwoodmgsbtsoy*: 'Now is the winter of our discontent made glorious summer by this sun of York.' Acronyms may remotivate existing terms or titles*. Ex: 'The Foreign Office is not popular throughout the rest of the Civil Service, and it is widely held that the CMG [Cross of St Michael] stands for "Call Me God," the KCMG [Knight Commander of St Michael and St George] for "Kindly Call Me God" and the GCMG [Grand Cross of St Michael and St George] "God Calls Me God" ' (J. Lynn and A. Jay, *The Complete 'Yes Minister,'* p. 239).

Acrostics*: Players choose a word at random and write a telegram using words whose order comes from the initial letters of the word agreed upon. Tony Augarde (pp. 32–51) proposes variants of acrostic games, including double acrostics and word squares which, unlike crossword puzzles, have no black squares. (Other literary games listed by Augarde include scrabble, anagrams*, charades, enigmas and riddles*, rebuses, and epigrams*. See also: W.R. Espy, *The Game of Words*; P. Hutchinson, *Games Authors Play*; L. Hesbois, *Les Jeux de langage*; D. Grambs, *Literary Companion Dictionary*, pp. 84–7.)

Bouts-rimés (verses composed to set rhymes): In such competitions in verse, the group chooses the rhymes and their number at the outset. (Nonsense verse, short poems of low intelligibility or meaning, parody some other poem while keeping its rhymes. Ex: 'You Are Old Father William,' by Lewis Carroll, parodies Robert Southey's 'The Old Man's Comforts.')

Consequences: The surrealist game of the 'cadavre exquis' ('exquisite corpse') is a form of this game, in which a player writes a word on a piece of paper which is then folded and handed to the next player, who repeats the process. The categories of words (general semantic content or parts of speech) may be specified in advance. At the end of the round, contestants examine the results and choose the most amusing. (See Aragon et al., *Dictionnaire abrégé du surréalisme*.)

Word chase: A competition for story-tellers who invent narratives* in which a previously listed group of incongruous words must appear in the agreed order. Ex: see 'word-game' in Queneau, *Exercises in Style*, pp. 33–4.

Transaddition: Adding a letter to a word whose letters are then rearranged to make a new word. Ex: sham + s > smash (Grambs, p. 87).

Word deletion: The removal from one word of a second word concealed in it produces a third word. Ex: patient – tie > pant (ibid.).

Conundrums: See riddle*, 3.

LITOTES Ironical understatement, especially one expressing an affirmative by the negative of its contrary (e.g., 'no small' for 'great') (see *Concise Oxford Dictionary*). See also Abrams, Beckson, Corbett, Cuddon, Fontanier, Gray, Lanham, Lausberg (a combination of periphrasis* and irony*), Marouzeau, Morier, Preminger, and Quillet.

Exx: 'Not half bad'; 'I'll bet you don't' meaning 'I'm sure you do'; 'It is no coincidence that ...'

Ex: The title of the comedy program 'Not! the Nine o'Clock News' is litotic: exposure to only a few seconds of its irreverent comments on current events reveals the impossibility of believing it to represent the official views of the BBC or any other network.

Other definition: Morier adds a second definition: a synonym of laconic, sober speech; much is said in few words; the speaker remains well within the substance of what is to be expressed. **Exx:** the styles of Stendhal, Pinter, or Beckett. See baroquism*, R1.

Synonyms: *diminutio* (Fontanier, Lanham); false attenuation*; meiosis* (Preminger: 'treating a thing as less important than it is'). In general, Anglo-Saxon critics treat meiosis as the *genus* of which *litotes* is a negative species.

R1: Litotes is attenuation recognized as false or simulated. The reader immediately reverses its effect and, by imagining what is missing, may exaggerate (hence the paradoxical definition: to say less in order to convey more). But readers must remain alert, or alternatively, the author may alert them by foregrounding the device in an inserted segment of pure enunciation*. Ex: 'As to the friendship evinced by these first people, *I will only say that* it has already proved to be unreliable' (A. Camus, *Essais*, p. 978).

R2: As in the case of antiphrasis*, context and intonation* reveal litotes, which is pronounced in a tone of minimal but undeniable assertiveness, implying that much more could be said. **Ex:** ' "It may be remotely conceivable," *he stage-whispered with precise delivery*, "that not every single syllable is absolutely beyond all hope of redemption" ' (Kingsley Amis, *The Old Devils*, p. 286). The role of context is the determining factor, as it is in the classical example provided by Chimène's remark to Rodrigue, her suitor: 'Je ne te hais point' ('I don't hate you') (Corneille, *Le Cid*, 3.4). Rodrigue has just killed Chimène's father in a duel, in which (extreme) case her statement must clearly imply her great love for Rodrigue.

And so litotes has created a kind of style, laconicism, which consists in the reduction of expressive flourishes in favour of 'maintaining expression within the emotion to be communicated' (V. Larbaud, *Sous l'invocation de Saint Jérôme*, pp. 166–7). Thus 'boar-hunting' will be referred to as 'pig-sticking.' **Ex:**

About suffering they were never wrong,
The Old Masters: how well they understood
Its human condition; how it takes place
While someone else is eating or opening a window or just walking
    dully along;
...
In Brueghel's *Icarus*, for instance: how everything turns away
Quite leisurely from the disaster; the ploughman may
Have heard the splash, the forsaken cry,
But for him *it was not an important failure*; the sun shone
As it had to on the white legs disappearing into the green
Water; and the expensive delicate ship that must have seen
Something amazing, a boy falling out of the sky,
Had somewhere to get to and *sailed calmly on*.
                    W.H. Auden, 'Musée des Beaux-Arts'

Camus's *L'Etranger* and Juliette Gréco's voice were French prototypes of the style which the existentialists also practised, precisely because such a style places the emphasis on context. This is 'white or blank writing,' the 'zero-degree writing' that Barthes spoke of.

R3: Litotes employs all forms of attenuation* (see euphemism*, R1) but most particularly that of the negation* of the contrary, a form popular in speech. **Exx:** 'It's not often that ...'; 'It's no joke'; 'This is not the ideal way to ...'; 'He didn't come up smelling of roses'; 'I don't have to be told twice.' A literary example: 'No capon priest the Goodly Fere / But a man o' men was he' (E. Pound, 'Ballad of the Goodly Fere,'

15–16). Litotes has become a type of emphasis* found also in written language. Ex: 'A role no less important for being behind the scenes.'

R4: When too original, litotes degenerates into phoebus*. Exx: 'Harmonious ego, *different from dreams*' (Valéry, 'La Jeune Parque'); 'Each one *immolates her / Silence* in unison' (Valéry, 'Cantique des colonnes'). Litotes also runs the opposite risk, that of falling into truism* through lack of originality. Ex: 'It is *no bad thing* to be young, handsome and a prince' (J. Giraudoux, *Electre*, 2.3).

LOGATOM A meaningless syllable formed arbitrarily, usually from initial and final consonants and a vowel, for use in testing telephone systems, or for testing hearing and memory. See *OELDS*.

Exx: lan, nal, tal, etc.

Analogous terms: trigram, paralog. J. Jung writes: 'Nonsense syllables and other laboratory learning materials, such as trigrams and paralogs. Trigrams are nonsense syllables, that is, a trigram is any three-letter combination which does not form a word. Paralogs or dissyllables are verbal units containing two syllables and range from meaningless units to actual words' (J. Jung, *Verbal Learning*, p. 30).

R1: Arbitrary *découpage** produces a kind of semi-logatom in which the elements are not necessarily consecutive. Ex: *infinitesimal* if cut up into bits like *itl* or *tesima*.

LOOP (neol.; Fr. *boucle*) A text which, by returning to its starting point, suggests that everything is beginning again, and will continue to begin again in exactly the same way, once the end is reached.

Exx: Ionesco's two plays *La Leçon* and *La Cantatrice chauve*

The loop figures in some songs and counting rhymes. Ex: 'In what should I get it [water], dear Liza, dear Liza ... In a bucket. There's a hole in my bucket ... Block it ... With what should I block it? ... With straw ... The straw is not cut ... Cut it ... With what should I cut it? ... With a sickle ... But the sickle isn't sharp ... Sharpen it ... With what shall I sharpen it? ... With a grindstone ... But the stone isn't wet ... Wet it then ... With what shall I wet it? ... With water ... In what shall I get water, dear Liza ...' (*da capo*).

R1: The loop is an inclusion* combined with repetition*. See also staircase*, R1, and parenthesis*, R4.

R2: The word comes from data processing, in which it designates a part of a program which can be begun again indefinitely.

R3: In music, the conclusion often reprises the first phrase, to which the initials d.c. (Italian, *da capo,* 'from the top') refer and whose end is then marked by a colon* and heavy dash. Literature has no equivalent convention.

M

MACARONICISM A noun derived from the adjective 'macaronic.' Macaronic verses are 'of burlesque form containing Latin (or other foreign) words and vernacular words with Latin etc. terminations' (*Concise Oxford Dictionary*). See also Augarde, Bénac, Cuddon, Frye, and Lausberg.

Exx: 'Puffus eliminus' [notice by Voyageur Coach Lines announcing smoke-free routes]; 'Muchibus thankibus' (Joyce, *Ulysses,* p. 115); [Stephen is speaking of Shakespeare]: 'Like John o'Gaunt his name is dear to him, as dear as the coat and crest he toadied for, on a bend sable a spear or steeled argent, honorificabilitudinitatibus, dearer than his glory of greatest shakescene in the country' (ibid., p. 172).

Other definition: sentences interrupted and jumbled up 'like a plate of macaroni.' Ex: Lucky's monologue in Beckett's *Waiting for Godot.*

Other name: 'dog' or ('lacerated') Latin. Ex: '*Caesar adsum jam forte* or Caesar had some jam for tea' (G. Willans and R. Searle, *Down with Skool!,* p. 47).

R1: Macaronicisms are related to parody*. Ex:

JOYCE: (Dictating to GWEN) Deshill holles eamus ...
GWEN: (Writing) Deshill holles eamus ...
JOYCE: Thrice.
GWEN: Uh-hum.

Tom Stoppard, *Travesties,* act 1

See also humour*, R1.

MAXIM A general assertion* expressed in a single sentence and formulated in a striking way. See Bénac, Cuddon, Frye, and Grambs.

Exx: 'Work expands to fill the time available'; 'Expenditure rises to meet income – and tends to surpass it'; 'Delay is the deadliest form of denial' (C.N. Parkinson, *The Law Complete,* p. 151).

Other definition: a 'rule of conduct or morality' (Robert). This is a restricted meaning added to earlier usage (*maxima propositio,* a sentence of the greatest generality).

Meaning

Analogous terms: sentence (archaic), aphorism, *pensée*, truth, saying, (moral) precept, principle (of conduct), (scientific) axiom or postulate, apophtegm or apothegm

Adjective: gnomic (gnomic poetry presents maxims in verse [Bénac])

R1: A *chria* is a maxim put into a dramatic or narrative situation and attributed to a character (Quintilian; Isidore of Seville, quoted by Lausberg, sect. 1117–20; see also Joseph, pp. 103, 311). *Historical sayings*, authentic or not, are types of chria. Although its name is no longer used, the device still remains active. Ex: 'Mme Flaubert [to her son, Gustave]: 'your mania for sentences has dried up your heart' (J. Barnes, *Flaubert's Parrot*, p. 156).

R2: By their generality maxims seem to be an appropriate means of remaking the world, and so characters may use them in answer to a complaint or to indicate some neurotic complex. **Ex:**

> F...: I am not a nobleman. My mother is a laundress. It's true she only washes the finest linen.
> ALARICA: Nobility lies in ambition and energy.
> Audiberti, *Le Mal court*, act 3

MEANING No one will be surprised to be told that there are many different kinds. After completion by their authors, texts remain no more than artefacts until they are read. For the reader, meaning is an effect produced by the text. The effect is either immediate, or deferred by reflection or analysis. It is diversified not only by a multiplicity of cultural differences, but also by the different approaches taken by readers both to a text's individual elements and to its entirety. The author may have foreseen these angles of approach, or decoding procedures, in order to communicate his meaning. The study of the modalities of signification is therefore essential to that of the devices.

1. Fundamental meaning / specific meaning. The fundamental meaning of a word is an ancient concept which Bloomfield called the word's 'head' meaning and defined as 'what you would think of first if the context did nothing to define the word' (quoted by W. Empson, in *The Structure of Complex Words*, p. 47). Synonyms: the *dominant* or *major* meaning.

Empson observes that the concept may cover quite diverse ideas: the *main* meaning, that is, the most frequent one; the *central* meaning, 'the one from which others are felt to branch out'; the *etymological* or 'root' meaning, 'suggested by derivation'; and the *primary* meaning, 'which actually came first in history' (ibid., p. 48).

The preceding definition is primarily of interest to the lexicologist. The semiotician prefers the concept of *classeme*, defined by Bernard

Pottier as a part of the sememe which organizes the generic semes (*seme*: 'a semantic trait or characteristic'; generic semes: those which indicate membership within a class; e.g., the seme 'colour' for the word *red*). *Semic* or *componential* analysis isolates semes by comparing them with each other (see Thomas A. Sebeok, gen. ed., *Encyclopedic Dictionary of Semiotics*, and Jean Dubois et al., *Dictionnaire de linguistique*). Pottier contrasts the classeme with the semanteme or set of specific semes (e.g., the semes which distinguish *red* from *green* and *purple*) and also with the virtueme or set of occasional semes dependent upon context. Neither concept was unknown in classical philology. Beauzée spoke of the *specific meaning*, that is, the one which a word shares with its synonyms, a concept not far removed from the notion of semanteme. He also spoke of *accidental meaning*, that is, the particular values adhering to a word used in a specific context; this concept is close to that of the virtueme (for examples, see catachresis*).

Specific meanings may alter. Ex: the word *gay*. It may even happen that the specific meaning of a word comes to signify the opposite of its fundamental meaning, and thus becomes a source of misunderstanding. *Classical* when used of French literature of the seventeenth and eighteenth centuries risks confusion with literature of the Graeco-Latin period. Even more frequent: the use of *modern* in the expression 'the modern period' to designate the time-span encompassing the seventeenth to the twentieth centuries may well be replaced by the fundamental meaning of *modern*, meaning the present century, as in 'modern art,' or, for that matter, *Modern Times*, the title of a film by Chaplin.

In dictionaries, the multiplicity of meanings often derives from the distinctions made between the specific and fundamental meanings of a word. Ex: 'Link. 1. One ring or loop of a chain; 2. Torch of pitch.' The first, fundamental meaning encompasses the second specific meaning (links were torches which formerly made up a 'chain-system' for lighting people along streets).

2. Denotation and connotation. Denotation, which unites essential semes, should be defined as the set formed by what Pottier calls classemes and semantemes, or what used to be called fundamental and specific meanings. Other semes, which are context-dependent, such as virtuemes or accidental meanings, may be seen as constitutive elements of connotation. (The mathematical meaning of extension concerns the referent rather than connotation. For the use made of *connotation* by logicians, see Lalande.) Analogous term: *usage-value*.

Among the semes complementary to an essential idea, according to Bally, we may distinguish those which reveal one of the author's attitudes (the *expressive* meaning) and those intended to produce a given effect on the reader (the *impressive* meaning). Both together form the set of *affective effects* with which we generally identify connotation.

The search for affective effects involves choosing between para-synonyms. Ex: *content/ecstatic*. Connotation is laudatory (or *meliorative*) when the term chosen presents a person or thing in a favourable light, pejorative in the opposite case. Ex: *freedom fighter / terrorist*. See *compensatio**, R1.

To the notion of affective effects, Bally adds that of *evocative effects*, since some words carry along with their specific meaning a whole implied ambiance, that of their natural environment. Ex: '– Is it that whiteeyed kaffir? says the citizen, that never backed a horse in anger in his life?' (Joyce, *Ulysses*, p. 274). It's not difficult to imagine that we are eavesdropping on a pub conversation. Reciprocally, as far as the lexicologist is concerned, context contributes to our decisions on meaning. Empson (*The Structure of Complex Words*) speaks of the *topical* meaning as being the one imposed by the context of a whole work. Ex: *post* in an article about the Post Office. Using a different example, he distinguishes this from the *probable* meaning, the one imposed by the real context. Ex: *saddle*, which, in mountainous country, may refer to a ridge between two summits.

Beauzée's accidental meaning was also called the *divided* meaning by Dumarsais (*Des Tropes*, p. 249). An implicit semic analysis may have presided over his choice of the term. Some contexts nullify essential semes in favour of secondary ones, thus 'dividing' the sememe! Ex: 'An Oxford don has just died. There is therefore a chair.' Only the notion of a professorial 'vacancy' remains. The complement of divided meaning is *compound* meaning, in which all the semes come into play. Ex: 'If we were to engage more professors, we would be short of chairs.'

Accidental meanings may with usage become essential. In that case they take the name of *derived* meanings, whereas the specific meaning from which they accidentally derive are called *primitive* meanings. Exx: *crucial*: primitive meaning, 'shaped like a cross'; *impact*: primitive meaning, the 'shock of a projectile'; derived meaning, 'strong effect, influence.'

3. Strict sense and broad sense. The prestige enjoyed by some terms following certain socio-cultural events, or more simply the use made of them by non-specialists, confers upon them greater and greater breadth or extension, with the result that they lose some of their specific semes. They take on a *broad* or extended meaning while still continuing to offer themselves for possible use in their *strict* or restricted meaning. Ex: *metaphor**, frequently used in the broad sense of literary image*, whereas it designates only images with a single vehicle, combined syntactically with the rest of the sentence.

It sometimes happens that the strict sense was established later than the broad one. Ex: *structure*, which used to mean simply a 'form, or organization,' has acquired the stricter meaning of a 'system of forms defined by their mutual differences.' In this case, we speak rather of a *restricted* or *limited* meaning (particularly if the sense is not current).

4. Literal and figurative meaning. Fontanier (p. 57) calls *figurative* or *tropological* (or *tropic*) a meaning which results from a particular case in which several semes lose their relevance, with the result that there occurs a voluntary abandonment of the term's literal meaning. *Tropes* are figurative devices. See image*, 2; metaphor*; metonymy*; synecdoche*; antonomasia*; and, for whole propositions, allusion*.

Semanticists like Darmesteter and Bréal see in metaphor* and metonymy* (if the latter is taken to include synecdoche*) the basis for any shift in meaning (P. Guiraud, *La Sémantique*, pp. 37–8). But Jakobson, by conferring a broader meaning on these terms, encouraged the replacement of logic and rhetoric by semiology. Semic analysis makes the notion of figure more precise by showing that changing the lexical signifier entails within the signified a change not merely of connotation, but of denotation, for a referent (an extra-linguistic object) which does not change. Lexemes, which only designate referents by means of a secondary seme, present gratis all of the essential semes possessed by such referents. Gide skilfully illustrates this overturning process by writing: 'Spring, dawn of summer! The spring of each day, dawn!' (Gide, *Romans*, pp. 220–1). In the first case, it is 'dawn' which is figurative; in the second, it is 'spring.' Tropes multiply synonyms without increasing the number of words.

5. Before going on to meanings which involve not single words but groups of words, we would like to call attention to the following:
– the *extended* meaning (Fontanier, p. 58), a figurative meaning which has become a specific meaning and has come into common usage after undergoing some tropic process. Ex: 'Mug' as in 'ugly mug!' See cliché*, R4, and image*, R4.
– the *abstract* meaning, which situates the sememe in the world of ideas and differs from the *concrete* meaning, which displaces it in the direction of individualization (Dumarsais, *Des Tropes*, p. 251; Fontanier, p. 57). Ex: (Either) the soldier's bravery, (or) the brave soldier ... rallied the platoon.
– the *collective* meaning, which only applies to groups of referents, while the *distributive* meaning applies to each element in the set. See R. Blanche, *Introduction à la logique contemporaine*, p. 176; and Fontanier, p. 56. Ex: 'Men are numerous. Socrates is a man. Therefore Socrates is numerous!' *Numerous*, because of its collective meaning, can only serve as predicate for a collective subject.
– the *undefined* or *indeterminate* meaning, which applies to a lexeme situated unclearly (some, certain ...), whilst it is *defined* or *determined*

Meaning

when the link between a lexeme and its environment is specified (the, this, our). Markers of indetermination for the verbal syntagm* are the indefinite pronouns, including the indefinite personal pronoun, one. See Fontanier, p. 56. Indetermination may derive, however, from the absence of a context. Thus Ducrot, in Dire et ne pas dire (p. 136), shows that a simple notice such as 'Open on Tuesdays' may mean 'even on Tuesdays' or 'only on Tuesdays,' depending on the customary practices of the establishment in question. See ambiguity*, R3.

– the implicit meaning, which is attributed without a specific marker, owing to the rudimentary state of expression in comparison with content. Thus, spokespersons whose job it is to comment upon declarations made by politicians strive to explain formulas that are left purposely vague. Implicit meaning may be revealed by means of a periphrasis* which explains the semes in question. Ex: 'From his cradle to his grave, a gale of blandest prosperity bore [Ellison] along. Nor do I use the word Prosperity in its mere worldly or external sense. I mean it as synonymous with happiness' (E.A. Poe, 'The Landscape Garden,' in Collected Works, 2: 702–3).

In chapter 8 of his Philosophy of Grammar, Jespersen identifies two types of implicit relationship between lexemes within the group substantive + complement: junction and nexus. Ex (proposed by Empson, The Structure of Complex Words, p. 65): 'The doctor's cleverness was great.' Some readers will judge that 'doctor' and 'clever' are simply joined together and that the sentence means that 'the doctor was very clever.' The semes are simply added together. Others will see the sentence as an assertion*. 'Doctor' and 'cleverness' form a nexus, that is, they have common semes since all doctors are necessarily clever. The sentence means in that case: 'The doctor was clever, very clever indeed.'

– the pregnant meaning, which remains implicit but is devoid of ambiguity since a simple appeal to verisimilitude serves to remove all doubt. Ex: 'in their wide arms' [i.e., 'wide open']. Analogous: proleptic meaning (see prolepsis*).

6. Literal and symbolic meaning. Among the ways of approaching whole texts, the most important is the one which consists in establishing some general isotopy* different from the one indicated by the theme*. The isotopy is frequently abstract, or 'profound,' and does not necessarily contradict the work's theme but sheds new light on it and may come to replace it. See symbol*, 1. Analogous: the spiritual meaning; the moral meaning (Fontanier, p. 59); the allegorical, analogical, or anagogical meaning. Meaning is allegorical or analogical, whatever the isotopy, as soon as it is no longer literal. It is moral if it involves morality; spiritual if it involves mysticism; and anagogic if it involves the eternal life. Ex: 'And it seems to me that, by the grace of God, I can be transported from this lower world to that higher world by anagoge ...'

(U. Eco, *The Name of the Rose*, p. 144). Non-symbolic language is said to be *literal*, or *logical*. See Dumarsais, *Des Tropes*, p. 251f.

7. Original and accommodated meaning. Although the influence exerted by the content of a paragraph on that of a sentence has never been studied, it is obvious that a simple modification of the context or situation of a sentence serves to modify its meaning. The new meaning produced by quotation* out of context (whether literary or real) is called the *accommodated* or *adapted* meaning (see Dumarsais, *Des Tropes*, ch. 3). In the following example, Zola foregrounds the accommodating or adapting process: 'I will quote once again the image from Claude Bernard which greatly impressed me: *"The experimenter is Nature's examining magistrate."* We novelists are the magistrates who examine men and their passions' (E. Zola, *Le Roman expérimental*, p. 65).

Almost all quotations must be taken *mutatis mutandis* (with due alteration of details), even *cum grano salis*. Rabelais, for example, skilfully exploits one of Saint Paul's axioms, 'Charity believeth all things' (1 Corinthians 13:2), in order to get the reader to believe him when he recounts how Gargantua entered the world through his mother's ear.

Accommodation may become reactualization*. Ex: 'Hail Mary, full of grace ...' These words, attributed to the archangel Gabriel in his address to the virgin Mary, take on quite a different sense when recited by Catholics. They no longer contain an announcement*, for example. (Their meaning is different again in a poem Victor Hugo addressed to Marie, one of his mistresses, whose 'graces' he 'hails.')

The original context often restricts the meaning while isolated quotation* dilates it. In the latter case, the accommodated meaning is called the *plenary* sense (from the Latin *plenior*). Most authors' ideas would be distorted by attribution of a plenary sense to every sentence they wrote. 'Give me a single line written by a man and I guarantee to get him hanged,' says the proverb. Some authors, however, seem deliberately to choose ideas with multiple applications. See authorism*.

The validity of an accommodated meaning depends on the user. Instead of being plenary, it may be restrictive. Ex: Bossuet, who, like many others, cites Ecclesiastes 1:2 – 'Vanity of vanities; all is vanity' – carefully omits to include among his examples the vanity of wisdom itself according to the prophet. On the contrary, Bossuet undertakes the praise of wisdom.

The adaptation of texts is a reader's right.

8. Manifest and subjective meanings. Between its expression in writing and its perusal, content may suffer distortions. Each person, in theory, alone knows what he or she 'means.' Next to manifest meaning, there is a place for *subjective* meaning, however infinitely diversified, even though it may become the subject of much onerous commentary from authors. Montherlant, for example, wrote several 'afterwords' to his play *Le Maître de Santiago*, taking readers to task for their interpretations. More recently, exponents of 'reader-response' criticism (Stanley Fish, for example) have posited meanings attributable to specific hermeneutic communities. And Frank Kermode has asked whether we 'can ... say absolutely anything we like' about literary texts (see his *Essays on Fiction*, pp. 156–67).

One interesting manifestation of the coupling of complementary notions is the opposition between the *obvious* and *intended* meanings of a text. The opposition surfaces very clearly in texts whose content is to be interpreted in a single more or less obligatory way, as in a discourse of command or instruction, such as the teaching or indoctrination of disciples, for example, in which liberty of interpretation is reduced to a few fleeting connotations, or is limited by the whole culture of a period. The intended meaning is in that case 'what the text means, its expressive intention, which supplies its motive force, above and beyond the current meaning of the words used' (J.-P. Audet in a private communication to B. Dupriez).

We might say that the subjective meaning is an intentional meaning that is not at all manifest. We become better able to perceive it by familiarizing ourselves with the whole of an author's work. This is the cross-checking method. Ex: 'Cela s'est passé / Je sais aujourd'hui saluer la beauté' ('That did happen / Today I know how to salute beauty') (A. Rimbaud, *Une Saison en enfer*). Rimbaud seems to mean, not that he has acquired respect for beauty, but that he has just learned to resist the excessive ecstasy beauty had previously caused him, and is now able simply to 'hail' or 'salute' it from a distance.

On the reader's side, subjective meaning is also a fairly frequent phenomenon (more frequent than might appear), even one to be recommended. In such a case, we speak of *extrapolation*, and if there is a deliberate attempt made to pass off a reader's subjective meaning for the author's, we speak of *distortion* of the text.

Besides intended and subjective meanings, we distinguish, on the author's side, a meaning we might call *subjectal*, that is, one lived by the subject: it is the author's manner of existence and self-expression, the author's *style* in the word's strict sense. Research into the markers of personal style appears easier thanks to the literary method of substitution, that is to say, by the establishment of variants which the analyst considers appropriate. Other techniques include: the study of stylemes or pairs between which the author had to make choices; the interpretation of these choices, that is, the offering of hypotheses as to the author's motives; and the integration of overlapping hypotheses. Details concerning this method, which is able to preserve its objectivity even in the case of research into a subjective phenomenon, is presented in B. Dupriez, *L'Etude des styles*.

9. Attention should be given to:
– *forced* meaning, which presses the text to say more than it does, or which shows something other than the *natural* meaning.
– *equivocal* meaning, a double meaning based upon the polysemic nature of words. Ex: *The Broken Window*, by Eva Brick.
– the *double* or *ambiguous* meaning, which is equivocal because of some mistake of syntax or grammar. Ex: 'It was said that Cluny rivaled Saint Peter's in Rome until it was rebuilt in the sixteenth century ...' (John James, *The Traveller's Key to Medieval France*, p. 201). Only knowledge of the context allows identification of the church to which the second 'it' refers.
– the *principal* meaning, which Fontanier contrasts with the *accessory* meaning; the *exemplifying* meaning (Mr Smith / a certain someone); etc.

MEIOSIS A figure which uses ironic understatement to represent something as in some way less than it is: a form of ironic emphasis (see Grambs). See also Abrams, Beckson, Corbett, Cuddon, Gray, Joseph, Lanham, Preminger, and Puttenham.

Ex: The final statement in Dante's Paola and Francesca episode – 'quel giorno più non vi leggemmo avante' ('That day we read no more') – understates the importance of the lovers' interruption.

Ex (ironic meiosis produces the following 'epitaph'):

He was found by the Bureau of Statistics to be
One against whom there was no official complaint
...
He worked in a factory and never got fired
...
And our Social Psychology workers found
That he was popular with his mates and liked a drink.
W.H. Auden, 'The Unknown Citizen'

R1: Group MU demonstrate (pp. 132–8) that as a metalogism or 'figure of thought,' meiosis functions, like hyperbole*, litotes*, irony*, and paradox*, by implicit reference to an ostensive situation; that is, to an utterance's extra-linguistic, pragmatic context. In order to understand *under*statement, some reference to a 'norm,' such as faithful description or veridical language or 'truth mirror,' must be invoked. Meiosis differs from litotes*, which functions by negating the contrary, as in expressions like 'not bad' [= 'very good'], 'modesty is not her strong point,' etc.

R2: Recently, meiosis in English prose (and therefore *a fortiori* in poetry) has come under attack from some authorities, as in the follow-

ing historical summary (which confuses meiosis with litotes): 'What
was a rhetorical device in the Classical schools of oratory – *meiosis* or
under-emphasis – and came into facetious use in Victorian times (e.g.,
"Pedestrianism in November is a matter of not a little unpleasantness")
is now second nature to most Englishmen, and has lost its original
ironic purpose. It now means modesty ... Conversationally this style
can be charming, but in prose it makes for irrelevancy, material omission, faulty connexion, logical weakness, and, eventually, boredom'
(Robert Graves and Alan Hodge, *The Reader over Your Shoulder*,
pp. 27–8).

METABOLE An accumulation of several synonymous expressions in
order to depict with greater force the same thing or idea (see Fontanier,
p. 332). See also Quillet and Robert (meaning 2).

Exx: 'At her feet he bowed, he fell, he lay down: at her feet he bowed,
he fell; where he bowed, there he fell down dead' (Judges 5:27); 'To dig
down deep enough to find the truth, / To penetrate and check, balance
and sift' (Howard Nemerov, 'The Private Eye,' in *Collected Poems of
Howard Nemerov*).

Other definitions: 1. 'Repeating the same words, but in a different
order' (Robert, meaning 1). See antimetabole*.
2. According to Quintilian and Longinus, a change in a (syntactic) turn
of phrase, figure, or rhythm* (see tempo*, R3). The *OED*, Littré, Lausberg, and Group MU give the term an even wider meaning: 'any kind
of change of whatever aspect of language' (Group MU, p. 18). We
would prefer to distinguish changes in the *paradigmatic axis* (not including repetition*), which are synonymous with stylistic deviation, from
metaboles in the narrow sense, in which two states (the second being
the transformation of the first) are expressed (successively) along the
syntagmatic axis.

R1: Metaboles differ from synonymy* in that, rather than affecting
single words, they affect word groups (while still employing synonyms
or equivalents). They are the opposite of mistakes* like redundancy*
and battology*, because rather than being pointless repetition*, they
attach new content to the same general idea. They are not figures of
words or of style, but of 'thought.' They satisfy the concern for clarity
in communication, sometimes expressing a speaker's change of mind.
Ex: 'MA UBU: But I'd like to know what has become of my fat Punch, I
mean my most respectable husband' (A. Jarry, *Ubu roi*, 5.1). See also
epanorthosis*, 'accumulation by negation' (Quinn, p. 68).

R2: Excessive use of metaboles is (obviously) a mistake* (see parastasis*).

METALEPSIS 'The expression of one thing by means of another which precedes, accompanies or follows it, or which is ... attendant upon or attached or related to it, in such a way as to recall it immediately to mind' (Fontanier, pp. 127–8).

Ex: 'In *Measure for Measure* Shakespeare has a character say "My father's grave / Did utter forth a voice." It was not the grave, nor the body within the grave, but something that was once within the body that did the uttering' (Quinn, p. 54).

Ex: 'The morning I was to undergo the knife, word came that Beryl was *as one with Nineveh and Tyre*. I hurried home to Tulsa, where Beryl was to be interred' (Gore Vidal, *Duluth*, p. 43). By means of this complex figure combining simile* with an allusion* to Kipling's poem 'Recessional' (1897), the narrator reports the character's death.

Analogous definition: 'A figure which signifies a present effect by a remote cause: "The ship is sinking: damn the wood where the mast grew"' (Joseph, p. 336; cf. Lanham, p. 66). This restricted sense, to which Willem (p. 40), Lausberg (sect. 570), and Morier also refer, seems to preponderate in Anglo-Saxon definitions of metalepsis.

R1: Metalepsis resembles metonymy* (see Fontanier, p. 127) and allusion*; it may also be a kind of euphemism*.

R2: Quinn (p. 54) describes metalepsis as 'double metonymy' and explains the figure as follows: 'At times the connection between two nouns in a metonymy might seem so remote that we are inclined to think that a double substitution has occurred, a metonymic two-step. For instance in *Genesis* it is written "they came under the shadow of my roof." Roof stands for house, but house stands for protection.' Quinn illustrates by a modern example the problems such a notion of metalepsis presents, particularly when it involves substitutions of parts of speech (verbs, for example) other than nouns. 'And when someone shouts "Thank you!" from one country club tennis court to another, he usually means "Please get my ball," and also "Every member of this club is polite."'

METANALYSIS An accident of communication: language units are divided up and analysed by listeners in ways other than the speaker intends. Term proposed by Jespersen.

Exx: The words *a napron* were metanalysed to *an apron*, with the result that the word *napron* became *apron* (see *OEDS*); 'I scream, you scream, everybody wants ice cream' (jazz vocal).

Other name: affix-clipping (Grambs)

R1: Metanalysis explains several linguistic phenomena such as agglutination (sometimes called proclisis); and aphesis, by which, for instance, *esquire* became *squire*.

R2: Metanalysis also forms the basis of many figures, most often humorous ones: puns*, equivoque*, allographs*, etc. Some examples of word-play* are obtained by metanalysis and mixing (see telescoping*). **Exx:** faction (i.e., fact + fiction); 'MORE NETWORK LESS NET WORK' (caption for computer ad selling communications software).

R3: Metanalytic stratagems produced hieroglyphic writing, which is composed of phonograms, signs which, like the rebus, sketch in outline the object whose name figures within the succession of sounds to be transcribed (and whose meaning is quite different). Redfern writes (p. 82): 'Puns may be pictorialized in the rebus, as in the one over the entrance to Blenheim House (a lion rending a little cock: *gallus* = cock, or Frenchman).' For a discussion of chronograms, hieroglyphic writing, and their use in cryptography*, see U. Eco, *The Name of the Rose*, p. 165.

R4: Metanalytic intervention allows the creation of riddles* when spoken aloud. **Ex:** Can you define wise? It's what kids are always asking, as in 'Wise the sky blue?'

METAPHOR The most elaborate of the tropes (see image*, 2). A transfer from one meaning to another through a personal operation based on an impression or interpretation which readers must discover or experience for themselves. See Dumarsais (ch. 10), Fontanier (pp. 99–104), Frye, Lanham, and Morier.

Although also used in a broader sense, the word *metaphor* is not, strictly speaking, a synonym for the literary image*, of which it is the most condensed form, being reduced to a single term. In fact, unlike allegory*, it has only one phore, or vehicle, although this may be evoked by several words. Unlike comparison* or simile*, the phore is dispersed syntactically throughout the sentence, in which the theme, or tenor, is enunciated.

Exx: 'A London taxi is a flying bomb ... The clatter as it barges into the crescent, the metric tick-tick as the bass notes die. The cut-off: where has it stopped, which house, when all of us in the street are waiting in the dark, crouching under tables or clutching pieces of string, which house? Then the slam of the door, the explosive anticlimax: if you can hear it, it's not for you' (John Le Carré, *Tinker Tailor Soldier Spy*, p. 295); 'Money is a language I speak better than you do. But you must learn something of the grammar of money ... Money illiteracy is as bad as any other illiteracy' (Robertson Davies, *What's Bred in the Bone*, p. 275); 'The psychoanalysts who are the great magicians of our day' (ibid., p. 401).

R1: Mallarmé: 'I am crossing the word *like* out of the dictionary.' In other words, 'I prefer metaphor to simile.' He tried to go even further, reducing the tenor almost to nothing, even trying to suppress it altogether. For instance, in 'Brise marine,' *birds, drunk, foam, skies, seas, steamer, masts, anchor, storms, shipwrecks,* and *fertile islands* all belong to the phore; only a few words – *books, heart,* and *empty paper* – refer to the theme. There is no sign to mark the analogy, and most of the elements in the vehicle have no particular link with the tenor. Ex: 'But, oh my heart, hear the song of the sailors.'

The deliberate suppression of the tenor risks a hermeticism sometimes achieved by the surrealists. Ex: '... the moment in which man, in order to concentrate upon himself all male pride and female desire, has only to hold on the tip of his sword the bronze mass with the bright crescent which really, and *suddenly* marks time' (A. Breton, *L'Amour fou,* p. 79). For the benefit of readers who have not solved this metaphorical riddle, Breton does supply the answer: 'the bull.'

Mallarmé dreamed of going all the way, of suppressing the vehicle as well. It was to have been the culminating quintessence, a poem which would say absolutely everything, using nothing, a book of blank, virgin pages ...

R2: Metaphors lose their power with use, evoking ever more immediately their tenor, until they lose their meaning* and become clichés*. Exx: green with envy; the scourge of war; etc. A literary example:

Happy he, who can on vigorous *wing*
Fly to bright and peaceful *fields*.

Baudelaire, 'Elévation'

Sublime or lofty style can accommodate conventional or stock metaphor quite well. To prove that one ought to prefer the ordinary term, Dumarsais recounts in chapter 10 of *Des Tropes* ('About Tropes') the case of the foreigner writing to his protector: 'You have for me the guts (*boyaux*) of a father.' He meant 'entrails' (*entrailles,* in French, metaphorically stand for 'affection').

R3: Metaphor and simile* may commingle, with tenor suddenly appearing in vehicle, and vehicle in tenor. Ex:

POLONIUS: In few, Ophelia,
Do not believe his *vows,* for *they are brokers,*
Not of that dye which their investments show,
But *mere implorators* of unholy suits,
Breathing *like sanctified and pious bawds*
The better to beguile.

Shakespeare, *Hamlet,* 1.3.126–31

Ex: ' "Exactly!" said Arthur. "That's exactly what we've been. As good

Metaphor

as gold. We've been the gold at the bottom of the whole thing." "Gold isn't really a bad part to play," said Dancourt ... "You and Maria are just gold – pure gold"' (Robertson Davies, *The Lyre of Orpheus*, p. 427).

The incoherence resulting from a clash of conventional metaphors should also be avoided. Ex: 'The Crusaders entered Constantinople, overturned the throne, and occupied it' [an uncomfortable seat!] (Jean-Charles, *Hardi! les cancres*, p. 27). Taking such metaphors literally can lead to some curious effects as well: 'He disappeared into the kitchen at the same time as a gust of icy wind. He always arrives like a gust of wind' (Guèvremont, *Le Survenant*, p. 99). 'Arriver en coup de vent' means to arrive, stay a moment, and then immediately leave again. Here the author is playing on the literal and figurative meanings of the expression.

Metaphor's degree of novelty is, then, one of its essential characteristics (see image*, R4).

R4: But a really new metaphor can be disconcerting. Working it out, however, consists merely in defining the tenor. Ex: 'I dip my pen not in an inkwell, but in life' (Blaise Cendrars, *L'Homme foudroyé*, p. 91). The tenor is *life* not *pen*. Ex: 'And the rain suddenly pours down the message's white oats on isles bathed in a pale golden light' (Saint-Jean Perse, *Amers*, p. 201). *Message* seems to be the tenor despite its abstractness; after all, abstract metaphors do exist. *Message* might evoke the shower's freshness. When asked by Pierre Van Rutten, the author confirmed that he was describing a spectacle he actually saw. *Rain* and *isles* are therefore to be taken literally.

R5: Personification* constantly relies on metaphors of action denoting persons. In the case of personification, however, the metaphoric entity is sufficiently complex to form allegory* or prosopopoeia*. Ex:

Bugles sang, saddening the evening air,
And bugles answered, sorrowful to hear
...
The monstrous anger of our taciturn guns.
The majesty of the insults of their mouths.

W. Owen, 'Bugles Sang'

Ex:

Thirty-six-hundred times an hour,
The Second whispers: Remember.

Baudelaire, 'L'Horloge'

R6: A brand-new metaphor frequently spreads over several words, remaining a metaphor so long as they remain part of a field of association, contributing elements to the evocation of a phore. Ex:

He began then, bewilderingly, to talk about something called entropy ... there were two distinct kinds of entropy. One having to do with heat-engines, the other to do with communication. The equation for one, back in the '30's, had looked very like the equation for the other. It was a coincidence. The two fields were entirely unconnected, except at one point: Maxwell's Demon. As the Demon sat and sorted his molecules into hot and cold, the system was said to lose entropy. But somehow the loss was offset by the information the Demon gained about what molecules were where. (Thomas Pynchon, *The Crying of Lot 49*, p. 77)

The Demon personifies the metaphor connecting 'the world of thermodynamics to the world of information flow' (ibid.).

R7: The semes on which an analogy is founded (see simile*, R3) are common both to the vehicle and the tenor. Consequently when metaphors accumulate, the area of intersection covered by the sememes is reduced. The result of such an analogy is to bring the expression into sharper focus. Ex: 'No, no, I saw him here in the cemetery, he was moving among the graves, a ghost among ghosts ... his face was a corpse's, his eyes already beheld the eternal punishment ... even at that moment I realised that there was a damned soul before me' (U. Eco, *The Name of the Rose*, p. 115).

METAPLASM The generic term for any alteration of a word by adjunction*, suppression, or inversion* of sounds or letters. See Dumarsais (ch. 2 and ch. 11), Group MU, Lanham, Lausberg (sect. 479–95), Marouzeau, *OED*, and Robert.

Other definition: Quinn (p. 19): metaplasmus, 'effective misspelling'

R1: Lanham, Lausberg, Littré, Marouzeau, *OED*, and Robert distinguish the following metaplasms:

1. By addition:	at the beginning of a word:	prosthesis*
	in the middle " " "	epenthesis*
	at the end " " "	paragoge*
2. By suppression:	at the beginning " " "	aphaeresis*
	in the middle " " "	syncope*
	at the end " " "	apocope*
3. By transposition		metathesis*
4. By dividing a syllable		diaeresis*
5. By fusion		synaeresis (see crasis*)

METASTASIS After an opponent has solidly established the facts, a speaker responds by placing the blame elsewhere. See Joseph, Lanham, Lausberg, Littré, and Robert.

Ex: 'It's not my fault, it's *his*.'

Ex [the arbitrarily banished Kent turns Lear's judgment against the king]: 'Fare thee well, King. Since thus thou wilt appear, / Freedom lives hence, and banishment is here' (Shakespeare, *King Lear*, 1.1.183–4).

Other definitions: 'passing over an issue quickly' (Lanham); 'a rapid transition from one point to another' (*OED*); 'change of tenses' (Legras, cited by Le Hir). The latter meaning designates more properly *metastasia*, 'a kind of hypotyposis* evoking past actions as if they were actually happening' (J. Morel, *XVIIe siècle*, nos. 80–1 [1968], p. 145 [glossary]). See enallage*.

R1: Fabri (2:155) presents the *rejection*, which consists of an excuse* for having spoken too long, by saying that 'it is my opponent's fault and he must answer for it.' This is *semi-metastasis*.

R2: See also intonation*, R2, and recrimination*.

METATHESIS Altering a word by transposing or rearranging letters or phonetic elements. See Robert.

Exx: *morden* for *modern*; *revelant* for *relevant*; 'A craving for carvings' [advertisement]

Ex: 'If Shakespeare's name for his ignoble savage, Caliban, is really a play on Cannibal, then perhaps we have syncopic metathesis' (Quinn, p. 23).

Synonyms: transposition (Lanham, Marouzeau); antisthecon (Lanham); transliteration (Dubois, p. 113). In linguistics, a *transliteration* is a 'letter-by-letter transcription of a word from a foreign language' (Dubois et al., *Dictionnaire de linguistique*).

Other definition: 'reminding listeners of past facts, introducing future facts, anticipating objections' (*Larousse du XXe siècle*)

R1: As a term of ancient grammar, metathesis could designate stammered words like '*insluter, Rébénice, Nomitauré*' [i.e., insult, Bérénice, Minotaur] (R. Ducharme, *L'Avalée des avalés*, p. 205).

R2: More frequent are metatheses within a syntagm* or sentence, that is, spoonerisms*.

R3: Applying the definition systematically, Queneau amused himself, writing: 'Un juor vres miid, sru la palte-frome aièrre d'un aubutos ...' ['Noe dya aobut dimday on teh rera platform of a sub'] (*Exercises in Style*, p. 154). This is lexical scrambling*.

METONYMY A trope which allows the designation of one thing

by the name of some element belonging to the same whole, on the strength of some sufficiently obvious relationship.

Exx: 'A traveller from the cradle to the grave' (Shelley, *Prometheus Unbound*, 4.551) for 'from birth to death'; 'The pen is mightier than the sword' (E.G. Bulwer-Lytton, *Richelieu*, 2.2) for 'Persuasion achieves more than violence'; 'The kettle is boiling; the buses are on strike' (see G. Lakoff and M. Johnson, *Metaphors We Live By*, pp. 35–40). See also euphemism*, R6.

Analogous definitions: Bary (p. 297), K. Burke (*A Grammar of Motives*, pp. 503f), Corbett, Fontanier, Lanham, Lausberg, Littré, Morier, *OED*, Preminger, and Robert

R1: Classical rhetoricians listed a variety of metonymies:
1. Cause for effect. A divine cause: *Bacchus* for wine; an active cause: *a Virgil* for a work by Virgil; a passive cause or instrument: *from his eloquent pen* for 'in his eloquent way'; an objective cause: *a marble Diana* for a marble statue representing Diana; a physical cause: *his star* for his destiny; an abstract cause: *her many kindnesses* for acts resulting from her kindness.
2. Instrument for user: *the second violin* for the second violinist.
3. Effect for cause: *to swallow death* for 'to drink hemlock'; 'And cuckoo-buds of yellow hue / Do *paint* the meadows with *delight*' (Shakespeare, 'Spring').
4. Container for contained: *take a glass*; Bless this *house*.
5. Place for a thing associated with it: *a fine Burgundy*; the *White House*; *Paris* is carefully reviewing the accords proposed by *London*.
6. Sign for thing associated with it: the *throne, sceptre*, or *crown* for royal power or dignity; *laurels* for glory; 'Why should I accept the *Garter* from his Majesty when his people have just given me the *boot*' (W. Churchill, after losing the 1945 election).
7. Physical for moral phenomena: 'You've gotta have *heart* [or *balls*]' for 'You must have courage'; a rat with a small *brain* for one with little intelligence.
8. The master for the subject: *penates* for house; *St Clair* for the lake placed under her patronage. The same applies to place names like St Andrews, St Margaret's Bay, etc.
9. Appropriate things for persons: *graybeards* for old men; '... *doublet and hose* ought to show itself courageous to *petticoat*' (Shakespeare, *As You Like It*, 2.4.6).

R2: The 'master tropes' (Burke), including metaphor*, metonymy, and synecdoche*, have been discussed and taught for some twenty-five centuries. They may once have formed a logical whole, but they are nowadays more easily defined extensionally than intensionally. Group MU, Le Guern, and Morier have noted that some semes are excluded from a metaphor* because they evoke an isotopy* incompatible with the one in the text. But distinctions between metonymy and synecdoche are harder to sustain. Le Guern (*Sémantique de la métaphore et de la métonymie*, p. 32) and Preminger attribute the confusion to Quintilian. Lakoff and Johnson, like Dumarsais, see synecdoche as 'a species of metonymy.' Most, however, consider the relationship between the literal term and the figurative term to be closer in the case of synecdoche than in that of metonymy. Fontanier speaks of connection, Genette of 'contiguity,' Morier of inclusion* (see inclusion, other def., 2).

In their *General Rhetoric* (pp. 120f), Group MU redefined synecdoche in broader but more useful terms. According to them, synecdoche is the minimal trope which takes the figurative term at a node in the semic tree on a different level from that (either more general or particular) of the literal term. A *sword* may be called either a *weapon* or a *point*; *wolves* may be called either *animals* or *furs*.

R3: It is possible to define metonymy (and some other tropes) without invoking logic or semic analysis. A trope's essential characteristic is the choice it makes of the most relevant lexeme (relevant because of its expressivity or popularity, or because it summarizes a situation in the briefest way, etc.). It also installs the lexeme with maximum terseness into the sentence, despite ellipsis* of some of the usual articulating factors of the idea in question, and relies on the context to ensure communication. (This definition excludes metonymies which have become conventional within a language; see catachresis*.) Ex: '*Watergate* changed American politics.' This kind of political metonymy uses popular allusions* in a kind of ideological 'shorthand,' usually in order to manipulate public opinion. Metonymy may be foregrounded:

> 'Who is there in the house!' said Sam, in whose mind the inmates were always represented by that particular article of their costume, which came under his immediate superintendence. 'There's a wooden leg in number six; there's a pair of Hessians in thirteen; there's two pairs of halves in the commercial; there's these here painted tops in the snuggery inside the bar; and five more tops in the coffee-room.' (Dickens, *The Pickwick Papers*, ch. 10)

The ellipsis* which accompanies any metonymy is evident in the following extract frm *Ulysses* (pp. 210, 211), in which Joyce takes up again at the end of the page the opening sentence of chapter 11, namely, 'Bronze by gold heard the hoofirons steelyringing,' and, by explaining the idea articulated in it, cancels out the metonymy: 'Bronze by gold, miss Douce's head by miss Kennedy's head, over the cross-blind of the Ormond bar heard the viceregal hoofs go by, ringing steel.'

R4: When one of the terms forming the metonymy is a proper name, the figure is called antonomasia*.

R5: Tropes which usage has made conventional are frequently called symbols*. Lausberg (sect. 568, 5) defines a symbol as 'a trope by which the name of a sign chosen by usage to designate a thing is substituted for the thing's name.' His example is: 'to give up robes for a sword' [to abandon the magistrature for the army].

It should be noted that metonymies which replace an idea or institution by some relatively trivial object become humorous devices. Exx: 'Gas and Gaiters,' a TV comedy series about gossipy Anglican clergymen; in French, 'le sabre et le goupillon' ('the sabre and the sprinkler') stand for the Army and the Church.

R6: As is well known, Jakobson extended the field of application of the complementary figures, metaphor and metonymy, to encompass more diverse categories: dreams, myths, psychoanalysis, various types of aphasia, tests, and so on. Even the original shapes of alphabet letters are metonymical (see graphism*, R1). Ordinal numbers are metonymic in relationship to cardinal numbers. From earliest antiquity metaphors exist in mathematics, where they are called the *proportional relationship* or simply *proportion* (a is to b as c is to d). As logical categories, metaphor and metonymy are in constant use.

Part of metonymy's function as a logical category is to attribute to leaders the credit or responsibility for national events, but the device becomes literary when the name of a prominent figure designates a historical period, or place, etc. Exx: the age of Pericles, or of Elizabeth; Cape Kennedy, Vancouver. This device has a special name: *eponymy* (see Cyril L. Beeching, *A Dictionary of Eponyms*).

MIMOLOGY (neol.) An imitation* of the human voice or of speech habits, or of a person's pronunciation. See Lausberg.

Exx: 'Grand Ole Opry'; 'Get on wi' t' turn!' (K. Waterhouse, *Billy Liar*, p. 120); 'To a speaker of Strine, "Air Fridge" is "something not extreme" as in "the air fridge person"; "Baked necks" is a popular breakfast dish; "Egg Jelly" is "in fact"; "Egg Nisher" is a mechanical device for cooling a room; "Flares" are blossoms; and "Furry Tiles" are stories beginning, "One Spawner time ..."' (Espy, 1971, p. 233); '– Now, baby, Cissy Caffrey said. Say out big, big. I want a drink of water. And baby prattled after her: – A jink a jink a jawbo' (Joyce, *Ulysses*, p. 284).

R1: Mimologies are produced by voicing or unvoicing consonants; by phonemic lengthening*; and by transcription of noises*. Joyce mixes in the text sounds of eating to evoke a conversation in a restaurant: 'I munched hum un thu Unchester Bunk un Munchday' (*Ulysses*, p. 139).

R2: Mimologies are also produced by diphthongization ([usually] tonic vowels become diphthongs by the addition in pronunciation of posttonic semi-consonants). Ex: In Shaw's *Pygmalion* (act 1), the flower girl pronounces the interjection *Ow!* as 'Ah-ah-ow-ow-ow-oo!' and the by-stander remarks: 'It's aw rawt: e's a genleman: look at his *bɔ-oots.*' Mimology serves also to foreground non-native pronunciation: 'No wonder the thousands of Roman extras cried "LEEZ! LEEZ!" instead of "Cleopatra!" when she did her triumphant entry' (M. Bragg, *Rich: The Life of Richard Burton,* p. 162).

R3: The specific meaning of mimology (according to the *OED*) is 'recitation of mimes.' The meaning indicated here is a 'derived' one.

MIRROR Two words possessing the same lexeme are subordinated one to another.

Exx: 'Who polices the police?'; 'Part of the new security force's function will be to spy on the spies.'

Other name: Paul Valéry, drawing his inspiration from mathematics, speaks of exponentiation (a x a = a^2). See also R5 below.

R1: Lexical mirroring is a kind of isolexism*. Sometimes it simply has a superlative effect. **Exx:** king of kings; the finest of the fine; *la crème de la crème.* Or it may simply be verbal extravagance: 'Who shaves the razor ... will erase the eraser' (Michaux, *Face aux verrous,* p. 60). Sometimes it reverses meanings: 'One short sleep past, we wake eternally, / And death shall be no more; death, thou shalt die' (John Donne, *Holy Sonnets,* no. 10).

R2: It may reflect its opposite, in which case it becomes a reversing mirror. **Exx:** 'The presence of absence' (the title of a collection of poems by Rina Lasnier); 'What to do in order to do nothing?' Valéry wonders (*Oeuvres,* 2:201); and Sartre offers: 'The terrible thing is, said Daniel, that nothing is ever very terrible. There are no extreme cases' (*Le Sursis,* p. 153). Reversing mirrors of this type are not isolexisms but examples of oxymoron* or of oxymoric* sentences.

R3: Valéry enjoys the lexical mirroring device because it is an image* of his own characteristic procedure, which consists in becoming conscious of his own consciousness: 'I am since I exist, and since I see myself; since I see myself see myself, and so on' (*Nouveau Dictionnaire de citations françaises,* no. 13412).

As in the logical or mathematical phenomenon of recursion, the mirroring process may multiply images endlessly and the images so reflected stretch off to infinity. A common visual case involves a picture of, for example, Mickey Mouse looking at himself in a picture of Mickey Mouse looking at himself in a picture of ...

A literary example:

There are born beginnings ...
which repeat

and ceaselessly repeat that I repeat that 'it repeats'
and that I repeat that I repeat that I repeat that 'it repeats'
echo of an echo of a never ending echo
H. Michaux, 'Paix dans les brisements'

Double mirrors reduce the complexity of the recursive mirroring device. **Exx:**

> What, reduced to their simplest reciprocal form, were Bloom's thoughts about Stephen's thoughts about Bloom and about Stephen's thoughts about Bloom's thoughts about Stephen?
> He thought that he thought that he was a jew whereas he knew that he knew that he knew that he was not. (Joyce, *Ulysses*, p. 558)

> 'Well, um, thinking back on what I said, and what you said, and what I said you said, or what they may say I said you said, or what they may have thought I said I thought you thought, or they may say I said I thought you said I thought ... I think I said you thought you were above the law.' (J. Lynn and A. Jay, *Yes Prime Minister*, p. 66)

R4: The subordinating conjunction (*that*) is not expressed in parataxis*, resulting in a kind of *semi-mirror*. **Ex:** 'I will know you know' (M. Duras, *Le Ravissement de Lol V. Stein*, p. 189). False mirroring also exists, as in the French expression 'blanc de blanc,' white wine made from white grapes.

R5: Lexical mirroring may resemble *mise en abîme*. (See Gide, *Journal 1889–1939*, p. 41, where he uses the spelling *abyme*; we have chosen the current spelling.) Group MU's translators call the device 'disappearing repetition' (*General Rhetoric*, p. 206). In Gide's usage, *abîme* refers to 'the heraldic image of an escutcheon bearing in its centre a miniature replica of itself' (L. Hutcheon, *Narcissistic Narrative*, p. 55). When Hamlet, for example, has the players mime the murder of his father, the king, the actors play the role of actors playing a different role. Tom Stoppard increased the complexity of the device in *Rosencrantz and Guildenstern Are Dead*, a play which takes place, as it were, in the wings of *Hamlet*, and whose action foregrounds the situation of the eponymous lords asked to spy on the prince.

Stories with a similar function may be inserted into a narrative* (see narrative, R4), like the story of Marcella and Chrysostom in chapter 12 of *Don Quixote*. This kind of mirroring device, in which a fictional story-teller tells a story about one of the fictional characters in the frame-narrative, has been called *second-degree narrative*. See G. Genette, *Narrative Discourse*, and L. Dällenbach, *Le Récit spéculaire*.

In second-degree narrative, *embedding*, by which the inserted story remains subordinate to the primary narrative, differs from *dovetailing*, by which the two are co-ordinated. In a film, narrative montage may alternate (shots and reverse-shots of a conversation, for example, succeed one another in the same temporal sequence) or may present a staggered series of shots within a broken temporal sequence. The narrative representation of a chase, for example, may focus alternatively on hunter and hunted. See James Monaco, *How to Read a Film*.

MISTAKE Mistakes occur in the text when the author – through ignorance or oversight – fails to recognize firmly established customs or structures, whether in content or form.

Exx: 'A friend of mine attributes to his gardener the remark that "She don't like me and I don't like her, so it's neutral"' (Espy, 1971, p. 160); 'But [Richard] Burton was not British, he was Welsh' (K. Turan, TV *Guide*, 25 Nov. 1989, p. 27) [presumably the author intends to distinguish between 'English' and 'Welsh']. See also lapsus* and blunder*.

Synonyms: error, howler, boo-boo (Amer. slang), *faux pas*, gem (a funny mistake, one worth 'treasuring')

R1: Numerous types of mistakes have been given specific names; notably the following:
– the spelling mistake or cacography, used to good effect in realistic literature. Ex: 'Dear sir ... while we was throwing a ten pence for luck onto back of Allergater corcodile ... it must have fell from my purse ... faithly, VIV' (Peter Reading, *Ukelele Music*, p. 16).
– printing errors, for which the technical terms include: misprints, or *literals* (see paragram*); doubles, or repetitions of a letter, syllable, or word; blanks, omissions, or *outs*; transpositions, or *pies*; and *friars*, blanks due to faulty inking.
– mistakes in pronunciation, transliteration of syllables, substitutions of phonemes. Ex: 'Mrs. Veller passed a very good night, but is uncommon perwerse, and unpleasant this mornin'' (Dickens, *The Pickwick Papers*, ch. 33). For mistakes in pronunciation, see below, R2.
– barbarisms* or mistakes in vocabulary.
– solecisms* or grammatical mistakes.
– cacologies* or mistakes in usage or in logical expression.
Discourse* must be free of such errors. For mistakes in translation, Valéry Larbaud proposed the name *Jhon-le-toréador* in which the *h* of *ohn* is misplaced, and the word *toreador* is misused in place of *torero* (*Sous l'invocation de Saint Jérôme*, p. 220).

R2: Many mistakes are not serious, being simply clumsy, involuntarily ambiguous, unharmonious, or obstructive to easy communication: these are textual deficiencies, infelicities, or weaknesses.
The occasional mistake in pronunciation is a matter of performance. Such mistakes include stammering*, *mumbling* (rapid, indistinct articulation), *spluttering* (uttering incoherent sounds), *stuttering* (weak, hesitant diction), and *muttering* (incomprehensible words spoken between clenched teeth). Other mistakes of pronunciation are constants.

Sigmatism deforms [s] and other fricatives; *rhotacism* is the use of the phoneme [r] instead of another, usually [l] or [s] (Pei and Gaynor); *lambdaism* is substitution of [l] (usually) for [r] (ibid.). *Lisping* is caused by the tongue being kept between the teeth during speech.

Unvoicing, which makes [b], [d], and [g] similar in sound to [p], [t], [k], and [z] and [v] similar to [s] and [f], derives from excessive muscle tension. *Closed rhinolalia*, which makes a speaker sound as if the nose is blocked, is the opposite of open rhinolalia, which affects sounds other than [n], [m], and [gn]. A *nasal twang*, or nasalization characteristic of the pronunciation of vowels in certain regions (Pei and Gaynor), occurs because the nasal cavity acts as a resonator. *Hoarseness* is caused by too much shouting.

Among psycholinguistic disorders: *aphasia* is a 'loss of speech, partial or total, or loss of the power to understand written or spoken language, as a result of disorder of the cerebral speech centres' (*OED*); *agrammatism* is a 'form of aphasia marked by an inability to form sentences grammatically' (*OED*); *ataxism* (neol.) fails to indicate the function of syntagms. *Amelodia* and *arhythmia* affect sound and rhythm of pronunciation, although such modification or amplification is often said to produce merely a 'strange' or 'foreign' accent. *Mutism*, a refusal to speak, contrasts with *tachylalia* or uncontrollable speech (see verbigeration*); *paragraphia* is substitution of letters, *paraphasia* is substitution of words, and *paragrammatism* of constructions. (See Ducrot and Todorov, pp. 161–6.)

When a text is read aloud, diction is seldom as natural as one might wish: too slow a delivery produces a drone. *Professorial delivery* consists in separating words one from another.

R3: Colloquial style, which consists of writing in a free-and-easy fashion, almost avoids being a mistake. Ex: 'In fact she had. Told Leonard what she was going to do. She was going to stay. Not "stay" precisely. "Not leave" is more like it' (Joan Didion, *A Book of Common Prayer*, p. 256).

R4: The mistake is a difficult concept to deal with. Novelists must allow their characters to speak 'in character,' and so they have them make typical mistakes (see epiphany* and mimology*). Besides correct usage, there exist long-accepted regional expressions, tricks of speech, professional and social sub-codes or parlances, various kinds of jargon* spoken or written by different coteries, idioms, and purely individual linguistic customs. So the notion of usage is itself not clearly defined. Even cases like the *hapax legomenon* ('word of which only one instance is recorded ["*hugger-mugger*" is *hapax-legomenon* in Shakespeare]' [*Concise Oxford Dictionary*]) are not without interest. Some texts resemble Princess Bolkowsky, whose 'little imperfection – the shortness of the upper lip and her half-open mouth – seemed to be a special form of beauty peculiarly her own' (Tolstoy, *War and Peace*, 1: 9).

We may suppose nevertheless that the choice of a term, construction, or graphic form brings with it obscurity or even misunderstanding, or in other words that the graphic, syntactic, or lexical structure is impaired. The concept of the mistake, evocative of the schoolmaster's cane, springs immediately to mind. But it is of greater relevance to point to the distinction between *performance* (the act itself, performed *hic et nunc*) and *competence* (knowledge of the language-system). Ex: the use of the adverb *hopefully* to mean 'we hope,' which 'Usage Panels' in two editions of the *Harper Dictionary of Contemporary Usage* have declared barely acceptable in speech and unacceptable in writing. However, this form of 'hanging adverb' (*Harper Dictionary*, 1985 ed., p. 289) seems to be a rising structure; 'thankfully,' for instance, having been recorded in *New York Times* movie reviews.

We may conclude that it will always be dangerous to underline a 'mistake' out of school, where the relationship between master and pupil involves an attempt by the latter to acquire greater competence, in terms of the socio-cultural criteria of the day.

R5: Mistakes, defects, and cases of lapsus*, unless voluntary, may be forms, but they are not devices. Does that mean that admitted mistakes are impossible in literature? Writing presupposes so many interdependent choices that it is impossible sometimes not to sacrifice some regions to get to others, as surgeons say. Automatic writing forms the most obvious example of this. Thus the surrealist Louis Aragon declared: 'I no longer wish to avoid the mistakes which my eyes or fingers make. I know now that they are not crude traps but curious byways towards a goal which only they can reveal' (Aragon, *Le Paysan de Paris*, p. 15). The validity of a mistake which makes possible the expression of something new has always been recognized as *poetic licence*. It was natural that the surrealists would extend it through automatic writing and writing dictated by the unconscious.

R6: See also flip-flop*, R2; foregrounding*, R2; enunciation*, R2; and truism*, R2.

MONODY Stanzas* sung or chanted on the same tune (see Verest, sect. 350). Preminger adds that monody was originally, in Greek tragedy, an ode* sung by a single voice. In English poetry, monody is frequently called 'elegy,' as is the case in critical works about *Lycidas*, for example, although Milton spoke in his epigraph* of a 'monody.' See Fowler, under 'Elegy.'

MONOLOGUE One person speaks aloud, normally in exclamatory fashion, without an addressee. In literature, this kind of discourse* is frequently simulated and might be described as a dialogue* with an imaginary addressee who sits in the audience.

Ex: 'TYRONE: Whose play is it? A stinking old miser. Well, maybe you're right. Maybe I can't help being, although all my life since I had anything I've thrown money over the bar for everyone in the house, or loaned money to sponges I knew would never pay it back' (Eugene O'Neill, *Long Day's Journey into Night*, act 4).

In the above example, double articulation is admitted: the character even addresses the audience as 'you,' while seeming to think aloud. On the other hand, since Edouard Dujardin's *Les Lauriers sont coupés* and particularly since Joyce's *Ulysses*, attempts have been made to transcribe pure *interior monologues* at the stage of endophasia (the internal verbal expression of unspoken thought), or what William James named the 'stream of consciousness' (*Principles of Psychology*, 1890) and what Michel Butor calls the 'internal tape recorder' (*Intervalle*, p. 60). Ex: 'now garters that much I have the violet pair I wore today thats all he bought me out of the cheque he got on the first O no there was the face lotion I finished the last of yesterday' (Joyce, *Ulysses*, p. 618). Since the words are pronounced only in thought, the sentence is barely sketched in, and many of the nuances remain in the tone used. (See also sentence* [types of], 5; interjection*; and nominal sentence*.) In literature, authors have striven to render this kind of expression in its original state by erasing all signs of a referential situation and all punctuation*. Ex: Virginia Woolf's *Jacob's Room*. The following is an extract from Beckett's *How It Is* (p. 10), in which we have inserted several caesuras* (see caesura, R4): 'life / life / the other / in the light / said to have been mine / on and off / no going back up there.'

Thus the presence of *holophrastic* (OEDS) textual segments becomes evident: syntagms* hardly integrated one with another and capable of subsisting alone. We hesitate to use in this sense the word *monorheme* (Bally, Cressot, Gray, Marouzeau, Morier, OED), whose meaning is controversial, but *word-sentence* exists (syntagm-sentence would be more accurate) and so why not say *holophrase* ('a single word used instead of a phrase, or to express a combination of ideas' [OEDS])?

The specificity of the holophrase or embryonic sentence is immediately obvious if one reads aloud Beckett's text, with its added caesuras and concluding melody. *As an utterance* (in direct discourse*; see narrative*), the same propositional content might become something like: *Real life, refused to me, living in the light, said to have been mine, off and on at least, there's no question of my going back to it.*

R1: Holophrases themselves rely on gestures*, pre-linguistic forms (i.e., non-codified inarticulate sounds; see noise*), and sign-language. With the development of the cinema and television, the study of such sign systems has made great progress, under various names: *kinesics* or *non-verbal communication*, formerly *physiognomy* (the study of facial expressions) and *chirology* (the study of speaking with the hands). J. Tardieu gives the following account of such phenomena: 'Don't forget the many meanings of lip movements, nor lowering the eyelids to denote scepticism, rubbing the hands together to denote satisfaction or malice, loosening the collar as if it were too tight (to suggest a short meditation before an important response)' (*Un Mot pour un autre*, pp. 15–16).

All the same, such gestures display conscious thought, whose moments of passivity may be invaded by real noises*, a fact that texts attempt to transcribe. Or thoughts may be disturbed by real images*, which some reproduce in photographs, paintings, or drawings. How may consciousness and perception be discovered at their point of origin? Is not such a phenomenon too individual to allow for communication as such? Can literary communication occur without recourse to the 'words of the tribe' and generalization?

R2: From primitive chaos first emerged gestures*, then lexemes (agrammatism; see ellipsis*, R3), then actualizers (morphemes which situate the lexeme in an environment: articles, pronouns, indefinite adjectives, etc.), and finally taxemes (syntactic markers). An example of the passage from holophrase to sentence:

> Music which leaves me hanging
> *its snares*
> *its snares*
> *which holds me in its snares.*
>
> Michaux, *Connaissance par les gouffres*, p. 7

R3: A monologue which occurs during a dialogue* is an aside. See *in petto*, R1. **Ex:**

> ESTRAGON: Here we go. Be seated, Sir, I beg of you.
> POZZO: No, no I wouldn't think of it! (Pause. Aside) Ask me again.
>
> S. Beckett, *Waiting for Godot*, act 1

R4: In a *soliloquy*, the speaker is really alone, saying thoughts aloud as though the speaker were the real addressee. The text thus has a finished appearance (unlike internal monologue), but is without the double articulation characteristic of monologue.

R5: See also *dubitatio**, R2; dialogue*, R3 (interior dialogue); nominalization*, R1; and *coq-à-l'âne*, R4.

MOTIF A unit of meaning* which may have a discursive function.

Analogous terms: *lexia* (Barthes): 'sometimes a few words, sometimes several sentences ... with an observable meaning' (*lexia* by analogy, apparently, with *lecture*: 'reading'); narrative predicate (Todorov)

Ex: 'Tyger! tyger! burning bright.' Blake employs the motif of the 'tyger' to suggest a number of deeper meanings, which a reader must interpret intuitively.

Other definitions: 1. theme*; archetype
2. 'A dynamic pattern imposing form and impulse on a whole poem. Victor Hugo's "A Villequier," for example, is constructed on these two movements: "*Maintenant que* ..." ["Now that ..."] and "*Considérez* ..." ["Consider ..."]' (P. Claudel, *Oeuvres en prose*, p. 14). This definition is akin to the definition of the motif in music (see also reprise* and anaphora*).

R1: The theme of a work is more general and often more abstract than a motif. Exx: the difference between Time (the theme) and the clock-motif in Poe's works; the white whale in Melville's *Moby Dick* is the motif for the theme of obsession. The same theme may have several motifs; the same motif may serve several different themes. The distinction resembles the one linking plot and action.

R2: 'Motifs ... which may be omitted without disturbing the whole causal-chronological course of events are *free motifs*' (B. Tomachevsky, 'Thematics,' in Lemon and Reis, eds., *Russian Formalist Criticism: Four Essays*, p. 68). Motifs which may not be so omitted Tomachevsky calls *bound motifs*, and Barthes *functions*.

MUSICATION (neol.) The accordance of priority to the text's sound patterns accompanied by a concomitant neglect of its other aspects, notably its meaning*.

> A land that is lonelier than ruin,
> A sea that is stranger than death:
> Far fields that a rose never blew in,
> Wan waste where the winds lack breath.
> A. Swinburne, 'By the North Sea'

Frances Stillman comments: 'One sometimes suspects, no doubt unfairly, that [Swinburne] did not care what he said, so long as it alliterated! For example, this quatrain from "By the North Sea" sounds very lovely, but means little' (*The Poet's Manual and Rhyming Dictionary*, p. 84). Clearly musication is often a matter of literary judgment.

R1: Musication may be described as multiple, compound alliteration*. But with alliteration, as with imitative harmony*, sounds remain secondary; they add emphasis*. In the case of musication, however, they play the primary role.

R2: Musication is left far behind by the French lettrists, who accord an absolute priority to sound over sense. ('*Lettrism*: Applied to a movement in French art and literature [c. 1945–57], characterized by a repudiation of meaning, and the use of letters [sometimes invented] as isolated units' [*OEDS*].) See noise*.

R3: Pseudo-language* goes further than musication, although incorporating it to prolong sentences. **Ex:** 'Tuesday will be the longest day. Of all the glad new year, mother, the rum tum tiddledy tum' (Joyce, *Ulysses*, p. 42).

R4: The systematic practice of paronomasia* results in musication. Tongue twisters, for example, give preference to sound-repetition over meaning. **Ex:**

Moses supposes his toeses are roses,
But Moses supposes erroneously;
For Moses he knowses his toeses aren't roses
As Moses supposes his toeses to be.

Quoted by Augarde, pp. 168–9

MYTH A symbolic narrative* (see symbol*, 1) in which characters, speeches, and action aim to establish a balance in spiritual and social values in which there is room for everyone and which offers an interpretation of human existence.

Ex: '[The ashes of a wicked couple] which flew away through the smoke-hole [of their tepee] turned into mosquitoes' (Cl. Mélançon, *Légendes indiennes du Canada*, p. 92). The story-teller thus explains both the nastiness of mosquitoes and what happens to the wicked.

Ex [modern literature may treat classical or traditional myth allusively and ironically]:

SATAN, n. One of the Creator's lamentable mistakes, repented in sackcloth and ashes. Being instated as an archangel, Satan made himself multifariously objectionable and was finally expelled from Heaven. Half-way in his descent he paused, bent his head in thought a moment and at last went back. 'There is one favor I would like to ask,' said he.
  'Name it.'
  'Man, I understand, is about to be created. He will need laws.'
  'What, wretch! you his appointed adversary, charged from the dawn of eternity with hatred of his soul – you ask for the right to make his laws?'
  'Pardon; what I have to ask is that he be permitted to make them for himself.'
  It was so ordered. (Ambrose Bierce, *The Devil's Dictionary*)

Not all narratives whose symbolic meaning simply illustrates some philosophical truth are myths (see apologue*). **Ex:** Baudelaire's

Albatross symbolizes the poet, but his Swan 'offers a symbol ... in which the hero is seen to come to grips with a god: [this is] a myth' (P. Clarac, *Le XIXe siècle*, p. 506). 'The specific social function of myth gives it two characteristics of its own. First, it defines a cultural area and gives it a shared legacy of allusion* (e.g. Homeric epics, the Old Testament) ... Second, [myths] link with one another to form a *mythology*, an interconnected body of stories that verbalizes a society's major concerns in religion and history particularly' (Frye et al., *The Harper Handbook to Literature*, under 'myth'). Bierce defines 'mythology' as 'the body of a primitive people's beliefs concerning its origin, early history, heroes, deities and so forth, as distinguished from the true accounts which it invents later' (*The Devil's Dictionary*).

Originally, in Greek, *myth* simply meant 'narrative,' but more recently the term's meaning has become more specific. In modern English and French definitions, the word's accidental meaning or virtueme ('the set of connotational semes, characteristic of an individual, social group or society' [Greimas, *Sémiotique: dictionnaire raisonné*, 1: 421]) has become the essential one: myth is a 'traditional narrative usually involving supernatural or fancied persons etc. and embodying popular ideas on natural or social phenomena' (*Concise Oxford Dictionary*); and it is a '[narrative] which presents dramatically beings who embody ... forces of nature, aspects of genius or of the human condition' (Robert, meaning 1). 'Myth' has even supplanted and replaced the classeme 'narrative' and acquired a pejorative connotation. Thus 'myth' also designates 'simplified, sometimes illusory images which some human groups elaborate or accept concerning an individual or a fact; such images play a determining role in their conduct or judgment' (Robert, meaning 5). Exx: the cowboy; the vamp; the Jaguar, Citroen DS (i.e., *déesse*, 'goddess'), or Mustang automobiles. See R. Barthes, *Mythologies*.

R1: The functions fulfilled by ancient myths were partially taken over by later oral literatures: 'The whole of this considerable body of fables, apologues*, tales, legends, and jokes takes up once again, on their own level, the function of myth. Like myths, each example from oral literature reveals a typical situation and also constitutes both an explanation of some real situation or pattern of behaviour and provides a model for imitation' (Raymond Queneau, *Histoire des littératures*, 1:9).

R2: The cosmogonic or creation myth concerns the origin of the world. Ex: 'Although the creation myths are numerous, a few basic types may be distinguished. One of these, found in almost all parts of the world, is the belief in a supreme creator deity, usually characterized as omniscient and omnipotent, as having existed alone prior to the world's creation, and having had a plan in creating the world, etc.' (*Encyclopaedia Britannica* [15th ed. 1974], under 'creation myth'). Like Genesis such myths frequently begin: '[In the beginning], there was ...'

Ex: 'There was nothing but myself. I hung in a timeless, spaceless, formless void that was neither light nor dark ... But, somehow, timelessness ceased. I became aware that there was a force: that I was being moved, and that spacelessness had, therefore, ceased, too. There was nothing to show that I moved; I knew simply that I was being drawn' (John Wyndham, 'Consider Her Ways,' in *Sometime, Never*, p. 63). Paul Eluard shows that personal cosmogonies also exist: 'To begin with, I will list the elements: / Your voice, your eyes, your hands, your lips' (quoted by R. Jean, *Eluard*, p. 59).

R3: Modern publicity finds the device of myth-creation an indispensable tool. A *brand name* sets in motion a 'halo of images, of ideas, sentiments, attitudes, beliefs, some deeper than others, some more conscious than others, and all having emotional content' (Denner, quoted in Fage and Pagano, eds., *Le Dictionnaire des media*). See also response*, R2.

N

NARRATIVE We create narrative (a generic term) by separating the action from the receiver, who can only learn about it by courtesy of the narrator and thanks to the act of narrating. Descriptions*, dialogues*, speeches, interior monologues*, etc. may reduce this separation, which is usually temporal in nature.

Narratives may be fictional, therefore, even though situated in the past, as is usually the case. In addition, narratives are frequently very elaborate kinds of texts since they present detailed accounts of actions involving characters, places, objects, circumstances, conversations, time-periods, and so on.

From earliest times, various kinds of narratives have existed: myths*, fairy-tales, fables, apologues*, epics. And narrative, which includes novels of all kinds, short stories, biographies, historical reconstructions, newspaper stories, etc., is still one of the most diverse genres.

Narrative's primary marker is dual temporal actualization created by the fact that the receiver was not present at the moment of the action. The present time of the action (also called *story, fabula, fiction,* or *the narrated action*) bears, superimposed upon it at least implicitly, the present time of the narration. The two temporal processes may occur without reference one to another or they may come together (see G. Genette, *Narrative Discourse*), but they may not be confused without the risk of narrative incoherence occurring when the reader slips out of the narrative into his or her own present time. **Ex:** At the beginning of *The Plague*, we encounter sentences such as 'Our citizens work hard, but solely with the object of getting rich' (A. Camus, *The Plague*, p. 5). The narrative proper begins some four pages further on with a precise indication of the time, which clearly marks off action from narration: 'When leaving his surgery on the morning of 16 April, Dr. Bernard Rieux felt something soft under his foot. It was a dead rat, lying in the middle of the landing' (ibid., p. 9). The citizens of Oran may well have had the right to express indignation concerning Camus's views about their city in the preamble, but they could not challenge the events within the narrative since these relate to a different kind of time, dis-

DIRECT UTTERANCE	NARRATIVE

VERB TENSES

anchor: the nunegocentric[1] present	anchor: the allocentric preterite
simple anteriority: the imperfect	simultaneity with the allocentric anchor: the imperfect
	anterior to the allocentric anchor: the pluperfect
the result of an anterior action within the nunegocentric anchor: the perfect	the result of an anterior action within the allocentric anchor: past anterior

PRONOUNS

speaker: I/we	characters: he/she, they
addressee: you	

TEMPORAL ADVERBS

today	April 16 (for example)
tomorrow/yesterday	the following day / the previous day
in a year's time / two years ago	a year later / two years previously
next Monday / last Monday	the following Monday / the previous Monday

ADVERBS OF PLACE

here	elsewhere

---

[1] The tense centred in the self and the here and now, as opposed to the other-centred (other person, time, and place) preterite.

tinct from time present, and consequently, in some cases, from reality.

This peculiar double temporality most frequently entails a second narrative marker: the use of the past tense. J. Dubois (*Grammaire structurale du français*, 2:209f) offers a diagrammatic representation of some of the markers which distinguish direct utterances from narratives (see table, p. 295).

The device called 'dialogism' (see dialogue*) reintroduces direct utterances into narrative as dialogues. Also, when narratives contain descriptions* or explanations*, they may lose their narrative form and become direct utterances or 'discourses.' Ex: 'The winter of 1879–80 was exceptionally cold. Flaubert's housekeeper made Julio a coat out of an old pair of trousers. They got through the winter together. Flaubert died in the Spring. *What happened to the dog [Julio] is not recorded*' (Julian Barnes, *Flaubert's Parrot*, pp. 62–3).

The action itself may even appear to occur in the present, called the 'historical present'; this temporal relocation may confer a greater feeling of reality on what happened. This type of present must however be structured more carefully than in the following example: 'He [the shoemaker] began [se mit] to hammer very hard on a sole and the other guy leaves [s'en va]' (Raymond Queneau, *Zazie dans le métro*, p. 83). Significantly, the published English translation contains 'departed.' (See Queneau, *Zazie in the Metro*, trans. Barbara Wright, p. 92.)

On the other hand, the simple construction of an utterance in 'indirect discourse' produces a narrative. Ex: 'Yet into this charming retreat York strode one evening a month after the quarrel, and, beholding Scott sitting there turned to the fair hostess with the query, "Do you love this man?" *The young woman thus addressed returned that answer – at once spirited and evasive which would occur to most of my fair readers in such an emergency*' (Bret Harte, 'The Iliad of Sandy Bar').

Dropping the main verb of expression ('he/she *said*,' for example) produces *free indirect* narrative, which repeats an utterance almost *verbatim*, retaining even exclamations* and intonation*, but modifying two markers: the pronouns and tenses. (See Brian McHale, 'Free Indirect Discourse: A Survey of Recent Accounts,' *PTL* 3:249–88.) Ex: 'Gabriel's warm trembling fingers tapped the cold pane of the window. *How cool it must be outside! How pleasant it would be to walk out alone, first along the river and then through the park! The snow would be lying on the branches of the trees and forming a bright cap on the top of the Wellington Monument. How much more pleasant it would be there than at the supper-table!*' (Joyce, 'The Dead,' in *Dubliners*, p. 224). Free indirect style (free, that is, from the introductory syntagm*) possesses a flexibility that almost confuses it with direct discourse, but its form reveals the presence of a narrator 'behind' the character. In the interior monologue*, or in dialogue, the narrator disappears.

The importance of these forms in the modern novel, where the use of the narrative present is frequent, may be explained by the modern reader's enhanced awareness of the nature of literary texts, which always remain in any case at some distance from reality. Such texts cannot coincide with the action they narrate, but aspire rather to reproduce it more or less completely and indirectly, in some deferred fashion, with a different, subsequent temporality. Ex: 'Cordelia and I are riding on the streetcar, going downtown, as we do on winter Saturdays' (M. Atwood, *Cat's Eye*, p. 4). In fact, the middle-aged narrator in this example is recalling events which took place long before the epic moment of narration.

Writers naturally take pleasure in foregrounding the artificiality of such narrative conventions. Ex: 'Gabriel ... pronounced these words: *"Being or nothingness, that is the question ... Gabriel is but a reverie (a charming one), Zazie the dream of a reverie (or of a nightmare) and all this story the dream of a dream, the reveries of a reverie, scarcely more than the typewritten delivery of an idiotic novelist (oh! sorry)"* ... Some travellers were standing in a circle round him, having taken him for a supplementary guide' (Raymond Queneau, *Zazie in the Metro*, trans. Barbara Wright, p. 100).

Thus, as long as typography makes possible distinctions between speakers, there is no real danger in switching the markers of narrative and direct utterance, in addressing one's characters as 'you,' for instance, as does Michel Butor in *La Modification*, or in making a character address the narrator as 'you.' ('You are the murderer,' says Poirot to the narrator of Agatha Christie's, *The Murder of Roger Ackroyd*.) The reader will be only more aware of his or her own activity: in the final analysis, what is being read is a literary text, and so the device of defamiliarization may simply encourage the reader to make even greater efforts at decoding.

R1: Just as the present is the unmarked tense in the nunegocentric system, the imperfect, the past tense of direct utterance, serves as an unmarked tense in narrative. Hence the usefulness of having a specific tense, the preterite, to mark the allocentric anchoring of narrative in the past. This explains why narrative in French, for instance, possesses a tense missing from direct utterance (the preterite or 'passé simple').

The distribution of pronouns may also seem surprising. Third-person pronouns have no specific role in direct utterances that unite third parties either to the speaker (the exclusive *you*) or to the addressee (the exclusive *we*). The use of *they* for people produces some distancing*, and the utterance begins to be narrative. On the other hand, first- and second-person pronouns have no specific function in narrative. When they appear, the narrative is tending to imitate a direct utterance. Ex: 'Catherine said they were asking too much. A sort of rage rose in her. *"It could have been so easy between us." "I'm tired,"* said Catherine' (Anne Hébert, *Les Chambres de bois*, p. 171).

Narrative

R2: A long narrative is made up of several *episodes* linked together to form a *plot*. The motive power for the plot is frequently the evolution of the characters' attitudes, called the *action*. Thus, the monolithic nature of characters like those of Hemingway, for instance, means that the psychological events take place outside the action, between *'takes,'* as they say in the cinema. Narrative rhythm (see rhythm* [of the action]) is determined by the duration of the episodes: 'in plays, then, the episodes are short; in epic poetry they serve to lengthen out the poem' (Aristotle, *Poetics*, 1455b 16). The *peripetia* reverses the action of a previous episode. The *rebound* is an added peripetia which puts off the *resolution* (the *dénouement* in French). *Diversions* are incidents which change the course of the action. *Coups de théatre* are sudden, unexpected, and spectacular modifications of the action. Ex: the resolution of Hemingway's *A Farewell to Arms*. The 'happy end' is a resolution favourable to the 'sympathetic' characters. *Epilogues* recount what has occurred since, or will occur after, the resolution.

From a functional viewpoint, narratologists distinguish between episodes (or *sequences*) necessary to intelligibility, and which have a *cardinal* function, and those with satellite functions which 'fill in the space between nodes' (Gerald Prince, *A Dictionary of Narratology*, p. 11).

R3: Either narrative is of the objective type, as in historiography, in which a narrator, although recounting events from his or her viewpoint, nonetheless remains outside the action; or else, there is *'focalization'* (Genette) on some character whose perspective shapes what is recounted. This character is frequently the hero (as in Salinger's *The Catcher in the Rye*, where Holden Caulfield is at the same time the focalized character, the hero, and the figurative narrator). In autobiographical narrative, the author recounts his or her own life, thereby playing the roles of author, narrator, and hero, and assuming responsibility for both the narrative and the perspective from which it is recounted. (Genette makes possible a distinction between observer and narrator by differentiating the person 'who speaks' from the one 'who sees'; see *Narrative Discourse*.)

Focalization may be seen in all its artificiality as a device in *August 1914*, where Solzhenitsyn situates a narrative, for which he himself assumes the ultimate responsibility, successively in the perspectives of a young man, Sania (chapters 1 and 2), a young woman, Irene (3 and 9) a young girl, Xenia (4 and 5), a kulak, Zakhar (8), General Samsonov (10, 11, etc.), a young dashing colonel, Vorotyntsev (12, 13, etc.), and so on. In order to give the reader a broad overview of military operations, he also from time to time introduces summaries, of an official kind, printed in small type (chapters 32 and 41, in particular).

R4: Nothing prevents one narrative from begetting another at some distance from itself, and so doubling the distance between it and a direct utterance: all that is required is that the first narrative be the narration of the second. For the second, Genette proposes the term 'metadiegesis' (and then quite correctly criticizes the term in *Narrative Discourse*). In fact, 'meta' is usually taken to mean 'about,' so that a 'metanarrative' would be a second-level narrative about the frame-narrative in which it is situated. This is clearly not always the case. Thus *The Arabian Nights* tells the story of Scheherezade telling the story of … The process repeats itself when Haroun-al-Raschid, the hero of one of her stories, has someone else tell him the story of Sidi Numan. See mirror*, R5.

Even third-degree narratives may be turned into direct utterances. Thus in *Les Conquérants* (pp. 134–7), Malraux shows Garine telling a story about Tcheng-Dai, who in his own narrative quotes his own words from twenty years earlier: 'Mr. Garine, he says (Garine almost imitates the old man's weak, measured, slightly learned voice) … I know that a life of honour may not escape calumny, which I disdain. But I once said to men worthy of respect and consideration, who had given me their confidence: "I hope you will believe that I am a just man …"'

Another way of producing two narrative levels is to foreground an implied process of enunciation*, which then becomes a first-degree utterance (with the other becoming a second-degree utterance). This is what Gide does throughout *Paludes*, and what John Fowles does in *The French Lieutenant's Woman* by asking the reader to choose between two possible endings.

R5: Several current short genres exist at the intersection of narrative and discourse*: newspaper stories, circulars, reports of proceedings, memoranda. Film *scripts* shorten narrative, partially suppressing *mimesis* (the attempt to reproduce the temporality of an action). They also summarize the *diegesis* (the story of past events). A film script (unless it is an original work) usually comes after the writing of a novel but (usually) precedes the making of a film. (Not by much when a director encourages improvisation or when, as in the case of Michael Curtiz's *Casablanca*, no finished script exists at the moment of filming.)

R6: As to the arrangement of narrative sequences, there exist various devices whose identification has begun:

EMBEDDING. A combination of narrative sequences (recounted in the same narrating instance or in different ones) such that one sequence is embedded (set within) another one … *Manon Lescaut* can be said to result from the embedding of Des Grieux's narrative into the one recounted by M. de Renoncourt.

ALTERNATION. A combination of narrative sequences (recounted in the same narrating instance or in different ones) such that units of one sequence are made to alternate with units of another sequence;

an interweaving of sequences. (Gerald Prince, *A Dictionary of Narratology*) [The celebrated murder scenes in Alfred Hitchcock's film *Psycho* intercut shots of the victim and killer (the shower and staircase sequences, for example).]

R7: See actant*, R1; allusion*, R4; anachronism*, R1; apocalypse*, R1; apostrophe*, R1; attenuation*, R3; definition*, R4; description*, R4; ellipsis*, R5; embedding*, other def.; enunciation*, R1; final* word, R2; flashback*; flash-forward*, R1; generalization*, R4; hiatus*, other def.; incoherence*; myth*; portrait*, R3; prophecy*, R1; prosopopoeia*, R2 and R4; repetition*, R5; reprise*, other def.; riddle*, 2; and symbol*, R3.

NEGATION A form of assertion* (see assertion, R1) in which the speaker's statement of a position includes a refusal of the asserted predicate or of a part of it. See Crystal, 1987, p. 243; *OED*; and Dubois et al., *Dictionnaire de linguistique*.

Ex: 'I am not aware that any community has a right to force another to be civilized' (J.S. Mill, *On Liberty*, ch. 4).

The attitude of refusal or disapproval manifests itself also in the choice of the appropriate lexemes which may be distinguished from negation in that they do not modify the form of an assertion*. Ex: 'The duty of an Opposition is to oppose' (Lord Randolph Churchill, 1830, quoted by W.S. Churchill, *Lord Randolph Churchill*, 1: 233).

Formal negation of the whole predicate affects the verbal syntagm* through the adverbial expressions *no, not, (n't), nothing, no one, never, no more*, etc. A part of the predicate may be denied: nominal syntagms may be negated by indefinite pronouns like *not one*; adjectival or adverbial qualifiers by *no* and *never*; sentences by *no, nay, not at all, by no means, not in the least, never!*, etc.

Negation may affect certain syntagmatic elements like prepositions (e.g., *without*) and conjunctions (e.g., *for fear that*). Nominal lexemes are negated by the use of privative prefixes such as *un-, ir-, a-, dis-, il-, non-*, and *ex-* (e.g., *unreal, irreducible, amorphous, dishonest, illegible, noncompliance, ex-friend*). Verbal lexemes are negated by the use of *mis-* and *dis-* (e.g., *misappropriate, disembark*). As may be seen, negation is also a form of adjacent, or even implicit, assertion* (see assertion, R3).

R1: It is important to distinguish the part of the sentence affected by negation, which tends to be placed in or near the verbal node even if the negative particle affects some other segment. Ex: 'It is not important that you leave' for 'It is important that you do not leave.' Such idiomatic ambiguity* may have a surprising effect, since the reader may understand the opposite of what is being said, until the rest of the text corrects the error. Ex: 'We shall not accept your invitation // to come at three o'clock; we shall come at two.' Negation may even affect

only virtual semes of the verbal lexeme. Ex: 'I shall not drink your brandy // I shall sip it.'
This type of surprise appears in antithesis*. Ex: 'She was never to have this dream again. // It was to become real, invading her whole life.' This is how Marie-Claire Blais announces Héloise's passage from convent to brothel in *Une Saison dans la vie d'Emmanuel* (p. 88). This kind of *pseudo-negation* is easily produced before any lexeme. Exx: 'I wouldn't call these works mediocre // they're the pits'; 'Did you like my performance?' 'Good is not the word for it.' This is the most artificial, so the most rhetorical, form of negation.

R2: Rather than being a sentence modality (see assertion*, R2), negation is only a grammatical form, which may therefore combine with any kind of sentence or assertion: exclamations*, injunctions*, and so on.
The case of negated questions* (see question, R1) produces curious results. When the negative interrogative form can change into a simple affirmative assertion* followed by *no?*, or *Isn't that so?* without the meaning changing, the negation is affecting not the utterance but only its interrogative form. In other words, one expects a positive response because the question is denied even as it is being asked. Ex: 'Haven't we just been out for a walk?' becomes 'Have we just been out for a walk, or not?' and both sentences imply a positive meaning* and the expectation of a positive response from the addressee.
That also explains the positive meaning which attaches to an exclamation like 'How much progress haven't we made since then!' We have already seen the morphological proximity between some questions and exclamations*. In this case, negation merely introduces into the verbal node a denied question (*Isn't that so?*) that predisposes the addressee to agree. As may be readily seen, all such exclamations may be transformed immediately into questions.
But if one answers no to a negative question, the result is ambiguity*. Exx:

Did you forget to feed the cat?
No.
You didn't feed it?
No, I didn't forget.

LEO: And this number three? Is it a myth? I mean it doesn't exist?
...
MADELEINE: No.
LEO: It does exist?
MADELEINE: No, Madame. It doesn't exist.

J. Cocteau, *Les Parents terribles*, p. 128

R3: Refusals may be expressed positively by means of negative lexemes. Ex: 'I oppose the use of violence to solve this dispute.'

Negation

Conversely, lexemes negative in meaning, if accompanied by grammatical negation, express agreement, albeit in a rather special way (see
attenuation* and litotes*). In short, double negation occurs, which – in
the absence of some perceptible intention in the context – expresses
only slight commitment. Ex: 'I shouldn't wonder if it didn't rain.'
It is only a step from such equivocal statements to the non-
committal *réponse de normand* or 'Norman answer.' (The Norman
peasant is notorious for his canniness, a fact exploited by, among
others, Maupassant in stories like 'La Ficelle' ['The Piece of String'].)
The Norman answer combines double negation with negation of an
affirmation. Ex:

> ANCESTOR: Do you recognize ... her? [Is she the one] we are waiting
> for?
> PEASANT: I'm not saying no but I can't say yes.
> H. Maeterlinck, *Les Fiançailles*, seventh tableau

The device may give access to some blurred, metaphysical other-world
widely used by 'negative way' mystics. Ex:

> Neither Non-Being existed then, nor Being.
> ...
> There existed at that time neither death nor non-death.
> ...
> The One breathed at his own impulse, without there being breath.
> Beyond That, nothing else existed.
> *Speculative Hymns of Veda*, 30: 1–2

No lexeme can resist such all-embracing negativity, the basic mystical
proposition being that the known must be left behind. Even language
itself is denied. Ex: The blurb on Marguerite Duras's novel *Le Ravissement de Lol V. Stein* affirmed: 'This, which has no name.' Such proclamations of nothingness may result from oxymoron* or oxymoric*
sentences in which contraries both become identical and cancel each
other out. Ex:

> FOURTH TEMPTER
>
> You know and do not know, what it is to act or suffer.
> You know and do not know, that action is suffering,
> And suffering action. Neither does the agent suffer,
> Nor the patient act. But both are fixed
> In an eternal action, an eternal patience
> To which all must consent that it may be willed
> And which all must suffer that they may will it,
> That the pattern may subsist, that the wheel may turn and still
> Be forever still.
> T.S. Eliot, *Murder in the Cathedral*, part 1

The cancelling of contraries resembles *dubitatio**. **Ex:** 'This creation, wherever it comes from, whether it represents an institution or not, – only the one who overlooks [this world] from the highest firmament knows, – *unless he doesn't know?*' (*Speculative Hymns of Veda*, 30: 7). Both of the negative markers may also be grammatical. If they are sufficiently far removed in the sentence from one another, they may cause surprise (see above, R1). **Ex:** 'I have no intention of passing your request for time off to the President // without informing him that I approve it totally.' (Sadistic office managers write this carefully on a little card, making sure that the second part is on the back.)

In the case of more than two negative markers, clarity may suffer. **Exx:** 'Were it *not* for its liking for game eggs, the badger could *not but* be considered other than a harm*less* animal'; '*No* rival is too small to be overlooked, *no* device is too infamous *not* to be practised, if it will ...' (Fowler, under 'negative mishandling').

R4: Semi-negation corresponds to semi-refusal (e.g., *scarcely* ...; *no longer* ...; *not yet* ...; *not so much* ...; etc.).

R5: A rhetorically interesting kind of negation is *no* / *none* / *no one* ... *but*, equivalent to *only*. **Ex:** 'No one but he really cares.' The form denies every subject except the one asserted, so conferring upon the latter an exclusive status, and is therefore the opposite of negating it. *No ... but* might be justly named *counter-negation*.

R6: If applied systematically, negation becomes an obvious device characteristic of 'contrariness.' But, as used by the surrealists, it is also a means of creating new meanings by modifying existing forms. Thus, in *Notes sur la poésie*, for example, Eluard and Breton seize upon some of Paul Valéry's reflections in *Littérature* and deny them systematically, thus turning them around. **Ex:** Valéry: 'Thought is bisexual; it both fertilizes and gives birth to itself' (*Oeuvres complètes*, 2:546). Eluard: 'Thought has no sex; [it] cannot reproduce' (*Oeuvres complètes*, 1:474). For the function of negativity, see response*, R4.

R7: When disapproval is overstated, it turns into *execration*, or *vituperation*, since the anger expressed emphasizes the initial refusal. When the grounds for complaint remain unformulated, whether relating to the whole situation or to precise persons or objects, the result is *contestation* (see epigram*, R2).

R8: A *disavowal* is a refusal of something one has previously approved. A *palinode* is a work in which one attacks what one had previously praised (or vice versa).

NEOLOGISM A recently created word, often formed in conformity with existing lexical structures. In literature, neologisms are frequently *hapax legomenon*, nonce-words (coined and used only once for a particular text) which the language does not ratify. See *OED*, Lausberg (sect. 547–51), and Leech (pp. 42–4).

Exx: 'conversationmanship' (R. Ebert, *Two Weeks in the Midday Sun*, p. 41); 'slithy' [< lithe + slimy] (Lewis Carroll, 'Jabberwocky')

Other names: neology (*OED*, Lausberg, Littré); nonce-formation (Leech, p. 42). Lausberg calls derived terms and compound* words created in conformity with a language's existing structures (even though the latter may no longer be current) 'invented [or] artificial words.' Ex (quoted by Leech): 'And I Tiresias have foresuffered all' (T.S. Eliot, *The Waste Land*, part 3).

R1: Neologisms are produced by derivation*, by compounding (see compound* word), by imitation of noises* or natural sounds (see onomatopoeia*), by gratuitous invention (see coinage*), or by blending or amalgamation (see portmanteau* word). It is not always possible, however, to determine which of these procedures was used, particularly in a text like Joyce's *Finnegans Wake*, which exploits all of them and more (see pun*). (W. Redfern describes as follows Joyce's foregrounding of neologisms: 'The whole of *Finnegans Wake* is a vast neologism born of the desire to make new, to make strange' [*Puns*, p. 167].) Ex: 'Sansglorians ... Jungfraud's Messonge book ... commodius vicus of recirculation ... gobbledydumped turkery ... Etruscan stabletalk ... prepronominal funferal, engraved and retouched and edgewiped and puddenpadded ...' (Joyce, *Finnegans Wake*, passim).

R2: Normally, an original meaning* corresponds to a lexical neologism. Leech (p. 44) calls this the ' "concept-making" power of neologism': 'If a new word is coined it implies the wish to recognize a concept or property which the language can so far only express by phrasal or clausal description. Eliot's *foresuffered* is not just a new word but the encapsulation of a newly formulated idea: that it is possible to anticipate mystically the suffering of the future, just as it is possible to *foresee*, *foretell* or have *foreknowledge* of future events' (ibid.).

NEOLOGISM (SEMANTIC) A new meaning given to an existing word.

Exx: 'No plant in the world has shown that it can *recuperate* plutonium on an industrial scale from oxide-bearing fuel' (*Guardian Weekly*, 7 Aug. 1977, p. 11) [example quoted in *OEDS* under 'recuperate']; 'bug' ('a concealed microphone' [*OEDS*]) – hence 'bugged' and 'bugger' (one who bugs); 'The best bugger in the business' (in Francis Ford Coppola's film *The Conversation* [1974]).

R1: Inevitable semantic neologisms resemble catachresis*. Catachresis seems often to be metaphorical in nature, whereas semantic neologisms are metonymical, which may increase their chance of survival.

R2: The meaning* of any word evolves, a fact making the consultation of specialized dictionaries indispensable to the reading of ancient (and not so ancient) texts. Ex: 'JULIET: O happy dagger / This is thy sheath, there rust and let me die' (Shakespeare, *Romeo and Juliet*, 5.3.169–70). Of the double meaning possessed by the verb to *die* in Elizabethan England (to expire and to achieve orgasm), Mahood comments: '[In Juliet's final cry] *happy* implies not only "fortunate to me in being ready to my hand" but also "successful, fortunate in itself" and so suggests a further quibble on *die*. Death has long been Romeo's rival and enjoys Juliet at the last' (*Shakespeare's Wordplay*, p. 58).

NOISE   The attempt to transcribe ambient or background sounds, even metaphorical ones, becomes onomatopoeia* if lexicalization* occurs. Otherwise, there is only transcription of noises.

Exx: 'Rtststr. A rattle of pebbles' (Joyce, *Ulysses*, p. 94); 'Listen: a fourworded wavespeech: seesoo, hrss, rsseeiss, ooos' (ibid., p. 41). See also R. Benayoun, *Le Ballon dans la bande dessinée: Vroom, Tchac, Zowie*. G. Jean published in *Poésie*, no. 66 (July 1979), pp. 194–9, a list of noises and screams used in cartoon strips; he also included 'translations.'

The problem is to provide, using vowels and consonants, an equivalent of noises having only a very tenuous connection with coded sounds. There is a kind of *s* sound in hissing, of *p* in explosions (Pow!); the *i* sound lends stridency ('Aye! Aye! What's all this then!'); *r* vibration, and so on. But dead wood, when dry, does not 'crack'; it goes *zpiessats* or *Ptkeeiett* or whatever. A sneeze makes a noise like: *chtzsm* or *eiettschtuuf* (English *atishoo* and French *atchoum* are literary renderings).
     Noise becomes onomatopoeia* when it enters the lexical system, in which case it receives a spelling. In French, the noise made by a clock is spelled *tic-tac*, not *tique-taque*; in the same way, 'gurgle' has an accepted spelling in English. Onomatopoeia may be inserted into a nominal syntagm* (*their tick-tock*) or a verbal one (*to gurgle*), and the link with the original noise may become blurred. See also monologue*, R1.

Other definitions: a concurrent acoustic event; unwanted information (*white noise*, a mixture of various frequencies, is used in experiments in the *masking* of communication; see H. Hörmann, *Introduction à la psycholinguistique*, p. 69). This might also be called *sonic scrambling*, a procedure used currently in radio transmissions and in the literary context of the theatre: the hubbub of crowds, or guests covering the hero's voice, and creating ambience, what the *Dictionnaire des media* calls 'the unity of place, of material or moral atmosphere.'

Nominalization

Background noises due to amplifiers include such *crackling* noises as *oom* and *ssch*, and hi-fi enthusiasts employ devices like 'woofers' and 'tweeters' to overcome them. Other bits of static interference, coming from electric sparks for instance, may disturb radiophonic reception.

R1: In onomatopoeia*, the noise is obliterated by the word. The simple device of changing the usual word causes the noise to reappear. Thus *cock-a-doodle-doo* was revived by Joyce as 'keekeereekee' (*Ulysses*, p. 420), and French *cocorico* as '*cou que li cou que li*' (M.-Cl. Blais, *Une Saison dans la vie d'Emmanuel*, p. 99).

R2: Noises intervene in other figures: see imitative harmony* and alliteration*.

R3: Other noises include the whole range of human, non-buccal sounds: the finger-snapping of the student who wants to answer a question; the different ways of knocking on or scratching at a door; applause; foot stamping; the tapping of pencils on desks; etc. To concrete sounds we must add musical sounds, either pure or synthetic ones. Whether concrete or musical, sounds may be generated electronically, recorded, modified by filters and reverberators, extended or condensed, harmonically displaced, and combined with others in synthesizers. This is the process of *sound-effects*, supplying the action with active sound, productive of effects. See Crystal, 1987, chapters 24–6; and Fage and Pagano, eds., *Dictionnaire des media*.

R4: *Lettrism*, the French literary and artistic movement founded in 1945 by Isidore Isou, extolled verse composed of noise (which does not necessarily exclude meaning*) rather than that which uses language. See pseudo-language*, glossolalia*, and musication*.

R5: The context confers a host of meanings on noises (see, for instance, injunction* and mimology*, R1).

NOMINALIZATION Substitution of a noun or noun phrase for an assertion*. An assertion* reduced to a simple notation*, in which the embedded predicate is identified with the subject, thus giving the text an appearance of irrefutability.

Ex: 'The man in the street enjoys television plays' becomes 'The man in the street's enjoyment of television plays [is on the increase]' (G. Leech, *Semantics*, p. 186).

Ex: 'Season of mists and mellow fruitfulness, / Close bosom-friend of the maturing sun' (J. Keats, 'To Autumn').

R1: The device differs from holophrases, in which a single word expresses an entire sentence or idea, and which are also frequently substantival (e.g., 'Silence!') but exclamatory and/or imperative in nature. Nominalization is not the spontaneous expression of feelings, ideas, or impressions by the use of nouns or other grammatical forms of reduced or implied syntax; rather, nominalization is a false kind of notation* whose function is referential but whose form corresponds to that of utterances which simply specify situations. Ex: 'Misfit in any space. And never on time. / A wrench in clocks and the solar system' (John F. Nims, 'Love Poem,' in *The Iron Pastoral*). See enunciation*.

R2: The word *nominalization* is borrowed from structural grammar, where it designates the corresponding grammatical phenomenon: the transformation of a proposition into a nominal syntagm*. The present definition deals with assertions*.

R3: The device differs from the use of substantivized forms, which is a form of transference*. Ex: 'It's all *the young* can do for *the old* to shock them and keep them up to date' (G.B. Shaw, *Fanny's First Play* [1911], introduction).

R4: The creation of new substantives from existing adjectives, verbs, etc. is a form of derivation* much favoured by recent structuralist and post-structuralist critics and ridiculed by their opponents. Exx: narrativity, interdiscursivity, transcodification, intertextuality, etc.

NONSENSE Assertions* or situations which communicate to readers their inability to make sense of them.

Ex:

> He thought he saw a Rattlesnake
> That questioned him in Greek:
> He looked again and found it was
> The Middle of Next Week.
> 'The one thing I regret,' he said
> 'Is that it cannot speak!'
>
> Lewis Carroll, 'The Mad Gardener's Song'

Ex: 'Fit from the neck up: Facial Yoga for all. This remarkable art was developed by the Guru in Korea from a technique evolved over thousands of pounds of enrolment fees. It uses only the muscles of the part of the body above the tie, and can be practised anywhere with hardly any discomfort ... But be warned, watch out for sloppy (or worse, *dangerous*) misuse of the technique by so-called "experts" ' (Hardie and Lloyd, eds., *Not! the Nine o'Clock News*, p. 52).

Analogous term: absurdity

R1: Nonsense is a kind of wit*, not unlike that found in conceits*, with the absence of sense being seen as a roundabout demand for a kind of meaning* at once logical and impossible. What is there to say about a bald soprano except to agree with Ionesco that she always does her hair the same way? It was doubtless the impossible probability of the following sentence from Lewis Carroll that led Eluard and Breton to quote it, under the rubric 'Smile,' in their *Dictionnaire abrégé du surréalisme*: 'If he smiles a little more, the ends of his mouth will join up at the back ... and then what will become of his head? I am very much afraid that it will fall off.'

R2: Other figures made comical by a nonsensical or semi-nonsensical context: oxymoron*, allograph*, antilogy*, dissociation*, *coq-à-l'âne**, and erasure* (of subject).

R3: For the relationship between nonsense and onomatopoeia*, see Crystal, 1987, p. 175.

NOTATION Scarcely actualized textual segments, isolated and having no predicative or syntactic function (see monologue*, R2), but without ellipsis* or brachylogia*. This is the type of sentence which corresponds to the function called by linguists 'situational' (see enunciation*, 4).

Exx: 'Wednesday March 30th 3 p.m. Watford Gap Service Station. M1 Motorway' (Sue Townsend, *The Growing Pains of Adrian Mole*, p. 179); 'Wagon Number 477047, First Class Compartment Number Seven' (Tony Foster, *Rue du Bac*, p. 185).

Letters* begin with a short notation of place and time. Titles* of works and names of persons, when enunciated as such in an appropriate tone of voice, are notations. **Exx:** *Tristram Shandy*; Mr George Brown.

R1: Notations referring to the subject: Designations of the person(s) performing an act of communication may accompany notation of its situation. Signatures and superscriptions (the address, the postal code on envelopes) are formal notations. (Subscriptions are signatures appended at the end of official documents; metonymically, subscriptions also refer to money, etc., subscribed.) The same is true of visiting cards, and of the *call signs* of radio or television stations (e.g, 'This is the CBC Network'), announcements* often followed by the time ('It's nine o'clock in Toronto, nine-thirty in Newfoundland'). References that follow quotations* are also notations of the author, title, edition, editor, place and date of publication, volume, page, and so on. Similarly, epitaphs, inscriptions on tombstones ('Here lies [followed by first name, then surname], born in [birthplace], on the [date], deceased the [date]') accompanied by an address to the dead person ('To the memory of our much regretted ...'; see apostrophe*), or by good wishes ('R.I.P.').

R2: Notations of distinctions: These are almost always laudatory remarks added to certificates, degrees, or testimonials; their use in publicity is widespread. **Exx:** '[This record won the] Charles Cros Award for Best Recording in 1990'; 'Academy Award for Best Actor in a Supporting Role.' A parodic notation of a distinction: 'B.A. Oxon. (failed).'

R3: Amplified notations figure before signatures at the end of notarized documents. **Ex:** 'Signed, under my hand, in Ottawa, this twenty-first day of October nineteen hundred and ninety-nine.'

R4: Notations appear in literary texts. **Ex:** 'A hackneycar, *number three hundred and twentyfour*, with a gallantbuttocked mare, driven by *James Barton, Harmony Avenue, Donnybrook*, drives past' (Joyce, *Ulysses*, p. 460). In the margin to the same text, the notation *3730* appears, which refers to the number of lines since the beginning of the chapter [i.e., chapter 15].

R5: Lists, calendars, maps, nomenclatures, glossaries, telephone directories, catalogues, indexes, tables, bibliographies, etc., are collections of some possible notations. *Necrologies* are lists of the dead, notices of death and obituaries giving biographical details of persons recently deceased.

R6: Introductions made by a third party when strangers meet are not, despite their appearance, notations. **Ex:** 'Ted, Bill.' The first word is an apostrophe* having a phatic function, the second an ellipsis* of a predicative sentence ('This is Bill.'). In introducing oneself (particularly when speaking into a microphone), frequently *I am* is elided.

O

OBLIQUE STROKE A punctuation* mark signalling a break; for example, the end of a line in the text quoted.

Ex: 'Descend from Heaven Urania, by that name / If rightly thou art called ... / ... for thou / Nor of the Muses Nine, nor on the top / ...' (Preminger, under 'Muse,' quoting Milton's *Paradise Lost*, 7.1ff).

R1: The French structuralists assigned a specific usage to this device; they made it the equivalent of the English abbreviation* *v.* (*versus*, against). **Ex:** 'signifer/signified, spoken/written, writing/reading, author/work, etc. ("*External/internal, image/reality, representation/presence, this is the old pattern to which we entrust the task of outlining the field of a certain science*")' (M. Pleynet, in *Tel Quel: théorie d'ensemble*, p. 98; the internal quotation comes from J. Derrida, *De la Grammatologie*).

R2: Obliques are also often used as situational* signs (see situational signs, R7). They may indicate pauses* (see 'vers libre,' R2, under line* [of poetry or verse]) and occasionally caesura* (see caesura, R4). See also seriation*, R1.

R3: See double* reading. Obliques are not infrequently confused with hyphens* despite their different usages. This may be because obliques still remain little used. Ex: 'the dialectics of violence-tenderness in Yves Thériault's works.'

ODE 'Lyric, usually rhymed, often in the form of an address, usually of exalted style, often in varied or irregular metre, and usually between about 50 and 200 lines in length' (*Concise Oxford Dictionary*). John D. Jump adds: 'In the nineteenth and twentieth centuries the word has been used to refer to lyrical poems which, originating in personal impulses, rise to the presentation of general ideas of some gravity and substance. Most of these poems are of moderate length and are fairly elaborate in structure and in style. Many of them take the form of addresses, although this is less common than it was when the Classical influence was more potent' (*The Ode*, p. 59).

The Greek ode was sung but had no rhyme* scheme since Greek poetry was not rhymed. The Pindaric ode had a set, triadic progression of stanzas, called the strophe, the antistrophe, and the epode (Preminger, Stillman).

ONOMATOPOEIA The formation of a word whose sound imitates the thing signified. See Crystal, 1987, pp. 174–5, Frye, Lanham, Lausberg, Littré, Morier, *OED*, Preminger, and Robert.

Exx: 'cuckoo'; 'The crooked skirt swinging, whack by whack by whack' (Joyce, *Ulysses*, p. 48).

Ex:

> Hark, hark!
>   Bow-wow.
> The watch-dogs bark!
>   Bow-wow.
> Hark, hark! I hear
> The strain of strutting chanticleer
> Cry, 'Cock-a-doodle-doo!'

Shakespeare, *The Tempest*, 1.2.382–6

Synonyms: imitative or echoic word; phonic symbolism (Dubois et al., *Dictionnaire de linguistique*)

A partial list of onomatopoeic words: atishoo, bang, biff, blare, boom, brr, buzz, caw, cheep, chirrup, click, click-clack, clickety-click, cock-a-doodle-do, coo, crack, crash, ding-dong, flop, froufrou, glug-glug, gobble-gobble (of a turkey), grr, growl, gurgle, hee-haw, hum, knock-knock, mew, miaow, moo, pit-a-pat, plop, pom pom pom, puff-puff, purr, quack, rataplan, rat-tat, rustle, sizzle, slap, smack, snap, sniff, snore, splash, squeak, swish, thud, tick-tock, ting-a-ling, tinkle, vroom-vroom, wallop, whack, yum-yum.

R1: Onomatopoeic words are indeed words (and not noises*) just like any others since they involve codification of pronunciation and graph-isms*, as well as of grammatical form and meaning*. But the line between onomatopoeic lexemes and noises is difficult to draw. Accord-ing to Grammont (in his *Traité de phonétique*, p. 395) there are many words whose phonic motivation may cause them to resemble onomato-poeia. And Laurence Perrine points to 'phonetic intensives' as a class of words 'whose sound, by a process as yet obscure, to some degree suggests their meaning. An initial *fl-* sound, for instance, is often associated with the idea of moving light, as in *flame, flare, flash, flicker, flimmer*' (*Sound and Sense*, pp. 204–5). But do we all experience sound phenomena in the same way, even when constrained by meaning? Both Grammont (loc. cit.) and Perrine (in Preminger, under 'onomatopoeia') point to the device's subjective nature, even though there may exist a fairly wide consensus on some examples. The device is important in both poetry and prose for it may influence the choice of words or suffixes (*glug-glug* or *gurgle*, for example). The above list is very limited and many words could be added (murmur, tittle-tattle, etc.).

R2: *Counter-onomatopoeia* consists in turning words into sound-effects. Ex: In some strip cartoons, storms are represented by threatening graphisms*; that is, words like *GROWL* or *CRACK* are written in enormous and distorted characters.

OXYMORIC SENTENCES The figure consists in making two suc-cessive assertions* contrary to, but not incompatible with, one another.

Ex: 'I believe in them [the dead people] and I don't believe in them, both at the same time' (M. Atwood, *Cat's Eye*, p. 80).

The assertions may be adjacent (contained in distinct syntagms* not necessarily in distinct sentences), co-ordinated one with other, indeed even subordinated one to another. Exx: '[What an author actually writes, compared to what he thinks] is richer and less rich. Longer and shorter. Clearer and more obscure' (P. Valéry, *Oeuvres*, 2: 569); 'It's not important, there are doubtless better things to do or not to do' (A. Breton, *Manifestes du surréalisme*, p. 43).

R1: Oxymoric combinations of contradictory words or sentences differ from other contradictory combinations of signifieds because the opposi-

tions created are only apparent and remain confined to the level of signifiers. (See oxymoron*, R1.) Ex: 'If he is cold, he does not feel cold. He
is hot without feeling the heat' (H. Michaux, *L'Espace du dedans*, p. 150).
Here the poet is describing a state of almost ascetic indifference. Compare this with: 'But this I say, brethren, the time *is* short: it remaineth
that those that have wives be as though they had none; And they that
weep, as though they wept not; and they that rejoice, as though they
rejoiced not; and they that buy, as though they possessed not; And
they that use this world, as not abusing *it*: for the fashion of this world
passeth away' (1 Corinthians 7: 29–31). Extreme positions thus neutral-
ize one another in a new and unique 'reality.' (See also negation*, R3.)
In the previously quoted examples, 'reality' is non-oxymoric, dual or
alternating (see alternative*), or multi-levelled, as in the case of assertions suborindated one to another.

OXYMORIC SENTIMENTS A clash of two contrary sentiments in
the same character.

Ex: 'Gargantua ... seeing on the one hand his wife Badebec lying dead,
and on the other his new-born son Pantagruel ... wept like a heifer, and
then suddenly guffawed life a calf' (Rabelais, *Pantagruel*, ch. 3).

R1: Oxymoric sentiments sometimes take the form of contrasting
images*. Ex: 'During the whole day's journey, the situation remained
unchanged, she was beside me but separate from me, at once a gulf of
loneliness and my soul sister' (M. Duras, *Le Ravissement de Lol V. Stein*,
p. 192).

R2: *Compensatio*, whose only purpose is to redress effects made by
certain connotations, is a 'false' example of oxymoric sentiments.

R3: A similar device alternates assertions concerning oxymoric actions,
the general theory of which may be illustrated by the following example: 'Solange had satisfied both Costals' carnal appetite and his
"rigorism." She had displayed herself to him both as whore and as
society-woman, and only such alternations interested him' (Montherlant, *Romans*, p. 1245).

OXYMORON The combinatin of two words whose meanings *seem* to
be mutually contradictory. See Group MU, Jacobs (pp. 113–14), Lausberg (sect. 807), and Preminger.
   Le Clerc (p. 240) cites Agamemnon's 'haughty weakness' in Racine's
Iphigénie with the comment that the oxymoron expresses 'two ideas
which seem incoherent but which in fact complement each other precisely.' Ducrot and Todorov (p. 278) describe oxymoron as the 'establishment of a syntactic relationship (co-ordination, determination)
between two antonyms. E.g.: "Eternity, thou *pleasing, dreadful* thought"
(Addison).'

Exx: Warren S. Blumenfeld quotes such examples as: working vacation, planned serendipity, gourmet hamburger, acid rock, loyal opposition, and a metal wood (golf club) (*Jumbo Shrimp and Other Almost Perfect Oxymorons*).

Exx: 'A Clockwork Orange'; 'A dungeon horrible, on all sides round / As one great furnace flam'd; yet from those flames / No light, but rather *darkness visible*' (Milton, *Paradise Lost*, 1.60–2); 'Cette *obscure clarté* qui tombe des étoiles' ('This *dark light* which falls from the stars') (Pierre Corneille, *Le Cid*, 4.3).

R1: The two contradictory words must refer to opposing qualities belonging to one definite object. This property distinguishes oxymoron from dissociation*.

R2: The words conjoined oppose their meanings one to another without reference to context. The result is that the paradox* remains latent, and there is therefore no antilogy* because, in reality, the meanings are not incompatible with one another. Gérard de Nerval's 'Black melancholic sun' is a figurative, not an existential star. Walter Redfern, discussing puns about death, remarks: 'Related terms to gallows humour are: black comedy, sick humour, *rire jaune*. In all, pain and pleasure are mixed, perhaps the definitive recipe for all punning' (*Puns*, p. 127). The same might be said of oxymoron.

When oxymoron accompanies an opposition of contextual meaning* there occurs a combination of contradictory ideas. Exx: real artificial turf; tulips in natural plastic. See mirror*, R2.

P

PALINDROME A word, sentence, or verse that reads the same backwards as forward (*Concise Oxford Dictionary*). See also Espy, Preminger, and Robert.

Ex: According to Noah Jacobs, our first parents introduced themselves to each other by means of palindromes: ' "Madam I'm Adam," he said, and she replied, "Eve" ' (*Naming Day in Eden*, pp. 46, 54).

Exx: 'Able was I ere I saw Elba'; 'A man, a plan, a canal – Panama.' For these and many other see Augarde, pp. 97–104.

R1: We may name *false* those palindromes which reorder words rather than letters. Ex: 'Girl, bathing on Bikini, eyeing boy, finds boy eyeing bikini on bathing girl' (J.A. Lindon, quoted by Augarde, p. 103).

R2: In his 'glossary for palindromists,' Frye (pp. 332–3) distinguishes between 'symmetrical' palindromes such as the ones quoted above, and 'asymmetrical' ones, which, when read backwards, do form a word, but not the same one. Exx: gnat, pin, remit, etc.

R3: To produce successful sentences or verses, palindromists ignore capitals* and punctuation*. Georges Perec made one lasting one hundred lines (see Oulipo, *A Primer of Potential Literature*). See also boustrophedon*, anagram*, and antimetathesis*.

PARABASIS In ancient Greek comedy, a speech made by the chorus, a sort of digression* which revealed to the spectators the author's intentions, personal opinions, etc. See Beckson and Ganz, Cuddon, Frye, and Littré.

Other definition: There is no reason to restrict the definition to Greek comedy. The word *parabasis* appropriately designates authorial *intrusions*: the device by which some modern authors step outside their chosen literary fictions to address readers directly. Ex: 'Reader, I think proper, before we proceed any farther together, to acquaint thee that I intend to digress, through this whole history, as often as I see occasion, of which I am myself a better judge than any pitiful critic whatever' (Henry Fielding, *Tom Jones*, ch. 2). Thackeray, at the end of *Vanity Fair*, indicates clearly the status he accords to readers: 'Ah! *Vanitas Vanitatum!* Which of us is happy in this world? Which of us has his desire? or, having it, is satisfied? – Come children, let us shut up the box and the puppets, for our play is played out.'

R1: Parabasis is a figure of enunciation*. See excuse*; authorism*, R2; and intonation*. Semi-parabasis also exists: see epiphonema*, R1, and epiphrasis*, R1.

PARADOX An assertion* which runs counter to received opinion, and whose very formulation contradicts current ideas. See Lanham, Lausberg, Littré, and *OED*.

Exx: 'All you ever wanted in a beer, and less' (ad for low-calory beer; see implication*); 'Nothing succeeds like excess'; 'The primary purpose of our arms is peace' (John F. Kennedy, speech); 'Plus ça change, plus c'est la même chose' ('The more things change, the more they remain the same').

Literary texts contextualize paradox by attributing it to different speakers. Ex: In Orwell's *Nineteen Eighty-Four* (ch. 1), the following paradoxes represent the official slogans* of 'Big Brother's' regime: 'War is peace, freedom is slavery, ignorance is strength.'

Synonyms: oxymoron* ('G[reek] "a witty paradoxical saying"; lit. "pointedly foolish," *Synaeceosis*. A condensed paradox, Milton's "darkness visible" for example' [Lanham]); paradoxism (Fontanier, p. 137)

R1: It is oxymoron which permits one to consider paradox as a literary device and not as a mental quality, namely, originality. The two contradictory words joined together must nonetheless form respectively the subject and the psychological predicate for there to be an oxymoric assertion. A 'wise fool' needs at least to become 'Here is a wise fool.'

R2: Successful paradoxes appear true, upon reflection, and must therefore be carefully constructed. Ex: '[English poets visiting America find themselves] up against the barrier of a common language' (D. Thomas, *Quite Early One Morning*, p. 146). False paradoxes are those which convince no one. Ex: 'A one-eyed man is even more incomplete than a blind man. The former knows what he lacks' (V. Hugo, *Notre-Dame de Paris*, ch. 5). If, however, such paradoxes parade their falseness, they produce surreal effects akin to those of antilogy*. Ex (the 'Catch-22' situation): '[According to doc Daneeka] "[Pilot] Orr was crazy and could be grounded. All he had to do was ask; and as soon as he did, he would no longer be crazy and would have to fly more missions. Orr would be crazy to fly more missions and sane if he didn't, but if he was sane he had to fly them. If he flew them he was crazy and didn't have to; but if he didn't want to he was sane and had to"' (Jospeh Heller, *Catch-22*, p. 46).

Ken Kesey's *One Flew over the Cuckoo's Nest* also presents a world reversed in which the asylum inhabitants appear to behave more rationally than the doctors and nurses responsible for them. For his transgressions against official unreason, the leader of the patients is lobotomized.

R3: Paradox produces outrageous ideas by creating oppositions between certain elements in an effort to force the public to reflect upon them. Ex: 'Instead of saying, for example: *Every member of society must do what (s)he is best at,* one says: *In a hierarchy, every employee tends to rise to his level of incompetence*' (L.J. Peter, *The Peter Principle*, p. 27).

The opposition between the terms may remain implicit as in the common *aporia* 'There are no words to describe ...' followed by a more or less detailed description. The more paradox is founded on reality, the less it needs to be formalized. Ex: 'It was all very well for Napoleon to write a *code of laws* protecting human life and property!' (A. Allais, *Plaisir d'humour*, p. 179).

R4: Paradox seems to spring spontaneously from any contact with the absolute and appears frequently in the words attributed to Christ and in popular piety. Exx: 'The meek shall inherit the earth' ('But the brazen shall contest the will' [W. Redfern, *Puns*, p. 138]); 'The first shall be last'; etc.

R5: The simplest way to create a successful paradox is to overturn a truism*. **Ex:** 'LORD DARLINGTON: I couldn't help it. I can resist every-thing except temptation' (Oscar Wilde, *Lady Windermere's Fan*, act 1). The effect rapidly becomes humorous. **Ex:** 'Line up alphabetically according to height' (Blumenfeld, *Jumbo Shrimp*, p. 69).

PARAGOGE Adding a letter or syllable to the end of a word (Lanham). See also Frye, Jacobs (p. 123), Lausberg (sect. 484), and Robert.

Exx: 'against' from Middle English *ageines*; to 'dampen' for to 'damp'; 'The vasty hall of death' (M. Arnold, 'Requiescat')

R1: Paragoge is a term taken from antique grammar, serving only to designate a trick used by classical poets who needed an extra foot in a line of verse, as in the following chiasmus* by James Thomson: 'Oh! Sophonisba! Sophonisba! Oh!' (*Sophonisba*, 1730, 3.2). See apocope*, R2, echolalia*, and metaplasm*.

PARAGRAM 'A play on words involving the alteration of one or more letters – one of the commonest forms of punning' (Redfern, p. 18).

Ex: 'People who live in grass houses shouldn't stow thrones.'

R1: Some so-called printer's errors are in reality paragrams. **Exx:** 'Master of Ars'; 'Sa Majesté la ruine [reine; i.e., 'ruin' v. 'queen'] d'Angleterre.'

R2: Pons (p. 11) calls Swift's complex paragrams (e.g., 'rettle' for 'letter' and 'lole' for 'love') 'consonantal substitution.' The following is an example of vocalic substitution: 'Ma *patate* maman' for 'petite' (Ionesco, *Jacques ou la soumission*, in *Théâtre*, 1:115).

R3: International paragrams are related to cryptography* (see cryptography, R2), portmanteau* words, approximations*, and lexical scrambling*. Unintentional paragrams are examples of lapsus*. The following paragram from Joyce is an example of verbigeration*: 'Sinbad the Sailor and Tinbad the Tailor and Jinbad the Jailer and Whinbad the Whaler and Ninbad the Nailer and Finbad the Failer' (*Ulysses*, p. 607).

R4: Semioticians have taken up the paragram in a very positive way. Julia Kristeva, in *Sémeiotikè*, generalized Saussure's hypotheses about the role played by anagrams* (see anagram, R4) in poetic texts and proposed a tabular (rather than a linear) reading of the text's paragrammatic network or system of letters: ' "We call paragrammatic network the *tabular* (not linear) *model* of elaboration" of textual language. "The term *network* replaces univocity (linearity) by encompassing it, and suggests that each set (sequence) is both end-point and beginning of a multivalent relationship." The term "paragram" indicates that each element functions "as a dynamic mark, *as a moving gram which makes a meaning* rather than expressing it" ' (J. Kristeva, quoted by Ducrot and Todorov, p. 359). Many words might be written with the letters which form the words in a given text! Beneath the surface a kind of 'poly-graphy' begins to take shape which psychoanalysis deciphers quite freely. In such a case, *paragram* acquires the meaning of a disposition of letters in accordance with some unconscious principle, capable of sustaining a plurality of readings.

PARAGRAPH A textual unit comprising several sentences separated from the previous and subsequent units by two extended pauses* consisting of one or more blank lines, or sometimes of special signs (asterisks, for example).

R1: Paragraphs are often confused with the device of the first indented line, their first distinguishing mark.

Like *chapters* (units made up of paragraphs), which form superior units along the combinatory axis, paragraphs may be numbered, indexed (alphabetically, for instance), or given titles* (or rather, subtitles). Capitalized titles form chapter headings, whereas the titles placed on paragraphs (more accurately, *subtitles* or *inter-titles*) are usually in lower case and end with a period, like accentuated sentences rather than inscriptions on display. See also punctuation*, R1. When a subtitle is a secondary element in a title, it is presented in the same way as the title, but in smaller, more distinct characters.

In poetry, which condenses the message, paragraphs are reduced to stanzas*, and the first indented line is made the same length as the other lines*.

In the theatre, a paragraph, or set of lines exchanged by the different characters, is a scene or tableau, with each separate intervention corresponding to an indented line.

R2: According to G. Genette (*Figures*, 2:38), the paragraph is the 'rhetorical cell' out of which essays are constructed, a unit defined by its function in the overall plan*.

R3: Journalists use the term *subtitle* to refer to titles within fairly long texts introduced more often than not by editors rather than by authors. A *caption* may be a short introductory paragraph at the beginning of an article.

R4: See situational* signs, 2; successive approximations*, R2; epanalepsis*, R4; interruption*, R3; pause*; point*; and plan*, R4.

PARALLEL The comparison* of the physical or moral relationship between two objects in order to show their similarities or differences (see Fontanier, p. 429). See also Bénac, *OED*, Quillet, and Robert.

Ex: 'The most obvious division of society is into rich and poor, and it is no less obvious that the number of the former bear a great disproportion to those of the latter. The whole business of the poor is to administer to the idleness, folly and luxury of the rich, and that of the rich, in return, is to find the best methods of confirming the slavery and increasing the burdens of the poor. In a state of nature it is an invariable law that a man's acquisitions are in proportion to his labours. In a state of artificial society it is a law as constant and as invariable that those who labour must enjoy the fewest things, and that those that labour not at all have the greatest number of enjoyments' (Edmund Burke, 'A Vindication of Natural Society' [1756]).

Other names: comparison (*OED*, Robert); *compensatio* (Lanham); *antisagoge* ('1 Contrasting evaluatons ... 2 Stating first one side of a proposition, and then the other, with equal vigor' [Lanham]); similitude (*OED*: 'talk in similitudes') when points held in common are discussed; dissimilitude (*OED*). Littré also speaks of dissimilitude when discussion centres upon 'the differences between two objects at first thought analogous.' Ex: 'The great Swiss novelist [Charles-Ferdinand] Ramuz devoted a whole book to the description of a storm approaching through the mountains. But a poet's storms, when compared to those of a painter, suffer from one great inferiority: they pass over. A painter's storms do not pass over. They last forever, they are eternally contemporary. The painter stops time, for his own benefit' (P. Claudel, *Oeuvres en prose*, p. 252).

R1: Parallels frequently take the form of parallelisms*. Dissimilitude is useful for refutation*.

PARALLELISM Correspondences* between two parts of an utterance are emphasized by means of syntactic and rhythmic repetition. (See rhythmic echo*, R3.) The device produces binary sentences or groups of sentences and used to be particularly recommended for the construction of periods*. See Cuddon, Leech (pp. 62–9), *OED*, Robert, and Turco.

Ex:

> Was it cowardice, that I dared not kill him?
> Was it perversity, that I longed to talk to him?
> Was it humility, to feel so honoured?
> I felt so honoured.
>
> D.H. Lawrence, 'Snake'

Other names: antapodosis (Lausberg, sect. 735). Turco (pp. 8–11) speaks of *grammatical*, *synthetic* (the second half of a sentence gives the consequence of the first), and *antithetical* parallelisms. He also lists (pp. 71–3) seventeen 'repetitional schemas' or 'reiterative constructions' useful in creating parallelism: anadiplosis*, anaphora*, antanaclasis*, antimetabole*, antistrophe, echoics (see rhythmic echo*), emphasis*, epanalepsis*, epanodis, epimone, epiphora*, epizeuxis, hypozeuxis, ploce, polyptoton, polysyndeton*, and symploce*. See also antimetathesis*.

R1: A reprise* is an elaborate but purely formal parallelism. For parallelism to occur, there needs to be made between two objects (or beings) a comparison* in which some syntactic or rhythmic elements are repeated. Ex: 'On our right is the house of the Duke of Wellington, on our left a statue of Achilles, both reminders of the importance of boots' (Tom Stoppard, *Lord Malquist and Mr. Moon*, p. 154).

R2: Oppositions between two kinds of content also produce parallelisms. Ex: 'As love, if love be perfect, casts out fear, / So hate, if hate be perfect, casts out fear' (Tennyson, 'Merlin and Vivien').

R3: Anaphora* may reinforce a purely gratuitous binary structure. Ex [a description of an amusement park]: 'Here you are turned around and there you fall a long way down, here you go very fast and there you go completely the wrong way round, here you are jostled and there you are knocked about, everywhere your stomach turns over and you laugh ...' (R. Queneau, *Pierrot mon ami*, p. 20).

R4: See also disjunction*, R3; regrouped* members; paronomasia*, R6; and period*.

PARALOGISM Illogical reasoning*, especially of which the reasoner is unconscious (see *OED*). See also Quillet, Robert, and C.H. Greenstein, *Dictionary of Logical Terms and Symbols*, p. 159: 'any type of fallacious reasoning.'

Ex: 'I asked him [Salvatore, a simpleton], however, whether it was not also true that lords and bishops accumulated possessions through tithes, so that the Shepherds were not fighting their true enemies. He replied that when your true enemies are too strong, you have to choose weaker enemies' (U. Eco, *The Name of the Rose*, p. 192).

Analogous terms: sophism, paralogia

R1: Paralogism is unintentional sophistry*. Ex: 'I could no more be grateful to "God" for creating me than I could hold a grudge against Him for not doing so, – if I did not exist' (Gide, *Romans*, p. 168). The author seems convinced that his argument* is solid, not realizing that the reason given, although final in the non-existence hypothesis, is weaker in the other case: anyone thinking about one's own existence may have whatever ideas and feelings one pleases.

R2: Aristotle, for whom a conclusion's truth is a function not only of the validity of the arguments used but also of their logic, described several kinds of fallacies that remain current:

– the *illicit or undistributed major*. Ex: '... exiles can live wherever they please ... such privileges are at the disposal of those we account happy; and therefore every one might be regarded as happy if only he had these privileges' (Aristotle, *Rhetoric*, 2: 24). Wherever they like ... except in their own country. The major premise is not universally true.

– *converse accident* (or hasty generalization), which consists in applying an assertion* generally true to a particular (or 'accidental') case that contradicts it. **Exx:** 'To imprison a man is cruel; therefore, murderers should be allowed to run free' (Lanham, p. 90); 'Some readers may find that Musidora gave herself to Fortunio very quickly ... Let's just say ... that passion is prodigal, and that loving is giving' (Th. Gautier, *Fortunio*, ch. 17).

– *false cause* (*post hoc ergo propter hoc*), which consists in thinking that it is the smoke that moves the train. Ex: 'There was a book of secrets written, I believe, by Albertus Magnus ... I read some pages about how you can grease the wick of an oil lamp, and the fumes produced then provoke visions' (U. Eco, *The Name of the Rose*, p. 90). On this general 'causal' basis, the speaker, Nicholas of Morimondo, makes a specific prediction: 'You know, if you take the wax from a dog's ear and grease a wick, anyone breathing the smoke of that lamp will believe he has a dog's head' (ibid.). Any criticism of causal links leads back to consideration of facts and to the possibility that there may exist more immedite, or more remote, 'first' causes.

– *denying the antecedent*. Ex: 'If Carl embezzled the college funds, then Carl is guilty of a felony. Carl did not embezzle the college funds. Therefore Carl is not guilty of a felony' (Irving M. Copi, *Introduction to Logic*, p. 226).

– *conjunction of irreconcilable arguments*. Ex: '... two and three be even and odde, but five maketh two and three, therefore five is both even and odd' (Thomas Blundeville, quoted by Joseph, p. 369). Joseph also comments as follows on a literary example: 'This fallacy seems to underlie Malvolio's attitude in wanting to bind his Puritanical ideas on all. Sir Toby objects: "Dost thou think, because thou art virtuous, there shall be no more cakes and ale?" (Shakespeare, *Twelfth Night*, 2.3.123).'

– the *vicious circle*, in which arguments, instead of justifying facts, merely restate them. Saint-Exupéry provides a flagrant example in the conversation between the Little Prince and the drunkard: 'Why do you drink? – To forget. – To forget what? – To forget that I'm ashamed. – Ashamed of what? – Ashamed of drinking' (Saint-Exupéry, *The Little Prince*, p. 43).

The vicious circle is a form of tautological reasoning*. Ex: 'The poet George Barker, in his short novel *The Dead Seagull*, has the following real or pretended quotation: "They cut down elms to build asylums for

people driven mad by the cutting down of elms"'' (Espy, 1983, p. 43).
Synonyms: diallelon, diallelus (*OED*).

– *begging the question (petitio principii)*, which is closely related to the
vicious circle and consists of a proof that uses as a premise the argument intended to serve as conclusion and upon which the latter depends. So, for Nietzsche, all metaphysics rests on a *petitio principii*: the
only way of defining being demands the use of 'it *is*' (see Rey, *L'Enjeu
des signes*, p. 92). Reasoning* based on hypothetical deductions (see
supposition*, R2) is also founded upon such an assumption until
experiments justify (or modify) it. In the absence of such verification,
the conclusion is only an *artefact* that remains presupposed by the
method used.

– *tautology** pure and simple, in which the demonstration is merely a
metabole* of the thesis. The following example foregrounds the device
by restating the thesis in exactly the same words: 'The more people
buy Honda, the more people buy Honda.' C. Saint-Laurent taxes Sartre
with tautology in the following summary of a page of the latter's *What
Is Literature?*: 'Only actions count; since only actions count, the proof is
that the rest doesn't count, or very little, at any rate; which is quite
normal since only actions count; therefore only actions count' (C. Saint-
Laurent, *Paul et Jean-Paul*, p. 27).

But is it not common practice, not to say only natural, to dress up as
ideas and arguments what are only intuitions and convictions based on
personal experience? And so we may quite willingly accept semi-
tautology, which is a kind of truism*. Copi argues: 'There is an important relationship between tautologies and valid arguments. To every
argument there corresponds a hypothetical statement whose antecedent
is the conjunction of the argument's premises and whose consequent
is the argument's conclusion ... Thus for every valid argument of the
truth-functional variety ... the statement that its premises imply its
conclusion is a tautology' (Copi, *Introduction to Logic*, p. 268).

– *complex ('loaded' or 'rigged') questions*: a hidden presupposition by
means of which confessions are obtained implicitly, without one's
opponent clearly realizing what is happening. Ex: 'When did you stop
beating your wife?' Or, to a witness claiming not to know the accused:
'Would you swear that you never saw him again from that time on?'
(Whether the witness answers yes or no, self-contradiction is still the
result.)

–the *'kettle,'* a case of paralogism in which the contradictory presuppositions of various propositions produce the same conclusion. Freud
discusses the following typical example: 'A. had borrowed a copper
kettle from B., and upon returning it, was sued by B. because it had a
large hole which rendered it unserviceable. His defense was this: "In
the first place, I never borrowed any kettle from B., secondly, the kettle

had a hole in it when I received it from B., thirdly, the kettle was in perfect condition when I returned it" ' (S. Freud, 'The Technique of Wit,' in *The Basic Writings of Sigmund Freud*, p. 667).

R3: Fallacies of ambiguity* or equivocation, when too obvious, are treated as comic devices. **Exx:**
– *shifts in the principal meaning.* Boris Vian foregrounds the device: 'I like sleeping with the shutters open because it prevents me sleeping and I don't like to sleep' (N. Arnauld, *Les Vies parallèlles de Boris Vian*, p. 130). As may be seen, discussion of the point at issue is resolved by modification of the thesis.
– the *red herring* or *ignoratio elenchi*, a diversionary tactic, a device for avoiding or ignoring the issue (Corbett, p. 92). **Ex:** The traditional 'whodunnit' functions by introducing a number of characters all of whom may have had a motive and an opportunity to kill the victim. Red herrings function as the principal technique by distracting the attention of the detective and reader away from the guilty and towards the innocent. One enigmatic set of clues succeeds another, pointing in each case to a different character. See Hutchinson, pp. 111–14.
– the *(false) analogy* (see reasoning*, R3). **Exx:** 'I caught a cold in the park. The gate was open' (Joyce, *Ulysses*, p. 111) [as if the park were a house]; 'The proof that Shakespeare did not write his plays is that [his friends] called him Willy' (A. Allais) [as if the normal familiarity existing between ordinary people did not apply to the great]. The absurdity of such analogies is even clearer when the thing compared and the comparing expression are amalgamated. **Exx:** 'My beard is a living thing, because it is growing, and if I cut it, it doesn't cry out. Neither does a plant. My beard is a plant' (Boris Vian, *Les Bâtisseurs d'empire*, in *Théâtre*, pp. 84–5); 'A woman without a man is like a fish without a bicycle.'
– *logic-chopping*: an excess of logic in the terms used produces error. **Ex:** 'Besides, you admit the disadvantage without searching for a solution, and how right you are! A disadvantage removed no longer is one' (A. Allais, *Plaisir d'humour*, p. 29).
– the *logical illogicality*: despite its logical form, the proposition is illogical. **Ex:** 'ROSENCRANTZ: And a syllogism: One, he had never known anything like it. Two, he has never known anything to write home about. Three, it is nothing to write home about ...' (Tom Stoppard, *Rosencrantz and Guildenstern Are Dead*, act 1).

PARAPHRASE Rewording or recapitulating to express the same meaning*; a restatement in different words, as to clarify the meaning. See Grambs.

Ex: 'In the course of the book old Mr Dupret dies and his son succeeds him as head of the business. Young Mr Dupret falls in love with a girl in London society but fails to make any impression on her; she in turns falls in love with a genial bounder called Tyler and fails to make any lasting impression on him' (E. Waugh, review [published 14 June 1930] of *Living*, by Henry Green, in *The Essays, Articles and Reviews of E. Waugh,* p. 81).

Analogous: gloss (Frye, Morier); annotation (Grambs, Robert); marginalia (Beckson and Ganz, Souriau, p. 187); scholium, 'an explanatory note or comment' (*OED*)

Other definitions: 1. 'Free rendering or amplification of a passage, expression of its sense in other words' (*Concise Oxford Dictionary*). In *The Well Wrought Urn* (pp. 176–238), Cleanth Brooks condemns what he calls the 'heresy of paraphrase,' the belief that a poem's meaning may be stated in other words. This pejorative connotation seems to us nonessential since other terms (perissology*, battology*) exist to emphasize such abuses. A bad paraphrase adds no new clarity to the original, agreed; but neither do ironic or baroque (etc.) paraphrases clarify it. Ex: 'In Dr. Johnson's famous dictionary patriotism is defined as the last resort of a scoundrel. With all respect to an enlightened but inferior lexicographer I beg to submit that it is the first' (A. Bierce, *The Devil's Dictionary*).
2. 'A kind of oratorical amplification* by which [a speaker] develops and accumulates several secondary ideas in the same sentence' (Fontanier, p. 396). This view considers only paraphrases which appear within the primary text, rather than those added by other commentators. See also periphrasis*, other def.

R1: Lausberg distinguishes paraphrases from *metaphrases*. The latter constitute a form of rewriting by which texts are not extended but merely modified (sometimes shortened, but not reduced to summary form) in order to make them clearer or more accessible to a specific audience. Ex: short versions of classic texts (particularly adventure novels) rewritten in simple vocabulary for young readers.

R2: Paraphrases occupy separate sections within a work, along with references. They appear either at the bottom of the page with the footnotes, or in parentheses* or square brackets. If they do form part of the text itself, they begin with some introductory syntagm* like *i.e., that is to say, in other words*, etc.

PARASTASIS An accumulation* of sentences repeating the same idea.

Ex: 'I could have been a judge but I never had the Latin. I just never had the Latin for the judging. I just never had it, so I'd had it as far as being a judge was concerned. I hadn't got enough of it to get through the rigorous judging exams. They're very rigorous, the judging exams, very rigorous indeed. They're noted for their rigour. People come out of them saying, "My god, what a rigorous exam!" And so I became a miner, instead. I managed to get through the mining exams, they're not very rigorous. There's no rigour involved really. There's a complete absence of rigour involved in the mining exams ...' (A. Bennett, P. Cook, J. Miller, and D. Moore, 'Sitting on the Bench,' in *Beyond the Fringe,* Capitol Records W-1792, 1961).

Synonyms: commoration (Scaliger, 3: 46; Joseph [*commoratio*], pp. 220, 383; Lausberg); epimone (Fabri, 2: 160; Joseph, pp. 220, 384; Lanham; Lausberg)

Analogous: rambling, maundering (*Concise Oxford Dictionary*); anecdotage (Marchais); epexergasia, gorgious (Lanham); *expolitio* (Fontanier, p. 420; Lanham; Lausberg; Morier). In his definition, however, Morier compares *expolitio* to metabole*: 'a clearer, more vivid repetition of an idea.'

R1: When unconscious or superfluous, parastasis is a defect of style. Ex: Tolstoy, *War and Peace,* volume 2, part 2, chapters 1–12. Most of the passages devoted to developing the single idea that historical events occur as a result of the collective will of peoples rather than because of 'geniuses' like Napoleon seem tautological to us. Sometimes parastasis has a purpose, as in the parody* quoted above, or in Beckett's novels (*Molloy,* for instance), where its function is to reveal the hero's state of mental stupor.

PARATAXIS 'Placing of clauses, etc., one after another, without words to indicate co-ordination or subordination, as *Tell me, how are you?' (Concise Oxford Dictionary*). See also Lanham (e.g., 'I came, I saw, I conquered') and Morier. Frye points out (under 'hypotaxis') that 'Erich Auerbach proposes a crucial and historic distinction between *paratactic* style (*and ... and ... and*) and *hypotactic* style (*although ... after ... because ... if*) in his *Mimesis: The Representation of Reality in Western Literature* (1946)'.

R1: The use of parataxis involves the erasure of *taxemes,* a term which designates discursive segments (prepositions, conjunctions, copula verbs, etc.) whose function is to indicate relationships between syntagms*. The sentence 'You will come, I hope' omits the conjunction *that* of hypotactic style: 'I hope that you will come.' See also ellipsis*, syntactic juxtaposition*, and mirror*, R4.

R2: However, parataxis possesses other means as well as syntactic erasure*. It has recourse to morphological erasure (see ellipsis*), dislocation*, and adjunction*. Ex: '[Mr Jingle]: ''Terrible place – dangerous

work – other day – five children – mother – tall lady, eating sandwiches – forgot the arch – crash – knock – children look round –
mother's head off – sandwich in her hand – no mouth to put it in –
head of a family off – shocking!"' (Dickens, *The Pickwick Papers*, ch. 2).
Parataxis even uses lexical erasure*. When a word is lacking in spoken
language, gestures, interjections*, or stereotyped sentences* may come
into play.

PARECHEMA 'A defect of language by which syllables having the
same sound are placed side by side, as *dorica castra*, and *fortunatam
natam*' (Lausberg).
   This term does not exist in English, where *parechesis* includes both
meliorative and pejorative senses of such syllabic juxtapositions.

R1: *Parechema* is a kind of cacophony*.

R2: In French, *parechema* at the end of a line was used by the Grands
Rhétoriqueurs to form *rimes couronnées* or 'crowned rhymes.' Ex: 'Mon
astre m'en*dort d'or*' (Alain Grandbois, quoted in Brault, ed., *Alain
Grandbois*, p. 94).

R3: Change of construction, or occasionally haplology*, 'cures' *parechema*.

PARECHESIS 'The repetition* of the same sound in words in close
or immediate succession' (Smyth, *Greek Grammar*, p. 680).

Ex: 'Gaunt as the ghostliest of glimpses that gleam through the gloom
of the gloaming when ghosts go aghast' (Swinburne, *Nephelidia*, quoted
by Lanham).

Ex: Jacobs, *Naming Day in Eden*, p. 51, suggests: 'Madam, I am Adam.'
That is, changing *I'm* to *I am* converts an example of a palindrome* into
one of parechesis.

PARENTHESIS The insertion of a segment, complete in meaning*,
and relevant or irrelevant to the subject under discussion, into another
segment whose flow it interrupts. See Lanham, Lausberg, Littré, and
OED.

Ex: 'Furthermore, this is his first flight over water (yes, Morris Zapp
has never before left the protection of the North American landmass, a
proud record unique among the faculty of his university) and he
cannot swim' (David Lodge, *Changing Places*, p. 11).

Synonym: dialysis (Le Clerc, p. 271). See also hyperbaton*, R1.

R1: The graphic signs, [( )], which open and close a parenthesis are
situational* signs. They may be replaced by hyphens* or even by

commas. **Ex:** 'If it made any real sense – and it doesn't even begin to – I think I might be inclined to dedicate this account, for whatever it's worth, especially if it's the least bit ribald in parts, to the memory of my late, ribald stepfather, Robert Agadganian Jr. Bobby – as everyone, even I called him – died in 1947, surely with a few regrets, but without a single gripe, of thrombosis' (J.D. Salinger, 'De Daumier-Smith's Blue Period,' in *Nine Stories*, p. 96).

R2: Fontanier, Lausberg, and the *OED* point out that a parenthesis relating to the subject used to be called a *parembole*. The distinction has not survived, probably because even epiphonema*, parabasis*, and digressions* always bear some relationship to the subject. The word *parembole* might be reclaimed as meaning a parenthesis which is syntactically bound to the rest of the sentence. In contradistinction, Marouzeau proposes that we define the parenthesis as an 'insertion into the course of a sentence of an element not syntactically attached to it.' To make the distinction clearer, one might say that, in the case of a parenthesis, the element in question must be removable without loss or change to the remainder's grammaticality or specific meaning*. In the case of parembole, on the other hand, removal would affect grammaticality and specific meaning. This criterion may be verified in the case of any parenthesis.

When, by means of this criterion, we examine, not the rest of the sentence, but the segment inside the parenthesis, we see that it is sometimes independent, sometimes not. If it, too, may be isolated without changing its grammaticality or specific meaning, we can speak properly of a parenthesis. **Ex:** 'But she was splendid at the moment, walking in the schoolyard with her attendants (it was actually Donna with the pale oval face, the fair frizzy hair, who came closest to being pretty), arms linked, seriously talking' (Alice Munro, *Who Do You Think You Are?*, p. 23). On the other hand, if the parenthetical segment depends syntactically upon the rest of the sentence, we have a parembole (a syntactically dependent parenthesis). **Ex:** 'Flo came to the school to raise Cain (her stated intention) and heard witnesses swear Rose had torn it on a nail' (ibid., p. 29). For syntagmatic paremboles, commas may suffice. Other paremboles may be lexemes, syllables, or even single letters. See double* reading.

R3: In reading aloud, the marks of parenthesis are two pauses*.

R4: Very long, dry parentheses, like references for example, or those which would be out of place in the main text, are banished to the footnotes. 'Second-degree' notes are possible, necessary even, in some critical editions. The following literary example appears in Hubert Aquin's *Trou de memoire* (p. 49):

The decayed piers created by Bernini[1] ...

...

1. Bernini was a great baroque architect ... Editor's note[2].
2. This note reveals the editor's lack of culture ... This note is by RR.

RR is the heroine. Aquin thus produces a kind of *mise en abîme* (see mirror*) within the primary process of enunciation*, plus a loop*: as author, he invented both RR, the character, and the editor whose cultural shortcomings RR points out. We may assume that this example expresses more than a joke; it provides a paradoxical way of pointing out that every statement in the text derives from its author.

R5: Parentheses opened and forgotten are digressions, as are second-level parentheses, or sentences divided by hyphens, parentheses, and commas. Ex: 'Yorick was this parson's name, and what is very remarkable in it (as appears from a most ancient account of the family, wrote upon strong vellum, and now in perfect preservation), it had been exactly so spelt for near, – I was within an inch of saying nine hundred years; – but I would not shake my credit in telling an improbable truth, however indisputable in itself; – and therefore I shall content myself with only saying, – It had been exactly so spelt, without the least variation or transposition of a single letter, for I do not know how long; which is more than I would venture to say of one half of the best surnames in the country; which in the course of years ...' (Laurence Sterne, *Tristram Shandy*, vol. 1, ch. 11).

The interior monologue* contains many parentheses not even indicated, because in this type of discourse* the character 'understands' his or her own thought processes without the necessity of such situational* signs. Ex: 'my dearest Doggerina she wrote on it she was very nice whats this her other name was just a p c to tell you I sent' (Joyce, *Ulysses*, p. 621).

R6: Parenthetical remarks constitute adjacent assertions* whose values are sometimes quite curious. See assertion*, R3; quotation*, R7; epiphonema*, other def.; epiphrasis*, R1; explanation*, R2 and R4; excuse*, R1; irony*, R2; paraphrase*, R2; and expressive punctuation*.

PARODY Conscious and deliberate imitation, either of content or form, which intends to achieve a mocking, or simply a comic, effect. See Cuddon, Frye, and Preminger. For a more complete discussion of the definitions of parody, see Linda Hutcheon, *A Theory of Parody* (1985).

Exx: 'The way to a man's heart is through his ears' (Xerxes, in Herodotus, 7.39); 'The way to a man's heart is through his stomach' (proverb); 'In the beginning, California was without freeways and water covered the land' (*Northern California*, ed. J. Carroll and T. Johnston, p. 11); 'The history of Catholicism shows that you can't make an omelette without breaking eggheads' (Ken Tynan, in Brett, ed., *The Faber Book of Parodies*, pp. 179–80).

Exx:

> When lovely woman stoops to folly
> And finds too late that men betray,
> What charm can sooth her melancholy,
> What art can wash her guilt away?
>> O. Goldsmith, *The Vicar of Wakefield*, ch. 29

> When lovely woman stoops to folly and
> Paces about her room again, alone,
> She smoothes her hair with automatic hand,
> And puts a record on the gramophone.
>> T.S. Eliot, *The Waste Land*, part 3 ('The Fire Sermon')

> When lovely woman stoops to folly
> The evening can be awfully jolly.
>> Mary Demetriadis, in Brett, ed., *The Faber Book of Parodies*, p. 174

Analogous: satire ('a poem in which wickedness or folly is censured' [Dr Johnson]); pastiche (entertaining compilations or imitations); caricature* (in the broad sense); skit; revue (a satirical set of sketches on contemporary themes)

R1: Literary parody (see burlesque*, R1) employs various devices from the parodied text, which it exaggerates or misuses. Parody is therefore a genre rather than a device. Examples of parodies of works: the *Battle of the Frogs and Mice*, a parody, attributed in antiquity to Homer, of an epic poem; the *Satyricon* of Petronius, which contains a long poem in hexameters parodying Lucan; Scarron's *Le Virgile travesti*; Fielding's *Shamela*; and the poems making up *The Faber Book of Parodies*. Foregrounding* the devices parodied defamiliarizes them. See particularly epitheton*, other def. Parody forms an effective kind of 'applied' or second-level rhetoric (see false –*, R1) which reveals itself by its tone (see intonation* and irony*, R1).

R2: Parody is only perceptible to those who know the model; hence the need to parody celebrities, notably politicians who invite caricature*. There are also many parodies of texts and styles. See Hutcheon and *The Faber Book of Parodies*. See also macaronicism*, R1; translation*, R2; and insult*, R3.

R3: Parody may be affectionate or biting. See persiflage*, R1.

PARONOMASIA 'A playing on words which sound alike; a word-play; a [type of] pun' (*OED*); 'playing on the sound and meaning of words: punning' (W. Taylor, *Tudor Figures of Rhetoric*, p. 117). See also Frye, Lanham, Lausberg, Littré, Morier, Preminger (who includes paronomasia under 'pun'), and Redfern (pp. 18, 49, 101–2).

Ex: 'They went and told the sexton and / The sexton tolled the bell' (Thomas Hood, 'Faithless Sally Brown').

Synonyms: paranomasia (Espy, 1983, p. 120); *agnominatio** (Lanham, Lausberg, Marouzeau, Scaliger); *allusio* and *prosonomasia* (Sonnino)

R1: It is easy to confuse paronomasia with isolexism*, which brings together words belonging to the same lexeme. Ex: 'To say unpleasant things unpleasantly.' As Marouzeau explains, however, we may accept as examples of paronomasia words etymologically similar. Ex: 'Man proposes but God disposes' (Proverbs 19:21).

R2: Paronyms (words which are practically homonyms) naturally provide the best examples of paronomasia, but not the only valid ones since paronomasia extends to the (fairly fluid) borders it shares with alliteration*. Ex: 'The end of the plain plane, explained' (ad for Braniff International, quoted by Corbett, p. 483).

R3: Morier proposes a subtle variation of paronomasia which he calls 'apophony' ('variation in vowel quality in the formation of grammatically related words, as in English give, gave, G. sprechen, sprach. Also called *ablaut* and *vowel gradation*' [*OEDS*]).

R4: Paronomasia leads to word-play*, which is why Preminger, Mahood (pp. 92, 141), and Redfern (pp. 17–18) classify it as a kind of pun*. Ex: 'a pornographer is one who offers a vice to the lovelorn' (J. Crosbie, *Dictionary of Puns*, p. 245).

R5: Involuntary paronomasia exists and may turn into cacophony*. Ex: 'In the inn, we went into dinner.'

R6: In general, the terms are coupled together, that is, they form examples of syntactic parallelism* which draw attention to the device. Ex: 'Not Angles, but Angels' (attributed to Pope Gregory at the sight of English slaves brought to Rome).

R7: When pushed to extremes, paronomasia (like antimetabole*, mirror*, etymology*, etc.) becomes a way of creating new meanings*, or at least of creating ambiguity* (see musication*). Ex: 'No worst, there is none. Pitched past pitch of grief / More pangs will, schooled at fore-pangs, wilder wring' (G. Manley Hopkins, 'No Worst, There Is None').

R8: Modern thinkers have not disdained the use of paronomasia. Exx: 'While I am engaged upon the formation and formulation of the idea of the subject and of the object ...' (Merleau-Ponty, *Phénoménologie de la perception*, p. 253); 'What [Bergson] believed to be coincidence is coexistence' (Merleau-Ponty, *Eloge de la philosophie*, p. 31).

R9: Examples of paronomasia involving proper names are easily constructed and are therefore very common. Not all are as clever as the following which also involves metanalysis*: 'Tailor to man who brings in torn pants: "Euripides?" Man: "Yes; Eumenides?"' (Espy, 1983, p. 121). See also assonance*, R2; distinction*, R4; echo* effect, R1; musication*, R4; pun*; antimetathesis*, R1; and antanaclasis*, other def.

PARTITION A word is given not only in its entirety but also syllable by syllable and in its possible syllabic groups.

Ex: 'Constantinople: *C* with an *O* and with an *N* spells *CON, S* with a *T*, with an *A* and an *N* spells *STAN, T* with an *I* spells *TI, N* and *O, P, L* and *E* spell *NOPLE, CONSTANTINOPLE.*' See Iona and Peter Opie, *Children's Games in Street and Playground* (1969) and *The Lore and Language of Schoolchildren* (1959).

R1: Partition plays on the signifer and possibly on the signified as well when the elements are presented as so many distinct objects (not the case in the above example).

PAUSE In oral speech, pauses occur as we inhale (which intervals mark the limits of *breath-groups*), or at momentary breath-stoppages, or, at the least, at interruptions in the sentence's melodic curve, or, of course, at periods of silence, of whatever duration. Graphically, pauses are shown by semicolons, periods, or blanks, so as to separate detachable parts (finished or not) from the spoken or written chain.

Varying amounts of *blank space* surround titles* and separate paragraphs*: for example, one or more blank lines between paragraphs. Blanks between elements within a sentence are rarer but form a principal device in the creation of the *rebus*. Ex:

rebellion		rebellion
	In 1789	
	FRA NCE	laws
	monarchy	uoıɓıləɹ
	thrown	
rebellion		rebellion

'This means: "In 1789 France was divided, monarchy overthrown, laws set aside, religion turned upside down, and rebellion at every corner' (Augarde, p. 88).

R1: Pauses play analogous roles in poetry and prose. In poetry, pauses should occur at rhythmic divisions like the caesura*. They may occur within the line* (see below), are more usual at the end of a line, and always appear at the end of a stanza*. In prose, pauses may appear within sentences, where they determine the length of rhythmic groups; they usually occur at the end of a sentence, and almost always between paragraphs.

Rhythmic pauses: In music, as is well known, the duration of pauses is exactly defined. A crochet rest is twice as long as a quaver rest. Ricardo Güiraldes proposed the insertion into literary texts of the musical signs for crochet and quaver, in order better to define rhythms*. Very rhythmic texts possess an exact duration for each pause (see line* [of poetry], 1, R2; 2, R2; 3). It should be possible to transcribe each duration. We might, for example, borrow the conventions used by phoneticians: one, two, or three vertical or horizontal lines, according to the length of a pause, or the signs ↑, ↓ accompanied or not by the figures 1 to 4 placed above the line, as in Hockett's system outlined in the *Dictionnaire de linguistique*; or again, we might indicate where pauses occur with ˘ for 'short' or ¯ for 'long,' according to the approximate duration of each.

Procephalous pauses before the line are called *anacrusis*. Morier named pauses after lines of poetry 'sighs' [*soupirs*]. See also enjamb(e)ment*, R2.

Pauses in prose: Their duration is unpredictable and all the more variable as a speaker loses control of the means of communication. Ex: 'Well then, I ... Er ... In the beginning ...' Periods disappear with the result that in such 'sentences' pauses become slips from one kind of duration to another. We abandon the text's duration as we search for the kind of duration appropriate to the speaker, whom we see struggling to work out how to think and speak at the same time. The presence of this actual, subjective background underlying verbal expression explains why pauses almost disappear when we adopt the text's viewpoint: texts in prose seem constantly to be beginning again from zero. See paragraph*, R1; sentence* (types of), 1. Interruptions* are the opposite of pauses because two people talk very briefly at the same time, but the device of *reticentia* (or aposiopesis*), by which we halt voluntarily, is a kind of expressive pause, whose silence is amplified by what listeners might be expecting in its place. See also reactualization*, 7.

Hyphens or dashes (see situational* signs, 3[a], and caesura*, R4) may transcribe special pauses, during which the speaker seems to be gaining confidence, and so help to emphasize the segment that follows. See also emphasis*, R1.

R2: Morier proposes the term *ligature*, or binding, to designate the suppression of a pause at the end of a sentence or paragraph which aims to keep the listeners' attention. Here is his definition: 'A strategy in eloquence by which the orator, once he has arrived at the end of a period, at the moment when his voice is dropping and slowing, suddenly carries on speaking, uttering quickly and emphatically the first word or phrase of the next sentence. E.g.: "Maupassant denounces ironically the atmosphere of depravity, the political and financial thieving and ... inflation." ' The pause carries over after the second *and*,

and is prolonged. Rhythmically speaking, arsis accompanies the word thus bound and the ictus occurs during the suspensive silence that follows. (Arsis: 'stress of a syllable or part of a metrical foot' [*Concise Oxford Dictionary*]; ictus: 'rhythmical or metrical stress' [ibid.].)

R3: There is usually a pause before appositions* (see apposition, R2), parentheses* (see parenthesis, R3), reminders*, and hyphens* (see assertion, R3).

PEREGRINISM The use of linguistic elements borrowed from a foreign language. Elements include: the sound system, graphy*, and sentence-melodies as well as grammatical, lexical, or syntactic forms, and even meanings* and connotations. See Pei and Gaynor.

Analogous definition: Fontanier, under 'imitation' (p. 288)

Synonyms: 'foreignism' (Pei and Gaynor); garble; interference

R1: We may distinguish, by the country of origin, between:
(a) Gallicisms*: French forms introduced into English.
(b) Anglicisms*: English forms introduced into French.
(c) Italianisms: '*Sacrifizio incruento*, Stephen said smiling, swaying his ashplant in slow swingswong from its midpoint, lightly' (Joyce, *Ulysses*, p. 188).
(c) Latinisms: 'Then this description, passing from *auctoritas* to *auctoritas*, was transformed through successive imaginative exercises, and unicorns became fanciful animals, white and gentle' (U. Eco, *The Name of the Rose*, p. 316).
(e) Hebraisms: 'Kaddish for Naomi Ginsberg' (Allen Ginsberg).
(f) Germanisms: '*Ehrebung* without motion, concentration / Without elimination ...' (T.S. Eliot, 'Burnt Norton').

R2: Peregrinisms become a literary device when foregrounded. In *The Name of the Rose*, for example, Eco constructs a character, Salvatore, on the device: '... he said: "Penitenziagite! Watch out for the draco who cometh in futurum to gnaw your anima! Death is super nos! Pray the Santo Pater come to liberar nos a malo and all our sin! Ha ha, you like this negromanzia de Domini Nostri Jesu Christi! Et anco jois m'es dols e plazer m'es dolors ... Cave il diabolo! Semper lying in wait for me in some angulum to snap at my heels' (p. 46). Adso, the narrator, goes on to explain the device: '... I could never understand what language he spoke. It was not Latin ... I realized Salvatore spoke all languages, and no language. Or rather, he had invented for himself a language which used the sinews of the languages to which he had been exposed ... I also noticed afterwards that he might refer to something first in Latin and later in Provençal, and I realized that he was not so much inventing his own sentences as using the disiecta membra of other sentences, heard some time in the past' (ibid., pp. 46–7). See pseudo-language*.

R3: Peregrinisms can be more or less complete (see anglicism*, R1). Many gallicisms used by anglophones (just like many anglicisms used by francophones) without respect to number, gender, grammar, or morphology betray the snobbery behind the device. Ex: 'Each balcony is equipped with chaise loungers' (ad for condominium). Gallicisms may be parodied: '... Sergeant Bird, so wittily nicknamed / Oiseau' (D. Thomas, *Quite Early One Morning*, p. 50). The game of 'Fractured French' consists in deliberately mistranslating French words and expressions: '*coup de grâce*: lawn-mower; *c'est-à-dire*: she's a honey' (Espy, 1971, p. 112).

R4: *Pidgins* are combinations of two languages; they are also referred to as *creolized* languages. Pei and Gaynor (p. 50) define the latter term as 'a trade language or "contact vernacular" which has become the only language used for daily speech and communication by an economically, socially or politically subject group, class or race; characterized by extreme morphological simplification of the language of colonization from which it is derived.' Their definition of *pidgin* makes it a generalized use of the more specific form, pidgin English: 'a creolized version of the English language, used by traders for communication with the Chinese and other Orientals. The word *pidgin* (a corruption of the English word *business*) is often used popularly as an adjective to designate hybrid forms of other languages' (p. 170). Ex: 'There are said to be more than 700 linguistic groups in Papua New Guinea ... Pidgin is the common tongue, the passport between tribes. It is a marvelous mélange of English, Australian slang, onomatopoeia, and local lore. The word "piano," for example, is *Bigfellabockus, teeth alla same shark, you hitim he cry out* – a big box, with teeth all the same size, and if you hit it, it makes a noise' (P. Benchley, 'Ghosts of War in the South Pacific,' *National Geographic*, April 1988, p. 451).

Similarly, Anglo-Indian, the vernacular used by British soldiers, government officials, and civilians in India, became known as *Hobson-Jobson*. Noah Jacobs explains the derivation of the term and gives examples indicating the term's generalized application to other language mixtures: 'When [the] association of sounds is confused in the popular mind from one language to another and unfamiliar words are rendered meaningful by being melted into familiar ones, it is known as Hobson-Jobson. This name is a mishearing of *Ja Hasan, Ja Hasan*, the cry of the Mohammedans in religious processions, as heard by the English ear, and although now used in a technical sense only, is itself an example of many such words that have been assimilated into language – e.g., *hoosegow* from the Sp. *juzgado*, tribunal; *sponge cake* (originally *Spanish cake*) is in Jap. *kasuteira* (which is clearly Castile); ... Russ. *voksal*, railroad station, from Eng. Vauxhall ...' (N. Jacobs, *Naming Day in Eden*, pp. 114–15).

R5: Regionalisms and provincialisms, expressions borrowed from local dialects, are not true peregrinisms. Ex:

Wee, sleekit, cow'rin, tim'rous beastie,
O what a panic's in thy breastie!
Thou need na start awa sae hasty,
Wi' bickering brattle!

R. Burns, 'To a Mouse'

R6: The successful use of peregrinisms or provincialisms in literature depends on the desired effect. Aristotle recommended them: the Athenians appreciated them (as do Londoners today) as long as they are clearly marked, which means intentional. They produce curious textual effects of which only the narrow-minded are afraid. Ex:

'The bellula?'
'Oc! Parvissimum animal, just a bit plus longue than the rat, and also called the musk-rat. And so the serpe and the botta. And when they bite it, the bellula runs to the fenicula or to the cicerbita and chews it, and comes back to the battaglia. And they say it generates through the oculi.' (U. Eco, *The Name of the Rose*, p. 308)

PERIOD A well-rounded, well-articulated, and harmonious sentence. The parts group connected ideas in balanced clauses whose grammatical shape and rhythmic structure emphasize their meaning*.

Ex: 'As the happiness of the *future* life is the great object of religion, we may hear without surprise or scandal that the introduction, or at least the abuse, of Christianity had some influence on the fall of the Roman empire. The clergy successfully preached the doctrines of patience and pusillanimity; the active virtues of society were discouraged; and the last remains of military spirit were buried in the cloister' (Edward Gibbon, *The Decline and Fall of the Roman Empire*, as quoted in G. Seldes, *The Great Thoughts*, p. 159).

Synonym: hypotactic style (hypotaxis is the opposite of parataxis*; see also hyperhypotaxis*)

Analogous definition: 'The word περίοδος in Greek meant a going-around, a circuit, and thus came to mean a well-rounded sentence, an extensive survey, and one with shape' (R. Lanham, *Style: An Anti-Textbook*, p. 123).

Other definition: 'Periodic sentence: in rhetoric, a sentence in which the most significant element or part occupies the final position' (Pei and Gaynor, p. 164).

R1: Periods have a *protasis*, or first part, and an *apodosis* or second part, divided by a peak, or a kind of median caesura*. Intonation* and sometimes meaning* mount in the protasis and descend in the apodosis (see assertion*). Periods may be binary or ternary (composed, that is, of two or three parts; see sentence*). An *antapodosis* is a phrase or clause which may be paired with the protasis in the middle of the period. The final proposition is called a 'clausula' (Lanham). See punch* line. Ex: 'Socialism is bound sooner or later to ripen into Communism [protasis] whose banner bears the motto [antapodosis]: "From each according to his ability [apodosis], to each according to his needs [clausula]' (V.I. Lenin, *The Task of the Proletariat* [1917], as quoted in G. Seldes, *The Great Thoughts*, p. 240).

R2: Bénac makes an analogical distinction between what he calls 'square' periods, composed of four parts, and 'round' periods, 'whose parts are tightly bound together producing a harmonious impression' (sometimes at the expense of relevance; hence the pejorative sense of the expression 'well-rounded periods'), and 'crossed' periods, 'whose clauses are opposed in pairs of antitheses.'

'Well-rounded' periods are frequently binary, with parallel clauses and repetition*. 'The art of making the parts of a sentence equal in length and similar in form' used to be called *parisosis* (Chaignet, p. 19). Ex: the sentence by Lenin just quoted. In such sentences, the parts of equal length are *isocolons* (Lausberg, Littré, Peacham, Joseph, *OED*, Quinn), and the rhythm* is *concordant*, whereas lack of balance between protasis and apodosis produces *discordant* rhythm. However, rhopalic periods, in which the members gradually increase in length, form an exception (from the Greek ροπαλου, a club or bludgeon; because this kind of club widens from handle to tip).

As Joseph points out (p. 297), Peacham, in showing how the figure *isocolon* can be used to emphasize the topics of logic, introduces a possible source of confusion in the term's definition. Thus 'isocolon' means for Peacham both clauses of equal length and a means of 'coupl[ing] contraries' (*The Garden of Eloquence* [1593], p. 58). Quinn (pp. 77–9) shows how its 'repeatedly balanced phrases' may be both 'stuffy ... the port-and-oak-panelled-study style of an Edward Gibbon' and also suitable for a boxer's verbal fisticuffs, as in the boast: 'The bigger they are, the harder they fall.'

Mestre makes a distinction between different parts of a period: *members* being clauses which 'end with a partial rest' and *interpolated phrases*, 'member-segments without meaning except in liaison with the rest of the member' (p. 93). *Jerky* or *incisive* style is one in which interpolated elements abound.

R3: Theoretically, the meaning* of each period is complete in itself. In practice, periodic sentences come in groups which form paragraphs* complete in meaning. (See Churchill's speeches, for example.)

R4: Periods represented the ideal form of writing in antiquity (atticism) because they constitute a victory over the incoherence of spontaneous thought and expression (see baroquism*, R1). '[Periods] are oratorical stanzas. We see the point at which they begin; we feel in advance their endings; our ears follow both the suspensive, climactic, and the falling, resolved melodies, and also the intermediate partial movements leading gradually to the end ... [Periods] are harmonious' (Chaignet, p. 441).

R5: Periods employ parallelism* (see cadence*, and anacoluthon*, other def.), epiphora*, hypotaxis, epitheton* (see epitheton, R1), antepiphora*, similes* (see simile, R2), *gradatio** (see *gradatio*, R4), and suspension*. They avoid homoioteleuton* (see homoioteleuton, R4). See also grandiloquence*, R1, and sentence* (types of). For periods intended to be read aloud, see hyperhypotaxis*, R1 and R4.

PERIPHRASIS The replacement of a single word by several which together have the same meaning*. See Lanham ('circumlocution'), Lausberg (sect. 589), Morier, Preminger, and Quinn.

Exx: the 'bird of night' for the 'owl'; the fourth estate; the gentlemen of the press; 'the love that dare not speak its name' (Oscar Wilde)

Exx: Winston Churchill is said to have replied to a question he judged impertinent: 'The answer to your question, sir, is in the plural, and they bounce'; '... they will suffer death before they give Information of any of their Accomplices: and when brought to *the fatal tree*, will deny their guilt with their last breath' (Reverend Samuel Marsden, quoted by R. Hughes, in *The Fatal Shore*, p. 352); 'Wondrous machines are now made ... with which the course of nature can be predicted ... I am told that in Cathay a sage has compounded a powder that, on contact with fire, can produce a great rumble and a great flame, destroying everything for many yards around' (U. Eco, *The Name of the Rose*, p. 88).

Other definitions: Corbett (p. 485) identifies periphrasis with antonomasia*; 'substitution of a descriptive word or phrase for a proper name or of a proper name for a quality associated with the name. [E.g.:] 'Pale young men with larded and *Valentino-black* side whiskers' (D. Thomas, 'Holiday Memory' [in *Quite Early One Morning*, p. 27]).' Fontanier, on the other hand, introduced (pp. 326, 361, 396) a distinction between *pronomination* (the designation of a noun, or thing, by a complex expression in several words), periphrasis (the more extended expression of an idea in a sentence), and paraphrase*. For him, the 'bird of night' would thus be an example of pronomination; Wilde's euphemism* would be periphrasis.

R1: Some of the uses of periphrasis: the avoidance of too precise a term; the designation of a person by his or her qualities; the creation of metaphors* (see abstraction* and baroquism*, R2); the replacement of something unpleasant (euphemism*) or neutral by a description*, a riddle*, or intellectual game (see pun*, R1). Ex:

– And how is Dick, the solid man?
– Nothing between himself and heaven, Ned Lambert answered.
– By the holy Paul! Mr Dedalus said in subdued wonder. Dick Tivy bald? (Joyce, *Ulysses*, p. 84)

It should be added that a speaker may have recourse to periphrasis quite naturally when the proper word either does not come to mind or does not exist. Ex: 'There is no word to describe the feeling of marching on the enemy, and yet it is as specific, as strong as sexual desire or anguish' (A. Malraux, *Antimémoires*, p. 312). See description*, R5.

R2: Examples of periphrasis may involve mythology, allusions*, or definitions*. Lausberg considers *anthorism* ('a counter-definition; a description or definition differing from that given by one's opponent' [*OED*]) as an example of aggressive periphrasis. Ex:

IAGO: You would be satisfied?
OTHELLO: Would? Nay, I will.

Shakespeare, *Othello*, 3.3.391–2

See epanorthosis* and self-correction*. Ex: 'Give me chastity, but not yet' (Augustine).

R3: See litotes*; self-correction*, R4; circumlocution*, R1; *compensatio*, R1; denomination*, R1; epitheton*, R3; phoebus*, R4; meaning* (implicit); translation*, R3; hyperbole*, R3; remotivation*, R1; and title* (of work), R5.

PERISSOLOGY Redundance or superfluity of speech; use of more words than are necessary; pleonasm (see *OED*). See also Fabri (3:126), Fontanier (p. 299), Grambs, Lausberg, and Pei and Gaynor. These authors all consider perissology to be a stylistic defect. Some make a distinction between it and pleonasm*, the corresponding stylistic figure. See also etymology* and paraphrase*, other def. 1.

Ex: 'as sure as eggs are eggs' ('a corruption of the logical formula, x = x' [N. Jacobs, *Naming Day in Eden*, p. 130]).

Synonyms: redundance (Fontanier, p. 302; Pei and Gaynor); incorrect, corrupt pleonasm (Fontanier; Robert)

R1: Although perissology is a defect of style, it has its uses in literature; for example, as a source of comedy: 'the voracious have completely eaten *and devoured* the coriaceous' (A. Jarry, *Ubu roi*, p. 156).

R2: Grammatical perissology exists. Ex: 'the grass you should keep off *of*' (D. Thomas, *Quite Early One Morning*, p. 54).

R3: Perissology is one of the principal devices used by the media in their production of *filler* or *padding*. Henry Peacham, the sixteenth-century English rhetor and logician, quotes Quintilian on the subject:

'*Perissologia*, like unto *Pleonasmus*, when a clause of no weight is thrust into a construction. Quintilian taketh this example out of Livius: "The Ambassadors, peace not having been obtained, returned home again from whence they came." Here the latter clause is superfluous, for it had been sufficient to have said, "The Ambassadors, peace not having been obtained, returned home again"' (*The Garden of Eloquence* [1593], quoted by Espy, 1983, p. 198).

PERMISSIO Pretending to allow what we would prefer to prevent, or to request what will be refused. See Girard, p. 285; the *OED* gives this sense of reluctant permission as rare in English.

Exx: 'Go ahead!, if you must ...'; 'You may laugh, but ...'

Ex:

> PARIS: You know that if you kiss Helen, I will kill you!
> HELEN: He doesn't mind dying, several times over even.
> PARIS: What's wrong with him? Is he getting ready to leap upon you? He's too polite for that ... Troilus, give Helen a kiss, you have my permission.
> J. Giraudoux, *La Guerre de Troie n'aura pas lieu*, 2.2

Synonyms: epitrope ('ironical permission' [Peacham, *The Garden of Eloquence*, in Espy, 1983, p. 174]; Joseph, p. 325; Fontanier, p. 149); *concessio* (Lanham). The figures licence* and parrhesia include a request for permission to speak candidly of unpleasant things.

R1: The device is sometimes a form of simulation*, sometimes of pseudo-simulation*, like irony*, to which it is related. See false –*.

R2: The device has its own intonation*. It usually takes the imperative form. **Ex:**

> Yet let him keep the rest,
> But keep them with repining restlessness;
> Let him be rich and weary, that at least,
> If goodness lead him not, yet weariness
>   May toss him to my breast.
> George Herbert, 'The Pulley' (from *The Temple*)

PERMUTATION The device consists in varying the order, not of words, as in the flip-flop*, nor of functions, as in hypallage*, nor phonemes*, as in spoonerisms*, but of syllables, which, in most cases, produces nothing more than a kind of scrambling*.

Exx: 'Ma vie est serdame' for 'Madame est servie' (B. Vac, *Saint-Pépin P.Q.*, p. 226) [an unintentional slip of the tongue caused by nervousness]. However, André Breton's 'Ecusette de Noireuil' in *L'Amour fou* is an intentional permutation by means of which he raises his grand-daughter to the peerage by permuting the syllables of *écureuil* (squirrel) and *noisette* (hazel nut). Similarly, Raymond Queneau permutes groups of letters of increasing length, some of them syllables in one of his *Exercises in Style*.

R1: We here use the word *permutation* in a special, restricted sense produced by ellipsis* of the more comprehensible phrase 'permutation of syllables between two words.' See also cryptography*, R2.

PERSIFLAGE 'Light banter or raillery; a frivolous manner of treating any subject' (*OED*).

Ex:

George the Third
Ought never to have occurred.
One can only wonder
At so grotesque a blunder.

> E.C. Bentley, *More Biographies,*
> as quoted in Espy, *The Game of Words,* p. 74

This is a clerihew (see poem*). See also graphy*, R2; and etymology*, R1.

Analogous: raillery; mockery; derision; diasyrmus ('disparagement of opponent's argument through a base similitude' [Lanham]; 'sarcastic irony' [Morier]); banter (Grambs); repartee (Redfern, p. 123)

Antonym: charientismus: 1. witty irony aiming to flatter; 2. 'clothing a disagreeable sense with agreeable expressions; soothing over a diffi-culty, or turning aside antagonism with a joke' (Lanham). Ex:

> KING: Have you heard the argument? Is there no offence in't?
> HAMLET: No, no, they do but jest, poison in jest; no offence i' the world.
>
> Shakespeare, *Hamlet,* 3.2.242–3

R1: Sarcasm* is bitter or virulent and therefore an obvious form of mockery*, whereas persiflage is less direct, closer to irony* in that it frequently takes a witty form. Exx: 'Full-frontal nudity – and there's as catch-penny an opening as you'll ever see – has now become accepted by every branch of the theatrical profession with the possible exception of female accordion players. There is, however, one group of per-formers whom it threatens to relegate to the status of an endangered species. Conjurors' (Fr. Muir and D. Norden, *The 'My Word!' Stories,* p. 80); 'He [Bernard Shaw] hasn't an enemy in the world, and none of his friends like him' (quoted in Shaw, *Sixteen Self Sketches,* p. 117). This is chleuasmos*.

Personification

Persiflage may include antiphrasis*. Ex: 'You're looking well, this morning' (to someone suffering from a hangover). It may also take the form of grandiloquence* or parody*, or be concentrated in a sobriquet or nickname. See also caricature*, R2, and intonation*.

PERSONIFICATION Endowing inanimate objects or abstractions with life and human characteristics (see Preminger). See also Fontanier (p. 111), Lanham, Lausberg, *OED*, and Robert.

Ex: 'As every hammerer at a typewriter knows, QWERTYUIOP is the blazon on the second bank of the keyboard from the top ... Without Qwert Yuiop's willingness to submit to my punishing fingers I doubt if I could have sustained the profession of author ... Qwert Yuiop in his traditional form, which is not much different from the way he was in the pioneering Remington days ... not only relates authorship to artisanship; he separates the written from the writer ...' (A. Burgess, *But Do Blondes Prefer Gentlemen? Homage to QWERT YUIOP and Other Writings*, pp. xii–xiii).

Synonym: animism (*OED*)

R1: Fontanier adds that the device may take the form of metonymy*, metaphor* (see metaphor, R4), or synecdoche*. It has a (nonpersonal) tenor and a (personal) vehicle, linked by analogy, logic, or contiguity. If the tenor is a person, the device is antonomasia*. If the vehicles are multiple, it is allegory* (see allegory, R3). Fontanier also mentions (p. 118) subjectification, synecdoche of persons ('my pen' for 'myself as author'; 'your arms will fight' for 'you will fight'; he may be invoked 'by our tears' for 'by our grief'). In our view, the word *subjectification* would be better employed to describe speaking personifications which are introduced as subjects into things or ideas, which they then represent 'from the inside,' as it were. Henri Michaux constantly uses the device in his poetry. Ex: 'In the tepid breath of a young girl have I taken my place' (*L'Espace du dedans*, p. 102). Thus, a thing or idea may not only be personified but made identical with the enunciating *I*. The result is a negative isotopy*, and the effect hallucinatory. Ex: 'Through suffering, I lost consciousness of my body's limits and grew irresistibly larger. I became everything: ants particularly ... Frequently I turned into a boa constrictor and, although somewhat embarrassed by my new length, I would prepare for sleep, or else I was a bison and getting ready to browse, but soon from my shoulder came a typhoon' (H. Michaux, *Encore des changements*, in *L'Espace du dedans*, pp. 48–9).

R2: Personification markers vary, with the only indisputable ones being identification with the person of the speaker (see prosopopoeia*) or receiver (see apostrophe*). Capital letters, which stand as markers for proper names or as signals of the beginnings of sentences*, may play a role in emphasizing personifications (see emphasis*, R2). But in Queneau's sentence 'The Ideal is the Family, the Homeland, Art' (*Le Chiendent*, p. 193), there is only emphasis without personification. When, on the other hand, Hilaire Belloc writes, 'Strong Brother in God, and last Companion: Wine' ('Heroic Poem in Praise of Wine,' in *Complete Verse*, p. 86), the capitals personify because the context invites personification. They emphasize as well, of course, and that is possibly their principal function because personification does not need capital letters. Ex: 'Canada the wide-eyed farm boy was becoming street-wise, though not truly wise' (Robertson Davies, *What's Bred in the Bone*, p. 495).

Another personification marker, syntactic in this case, is the subjective function of verbs requiring an animate, or human, subject. But this makes an uncertain marker because it is used particularly for abstract terms without personification. See dialogue*, R4. Ex: '[Sir Philip Sydney's sonnets] are about love, they *are not in love*; they *address* love, they *do not speak out of* it' (D. Thomas, *Quite Early One Morning*, p. 91). The metaphor* (see metaphor, R4) here is verbal. It is sometimes sufficient merely to add a more reliable marker, or to multiply such verbs, for the isotopy* to be inverted, which results in the noun appearing to be a personification. Compare, for instance, 'Ingratitude, more strong than traitors' arms, / Quite vanquished him' (Shakespeare, *Julius Caesar*, 3.2.188–9) with 'Mischief, thou art afoot, / Take thou what course thou wilt' (ibid., 3.2.265–6).

R3: Classical and neo-classical authors exploited decorative Olympian personification. Fontanier (p. 120) calls the device 'mythologism,' offering the following example from La Fontaine: 'Once Thetis had chased away golden-haired Phoebus.' He goes on to explain: 'Now, who can be unaware that ... Thetis is the goddess of the sea? that Phoebus, otherwise known as Apollo, is the sun, the god of light? that the sun, when it sets, goes to rest in the depths of the sea, next to Thetis? and that, when Apollo rises, he is chased away by Thetis so that day may return to the wordl?' The device of mythologism is now considered archaic.

R4: Identification (see definition*, R2), which raises persons to the level of ideas, is the opposite of personification, which animates ideas by personalizing them. See also denomination*, R3, and title* (of work), R3.

PHOEBUS ('An epithet of Apollo, particularly in his quality as the god of light. The name often stands for the sun personified' [*Benét's Reader's Encyclopedia*, 1987, 3rd ed.]. The name of the character becomes, metonymically, that of the device.) A text rendered barely intelligible by the brilliant but incomprehensible presentation of simple ideas. The closest term used by the English rhetors seems to be *bomphilogia* (Joseph, Lanham). However, where the French term emphasizes *brilliance*, the English discerns only boasting.

Ex (of bomphilogia, quoted by Joseph, p. 71): 'FALSTAFF: I am a rogue if I were not at half-sword with a dozen of them two hours together. I have scap'd by miracle. I am eight times thrust through the doublet, four through the hose; my buckler cut through and through; my sword hack'd like a handsaw – ecce signum! I have never felt better since I was a man ... if I fought not with fifty of them, I am a bunch of radish! If there were not two and fifty upon poor old Jack, then am I no two-legg'd creature' (Shakespeare, *Henry IV*, Pt 1, 2.4.182–208).

Analogous terms: rodomontade (from a character called Rodomonte, a boastful Saracen king in Ariosto's *Orlando Furioso*); amphigouri (a term less archaic than phoebus but also more pejorative); nonsense* (pejorative); gibberish* (pejorative)

Same definition (emphasizing brilliance, rather than boasting, in French): Girard, pp. 132, 244 ('Excess ornamentation produces obscure ideas').

Other definitions: See literary* games.

R1: Phoebus is a form of baroquism* (see baroquism, R3). If the text's difficulty springs from meaning* (see abstract, analogical meaning*, etc.), hermeticism replaces phoebus. Properly speaking, hermetic philosophy goes back to the sacred texts of ancient Egypt.

R2: If the hidden sense does not in fact exist, we have verbigeration*.

R3: The term *gibberish* should be reserved for the kind of frequently encountered obscurity which is involuntary. Ex: 'These love affairs seem more or less normal to us.' (Does this mean that they are fairly normal, or fairly abnormal?)

R4: The phoebus exploits tropes, ellipsis*, periphrasis*, litotes* (see litotes, R4), and riddles* (see riddle, R4). One easy way to produce phoebus is to use double figuration (figures within figures). Puns* are a type of phoebus because they are composed of equivoque* combined with concomitant periphrasis* (see pun*, R3). Other devices placed one upon another produce phoebus. Ex: 'No pity for the Marly maze.' In order to decode this, one has to refer to the slogan* (considered typical of middle-class sentimentality): 'Pity the Marly horses [*les chevaux de Marly*].' The muddled middle-class mind may also call up the notion of 'maze' [*écheveau*]. The expression's obscurity springs initially from its superposition of an allusion* (to the slogan) onto an equivoque*. Less obscure is the following ad in a dentist's office: 'Ignore your teeth and they'll go away.' The axiom combines irony* with a possible allusion* to such optimistic proverbial saws as 'Ignorance is bliss' and 'Ignore a problem and it will go away.'

PICTOGRAM 'A written symbol* which denotes a definite object, of which it is a complete or simplified picture' (Pei and Gaynor).

Exx (used in publicity):

In literature, the term might be applied to drawings accompanying the text, to graphisms* (see graphism, R1) whose shapes evoke the thing referred to. Ex: Old S❀L

Ex: Eco uses pictograms in *The Name of the Rose* for cryptographic purposes ('Second Day: Compline') and also to enable readers to follow William of Baskerville's topographical analysis of the monastery library's cataloguing system ('Fourth Day: After Compline').

Analogous terms: drawing, picture, icon (Peirce), ideogram. See also graphy*, R5.

Other definitions: In its more restricted sense, the pictogram is a drawing which transcribes a sentence*, whereas a drawing of a single word is an ideogram (see Crystal [1987] and Dubois et al., *Dictionnaire de linguistique*). But the possible opposition between these two words is sometimes used differently. According to Etiemble (*L'Art d'écrire*, pp. 32–3), pictograms are figurative, whereas ideograms are coded (see symbol*, 3).

R1: *Calligrammes** resemble pictograms, as does the rebus (see allograph*, R1).

R2: *Vignettes*, 'ornament(s) round capital letter etc. or in blank space,' complete a printer's *font* or 'set of type of same face and size' (*Concise Oxford Dictionary*).

PLAN The arrangement of the parts of a work.

The plan, when there is one, varies according to literary genre. But long, complex genres usually require an introduction or exposition, a development – logical, chronological, or organic – and a conclusion, peroration, or *dénouement*, according to whether the genre used is essayistic, oratorical, or dramatic. That is the 'natural order' (Lausberg, sect. 446).

Rhetoric, which came into being with democracy, gave particular attention to the production of detailed plans for public discourse*, in the forensic, deliberative, and ceremonial genres (e.g., academic addresses or those made on special occasions), and later in religious eloquence. The following are the parts outlined by ancient and modern rhetors.

The *exordium*, often supported by a *text*, consists of the proposition or enunciation of the thesis to be defended (Corbett, p. 303). (When pleading at the bar, barristers may have a *narratio* precede the introduction.) A *divisio* follows which outlines the different points to be developed. An *invocation*, addressed to some human, divine, or mythological person, may be inserted at this point.

The main body of the discourse includes the proofs of the proposition; that is, after a skilful *narratio*, the arguments*. The positive arguments forming the *confirmatio* come first (Corbett, Lanham); then comes the defensive strategy: the confutation or refutation* of the opponent's arguments by pointing out objections to them. See Lausberg, sect. 430, and Suberville, pp. 406–10.

The *peroratio* contains a recapitulation of the proposition and its parts, or communicates the emotions aroused by it: indignation, pity, hope, resolve, etc.

R1: We need still to consider what these discursive subdivisions become in literary genres, where they are not codified. The *divisio* is to be found in any scientific treatise; the final emotional appeal appears at the end of personal correspondence. The absence of any kind of subdivision makes of a work a *monobloc*.

R2: Even if its chapters are preceded by an introduction, a book may begin with a *preface* (or set of introductory remarks, sometimes addressed to an authority in the field), or *foreword* (a short discourse*), or a short *notice* from the editor. It may end with a *postface*, even though there is already a conclusion.

R3: *Transitions* between the different parts are presented in order to ensure a better *texture*, or liaison between them (Lausberg). Ex: 'What were the consequences, and what was Yorick's catastrophe thereupon, you will read in the next chapter' (L. Sterne, *Tristram Shandy*, vol. 1, ch. 11).

R4: Balance and naturalness are the two qualities of a plan, but they are difficult to reconcile. Michelet quite justly denounces the speech made by Jean Petit after the assassination of the Duke of Orléans in 1408: 'Exordium: twelve qualities of the Duke of Burgundy; syllogism: major subdivided into three "truths," each in six parts, with eight corollaries, all to say that covetousness deserves death; then the minor: the sin of Orléans was covetousness, which deserves death because covetousness caused four cases of apostasy (plus narratives). Then twelve "proofs" drawn from authorities going from Saint Thomas to the noble Tullius [Cicero]' (Payen, p. 41). This kind of plan has been compared to Gothic architecture; in both, artifice reigns triumphant.

If we wish to avoid an imbalance between parts which are logically articulated but which call for subdivisions and presentations of unequal lengths, the *numbering* of sections (1, 2 ...), subsections (1.1, 1.2 ...), and so on (1.1.1, 1.1.2 ...) offers greater flexibility than the labelling of chapters by Roman numerals (I, II ...), paragraphs by Arabic numerals (§1, §2 ...), points covered by letters (A, B ...), and other divisions by smaller or less bold letters and numerals. Harmony of proportion in architecture or in a discourse* is called *eurhythmy* (*OED*).

R5: See also amplification*; imitation*, R8; letter*; and paragraph*, R2.

PLEONASM 1. A superabundance of words which strengthen what is expressed. See Espy, 1983, p. 124; Fontanier, p. 302; Marouzeau; *OED*; and Quinn, pp. 61–3.

Ex (of double pleonasm): 'I saw with my own eyes, I heard with my own ears.'

2. Redundancy*, using useless words, a defect tending towards battology*. See Lanham, Quinn ('pleonasmus'), Marouzeau, and *OED*.

Ex: 'To be inundated is to be overwhelmed by a wave, and to be redundant is to be overflowing, unnecessarily wordy, tautologous, overabundant, excessive, or using too many synonyms in a single definition' (William Safire, 'On Language,' *New York Times*, 12 Nov. 1983). See also punch* line.

Analogous: perissology* (incorrect pleonasm), tautology*, redundancy*, battology*, asterismos (Quinn, p. 63)

R1: Confusion reigns concerning the terms *pleonasm, perissology*, *redundance* (or *redundancy**), and *battology**. The following distinctions are possible:
1. Pleonasm: repetition* of an idea by the use of two or more different words within the same member of a sentence.
2. Perissology: an (involuntary) pleonasm which produces a mistake*.
3. Redundance/redundancy: repetition of an idea in two separate sentences or two separate members of the same sentence.
4. Battology: excessive, unjustified redundance.
Only pleonasms and redundancy are considered stylistic devices; perissologies and battologies are mistakes* and can only be used as such (in ironical or comic texts).
   Strictly speaking, pleonasms presuppose repetition of the signified without isolexism*. They are one of the most natural forms of emphasis* (e.g., 'He added several supplementary details') which only seems wrong (see perissology*) when blatant (e.g., 'progressively better and better' or 'to foresee in advance'). An example from contemporary literature [from a review of *The Holy Blood, the Holy Grail*, by M. Baigent, R. Leigh, and H. Lincoln]: 'Alternatively, there was no grail: the *sangraal* is the *sang royal*: the title of the book is a pleonasm' (A. Burgess, *But Do Blondes Prefer Gentlemen?*, p. 33).

R2: Both Morier and Quinn criticize pleonasm 'phobia.' Morier distinguishes the 'semi-pleonasm' (e.g., 'a pool of water,' since *pool* alone evokes water despite the fact that pools of oil or blood exist) from 'false pleonasm' (e.g., 'to light a fire,' 'to go up to the attic'). A fire must be lit in order to burn, and despite the fact that an attic is an upstairs room, it is not the only one. In either case precision is needed: we can light other things than fires (candles, passions, etc.) and go upstairs to bed. See also etymology*, other def.

R3: In poetry, enallage* permits one to 'cure' pleonasm. Otherwise, pleonasm seems best avoided. See epitheton*, R1.

POEM (FORMS OF) In antiquity poems were classified in most cases by their content or tone: epic was legendary; eclogue, pastoral; elegy, plaintive; satire, critical; and so on.

In the fourteenth century, the Grands Rhétoriqueurs defined fixed-form poems in French by length of line* and stanza*, rhyme* scheme, and other formal elements. English and North American prosody adopted and adapted antique and modern forms from around the world and originated as well their own in accordance with their own demands and constraints.

Descriptions and examples of all the following poetic forms may be found in Lewis Turco's *The New Book of Forms: A Handbook of Poetics*, Henri Morier's *Dictionnaire de poétique et de rhétorique*, Miller Williams's *Patterns of Poetry*, Frances Stillman's *The Poet's Manual and Rhyming Dictionary*, Philip Davies Roberts's *How Poetry Works*, and Alex Preminger's *Princeton Encyclopedia of Poetry and Poetics: alba, ballade*, ballade royale, blues, calligramme*, cancione, canso, carol, catalog poem, chant royal, chantey, cinquain, clerihew, complaint, double ballade, eclogue, elegy, englyn, epithalamium, hymn, kyrielle, lay* (or *lai, virelay* or *virelai,* plus *virelai nouveau*), *limerick, Little Willie, madrigal, ode** (Pindaric, Horatian, irregular), *rhyme royal, rondeau* (of 10 or 15 lines), *rondeau redoublé, roundel* (French or Chaucerian), *rondelet, sapphic, sestina* (rhymed or unrhymed), *sonnet** (Italian or Petrarchan, English or Shakespearian, Spenserian, Miltonic), *terza rima, triolet, villanelle.*

From the Orient have come the *pantoum* of Malay origin, the *haiku,* a Japanese form in three lines (of 5, 7, and 5 syllables) counting 17 syllables in all, and the *tanka,* also Japanese (5 lines containing 31 syllables: arranged 5,7,5,7,7). From Persia came the *rubai* or *'Omar Khayyam Quatrain'* (Preminger).

The progressive disappearance of fixed forms, a process begun in the nineteenth century, has accompanied the replacement of regular verse forms by free verse. The form chosen no longer predetermines, by convention, versification, spatialization, and theme* (and vice versa). Each poem nowadays possesses its own structure. The task of the stylistic analyst is by no means made easier by the new freedom, and we have much to learn in this field.

Point

In *prose poetry* (or *poèmes en prose*) too, the finished quality of some overall structures, which are being continually renewed, remains scarcely more than intuitively accessible. Observations concerning free-form poetry may be found under rhythm*; line* (of poetry or verse); dialogue*, R1; accumulation*, R4; noise*; *calligramme**; correspondences*; echo* effect, R3; graphic juxtaposition*; letter*, R1; metaphor*, R1; prosopopoeia*, R3; stanza*, R5; and tempo*, R3.

R1: See also acrostic*; epanalepsis*, R3; epanorthosis*, R4; inclusion*; motif*, 2; rhyme*, 2; well-wishing*, R4; metrical verse (under line* of poetry); adynaton*, R1; assonance*; maxim*; tempo*; and harmony*.

POINT 'Subtle ideas (generally very short and witty presented in antithetical form) aiming to challenge the reader's wit' (M.W. Croll, *Style, Rhetoric and Rhythm*, p. 29).

Exx: 'What oft was thought, but ne'er so well expressed' (A. Pope, *An Essay on Criticism*, l. 298); 'In this abbey something has happened that requires the attention and counsel of an acute and prudent man such as you are. Acute in uncovering, and prudent (if necessary) in covering' (U. Eco, *The Name of the Rose*, p. 29).

Other definition: Lanham (p. 78) speaks of the 'pointed style,' adding that the expression was used in discussions of seventeenth-century prose style to refer to 'a style usually *Senecan* [curt, paratactic sentences expressing *sententiae* or aphorisms] in which rhetorical figures (often schemes, especially those of balance and antithesis*, of word- and sound-play) are used to clarify, reinforce, "point" a meaning. The effect is often epigrammatic ... The noun "point" often means the *Sententia*, or meaning, which was thus epigrammatically expressed.'

R1: In its purest form, the point is an irresistible quip used for ending a paragraph* (just as the hit completes a series of passes in fencing). Ex: '*Interpreter*, n. One who enables two persons of different languages to understand each other by repeating to each what it would have been to the interpreter's advantage for the other to have said' (Ambrose Bierce, *The Devil's Dictionary*). Points may take the form of aporia (see riddle*, R1). They presuppose wit* in both producer and receiver.

R2: Modern points quite readily replace reasoning* with word-play*, antimetabole*, etc. Ex: 'The weapon of criticism certainly cannot replace the criticism of weapons' (K. Marx, *Critique of Hegel's 'Philosophy of Right'*, p. 137). Bierce's stories and short pieces frequently end with a formal point of this kind. Ex: '*Christianity in Action*. On last Monday two little Christians (with a big C) were up before his Honor (with a big H) for pelting a Chinaman with rocks. On account of their youth, good character, color, nationality, religion and the politics of their

347

Polysyndeton

fathers, they were let off with a reprimand' (*The Devil's Advocate: An Ambrose Bierce Reader*, p. 109).

R3: Like conceits*, which they resemble, points may combine metaphor* with antimetabole*. Ex: 'And he answered that the beauty of the cosmos derives not so much from unity in variety, but also from variety in unity' (U. Eco, *The Name of the Rose*, p. 16).

POLYSYNDETON The repetition* of conjunctions more frequently than grammatical order demands (see Littré). See also Lanham, Lausberg, and Preminger.

Ex: 'And the basement kitchen in nipping February, with napkins on the line slung across from door to chockablock corner, and a bicycle by the larder very much down at wheels, and hats and toy engines and bottles and spanners on the broken rocking chair, and billowing papers and half-finished crosswords stacked on the radio always turned full tilt, and the fire smoking, and onions peeling, and chips always spitting on the stove, and small men in their overcoats talking of self-discipline and the ascetic life until the air grew woodbine-blue and the clock choked and the traffic died' (Dylan Thomas, *Quite Early One Morning*, pp. 40–1).

Other name: polysyntheton (Lausberg)

Antonym: asyndeton*

R1: According to Quintilian (9.3), polysyndeton and asyndeton* are complementary: the two figures are no more than an accumulation* of words or sentences piled one upon another; the only difference is that conjunctions are sometimes added and sometimes omitted. In 'normal' accumulations, in both English and French, a single *and* or *et* suffices (e.g., 'The tailor, his son, and the dog'). This practice is intermediate between the two figures.

R2: According to Corbett (pp. 470–1) and Quinn (p. 13), polysyndeton, by slowing down a sentence, may add 'dignity' to it, produce an incantatory effect, or 'produce the flow and continuity of experience' (Corbett, p. 470). According to Cressot (see *Le Français moderne* 9 [1941], pp. 82–3), the repetition of *et* has rather a disjunctive than a conjunctive function. The example from Dylan Thomas quoted above seems equally to illustrate that the English *and*, when used in enumerations, tends to produce a catalogue or inventory of discrete items, be they objects, persons, or actions.

R3: Polysyndeton produces binary or ternary structures by using *and*, *or*, etc. to group elements in pairs, triplets, and so on. Other conjunctions may be repeated: 'After the sunsets and the dooryards and the sprinkled streets, / After the novels, after the teacups, after the skirts that trail along the floor' (T.S. Eliot, 'The Love Song of J. Alfred Prufrock,' ll. 101–2).

R4: We speak of polysyndeton in the case of co-ordinating conjunctions, but it seems also to exist in that of *sub*ordinating conjunctions, and even in that of connecting adverbs. Ex: '*If* both of the lines A and C are parallel to the line B, *then* the lines A and C are parallel to one another.'

PORTMANTEAU WORD
The amalgamation of two words on the basis of partial homophony, with the result that each retains enough of its original lexical physiognomy to remain recognizable.

Exx: 'brunch' (< breakfast + lunch); 'steakwiches' (< steak + sandwiches); 'smog' (< smoke + fog)

Ex: 'When a man fell into his anecdotage it was a sign for him to retire from the world' (B. Disraeli, *Lothair*, ch. 28) (< anecdote + dotage). See also 'conversationmanship' (R. Ebert, *Two Weeks in the Midday Sun*, p. 41) (< conversation + one-upmanship, an allusion* to Stephen Potter's *OneUpmanship* [1952]).

Synonyms: blend, lexical interlocking, centaur-word (Redfern, p. 88), telescope word, semantic conflation

Antonyms: etymology*; deportmanteau word ('the division of a portmanteau word into its original constitutive elements' [Oulipo, *A Primer of Potential Literature*, p. 198])

R1: The device usually aims at creating semantic syllepsis*. Ex: '*Time* magazine and theatrical columnists are well known for the technique of intentionally combining two words to form the new blend: *slanguage*, *sextraordinary*, and *alcoholidays*' (Peter Farb, *Word Play*, p. 307).

R2: Michaux indicates one of the device's psychic origins: 'Some insane people for whom there are impressions ... which impose themselves uncontrollably, which attain consciousness impetuously and *all at the same time* ... create, out of necessity, new words ... Thus, a mentally sick person may repeat endlessly "*penetraversed*," i.e., penetrated at the same time as traversed' (H. Michaux, *Connaissance par les gouffres*, p. 128). Michaux himself experimented with the phenomenon, creating among others the word *monstruellement* (< *monstrueusement*/monstrously + *cruellement*/cruelly) in *Paix dans les brisements*. See also lapsus*.

R3: If a word invented in this way enters the language, linguists speak of a blend word, or one obtained by blending (Adams, Bauer), or by contamination (Pei and Gaynor). The phenomenon also exists in nature: crossing a horse with a donkey produces a mule.

R4: Modelled on children's counting-out rhymes (e.g., 'Eeny, meeny, myny, mo'), there is a game which consists of inventing potential portmanteau words or telescoped sentences (see telescoping*).

R5: Portmanteau words are not far removed from coinages* and paragrams.

PORTRAIT 'A physical and moral description* of an animate being, either real or fictional' (Fontanier, p. 428). See also Lausberg, Littré, Quillet, and Robert. In English, definitions of *portrait* refer more specifically to graphic representation than to written descriptions; nor do they usually make the distinction between physical and moral traits; see *OED*.

Ex: 'Her nose must once have been what was called cute but now was too small for her face. Her face was not fat but it was large. Two lines led downwards from the corners of her mouth; between them was her chin, clenched like a fist' (Margaret Atwood's *The Handmaid's Tale*, p. 15).

Analogous: *prosopographia*, physical description (Fontanier, Joseph, Lanham, Lausberg); *effictio* or *blazon* ('the head-to-toe itemization of a heroine's charms' [Lanham]); *ethopoeia*, moral description (Fontanier, Joseph, Lanham, Lausberg); character-study. The French term *portrait-charge* indicates an unkind character sketch or caricature*.

R1: Like any form of description, portraits may be drawn from a character's viewpoint, with or without identification occurring between author/narrator and character, or between reader and character. The narrator of Robertson Davies's *What's Bred in the Bone* comments on the subjective use of portrait-making made by creator, sitter, and receiver: '... Francis [an artist] learned ... that a portrait is, among other things, a statement of opinion by the artist, as well as a "likeness," which was what everybody wanted it to be' (p. 107).

R2: The physical and moral portrait has long had the dignity of a literary genre and, as a principal means of representing character, has often been used as a criterion for judging fiction. See R. Fowler, 'Character,' in *A Dictionary of Modern Critical Terms* (1987). Joyce's *Portrait of the Artist as a Young Man*, as well as Dylan Thomas's *Portrait of the Artist as a Young Dog*, might be taken as incorporating exemplary modern forms of the humorous portrait. The following displays a dramatic shift of viewpoint: 'One minute I was small and cold, skulking dead-scared down a black passage in my stiff, best suit, with my hollow belly thumping and my heart like a time bomb, clutching my grammar school cap, unfamiliar to myself, a snub-nosed storyteller lost in his own adventures and longing to be home; the next I was a royal nephew in smart town clothes, embraced and welcomed, standing in the snug centre of my stories and listening to the clock announcing me' (D. Thomas, 'The Peaches,' in *Portrait of the Artist as a Young Dog*, p. 4).

R3: Portraits may also be 'dramatic' in another sense: produced, that is, by 'showing' rather than 'telling.' The change in perspective in the previous example might have been achieved by a narrative* of action or through dialogue*. See hypotyposis*, R4.

PRAEMUNITIO (L. 'strengthening beforehand') Preparing one's hearers to receive some proposition that might offend them, if it were introduced too abruptly. See Littré.

Exx: 'For the most wild, yet most homely narrative which I am about to pen, I neither expect nor solicit belief. Mad indeed would I be to expect it, in a case where my very senses reject their evidence ... Hereafter, perhaps, some intellect may be found which will reduce my phantasm to the common-place ...' (E.A. Poe, opening lines of 'The Black Cat'); 'Let me light another Schimmelpenninck and be coarse. A friend of mine slept with one of these exquisite dream figures [i.e., mannequins] and said it was like going to bed with a bicycle' (A. Burgess, *But Do Blondes Prefer Gentlemen?*, p. 86).

Analogous: *'procatasceue* (G. "prepares beforehand"): giving an audience a gradual preparation and buildup before telling them about something done; *diorthosis; prodiorthosis; praecedens correctio'* (Lanham). See also response*, R2.

R1: The *praemunitio* frequently forms part of the preface or 'notice' to the reader.

PRAYER Texts, either private or officially recognized by some religious denomination, by means of which one addresses some transcendental or immanent being, greater and more powerful than oneself.

Exx:

Now I lay me down to sleep;
I pray the Lord my soul to keep.
If I should die before I wake,
I pray the Lord my soul to take.
> Anon. First printed in the *New England Primer*, 1781

O God, if there be a God, save my soul, if I have a soul!
> Anon. Prayer of a common soldier before the battle of Blenheim.
> Quoted in Newman's *Apologia pro Vita Sua*, 1864

O Death, where is thy sting-a-ling-a-ling,
O Grave, thy victoree?
The bells of Hell go ting-a-ling-a-ling
For you but not for me.
> Anon. Song popular in the British Army in France, 1914–18

Prayer

Analogous: orison (archaic), meditation (reflection rather than adoration), paternoster, rosary

R1: Prayers generally begin with an invocation in the form of an apostrophe* which performs the phatic function of establishing 'contact' (see enunciation*). Ex: At the beginning of the psalms, we read formulas like 'How lovely is thy dwelling place, O Lord of Hosts!' (Psalm 84). The formula of address has become fixed, an interjection* almost devoid of meaning*, as in current forms like 'My God, how she's changed!'

After the apostrophe*, there may follow one of the many forms of entreaty (see supplication*, R1, and exorcism*) or a benediction (see celebration*), a curse (see well-wishing*), or a dialogue*. **Ex:**

Glory be to God for dappled things.
...
All things counter, original, spare, strange;
Whatever is fickle, freckled (who knows how?)
With swift, slow; sweet, sour; adazzle, dim;
He fathers-forth whose beauty is past change:
> Praise him.
>> Gerard Manley Hopkins, 'Pied Beauty'

Protests are not ruled out, though they may be softened, as in Milton's sonnet 'On His Blindness':

'Doth God exact day-labor, light denied?'
I fondly ask. But Patience, to prevent
That murmur, soon replies, 'God does not need
Either man's work or his own gifts.'

The ending of a prayer has a marker: *Amen*. See punch* line, R2.

R2: The Being, of whatever nature, addressed by what are called the 'religious' figures of speech, need be only very broadly identified as something or someone greater and more powerful than the speaker. Such a Being must be thought to be more capable of bringing to fruition some plan involving either the world, in general, or merely the speaker. The transcendental nature of such a Being, to which we will refer simply as the *source of Power*, becomes particularly clear in requests made for victory over an enemy, or for the turning aside of some disaster, etc. The immanence, or innate power of such a Being, seems to be some form of inner strength. Ex: 'Blessed be He in homosexuality! Blessed be He in Paranoia! Blessed be He in the city! Blessed be He in the Book! Blessed be He who dwells in the shadow!' (Allen Ginsberg, 'Hymmnn,' in Ellmann, ed., *The Oxford Book of American Verse*, p. 928).

R3: According to J. Ladrière ('La Performativité du langage liturgique,' *Concilium* 82, nos. 7–8 [Feb. 1973], p. 58f), liturgical language, particularly in the Christian variety, is *performative* from three points of view. (1) It 'arouses a certain affective disposition' [in the listener], such as 'confidence, veneration, gratitude, submission, contrition, etc.' (2) It creates a community of speakers, who speak of themselves as 'we' and 'us,' and who, as they participate in the communion service, become 'members of Christ's body.' (3) By repeating the historical words uttered by Christ, by testifying in unison to the accomplishment of the mystery, and by accomplishing again the sacrament of the Last Supper, speakers cause a particular eschatological event from the past to recur in the present.

PRETERITION 'A figure by which summary mention is made of a thing, in professing to omit it' (*OED*). See also Lanham, Lausberg, Littré, and Morier. Both Quinn (pp. 70–1) and Fontanier (p. 143) add that such a declaration of omission is in fact a way of emphasizing the allegedly omitted material.

Exx: 'If I were to call any figure inherently disreputable (which, of course, I will not), this would be the one. Nor will I mention that the only American president who repeatedly used the praeteritio was also the only one who had to resign' (Quinn, p. 71); 'The giant rat of Sumatra, a story for which the world is not yet prepared' (Conan Doyle, 'The Sussex Vampire,' in *The Case Book of Sherlock Holmes*).

Ex:

> He won't talk any more of the distant days
> Of his childhood in the coalface and the tavern
> And all his cronies who had left him behind
> In the ragged little hut by the river
> W.H. Davies, 'The Angry Summer,' in Collected Poems

Synonyms: paralipsis (Corbett, p. 490, Joseph, p. 325, Lausberg, Morier, Robert); paralepsis (Lanham); pretermission (Fontanier, Lausberg, Littré, Morier, OED, Robert). Lanham also gives: *occupatio, occultatio,* and *parasiopesis.*

R1: As already pointed out, the device is eminently rhetorical (see false–*, R1). It draws attention to the interplay between enunciation* (uttering) and *utterance* (content, *lexis*, or *dictum*; in logic, the latter two terms indicate what is said independently of a thing's truth or 'virtual value'). When enunciation ceases to be implicit (an utterance being preceded by 'I say'), it becomes possible for it to contradict itself ('I am not saying that ...'), which may shake its authority, reducing the force of an affirmation to that of an uncertain idea. The device may begin with attenuation*, though not with litotes*. Ex: 'I'm not saying that you get a load of riffraff down the mine, I'm just saying that we had a load of riffraff down *my* mine' (A. Bennett, P. Cook, J. Miller, and D. Moore, 'Sitting on the Bench,' in *The Complete Beyond the Fringe*, p. 97). Or else the expression conceals an apodioxis (see argument*, R2): 'It would take too long to demonstrate here that ...,' (the conclusion of which statement implies nonetheless that the demonstration has indeed taken place).

Apparent preterition is sometimes only a summary: 'I will not say that he is the author of twelve books ...' In other words, 'I will not spend much time on this fact, important though it may be.' Expressions like 'I don't need to tell you that ...,' 'I won't remind you how ...,' as well as 'not to mention ...' and 'to say nothing of ...' (Quinn, p. 71) are also semi-preteritions which hardly emphasize an utterance, except in certain contexts. Others draw attention to the speaker's hesitation: 'Mr Sicaro, without wishing to name him.' The expression is normally a kind of excuse* which means the person in question must be named, or that some (disagreeable) words must be used. Ex: 'I have said these things to you, Brother William, obviously not to gossip about the abbot or other brothers. God save me, fortunately I do not have the nasty habit of gossiping' (U. Eco, *The Name of the Rose*, p. 125). Semi-preteritions may also foregound euphemisms*. Ex: '... the morgue (a not very enticing locality, not to say gruesome to a degree, more especially at night)' (Joyce, *Ulysses*, p. 502). True preterition is a form of pseudo-simulation, concealing the better to display. This is particularly useful in discussion, but the reason may also lie in a lack of the appropriate term. Ex: 'O charms of love, who could describe you!' (Constant, *Adolphe*).

Alphonse Allais foregrounds preterition in order to ridicule the device: 'Professional ethics prevent me from revealing my patient's identity, and so I will not name him in this letter. However, not wishing to seem a joker, I will simply say that the said sick man is called A. L..., a grocer in St H... on S... (Hautes-Alpes), who should be contacted for information. (All the proper names contained in parentheses are given fully. The editors of *Sourire* decided, however, that the initials alone would be amply sufficient)' (A. Allais, *La Barbe et autres contes*, p. 109).

R2: Another kind of preterition consists in the pretence that one has no wish to do what one then proceeds to do. Ex: 'I am not trying to discourage (or offend, disillusion, bore) you, but ...' Compare the expression 'Allow me to play devil's advocate.' Whether such expressions are made sincerely or whether, on the contrary, speakers are simply using litotes* makes no great difference to their effect. Ex: 'FIRST FURY: I have no ulterior motive, nor any wish to influence you ... But if a word such as this one [i.e., "yours"] were to kill your sister, we would be very happy!' (Jean Giraudoux, *Electre*, 1.12). See also aposiopesis*, R2.

R3: We might call the opposite device, namely, reminding the reader that one has already said something before repeating it, *counterpreterition*. Ex: 'But I remember, I think, that I have already offered this description; I have already told you of the high wall of hedges which end by imprisoning you, this path ...' (Goethe, *The Sorrows of Young Werther*, trans. E. Mayer and L. Bogan, p. 83).

R4: Preterition may be compared to *dubitatio**. Ex: 'Dare I speak of Chronology ... Dare I disturb your youthful notion of causality ... Will I tell you that the passing years ...' (P. Valéry, *Oeuvres*, 1:1131). See also transition*.

R5: Umberto Eco points out the use made of preterition by narrators of historical novels: the device serves to communicate the 'background' information necessary to the reader's understanding of the action: 'Adso's narrative style is based on that rhetorical device called preterition or paralepsis, or "passing over" ... The speaker, in other words, claims he will not speak of something that everyone knows perfectly well, and as he is saying this, he speaks of the thing. This is more or less the way Adso mentions people and events as being well known but still does speak of them' (U. Eco, *Postscript to 'The Name of the Rose,'* p. 39).

PRETEXT An irrefutable argument* whose only defect, one difficult to denounce flatly, is that it is false or irrelevant to the point at issue.

Ex: a political party claiming to rise above party politics. See abstraction*, R6.

Ex: 'By being so long in the lowest form [at Harrow] I gained an immense advantage over the cleverer boys ... I got into my bones the essential structure of the ordinary English sentence – which is a noble thing' (W.S. Churchill, *My Early Life*, ch. 2). In order to prove his point (that is, that being a dunce is no bad thing), he shifts the question. See also concession*, R3.

Synonym: pareuresis

R1: In riddles* or conundrums, word-play* supplies pretexts as solutions. Ex: 'What has four legs and flies? A dead horse.'

PROLEPSIS 'A figure in which objections or arguments* are anticipated in order to preclude their use, answer them in advance, or prepare them for an unfavourable reaction: = *Procatalepsis*' (OED). See also Fontanier (p. 410), Grambs, Lanham, Lausberg, and Morier (sense 2).

Exx: 'I know it will be said, continued my father (availing himself of the Prolepsis), that [sex] in itself, and simply taken – like hunger, or thirst, or sleep – 'tis an affair neither good or bad – or shameful or otherwise' (Laurence Sterne, *Tristram Shandy*, vol. 9, ch. 33); 'I must declare an interest. Jeffrey Cook's book on Romantic drama sets out to refute (most courteously) one of the central proposals in *The Death of Tragedy*. In that book I argued ...' (George Steiner, *TLS*, 12–18 Feb. 1988, p. 168).

Synonymous: procatalepsis (Peacham); 'anticipation and answering of an opposing argument or objection' (Grambs); 'pre-emptive strike in argument' (Cuddon); anticipated refutation* or prevention; anticipation (Lanham [*anticipatio*], Scaliger, Bary, 1:426); *praeoccupatio* (Lanham, Fontanier); *praeceptio, praesumptio, presumptuous* (Lanham); *ante occupatio* (Fontanier, Lanham, Littré)

Other definitions: *anticipation* in the term's several senses, including narrative flash-forward* (Cuddon, Genette, *OED*, Littré); dislocation*; pregnant meaning (Marouzeau, Morier; see meaning*, 5)

R1: Prolepsis has two parts. The first puts words into the opponent's mouth by expressions like 'You will say ...,' 'You will object ...,' etc. According to Lamy (see Le Hir, p. 136), this is the prolepsis proper. The second part refutes the putative objection. Lamy calls this the *upobola*.

A more detailed scenario includes anticipated dialogue*. But we should distinguish clearly between prolepsis and *subjectio* (responding in the place of an accused person; see question*, R3) since prolepsis is not concerned with an opponent's real objection.

The second part may take any form of refutation*, including apodioxis and disqualification (see argument*, R2), or excuses*. Ex: 'I apologize in advance for the weakness of my case, to which you will object ...'

PROPHECY The confident announcement* of some future event by an individual vouchsafed knowledge of it by some transcendental Being on whom the future may depend.

Ex [An eagle passes overhead; Helen stands up and says]: 'Listen, while with such inspiration as I have I explain this omen and what I feel sure it portends. Just as this eagle came down from his native mountains and pounced on our home-fed goose, so shall Odysseus, after many hardships and many wanderings, reach his home and have his revenge' (Homer, *The Odyssey*, trans. E.V. Rieu, book 15).

Ex (from modern publicity): 'Try brand X, and you'll find it will reduce the work by half.'

Synonymous: foretelling, oracle (see riddle*), vaticination, prognostication, diabole (Lanham)

R1: The temporality of the utterance coincides with that of its enunciation* thus conferring upon the device its considerable illocutionary power. Prophecies simulate or postulate future accomplishment. Such power is impossible in narrative* save by the introduction of some second-degree utterance. A similar reduction of illocutionary force occurs when prophecy becomes merely the announcement* of some future consensus. Ex: 'Those who love beauty of language will continue to denigrate such neologisms' (Greimas). Michaux's striking paradoxes* are too universal in scope to be prophecies: 'In the darkness we shall see clearly, my brothers / In the labyrinth, we shall find the true path' (*L'Espace du dedans*, p. 152). But the use of the future tense with precise, unique temporal actualization is sufficient to make the most banal of texts into a prophecy. Ex: 'You will see him a little later ... A friend will be with him, and you will hear these words' (Queneau, 'Prognostication,' in *Exercises in Style*, p. 15). The only thing missing is the claim to be divinely inspired. It is the making of such a claim which distinguishes prophecy from mere forecasts, declarations of intent or conviction, and promises. See flash-forward*, R1.

Future time is sometimes only implied, as in the following title* of a report on pollution: 'The Final Thirty Years of the Earth.'

R2: *Curses* are prophecies of disaster. Ex [The Lord will say on the seventh day after the coming of the Antichrist]: 'Far from me, ye accursed, into the eternal fire that has been prepared for you by the Devil and his ministers! You yourselves have earned it and now enjoy it! Go ye from me, descending into the eternal darkness and into the unquenchable fire!' (U. Eco, *The Name of the Rose*, p. 405). As the example shows, prophecies may take apocalyptic form. See apocalypse* and supplication*, R1.

R3: Different from prophecy is *kerygma*, evangelical proclamation or preaching (*OED*), in which what is proclaimed in the name of the Deity is some quasi-present event. Ex: 'You know the word which he [God] sent to Israel, preaching good news of peace, preaching good news of peace by Jesus Christ (he is Lord of all), the word which was proclaimed throughout all Judea ...' (Acts of the Apostles, 10:36–7).

R4: Unlike prophecies proclaimed to all hearers, *premonitions* are confused glimpses of what may occur at some future time.

PROSOPOPOEIA The 'presentation of absent, dead, or supernatural beings, or even inanimate objects, with the ability to act, speak, and respond' (Fontanier, p. 404). See also Espy (1983), Lanham, Lausberg, Littré, Morier, *OED*, and Preminger.

Ex (quoted by Fontanier): 'O Fabricius! What would your great soul have said ...? Gods! what would you have said, what have they become, these thatched cottages and rustic hearths where used to live moderation and virtue?' (J.-J. Rousseau, *Discours sur les Sciences et les Arts*).

R1: Prosopopoeia is a figure of elevated or 'sublime' style (see grandiloquence*, R1). Fontanier adds (as do many other collectors of rhetorical tropes and figures) that prosopopoeia should not be confused with personification*, apostrophe*, or dialogism (see dialogue*). But the three figures often go together. Ex: 'With how sad steps, O Moon, thou climb'st the skies' (Sir Philip Sidney, *Astrophel and Stella*, l. 31). Dialogism involves giving speech to an absent being or to a personified inanimate object who then converses; apostrophe involves an address to the being or object; and personification only occurs if the being presented is not already a person.

R2: Prosopopoeia is an odd figure. A narrative* figure, since that is where one usually finds it, it nonetheless rejects the double actualization implicit in narrative (what is told in the past being lived in the present by characters and readers). It does so by striving to present as direct enunciation* what is being recounted at second hand. Characters become real speakers; hence the use of apostrophe* and dialogism. Absent persons or objects take their place in the present. The following examples show the figure's capacity to suggest effects close to *hallucination*, as the personifying details produce 'human' figures from an inanimate object, and then from an abstraction*:

Thou still unravished bride of quietness,
Thou foster-child of Silence and slow Time,
Sylvan historian, who canst thus express
A flowery tale more sweetly than our rhyme.
Keats, 'Ode on a Grecian Urn'

Who hath not seen thee oft amid thy store?
Sometimes whoever seeks abroad may find
Thee sitting careless on a granary floor,
Thy hair soft-lifted by the winnowing wind;
Or on a half-reaped furrow sound asleep,
Drowsed with the fume of poppies, while thy hook
Spares the next swath and all its twinèd flowers:
And sometimes like a gleaner thou dost keep
Steady thy laden head across a brook;
Or by a cider-press, with patient look,
Thou watchest the last oozings hours by hours.
Keats, 'Ode to Autumn'

Unexpected or unconventional (see false –*, R1) prosopopoeia may produce *delirious exaltation* (see reactualization*, 7).

R3: Does prosopopoeia share with other figures, hypotyposis* for example, the characteristic of making present what is absent? Besides characters, might not places, scenes, and events be made present? But hypotyposis, by describing things *as if* we could see them, remains within a narrative* framework, whereas Keats's personification* of Autumn dramatizes the absent abstraction* in a present setting by the use of the present tense. See also metaphor*, R4.

We call *evocation* the general device which takes some element of a distant or past content and installs it in a present enunciation*. Hypotyposis* is purely formal or rhetorical evocation, whereas evocation in the strong sense possesses a surrealistic or obsessive nature. Ex: Michaux's poem entitled 'Projection' (*L'Espace du dedans*, pp. 58–9). *Delirious exaltation* is an evocation of imaginary things. Evocation also occurs when we see a past event for a second time. Ex: ' "There's the saucepan that the gruel was in!" cried Scrooge, starting off again, and frisking round the fire-place. "There's the door, by which the Ghost of Jacob Marley entered! There's the corner, where the Ghost of Christmas Present, sat! There's the window where I saw the wandering spirits! It's all right, it's all true, it all happened" ' (Dickens, *A Christmas Carol*, stave five).

In the cinema, *special effects* are means used to make the fantastic* seem true (the hero 'climbs' a cliff-face, which in reality is a horizontal mock-up). In the same way, we might identify in literature the (false*) means serving to 'authenticate' a narrative*. One example is the letter to the editor declaring that the text was 'found' among the papers of a dead character (e.g., Benjamin Constant's *Adolphe*) or in a bottle rescued from the sea (e.g., Poe's 'MS. Found in a Bottle').

R4: The use of prosopopoeia as a rhetorical argument* is risky. When L. Pauwels, in his 'Lettre ouverte aux gens heureux' ('Open Letter to the Fortunate'), puts words into Lenin's mouth, the style remains that of Pauwels.

PROSTHESIS The addition of a letter or syllable at the beginning of a word (see *OED*), without changing the latter's meaning* (see Littré). See also Jacobs (p. 123), Joseph, Lanham, Lausberg, and Thomas Wilson (*The Arte of Rhetorique*).

Exx: grudge/begrudge; weep/beweep (Quinn)

Synonym: prothesis (*OED*, Marouzeau, Robert)

R1: As the definition reveals, English and French usages differ. English does not insist that the additional element bring no change to the word's meaning or value. Thus Lanham quotes, for example, the word *irregardless*, in which the addition of the redundant prefix *ir-* makes the term grammatically incorrect.

R2: Prosthesis is a term from ancient grammar corresponding nowadays to a device classified among metaplasms*. **Exx:** 'yestereve'; 'Horhot ho hray ho rhother's hest' (Joyce; see Group MU, p. 51).

R3: Gemination* is a form of prosthesis. **Exx:** geegee; ack-ack.

PROVERB A maxim* in common use, applicable in various contexts.

Ex:

> POLONIUS: Be thou familiar, but by no means vulgar.
> ...
> Give every man thy ear, but few thy voice.
> Take each man's censure, but reserve thy judgement.
> Costly thy habit as thy purse can buy
> ...
> For the apparel oft proclaims the man
> ...
> Neither a borrower nor a lender be
> ...
> This above all: To thine own self be true
>
> Shakespeare, *Hamlet*, 1.3.61–78

Here the use of proverbs, although it may be ironic, does not turn clichés* into 'perverbs,' or perverted proverbs. Jacobs lists the following: 'Familiarity breeds children; Time wounds all heels; Flatulence is an ill wind that blows good to nobody; She is every yard a queen; He is every other inch a gentleman; A straight line is the shortest distance between two joints; Many are called but few get the right number; Scratch a Russian and he'll appreciate the favour; Hitch your wagon to a movie star' (*Naming Day in Eden*, p. 132).

Analogous: adage, dictum, tag

Other definition: See riddle*, 5.

R1: We may consider proverbs to be well-known expressions, about the length of a simple sentence*, which function in conversation as do clichés*, other fixed expressions shorter than proverbs. Indeed, although proverbs may seem to have a fixed meaning*, they may in fact take on meanings which depend on their context; and texts may be adapted and substitutions* made, as Jacobs's list clearly shows. See also simile*, R3.

R2: Expressions become proverbial through quotation*. They come from ancient collections of wise sayings (e.g., 'Man does not live by bread alone') or from celebrated statements, which may be of recent date (e.g., 'I shall return' [General MacArthur]). Paroemiologists study them and paroegraphers prepare collections of them. Turco (p. 59) defines *parimia* as 'speak[ing] by means of proverbs ("An apple a day keeps the doctor away." That's true – he'd rather have money as pay).' See *The Oxford Dictionary of English Proverbs* (1970).

R3: As a form sedimented by diverse cultures, proverbs cannot refer to any single coherent or non-contradictory system of thought. Exx (two French proverbs): 'Father a miser, son a waster' versus 'Like father like son.' And John Ferguson reminds us, by means of a pun*: 'Proverbial saws, for example, make dangerous major premises: many hands make light work, but too many cooks spoil the broth. And many arguments have fallen apart because the disputants, as Mark Pattison said of the cleaning-women shouting at one another from opposite doorways, have been arguing from different premises' (John Ferguson, *Aristotle*, p. 40).

R4: See also semantic syllepsis*, R4, and literary* games.

PSEUDO-LANGUAGE Pseudo-language occurs in a segment of a text which possesses clarity of form from the viewpoints of sound, rhythm*, and melody, and even from a graphic perspective, and thus seems to be made up of words, but which has no lexeme in current use, no accepted grammatical form, nor any clear syntactic function. Pseudo-language imitates regularly constituted and officially recognized language. It transmits, for example, a sung melody (e.g., 'hi ho'; 'la lalala la'), notably in children's counting-out rhymes.

Exx: 'Yan, tan tethera, pethera, pimp, sethera, lethera, hovera ...' (Lincolnshire rhyme quoted by Augarde, p. 168); '... Tuesday will be the longest day. Of all the glad new year mother, the rum tum tiddledy tum' (Joyce, *Ulysses*, p. 42).

Synonymous: sounds without meaning; a string of meaningless syllables; metalalia (neol.)

R1: Pseudo-language is the privileged mode for emphasizing the phatic function of communication (see enunciation*, 2). Here, for example, is the preamble by which the story-teller, during an evening spent around the fire in French-Canadian homes long ago, would get the attention of a noisy group: 'Cric, crac, les enfants! Parli, parlo, parlons! Pour en savoir le court et le long, passez l'crachoir à Jos Violon. Sacatabi, sac-à-tabac! A la porte les ceuses qu'écouteront pas!' ('Snap, crack, children! Parla, parly, let's palaver! To know the long and short of it, give an ear to Violon Joe. Sackbacky, backysack! Outside them as won't listen!') (L. Fréchette, 'Tom Caribou,' in *Contes de Jos Violon*, p. 35).

The function of the interjection *nuhh nuhh nuhh* (frequently accompanied by a discouraging gesture*) is to prevent a speaker from continuing.

R2: Pseudo-language may separate itself from regular language, thus prolonging it, or slip back into it. See musication*, R3. It may derive from some mental disturbance (see mistake*, R2).

R3: *Lallation* ('childish utterance' [*OED*]), a vocalic emission made without expressive intent by a baby at the breast, is the first form of pseudo-language. *Glossomania* or imitation* of the sounds of language is the final stage, which interjections* (see interjection, R4) may approach. Glossolalia* differs from lallation and glossomania because it possesses a definite intended meaning.

PSEUDO-SIMULATION Pretence which is foregrounded or explained in the text in which it appears. The simulation* thus becomes obvious, since it makes no attempt to conceal itself. It would be redundant to 'expose' it as such since it cancels itself out, while still remaining effective.

Exx:

HITLER ARRESTED IN TORQUAY
Neighbours of the Hitlers in exclusive Brazilia Drive, were shocked to learn that the quietly-spoken, retiring man who they knew simply as 'Der Fuehrer,' was a wanted criminal. (Richard Ingrams, ed., *The Life and Times of Private Eye, 1961–1971*, p. 212)

– 'Are you a strict t.t.?' says Joe.
– 'Not taking anything between drinks,' says I. (Joyce, *Ulysses*, p. 241)

Other name: counter-simulation. Any defamiliarizing device of narrative* or pictorial representation which exposes the mimetic illusion is a form of counter-simulation. Thus René Magritte's picture of a pipe entitled *Ceci n'est pas une pipe* ('This is not a pipe') reminds us that it is a picture of one. Similarly, Nabokov's short story 'The Vane Sisters' came accompanied with a note suggesting that 'puzzle-minded readers may be interested in looking for the coded message [an acrostic*] that occurs in the last page of the story' (example cited by Hutchinson, p. 36).

R1: The theory of pseudo-simulation was outlined by Jean Simeray ('Erreur simulée et logique différentielle,' *Communications*, no. 16, pp. 36–59), who upheld that the device is important in all forms of literature, including poetry, where it takes the form of metaphor*. Clearly, any kind of theatrical performance routinely employs pseudo-simulation.

In order that the examples quoted remain brief, we need to take them from among fairly obvious deliberate mistakes. Thus the 'yelling of a toothless baby' (R. Queneau, *Le Chiendent*, p. 119) gives us to understand that the reason for the newborn child's lack of teeth comes from its having lost them. Also expressions like 'I was receiving congratulations from the four corners of the circular globe' or 'Stop those carefully rehearsed and written *ad libs*' ('Tales of Old Dartmoor,' in *Best of the Goon Shows*, BBC recording, 7 Feb. 1956 [Parlophone Records]) call attention, by means of a contradiction in terms, to much-used but illogical or misused clichés*.

R2: A particularly indirect form of pseudo-simulation involves the speaker's pretending to believe that the receiver will imagine something incorrect, or even impossible, and that the receiver therefore needs to have his or her eyes opened. Ex: 'Bombs do not have homes to go to. They are always in a hurry all the same' (H. Michaux, *L'Espace du dedans*, p. 278). The pretended mistake involves the presupposition that the receiver will try to understand bombs in terms of selfish people. Singularization* simulates ignorance of certain prejudices.

R3: Preterition*, *permissio**, and truisms* are almost always cases of pseudo-simulation. Morier mentions a figure, *paryponoian* (a French form of the Greek *par 'uponoian*), by means of which we 'pretend to believe that an idea springs from its opposite (e.g.: his eyes sparkled with stupidity)'. See blunder*, R3.

R4: Jokes may incorporate pseudo-simulation. Ex: 'Malaises have been sighted in different parts of the country ... almost all described as "deep-seated" ... One man said "I have seen no Malaise, matey. Deep-seated or the other. Malays, yes, quite a lot of them about"' (R. Ingrams, ed., *The Life and Times of Private Eye, 1961–1971*, p. 161).

R5: See also humour*, R2 and R5; blunder*, R3; and false –*, R2.

PSITTACISM 'The mechanical repetition* of previously received ideas or images* that reflects neither true reasoning* nor feeling; repetition of words or phrases parrot-fashion, without reflection, automatically' (OEDS).

Exx:

He accepted everything. The past was alterable. The past never had been altered. Oceania was at war with Eastasia. Oceania had always been at war with Eastasia. Jones, Aaronson, and Rutherford were guilty of the crimes they were charged with. He had never seen the photograph that disproved their guilt. It had never existed; he had invented it. (George Orwell, *Nineteen Eighty-Four*, p. 228)

'I and the Government of which I am a member want you to regard us as friends. Yes, friends. We have put you right, yes? You are getting the best of treatment. We never wished you harm, but there are some who did and do. And I think you know who those are.'

'Yes, yes, yes,' he said, 'there are certain men who wanted to use you, yes, use you for political ends. They would have been glad, yes, glad for you to be dead, for they thought they could blame it all on the Government.' (A. Burgess, *A Clockwork Orange*, p. 138)

Synonymous: knee-jerk verbosity; the parroting (hence the word *psittacism*) of ill-assimilated, practically rote-learned terms for the purpose of terrorizing the uninitiated rather than of communicating with them.

R1: Psittacisms are imitations* (see imitation, R7) rather than quotations*, and they have their own more or less automatic intonation*. See also slogan*, R1.

PUN A play on words which resemble each other in sound but differ in meaning*. See also Empson (*Seven Types of Ambiguity*, ch. 3), Joseph, Littré, Robert, Lausberg (sect. 1244), Preminger, Mahood (*Shakespeare's Wordplay*), and Redfern (*Puns*).

Ex [spoken by the dying Mercutio]: 'ask for me tomorrow, you shall find me a grave man' (Shakespeare, *Romeo and Juliet*, 3.1.101). The same pun in a modern context: 'Drinking and driving is a grave mistake.'

Ex:

Even the bright extremes of joy
Bring on conclusions of disgust,
Like the sweet blossoms of the May,
Whose fragrance ends in must.

Thomas Hood, 'Ode to Melancholy'

Other definitions: 'Pun' is often used in the broader sense to designate an example of ambiguity* and so may refer to a number of devices such as approximation*, syllepsis*, blend or portmanteau* word, etc. Both Preminger and Joseph also classify among 'puns,' antanaclasis*, paronomasia*, syllepsis*, and asteismus* because they may serve a comic function.

R1: In one precise meaning of the term given by Littré, a pun is a periphrasis*, which at first sight seems hermetic, but which may be clarified by considering it to be an allusion* to an ambiguous or homophonic referent (see homonymy*, R3); or sometimes to a case of metanalysis* (see metanalysis, R2).

R2: Puns occur more frequently in colloquial language, where the situation renders decoding easier than in literature. **Ex:** 'Garçon, ce steak est innocent' (i.e., *innocent*, instead of *pas coupable*, which is both 'not guilty' and 'uncuttable'). They are also found in definitions given as clues in crossword puzzles and in charades. Ex:

Execration perhaps – though it seems very wrong
On request to the dog to oblige with a song.

Answer: cur-sing.

Hubert Phillips, quoted in Espy, 1971, p. 70

R3: When combined with allographs*, puns make good cryptograms. Ex: 'La société des amis de l'ABC' (V. Hugo, *Les Misérables*, part 3, book 4) refers to a revolutionary group, since 'the ABC' designates phonetically the people, *abaissé* (downtrodden) by the bourgeois. The pun here derives from phonetic ambiguity*. See also phoebus*, R4. It is the principal device in the charade. Ex:

My first wears my second; my third might be
What my first would acquire if he went to sea.
Put together my one, two, three
And the belle of New York is the girl for me.

Answer: Manhattan.

Hubert Phillips, quoted in Espy, 1971, p. 70

R4: Most puns have a comic effect decodable by reference to their context. For example, a court jester is said to have remarked of Archbishop Laud: 'Great praise to God, and little laud to the devil.' More recently, an opponent of Britain's entry into the European Economic Community coined the following, which Redfern (p. 24) calls 'an example of splitting, of fission, and near the knuckle: "Britons never shall be slaves, only Europe peons."' Other modern examples: 'In Canada, the left is more gauche than sinister' (a trilingual pun if etymology* is taken into account). The legend on a publicity poster for a photocopier: 'Bye Canon. Bye Xerox. Buy Gestetner Copiers.' During the 'Irangate' hearings in 1987, the two following puns appeared on the cover of *People* magazine (July 27): 'Oliver North: True or just Magnetic.' Puns may serve as vehicles of irony*.

R5: See also denomination*, R2, and etymology*.

PUNCH LINE We propose to extend this term to cover any kind of conclusion or *clausula*, including the rounding-off of a sentence. Like the ancients, some modern writers have lavished particular care on the endings of sentences* or paragraphs*. Far from allowing a thought to end conventionally, they emphasize some aspect of it through the use of metaphor* or paradox* and draw attention to the ending by a special rhythm*: the result is a punch line.

Exx:

ORONTE: Beautiful Philis, one despairs
Yet one still hopes.
PHILINTE: The ending is pretty, loving, admirable.
ALCESTE: A plague on your ending, poisoner, to the devil with it.
Molière, Le Misanthrope, 1.2

No ups and downs my pretty,
A mermaid, not a punk;
A drunkard is a dead man,
And all dead men are drunk.
W.B. Yeats, 'A Drunken Man's Praise of Sobriety'

Antonym: epanorthosis* (see epanorthosis, R4)

Synonyms: *chute* (Fr.); *clausula* (L.); clausule (*OED*; see 'period'); 'apoth-esis' (Lausberg). A cadence*, the 'fall of voice, esp. at end of sentence' (*Concise Oxford Dictionary*), represents a conventional type of finale; see Littré; Verest, sect. 92; and Robert.

Analogous terms: explicit ('word used by scribes in indicating the end of a book, or of one of the separate pieces contained in a MS ... "Here ends" ' [*OED*; see also Littré]); cursus ('a Latin word designating the clausule from the viewpoint of rhythm [*cursus planus, velox, tardus,* etc.]' [Lausberg, sect. 1052])

R1: A short final clausule, or *minor cadence*, differs from a long *major cadence*. **Ex** (of a minor cadence): 'The sea changed, the fields changed, the rivers, the villages, and the people changed, yet Egden remained' (Th. Hardy, *Tess of the D'Urbervilles*, ch. 1). **Ex** (of a major cadence): 'And all her shining keys will be took from her, and her cupboards opened, and things a' didn't wish seen, any body will see; and her little wishes and ways will all be as nothing' (Th. Hardy, *The Mayor of Casterbridge*, ch. 18). See sentence* (types of), 2.

R2: According to Philippe Hamon ('Clausules,' *Poétique*, no. 24, p. 509), clausules (he extends the term's meaning to include not only the final member of a period* but also the finale of any work) may or may not be predictable, emphatic, stereotyped, anticlimactic, in conformity with the genre of the work in question, *open* (i.e., provoking either the reader's expectation of a sequel, or leaving the work open to diverse interpretations), or, in the case of a part of a work, internal. **Exx** (Hamon, ibid., p. 501): 'They lived happy ever after and had lots of children' (fairy story); 'Yours sincerely' (letter*); 'Remove and serve hot' (recipe*). The moral of a fable, the ballad's *envoi*, the charade's 'My whole is ...,' the etymological tale's 'And it was from that time that ...,' the prayer*'s 'Amen,' the news item's 'The victim was taken to hospital where he died soon after,' the serial's happy end, the song's 'Bis/ repeat/*da capo*,' etc.: all are examples of clausules in Hamon's view. See also final* word.

PUNCTUATION We may divide punctuation marks into three categories.
1. Commas, semicolons, periods, colons*, dashes, and oblique* strokes usually mark pauses*; in all cases, they are articulating devices within texts. See syntagm*, assertion*, and caesura*.
2. Question* marks, exclamation* marks, and points of suspension*, or lines of (three or more) dots, indicate affective variants of periods or form very approximate markers of enunciation*. See expressive punctuation.
3. The remaining signs 'of punctuation' indicate a sentence's position within its context and real environment; we call them 'situational* signs.'

R1: The typographical characters used for display (in posters, for example), which are free and varied in shape, create their own norms for punctuation. Hyphens may be round in shape; final periods, if used at all, may look like hyphens, and so on.

R2: See adjunction*, R3.

R3: In the following anecdote, punctuation marks function as a short-hand code:

> In 1861, [Victor Hugo] completed *Les Misérables*. There is a famous story that, after publication of the first volume, Hugo sent a tele-gram to his publisher. It said, simply:
> '?'
> The answer came back by return:
> '!'
> His publisher made more than half a million francs out of the first six years' sales. (*Les Misérables*, souvenir brochure to the musical version)

PUNCTUATION (EXPRESSIVE) Affective variables of periods (such as ?, ! and ...) guide the reader to one of the three types of enunciation* whose melody alone (see intonation*) would otherwise permit identification.

Ex: 'She knows?'; 'She knows!'; 'She knows ...' See question*, exclama-tion*, interjection*, interruption*, and aposiopesis*.

Expressive punctuation is the graphic marking of intensity by means of more than one graphic sign. **Exx:** 'When we've finished burning all the books!!!' (A. Gide, *Romans*, p. 164); 'CARR: Silly place to put it, really ... (*sips*) Is this the Perrier-Jouet, Brut, '89???!!!' (Tom Stoppard, *Travesties*, act 2).

Some combinations are quite usual: ! ... ? ... ?! When placed in parentheses*, question marks express doubt (?); exclamation marks in parentheses express irony* (!); suspension points indicate passages omitted (...).

R1: Melodies that correspond to graphic signs: Of all the different types of intonation*, written language conserves almost nothing. To the period or full stop corresponds a simple kind of intonation that Delattre (*French Review*, 1966, p. 6) calls 'finality,' extending from the medium (an individual's static average tone) to low. From medium to sharp or extra-sharp, we have minor or major continuations* (i.e., commas, suspension points), which indicate that the sentence is not finished. The mark of an exclamation* is a rise in the voice during the syntagm* concerned; the rise marking a question* is steeper but briefer.

R2: Affective variants of a final period, because they combine with it, are always graphic markers that appear at the end of the sentence*. This fixed position prevents their use to indicate which particular segment is interrogatory or exclamatory. To the written sentence 'Jane stayed all afternoon?' there really correspond four spoken sentences, each with a different meaning. In the first, the voice rises on 'Jane,' thereby posing a question about the subject; in another, the voice may rise on 'stayed'; in another, on 'all'; and so on. Intonation* makes all these meanings* quite clear, whereas the written form confuses them, unless its syntax is altered for each one. In order to make written expression more similar to oral, we might invent *interrogative* and *exclamative commas*. Such commas would take their appropriate place after each speech act. It would be even more accurate to print in bold the lexeme stated or emphasized. See assertion*.

R3: Although they transcribe a suspensive melody, points of suspension* merely indicate that everything is not being said. They may occur in the course of a sentence to announce the unfinished nature of the thought expressed and that the speaker is offering it in some other form. They may also indicate prevarication or evasion. Ex (of the latter): 'As I was saying, I'm glad you asked me that question. Because ... well, because it's a question that a lot of people are asking. And Why? Because ... well, because a lot of people want to know the answer to it' (J. Lynn and A. Jay, *The Complete 'Yes Minister,'* p. 81). See interruption*, R4, and counter-interruption*.

R4: Queneau suggests (in *Le Chiendent*, p. 240) the introduction of an 'indignation mark,' to be represented by a reversed question mark.

R5: In linguistics and in logic, sentences* which are untrue or invalid are preceded by an asterisk, and sentences represented as being of 'doubtful' accuracy or veracity by a question mark.

Q

QUESTION An assertion* whose predicate seeks completion or confirmation from the addressee.

Exx: 'Who's there?'; 'Is that you, John?'

Other definition: 'subject being discussed or for discussion' (*Concise Oxford Dictionary*). Common expressions: 'that is not the question'; 'the question is ...'; 'out of the question'; 'there is no question that ...' See pretext*; ambiguity*, 3; and flashback*, R1.

R1: The melodic marker for the interrogative form is a steeply rising tone of voice at the end of the phonetic word to which the question may reduce. (See expressive punctuation*.) The graphic marker is almost universal: ?

'Total' interrogation applies to the whole verbal node and is marked by the inversion* of the subject, noun or pronoun, and the verb or even by intonation* alone. Ex: 'Is he leaving?'; 'Is John leaving?'; 'John's leaving?' In this case, it is the accomplishment of the action (or effectivity of the state) expressed by the verb which is called in question.

Interrogation is 'partial' when some part of the assertion* is tacit, that is, implied without being stated: an interrogative morpheme ('how?'; 'for whom?' etc.) suffices in such a case.

The same assertion*, in reversed or completed form, forms the response*. Both questions and answers may be elliptical Ex: 'You?' 'No!' 'Who?' 'Him.'

R2: Questions do not only have a referential function. They may serve the emotive, phatic (concerned with establishment of contact), and injunctive functions of communication, as dialogue* reveals.

The injunctive function is predominant in an *interrogation session*, during which a speaker seeks, by a barrage of questions, to gain the upper hand and to force the person being interrogated to reveal information he or she seems anxious to hide. Ex: ' "Who gave you the message for Jim about Tinker, Tailor? Did you know what it meant? Did you have it straight from Polyakov, was that it?" ' (John Le Carré, *Tinker Tailor Soldier Spy*, p. 275). The victim may attempt to evade the questions. One of the best methods of evasion is to reply with a question. Ex: ' "All right, come on, so what happened to the networks? ...

Question

Why didn't you come and see me at home when you got back? You could have done. You tried to see me before you left, so why not when you got back? Wasn't just the rules that kept you away?" "Didn't anyone get out?" Jim said' (ibid., pp. 240–1). See also injunction*, R1.

On the other hand, questions addressed to no one in particular indicate, by their betrayal of the speaker's distress, that the emotive or expressive function is predominant. Ex:

'Who called?' I said, and the words
Through the whispering glades,
Hither, thither, baffled the birds –
'Who called? Who called?'

Walter de la Mare, 'Echo'

The speaker goes on to reveal his frustration, or loneliness, by a further emotionally charged question that comes back to haunt him:

'Who cares?' I bawled through my tears;
The wind fell low:
In the silence, 'Who cares? Who cares?'
Wailed to and fro.

But we may ask ourselves real questions. Ex: 'If he [Mr. Kauderer] had come back, why could we not meet as we had every day? And if he had not come back, whom was I on my way to meet at the cemetery?' (Italo Calvino, *If on a Winter's Night a Traveller*, trans. W. Weaver, p. 65). See also interior dialogue*.

R3: The most manipulative interrogatory form is really a disguised assertion*, and is justly called a *rhetorical question*. Fontanier (along with many other rhetorical theorists) sees it as an interrogative figure which challenges the addressee to dare to deny anything or even to reply at all (p. 368). He also calls our attention to the affirmative value possessed by negative expressions, and vice versa. Ex: 'What is the purpose of the holy cleansing of confession, if not to unload the weight of sin, and the remorse it involves, into the very bosom of our Lord, obtaining with absolution a new and airy lightness of soul, such as to make us forget the body tormented with wickedness?' (U. Eco, *The Name of the Rose*, p. 277).

Rhetorical questions, or pseudo-interrogations, appear frequently in literary discourse* when the need arises to communicate impressions. Ex: 'O Wind, / If Winter comes, can Spring be far behind?' (P.B. Shelley, 'Ode to the West Wind'). Or they may have a disguised conative function, inviting the hearers to action. Ex: 'Will no one revenge me of the injuries I have sustained from one turbulent priest [i.e., Thomas Becket]?' (King Henry II, quoted in *The Oxford Dictionary of*

Quotations, 3rd ed., p. 246). The interrogative form may even appropriately communicate physical sensation. Ex: 'Can't you see how still and beautiful it is this evening?' (J. Hébert, *Le Temps sauvage*, p. 45).

Another function of pseudo-questions is to undermine a position by casting doubt upon it; naturally, such a procedure is subject to abuse. Ex: 'Soft contact lenses? Should PRICE be your major concern?' (advertisement, which Bausch and Lomb, makers of lenses, describe in one of their publicity brochures as 'a public service message'). Ex: 'In *The Plug-In Drug*, author Marie Winn asks: "Is it merely a coincidence that the entry of television into American homes brought in its wake one of the worst epidemics of juvenile violence in the nation's history?" One of that book's critics was tempted to reply: "Is it not possible that these kinds of disguised assertions [accusations made by means of rhetorical questions] are poor substitutes for research?" ' (*TV Guide*, 21–7 May 1983, p. 5).

Such oratorical questions come with their own intonation*, which seems to imply the answer. Classical rhetoric recommends a kind of pseudo-interrogation procedure, consisting in presenting several assertions in the alternating forms of question and answer, and since the speaker responds for the opponent, the pretence is that the latter's confession or agreement has been obtained. This is *subjectio* (Fontanier, p. 374; Lanham; Lausberg) or *hypophora* (Lanham). Ex: 'FALSTAFF: What is honour? a word. What is that word, honour? Air. A trim reckoning! Who hath it? He that died o' Wednesday. Doth he feel it? No. Doth he hear it? No ... [etc.]' (Shakespeare, *Henry IV*, Pt 1, 5.1.135)

Another form of pseudo-interrogation is deliberative, when we pretend to question the listeners, whereas in reality we are pressing them to make a decision (see *deliberatio**). Or we pretend to ask ourselves questions, although we are really proposing objections in so doing. (This is a particularly useful figure in learned discussions; see *dubitatio**.) When trying to get a student to think of what we wish to teach, we may use the Socratic method, also called the *maieutic* method.

To summarize: questions offer a form by which we may express almost anything, including:

– *suppositions**. Ex: 'FIRST VOICE: In Mirador school he learned to read and count. Who made the worst raffia dollies? Who put water in Joyce's galoshes, every morning prompt as prompt?' (Dylan Thomas, *Quite Early One Morning*, p. 53).

– *word-play**. Ex: 'When is a door not a door? When it's ajar.'

– simple-minded *blunders**. Ex: 'What must a soldier put in his gun? Complete confidence' (Jean-Charles, *Les Perles du facteur*, p. 205).

– even part of the action of a novel (see Joyce, *Ulysses*, pp. 544–607). Ex: 'How was the irritation allayed? He removed his collar' (p. 583).

R4: A question may fill a whole paragraph* and necessitate many separate assertions* as answers: in such a case, we speak also of *problems*. *Problematics* is the art or manner of posing a set of problems; *dialectics*, the art or manner of discussing them. Thus, in Plato's works, dialectical discussion takes the form of question and answer. More accurately, we call *dialectical* an exposition (of facts, for instance) which is articulated so as to form a proof, an objection, a discussion, or conclusion and which pretends to be the dialogue* it would only become if the opponent faced the speaker. See also *deliberatio*.

The mere calling in question of one of the opponent's propositions is sufficient to arouse suspicion. The simplest of questions is charged with all kinds of perlocutionary values, and possibly of hidden presuppositions. (See enunciation*, R3; paralogism*, R2; and refutation*, R4.)

R5: For complex (or 'loaded') questions, see finesse* and paralogism*, R2. For negative questions, see negation*, R2. For an accumulation of short questions, see epitrochasmus*.

QUIBBLE An insubstantial or merely verbal argument* by which a speaker attempts desperately to prove that he or she is right. See *OED* and Robert.

Ex: 'PLAYER: We keep to our usual stuff, more or less, only inside out. We do on stage the things that are supposed to happen off. Which is a kind of integrity, if you look on every exit being an entrance somewhere else' (Tom Stoppard, *Rosencrantz and Guildenstern Are Dead*, act 1).

Synonyms: cavil, hair-splitting, logic chopping

R1: Quibbles may be detected by their intonation*.

QUOTATION 'A passage taken from an author who may be an authority' (Littré). See also Grambs, Lausberg (sect. 1244), Quillet, and Robert.

Ex: 'If we turn to Flaubert's letters, we discover him ... writing to his mother ... "And to think that I had specially brought that card all the way from Croisset and didn't even get to put it in place"' (Julian Barnes, *Flaubert's Parrot*, p. 70).

Other names: quote, extract, pericope (an extract chosen for a public or liturgical reading). In English, *citation* has come to mean a citing, or mention in an official dispatch, or the descriptive note accompanying the announcement of an award (*Concise Oxford Dictionary*). See also epigraph*.

The art of introducing maxims* into a speech was so much studied in the past that it received a name, *gnomology* ('the collecting of gnomes, sayings, maxims' [*OED*]). The *cento* (L. 'patchwork') was a work entirely composed of quotations. Modern examples: Eluard, *Premières vues anciennes*; Alvarez, *The New Poetry* (1962), cited by Cuddon (p. 107). See Dumarsais, *Des Tropes*, p. 275. Recent (and not so recent) collections of quotations arranged alphabetically include those by Dupré, P. Oster, John Bartlett, and the compilers of *The Oxford Dictionary of Quotations*.

Anthologies, morceaux choisis, analects (Robert, *Concise Oxford Dictionary*), and *catalects* (Littré, Cuddon) reproduce extensive quotations from authors and may offer them as *models* for imitation*. Indeed, quotation was a principal figure in oratorical amplification*.

Other definitions: Littré's definition of quotation has been extended in more recent times. Authorities, spiritual or not, no longer form the only source of quotations; rather, adduced documents of all kinds give objectivity to a text.

Jakobson (p. 177) gives maximal extension to the quotation by defining it structurally: M/M; that is, 'a message inside the message,' even 'a message about the message.' He explains the latter meaning thus: 'We quote others, or our own past words, and we are even inclined to present certain of our experiences in the form of self-quotation.' Self-quotation is natural in current speech (e.g., 'As I said before ...'; 'so I says, says I'; 'que j'dis'). In a published text, self-quotation is a form of autism* and risks appearing out of place, except in certain cases, when, for example, it is a matter of justifying one's intentions (see the notes Montherlant appended to his play *Le Maître de Santiago*). In scientific texts, it is current practice to give references to one's previous publications.

R1: The signs of quotation are the separation of quoted matter from the text, and/or quotation marks (see situational* signs, 5), and the *reference* to the work quoted (see notation*, R1). Oral quotation has a special kind of intonation*. The expression 'so they say' points out a quotation without a direct reference (or transforms an utterance into a *false quotation*).

The text quoted must correspond to the original; or, at a pinch, be in free indirect style. In indirect discourse*, it is no longer a quotation but a summary or *resumé*. 'I am quoting from memory' draws attention to one's uncertainty concerning a quotation's accuracy.

R2: When the text quoted is in another language, a translation* is usually given, possibly with the original in a footnote. Quotation in a foreign language (real or invented) allows for all kinds of translations. Ex [taking his inspiration from Molière's *Le Bourgeois gentilhomme*, 5.1, Alfred Jarry caricatures an official visit to North Africa]:

MR. LOUBET (in the language of the country): Ha la ba, ba la chou, ba la ba, ba la da.

Which means: France protects all those, French or native, who live on her soil; but, in return, she expects from them absolute devotion. (A. Jarry, *La Chandelle verte*, p. 371)

This is *false translation*, almost pseudo-language*.

R3: Snobbery in quotation exists, which involves larding one's speeches with trendy names, often unnecessarily. Ex: A linguist quotes Jakobson merely to say that 'the decoding goes from sound to meaning.' Words attributed to a recognized authority may also be used to cut short a discussion: this is the argument* from authority.

R4: Quotation receives from simulation, change of context, or merely from present reality a different, adapted meaning* (see meaning, 7). The occasion confers intensity and force on certain liturgical texts, patriotic anthems, etc., however threadbare and formulaic. Ex [Malraux is recounting events in France in 1944; double quotation marks identify extracts from the French national anthem]: '*La Marseillaise* rediscovered the force of its prophetic outcry: the "day of glory" was the Liberation, the "tyranny" in question, we knew it well, "do you hear in our country places" the tanks which were perhaps getting closer' (A. Malraux, *Antimémoires*, p. 257).

If need be, quotations are modified or adapted (see substitution* R2). A text may be quoted, however, without the secondary narrator or speaker assuming responsibility for its message. In such a case, the quotation is a pure signifier, which may form the basis for a discussion or a vote, for example. Such a quoting procedure contains no interpretation; there is only autonymy or self-reference (see short* circuit).

R5: The *false quotation* (e.g., under R2, above) differs from the *half-quotation*, which is given without acknowledgment or reference (see imitation*, R8), and from the unconscious quotation, which is the presence in any discourse* of many previously consumed texts, that is, of *intertextuality*. Ex: In Eco's *The Name of the Rose*, the 'detective,' William of Baskerville, reconstructs intertextually the 'lost' section of Aristotle's *Poetics* on 'Comedy,' as his opponent, Jorge of Burgos, deduces: '[William:] "Truth reached by depicting men and the world as worse than they are or than we believe them to be, worse in any case than the epics, the tragedies, lives of the saints have shown them to us. Is that it?" [Jorge:] "Fairly close. You reconstructed it by reading other books?" ' (p. 472). For pseudo-quotations, see situational* signs, 5. See also psittacism*, R1.

R6: *Relayed* or *displaced* words (Bloomfield, quoted by Jakobson, p. 177) are texts torn from their context, without being inserted in another (not to be confused with 'out of place or unwarranted comments'). Out of context, the meaning* of a quotation becomes more general.

R7: Quotation is motivated, and the quoter sometimes feels the need to underline certain passages (as in the present work, where such passages appear in italics). It is then usual to warn the reader parenthetically that the emphasis is not in the original. See also end* positioning, other def., 2; and counter-interruption*, R1.

R

REACTUALIZATION Actualization of a syntagm*, which the use of pronouns achieves unproblematically, establishes for each sentence* the relationship between speaker and addressee, and more exactly that between the diverse factors in communication. (See enunciation*.) While it is normal, in a single set of sentences, to have the same actualizing process, we may sometimes observe changes in one or more of these factors. In such a case, reactualization occurs.

1. A change of speaker. This is the case in plagiarisms, psittacisms*, and adapted quotations* (see meaning*, 7). It occurs within the sentence itself when another person's words are reported in indirect speech (when, that is, we pass from the process of enunciation* to the utterance itself). Changes of speaker occur naturally in dialogue*, in which the addressee 'replies,' thus becoming the speaker, and so on. This kind of reactualization may occur within a sentence. Ex:

CARR: It's worth fifty tanks
JOYCE: Or twenty-five francs

Tom Stoppard, *Travesties*, act 1

Authorisms*, in which the speaker is at the same time character and author's representative, are examples of *double actualization*.

2. A change of addressee. Ex:

JOYCE: Top o' the morning – James Joyce!
I hope you'll allow me to voice
my regrets in advance ...
CARR: I ... sorry ... would you say that again?
JOYCE: Begob – I'd better explain
I'm told that you are a –
TZARA Miss Carr!
GWEN: Mr. Tzara!
JOYCE: (seeing Tzara for the first time) B'jasus'. Joyce is the name.

Stoppard, *Travesties*, act 1

Reactualization

Markers of reactualization include changes of pronoun; stage directions emphasize the process (as do gestures*, during a performance).

3. A change in the contact. This factor, corresponding to the phatic function of communication, establishes attitudes (of superiority, equality, distance, intimacy, etc.) and is modified by changes in tone of voice. Ex:

> LADY BRACKNELL [who has just voiced opposition to her nephew Algernon's desire to marry Miss Cardew]: As a matter of form, Mr. Worthing, I had better ask you if Miss Cardew has any little fortune?
> JACK: Oh! about a hundred and fifty thousand pounds in the Funds ...
> LADY BRACKNELL (sitting down again): A moment Mr. Worthing. A hundred and fifty thousand pounds! And in the Funds! Miss Cardew seems to me a most attractive young lady, now that I look at her.
>
> Oscar Wilde, *The Importance of Being Earnest*, act 4

4. A change of referent. Usually, discourse passes from subject to subject by means of transitions*, banal or otherwise. Ex: 'LENIN: You must disappear from Geneva for at least two or three weeks, until you receive a telegram from me in Scandinavia ... Your Lenin. *P.S.* ... I write to you because I am convinced that everything between us will remain *absolutely* secret' (Stoppard, *Travesties*, act 2). The transition occurs when the character says 'P.S.,' which indicates a change of subject. Reactualization occurs when such changes are made suddenly. See *coq-à-l'âne**.

5. A change of code. The speaker goes from one language to another. Ex: 'TZARA: I began, *"Boum boum boum il déshabille sa chair quand les grenouilles humides commencèrent à brûler."* Hulsenbeck began, *"Ahoi ahoi des admirals gwirktes Beinkleid schnell zerfallt"* ' (Stoppard, *Travesties*, act 1). Reactualization also occurs when the change involves only grammar. (See correction*.) Ex: 'Does he drink a lot, your dad? – Did he drink, you mean. He's dead' (R. Queneau, *Zazie dans le métro*, p. 51).

6. A change of form. This can involve a change of prose for poetry, for example, or vice versa. Stoppard's characters, James Joyce and Tzara, frequently switch to poetry in *Travesties*, either reciting Shakespearian sonnets and limericks, or satirical verses of their 'own' devising.

7. A change of situation (in time or space). The time and place of communication, as well as its referents, may change when a speaker, in the throes of *delirium*, or some form of *exaltation* or anamnesis*, is projected into an imaginary world. In *Travesties*, Stoppard employs what he calls 'time slips,' since 'most of the action takes place within [Henry] Carr's memory' (p. 17). This allows movement between Carr's apartment in Zurich in March 1918, where Joyce, Lenin, and Tzara meet during the preparations for a performance of Wilde's *The Importance of Being Earnest,* and the same apartment many years later, where Carr still lives as an old man. Ex:

> BENNETT: The war continues to dominate the newspapers, sir.
> CARR: Ah yes ... the war, always the war ... I was in Saville Row when I heard the news, talking to the head cutter at Drewitt and Madge in a hounds-tooth check slightly flared behind the knee, quite unusual ...

> Stoppard, *Travesties,* act 1

Without any transition, Carr's 'not notably reliable' (Stoppard, *Travesties,* p. 27) memory slips back to relive nostalgically pre–World War I life.

REASONING A set of arguments* arranged so as to lead to a conclusion. See *OED* and Robert.

Ex: 'The man's business was a small one, and there was nothing in his house which could account for such elaborate preparations, and such an expenditure as they were at. It must, then, be something out of the house. What could it be? I thought of the assistant's fondness for photography, and his trick of vanishing into the cellar. The cellar! That was the end of this tangled clue' (Conan Doyle, 'The Red-Headed League,' in *The Complete Sherlock Holmes,* 1:190).

Analogous: argumentation; syllogism; formal, regular argument*; ratiocination

R1: The syllogism or process of formal reasoning in ancient logic included two arguments* (the major and minor premises) entailing a conclusion. The three assertions* must logically follow: Ex: 'A sense of timing was at work, almost an instinct [the minor]. But then, timing is made by the man, I think [the major], and therefore man creates his own destiny [conclusion]' (Laurence Olivier, *On Acting,* p. 113).

In practice, even in formal argument, we rarely give the syllogism in its full form, so as to avoid clumsy repetition*. One of the premises (the premises are the arguments* forming the syllogism) or even the conclusion remains understood. This type of reasoning process with apparently only one argument is an *enthymeme* (*redditio causae, etiologia*). Ex: 'And besides, if it is evil to handle certain books, why should the Devil distract a monk from committing evil?' (U. Eco, *The Name of the Rose,* p. 89). Enthymemes occur constantly in philosophy (e.g., 'I think, therefore I exist') as they do in literature. Ex: 'Where there are horses there must be smiths' (Robertson Davies, *What's Bred in the Bone,* p. 108). See truism*, R2.

Fontanier (pp. 382–4) names *enthymemism* the particularly lively and striking formulation of enthymemes. Ex: 'If you haven't the vitality, don't act. If you can't do it, don't do it' (L. Olivier, *On Acting*, p. 327). This figure frequently comes concealed in an illogical form. Ex: 'A little is really quite a lot.' This is only an apparent contradiction (or anti-logy*), which we can sort out by positing a major premise such as 'It is sometimes impossible to succeed fully' and a minor such as 'Well, we succeeded in part at least.'

Enthymemes lose their effectiveness when the implied argument* is not immediately clear. Ex: 'Carnivorous plants exist because flies are animals.' It would have been better to imply the major and express the minor premise: 'There exist plants which eat flies.'

The *sorites* or polysyllogism is a chain of arguments whose conclusion repeats one term from the first syllogism and one from the last. Ex: 'In reality, however, England owed its superiority to its old maids, as a distinguished British biologist has pointed out. For good English beef, his argument runs, depends upon the industrious bumblebee which pollinates red clover eaten by cattle, and the number of bumblebees in turn is determined by the number of cats, since the mice rob the nests of the bumblebees, and mice are killed by cats. Hence, few cats mean many mice, few bumblebees, little clover and bad meat. Because old maids are fond of cats as pets, ergo England's power depends on the number of its old maids' (Noah Jacobs, *Naming Day in Eden*, p. 10). As this example shows, sorites may, even more easily than enthymemism, produce unexpected conclusions.

But arguments usually need the support of some proof which may be presented contiguously: this is the *epicheireme*. Ex (analysed by Barthes in his article 'L'Ancienne Rhétorique' ['Ancient Rhetoric'], *Communications*, no. 16 [1970], p. 205): the Soviet note sent to the Chinese government, who had protested following the suppression by the Russian police force of a demonstration by Chinese students in front of the American embassy in Moscow. *Major*: There exist diplomatic norms respected by all countries. *Proof of the major*: In their own country, the Chinese themselves respect these norms. *Minor*: But the Chinese students in Moscow violated the norms. *Proofs of the minor*: the narrative* incorporating details of the demonstration (insults, acts of violence, and the like liable to penalties under the law). The conclusion, though left unstated (the form is therefore enthymematic), is clear.

R2: The premises, particularly the major, are frequently general laws. In such cases, whether the conclusion is a categorical proposition (true *de jure*) or an assertorical proposition (true *de facto*), the reasoning is deductive. An inference drawn from a general principle is a *deduction*, whereas one drawn from particular observation is an *induction*. Indeed, the 'facts' may serve as the strongest argument of all (as Sherlock

Holmes and police-sergeant Joe Friday [of TV's 'Dragnet'] never tired of reminding us). **Ex:**

> The only real beauty is useless; whatever has a function is ugly, because it expresses some need, and man's needs are ignoble and disgusting, as is his poor, weak nature. – The most functional place in a house is the latrine. (Th. Gautier, *Mlle de Maupin*, preface)

But that does not immediately make for an induction: we need to see what role facts play in this reasoning process. Do they form the conclusion or the argument? In the latter case, we may feel unsure because the 'art for art's sake' principle which Gautier is here expounding is not drawn from the observation concerning the functional value of latrines! Nor is this observation drawn from the general principle except 'for the sake of argument' and as an example, as we say. *Exempla* do not then form part of a logically constructed argument; as proofs, they are only illustrations, capable only of *showing* rather than demonstrating. **Ex:**

> ' "Marginal images often provoke smiles, but to edifying ends," he replied. "As in sermons, to touch the imagination of devout throngs it is necessary to introduce exempla, not infrequently, jocular, so also the discourse of images must indulge in these trivia. For every virtue and for every sin there is an example drawn from the bestiaries, and animals exemplify the human world" ' (U. Eco, *The Name of the Rose*, p. 79).

In the case of a single assertion and many examples, we have a vivid type of amplification*. **Ex:**

> The hand that signed the paper felled a city;
> Five sovreign fingers taxed the breath,
> Doubled the globe of dead and halved a country;
> These five fingers did a king to death
> Dylan Thomas, 'The Hand That Signed the Paper'

The whole poem develops the idea that absolute power is invested in one person. Concretization* offers an (extravagant) way of replacing this type of argument.

R3: Conclusions obtained by deduction will only be as true as their most general premise, and it is rare that such generalities are completely reliable. When obtained by induction, they depend upon the number of facts it was possible to observe. When such a procedure offers insufficient evidence to serve as proof, we have recourse to argumentative transposition, or analogical reasoning, argument from comparison*, from similarity and assimilation. **Ex:**

> Sometimes ... I thought that the idea that one person's mind is accessible to another's is just a conversational illusion, just a figure of speech, an assumption that makes some kind of exchange between basically alien creatures seem plausible, and that really the

Reasoning

relationship of one person to another is ultimately unknowable.
(Robert M. Pirsig, *Zen and the Art of Motorcycle Maintenance*, p. 269)

Because of the difficulty inherent in any attempt to formulate axioms to explain the functioning of the brain, the speaker compares such explanations to other figurative uses of language. From there the induction follows: such explanations depend on the previously accepted convention that all communication is mysterious and unsure. Such analogical reasoning functions as does metaphor*, using the same kind of transposition. Because of their double movement, from position to transposition, demonstrative comparisons* are more flexible than more simple types of reasoning.

But such transfers of meaning* can be dangerous. Ex: 'MR SMITH: A conscientious doctor must die with his patient if they can't get well together. The captain of a ship goes down with his ship into the briny deep, he does not survive alone' (Eugene Ionesco, *The Bald Soprano*, in *Four Plays*, trans. D.M. Allen, p. 11). Even more obvious are cases involving paralogism* (see paralogism, R3) which present as arguments simple metaphors*, rather than comparisons* permitting one to examine at leisure the proposed equivalences. Morier suggests that such metaphorical 'arguments' should be called '*epitropes*.' He gives an example from the nineteenth-century French thinker Ernest Renan: 'Catholicism? Catholicism is an iron bar; you don't try to reason with an iron bar.' (According to Lanham, *epitrope* is a type of concession: 'permission or submission to an opponent or disputant, either earnest or not'; Lausberg agrees [sect. 856–7]: 'concession' or 'permission.' See *permissio** and concession*.)

Distrust of the argument by analogy appears in the adage 'Analogic is not logic.' And yet, in certain cases there is nothing more expressive or convincing than a comparison*. Ex: 'A meal without wine is like a day without sunshine.'

R4: For other forms of reasoning, see paralogism*; refutation*; supposition*; alternative*, R2; and wit*.

R5: To Aristotle and other writers in the classical tradition, the truth of a conclusion depends upon that possessed by the arguments and upon the logic of their articulation. The modern age has witnessed a progressive development of formal logic. Modern symbolic logic has incorporated mathematical set theory, while abandoning classical logic. In the sciences (including some social sciences like economics and sociology), automated logic reigns. In everyday political, judicial, or literary reasoning, there is deep distrust of 'logic': reasoning is frequently considered to be an *a posteriori* arrangement of material, able to conceal as well as to confirm; an artificial tool, and therefore not as true as direct *testimony*, organized, like 'oral history,' for example, so as to offer a microcosm of an entire situation or set of events.

Testimony differs from reasoning in somewhat the same way as facts differ from explanations*. See remotivation*, R2.

RECAPITULATION The repetition* in condensed form of the different points made in a report or exposition of facts.

Ex: ' "You're kidding," said Hartwood, disbelief in his voice. "A major United States businessman commits suicide and less than forty-eight hours later his personal aide is killed under mysterious circumstances. It turns out that the aide was once in the C.I.A. and all you do is leave the file open?" ' (Christopher Hyde, *Whisperland*, p. 99).

Analogous: anacephalaeosis (Morier). Lanham believes this to be synonymous with enumeration*, whether repeated at the end of a discourse* or not.

R1: Recapitulation is one of the essential parts of classical discourse; see plan*. (Cicero even advises recapitulation of the arguments* making up the proof*, albeit in a different style.) Ex: 'In summary, I have argued that ...' But literary texts also present the device in their conclusions. Limited to a single sentence*, recapitulation is the opposite of regression*.

R2: Recapitulation differs from both *division* and *summary*. The first two are attached to the body of the discourse*: division precedes and recapitulation follows it. The summary remains independent of it.

If a summary covers a whole work, it is called an *abridgement*, a *précis, memorandum, digest*, or *condensation* of a book. An even briefer summary simply lists, in the form of an enumeration*, the topics treated in a chapter. The *argument* or *synopsis* of a film script, opera, essay, or speech is a brief analysis of the essential points.

R3: Because recapitulations bring together several elements, they often become enumerations*. The elements themselves lead normally to a general conclusion or *synthesis*.

RECIPE A summary of the ingredients and actions by means of which something is made.

Ex: 'EGGS BERCY: 4 eggs; 2 tablesp. tomato sauce; 1/2 teasp. salt; 4 small pork sausages cooked; 1/4 teasp. freshly ground pepper. Butter a pie dish. Break eggs in dish. Add salt and pepper. Bake at 400 degrees F. for 15 minutes. Arrange tomato sauce and sausages between yolks. Continue baking for 5 minutes. Serve hot in baking dish. Serves 4' (Fernande Garvin, *The Art of French Cooking*, pp. 48–9).

Ex: 'TO PAINT A PORTRAIT OF A BIRD: First paint a cage / with an open door ...' (Jacques Prévert, *Paroles*, p. 151).

R1: The list of dishes or courses is the *menu*, which accords them titles*: *poulet chasseur* (literally 'hunter['s] chicken') is chicken with green peas; *truite meunière* ('miller['s] trout') is trout fried in butter and garnished with parsley. The qualifier indicates the garnish or sauce.

R2: Recipes have a marker at the end (see punch* line, R2): 'Serve hot' or some similar form.

RECRIMINATION The resort to counter-charges against an opponent, rather than to an attempt to clear oneself. See *OED* and Robert.

Ex: 'He did it to me first!' See also excuse*, R1.

Other definitions: Lausberg and Littré define recrimination as 'metastasis*.' However, English rhetors, at least since Tudor times, consider metastasis to be a 'rapid transition from one point to another' (*OED*).

Synonym: antanagoge: 'when, not being able to answer the Adversary's accusation*, we return the charge, by loading him with the same crimes' (*OED*).

R1: Recriminations have their own intonation*.

REDUNDANCY Repetition* of an idea in two or more closely rephrased forms.

Ex: 'Match'd with an aged wife, I *mete and dole* / Unequal laws upon a savage race' (Tennyson, 'Ulysses').

Same definition: Several parts of the message transmit the same thing (information theory).

Synonym: duplication (*OED*)

Other definitions: For the ancients, and for Webster and Lausberg, the word has a broader meaning: 'exceeding what is natural, usual, or necessary; superfluous; as, a redundant foot in a verse; redundant words in a statement' (Webster). See battology*; baroquism*; grandiloquence*; metabole*, R1; sentence* (types of), 5; and verbiage*.

Fontanier also considers it a mistake*. 'Redundancy, an incorrect pleonasm* or perissology*: all three are the same thing' (p. 302).

R1: If redundancy involves the use of the same terms, we have *homiologia* (Lanham); if it involves different terms, *macrologia* (Fabri, Lanham).

R2: Redundancy seems justified when we wish to emphasize the strangeness of, for example, an assertion*. Ex: 'The greater part of the fearful night had worn away, and she who had been dead, once again

stirred – and now more vigorously than hitherto ... The corpse, I repeat, stirred, and now more vigorously than before' (E.A. Poe, 'Ligeia').

R3: Redundancy may take antithetical form. Ex: '... part three after Pim
not before not with' (S. Beckett, *How It Is*, p. 21).

REDUPLICATION Consecutive repetitions*, in the same clause of a
sentence*, of words having a particular interest (see Littré). See also
Fontanier (p. 330), Marouzeau, Quillet, and Robert.

Ex: 'Tears, idle tears, I know not what they mean' (Tennyson, *The
Princess*, 1.21).

Other names: *redoublement* (Marouzeau, Quillet, Robert); *conduplicatio*
(Fabri, 2:175; Lanham); epizeuxis (Morier, Quinn); palillology (Morier,
OED). See also gemination*, other def.

Other definitions: *Reduplication* is another term on which French and
English rhetorical usage seems to differ. The OED lists the following
two rhetorically significant meanings: '1. The action of doubling or
folding. 1589 PUTTENHAM *Eng. Poesie* III, xix: "The Greeks call this figure
Symploche, the Latin *Complexio* perchaunce for that he seemes to hold in
and to wrap up the verses by reduplication, so as nothing can fall out'
... 3. The repetition of a term with a limiting or defining force; hence,
the addition of some limiting term to one already used, or the sense of
a term as thus limited. *Obsolete* [e.g.: "Every good thing is to be desired, as it is good"].' Ex: 'He [the professional golfer] not only makes
your golf game better, he makes golf a better game' (ad by the US
Professional Golfers' Association).
    In 1521, Pierre Fabri (2:73) defined reduplication as: 'Saying twice
what one has to say, in two different ways as: "Toby was a young man
and not an old one." ' This is redundancy* in antithetical form. See also
polysyndeton*.

R1: Reduplication is a kind of repetition*. When a term is repeated for
emphasis*, but not immediately, we have semi-reduplication or *diacope*
(Quinn, pp. 81–2). Ex: 'And then a small, dry voice, like the voice of
someone who has not spoken for a long time, joined our singing: a
small, dry eggshell voice from the other side of the door: a small, dry
voice through the keyhole' (Dylan Thomas, *Quite Early One Morning*,
p. 20).
    If syntax demands repetition, the effect almost disappears and we
have *false reduplication*. Ex: 'This committee is called the Organizing
Committee.' Immediate repetition is not always syntactically possible,
particularly in the case of pronouns. See isolexism*, R4.

R2: If the repeated syntagm* can be isolated as a separate but complete
syntagm, we have epanalepsis* (see epanalepsis, R1).

R3: Reduplication may easily become an abuse. Ex: 'This program will show viewers the beauty, the beauty of the flora, of the flora in the tundra, in the tundra of James Bay.'

REFRAIN 'Recurring phrase or line especially at end of stanzas' (*Concise Oxford Dictionary*). See also Abrams, Cuddon, Frye, Preminger, and Turco.

Exx: In his poem 'The Raven,' Poe repeats as a refrain the single word 'Nevermore'; Tennyson repeats the refrain 'The Lady of Shalott' after twelve of the nineteen stanzas* of his poem of the same title.

Other names: ritornello (Preminger); kyrielle (*OED*; 'archaic' [*Harrap's*]); *rebriche* (Morier)

R1: A *litany* is a type of refrain in which the subject changes and the predicate remains the same. Ex: 'Through the open window of the church the fragrant incense was wafted and with it the fragrant names of her who was conceived without stain of original sin, *spiritual vessel, pray for us, honourable vessel, pray for us, vessel of singular devotion, pray for us, mystical rose*' (Joyce, *Ulysses*, p. 292 [emphasis added]). See insult*, R3; and title* (conferring of), R4. *Cantillation* is 'chanting, intoning, musical recitation; *spec.* that used in Jewish synagogues' (*OED*).

R2: In his poem 'And Death Shall Have No Dominion,' Dylan Thomas uses the title* as the first and last line of each stanza*.

R3: Refrains may achieve comic effects as choruses in comic songs. Chaucer, as well as Gilbert and Sullivan, used comic refrains, as in his 'Complaint to His Purse,' which repeats the line 'Be heavy again, otherwise I may die!' At least seven of the songs in Gilbert and Sullivan's comic operetta *The Mikado* employ refrains of varying lengths, including: 'And I am right / And you are right ...'; 'They'd none of them be missed!'; 'Three little maids from school'; 'To his daughter-in-law elect'; 'My object all sublime / I shall achieve in time – / To let the punishment fit the crime ...'; 'Oh willow, titwillow, titwillow!'; and so on.

R4: A *leitmotif* is a sentence* or idea, usually associated with a character in narrative* or Wagnerian opera, which is repeated constantly. Ex: In Dickens's novel *David Copperfield*, at least four characters are provided with such tags which recur in their conversation and in fact serve to identify them. Barkis constantly repeats, 'Barkis is willin' '; the word 'humble' (or, more properly, 'umble') identifies Uriah Heep; and Mr and Mrs Micawber are determined respectively to wait for 'something to turn up' and never to 'desert Mr Micawber.'

R5: See epanalepsis*, R5; inclusion*, R1; and rhyme*, R3.

REFUTATION A line of reasoning*, or set of arguments*, whose function is to overturn an adversary's conclusion by undermining his or her arguments.

Ex: 'But the argument that, because the government believes a man has committed a crime, it must prosecute him is much weaker than it seems. Society "cannot endure" if it tolerates all disobedience; it does not follow, however, nor is there evidence, that it will collapse if it tolerates some' (Steve Dworkin, 'On Not Prosecuting Civil Disobedience,' quoted by Corbett, p. 5).

R1: Thomas Kuhn explains the relationship he finds between the notions of 'proof,' 'refutation,' and 'falsification' in the following response to Popper's criticisms of his theory concerning revolutions in science: 'But Sir Karl [Popper] describes as "falsification" or "refutation" what happens when a theory fails in an attempted application, and these are the first of a series of related locutions that again strike me as extremely odd. Both "falsification" and "refutation" are antonyms of "proof." They are drawn principally from logic and from formal mathematics; the chains of argument to which they apply end with a "Q.E.D."; invoking these terms implies the ability to compel assent from any member of the relevant professional community. No member of this audience, however, still needs to be told that, where a whole theory or often even a scientific law is at stake, arguments are seldom so apodictic. All experiments can be challenged, either as to their relevance or their accuracy. All theories can be modified by a variety of *ad hoc* adjustments without ceasing to be, in their main lines, the same theories' (Thomas Kuhn, in *Criticism and the Growth of Knowledge*, ed. I. Lakatos and A. Musgrave, p. 13).

R2: Le Clerc proposes a form of refutation based on a search for the weaknesses of the antagonist's arguments: 'If he proved something irrelevant to the matter in hand, if he abused the ambiguity of words, if he drew an absolute, unrestricted conclusion from something true only accidentally or in certain respects, if he declared clear what is doubtful, confessed what is contested, declared relevant to the case what is merely idle speech' (*Nouvelle Rhétorique*, p. 137). But the principal topics of refutation belong among the 'commonplaces' (see argument*). Angenot specifies some additional ones:
– *contradiction* (Perelman, 1:262), by which we show that our adversary did not remain within his or her own logic
– *incompatibility*, by which we say that our adversary is trying to prove two irreconcilable things (one cannot at the same time be a have and a have-not)
– *dilemma* (Kibédi-Varga, pp. 65–6; Lanham), by which we oblige our opponent to choose between two equally disadvantageous options (you're damned if you do, and you're damned if you don't)

– *pseudo-dilemma*, by which we reconstruct two contrary sets of arguments both of which, we claim, were advanced alternately by our opponent and tend to support the same conclusion (Perelman, 1:319)
– *dissimilitude*, by which we show that our opponent confuses quite distinct cases, by practising amalgamation of opposites, for example
– *counter-example*, whose aim is to reduce a general truth to an occasional one
– *redefinition of the question*, with quotation* of supporting authorities. Ex: 'I define a Republic, said Rousseau, as any State ruled by laws under any form of administration, because only then does the public interest rule and does the public good count for anything' (quoted by R. de Jouvenel, *La République des camarades*, p. 265).
– *probable partiality*, by which we show that no one can fairly judge a dispute in which one is involved. Ex: 'The servant of received opinion (alias the professor) defends himself against the charge that his ideas are controlled by his social superiors: no one likes to admit to his role in the thought-police' (Paul Nizan, *Les Chiens de garde*, p. 96).
– *absence of proof* in support of some affirmation. Ex: 'All these things – let's admit their importance – are proposed without a shred of proof. And it is upon them that the whole edifice rests' (J. Benda, *Le Bergsonisme*, p. 22).

For the refutation of a dilemma, see alternative*, R2.

R3: Apodioxis, evasion, and other less reputable types of refutation are described under argument*, R2. See also sophistry*, R3, antiparastasis*, R1; concession*, R3; counter-litotes*, R2; and excuse*, R1.

R4: Traditionally, refutation has its place in the second part of the development of a speech (see plan*). It helps to characterize the relationship between speaker and addressee (see enunciation*, R1). It has its own intonation*. It takes the form of dissimilitude (see parallel*, R1) and may be simulated (see false –*, R1). An anticipated refutation is a prolepsis*.

R5: *Counter-refutation* consists in refuting a refutation. If an argument* which opposes a line of reasoning* is presented ahead of time as being susceptible of possible refutation, it is no more than an *objection*. Objections are characteristic of honest discussion in which speakers seek to understand rather than to refute. Objections are therefore usually made in the form of questions*. Ex: 'What about the workers!' They too may be simulated (the *ab absurdo* argument). See supposition*, R1.

REGRESSION 'Return to a subject ... recurrence or repetition* (of a word or statement)' (*OED*); repetition of words from the beginning of a sentence, with detailed explanation of them (see Littré). For the latter definition, see also Lausberg (sect. 798), Morier (sense 2), and Quillet.

Ex:

Treason doth never prosper! what's the reason?
For if it prosper, none dare call it treason.
John Harington (1561–1612), *Epigrams*, books 4, no. 5

Ex: 'For we are unto God a sweet savor of Christ, in them that are saved, and in them that perish. To the one we are the savor of death unto death; and to the other the savor of life unto life' (2 Corinthians 2:15–16).

Other name: *epanodos* (Espy, 1983; Jacobs, p. 131; Lanham; Peacham)

Other definition: 'repetition in inverse order of ... the words at the beginning of a sentence' (Littré; see also Morier [sense 1]). See *reversio**.

R1: Regressions are examples of anticipated recapitulations*.

REGROUPED MEMBERS Analogous functions (for example, subjects on the one hand and verbs on the other) are regrouped (within a sentence) into a set of consecutive, syntactically parallel clauses, despite the confusions in meaning which may result. See Morier.

Ex:

Ever the hard unsunk ground,
Ever the eaters and drinkers, ever the upward and downward sun,
 ever the air and the ceaseless tides,
Ever myself and my neighbours, refreshing, wicked, real.
Walt Whitman, 'Song of Myself,' ll. 42–4

Ex: '... and in administrative committee rooms, assemblies of Jesuit fathers, of illiterate aristocrats and of bankers from the City of London ... represent in equal parts the indispensable contribution made by the common herd, by the landed gentry and by capitalism' (Claude Simon, *Histoire*, p. 165).

Other names: respective enumeration* (H.R. Diwekar); parallelism* (Fowler)

R1: The device, which may admittedly reduce clarity, seems to be unknown in classical rhetoric. It nevertheless occurs frequently in the Buddhist poetry of India and occasionally in sixteenth-century French texts when they are both poetic and abstract.

R2: A simple regrouping of functions will not do; they must require parallel decoding. Thus, the following example is a disjunction* in which the members are not regrouped since the verbs fit all the subjects:

> French, English, Lorrainers, in a furious muster
> Advanced, fought, struck and died together.
>
> Voltaire, *Henriade*, VI

R3: The device denotes a type of thought which is at the same time both synthetic and analytic. **Ex:** 'In the case of both spiritualism and materialism, through excess of admiration or through lack of esteem for them, Man remains floating above, or stranded upon, the margins of the Universe – without roots, a mere accessory' (P. Teilhard de Chardin, *Oeuvres*, 6:26).

REMINDER In response to a listener's unasked question*, whether real or merely supposed, the speaker inserts between two pauses* an explanatory segment which repeats an idea or word already uttered or left implicit.

Ex: 'It will (the air) do you good ...' (Joyce, *Ulysses*, p. 539).

Other meaning: see flashback*, R2; and repetition*, R4.

R1: Syntactic reminders also exist. See restart*.

R2: Reminders are a feature of spoken language. In serious written language they may appear careless or have a comic effect. They may draw attention to enunciation*. **Exx:** 'I'm sure (at least I *think* I'm sure)'; 'I couldn't tell as I read this (and tonight I still can't) if Humphrey were playing a practical joke' (J. Lynn and A. Jay, *The Complete 'Yes Minister,'* pp. 144, 192).

R3: Reminders are effective if their content has already been indicated; otherwise, they are simulated.

REMOTIVATION In linguistics, motivation is the relationship which the mind establishes between a form and its meaning*. Remotivation consists in changing the relationship.

Ex: Concrete poetry as well as such French forms as the *calligramme** produce poems whose meaning is revealed by their shape rather than (or as well as) by what the words mean (see p. 389).

R1: Motivation is often unconscious. It compensates for the sign's arbitrary nature, because the relationship established between signifier and signified is never characterized by absolute necessity. As Saussure showed, there is no reason why a particular signified receives its signifier (proof: the differences between languages). Motivation is a psychic phenomenon which attaches itself onto some pre-existing link between signifier and signified.

au pair girl

pair gі
rl au pair
ɔair girl au
au pair girl
ɹu pair girl aι
ιrl au pair girl a
ɹair girl au pair girι
ɹirl au pair girl au pair
ɔair girl au pair girl au pa
air girl au pair girl au pair
pair girl au pair girl au pa
ιu pair girl au pair girl aι
ιirl au pair girl au pair
ᴎirl au pair girl ⁻

Ian Hamilton Finlay, in *Twentieth-Century Poetry and Poetics*, ed. Gary Geddes, p. 398

It is achieved in different ways: onomatopoeia*, tricks of sound (see word-play*), graphisms*, associations within a family of words, etymology*, and metanalysis* in the case of longer segments. Sometimes it is the general shape of the word we associate with the thing, which explains, incidentally, the evocative power of some portmanteau* words.

The opposite, the *deportmanteau word*, is more subtle since we suppose that in reality an ordinary word results from the contraction of several words which form its periphrastic equivalent. Ex: The *Spectator* of 9 April 1887 (see *OEDS*) spoke of the ' "Torrible Zone" [i.e., torrid + horrible] which is one of the most beautiful of portmantologisms,' thereby positing for those wishing to understand its neologism* the periphrasis 'data studied by portmantologists, i.e., by those who study portmanteau words.'

Not so difficult to bring off is syntactic remotivation which restores a grammatical category to what it was in the past, or throughout its history, that is, *diachronically*. (Diachronic comparison* of a phenomenon through its different historical stages is opposed to synchronic comparisons of a phenomenon with other similar ones in the same time period.) Adjectives or nouns which derive from present or past participles may be restored to their previous verbal forms. **Ex:** 'a student of revolution.' Use of the direct object revives the notion of study (as in '[s]he studies revolutions'), whereas use of the noun as subject sometimes implies a young person who may or may not do much studying. ('The pejorative kind of semantic change has always been commoner than the meliorative, human nature being what it is, and Mr. Howard shows how *student* is coming to mean irresponsible young layabout, just as *research* can signify the looking up of telephone numbers and the riffling through of old press cuttings' [Anthony Burgess, *But Do Blondes Prefer Gentlemen?*, p. 207].)

Remotivation also occurs when we go back from the generally accepted figurative meaning* of a term to its literal meaning, if the latter still exists. **Ex:** 'A moment ago ... I had been struck (what an astonishing word. How many words seem to have been invented by neurotics!) by the awful chair (in the shower room of a lunatic asylum)' (H. Michaux, *Connaissance par les gouffres*, p. 78). See also simile*, R3; and denomination*, R3.

R2: When a specific meaning* attaches to a term because of a process of reasoning*, its motivation may be uncertain. In statistics, for example, there is the case of *objective* and *subjective* averages. The objective average is the average based on different measurements of the same thing; the subjective average is that of the measurements of several analogous things. *Objective* seems to have been taken to refer to the unique character of an object, but a different argument would be just as plausible: in the case of a single object, the average relates to differences between estimates (their subjective aspect); in the case of several objects, calculations cover each variable as 'objectively' (!) unchangeable. In such a case, we would get two specifically opposite meanings.

REPETITION Using the same terms several times (see Fontanier, p. 329). See also Lausberg, Littré, and Preminger.

Fontanier's definition, although a narrow one in that it involves only 'terms,' nonetheless includes several specific figures. See reduplication*, triplication*, and tautology*. For other types of repetition, see alliteration*, antimetathesis*, assonance*, chiasmus*, echo* effect, gemination*, pleonasm*, verbigeration* and the double (a type of printing error; see mistake*).

R1: If several terms are involved, they may be repeated in a different order. **Ex:**

POLONIUS: That he is mad, 'tis true: 'tis true 'tis pity;
And pity 'tis 'tis true. A foolish figure!

Shakespeare, *Hamlet*, 2.2.97–8

R2: Repetition without purpose is usually judged to be careless.

R3: Figures of repetition for purposes of emphasis* include: amplification* (see amplification, R3); anaphora*; antepiphora*; and epiphora*. See emphasis*, R1.

R4: Victims of *palillalia*, a type of pathological repetition, say the same word over and over again; those suffering from *palimphrasia* repeat the same phrase or sentence. See also epanalepsis* and echolalia*. In Pierre Marchais's glossary of psychiatric terms, the quasi-mechanical repetition of an action is called *iteration*. In the Middle Ages, people used to make the sign of the cross before counting 1, 2, 3, 4 ... because they feared some (diabolical) automatism might force them to continue.

R5: In narrative*, episodes may be repeated as announcements of what will occur later, as reminders*, or as variations* of events recounted. Such narrative is 'repetitive' and is the opposite of the 'singulative' variety, in Genette's terminology (see *Narrative Discourse*, ch. 3). See also loop*.

REPETITION (HACKNEYED) Repetition of the same words a great many times.

Exx:

... the title of Daniel Hoffman's book (1972) is beyond satire. It is *Poe, Poe, Poe, Poe, Poe, Poe, Poe*. The rhythm, of course, is that of Poe's own 'The Bells' ... but there is a defiance there, like William Pitt in the House of Commons crying 'Sugar, sugar, sugar, sugar, sugar, sugar. Who will dare to laugh at sugar now?' (A. Burgess, *But Do Blondes Prefer Gentlemen?*, p. 295)

So when Humphrey brought me up-to-date this morning, I was appalled. I could hardly believe it at first. I told Humphrey I was appalled.
'You're appalled?' he said 'I'm appalled.'
Bernard said he was appalled too. (J. Lynn and A. Jay, *The Complete 'Yes Minister,'* p. 114)

Analogous idiom: to harp on the same theme or topic

R1: Such constant repetition has an emphatic or insistent function, but it may also signal mental aberration. **Ex:** 'MR. MARTIN: Well then, well then, well then, well then, perhaps we have seen each other in that house, dear lady?' (Eugene Ionesco, *The Bald Soprano*, in *Four Plays*, trans. D.M. Allen, p. 17). See also André Breton's poem 'Pièce fausse' in *Clair de terre*. A prototypical example of hyperbolic repetition is David's lamentation on the death of Absalom: 'O my son Absalom, my son, my son Absalom! my son, my son! ... O my son Absalom, O Absalom, my son, my son!' (2 Samuel 18:33; 19:4).

R2: Queneau identified one type of hackneyed morpho-syntactic repetition which consists of constructing all the sentences in a text in the same way. **Ex:** 'Then the bus arrived. Then I got on. Then I saw ...' (*Exercises de style*, p. 61).

REPRISE (GRAMMATICAL) We propose to restrict the meaning of this term to repetition*, not of lexemes, but of their grammatical environment, both formal and functional. This will therefore include articles, endings, prepositions, subordinating conjunctions, and so on.

Ex: 'What seas what shores what grey rocks and what islands / What water lapping the bow' (T.S. Eliot, 'Marina'). See also synonymy*, R1, and triplication*, R1.

Other definitions (more general meanings): 1. In music, a repeated passage or song in a musical program.
2. *Semi-variation*. In a narrative* or description*, a return to the same point using different but not incompatible terms. See variation*. **Ex:** 'If from the ginkgo tree a single little yellow leaf falls and rests on the lawn, the sensation felt in looking at it is that of a single yellow leaf. If two leaves descend from the tree, the eye follows the twirling of the two leaves as they move closer, then separate in the air, like two butterflies chasing each other, then glide finally to the grass, one here, one there. And so with three, with four, even with five; as the number of leaves in the air increases further, the sensations corresponding to each of them are summed up, creating a general sensation like that of silent rain, and – if the slightest breath of wind slows their descent – that of wings suspended in the air, and then that of a scattering of little luminous spots, when you lower your gaze to the lawn' (Italo Calvino, *If on a Winter's Night a Traveller*, trans. W. Weaver, p. 199).

R1: As a figure, it seems to be close to *homoioptoton*, in which identical declension allows comparison of lexemes having the same function (see homoioteleuton*, R1). See also parallelism*, R1, and period*, R2.

R2: If the lexeme is modified, but not its affixes, it is a *semi-reprise*, frequently accompanied by homoioteleuton*. See also isolexism*, R1.

R3: Because of the substitutions* it makes when lexemes are replaced arbitrarily, grammatical reprise is one of the devices of collage* recommended by Eluard (*Oeuvres complètes*, 1:991). If we were to take as model the children's song: 'If there were no soup, there would be no spoons. If there were no more sons, there would be no more mothers ...,' we would get by arbitrary lexical substitution: 'If there were no dreams, there would be no dark glasses. If there were no darkness, there would be no poets ...' See also seriation*, R2, and anaphora*, R1.

RESPONSE An utterance whose function is to complete, confirm, or weaken a question*.

Ex:

> GWEN: Do you know Mr. Tzara, the poet?
> JOYCE: By sight and reputation; but I am a martyr to glaucoma and inflation.
>
> Tom Stoppard, *Travesties*, act 1

Responses may begin by reformulating the question (i.e., by adapting the actualizers). They may also turn back the question on the speaker, or repeat the same words (if they change the terms' meaning*, we have antanaclasis*).

Idioms: to 'field questions'; 'to give an actor cues'; 'to play straight-man'; 'to feed a comedian lead-in lines to allow witty retorts.' Ex:

> [Mark] Twain and ... William Dean Howells were leaving church one morning as it started to rain heavily.
> 'Do you think [the rain] will stop?' asked Howells.
> 'It always has,' answered Twain. (Leonard Rossiter, *The Lowest Form of Wit*, p. 92)

Analogous: answer, rejoinder, retort, give tit for tat. Ex:

> FLORA: He wasn't worth it.
> AGNES (Sighs): I don't know. There never was another for me.
> FLORA: Plenty of fish in the sea, I say.
> AGNES: Different kettle altogether.
>
> Tom Stoppard, *Teeth*, in
> *The Dog It Was That Died and Other Plays*, p. 71

– *repartee*: 'making of witty retorts' (*Concise Oxford Dictionary*). Ex:

> (Young woman): 'There are two things I don't like about you, Mr. Churchill.'
> 'Yes, and what are they?' he asked.
> 'Your politics and your moustache.'
> 'Madam, from your appearance you are hardly likely to come in contact with either.' (Rossiter, *The Lowest Form of Wit*, p. 70)

– *retortion**: an answer made to an argument* by converting it against the person using it (see *OED*). Ex:

> 'I think you look pretty nifty.'
> 'Thank you, I wish I could say the same about you, but I don't lie.'
> 'Why not, I did.' (Bob Hope, in *A Masterpiece of Murder* [TV film, 1987])

– *responses*: 'responsary; any part of the liturgy said or sung in answer to a priest' (*Concise Oxford Dictionary*)

– *traverse:* in a lawsuit, a formal denial especially of an allegation concerning factual matters. See tautology*, R1.

R1: The alternating set *question/answer* (see dialogue*) is present in segments both shorter and longer than a sentence and is fundamental to simple asseveration. The latter is, after all, divided between presuppositions, on the one hand, and statements, on the other. *Presuppositions* form the more or less implicit content of questions (which usually specify also which piece of the answer is missing). *Statements* serve to answer the questions. In longer texts, the posing of a question may require several paragraphs*, while the answer will be expressed as multiple arguments*, hypotheses, remarks, and conclusions.

We should also mention collections of brief exchanges, such as *catechisms,* 'collections of doctrinal verities,' which take question/answer form and which have to be learned by heart. Our own period has produced another way of collecting brief exchanges of this nature: the *opinion poll,* to which the addressee supplies the answers. In more didactic form, the *test* allows only for choices between ready-made responses. This is a kind of *examination* in which the answers are marked so as to permit a tabulation of results as a basis for rating candidates.

R2: Most texts participate in the self's dialogue* with the world. We ask questions of ourselves and of others, and we provide answers to both types. Responses always form the most impersonal kind of texts and may be understood better if they are replaced in their context. According to André Jolles (*Formes simples,* p. 104f), the primitive literary genre, myth*, is a response to an audience's implied questions, as opposed to riddles* or conundrums, which imply responses. Successful writers know how to guide their readers, how to lead them to ask those questions they will enjoy answering. Ex: 'He tried to read. It was evening. The lamplight lit up his book, his hands, the divan. But it was becoming difficult to read. Something somewhere was different. He glanced up from the text. The room had become bigger, remarkably so. It ... was in a big house he had sometimes gone to, a great lady's house. She might come in' (Michaux, *Les Grandes Epreuves de l'esprit,* p. 93). Even clearer is the key word kept back until the last line, as in Ambrose Bierce's story 'A Horseman in the Sky' or in Eluard's poem 'Liberté.'

In the theatre, the function of some sentences is to reveal to the audience data necessary to comprehension of the plot: the characters speak each other's names and exteriorize their preoccupations, for instance. This is expository dialogue (see explanation*, R1). Ex:

ESTRAGON: Nothing to be done.
VLADIMIR: I'm beginning to come round to that opinion. All my life I've tried to put it from me, saying, Vladimir, be reasonable, you

haven't yet tried everything. And I resumed the struggle. So there you are again.

ESTRAGON: Am I?

VLADIMIR: I'm glad to see you back. I thought you were gone forever.

ESTRAGON: Me too.

...

VLADIMIR: May one enquire where his Majesty spent the night?

ESTRAGON: In a ditch.

VLADIMIR: And they didn't beat you?

ESTRAGON: Beat me? Certainly they beat me.

VLADIMIR: The same lot as usual?

ESTRAGON: The same? I don't know.

Samuel Beckett, *Waiting for Godot*, act 1

R3: Responses convey the markers of the different types of contact between speakers. Sometimes such contacts change during a conversation (see reactualization*, 3). The identity of the public addressed becomes clear in the tone used, the 'most important thing,' according to Paul Valéry. The three kinds of style (grand, middle, low or plain [Lanham, p. 113]) offer little help in categorizing addressees, who in the past were classified socially. (See level* of language.) Nowadays, however, we distinguish between tones which are oratorical, intellectual, affective, and so on. When Valéry was preoccupied with the question of his readers' silent responses to his works, he invented categories for them: '... a group of people, a superficial youth who must be dazzled, stunned to be moved – or a distrustful individual, difficult of access – or one of those apparently deep types who allow you to say anything, actually welcome it; they grasp what you're saying, run on ahead even, but soon cancel out what you in fact wrote' (P. Valéry, *Oeuvres*, 2:577).

Some unavowed portion of a response is to be understood outside the utterance proper, particularly the way it serves to identify the speaker. For example, French people will speak French in Denmark, even though they may speak English, and even though they know English is more likely to be understood, simply because they prefer not to be *taken for* English. (This is an example of the *perlocutionary* value of an utterance.) The tone used also identifies the speaker's mood (threatening, discouraging, etc.).

R4: Another kind of response, not always expected (or welcome), is the *objection*, which we may make against our own arguments: this is the negative function of argumentation. Simply repeating some of the words of the question in the right tone is enough. Ex: ' "It was bound to happen." "*Bound!* ... *bound?* One never knows." '

Objections cannot be avoided, but a speaker may try to respond to them in advance by means of prolepsis* and *subjectio* (see question*,

R3). Prefaces, forewords, and afterwords may be proleptic or analeptic responses to possible objections from readers. In *discussions*, academic or otherwise, objections may take the form of questions*.

For evasive responses, see argument*, R2. For the exploitation of presuppositions, see finesse*, R1. For both responses expected to be positive and also the 'Norman' answer, see negation*. See also interjection*; literary* games; persiflage*; reminder*; tautology*, R1; and well-wishing*, R2.

RESTART (neol.) In order to reattach several groups of words to a segment central to the sentence's syntax, the speaker repeats it, at least in part.

Ex: 'The few – by which we mean those who think, in contradistinction from the many who think they think – *the few* who think at first hand, and thus twice before speaking at all – these received the play with a commendation somewhat less *prononcée* – somewhat more guardedly qualified – than Professor Longfellow might have desired, or may have been taught to expect' (E.A. Poe, 'The American Drama,' in *E.A. Poe: Selected Writings*, p. 464).

Synonym: syntactic reminder

R1: Restarts do not necessarily employ epanalepsis*. The repetition* in other terms of the pivotal syntagm* is more elegant. This is the device recommended by the ancient rhetors, who named it anapodoton (see anacoluthon*, R2). Ex: 'He is a mimetic man: unconfident, eager to please, infinitely suggestible' (David Lodge, *Changing Places*, p. 10).

R2: The pivotal syntagm* may change its grammatical form, but it retains the same function. If it does change its form, there is a type of anacoluthon*, as Marouzeau points out. Exx: 'Why don't I – but no, you should do it yourself'; 'He couldn't go, how could he?' Restarts are common in spoken language and give a very natural effect in mimetic reproduction of speech or interior monologue*. Ex: 'yes imagine Im him think of him can you feel him trying to make a whore out of me' (Joyce, *Ulysses*, p. 610). There may also be a syntactic stop and restart. Ex: 'I have seen the plain waiting; waiting for a little rain' (Gide, *Romans*, p. 161). See self-correction*, R2.

RETORTION 'An answer made to an argument* by converting it against the person using it' (*OED*). See also Lalande and Robert.

Ex: '... I am one of the writers rebuked by Mr. Howard of *The Times* for using gibberish ... [Mr. Howard writes,] "It is a paradox that it [the word *gay*] has been expropriated by one of the sadder groups of society" (does not Mr. Howard mean "appropriated") ...' (Anthony Burgess, *But Do Blondes Prefer Gentlemen?*, pp. 206–7).

Other definition: metastasis (Joseph, Lanham, Peacham)

R1: Another, quite current, type of retortion is the *ad hominem* (or *ad feminam*) retort that one's opponent does not apply his or her principles to his or her own conduct. Perelman (pp. 274–5) gives the following comic example: 'In a provincial theatre a policeman went on the stage, when the audience was standing to sing the *Marseillaise*, to announce that anything not mentioned in the poster outside the theatre was prohibited. "Are *you* mentioned in the poster?" interrupted a spectator.' Another example: 'A missionary blamed his African flock for walking undressed. "And what about yourself?" they pointed to his visage, "are not you, too, somewhat naked?" "Well, but that is my face." "Yet in us," retorted the natives, "everywhere it is face"' (Roman Jakobson, 'Closing Statement: Linguistics and Poetics,' in *Style in Language*, ed. Th. Sebeok, p. 377).

R2: A purely rhetorical form, *false retortion*, consists in countering with one of the opponent's own sentences by drawing attention to the opponent's failure to live up to his or her own expressed intention. Ex: 'Mr. [John] Simon is the first to admit that he is capable, like the rest of us, of bad writing, but he should not write badly when he is writing of bad writing' (A. Burgess, *But Do Blondes Prefer Gentlemen?*, p. 214). Antanaclasis* offers a more anodyne, and more astute, way of taking one's opponent at his or her word.

REVERSIO A troublesome term which is presented by Lanham as a synonym of anastrophe*, by Littré, Morier, Quillet, and Robert as a synonym of regression*, and by Fontanier and Lausberg as a synonym of antimetabole*. *Reversio* may reduce to the common denominator of the two latter figures: repetition* of a group of successive terms in reverse order.

Ex: 'Grossbooted draymen rolled barrels dullthudding out of Prince's stores and bumped them up on the brewery float. On the brewery float bumped dullthudding barrels rolled by grossbooted draymen out of Prince's stores' (Joyce, *Ulysses*, p. 96).

R1: Unlike antimetabole*, *reversio* does not create new meaning.

R2: The figure is easier to achieve in Latin, where word order is freer. In English and French, we reverse the order of syntagms* more easily than that of words.

R3: *Reversion* is 'translation back into the original language' (*OED*).

REWRITING Readers may receive various successive versions of the same text, versions which differ not simply because of a few variants, but because of occasionally quite considerable differences in content and form, even in intent and length.

Rewriting

Exx: John Fowles published a revised version of his novel *The Magus* in 1977 (the first version was published in 1966). Fowles also provided alternative ('happy' and 'unhappy') endings for his novel *The French Lieutenant's Woman* (1969). Flaubert produced (but did not publish) two versions of *L'Education sentimentale* (1843–5, 1869). In his edition *Wifred Owen: The Poems* (Penguin Books, 1985), John Silkin reproduces two versions of 'Strange Meeting' and also a photograph of the manuscript because of its 'ambiguity' (p. 143). François Hébert presents in *Holyoke* four versions or revisions of an unfinished text. Francis Ponge offers two successive versions of *L'Appareil du téléphone* (*Le Grand Recueil*, 3:1).

Analogous: recasting

R1: *Interlineation* and *marginalia* (*OED*) are written units added either between the lines or in the margins of a text. The devices are sometimes used in advertisements where appropriately manipulative handwritten adjectives or adverbs are added for emphasis. *Cancelling marks* cross out words or syntagms*. **Ex:** In the edition of Wilfred Owen's poems already referred to, Silkin reproduces (p. 140) the following cancelled line from 'Strange Meeting':

~~Yet slumber droned all down that sullen hall.~~

R2: *Alterations* or *second thoughts* are short modified passages an author adds or withdraws from a text before publication. (The French word is *repentir* – something repented and corrected; Morier found it among terms relating to painting.) If the changes involve correction of imperfections, we speak of *touching up* (a term from painting) or *retouching* (from photography). Morier writes: 'The study of alterations ... shows the author's craftsmanship, linguistic scruples, care for logic, [terminological] accuracy, coherence, precision, delicacy, reticence [*pudeur*] ... Sometimes loss of clarity is the result: *dark* grottoes become *unknown* (the change blurs the expression); often it becomes clearer, as in Baudelaire's *basaltic* grottoes (the change makes it needle-sharp)' (see 'repentir,' in Morier, *Dictionnaire de poétique et de rhétorique*).

R3: *Interpolations* are changes to an original text made by someone else, with the result that the meaning* is obscured by error or deception.

R4: In palaeography, to mark a letter for removal, a point is pricked below (or sometimes above) it; surrounding a word with points marks it for removal. This is called *expunging* (*OED*).

R5: A metaphrase is rewriting in summary form (see paraphrase*, R1).

R6: Complete texts are frequently rewritten in a different genre (e.g., novels adapted for the stage or cinema), or for a different public (children's editions, vulgarizations, digests, etc.). 'Remakes' in the cinema are newer versions of motion pictures already made. **Ex:** Lewis

Milestone's *Mutiny on the Bounty* (1962), starring Marlon Brando, is a remake of Frank Lloyd's *Mutiny on the Bounty* (1935), which starred Clark Gable.

RHYME Identity of a certain number of phonemes at the end of two or more lines* of poetry.

1. Rhyme quality. *Imperfect rhyme* (also called 'partial,' 'slant,' 'half,' 'approximate,' 'oblique,' 'off,' or 'near' rhyme) includes assonance* (the vowels of two stressed syllables sound alike; e.g., 'seem'/'clear') and consonance (agreement between the [esp. final] consonants of stressed syllables; e.g., 'dive'/'dove'). Ex:

It seemed that out of battle I escaped
Down some profound tunnel, long since scooped
Through granites which Titanic wars had groined.
Yet also there encumbered sleepers groaned.
Wilfred Owen, 'Strange Meeting'

See assonance*, R3.

Exact rhyme (also called 'complete,' 'perfect,' 'whole,' 'true,' or 'full' rhyme) is identity between the monosyllables (vowel and supporting consonant) or final stressed syllables of two or more words.

Leonine rhyme: 'Strictly used, the term means a disyllabic rhyme of the last syllable of the second foot and the first syllable of the third foot, with the two syllables of the sixth foot of a Latin hexameter. More commonly it indicates the rhyme of the word preceding the caesura* with the final word in both hexameters and pentameters' (Preminger).

Rich rhyme: repeating sounds with two senses. Ex: 'two'/'too'.

Holorhymes are rhymes so rich that the French call them 'millionaire' rhymes; they appear mainly in punning combinations like 'On demande *une pan*ac*é*e *universelle* / Pour guérir *une panne universelle*' ('Required a universal panacea to repair a fairly common breakdown'; example cited by Redfern, p. 100). If too rich, rhyme tends to become word-play*. See equivoque*. Ex:

Then I can write a washing bill in Babylonic cuneiform,
And tell you every detail of Caractacus's uniform;
In short, in matters vegetable, animal and mineral,
I am the very model of a modern Major-General.
W.S. Gilbert, *The Pirates of Penzance*

For a detailed discussion of rhyme, see Frances Stillman, *The Poet's Manual and Rhyming Dictionary,* and Philip Davies Roberts, *How Poetry Works.*

2. Rhyme schemes. Rhymed couplets are two successive lines rhyming with each other (*aabb*); alternate rhymes are made up of two couplets, one of which may be masculine and the other feminine (see below, 3), which are interwoven (*abab*). Introverted or enclosing rhymes have one rhyming couplet inserted within another (*abba*). Rhyme may also occur randomly.

End-rhyme may combine with *in-rhyme*, repetitions* of identical sounds at the end of a line and at the hemistich, so that the hemistiches rhyme with one another. Or, as in *cross-rhyme*, the end of one line is matched with the middle of the next, or vice versa.

The game may be pursued further: poems may still retain meaning* when only the first hemistiches (which may rhyme, thanks to in-rhymes) are read. The device received a name in Greek, *asynartete*, although the definitions (*OED*, Cuddon) point out that the hemistiches differ rhythmically, with a single line being composed of 'two members of different rhythms ... combinations of dactyl, trochee and iambus' (*OED*).

3. Masculine and feminine rhymes. Masculine rhymes involve only one stressed syllable, as in 'fail'/'wail' and 'mine'/'thine'. Feminine rhymes consist of a stressed syllable followed by an unstressed syllable; for example, 'landing'/'standing'. In French prosody between the fourteenth and sixteenth centuries, custom established alternation of what constitute sexed rhymes in that language: a feminine rhyme ends in a so-called mute *e*. However, since the *e* gradually lost its value in non-poetic pronunciation, a new kind of rhyme in which masculine endings were allowed to rhyme with feminine became possible. This is especially noticeable in the poems of the late nineteenth-century symbolist Paul Verlaine and in those of the surrealist Louis Aragon (who makes *rue* rhyme with *disparu*, for instance). The rule prescribing alternation of masculine and feminine rhymes is now only respected in fixed-form poems*.

R1: Adoption of a traditional, or fixed, form (see poem*) involves acceptance of a predetermined rhyme scheme. If stanzas* are heterometric (see syllabic line*), lines of the same length usually rhyme with each other, but the opposite system is, of course, possible.

R2: For rhymes in prose texts, see homoioteleuton*.

R3: The word *rhyme* has the same origin as *rhythm** (the Greek word *rythmos*), and its meaning only became separated from rhythm over time. In England and France the separation was already occurring in the fourteenth and fifteenth centuries and was completed by the seventeenth (Cuddon).

R4: Modern experiments with rhyme generally involve near-rhyme in English, where non-rhyme ('the total absence of rhyme found in blank verse and free verse' [Stillman, p. 83]) is more important than in modern French poetry. This despite the surrealist poetic endeavour, which affected both form and content and reopened the way to the universal devices of poetry. In surrealist poems, syllable counting and rhyme are succeeded by a greater rhythmic diversity, and rhyme itself is replaced by echo* effects in undefined, nuanced combinations.

RHYTHM In the broad sense, rhythm involves the respective duration of segments of *discourse** of whatever dimensions. We may just as easily speak of the *rhythm** *of the action* of a narrative as of the binary or ternary rhythm of a *sentence**.

In the strict sense, prose rhythm is the organization of phonetic words into *rhythmic groups*. Prose poetry, or poetic prose, is characterized by some degree of regularity in its *accents**.

Rhythm in poetry is more elaborate.

R1: Poetry is to prose what dancing is to walking: it has a particular rhythm which we can understand by beating time. Morier points out that this may be done 'by making circular hand-movements' and that 'this was perhaps how verses were scanned in ancient times.' To confirm his hypothesis, Morier proposes a new etymology* for *versus* (verse), which in his view is related, by the circular movement which may have accompanied diction, to the Latin *vertere* (to turn). By recalling that verse was spoken before it was written down, he has no difficulty in refuting traditional etymology, which sees verse deriving from *versus*, meaning a line, row, or furrow. 'In this more flexible manner of beating time,' Morier continues [more flexible, that is, than raising and lowering the hand or foot, for instance], 'the *ictus* or stress is indicated by arrival at point zero, the nadir of the circle made' (Grammont, *Le Vers français*, p. 86). Binary rhythm is divided into weak and strong time (arsis and thesis; that is, rise and fall in stress: *yi ts'ing yi tchouo* in Chinese). The nadir of the circle corresponds to strong time. The advantages of this method of marking rhythm are obvious: spontaneity, naturalness, rapidity, and flexibility.

This method is particularly appropriate for scanning rhythmic verse in which the rhythmic divisions may not be entirely tied to accent*. We thus preserve the interplay of long syllables placed either at the beginning or end of a measure, and also that of expressive accents. Beating time in this circular fashion allows one to feel regular, measured duration even in the case of changes to the number and duration of syllables, or silences. The ictus may also be displaced onto the arsis by a kind of *change of step*, as in dancing. René Char achieves this in both *La Sorgue* and *Jacquemar et Julia*.

If rhythmic divisions are made to coincide too frequently with the ictus, the result is military marches rather than lines of poetry.

R2: Francis Poulenc, who set many poems* to music, explained in an interview on French radio on 10 November 1968 how he went about establishing rhythm: 'When I have chosen a poem, whose musical transposition I may accomplish only months later, I examine it from all angles. If it is by Apollinaire or Eluard, I attach the *greatest* importance to the way the poem is laid out on the page, to the blank spaces and margins. I recite the poem to myself frequently, listen to it, look for the traps ... I note down the breathing periods, and try to discover its internal rhythm from one of its lines, *not* necessarily the first one ... When some detail of prosody slows me down, I never try to rush it. Occasionally I wait for days on end, trying to forget the word, until I see it in a new light.'

R3: See also apocope*, R5; cadence*, R1 and R2; typographical caesura*; rhythmic echo*; enjamb(e)ment*, R1; imitative harmony*; mistake*, R2; ode*; parallelism*, R1; pause*, R1; period*; punch* line; stanza*; tempo*, R3; and triplication*, R1.

RHYTHM (OF THE ACTION) Because it lacks a standard measure, the tempo* of events has scarcely been analysed. In the mystery novel, for example, periods of slow searching for clues alternate with sequences of rapid action. How may one gauge acceleration and deceleration of the plot-rhythms? The most natural intrinsic criterion remains the work's first episode, to which we may successively compare the later ones. In novels of action, general tempo usually increases in speed. Conversely, in the final volumes of Proust's *A la recherche du temps perdu*, the action dissolves into a series of meditations.

R1: Narrative* rhythm has been studied in comparison with story or narrated time and with telling or narrator's time. G. Genette (*Narrative Discourse*, ch. 2) distinguishes among: *scene*, in which narrative duration seems to coincide with story time; *summary*, in which action is recounted briefly; *pause*, either descriptive or explanatory, in which telling and action are suspended; and *ellipsis*, when narrative elements are skipped over while the action continues.

Ellipsis* is implicit when narrative stops and then takes up again without revealing what happened in the interim. The duration of an ellipsis may be clearly or obscurely defined (e.g., 'two years passed' or 'a few years went by'), and it may be qualified (e.g., 'after several years *of happiness*').

There are several intermediate stages between summary and scene. In a single chapter of *War and Peace*, Tolstoy's narrator gives a general overview of Napoleon's retreat from Moscow, summarizes the activities of a military squadron, describes the morning spent by one of the heroes, and transcribes a conversation before finally returning to the development of his own ideas and to the explanation of his feelings.

It seem difficult, as well, not to consider some pauses as parts of the action's *narration*. Descriptions* often occur when a character is contemplating the person or place in question because the character's thoughts and impressions are important at that particular moment in the action. In Nathalie Sarraute's novel *Le Planétarium*, for instance, the hero's slightest impressions receive developments in the form of imaginary descriptions, explanations, and particularly dialogues*, all of which make the duration of the narration longer than that of the action narrated. The same is true in William Golding's *Pincher Martin* and Horace McCoy's *They Shoot Horses, Don't They?* Rather than speaking of *deceleration*, which would concern the action itself, we will call this process *dilatation* or expansion. Dilatation resembles amplification* and lengthening*, which involve expression rather than content. Action becomes drawn out and slowed down in opera, in which singing causes a libretto that can be read in a few minutes to last several hours. Although desirable in lyric passages, increased duration seems awkward when the action speeds up; hence the presence in grand opera of dramatic vocal crescendos with musical accompaniment. The solution in operetta or modern musicals, staged or filmed, is spoken passages. See also accumulation*, R5; definition*, R4; generalization*, R4; and narrative*, R2.

RHYTHMIC MEASURES Units for measuring rhythm* in classical prosody. See metric verse under line* (of poetry or verse).

Synonym: 'metric foot: a division of a verse, consisting of a number of syllables one of which has the ictus or principal stress' (*OED*)

R1: Commonly, feet have two syllables. Calling the French alexandrine, for instance, a line of twelve feet confuses metric measure with syllables, units of intonation*. The only case in which measure and syllable may be equated is that of catalectic lines. These lack a syllable (usually) in the last foot but may include silences at the beginning of a line (*anacrusis*), or at the caesura*.

R2: Preminger (pp. 285–6) offers the elements listed in the following table of feet:

IAMB (iambus); iambic x / de\u0301stro\u0301y

ANAPEST (anapaest); anapestic x x / interve\u0301ne

TROCHEE (choree); trochaic / x to\u0301psy

DACTYL; dactylic / x x me\u0301rrily

SPONDEE; spondaic / / ame\u0301n

PYRRHIC (dibrach) x x the\u0301 se\u0301aso\u0301n o\u0301f mi\u0301sts

TRIBRACH x x x

MOLOSSUS / / /

ANTIBACCHIUS / / x

AMPHIBRACHIC / / / *There wás a young láby in Spáin*

APHIMACER (cretic) / x /

BACCHIUS x / /

Longer feet are more complex and fairly rare:

DIPYRRHIC x x x x		
DISPONDEE / / / /		
PAEON 4 x x x /	EPITRITE 4 / / / x	
PAEON 3 x x / x	EPITRITE 3 / / x /	
LESSER IONIC x x / /	GREATER IONIC / / x x	
PAEON 2 x / x x	EPITRITE 2 / x / /	

DIAMB (iambic dimeter) x / x /   x / x / *And so to bed*

ANTISPAST / x x /

CHORIAMB / x x /   / x x /   / x x / *lilies without, roses within* (Marvell)

EPITRITE 1 x / / /   PAEON 1 / x x x

(IMPURE) CRETIC x x x x x (2 long replaced by 2 short)

RIDDLE 1. In the past, the Pythian sibyls gave their oracles (see prophecy*) in the form of allegories* whose meaning* remained hidden. As a result, the riddle is an obscure allegory, according to Quintilian.

Ex: '[Croesus consulted the oracle at Delphi about a war he intended to undertake against Cyrus.] Pythia replied: "When a Mule is King of the Medes, then ... flee ... do not stay where you are and do not be ashamed to be a coward" ... Croesus was overjoyed ... thinking that it was impossible for a Mule to rule over the Medes ... And that consequently neither he nor his descendants would cease to be masters there. [After his defeat, Croesus sent a messenger] to lay his chains on the threshold of the temple and to ask the gods whether they did not blush at having encouraged him. [Pythia replied that his recriminations were without reason]: "Cyrus was the Mule; because he was born of parents belonging to two different races; while his mother was noble, his father was of more modest lineage" ' (Herodotus, *Histories*, 1.55.90–1).

2. The riddle, which is no longer short, has invaded narrative* and dramatic action, flourishing nowadays in the detective novel.

Ex: the riddle of the closed room, invented by Edgar Allen Poe in 'The Murders in the Rue Morgue': 'The closed room is the place which is guarded, forbidden, where the killer could not enter and where, despite all, he kills. The closed room is a problem *par excellence*' (Boileau and Narcejac, *Le Roman policier*, p. 48).

3. Composing and deciphering riddles also form literary or 'parlour' games: 'The riddle is scarcely more than a conundrum. Unlike logogriphs, charades and the rebus, in which symbols* and definitions* help the searcher, the riddle must be solved from a text providing clues as obscure and bizarre as possible' (Claude Aveline, *Le Code des jeux*, p. 303).

Ex: 'A gentleman with a neck, and no head, two arms, but no legs? A shirt' (Paul Eluard, *Poésie involontaire et Poésie intentionnelle*, in *Oeuvres*, 1:1168).

Aveline (pp. 303–4) distinguishes between riddles which are comical, or double, or homonymous, etc. For riddles based on sound, see metanalysis*, R4.

Mention should also be made of *false riddles*, which are intended to be easily solved and are a kind of emphasis*. Ex: 'They are in full swing and will last for a few weeks yet. What? The holidays' (from a French weekly).

A *charade* is 'a kind of riddle, in which each syllable of the word to be guessed, and sometimes the word itself also, is enigmatically described, or (more recently) dramatically represented' (*OED*). 'I am a word of twelve letters. My 12, 4, 7, 2, 5 is an Eastern beast of burden. My 1, 8, 10, 9 is a street made famous by Sinclair Lewis. My 11, 3, 6 is past. My whole is a person suffering from delusions of greatness. Solution: Camel, Main, ago: megalomaniac' (Espy, *The Game of Words*, pp. 69–70).

Charades are a form of *logogriph*, riddles in which one is asked to guess a word, frequently from a process of 'acting out.' Ex: 'See blank tee what domestic animal? Tee dash ar most courageous mariner' (Joyce, *Ulysses*, p. 233; i.e., *cat*, *tar*). Crossword puzzles are often collections of comic logogriphs. Ex: 'Honeyed tones from Labour Leader – I'm no less useful (15 letters).' Solution: mellifluousness: anagram* of the fourteen letters forming the second half of the clue, plus the 'leader,' namely, the first letter of the word 'Labour.' Ex: 'Heureusement il ne manque pas de tact' ('Fortunately he does not lack tact'; 7 letters). Solution: *aveugle* (the blind man): a pun* on the sense of touch and politeness. See A.J. Greimas, 'L'Ecriture cruciverbiste,' in *Du Sens*, p. 290. See also semantic syllepsis*, R2.

The solving of riddles is a characteristic narrative device in the plots of folktales. As Queneau explains (*Histoire des littératures*, 1:8): 'Riddles appeal to a hero's intelligence and skill, and intelligence, like physical courage, is a means of passing tests of initiation.'

Dramatized proverbs*, which Musset raised to the dignity of a literary genre, were originally riddles presented in the form of improvised comedy. Spectators were expected to guess the proverb which the comedy illustrated.

Riddle

4. Literary riddles, serving to attenuate, underline, or singularize, are similar to phoebus*. Ex: 'The sky moved back by at least ten metres' [the character has jumped down from the prison wall] (beginning of A. Sarrazin's *L'Astragale*).

R1: Aporia, the unsolvable problem, refutes one hypothesis by absurdity, pointing out the opposite. Ex: Would Buridan's ass, if placed between two identical bundles of hay, die of indecision? (This aporia serves to prove that the will is not exclusively prompted by external considertions.) Ex: 'The earth is blue like an orange.' This line by Eluard proves, in our view, that commas may not be suppressed without penalty. Indeed, the surrealistic image of a blue orange would lose all its force if one were merely to suppose that a comma has been suppressed after 'blue.' 'The earth is blue, like an orange' = 'it is blue and it is like an orange (i.e., round)'. Only by retention of commas in 'normal' usage can one indicate that a comma is not wanted in this case.

It is advisable to place the aporia either at the beginning or end of a text (see point*). A didactic example: 'In contemporary views of the unconscious, the father is castrated by the mother' (G. Mendel, *La Crise des générations*, p. 193). This example strikingly presents the idea that, in the view of a new generation, technical omnipotence has changed social power, once essentially paternalistic, by attaching to it maternal images of childhood.

R2: The creation of riddles involves a double displacement: abstraction* followed, conversely, by concretization*; this process causes them to resemble tropes.

R3: The *shibboleth* is a 'test word or principle or behaviour or opinion, the use of or the inability to use which reveals one's party, nationality, orthodoxy, etc.' (*Concise Oxford Dictionary*). For instance, during the 'Bruges matins' on 17 May 1302, the Flemish people massacred their French occupiers, whom they identified by their inability to pronounce the Flemish words *schild* and *vriend*.

R4: Some conundrums are deceptive (see anticlimax*, R4). The enigmatic nature of any utterance marks the existence of an intended meaning*. See symbol*, 1, R1. Riddles have their own intonation*.

R5: Like any other genre, riddles are open to parody*. One common form of riddle – 'What's the difference between X and Y?' – was reduced to a nonsense in Robert Altman's film *Images* (1972): 'What's the difference between a rabbit? Nothing, it's both the same.'

S

SARCASM Aggressive, frequently cruel, mockery.

Ex: 'Sarcastic references to other nationalities are common: German humour in Rumanian is a lack of humour (*humor nemtesc*), a German joke in Spanish means stale wit (*chiste aleman*) ... A petty quarrel over nothing is in French a German quarrel (*querelle d'Allemand*); inefficient management in German is Polish economy (*polnische Wirtschaft*); inept diplomacy in Rumanian is Bulgarian diplomacy (*diplomatie bulgareasca*), and empty threats are characterized by the proverb 'Beware the Bulgarian fleet and the Greek cavalry' (*Ferestete de flota bulgara si de cavaleria greceasca*). The funny bone is in French *le petit Juif*. The Lat[in] *Teutonici sunt nati venerunt de culo Pilati* (The Teutons were born coming out of Pilate's fundament) is perhaps the unkindest cut of all' (Noah Jacobs, *Naming Day in Eden*, pp. 62–3).

Analogous definitions: Lanham, Lausberg, Littré, *OED*, and Scaliger, 3:86

Other names: diatribe, satire, libel (short, false, and defamatory written statement [Bénac]), pamphlet (brochure attacking an institution). These parasynonyms designate more fully developed examples of sarcasm, sometimes even literary genres. See also irony*.

R1: Among attitudes towards the addressee, those which destroy trust and mutual understanding through unfair treatment are persiflage*, sarcasm, and insults*. The rhetorical type of reproach is *objurgation* (Jacobs, p. 101, Littré, *OED*, Robert).
    Such attitudes provoke ripostes in the same vein. **Ex:**

'You know very well that charity, not poverty, is the principle of the perfect life!'
'That is what your glutton Thomas said!'
'Mind your words, villain! The man you call "glutton" is a saint of the holy Roman church!'
'Saint, my foot! Canonized by John to spite the Franciscans!' (U. Eco, *The Name of the Rose*, p. 347)

Another even more radical way of destroying mutual understanding is the curse, or *anathema*, which excommunicates a person or condemns a doctrine or intellectual attitude. In this case, as in those exemplified by judicial condemnation, or by blows and wounds, we have left rhetoric far behind.

R2: Sarcasm may combine with apostrophe* and exclamations*. **Ex:**

'Ah! Malraux! How many stupid, empty sentences you are responsible for – not to mention those you wrote' (J.-Fr. Revel, *Contrecensures*, p. 40). In fact, this is a rhetorical apostrophe because the real addressee was the reading public. A speaker may wish to instruct such a public rather than to accuse the victim, who, in such a case, has even less connection with the subject under debate and is sometimes designated merely by allusion*.

Other sarcastic remarks resemble wisecracks, which Dorothy Parker differentiated from wit*: 'Wit has truth in it, wisecracking is simply calisthenics with words' (quoted in L. Rossiter, *The Lowest Form of Wit*, p. 62). Parker made one of the many sarcastic jibes for which she remains famous on being told of the death of the not over-energetic ex-President Calvin Coolidge: ' "How can they tell?" ' (ibid., p. 48). The same source recounts (p. 19) a similar throwaway sneer: 'And Somerset Maugham, watching Spencer Tracy on set during the filming of *Dr Jekyll and Mr Hyde* asked a friend behind him: "Which is he playing now?" '

R3: Sarcasm has its own intonation*. Epigrams* are frequently sarcastic. See also chleuasmos* and ambiguity*, 1.

R4: The opposite of sarcasm is praise. See celebration*, R2, and false –*, R1.

SCESIS ONOMATON (Gr. 'relation of words') Leaving the sentence without a verb. See Joseph, Lanham, and Quinn.

Ex: 'When a sentence or saying doth consist altogether of nouns, yet when to every substantive an adjective is joined, thus: A man faithful in friendship, prudent in counsels, virtuous in conversation, gentle in communication, learned in all learned sciences, eloquent in utterance, comely in gesture, pitiful to the poor, an enemy to naughtiness, a lover of all virtue and godliness' (Henry Peacham, *The Garden of Eloquence* [1593], quoted by Espy, 1983, p. 203).

R1: As well as pointing out (p. 33) that scesis onomaton represents a form of absolute ellipsis*, Quinn emphasizes that far from being an antiquated, forgotten figure in the twentieth century, it has become a 'conventional way to indicate either the apprehension of immediate particulars or the flow of consciousness.' Ex (quoted by Quinn):

> Hog butcher of the world
> Tool maker, stacker of wheat,
> Player with railroads and the nation's freight handler;
> Stormy, husky, brawling,
> City of the big shoulders.
>
> Carl Sandburg, 'Chicago'

SCHEMATIZATION Instead of recounting, describing, or representing an action dramatically, we give a schema or outline of a work.

Ex: '1885. The eyes of the world are fixed on France. An obscure, Jewish artillery officer is accused of selling military secrets to Germany. Convicted by court martial, he is degraded by his regiment and deported, vilified by the press and condemned to a living death on the notorious Ile du Diable ... A desperate message is delivered to "the court of final appeal" at a famous address in London's Baker Street ...' (Michael Hardwick, *Prisoner of the Devil*, 'blurb' on the book jacket).

Ex: 'Captain de Courcy Foulenough, the well known clubman, has succeeded, by using the names of prominent London hostesses, in obtaining credit at some of the more shady whelk stalls at Brighton' (J.B. Morton [Beachcomber], quoted in *The Best of Modern Humor*, ed. Mordecai Richler, p. 101).

R1: In most novels, some episodes are recounted rapidly, in indirect style. They are summaries of part of the action (see rhythm*, R1) without being necessarily schematizations. Ex: 'So off they started about Irish sports and shoneen games ... and building up a nation and all to that' (Joyce, *Ulysses*, p. 260). In order for schematization to occur, the text must present itself as a blueprint or diagram of some other text which is the true one and which it is replacing. Its author must also be presented as a commentator of a work already completed or still to be written. The device is part of the movement to dissolve, distort, or displace a work in order to destroy its resistance as a perfected, totally finished object, and to open the imaginary world to a plurality of readings.

R2: Too schematic a summary risks banality. The opposite is hypotyposis* (see hypotyposis, R2).

R3: Summaries may take the form of notations*. Ex: 'Cut to: Whole luxurious office, Mott a man of fifty-five, Frost thirty' (J.P. Donleavy, 'The Interview' in *The Beat Generation and the Angry Young Men*, ed. G. Feldman and G. Gartenberg, p. 272).

SCRAMBLING (LEXICAL) Replacing a letter to distort the meaning of a word. See paragram*.

Exx: *dangir* for *danger* (R. Ducharme, *L'Avalée des avalées*, p. 265); 'There's a *vas deferens* between children and no children' (W.A. Redfern, *Puns*, p. 18).

R1: If the result is an equivoque*, lexical scrambling is an approximation*. See also spoonerism*, R3.

R2: Letters may be reversed rather than replaced. See metathesis*, R3.

SCRAMBLING (SYNTACTIC) Syntactic disruption rendering the sentence unintelligible.

Ex: 'Arrogant and snivelling in tone [1], who happened to be next to him [2], with the man to remonstrate [3], he started [4]' (R. Queneau, *Exercises in Style*, p. 16). Reading the syntagms* in the order 1/4/3/2, and reversing pronoun and verb in syntagm 3, make the meaning clear.

Other names: *synchisis* ('a figure of construction or defect of style which makes a sentence difficult to understand by reversing the natural order of words' [Lausberg, p. 951]); '*mixtura verborum*' (ibid.; 'deliberately jumbled word order to indicate a confused state of mind' [Grambs])

R1: For semi-scrambling, see hyperbaton*, other def.

SELF-CORRECTION 'The speaker appears to retract purposely what he has just said in favour of something stronger, more decisive or appropriate' (Fontanier, p. 366, under 'correction'). See also Littré.

Exx: '*Of Mice and Men* is, I think, a fine novella (or play with extended stage directions) ...' (A. Burgess, *But Do Blondes Prefer Gentlemen?*, p. 376); '[An enormous head] nourished on itself, or rather on my immense grief, yes, yes, grief about I'm not sure what, but in which a whole age collaborated, no, *three ages*. And all of them bad' (H. Michaux, 'Têtes,' in *Peintures*); 'I once had a girl, / Or should I say / She once had me' (J. Lennon, 'Norwegian Wood' [MacLen Music Inc. BMI]).

Other names: *correctio* (Lanham). See also epanorthosis*.

Other definition: a correction which the receiver of the message makes unaided (information theory)

R1: Self-correction is obviously a species of the genus, correction, which may be addressed to others as well as to oneself. Ex: 'An accident. You mean an attempt on your life' (Hergé, *Tintin* [cartoon strip]). Corrections may be made purely as a matter of form. Ex: 'The officer consulted his list and said: "Ter-*ro*-rist." The next man in line ... took one step forward, raised a philological index-finger and said respectfully: "Not a terro-rist: a *tou*-rist"' (A. Malraux, *Antimémoires*, p. 247). Simulated correction is a form of emphasis*. Ex: 'I'm told it [Irish] is a grand language by them that knows. – Grand is no name for it, said Buck Mulligan. Wonderful entirely' (Joyce, *Ulysses*, p. 13). So there are *pseudo-corrections*. See also periphrasis*, R3.

R2: The marks of self-correction are expressions like 'What am I saying,' 'I mean,' 'or rather,' 'but,' 'no,' and 'yes'; or a restart*; or simply a stop followed by a *new beginning*. Ex: '*Just like before*, he thought, *like* *being in a prison – no, security in a prison is nothing compared to this'* (Tom Clancy, *Patriot Games*, p. 215). Some new beginnings are purely syntactic. Ex: 'I, I have, I am / Elsewhere' (H. Michaux, *Epreuves, exorcismes*, p. 11). They are, nonetheless, forms of self-correction to the extent that they return to a just enunciated text in order to correct it. It is, moreover, this type of readjustment which serves to define the device because disavowal of what was said is not essential; revision is sufficient, if for no other reason than merely to approve the original version. That is the meaning* of certain forms of reduplication* or of apparently gratuitous insertions of the word *yes* or the syntagm* 'I mean' into the process of enunciation.

If self-correction applies only to the signifier (see lapsus*, R3), the speaker may add 'I should say.' Ex: '[The name] of the island, or of the town, I should say ...'

R3: Although rhetorical self-corrections do exist, the device in itself forms a sign of sincerity. Ex: 'What does it mean, the kind looks she often gave me (often, no, but sometimes)?' (Goethe, *The Sorrows of Young Werther*, p. 126). In written texts, where authors have always been at liberty to make changes, self-correction is a deliberate device and must therefore have a *perlocutionary* value. (The author pursues a goal beyond that of enunciation. See Ducrot and Todorov, p. 343.) It might, for instance, be used to make a character reveal his true feelings. Ex [Alun muses about his daughters]: 'The girl was even worse in this respect than her elder sister, now safely married, or rather safely out of the way most of the time on that account' (Kingsley Amis, *The Old Devils*, pp. 101–2). It may also be a matter of indicating that the text is a spontaneous transcription of spoken language and not a written composition. Ex: 'She knows the twelve parts of the may-bug. She's a botany freak. A zoology freak if you prefer' (R. Ducharme, *L'Avalée des avalés*, p. 147). The incorrect word (*botany*) is both displayed and corrected.

R4: **Other uses:** Self-correction serves:
1. to limit an assertion* (see assertion, R3) without modifying it. Ex: 'A certain number of affairs, complicated in appearance – but only in appearance' (G. Bernanos, *Oeuvres romanesques*, p. 768);
2. to insert a distinction*. Ex: 'His glass was empty and he poured himself a treble, or another treble' (K. Amis, *The Old Devils*, p. 341);
3. to juxtapose two lexemes. Exx: 'His unprejudiced outsider's perspective had worked before and it might work again, he thought – hoped' (T. Clancy, *Patriot Games*, p. 323); '[the fleeing General Staff invites its leader to take off his insignia so as to hide his rank] My epaulettes? – growled, *no, roared* Samsonov' (A. Solzhenitsyn, *August 1914*, p. 381). Joyce might have preferred a lexical juxtaposition*: something like *growlroared*;

4. to translate a simile* or metaphor*. **Ex:** 'It's a bird? It's a plane! No ... it's Superman!';
5. to emphasize a word. **Ex:** 'With all this lightness I do not rise, I descend. Or rather I am dragged downward, into the layers of this place as into liquefied mud' (M. Atwood, *Cat's Eye*, p. 13).

R5: Self-correction has its own intonation*. It is similar to the restart* (see restart, R3); it may lead to extravagant* comparisons (see extravagant comparison, R4) and serve as a transition*. In more developed form, it become epanorthosis* (see epanorthosis, R1).

SENTENCE (TYPES OF) Most long sentences possess a complex rhythmical structure and are only typical in some of their parts. We are considering in the present instance relatively simple models. A more advanced study might begin with an analysis of the constituent members, separated by square brackets, etc. (see syntagm*).

1. We might call sentences composed of a single member *unary* (a neologism* common in logic and formed by analogy with *binary*). We would also be conforming to etymology* if we used the term *monorheme* to refer to them, but Marouzeau uses it to refer to one-word sentences (e.g., 'Come.') and so identifies monorhemes with holophrases (see monologue*). Wartburg and Zumthor, on the other hand, taking as their criterion the assertion*, call monorhemes those sentences whose theme* (or psychological subject) is implicit, despite the fact that there also exist short sentences in which the predicate is implied.
A sentence may be considered unary when it progresses without interruption by any factor articulating meaning* (such as a comma, or *a fortiori* a pause*), whatever the length of the single member. **Ex:** 'Modern writers show greater freedom than was once customary in what they place in that position [i.e., between one full stop and another]. *And what of the will to power? Finally on one small point. So far so good. So then. Now for his other arguments*' (Fowler, under 'sentence').

2. *Binary* sentences have two members. **Ex:** 'If the flights of Dryden therefore are higher, Pope continues longer on the wing. If of Dryden's fire the blaze is brighter, of Pope's the heat is more regular and constant. Dryden often surpasses expectation, and Pope never falls below it. Dryden is read with frequent astonishment, and Pope with perpetual delight' (Samuel Johnson, *Lives of the English Poets*, 3:223). Johnson's sentence also contains parallels* in structure and in the thoughts expressed. Neither is necessary to make a sentence binary. **Ex:** 'He went away, she came back.' According to the lengths of the respective members, we have minor or major cadences* (see punch* line, R1). Parallelisms* facilitate the production of binary sentences, particularly in the case of periods*.
Binary sentences are sometimes called dirhemes, but Marouzeau and

Wartburg and Zumthor take *dirheme* to mean a sentence in which both subject and predicate are expressed.

3. *Ternary* sentences have three members. Ex: 'The question, "What is the purpose of human life?" has been asked times without number; it has never received a satisfactory answer; perhaps it does not admit of such an answer' (Sigmund Freud, *Civilization and Its Discontents*, p. 26). (The first member of Freud's sentence is itself ternary.) We find the same elementary structures within the members themselves. If a member does not include repetition*, tmesis*, inversion*, apposition*, etc., it is unary. Binary members are quite common. Ex: 'When I was a soldier I was taught: "If it moves, salute it; if it doesn't move, white-wash it." Today's militant, if unsoldierly, extremists have a simpler philosophy: whether it moves or not, kidnap it' (A. Burgess, *But Do Blondes Prefer Gentlemen?*, p. 17).

4. In most sentences, there is an irregular alternation of long members (or colons) and short (commas). In the period, which was for long the model sentence for finished prose, an excess of short members or *commatism* (Lausberg, sect. 939) was not recommended. The result was that the period* tended towards redundancy* (every nominal syntagm* received its own epithet, for example). Ex (of commatism): 'But the real source of the depression, as the conferees gathered for the sherry, and squinted at the little white lapel badges on which each person's name, and university, was neatly printed, was the paucity and, it must be said, the generally undistinguished quality of their numbers' (David Lodge, *Small World*, p. 4).

Absence of organization in the ideas expressed in some modern texts produces sentences christened in French 'invertebrate' or unarticulated. Ex: 'The Elizabethan translation uses a pleonasm *trample them under their feet* which the modern translation cleans up to *trample*. Is the modern translation better prose? *Better prose for the purpose?*' (R. Lanham, *Style: An Anti-Textbook*, p. 36). The next logical step, albeit a long one, is interior monologue*: 'I wonder is he awake thinking of me or dreaming am I in it who gave him that flower he said he bought he smelt of some kind of drink not whisky or stout' (Joyce, *Ulysses*, pp. 610–11). For other types of sentences, see hyperhypotaxis*, R3, and macaronicism*, other def.

R1: For sentence modalities, see enunciation*.

SERIATION 'Succession in series; serial succession; formation of or into a series' (*OED*).

Ex: 'A French *philosophe* recently pointed out that, while the French love triplets (*Liberté, Egalité, Fraternité*, for instance), the British prefer pairs – eggs and bacon, Fortnum and Mason, Crosse and Blackwell,

Dieu et Mon Droit, Burgess and Maclean, Gilbert and Sullivan' (A. Burgess, *But Do Blondes Prefer Gentlemen?,* p. 569).

R1: Such classifications may be marked by juxtaposition (of series of co-ordinated elements) or by co-ordination (of series of juxtaposed elements). **Ex:** 'Han Suyin speaks of France and China, of women and love.' Disjunctions* accompanied by antinomic, or paradoxical, terms often serve to introduce each series. **Ex:** 'Over here, flower, sugar, pasta, jam, ready made sauces; over there, fresh fruit, vegetables in season, citrus fruits.' A change of tone serves to mark the two different series; in writing, oblique* strokes might be used.

R2: Like the reprise*, which is similar in form, seriation may simply be a pretext* ('an absurd formal justification'; see image*, R1) for stringing together inconsequential elements. **Ex:**

> MR. MARTIN: Paper is for writing, the cat's for the rat. Cheese is for scratching.
> MRS. SMITH: The car goes very fast but the cook beats batter better.
> Eugene Ionesco, *The Bald Soprano,* in *Four Plays,* p. 39

SEXISM A term which implies or states that one sex is superior to the other and which thus perpetuates the discrimination practised against the members of the supposed inferior sex. Such terms encourage conformity with the traditional stereotyping of social roles on the basis of sex. See *OEDS.*

Ex: During 1985–6 expressions of public concern caused the name of the new Canadian anthropological museum to be changed from 'The Canadian Museum of Man' to 'The Canadian Museum of Civilization.'

R1: Awareness of sexual discrimination in a male-oriented view of the world has affected both the vocabulary and grammar of English. 'Neutral' or non-sexually specific substitutes for 'male' words include: 'business executive' for 'businessman,' 'artisan' for 'craftsman,' 'supervisor' for 'foreman,' 'representative' for 'spokesman,' and 'worker' for 'workman.' Among verbs, to 'staff' replaces to 'man,' and among adjectives 'diplomatic' replaces 'statesmanlike.' The realization that the use of sexually neutral language has become a requirement in business as well as in social intercourse has produced a series of handbooks. See, for instance, *The McGraw-Hill Style Manual: A Concise Guide for Writers and Editors,* ed. Marie M. Longyear; and Casey Miller and Kate Swift, *The Handbook of Non-Sexist Writing for Writers, Editors and Speakers.*
  Perhaps the most difficult grammatical problem derives from the absence in English of a sex-neutral third-person singular pronoun when

used in combination with sex-neutral nouns or indefinite pronouns. **Exx:** 'A teacher who owns *his* own computer'; 'Anyone may come if *he* buys a ticket.' Use of the plural solves the first problem: 'teachers who own their own computers.' However, the use of a third-person plural pronoun, *they*, is grammatically incorrect after 'anyone.' Recasting the sentence in the plural produces: 'All those who buy tickets may come.' Another frequent device involves the use of doublets such as 'he or she,' as in 'The reader, when he or she must decide upon the merits of the case ...' Still another uses double* reading: 'The reader, when (s)he ...'

R2: The problem identified by the term *sexism* is far from resolution, but the trend away from the linguistic reductionism implicit in the use of 'male' pronouns, etc., to refer to groups composed of men and women is likely to continue. David Crystal distinguishes between the relative ease with which publishers may exercise control over sexism in written language, and the absence of such control in speech: 'If I inadvertently introduce a sexist pronoun into the draft of this book, I (or a sub-editor) will doubtless spot it and replace it. But there are no such controls available in the rush of conversational speech. How long it takes for spoken language to respond to fresh social pressures so that a new usage becomes automatic throughout a community, no one knows' (David Crystal, *The English Language*, p. 257).

SHORT CIRCUIT Language, being a subset of the universe which it must express, possesses the faculty of self-designation, not only in abstract terms, by means of appropriate lexemes (metalanguage, linguistic jargon*), but also directly, by *autonymy* (neol.). **Ex:** '*Word* is a word. I say *word* and not *whirred* ...' Autonymy is marked, orally, by a pause* (or a glottal stop) and by special intonation*; graphically, by italics and sometimes by quotation* marks (see situational* signs, 2).

In any case, we should note that when names form the predicate of a verb of appellation, they are autonymical, needing no distinguishing mark. **Ex:** 'She was called Agnes.' The same is true if the name forms the subject of an appellative predicate. **Ex:** 'Agnes was her baptismal name.'

The faculty of self-designation, that is, of turning language's denotative aim from the signified to the signifier, holds true even for more extended segments (see quotation* and reported speech or indirect discourse*). See also J. Rey-Debove, 'Autonymie et métalangage,' *Les Cahiers de lexicologie* 11 (1967).

In literature, comic, ironic, or absurd effects derive from this peculiarity which inheres in the very nature of language. Examples always involve play on the distance which can be established between signifier and signified, either when the one replaces the other, or when they are made identical (in which case the sentence has two meanings* depending on the decision to read the terms as having an autonymical function or not), or when they are mutually contradictory. A spark jumps between the poles of the sign; hence the name, *short circuit*, which might be used to designate such devices.

Exx: 'This character was also reading a journal, *The Journal*' (R. Queneau, *Le Chiendent*, p. 25); 'Four months later, they started another operation, which they called The Other Operation' (Chapman et al., *Monty Python's Flying Circus*, 1:186).

Transphrastic examples (i.c., 'referring to a text longer than a single sentence'): Some chapters of Gide's *The Coiners* are pages from a novel written by one of the characters, Edouard; naturally his novel is also called *The Coiners*.

R1: Short circuits also occur between what is said and what is done. **Ex:** 'FIRE CHIEF: I should like to remove my helmet, but I haven't time to sit down. [He sits down, without removing his helmet]' (Ionesco, *The Bald Soprano*, in *Four Plays*, p. 27). This type of short circuit may be simply accidental, or 'false'; that is, rhetorical. **Ex:**

GARCIN: Let's carry on then.
(The curtain falls)
> J.-P. Sartre, the ending of *Huis-clos* [*No Exit*]

R2: Contradictions between a character's signifiers and signifieds are subtler. A character may represent someone (among others the author, indeed even the author in the role of novelist) or merely be himself (or herself). **Ex:**

'I see a man.'
'What? A novelist?'
'No. A character.' (Queneau, *Le Chiendent*, p. 25)

R3: André Morel is neither the first nor only editor to have extended the short circuit to include a complete work, as he did when he published a celebration of silence, containing only blank pages. Also extant are the *Mémoires d'un amnésiaque* and the (frequently untitled) books of blank pages meant to be completed by their readers.

R4: Autonymy cancels out tautology* (see tautology, R2).

SIMILE A comparison* in which the comparing element (the *phore* or *vehicle*) is joined to the explicit or implicit notion being compared (the *theme* or *tenor*) by 'like' or 'as.' See Fontanier, p. 337, Frye, Morier, and Preminger.

Exx: 'When the evening is spread out against the sky / Like a patient etherized upon a table' (T.S. Eliot, 'Love Song of J. Alfred Prufrock');

'And then to wake, and the farm, like a wanderer white / With the dew, come back, the cock on his shoulder' (Dylan Thomas, 'Fern Hill'). See also allegory* and apologue*.

R1: The presence of the vehicle constitutes the literary image*. Similes are images in which both tenor and vehicle are expressed (the latter by a syntagm*) and separated syntactically by a mark of analogy. The marks of analogy include *like, as, such, similar, better than, more than, seem(s) like, resemble(s),* and *simulate(s),* as well as apposition* (see apposition, R3) or what Group MU calls 'pairing' (see *A General Rhetoric,* 4.3.2.2). Pairing consists in replacing *like* by a lexical word having the same effect: sister, cousin, etc. **Exx** (quoted by Group MU): 'He is made one with nature' (Shelley); 'The earth and I make *a pair*' (Audiberti). If tenor and vehicle fulfil functions like those of noun complement / noun or subject/verb, they no longer oppose one another syntactically and the result is metaphor*.

R2: Simile may be extended throughout a proposition so as to form the protasis of a period*. Ex:

As those black granite pillars, once high-reared
By Jemshid in Persepolis, to bear
His house, now 'mid their broken flights of steps
Lie prone, enormous, down the mountain side –
So in the sand lay Rustum by his son.
Matthew Arnold, 'Sohrab and Rustum'

This very ample type is called 'Homeric' or epic simile. It easily gives way to baroquism* (see baroquism, R2). Or else, in more developed conversational form, it may become the basis of dramatic action. (See apologue*.)

But 'merely ornamental' (Bénac) simile has become exceptional. Most similes seek to clarify some aspect of the text's meaning(s)*, or to substitute for the absence of established terminology, or to moderate the novelty of the concepts introduced; in short, to improve communication. Ex: ' "If the animals leading the herd change, this happens because the collective will of all the cattle is transferred from one leader to another, according to whether the leader leads them in the direction chosen by the whole herd." *Such is* the reply of the historians who assume that the collective will of the masses is delegated to rulers on terms which they regard as shown' (L. Tolstoy, *War and Peace,* 2:1417).

If the comparing elements become confused with the entity being compared, the result is allegory* (see allegory, R4). If the former replace the latter, there is metaphor*.

R3: In English certain similes are clichés*: 'clear as a bell'; 'deaf as a post'; 'strong as an ox'; 'quick as a flash'; etc. Similarly, in French, more than a hundred similes have become clichés (see cliché, R4) which function as a means of emphasis*: 'vif comme la poudre' ('fiery-tempered'); 'battre comme la plâtre' ('beat someone to a pulp or jelly'); etc. (See M. Rat, *Dictionnaire des locutions françaises*, under 'vif'.) The *Similes Dictionary*, ed. E. and M. Sommer, lists more than sixteen thousand similes and comparisons* from some three thousand authors.

Remotivated and foregrounded proverbs* and clichés* possess the power held by familiar, and therefore already 'true,' texts (already true in a 'false' sense of that term, but that is the trickery inherent in the device). Ex:

Our love remains
As stubborn as a donkey
As sharp as desire
As cruel as memory
As stupid as regret
As tender as a souvenir
As cold as marble
As beautiful as daylight
As fragile as a child
It smiles as it watches us.

Jacques Prévert, *Paroles*, p. 137

SIMILITUDE A comparison* drawn between two things or facts and based on qualities held in common.

Ex: 'What special affinities appeared to him to exist between the moon and woman? ... her nocturnal predominance; her satellitic dependence ... her power to enamour, to mortify, to invest with beauty, to render insane ... her splendour, when visible; her attraction, when invisible' (Joyce, *Ulysses*, p. 576).

Other meanings: 'likeness'; 'parable,' 'allegory*' (*OED*). See paronomasia*, R1.

R1: Similitudes are a type of parallel* which may be used in a process of reasoning* (see reasoning, R3).

SIMULATION An attitude or declaration that tends to deceive the victim, addressee, or reader concerning what we are, or what we think, want, or feel, etc.

The following example saves readers from falling victim to the character's attempts to escape detection: 'First Jim described the recruitment of Max and the manoeuvres he went through in order to disguise his mission from the rest of the Circus. He let it leak that he had a tentative lead to a high-stepping Soviet cypher clerk in Stockholm, and booked himself to Copenhagen in his old workname, Ellis. Instead, he flew to Paris, switched to his Hajek papers and landed by scheduled flight at Prague airport at ten on Saturday morning' (J. Le Carré, *Tinker Tailor Soldier Spy*, p. 246).

Analogous: feint, sham, pretence, hoax, mystification, quackery, play-acting, posing (as opposed to *naturalness*)

R1: Simulation which deceives no one, because it is too obvious, is pseudo-simulation. All devices, even the least false* or rhetorical in that term's pejorative sense, ultimately belong under the heading of simulation or pseudo-simulation*, which are extremely widespread attitudes. Neither diplomacy nor even simple politeness escapes some degree of simulation. See ambiguity*.

R2: Verbigeration* pretends to be language; *assimulation*, a type of pretence (*OED*), is, according to Quillet, a type of sham ignorance used to get attention and is therefore similar to *communicatio**; an excessive or simulated enthusiasm is called *parenthyrsis* (Theodorus of Gadara, a rhetorician [fl. 30 BC], cited by Longinus, *On the Sublime*, ch. 3).

R3: Wit* may take the form of simulated error. Ex: 'BLAISE: If you live here, you will end up by catching medicine. Whereas I will be cured of it by the sick' (Audiberti, *L'Effet Glapion*, p. 233). The doctor is here treating medicine as a disease.

R4: Wit* itself can be simulated, as in the following anecdote concerning Gounod and Mme Strauss, noted for her wit. Gounod is said to have whispered to her at a première, 'Don't you find this music a bit ... octagonal?' ' "That's just what I was going to say," she retorted, scenting that he was teasing her' (Ch. Lalo, 'Le Comique et le spirituel,' *La Revue d'esthétique* [1950], p. 313).

R5: See also chleuasmos*, R1; quotation*, R4; *dubitatio**; enunciation*, R1; blunder*, R3; and *permissio**, R3.

SINGULARIZATION The presentation of an episode in a narrative* from a particular, unusual point of view, as seen by some uncomprehending third party, a child, for instance. The result is that the reader perceives details and values in an unfamiliar light.

Ex [Natasha's first visit to the Opera]: 'The third act took place in a palace ... At the front of the stage stood a man and woman – the king and queen, no doubt. The king was gesticulating with his right arm ... The damsel ... sang something dolefully, addressing the queen, but the king peremptorily waved his hand, and the men and women with bare legs emerged from the wings on both sides and began dancing together. Next the violins played very shrilly and merrily. One of the women, with thick bare legs and thin arms ... walked into the middle of the stage and began skipping into the air and kicking one foot rapidly against the other. Everyone in the stalls clapped, and roared "Bravo!" ' (L. Tolstoy, *War and Peace*, 1:666–7).

Analogous: *ostranenie*; 'defamiliarization' (Victor Shklovsky, 'Art as Device' [1917])

R1: Shklovsky writes: 'The purpose of art is to impart the sensation of things as they are perceived and not as they are known. The technique of art is to make objects "unfamiliar," to make forms difficult, to increase the difficulty and length of perception because the process of perception is an aesthetic end in itself and must be prolonged. *Art is a way of experiencing the artfulness of an object; the object is not important*' ('Formalism,' in *A Dictionary of Modern Critical Terms*, ed. Roger Fowler, p. 101). The device belongs among those we have grouped under pseudo-simulation*.

Singularization offers a means of clearing away received ideas so as to get to the things that matter. **Ex:** 'The Elizabethans were very American in some ways, particularly in their phonemes and the vague ebullience of their speech ...' (A. Burgess, *But Do Blondes Prefer Gentlemen?*, p. 261).

R2: The device occurs diffusedly in many novels, when characters view events. **Exx:** Henry James, *What Maisie Knew* (1897); William Faulkner, *The Sound and the Fury* (1929); L.P. Hartley, *The Go-Between* (1953); Umberto Eco, *The Name of the Rose* (1980).

SITUATIONAL SIGNS (neol.) Signs which transcribe the particular tone of a quotation*, a response*, the title* (of a work), etc., and which thus indicate the situation of a segment within its syntagmatic context or within the real context which it evokes.

In the text, such marks are additional to the usual signs of punctuation*, which shows that they form a category apart.

1. Emphasis* may be applied to a segment of the text by the use of signs existing on a sliding scale going from small capitals and bold type to large type. **Ex:** See graphy*, R5. Outside the text itself, such signs indicate its title, and the size of the characters used marks their relative importance and organization.

Michel Butor (in *Illustrations*) uses different typesettings and placements independently of the linear reading process to define poetic forms.

2. Italics form a separate case. In the text they serve to connote a meaning determined by the context. **Ex:** 'Elisa *found* [a euphemism* for

'stole'] a $10 sweater the other day' (M.-Cl. Blais, *Les Apparences*, p. 57). They indicate titles of books. **Exx:** 'Propaganda' is an article by Steve Neale in *Screen*; 'Enigmes de Perse' is an article by Jean Paulhan in *La Nouvelle Revue Française*. (The use of quotation marks to indicate titles of articles or parts of books, which is of Anglo-Saxon origin, has now spread to francophone countries.) Italics point out the use of foreign words. In a general way, they designate autonymical segments (see short* circuit). They may also serve to separate a paragraph*, a sentence*, or a word from the rest of a text set in roman type. In a text in italics, roman type serves the same function. **Ex:** '*One might think one was reading* human *articles on great* living *men*' (Villiers de l'Isle-Adam, *Contes cruels*, p. 73). In a hand- or typewritten text, continuous underlining indicates the use of italics (see emphasis*, R1 and R2).

3. (a) A dash is used to set off one element of a text from the rest. (The dash, typed as two hyphens, differs from the [single] hyphen.) **Ex:** 'Not sympathy, Nathanael, – love' (Gide, *Romans*, p. 156). The dash corresponds to the silence used in spoken language to increase anticipation.

Syntagms* may also be displayed by detaching them, using dashes, from the surrounding syntactic construction. (Dashes play a similar role to that assumed by parentheses*, but they have a contrary effect.) **Exx:** 'We're using a lot of closeups – something we haven't done before – and mixing them with middle and long shots' ('Talk of the Town,' *New Yorker*, 14 Feb. 1983); 'We're using only moving cameras – no fixed angles, and no zoom-lens shots' (ibid.).

(b) At the beginning of a French sentence, the dash may indicate the passage to the next point in a series. **Ex:** 'Avenues. – Moors, but not rough ones. – Cliffs. – Forests. – An icy stream' (Gide, *Romans*, p. 209).

If quotation marks indicate quotations* (see quotation, 5), a dash announces, in French, the speech of a character. **Ex:** 'Mais, dit Angèle, cela ne suffit pas pour faire une poésie ... – Alors, laissons cela, répondis-je' (Gide, *Romans*, p. 207).

4. The refusal to integrate into the surrounding text one of the segments mentioned leads to the use of parentheses*; this convention contrasts with the use of dashes to set apart a segment (see 3[a] above). Such a segment may be placed outside the text in marginal notes or footnotes, attached to the rest only by an asterisk or footnote number. On the other hand, a parenthesis* included in the text signals a digression* or a double* reading. When Queneau decided to insert one parenthesis in another he used square brackets, as in algebra. '– [... (...) ...] ...' See *Bâtons, chiffres et lettres*, p. 130. Common usage in English reverses this procedure: (... [...] ...). Gérard Bessette's use of double brackets for the transcription of a character's secret thoughts remains a

mannerism: '((constant fear of showing a petticoat))' (*Le Cycle*, p. 204). See also paraphrase*, R2, and syntagm*, R1.

5. Quotation* marks (' ') indicate the limits of a segment from a different source. There is the case of a text drawn from another work (see quotation*) or of a set of terms whose signified only is referred to. Ex: 'It's *awesome* means "it's very impressive."' See also dialogue*, R3.

Quotation marks exist even in conversation, as Proust noticed: 'When [Swann] used an expression which seemed to imply an opinion on a subject of importance, he was careful to isolate it by means of a special kind of mechanical and ironic intonation, as if he had placed it in quotation marks, seeming not to wish to take responsibility for it, saying: "the *hierarchy* (of the arts), you know, as ridiculous people say"' (*A la recherche du temps perdu*, 1:93). This example forms a *pseudo-quotation* and so quotation marks are particularly appropriate. Very common now in speech is the locution 'quote, unquote' at the beginning of a passage. Such warnings may be classified with formulas like 'so it is said,' 'so-called,' or 'alleged,' by which speakers distance themselves from a text, refusing to take full responsibility for it. Frequently, they permit a narrator to comment ironically upon over-emphasis or lack of insight in a character's discourse*. Exx: ' "So this – this is the kind of slough into which our democracy has declined," he said with much bitterness and gigantic quotation-marks where needed' (K. Amis, *The Old Devils*, p. 327); ' "Sorry," said Malcolm. He had forgotten to include sonic inverted commas in his run-through of Gwen's special voice-effects' (ibid., p. 383).

Jakobson isolated the phenomenon in his study of *shifters*, words whose meaning changes following the enunciation*'s co-ordinates. We prefer Dubois's more precise statement that such terms are *modal agents*, that is, marks specifying the speaker's manner of viewing his or her own discourse* (see Dubois et al., *Dictionnaire de linguistique*). See also end* positioning.

Jakobson calls this kind of modal agent a *testimonial*; it might also be named an *attestation*. It is sometimes transcribed by italics rather than by parentheses*, since these two situational signs are frequently confused (see above, 2).

Outside the text, the sign of a quotation* is its position, as an extratext, epigraph*, etc. This kind of distancing* or spatial highlighting occurs in the case of an introductory paragraph*, or sentence* of several lines, or single line* of poetry. The device calls for smaller type and format changes such as reduced justification (wider margins) and reduced line spacing.

6. Points of suspension between round or square brackets indicate in French the omission of text (a segment or segments, for instance). In English, brackets are not necessary. These are the conventions followed in critical editions. But Damourette proposes (*Traité moderne de ponctua-*

tion) a new convention to replace the use of brackets in French: five points, which, as a convention, is less marked. Three points would be enough as long as they are preceded and followed by a single space in order to distinguish them from points of suspension (which are not preceded and followed by a space).

In English, the standard set by the *Style Sheet* of the Modern Language Association of America (2d ed., p. 6) calls for 'three *spaced* periods [and] a space before the first period' to mark ellipsis* within a sentence*. Ellipsis after the conclusion of a sentence demands four periods (the sentence period plus three spaced periods). An omission of significant length may either be shown by a 'single typed line of spaced periods' or by 'three spaced periods after the last word before the ellipsis.'

A *cut* excises whole sentences and is marked in French by one or several lines of spaced periods. The cut may have expressivity. Ex: At the end of the fifth book of his *Nourritures terrestres*, Gide replaces a possible description by a line of periods, but the subject of the development is a plain, whose immensity is thus evoked (see also counter-interruption*).

7. The sciences also have their special situational signs. Square brackets serve to announce a transcription in the phonetic alphabet; oblique* strokes (//), the transcription of a seme; quotation marks mean that only the signified is being referred to; small capitals represent the referent or real thing referred to.

SLANG Cant or *argot* of a class or group, formerly especially of thieves.

Exx: 'front the gaff' for calling at the entrance of a large house; 'sham' for a gentleman (Cuddon); 'snow' for cocain; 'angel dust'; etc.

Synonyms: *argot*, cant, billingsgate (slang that pretends to be linguistically daring, crude, or vigorous). There are also regional *argots* like *mourmé* (used by masons in Haute-Savoie), *brusseleer*, cockney rhyming slang ('apples and pears' for stairs, 'trouble and strife' for wife, etc.). Robert Hughes says of nineteenth-century Australian convict slang: 'A woman was a *bat*, a *crack*, a *bunter*, a *case fro, cattle*, a *mort*, a *burick*, or a *convenient*. If she had a regular man, she was his *natural* or *peculiar*. If married, she was an *autem mott*; if blonde, a *bleached mott*, etc.' (*The Fatal Shore*, p. 258). See response*, R2.

Other definition: By extension *slang* also designates any jargon* restricted to a small group of initiates.

R1: Slang has its secret code words (see cryptography*, R2), but it always contains popular language (see level* of language) and often racy jokes. Exx: 'A tosheroon (25p) for the coat, two 'ogs (20p) for the trousers, one and a tanner (15p) for the boots, and a 'og (10p) for the cap and scarf. That's seven bob (35p)' (G. Orwell, *Down and Out in Paris and London*, p. 141); 'T'as de la merde dans les châsses [eyes] / Vous n'y voyez pas clair.' Thieves' and soldiers' slang, as well as more snobbish varieties, are based on popular language with added jargon*.

R2: Slang uses abridgement* and is readily caricatural (see caricature*, R1).

R3: Mixing slang and 'high' or 'lofty' style creates dissonance*.

SLOGAN 'Statement or expression adopted to bespeak a position, attitude or goal or to characterize or represent' (Grambs); 'short catchy phrase used in publicity' (*Concise Oxford Dictionary*). In other words, slogans employ formulas (see maxim*) considered to be rich in meaning* and in various connotative values, but which in reality are banal because of the triviality of their meaning (as in publicity) or because over-use makes them threadbare.

Exx: 'Players please'; 'I like Ike.'

Ex: 'FIRE CHIEF: I speak only from my own experience. Truth, nothing but the truth' (Eugene Ionesco, *The Bald Soprano*, in *Four Plays*, p. 29).

Analogous: motto, watchword, rallying cry

R1: Slogans share banality of content with commonplaces (see cliché*); like clichés, they are a kind of psittacism* which gives a definite and unique meaning to syntagmatic segments longer than a word. Eco writes: ' "Down with moonlight" – a futurist slogan – is a platform typical of every avant-garde; you have only to replace "moonlight" with whatever noun is suitable' (*Postscript to the 'Name of the Rose,'* p. 66).

R2: Originally, slogans were battle cries shouted by leaders and taken up by attackers. **Ex:** 'God for Harry! England and Saint George!' (Shakespeare, *Henry V*, 3.1.34). They still occur in sporting competitions, where they serve to encourage the participants. See also epigram*, R2.

R3: Slogans have as intonation* the high intensity characteristic of publicity hype.

SOLECISM 'Offence against grammar or idiom' (*Concise Oxford Dictionary*); 'misused word, impropriety or illiteracy' (Grambs); '*ignorant* misuse of cases, genders, tenses' (Joseph, p. 300). See also Crystal, Lausberg, Pei and Gaynor, and Robert.

Ex: 'People must not say "Between you and I" or use *like* as a conjunction or make *hopefully* do the job of the German *hoffentlich*. They must learn that *media* is a Latin and *criteria* a Greek plural and neither may be used as an English singular' (A. Burgess, *But Do Blondes Prefer Gentlemen?*, p. 212).

Other names: faulty concord (*OED*). *Antiptosis*, which Dumarsais gives (4:148) as a synonym of solecism in French, means in English simply the 'substitution of a prepositional phrase for an adjective: tower of strength' (Quinn, pp. 51–2). See also barbarism*, other def.

R1: See mistake*, R2, and grammatical syllepsis*, R1. Discussion of solecisms in English poetry tends to become confused with discussion of poetic licence. Geoffrey Leech (pp. 42–57), for example, in examining various types of 'deviation' (formal, grammatical, lexical, semantic, syntactic, etc.), acquits poets like Dylan Thomas of falling under the proscriptive term 'solecism.' He praises them rather for their success in escaping 'banality' by 'renewing' the language. Anthony Burgess makes the same point: namely, that today's 'solecism' is tomorrow's accepted usage and that writers are naturally among the first to sense the shift.

R2: In prose, few authors totally avoid censure, as Burgess again admits. His definition of language as (in part) 'deliberate lexical abuse for aesthetic ends' (*But Do Blondes Prefer Gentlemen?*, p. 208) clearly is intended to remove blame from writers who refuse to submit to a prescriptive theory of grammar. For intended solecisms, see enunciation*, R2.

SONNET The principal fixed form in English Elizabethan poetry, adapted from the Italian model. The change in versification gives the English sonnet six alternate rhymes* divided into three Sicilian quatrains and one heroic couplet (*abab, cdcd, efef, gg*). The French sonnet usually had two quatrains, which used only two rhymes, followed by a couplet and then by four lines employing alternate rhymes (*abba, abba, cc, dede*).

R1: See punch* line; imitation*, R3; and point*.

SOPHISTRY 'Specious but fallacious reasoning*; employment of arguments* which are intentionally deceptive' (*OED*). See also Corbett, Dumarsais, Joseph, Littré, and Perelman.

Ex: 'If you look at her because she is beautiful, and you are upset by her ... if you look at her and feel desire, that alone makes here a witch' (U. Eco, *The Name of the Rose*, p. 330).

Ex [Francis has painted a fake picture which is to be sold as authentic. Saraceni, his teacher, quells his doubts thus]: '*Drollig Hansel* is a student exercise, undertaken in the style of an earlier day ... If an expert ...

cannot tell that it is modern, what greater proof can you have of my achievement. But you are blameless. You did not paint to deceive, you signed nobody else's name to it, and you did not yourself send it to England' (Robertson Davies, *What's Bred in the Bone*, p. 392).

Analogous: sophism, paralogism*, captious argument*

R1: Sophisms are intended paralogisms, meant to deceive. The term, which derives from the Greek word for wisdom, *sophia*, acquired its pejorative meaning* from Socrates, who denounced the hypocrisy of the sages (or Sophists), logicians who, he claimed, were both mercenary and pretentious. The truly wise know that wisdom, like truth, is an ideal to be sought constantly; they are therefore friends of wisdom (philo-sophers).

R2: Sophistry employs the same forms as does paralogism* (see paralogism, R2) and may even extend to antilogy*.

R3: Revealing the sophistic arguments of an adversary is an excellent form of refutation*. So effective is it, that even a valid conclusion may not stand up to it. Ex:

> For example: a substance exists that blackens the fingers of those who touch it ...
> Triumphantly, I completed the syllogism: 'Venantius and Berengar have blackened fingers, ergo they touched this substance!'
> 'Good, Adso,' William said, 'a pity that your syllogism is not valid, because ... the middle term never appears as general.' (U. Eco, *The Name of the Rose*, p. 261)

Events later prove that Adso's conclusion was correct, although his formulation of it was illogical.

R4: If foregrounded, sophistry may turn into witty repartee.

SPELLING OUT Separate pronunciation, one after another, of the letters composing a word.

Ex: 'It's a note from Mr Boris. He can't come. – Mr Maurice? says the voice. – No, not Maurice: Boris. B as in Bernard, O as in Octave' (J.-P. Sartre, *L'Age de raison*, p. 225).

R1: Rapid spelling (a kind of oral scrambling) is a means of communicating secret information despite the presence of a third party.

R2: Spelling out may be accompanied by syllabification which consists in 'articulation by syllables' (*Concise Oxford Dictionary*). The device serves to emphasize. Ex: '*in fin i ty*.' Dictation also contains various exploitable devices: 'An infantile epistle, dated, small em monday, reading: capital pee Papli comma capital aitch How are you note of

interrogation capital eye I am very well full stop new paragraph ...'
(Joyce, *Ulysses*, p. 592).

SPOONERISM A metathesis* suggested by two elements belonging
in a syntagm* which would produce a new syntagm, often representing some gauloiserie*. See Cuddon, Frye, and Grambs; and under
'contrepéterie,' Angenot (p. 157), Marouzeau, and Robert.

Exx: 'a right mucking fuddle' (R. McCrum, W. Cran, and R. MacNeil,
The Story of English, p. 281). A classical example comes from Rabelais's
Pantagruel (ch. 17): 'Il disait qu'il n'y avait qu'une antistrophe entre
femme folle à la messe et femme molle à la fesse' (i.e., consonantal
inversion* between a woman crazy at mass and one soft in the ass).

In English, the device bears the name of the Rev. William Archibald
Spooner, Warden of New College in Oxford from 1903 to 1924, who is
supposed to have suffered from the habit of transposing letters at the
beginning of words. Tony Augarde, however, in *The Oxford Book of
Word Games* (p. 173), suggests that most of the well-known spoonerisms, like the later parallel group of semantic infelicities attributed to
Sam Goldwyn, were in fact coined by others. Among the examples
Augarde lists are: 'a well-boiled icicle'; 'our queer Dean'; 'the Lord is a
shoving leopard'; 'please sew me to another sheet'; 'noble tons of soil';
and so on.

Other names: In French *contrepret* (verb: *contrepéter*). Robert, relying on
Rabelais, also gives antistrophe, but wrongly, it would appear.

R1: The spoonerism involves ambiguity* and a subtle kind of approximation*. The permutations* may affect numerous sounds or
sound groups. See L. Etienne, *L'Art du contrepet*; Augarde; and Espy,
1971.

R2: The surrealists abandoned the device's trivial aspect and adapted it
to their needs. **Exx:** 'Martyr, c'est pourrir un peu' ('To be martyred is to
rot a little'), a deliberate distortion of the cliché* 'Partir, c'est mourir un
peu' ('Going away is a little death'); 'Clanche de Bastille' (J. Prévert,
Paroles, pp. 3, 27).

R3: When the new syntagm is unintelligible, there is only a *pseudo-
spoonerism*, which is close to mere mumbling, as is metathesis*. **Exx:**
'Clamn dever, Lenehan said' (Joyce, *Ulysses*, p. 113); 'Le boème de
Panville intilutée: Ma Lère' (R. Ducharme, *L'Avalée des avalés*, p. 83).
This might also be termed lexical scrambling*.

R4: The involuntary spoonerism, of the sort attributed in English to the
Rev. Oxfordian, is a comic form of blunder*. An actor supposed to say,
'Sonnez trompettes' ('Blow trumpets'), cried: 'Trompez sonnettes' (i.e.,

'Deceive bells'). Spooner, dismissing an idle undergraduate: 'You have hissed my mystery lectures; you have tasted a whole worm. You will leave Oxford on the next town drain' (Augarde, p. 174). Littré and the *Grand Larousse Encyclopédique* make no distinction between the permutation* of whole syllables, as in the last French example quoted, and the subtler permutation of two letters.

SQUIB A very short editorial, either paradoxical or humorous, on a contemporary news event.

Ex: 'After having welcomed American table tennis players to China, Communist China is now organizing a great Afro-Asiatic ping-pong tournament. The Chinese believe that, in inventing ping-pong diplomacy, they are innovators; in fact such diplomacy bears a striking resemblance to the traditional kind: settled around a green table, the participants continue to return the ball until the moment when one of them is eliminated by a backhand' (L.-M. Tard, in Montreal's *Le Devoir*).

Other meanings: See letter*.

R1: The *genre* has its rules, which L.-M. Tard defines as follows. Take a subject from the headlines. Invent a comic comparison with a dazzling punch* line. Centre the text on a single idea. First paragraph: exposition of the subject. Second: transition and punch line. Rework the text to produce concision and variety of terms and expressions.

SQUINT (SYNTACTIC) (neol.) A lack of clarity in the linking together of segments of the discourse*. A sentence* or syntagm* seems to refer to the preceding segment, whereas it refers to some other. Generally, reference to the global meaning* solves the equivoque*.

Ex:

Caesar entered on his head
his helmet on his feet
his sandals in his hand
his good sword in his eye
a furious glare

P. Thierrin, *Toute La Correspondance*, p. 321

The original text, which is not written as poetry, has commas after *entra* [entered], *casque* [helmet], *sandales*, and *épée* [sword].

Other names: squinting construction (Dumarsais); 'Janotisme' or 'jeannotisme' (Robert). A 'jeannot' is a simpleton to whom are attributed sentences such as: 'I put a stain on the jacket of grease which my woollen grandfather had had dyed before dying purple.'

R1: The term describes syntactic ambiguity*. A squinting construction is one in which a syntagm* seems to look in two directions at once.

R2: Overlong suspensions* and approximations* risk breaking the connections between syntagms and thus producing syntagmatic squints. **Ex:** 'A firm sent its bill with the following letter: *Dear Sir, We beg to enclose herewith statement of your account for goods supplied, and* being desirous *of clearing our Books to end May will* you *kindly favour us with a cheque in settlement per return, and much oblige.* The reply ran: *Sirs, You have been misinformed, I have no wish to clear your books'* (Fowler, under 'unattached participles'). The syntagm 'being desirous' squints backward to 'We' and forward to 'you.'

R3: The Grands Rhétoriqueurs used the syntactic squint at the hemistich to form ambiguous lines which, by incorporating equivoque*, could be read in two ways. They could thus attack their victims while seeming to praise them. See Morier, under 'rimes brisées.'

STAIRCASE The text reproduces several times a subordinating syntactic link. The simplest case is that of a noun governed by a relative pronoun, which in its turn is governed by a second relative pronoun, and so on.

Ex: 'On his father's side, my brother-in-law had a first cousin whose uncle on his mother's side had a father-in-law whose grandfather on his father's side had taken as second wife a young native girl whose brother had met, on one of his journeys, a girl he fell in love with and by whom he had a son who married an intrepid pharmacist who was none other than the niece of an unknown quartermaster in the British Navy whose adopted brother ...' (E. Ionesco, *The Bald Soprano*, in *Four Plays*, p. 51).

Other name: embedding (J. Dubois, *Grammaire structurale du français*, 3:14–15)

R1: Left alone, the figure might continue indefinitely. However, it must stop somewhere, unless it returns back to the beginning, in which case it becomes a loop*.

R2: Some small staircases are purely formal. **Ex:** 'The left hand transfers the fork to the right hand, which stabs the piece of meat, which approaches the mouth, which begins to masticate using contracting and extending movements which affect the whole face' (Robbe-Grillet, *La Jalousie*, p. 111).

R3: When the second link in the series undermines the character of the one preceding it (as an exception to an exception, is this the return to the rule?), the result is a shaky staircase. This is the case in sentences which feature many *buts*. **Ex:** 'But he did not follow up his threats by any prompt action against the young king, but went off to Germany to conclude the campaign against his brother Lewis of Bavaria. But on arriving in Bavaria he did not strike down his enemy, but made a six months' truce with him' (quoted by Fowler, under 'but').

R4: In the 'staircase plot,' the narrative* branches off at each succeeding episode, abandoning in the process the various plots already begun. Ex: Bunuel's film *The Phantom of Liberty*.

STAMMERING A mistake* (see mistake, R2) in pronunciation in which one syllable is repeated several times.

> KEN: You wwwant mmme to ggget a bbb ...
> *Otto is staring. Ken's stutter gets worse.*
> Bbbig ... cccar ... ffffor ... the ... ggg ... gggetaway?
> > John Cleese and Charles Crighton,
> > *A Fish Called Wanda: A Screenplay*, p. 7

Ex: 'Fafafafafafamous, stammered Pradonet' (R. Queneau, *Pierrot mon ami*, p. 37).

Approximate reproduction of the words of a stammerer is a form of mimology*. In French automatic poetry, it receives literary value. Ex: 'Il peut ppppeut! ppp eu peu!!' (C. Gauvreau,'Ravage cicatrice,' in *Oeuvres créatrices complètes*, p. 220).

R1: Stammering is distinguished from prosthesis* and from gemination* in which the added syllables are lexicalized. Stammering belongs only to the domain of performance (contingent production) and cannot affect the language. Its principal characteristic is less the redoubling of a syllable than a halt at any part of an utterance accompanied with staccato repetition*. If linked to psychological problems (see Crystal, 1987, p. 278), it becomes a sign of them, or of deep emotion. Ex: 'He had to punch me in the face because you had punched him. Otherwise, there was no equality and I wouldn't have been able to fra ... fra ... fratern ... fra ... ternize. I answered. He wants to fra ... fraternize' (W. Gombrowicz, *Ferdydurke*, pp. 252, 264).

STANZA A group of lines* of verse whose limits are marked by two extended pauses* of silence or blank space.

Ex:

> The grass is half-covered with snow.
> It was the sort of snowfall that starts in late afternoon,
> And now the little houses of the grass are growing dark.
>
> It is the morning. The country has slept the whole winter.
> Window seats were covered with fur skins, the yard was full

Of stiff dogs, and hands that clumsily held heavy books.
Robert Bly, 'Snowfall in the Afternoon,' in *Silence in the Snowy Fields*

Stanzas may contain anything from three to twelve lines; they may bear the following names: tercet, quatrain, quintain (or cinquain or quintilla), sextain (or sestet), septet, and octave (or octet). French adds: *neuvain, dixain, onzain,* and *douzain* for stanzas of nine, ten, eleven, and twelve lines. We should not forget the short, or the split, or the heroic couplet. **Exx:**

Watching the birds, I think of Bach,
each of the distant wheeling flock
> John Stone, 'January: A Flight of Birds' (short couplet),
> quoted in M. Williams, *Patterns of Poetry*, p. 23

A book is coming out I wrote somehow.
I could not now.
> Clement Long, 'Lines at Four in the Morning' (split couplet),
> quoted in ibid., p. 24

A little learning is a dangerous thing;
Drink deep, or taste not the Pierian spring.
> Alexander Pope, 'A Little Learning' (heroic couplet)

The monostich, or poem (and therefore stanza) one line long, is not unknown. Both Preminger and Turco list the Spanish form called a 'mote' or 'glose': a poem consisting of a single line containing a complete thought. See paragraph*, R1, and period*, R4.

Synonyms: strophe (Preminger, Turco). In French a group of four lines linked by rhyme* and metre is also called a *quartier* (see Morier).

R1: Preminger comments (under 'stanza') upon some of the distinctions between current stanza forms and French neo-classical or 'regular' variety: 'Although the essence of stanzaic composition lies in the regular repetition of the pattern, stanzaic verse often employs variation, not only by means of metrical substitution but also by introducing irregularities into the stanza's form.'

R2: In the Old French epics or *chansons de geste*, the stanza was called a *laisse*, which could contain any number of assonanced lines.

R3: The structure of the modern stanza, like that of *vers libre* and of the poem* itself, remains fluid (see 'vers libre' under line* [of poetry or verse]). It may be quite regular, as in Dylan Thomas's 'Fern Hill' (six stanzas of nine lines each), for example, or extremely varied both in length and rhyme, as in Peter Readings' *Ukelele Music* (1985), one of whose (untitled) poems contains stanzas of 19, 3, 10, 8, 8, 6, 5, 7, 8, 5, and 11 lines.

Substitution

R4: See also acrostic*; antepiphora*; ballad*; celebration*; epiphrasis*, R3; inclusion*, R1; ode*; and refrain*.

SUBSTITUTION The replacement, within some hackneyed phrase, cliché*, fixed syntagm*, proverb*, quotation*, or received idea, of certain lexemes by others opposite in meaning* or likely to cause surprise.

Exx: 'She heard her butler say, "What name did you say, sir?" and then a loud voice replied, "A Foulenough by any other name would smell as sweet. He droppeth as the gentle dew from Heaven"' (J.B. Morton [Beachcomber], in Richler, ed., *The Best of Modern Humor*, p. 95); 'The duplicate forms which denote contempt, like *fancy-shmancy*, and *Oedipus-shmoedipus* and *data-shmata*, are perhaps unique in their attaching so much semantic weight to a mere bound morpheme (excuse the expression; your response should be *morpheme-shmorpheme*)' (Anthony Burgess, *But Do Blondes Prefer Gentlemen?*, p. 183).

R1: The uncontrolled substitution of lexemes is a form of paraphasia, a language disorder, since the substituted lexeme is sometimes a coinage*. In such a case, the effect of the substitution is to erase the meaning*. See verbigeration*, R2.

On the other hand, substitutions in literature, when they are not simply examples of word-play*, pursue specific ends. The French poet and dramatist Jean Tardieu, when he wrote *Un Mot pour un autre* ('One word for another'), tried to show that lexemes do not have priority in communication: 'What, you here, my dear count? What a nice *tulip!* You've come to *replenish* your cherished *pittance?* ... But how did you *come aboard* then?' (p. 61). The place and sound of *tulip* call more or less consciously to mind a different word, namely *surprise; come aboard* might recall *get in*. See mistake*, R2, and humour*, R1.

Such substitutions became systematic with the surrealists, for whom they represented a creative or even recreational device. Ex: 'When reason is away, the mice dance' (152 proverbs adapted to modern tastes, in Eluard, *Oeuvres*, 1:153f). English has 'perverbs' or perverted proverbs* such as 'Familiarity breeds children,' etc. See also anaphora*, R1; false –*, R4; and reprise*, R3.

R2: Arbitrary substitutions may cause surprise, but there is another very common form of substitution which is content simply to rejuvenate clichés* and adapt quotations* to new contexts. One finds it in the most serious texts. Paul Valéry studied the process (see *L'Idée fixe*, in *Oeuvres*, 2:237–40) under the curious name *parrot*. 'Shooting down parrots' means taking up well-known phrases or expressions and bending them to some new meaning. 'Yes I am able to make distinctions ... I am the distinguishing animal' [adapted from the French cliché 'Man is the laughing animal'] (Valéry, *Oeuvres*, 2:238). The following is a 'plucked' parrot (see foregrounding*): 'Pascal said something very true: "*continuous eloquence is boring.*" I would be tempted to modify that by saying: "Continuous music is boring ... Continuous poetry is boring" ' (Paul Claudel, *Oeuvres en prose*, p. 152). For examples of the parrot in English, see parody*.

The power of natural substitutions derives from the presence, in the listeners' collective unconscious, of an almost identical signifying structure, so that the speaker's discourse* contains both new and already familiar material, plus the tacit invitation that listeners work out the trick. A clever literary example is the title of a work by Robert Desnos: 'Deuil pour deuil' ('A death for a death'), which comes from 'Oeil pour oeil et dent pour dent' ('An eye for an eye and a tooth for a tooth'). The extreme form of substitution is *alteration*. Ex: 'I'd rather lay an egg in a box than go and steal an ox' (Ionesco, *The Bald Soprano*, in *Four Plays*, p. 40). In this example, there is more than a mere parrot: the proverb* 'Who steals an egg today will steal an ox tomorrow' is recalled but in quite a different context, that of personal preferences, and also in a different mode, in the absurd one in which people 'lay' eggs. This alteration is really a case of the *subversion* of meaning.

R3: For graphic substitution, see paragram*. For substitutions of sounds, see mistake*, R1 and R2. For substitutions of proper names, see anachronism*, R1. Constructions may also be substituted; see mistake*, R2.

R4: Valéry also practised what he called 'rhumbs,' by which he meant substitutions of ideas or thoughts which 'present certain definite deviations in contrast to some constancy in the mind's deep and essential intentionality' (*Rhumbs*, p. 11).

R5: Substitutions of characters form one of the plot devices of classical drama, the mistake* or false inference. Ex: Jack and Algernon, in Wilde's *The Importance of Being Earnest*, each encounter identity problems because of misunderstandings arising out of their 'inventions': 'ALGERNON: You have invented a very useful younger brother called Ernest, in order that you may be able to come up to town as often as you like. I have invented an invaluable permanent invalid called Bunbury, in order that I may be able to go down into the country whenever I choose' (act 1). Tom Stoppard's *Travesties* (1974) presents rehearsals for a March 1918 production of Wilde's play in Zurich, in which roles are played or discussed by James Joyce, Tristan Tzara, and Lenin, all of whom lived in Zurich at the time. Substitutions occur at the level of both dramatic productions: at that of Stoppard's play and at that of the 'play within a play,' Wilde's *Earnest*. The false inference is traditionally resolved by the *recognition* scene (or *anagnorisis*), whose importance in classical or neo-classical drama probably derives from that accorded to it by Aristotle. False inferences produce misunderstandings, whether deliberately contrived or not, concerning a character's identity. *Misunderstandings* in the proper sense concern situations. Ex: (taken from act 3 of Georges Feydeau's *Occupe-toi d'Amélie*, adapted by Noel Coward as *Look After Lulu* [1959]): The godfather thinks he is at a real marriage ceremony; the other characters present, except Etienne and the mayor, think they are involved in a fake marriage and that the whole thing is a joke. Etienne and the mayor know that the ceremony is in fact a real one. Compare also the misunderstandings in Camus's play *Le Malentendu* ('The Misunderstanding'), in which a mother and daughter murder their son/ brother returned after many years' absence and whom they do not recognize.

R6: In the novel there may be sequences of substituted action we might call 'narrative relays.' Thus in one of his stories, Maupassant leaves the lovers, Henri and Henriette, at their love-making beneath a tree to describe the song of a finch, which is first langorous, then ardent, then shrill, and finally calm again.

R7: One modern way of making 'surrealistic'-type substitutions would be to submit the text to a process of automatic translation and re-translation by a computer. An aphorism like 'The spirit is willing but the flesh is weak,' having been passed through a Russian computer, apparently came back as: 'Spirits are quick, but meat is soft' (*C'est-à-dire: Bulletin du Comité de linguistique de Radio-Canada* 6, no. 3, p. 13).

SUPPLICATION A humble but insistent petition or request.

> PENELOPE: Darling ... play with me ...
> BONE: I can't ... I'm so behind ...
> PENELOPE: Oh, play with me.
>
> Tom Stoppard, *Another Moon Called Earth*, scene 2,
> in *The Dog It Was That Died and Other Plays*

Analogous: deprecation, an 'entreaty or earnest desire that something may be averted or removed' (*OED*). In English, deprecation, just like its French equivalent, *déprécation*, was a figure in judicial rhetoric by means of which counsel implored the judge's indulgence (see Verest, sect. 454). It later took on the broader sense of a 'figure of passion' (see Fontanier, p. 440, Lausberg, Littré, and Morier).

R1: *Epiclesis* (or epiklesis) is an *impetratory* prayer, one made to obtain something for which an individual or group feels a need. Ex: the decades of the rosary recited at the bedside of a sick person. To *implore* is to accompany a request with weeping. A *memorandum* may contain a request of a very general nature on behalf of someone else. The granting authority is requested to 'remember' some living or deceased person.

Obsecrations are 'earnest entreaties' (Lausberg, Littré, *OED*) by means of which we assume the invoked authority's power or strength. Ex: 'Domine ad adjuvandum me festina,' a liturgical leitmotif.

Imprecations are curses (see well-wishing*, R4) in the form of supplications. Ex: 'But thou, O God, wilt cast them down into the lowest pit; men of blood and treachery shall not live out half their days' (Psalms 55:23). This is close to prophecy*.

R2: It only needs the addition of apostrophe* for well-wishing* to become supplication. Ex: 'If only to my law, O Love, you could make her subject' (Racine, *Andromaque*, 2.1). See also blasphemy*, R1; celebration*, R4; exclamation*, R1; exhortation*, R1; injunction*, R2; and intonation*.

SUPPOSITION A modality of the assertion* consisting in positing something as possible. An idea introduced for consideration and subsequent verification; a pure possibility put forward by the imagination.

Ex: 'It may be that in the attenuation, desiccation, and death of religions the world over, a new religion is being formed in the indistinct hearts of men, a religion without a God, without prohibitions and compensatory assurances, a religion whose antipodes are motion and stasis, whose one rite is the exercise of energy, and in which exhausted forms like the quest, the vow, the expiation, and the attainment through suffering of wisdom are emptied of content, put in the service of a pervasive expenditure whose ultimate purpose is entropy' (John Updike, *The Coup*, p. 103).

Ex: 'Pause. If we were all suddenly somebody else' (Joyce, *Ulysses*, p. 91).

Synonym: hypothesis

R1: Even imagined suppositions relate to something real; there is, however, a kind of gratuitous, purely expressive supposition: the *pseudo-supposition*. Ex: 'If pigs could fly ...'

The type of reasoning* 'by means of familiarization' (Angenot) which invites the audience to put itself in the place of someone so as better to understand is half-way to a pseudo-supposition. Ex: 'What would we say if it were up to us ...'

Very different is *ab absurdo* or *apagogical* (OED) reasoning, which, although it takes the same route, in fact results in the refutation* of a hypothesis. Having pretended to accept it, the speaker, using deductive logic, draws from it the most ridiculous consequences possible. Ex: 'If my heart has been enticed to a woman, and I have lain in wait at my neighbour's door; then let my wife grind for another, and let others bow down upon her' (Job 31:9). Job expresses indignation at his misfortunes by supposing that he has committed certain sins. He then pours down upon his own head curses which in fact prove his innocence.

R2: Hypothetico-deductive reasoning, widely used in the sciences, consists in examining the consequences of a hypothesis with a view to its better verification by means of experiments. **Ex:** 'Things seem to happen as if ...' (and then the deductions follow). **Ex:**

> The walrus and the carpenter
> Were walking close at hand;
> They wept like anything to see
> Such quantitites of sand.
>
> ...
>
> 'If seven maids with seven mops
> Swept it for half a year,
> Do you suppose,' the Walrus said,
> 'That they could get it clear?'
>
> Lewis Carroll, *Through the Looking-glass*, ch. 4

R3: In literature suppositions open the door to flights of fancy, which Audiberti named the 'Glapion Effect' and which Blaise explains to Monique as follows:

> BLAISE: You ... There's someone at the door.
> MONIQUE: At the door? Usually I hear everything ...
> BLAISE: Calm down. I am supposing that someone is there. You open the door. You find a person about whom something strikes you as being unexpected, curious. From that impression you imagine a whole novel, enormous, instant, frenetic. That's the Glapion Effect!
>
> Audiberti, *L'Effet Glapion*, p. 141

Hypotheses may bear upon any subject; they may accumulate, create antitheses*, or be rejected, and so on. Ex: 'What was his frank judgement of so much of [his antenatal history's] ugliness, he asked himself, but a part of the cultivation of humility? What was this so important step he had just taken but the desire for some new history that should, so far as possible, contradict, and even if need be, flatly dishonour, the old? If what had come to him wouldn't do, he must *make* something different' (Henry James, *The Golden Bowl*, ch. 1).

Nothing remains more hypothetical than the intentions of others, a fact Henry James exploited to the full: 'Neither his speech nor his silence struck her as signifying more, or less, under this pressure, than they had seemed to signify for weeks past; yet if her sense hadn't been absolutely closed to the possibility in him of any thought of wounding her, she might have taken his undisturbed manner, the perfection of his appearance of having recovered himself, for one of those intentions of high impertinence by the aid of which great people, *les grands seigneurs*, persons of her husband's class and type, always know how to re-establish a violated order' (James, *The Golden Bowl*, ch. 35).

R4: Suppositions may take the form of questions* (see question, R3). For the argument* which proceeds by denying a supposition, see paralogism*, R2.

SUSPENSE Waiting anxiously for some dramatic outcome; 'state of usually anxious uncertainty or expectation or waiting for information' (*Concise Oxford Dictionary*). The state is closer to fear in the thriller, for example.

Ex: 'A curious person goes into someone else's room and begins to search through the drawers. Now, you show the person who lives in that room coming up the stairs. Then you go back to the person who is searching, and the public feels like warning him, "Be careful, watch out. Someone's coming up the stairs." Therefore, even if the snooper is not a likable character, the audience will still feel anxiety for him. Of course, when the person is attractive, as for instance Grace Kelly in *Rear Window*, the public's emotion is greatly intensified' (Alfred Hitchcock quoted in François Truffaut, *Hitchcock*, p. 51).

R1: Suspense has its own intonation*, which promises resolution of tension. It forms one sure way of keeping the reader's or spectator's attention in detective novels and adventure or mystery films. See also flashback*, R1.

SUSPENSION 'Instead of presenting straight away some expressive trait by which we aim to produce great surprise or a powerful impression, we make the listener wait until the end of the sentence or period to hear it' (Fontanier, p. 364). See also Dumarsais (5:286), Lausberg, Littré, Morier, Quillet, Robert, Willem (p. 36), and *OED*: 'The action of keeping or state of being kept in suspense (*spec.* in *Rhet*). [E.g.:] 1728 Chambers *Cycl* s.v., In Rhetoricke, suspension is a keeping the hearer attentive and doubtful. 1798 Edgeworth *Pract[ical] Educ[ation]* (1811) I, 123: You may exercise his attention by your manner of telling this story: you may employ with advantage the beautiful figure of speech called *suspension*.'

Exx: 'At the termination of this sentence I started, and, for a moment, paused; for it appeared to me (although I at once concluded that my excited fancy had deceived me) – it appeared to me that, from some very remote portion of the mansion, there came, indistinctly to my ears, what might have been, in its exact similarity of character, the echo (but a stifled and dull one certainly) of the very cracking and ripping sound which Sir Launcelot had so particularly described' (E.A. Poe,

'The Fall of the House of Usher'); 'Suddenly a corner was turned, a blaze of light burst upon our sight, and we stood before one of the huge suburban temples of Intemperance – one of the palaces of the fiend, Gin' (E.A. Poe, 'The Man in the Crowd').

Other meaning: interruption* (see interruption, R5). See also the expression 'points of suspension.'

R1: Morier has examined various forms of suspension: the insertion of one or more subordinate phrases or clauses; *reticentia*, followed by an address to the reader in which 'we tease him about his having to wait'; cryptic words or expressions intended to cause a listener to ask questions; the introduction of some independent phrase or clause which serves to announce the delayed dramatic element. We would like to add: digressions* (see digression, R2); accumulations*; and end* positioning (see end positioning, R1).

R2: Suspension may cause a syntactic squint* (see syntactic squint, R2).

SWEAR-WORD A coarse or obscene word or imprecation intended to shock.

Ex: 'Good. Let's not fuck around any more, Charles' (Eric Wright, *Death in the Old Country*, p. 146).

Analogous terms: crudity, curse, obscenity, expletive

R1: Swear-words are frequently not spelled out. Ex: 'If Byron f–d his sister he f–d her and there an end' (D.G. Rossetti, letter of 15 Sept. 1869, in *Letters of D.G. Rossetti*, 2:743). See abridgement*, R4.

R2: Swear-words may have an injunctive function (see injunction*) at once performative and anti-social. Michaux notes that in French 'the word m... [i.e., "merde," literally, "shit"] still expresses demoralization and moral collapse' (*Passages*, p. 171). In English, as examples in *OEDS* may be said to illustrate, phrases like 'in the shit' expressing 'misfortune, unpleasantness' seem to share the same function. Barthes began his *Le Degré zéro de la littérature* as follows: 'Hébert [the journalist and politician] never wrote an opening article for a number of the [Revolutionary newspaper] *Le Père Duchêne* without introducing a few examples of *fuck* and *bugger*. These obscenities had no meaning in themselves, but they were signals. Signals of what? A whole revolutionary situation.'

The obscenity is indeed intended to shock, to challenge the social system which is founded on an at least apparent respect for others. It breaks the link with the person addressed (see insult*) and loudly voices an indignant cry that special attention be given to the speaker or

the group the speaker represents (see interjection*, R5). Ex: 'To hell
with the bloody brutal Sassenachs and their *patois*' (Joyce, *Ulysses*,
p. 266).

SWEET TALK The use of one or more meliorative lexemes which,
by means of apostrophe*, form the predicate of an implicit assertion
whose object is the addressee.

Exx: 'Come on up, honey' (Alice Munro, 'Privilege,' in *Who Do You
Think You Are?*, p. 33); 'You're such a lovely audience we'd like to take
you home with us' (J. Lennon and P. McCartney, 'Sgt. Pepper's Lonely
Hearts Club Band').

Analogous: soft or fond words; billing and cooing; honeyed phrases;
pet names; flattery

Antonym: insult*

R1: Sweet talk may be lexicalized in the form of diminutives (see
gemination*, R1) or of 'hypocoristic' derivatives. Ex: 'My grandmother,
too, used to put other people's ailments into the diminutive: strokelets
were what her friends had. Aldo said he was bored to tearsies by my
grandmother's diminutives' (Renata Adler, *Speedboat*, quoted by
Grambs under 'diminutive'). A *hypocoristic* name is a 'pet' name, one
whose function is 'to express an intention to caress' (Marouzeau).

R2: Modesty transforms sweet talk by means of antiphrasis* or some
other trope. So my 'old love' is a hypallage* if said to a young girl or
wife; it is the relationship that is old.

R3: In intimate correspondence, pet names replace titles in apostrophes*. **Exx:** 'My love'; 'Darling'; 'My treasure'; etc.

SYLLEPSIS (GRAMMATICAL) 'The use of a single word, which
has grammatical congruence in only one syntactic construction, in more
than one' (Preminger).

Exx: 'My ladie laughs for joy, and I for wo' (George Puttenham, *The
Arte of English Poesie* [1589], ed. of 1970, p. 165); 'The captain and the
platoon *was* taken prisoner.'

Other name: synthesis (Fontanier, p. 308)

Other definitions: Most authorities (*OED*, Littré, Morier, Preminger)
define the phenomenon by opposing grammatical congruence to semantic accord, a distinction we find forced, given that the grammatical
accord is not intrinsically contrary to the sylleptic meaning*, but simply
involves a different way of conceptualizing it. In addition, speaking of

the absence of agreement between two terms conforms more accurately with the Greek etymology* of *syllepsis*, 'a taking together.'

R1: If the absence of agreement is not justified, either by usage, evocation (as in 'none of us *are* getting any younger'), or meaning (as in the above example in which captain and platoon are seen as members of a single captured group), the result is a solecism*.

R2: *Attraction* (see lapsus*, R2) is the opposite of grammatical syllepsis.

R3: Syntactic syllepsis may perhaps exist. It consists in giving to a single syntagm* two simultaneous but distinct functions in relationship to the verbal node. Ex: In chapter 8 of *Puns*, Redfern intends to follow in Hemingway's footsteps ' "across the river[s] and into the trees." ' The title of Hemingway's novel, with one small change, as well as supplying that of Redfern's chapter, also refers to the decision to follow the pun into the 'real' world outside the library. It is thus an adverbial phrase both in the two titles* and in the sentence quoted.

SYLLEPSIS (SEMANTIC) A figure by which a word or expression is used simultaneously in its literal and figurative senses. See Dumarsais (2:11), Fontanier (p. 105), Lausberg, and Preminger.

Exx: 'We go a long way to please you' (advertisement for a public transport system); 'Toshiba: We Mean Business'; 'At a word, hang no more about me. I am no gibbet for you' (Shakespeare, *The Merry Wives of Windsor*, 2.2.17).

R1: There is little agreement among rhetoricians on the difference between syllepsis and zeugma*. Corbett (p. 483), for example, classified the well-known lines from Pope's 'The Rape of the Lock' – 'Or stain her honour or her new brocade' and 'Or lose her heart, or necklace, at a ball' – as syllepsis, while admitting that they 'are often classified as zeugma.' We believe them to be cases of zeugma. Both Group MU (pp. 75–7) and Espy (1983, p. 134) differentiate the two figures solely on the basis of grammatical congruence. According to them, zeugma is grammatically incorrect syllepsis; in other words, they reduce all syllepsis to grammatical syllepsis*, which in our view is not a figure.

Synonym: oratorical syllepsis. Brian Vickers tells a 'cautionary tale' about the confusions between syllepsis and zeugma and correctly concludes that many of the reference works we rely upon today were produced in the nineteenth century when rhetoric was 'in eclipse,' and so prove unreliable when subjected to critical scrutiny. See Brian Vickers, *Classical Rhetoric in English Poetry*, p. vi.

R2: Syllepsis is one of the forms used in word-play*. Many riddles*, including some difficult crossword clues, involve passing from figurative to literal meanings* or vice versa. Ex: 'Why is a cat longer at night than in the morning? Because he is let out at night and taken in in the morning' (Espy, *The Game of Words*, p. 208).

R3: Fontanier distinguishes *metonymical syllepsis*, in which the container is given for the contained (e.g., 'hearts' for 'emotions'), *synecdochic syllepsis* (e.g., 'to out-Nero Nero'), and *metaphorical syllepsis*. Ex:

> PYRRHUS: I suffer all the evil deeds I committed at Troy
> Conquered, loaded with chains, consumed with regret,
> Burned by more fires than I set there.
>
> Racine, *Andromaque*, 1.4

Peter France (*Racine's Rhetoric*, p. 67) describes this example of syllepsis as point*. We would say that syllepsis is the finest form of point. Spitzer (*Etudes de style*, p. 266), who picks out numerous examples of this kind in Racine's plays, presents them as features of mannerism. See baroquism*. The following example, taken from Quinn (p. 31), is a sylleptic simile*: 'Bad prose, like cholera, is a communicable disease.'

R4: Some involuntary examples of syllepsis may be ridiculous; they create incoherence* because their figurative meaning, though dormant, springs too easily to life. Ex: 'He died on the guillotine but with his head held high.'

SYMBOL Symbols come in three forms.

1. They may be texts to which their authors attach meanings* within the framework of some more general isotopy*. Two isotopic levels are established in such a case; the first one obvious, the second symbolic (see meaning*, 6). The former is defined by a word or by one of the sentences used; the latter, by the set of sentences forming the whole work. Ex: The single word 'Tyger' as opposed to the whole of Blake's poem. The literal meaning* of Blake's poem is conveyed by a vivid physical image of the beauty, strength, and potential for destruction possessed by the tiger. Another probable meaning is suggested by the line: 'Did he who made the Lamb make thee?' This symbolic meaning, introduced by means of an apostrophe* to the animal, clearly concerns the moral problems implied by the co-existence of good and evil in the world, and also the believer's dilemma when asked to approve the Deity's partial responsibility for the latter. The symbol therefore calls attention to the resultant conflict between the theological notions of free will and moral determinism. Thus the symbol of the tiger serves to introduce at least some of these questions or meanings which the poem leaves unsolved.

R1: We distinguish between the *meaning* or *value* of a symbol and its *interpretation*. (See meaning*, 4 and 7.) We generally interpret literary works by searching in them for one or more symbolic meanings. We may, if we have recourse to psychoanalysis, literary sociology, or numerology, confer on a work diverse symbolic values. Even if the author did not seek them, such values are perhaps no less real than those the author did have in mind. But they remain posterior, perhaps even exterior, to the created work. A particular symbolic interpretation depends entirely upon its fabricator, the reader, whereas the symbol as a device depends upon the author of the text and has to be perceived by the reader.

Factors which reveal the presence of an intended symbolic meaning include:

(a) The inadequacy of the literal meaning within the context in question. Ex: 'The lion roars in the bush' (a Bantu proverb* quoted by M. Maloux, *Dictionnaire des proverbes, sentences et maximes*, p. 248). Native speakers, who use the proverb to speak of courage, immediately grasp the intended meaning: the hero achieves recognition on the field of battle.

(b) The hermetic, enigmatic, or absurd nature of the literal meaning. Ex: 'And death shall have no dominion' (Dylan Thomas). The poet has acquired immunity to death? (See meaning*.)

R2: The tropes which replace one signifier with another (see image*, 2) may produce symbolic relationships between the corresponding signifieds. See metonymy*, R4.

R3: For symbolic narrative*, see myth* and apologue*. In the modern novel, symbols acquire the status of interiorized *objective correlatives*, a status they have enjoyed for a much longer period in poetry. T.S. Eliot explained the process by which such symbols may configure a character's subjectivity, the support, that is, for sensations, feelings, and memories onto which, in the course of the action, are projected the character's criminal or sexual obsessions: 'The only way of expressing emotion in the form of art is by finding an "objective correlative"; in other words, a set of objects, a situation, a chain of events which shall be the formula of that *particular* emotion; such that when the external facts ... are given, the emotion is immediately evoked' (T.S. Eliot 'Hamlet' [1919], in *Selected Essays* [3rd ed., 1951], p. 145). **Exx:** Proust's *A la recherche du temps perdu*, which presents a narrative of Marcel's past life of 'lost' or 'wasted' time, but also configures his quest for redemption through art, the subject of which is his past life and its artistic meaning; Eco's *The Name of the Rose*, a metasymbolic narrative* which, by means of a medieval detective story, examines the nature of the signifying process itself and its relationship to onomastics.

R4: We distinguish symbols from correspondences*.

2. Also symbolic are gestures* or objects to which cultural traditions

attach a particular meaning* within some more general isotopy*. Exx: military salutes; the exchange of rings in the marriage ceremony; the 'Sign of the Cross'; the language of flowers; the symbolic system of numbers; etc. Morier lists objects which have such symbolic values under *symbole* in his *Dictionnaire de poétique et de rhétorique*. See also J.E. Cirlot, *A Dictionary of Symbols*.

In the case of this type of symbol, passage from one term to another occurs not only by means of analogy but also by means of metonymy* (see metonymy, R5) or synecdoche*, even by pure convention. Ex: Turtle-doves may 'stand for' fidelity in love. If the symbolic object represents a set of values, we speak of an *emblem*; if it indicates membership in some institution, we call it a *badge*.

3. Also symbolic are graphic signs to which specialists attach a meaning within the isotopy formed by their particular science or area of technical expertise. Exx: the signs of the zodiac; the code formed by road signs; the geographical legends on maps; ♂ for male and ♀ female; etc.

When the graphic sign reproduces, in a more or less schematized form but without codification, the shape of the signified, the result is a drawing not a symbol; in Peirce's terminology, it is an *icon*. But if an icon becomes part of a set of analogous signs, or if it is used frequently, the sign becomes simplified and turns into an iconic symbol. Ex: ✗ meaning a battle. When the shape of the signified is no longer clearly perceived, we have a purely graphic symbol. Exx: ⓚ or a trade mark, or shop sign, etc.

Not all symbols are iconic in origin. Scientists create symbols, as the need occurs, in order to shorten transcription and to write formulas. In so doing, they frequently use the first letter(s) of the technical term. Exx: H for hydrogen; kg for kilogram; db for decibel; Q for the set of fractional numbers (from the word *q*uotient). The origin of these symbols is lexical. The absence of a period distinguishes them from abbreviations* (see abbreviation, R1).

R1: The word *sign*, which is the generic term in the series which also includes *index*, *symbol*, etc., acquires a restricted meaning in opposition to the others. Erasure of the iconic relationship makes for a passage from symbols to simple *signs*. Ex: ∀, the bull's head, when stylized as an inverted capital *A*, loses its signified as it is used increasingly to designate a sound and as it is no longer inverted; this proves that the symbol has disappeared.

Letters are signs, as are numbers. In algebra, *a*, *b*, *x*, and *y* are not symbols but signs because they may represent any value.

The opposition between icon and sign is clearly evident in the symbol ⊂ from Cartesian mathematics, which means 'is included in.' It is to be deciphered iconically (the open end indicates possible inclusion); on the other hand, if used as a sign, namely, if it is considered as referring to *c*, the first letter in *contains*, we have the opposite meaning.

R2: Two types of icon are frequently distinguished. The first forms a message and replaces a sentence (the pictogram* or 'phraseogram'; see Dubois et al., *Dictionnaire de linguistique*). **Exx:** primitive Indian writing; the *x* at the bottom of a letter or card which means a 'kiss.' The second type of icon seeks to reproduce the content of a single word, as in Chinese writing (ideograms or logograms). **Exx:** the iconic symbols mentioned above under meaning (3).

R3: Peirce's legisigns include all kinds of signs, as opposed to realities, or 'documents,' which may also frequently take on signifying value from their context. (A real thing which habitually occurs at the same time as another to whose meaning it offers clues is not a sign but an *index* or *symptom*.) This distinction appears in the opposition between semiology and semiotics. *Semiology* is the science of signs in the broad sense, that is, of signifiers in relationship to their signifieds. *Semiotics* is the science of real things that have meaning*, of signifieds in their relationship to human society.

R4: See acronym*, R4.

SYMPLOCE A combination of anaphora* and epiphora*. See Joseph, Lanham, Lausberg (pp. 663–4), Leech, Morier, Preminger, Quinn, and Turco.

Exx:

I will recruit for myself and you as I go;
I will scatter myself among men and women as I go.
Walt Whitman, 'Song of the Open Road'

The yellow fog that rubs its back upon the window-panes,
The yellow smoke that rubs its muzzle on the window-panes.
T.S. Eliot, 'The Love Song of J. Alfred Prufrock'

Other names: *complexio* (Lanham, Lausberg, Littré, Preminger); variation (Bary). The following example uses symploce to form a sorites:

For want of a nail, the shoe was lost
For want of a shoe, the horse was lost
For want of a horse, the rider was lost
For want of a rider, the battle was lost
For want of a battle, the kingdom was lost.
Attributed variously to George Herbert (1593–1633) or Benjamin Franklin (1706–90) by James Gleick, *Chaos: Making a New Science*, p. 322, and the *Oxford Dictionary of Quotations* (3rd ed.) respectively

R1: See also antepiphora*, R1, and epanalepsis*, R6.

SYNCHISIS 'Confused word order in a sentence' (Lanham). See also Lausberg and Robert.

Ex:

Thine, O then, said the gentle *Redcrosse* knight,
Next to that Ladies loue, shalbe the place,
O fairest virgin, full of heauenly light.
                    Edmund Spenser, *Faerie Queene*, 1.9.17, cited by Lanham, p. 97

Other name: synchysis (*OED*)

R1: In classical rhetoric, synchisis consists in breaking the syntactic development by parenthetical additions which leave the sentence structure unresolved. For French examples of synchisis, see Lautréamont's *Les Chants de Maldoror*, 4.3.
Synchisis may be defined as faulty hyperhypotaxis*.

SYNCOPE The omission of letters or syllables from the middle of a word or expression. See Espy (1983), and Group MU, Lanham, Lausberg (sect. 489), Leech, Littré, and Oulipo.

Exx: 'Halloween' for 'all hallow even'; ma'am; bos'n; 'Ne'er cast a clout till May is out' (old English proverb*); 'Tronno' for 'Toronto'; 'Thou thy worldly task hast done, / Home art gone, and ta'en thy wages' (Shakespeare, *Cymbeline*, 4.2.258–9).

Other name: *abscisio de medio* (Group MU)

R1: Syncope is a term from ancient grammar corresponding to what is now a device. Ex: 'Yrfmstbyes. Blmstup' (Joyce, *Ulysses*, p. 235; which probably stands for: 'Yes, right, first must say the goodbyes. Bloom stood up').

R2: The device is not as artificial as it may appear. It occurs frequently in spoken language. Exx: missus (from mistress); Barbra.

R3: Syncope is a metaplasm*. See also caesura*, R5.

SYNECDOCHE A trope (see meaning*, 4) that permits the designation of something by a term whose meaning includes (or is included by) that of the literal term. (See inclusion*.)

Exx: 'hands' for 'men' or 'sailors'; '*Time Magazine* says ...' for 'a reporter writes in *Time Magazine*.'

Exx: 'Was this the face that launched a thousand ships, / And burnt the topless towers of Ilium?' (Christopher Marlowe, *Dr. Faustus*, ll. 1328–9);

'... at an age when many of our young poets are running away to Broadcasting House' (Dylan Thomas, *Quite Early One Morning*, p. 123).

Analogous definitions: See Abrams, Burke (*A Grammar of Motives*, pp. 503f), Corbett, Dumarsais (2:4), Fontanier, Joseph, Lanham, Lausberg, Littré, Morier, *OED*, and Preminger.

Synonyms: The type of synecdoche exemplified by twenty 'head' of cattle or 'a set of wheels' (the part for the whole) might be called a *close-up on a detail*. But close-ups are not always tropological. Exx: 'His lips sought her breast'; 'My eyes are weeping but I am not' (i.e., from peeling onions rather than from grief).

R1: Rhetoricians list various kinds of synecdoche:
1. *Part for the whole.* Exx: Among animate beings: 'vicious tongues' for detractors; 'Heart cries, "No"' ' (W.B. Yeats, 'The Folly of Being Comforted'). Among objects: 'The broken wall, the burning roof and tower / And Agamemnon dead' (W.B. Yeats, 'Leda and the Swan'). Among countries: 'Canada beat Russia at hockey.' Among human groups: 'Israel' for 'the Jewish people'; 'Ignatius' for 'the Jesuits.' Among abstractions*: 'one of the great *minds* of our day.' Among spiritual beings: 'Providence' for 'God.'
2. *Matter for beings or objects made from it.* Exx: 'You are the blood of Atreus' for 'his son'; 'Rome is in irons' for 'Rome is in slavery'; 'This is a good hotel, but they don't take plastic [i.e., credit cards].'
3. *Number.* Exx: Singular for plural: 'the enemy' for 'our enemies.' Plural for singular: 'wheels' for 'car' (an emphatic plural).
4. *Genus for species.* Exx: 'I saw her upon nearer view, / ... A creature not too bright or good' (W. Wordsworth, 'She Was a Phantom of Delight'); '... the vessel puffs her sail' (Tennyson, 'Ulysses').
5. *Species for genus.* Exx: 'Give us this day our daily bread'; 'Own the sword that crowned 25 kings' (ad for replicas of the sword of Charlemagne).
6. *Abstract for concrete.* Exx: 'The weaker sex, to piety more prone' (Sir William Alexander, Earl of Stirling, *Doomsday*, Hour v, lv); 'Crabbed age and youth cannot live together: / Youth is full of pleasance, age is full of care' (Shakespeare, *The Passionate Pilgrim*, no. 12).
7. *Common noun for proper name.* Ex: the 'little tramp' for Charlie Chaplin. Or vice versa. Ex: a 'little Hitler' for a petty dictator. Also one proper name for another, etc. See antonomasia*.

R2: For the distinction between synecdoche and metonymy, see metonymy*, R2.

R3: Synecdoche introduces distance that allows for various effects. Diplomats use and abuse it to say what may not be said. Ex: 'Paris denies all knowledge of the sinking of *Greenpeace.*' However, the effect is sometimes the opposite of the one intended, as the example shows, for such official disclaimers are rarely believed. For synecdoche in periphrases* employed by the French seventeenth-century *précieuses*, see baroquism*, R2. Synecdoche has its own isotopy* (see image*, 2), may make abstractions* concrete (see concretization*, R3), or personify them (see personification*, R1). See also definition*, R1; title* (of work), R1; and apposition*, R4.

SYNONYMY There is synonymy when several terms designate the same thing and when, in theory, we may use one of them in place of another. See also Crystal, Fontanier (p. 332), Lausberg (sect. 649–56), *OED*, and Robert.

Exx: kingly/royal/regal; pavement/sidewalk

Exx: 'Then you have a beautiful calm without a cloud, smooth sea, placid ... moon looking down so peaceful' (Joyce, *Ulysses*, p. 310); '[This parrot has] passed on! This parrot is no more! It has ceased to be! It's a stiff! Bereft of life, it rests in peace – if you hadn't nailed him to the perch, it would be pushing up the daisies! It's rung down the curtain and joined the choir invisible! THIS IS AN EX-PARROT!' ('Parrot Sketch' [from Monty Python TV show], quoted in R. Wilmut, *From Fringe to Flying Circus*, p. 205).

Synonyms: dittoism (*OED*); dittology (according to Lausberg, who cites Vossler, but both the *OED* and Marouzeau use *dittology* in a different sense; see gemination*)

R1: Synonymy is a type of amplification* which does not involve the use of a single synonym. It is a figure of expression which places in juxtaposition to a term several others, all having the same function, all appropriate also to the discursive theme, and all calling attention to various aspects of it. **Ex:** 'In trickery, evasion, procrastination, spolia-tion, botheration, under false pretences of all sorts, there are influences that can never come to good' (Dickens, *Bleak House*, ch. 1). We thus have accumulations of lexemes, plus reprise*. **Ex:** 'Teflon had a camera: Leica, procured half-legally overseas by a Navy friend' (Th. Pynchon, *V*, p. 9).

R2: If the sememes are identical (perfectly synonymous), the figure becomes gratuitous, useless, as we see more clearly from cases of co-ordination than from juxtaposition*. The result is perissology*. **Ex:** 'He is with and in the company of a friend and pal' (R. Queneau, 'Double Entry,' in *Exercises in Style*, p. 22). In any case, perfect synonymy is rarer than the imperfect kind called *parasynonymy*. **Ex:** prosperity/hap-piness. See meaning*, 5. Some terms have many synonyms. **Ex:** see mistake*.

R3: If the sememes are widely separated (i.e., analogous only), we can no longer speak of synonymy, but enumeration*, even accumulation*. Ex: 'English, let alone American, has no word that simply expresses sexual intercourse without implying an attitude. *Screw* is lewd, *make love* euphemistic, *fornicate* biblical, *copulate* clinical, *fuck* vulgar' (Richard Lanham, *Style: An Anti-Textbook*, p. 90). This is what Bary (1:369; 2:31) called *polysynonymy*. See also successive approximations*.

R4: Synonyms which appear within the same sentence or in different propositions may not only signal a desire for expressivity but for elegance: they represent an attempt to avoid repetition*. Ex:

Behold her, single in the field,
Yon solitary Highland lass!
Reaping and singing by herself.
> W. Wordsworth, 'The Solitary Reaper'

See counter-pleonasm*, R2.

R5: When they appear with different functions in the same sentence, synonyms form pleonasms*, even perissologies*. Ex:

Will no one tell me what she *sings*? –
Perhaps the *plaintive numbers* flow

...

Or is it some more humble *lay*.
> Wordsworth, ibid.

The French word *datisme* ('datism: broken or barbarous speech; a fault in speaking such as would be made by one not fully acquainted with the language' [*OED*]) means a 'fondness for the accumulation of synonyms where one word would suffice' (*Harrap's New Standard French and English Dictionary*).

R6: Literary texts sometimes employ inverted synonymy which involves grammatical categories. Ex: 'O filthy greatness! sublime ignominy!' The first adjective is synonymous with the second noun and vice versa. Sometimes inverted synonymy involves meaning* (e.g., 'very simple, unmysterious grief'), which produces antithesis* or oxymoron*. Synonymy may also involve syntagms* and employ metaphor*. Ex: 'The light from her pale eyes, bright lanterns, living opals' (Baudelaire, 'Le Chat').

R7: False synonymy consists in opposing a word's meaning in the *langue* (what Benveniste calls its *significance*) to the meaning expected in the context. (On this subject, see the different senses of the notion *fundamental meaning*. When a term has no synonym, we have recourse to periphrasis*.) 'Insecure' has one meaning in a psychological novel, another perhaps in a spy novel; only experience teaches the reader which meaning the word invokes.

R8: Some synonyms are intensive. See interjection*, R1. For synonymy which involves syntagms* or sentences*, see metabole*. Synonymy may also disguise tautology* (see tautology, R1). Synonyms may replace proper names; see conferring of titles*, R5. Tropes produce multiple synonyms. See meaning*, 4.

SYNTAGM A group of written words characterized by the fact that they play some role with respect to a verbal node, or that they have some function in a sentence. When we envisage the way speech progresses through time (the *linearity* of language or music differs from the *spatiality* of the plastic arts), a process which linear chains of written signs reproduce, the syntagm is intermediate between the word, an indivisible segment (into which no other segment[s] can be introduced), and the sentence*, or unit of expression.

We distinguish *nominal syntagms* (NS) from *verbal syntagms* (VS), also called clauses or propositions, and *qualifying syntagms* (QS). The latter is the least developed of the three categories, containing only adverbs and adjectives. The VS is the most fully developed, with its numerous grammatical morphemes (number, person, mood, tense) and its nominal, verbal, and qualifying expansions.

R1: Syntagmatic analysis begins with a division into syntagms and continues with the marking, by means of parentheses, tree diagrams, or square brackets, of their organizational hierarchy. We will show here the method which employs square brackets.

We proceed as for any analysis of immediate constituents, that is, by choosing to unite, among neighbouring terms, those most closely related by mutual dependence. We rewrite the syntagms on separate lines so that a single straight line in the margin unites them. We close the line with a right-pointing square bracket wherever the text, if spoken aloud, might stop or begin. Ex:

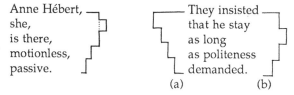

Anne Hébert, she, is there, motionless, passive.		They insisted that he stay as long as politeness demanded.
(a)		(b)

In the second example, the square brackets produce an ambiguity. We can attach 'as long ...' either to 'that he stay' (a) or to the whole formed by the first two previously united syntagms (b), which gives a very different meaning (they are happy to see him leave).

Tautogram

Left-pointing brackets indicate the possiblity of excluding one syntagm without modifying the meaning of the rest of the sentence. They almost always correspond to a comma. The relative rareness of excluded syntagms is one of the characteristics of Proust's style. They are remarkably frequent in Marie-Claire Blais's sentences, which are occasionally just as long as their Proustian counterparts.

R2: See abridgement*, R3; amphibol(og)y*; anastrophe*, R1; typographic caesura*, R1; colon*; *compensatio**; denomination*, R2; disjunction*, R2; *dubitatio**, R4; rhythmic echo*, R2; embedding*; enjamb(e)ment*, R2, R3, and R5; epanalepsis*, R1; erosion*, R1; head-to-tail*, R1; hendiadys*, R1 and R2; homonymy*, R2; hyphen*; graphic juxtaposition*, R1; lexical juxtaposition*; metanalysis*, R1; metathesis*, R2; mistake*, R2; monologue*; oxymoric* sentences; parataxis*, R1; parenthesis*, R2; psittacism*, R2; expressive punctuation*, R1; reactualization*, R3; regression*, R2; syntactic scrambling*; situational* signs, 3 (a); slogan*, R1; spoonerism*; syntactic squint*; grammatical syllepsis*, R3; synonymy*, R6; translation*, R2; and word-play*. For different types of syntagm, see the Index.

T

TAUTOGRAM A syntagm*, line* of verse or sentence* the words of which begin with the same letter.

Ex: 'These muttering, miserable, mutton-hating, manavoiding, misogynic, morose and merriment-marring, monotoning, mournful, minced-fish and marmalade masticating Monx' (Edward Lear, quoted by Hesbois, p. 69).

Synonyms: tongue-twister (Augarde, pp. 160–5); paronomeon (Fabri, 3:128)

R1: Joyce adapted as follows the best-known of these alliterative tongue-twisters: 'Peter Piper pecked a peck of pick of peck of pickled pepper' (*Ulysses*, p. 157).

R2: The device usually involves excessive alliteration*; hence its comic effect. It may also seem allusive if it involves the initial letter of someone's first name. If the effect fails, we have tautophony (see cacophony*).

R3: In late fifteenth-century France, the ludic possibilities of the device delighted the Grands Rhétoriqueurs. Fabri proposed names for tautograms beginning with *l, m, s* ... and so on.

TAUTOLOGY 'A logical error consisting in presenting as meaningful a proposition whose predicate says no more than its subject' (Robert).

Exx: 'That's the way things are'; 'Boys will be boys and our two twins were no exception to this golden rule' (Joyce, *Ulysses*, p. 285).

Synonym: identical proposition (in logic)

Antonym: antilogy*

Other definitions: 'a statement form which has only true substitution instances' (Copi, p. 265); 'a repetition of the same statement' (*OED*); 'a false demonstration in which the thesis is repeated in different words' (Robert); 'the repetition of traditional terms in legal language [as in] "a sale made and completed" ' (Marouzeau)

R1: Tautology does not necessarily take the form of a proposition with a grammatical predicate: all that is needed is that the psychological subject and predicate coincide. **Exx:** 'Ah! I was young too, in my youth, me too' (A. Maillet, *La Sagouine*, p. 53); 'I bought it where one buys such things' (a refusal to answer the question). Synonymy* disguises tautology but does not put an end to it. **Ex:** 'When three hens go into the fields, the first goes first, the second follows the first, the third comes along behind' (a child's counting-out rhyme in French).

R2: In theory, tautology is a mistake* (see paralogism*, R2). But some tautologies may be true. The existentialist philosopher V. Jankélévich (*Traité des vertus*, p. 108) has shown that tautological truth is a victory for existence over essence. Gertrude Stein's famous tautological axiom, 'A rose is a rose is a rose,' thus becomes, in Jankélévich's terms, 'a form of virtuous rather than vicious circle.' In the same way, the World War I soldiers' song 'We're here because we're here because we're here ...' forms a pertinent comment upon the futility of the conflict. And a commercial advertisement like 'The more people buy Hondas, the more people buy Hondas' may have a conative effect. The opposite form to this one is paradox*, as in 'Plus ça change, plus c'est la même chose' ('The more things change, the more they stay the same').

Tautological forms are also meaningful when one of the terms is autonymical, or self-designating (see short* circuit, R4). **Ex:** 'We must call things by their right name / a dog is a dog' (J. Prévert, *Paroles*, p. 111). Or again, when one of the terms is elliptical. **Ex:** 'Monday is a Monday' for 'Next Monday, we'll have the usual Monday schedule.' ('Monday is a Thursday' would be false antilogy*.)

Finally, almost all tautologies include a more or less clearly marked case of diaphora*, which is used to justify them. Thus when Paul Valéry (*Oeuvres*, 2:258) challenged the validity of Freudian psychoanalytical theory, he declared: 'I am not afraid to go so far as to think that a dream ... is a dream' (i.e., *and no more than that*). The following ad is designed to allay investors' fears of being turned away because they do not belong to the 'in house' group: 'You don't have to bank with us to bank with us.' The predicate's additional semes may be supplied by intonation* or by intensives. **Exx:** 'Thirty thousand, it's a *number*' (or 'it's *just* a number'); 'When I'm bored, I'm *bored*' (or 'I'm *really* bored'). It is also sometimes an advantage not to have to explain things too clearly. **Ex:** 'Things being what they are ...' (de Gaulle). On the other hand, tautologies may introduce explanations* (see explanation, R3), as is the case with truisms*, of which they form part. Tautology may fulfil a desire for attenuation* or understatement and come in the form of litotes*. **Ex:** 'The past is the past and the present the present.' This double tautology emphasizes the truism that the present differs from the past, which in litotic form becomes: 'The way things were done in the past is no longer valid today.' Such forms are *pseudo-tautologies*.

R3: While obvious tautologies are frequently false (they do not mean what they say), the worst ones, because they are true, are hidden. **Ex:** '[The city of] Florence is Florence because she corresponds to our expectations about her and because she behaves exactly as she should.' Scientists have a soft spot for such *semi-tautologies*. **Ex:** 'The poppy puts you to sleep because of its soporific properties.' Abstractions* (see abstraction, R2) encourage such cases. **Ex:** 'My sharp mind enabled me to find my thinking cap.'

R4: See intonation*; pleonasm*; and extravagant* comparison, R4.

TELESCOPING Condensing into a single sentence two others that have one identical syntagm*.

Ex: 'The cub-reporter, instructed to be concise, telescoped thus the escape of a mental inmate who raped a woman: "Nut bolts and screws" ' (Redfern, *Puns*, p. 120).

Redfern comments that the 'Surrealistic game of "*l'un dans l'autre*" ["The one is in the other, or in both"] suggests both the superimposing and telescoping found in all punning' and thereby indicates the device's rhetorical importance. Turco (pp. 49–53) mentions telescoped metaphor*'s role in producing obscurity in conceits* which may spread over several sentences.

Other names: sentence-mixing; the French term '*phrase-valise*' or 'portmanteau-sentence' derives from an analogy with *mot-valise* or 'portmanteau word.' Telescoping offers an effective means for renewing clichés*. **Ex:** 'Plain as the nose on your pikestaff' (Kingsley Amis, *The Old Devils*, p. 246). Telescoping here renews two frequently heard similes*: 'plain as the nose on your face' and 'plain as a pikestaff.'

R1: French surrealist poets like Paul Eluard showed that telescoping may produce dissociations*. Ex: 'La pendule sonne deux coups de couteaux,' which, translated literally, becomes: 'The clock strikes two knife-strokes' (P. Eluard, *Oeuvres*, 1:297). Frequent telescoping may cause meaning to drift into obscurity (see verbigeration*, R3).

TEMPO Frequency of rhythmic divisions; 'usually means "speed" ' (P.A. Scholes, *The Oxford Companion to Music*); 'relative rate of speech' (Crystal, 1987). See also Marouzeau, Morier, *OED*, and Robert.

Synonyms: movement (in the musical sense); cadence*

R1: To measure the different *tempi* for reading aloud literary texts in French, Morier proposed a scale similar to the musical one, but much less extensive (from 50 to 98 beats a minute as against from 40 to 120), with the same general divisions: (1) *largo*; (2) *larghetto*; (3) *adagio*; (4) *andante*; (5) *allegro*; and (6) *presto*. That is: (1) 'slow and dignified'; (2) 'slow and dignified but less so than *largo*'; (3) 'not so slow as *largo*'; (4) 'flowing, slowish but not slow'; (5) ' "merry," i.e. quick, lively, bright'; and (6) 'quick' (Scholes, *The Oxford Companion to Music*). We would add *agitato* ('agitated' [Scholes]).

R2: Souriau emphasized the importance of tempo in poetry: 'I am quite willing to believe that one of the first considerations conditioning, from a musical viewpoint, the choice of a particular poetic form is the fact that the poem itself suggests a given tempo which may bear some relationship to certain forms: sentimental, idyllic, or others more rapid or energetic, still others solemn and declamatory, and so on' (E. Souriau, in *Musique et poésie au XVIe siècle*, p. 349).

R3: The general movement of a text may contain more or less sudden intervening modifications. Ex: In his 'semi-' or 'dramatic' opera *King Arthur* (1691), Henry Purcell exploited the panting rhythm* of a line* of verse, 'Let me, let me freeze again to death,' to suggest the cold in the 'Frost' scene (act 3). Similarly, in Michaux's poem 'L'Avenir,' the same panting rhythm becomes evident: 'Quand les mâhahâhahâ.' We can speak in such cases of 'changes of speed' (Grammont, p. 103) or metabole* (Quintilian) and specify either sudden or gradual acceleration or deceleration.

Singers and composers possess great freedom in this respect. They may spread some syllables over several notes of varying lengths, as is frequently the case both in Handel's oratorios and in some modern folk-songs. The device occurs constantly on the final syllable, tightly uniting effect to effusion.

THEME Within a work, the theme is an idea repeated frequently (motif*, leitmotif), or a basic idea (thesis, obsessive image*), or an essential one (formal structure). Within a paragraph*, it is the topic treated (see isotopy*). In an assertion*, it is the subject predicated (the matter, or psychological subject). In a comparison*, it is the thing compared (see image*, 2).

R1: From the Greek *thema*, literally 'the thing posed.' In Ducrot's terminology (see assertion*, R5), 'the thing posed' figures in the predicate, whereas its complement, 'the thing presupposed,' is in the theme. Thus, there is a possibility of terminological confusion, which derives from semantic evolution.

R2: The idea of a 'theme' is associated with the idea of a 'starting-point which remains subjacent'; hence the meaning it still retains, that of an initial basis for subsequent variations*. See also allegory*, R1.

R3: To isolate the theme from the predicate, we have dislocation* (see dislocation, R2) and emphasis*. The theme is often implicit (see sentence*, 1), but it may also occupy half of the sentence (see sentence*, 2). In tautologies*, predicate and theme are identical.

R4: For the theme of a work, see also apocalypse*; apologue*; motif*; poem*; spoonerism*, R2; and lamentation*. For the theme of a paragraph*, see also ambiguity*; cliché*, R1; echo* effect, R3; reactualization*, 4; response*, R2; meaning*, 6; and variation*, R1. For the theme of an assertion*, see also apposition*; colon*; correspondences*; definition*; dislocation*, R2; enunciation*, 6; insult*; interjection*, R1; inversion*, R2; sweet* talk; negation*; nominalization*; paradox*, R1; sentence*; refrain*, R1; tautology*, R1; and truism*, R1. For the theme of a comparison*, see also allegory*; short* circuit; simile*; image*, 2; incoherence*, R1; metaphor*; and personification*, R1.

THREAD (DISCURSIVE) The unidimensional progress of a text, whether from a graphic perspective (see haplography*), from the point of view of sounds (see interruption* and *in petto**), from a grammatical viewpoint (see anacoluthon*), or from that of the utterance (see flashback*) or of its enunciation*.

Analogous terms: syntagmatic axis; combinatory axis (the combination of elements seen from one of the enumerated perspectives)

THREAT Anything which tends to create in the person addressed the fear that the speaker may harm him or her in some way.

Ex: ' "Watch that," I said ... "Do watch that, O Dim, if to continue to be on live thou dost wish" ' (A. Burgess, *A Clockwork Orange*, p. 26).

Analogous terms: commination (Morier, *OED*), adj. minatory; intimidation

R1: Common forms: 'What did you say!?'; 'Say that again!'; 'Watch it!';

etc. See injunction*, R5. Aposiopesis* (see aposiopesis, R2) is a useful figure in this context, since threats are the stronger for being imprecise: they allow the addressee to imagine the worst. This is the famous *Quos ego* ... ('I ought to ...') uttered by the angry Venus in the *Aeneid*. In the *Barber of Seville* we find: 'THE COUNT: "If you say a word ..."' (Beaumarchais).

Threats may be expressed ironically and indirectly, as in Theodore Roosevelt's 'Speak softly and carry a big stick' (speech, 2 Sept. 1901). A literary example: 'Listen, my little man, we may be soft, but there *are* two of us' (Sauvageau, *Wouf Wouf*, p. 17). See implication*, R1, allusion*, and antiphrasis*.

R2: Fabri (2:13) recommends the false threat or *admonition*: 'From the adversary's argument, we show that there may follow a most perilous disadvantage.' *Increpation* (chiding, reproach [*OED*]) is a kind of half-threat, which attaches acrimony to anything said. Bary presents it (apparently without irony*) as follows: 'Speaking to someone using exclamations, brusque movements and with an air of insult ... This figure is suitable for superiors, the old and the virtuous' (Bary, *Rhétorique française*, p. 342).

Literary criticism used threateningly produces 'intellectual terrorism' (see J. Paulhan, *Les Fleurs de Tarbe*) and its natural consequence, conformism.

R3: The *ad verecundiam* argument plays on an opponent's reverence for authority or respect for traditional human values. **Ex:** In *War and Peace* the nobles dare not refuse to pay the emperor extra taxes for fear of seeming to be lacking patriotism and generosity.

TIMBRE 'A sound's tonal quality, or "colour," which differentiates sounds of the same pitch, loudness, and duration (Crystal, 1987, p. 432).

R1: The printed word retains none of the markers which allow us to recognize an individual voice by its timbre. The only individual markers possible in the printed text would be the author's handwriting, if Lumitype were employed during the printing process to print special characters taken from each handwritten letter. See graphy*, R1. See also typographical variation*, R3.

R2: A list of adjectives used to describe the human voice: low-/high-pitched; strong/weak; sonorous/quiet; toneless; powerful/feeble; piercing/choking; full-throated, warm, rich, full, resounding, ringing / hollow, thin, fluting, cracked, faint, faraway; vibrant/shrill; brassy, thundering, booming, resounding, stentorian / cracked, quavering, trembling, hesitating, tremulous; male/senile; firm, rasping, dry, harsh, abrupt, curt, imperious, authoritarian, peremptory, sarcastic, ironic,

Title (Conferring of)

mocking / soft, tender, coaxing, flattering, insinuating, unctuous; low, deep, guttural, hollow, sepulchral / high-pitched, over-shrill, screechy, sour; crystal, clear, cool, distinct, pure / metallic, corn-crake, falsetto, nasal, ventriloquial.

R3: See dialogue*, R1. A change of timbre accompanies and indicates exaltation or delirium (see reactualization*, 7). See also mistake*, R2.

TITLE (CONFERRING OF) The attribution to persons (sometimes to institutions, or places, etc.) of superior or characteristic qualities which situate them, in a more or less durable way, within a social group.

Exx: Mr, Mrs, Miss, Sir, Your Excellency, Sire, the Honourable N., Reverend N., etc.

Exx: 'Amongst the clergy present were the very rev. William Delany, S.J., L.L.D.; the rt rev. Gerald Molloy, D.D.; the very rev. P.J. Kavanaugh, C.S. Sp. ...' (Joyce, *Ulysses*, p. 260); 'The chaste spouse of Leopold is she: Marion of the bountiful bosoms' (ibid., p. 262).

Nowadays, a title is often that of some social function (secretary, manager, attorney, etc.). That was also the case in the Middle Ages for noble titles whose meaning has more or less disappeared (e.g., Prince, Duke, Chief) to be replaced by military ranks. See also recipe*, R1.

R1: Titles form a special kind of *qualification* and may even take the qualifying forms of adjective or noun, epithet, attribute or appositional phrase, or of an apostrophe* (see insult* and sweet* talk, R3). Compare the following: 'Curious George'; 'George is curiosity personified'; 'George the curious'; 'Oh Curious One.' Titles may also characterize or define, even constitute in themselves an identity (see definition*, R2). They may be concrete or abstract; they may occasionally employ images* by means of synecdoche*, metonymy*, or metaphor*. Ex [Cedric is searching for a title for the new periodical he has founded]: 'Can you hear Cedric's mind churning away? "Vacuum," "Volcano," "Limbo," "Milestone," "Need," "Eruption," "Schism," "Data," "Arson." Yes, he's got it: "Chiaroscuro" ' (Dylan Thomas, *Quite Early One Morning*, pp. 130–1). Finally, like any image*, titles may fit a complex, usually positive isotopy*, one 'in equilibrium' if identification is involved, and even a negative one in the case of *reincarnation* which is common in Hinduism.

R2: Although titles possess a social function, that does not prevent them from originating very subjectively in some individual's mind. We may even replace a proper name with some more or less gratuitous title as does the Citizen when he expresses his opinion of Bloom: 'Virag from Hungary! Ahasuerus I call him. Cursed by God' (Joyce, *Ulysses*,

p. 277). The conferring of titles may thus become confused with naming. Ex: 'What's *your* name, trouble?' 'Trouble is his *middle* name.'

R3: Surnames too are proper names derived from titles. Lautréamont and the French surrealists liked sarcastic nicknames: Chateaubriand, the Melancholic-Mohican; Théophile Gautier, the Incomparable-Grocer; Lamartine, the Doleful Stork; etc. See also *agnominatio**, R3.

Capitalization of initial letters authenticates the device by attaching it to an ancient tradition. Livia, the wife of Augustus, for example, was venerated as the incarnation of Justice, Salvation, or Piety, and she was represented on imperial coins with the attributes of these allegorical abstractions*. In this case, we see the convergence of two devices: the personification* of an idea and the identification of a real person with the idea so personified.

R4: In the Middle Ages, the signifying nature of names was underlined by a mystical theory: the name's effusion. Saying a person's name aloud was thought to communicate his or her personal qualities to the hearers, which explains the reason for the recitation of litanies, decades of the rosary, and invocations to supernatural beings. Divine names were thought to provoke some immediate intuitive comprehension of the qualities they represent. Ex: 'For example, the name of *God* becomes liquid to mingle with that other name: *God with us* (Matthew 1:23). The *Admirable* fuses with the *Counsellor*; *God* and *Strength* (Isaiah 9:5) with *Father of future Ages* and *Prince of Peace*; and the *Lord our Justice* joins with the *Merciful One* and with the *God of Compassion* (Psalms 111:4)' (Bernard de Clairvaux, *Sermon* XV *on the Song of Songs*, sect. 1).

R5: Conferring titles is a simple way of adding synonyms to a proper name by means of antonomasia*, which may incorporate images* or employ periphrasis*. Ex: See Joyce, *Ulysses*, pp. 261–2, where Bennett is called successively 'Percy,' 'the welterweight sergeantmajor,' 'the artilleryman,' 'the soldier,' 'the redcoat,' 'the bulkier man,' 'the Englishman,' 'Pucking Percy,' 'the military man,' 'Battling Bennett,' and 'the Portobello Bruiser.' See also letter*.

TITLE (OF WORK) Most titles attempt to give some indication of a work's content, either abstractly (e.g., *The Plays of ...*, *The Complete Works of ...*), or more concretely (e.g., *Man and Music* [A. Burgess], *Alice in Wonderland* [Carroll]), or metaphorically (e.g., *The Grapes of Wrath* [Steinbeck], *Tinker Tailor Soldier Spy* [Le Carré]).

The title may simply be an *incipit*, taken, that is, from the work's first words ('And Death Shall Have No Dominion' [Dylan Thomas]). In such a case the title does not always appear above the text.

In the modern age of commercial labels, a title is more frequently 'consumed' than the rest of a work. (It is mentioned in conversations, catalogues, reviews, bibliographies, etc.) This very practical consideration explains the modern shortening of titles right down to a single word or even a single letter (e.g., *Maurice* [E.M. Forster], *V* [Thomas Pynchon]). Despite this, however, authors strive in their titles for maximum denotation and connotation; hence titles which are finely crafted from the point of view of rhythm*, or for evocative or affective effect: *A Clockwork Orange* [A. Burgess], *Portrait of the Artist as a Young Dog* [D. Thomas], *Life before Man* [Margaret Atwood], *Flaubert's Parrot* [J. Barnes].

Peter Weiss evoked lengthy titles from the past with *The Persecution and Assassination of Jean-Paul Marat as Performed by the Inmates of the Asylum of Charenton under the Direction of the Marquis de Sade* (1965), which soon became shortened to *Marat-Sade*.

R1: In the press, titles attempt to summarize collections of facts and specific ideas. Thus they are longer than literary titles, being frequently split into two parts. Ex: 'Taking the Pledge. The mudslinging begins as the candidates argue about patriotism.'

R2: Joyce, who did not append titles to the chapters of *Ulysses*, did entitle, however, each paragraph or section for about thirty pages (pp. 92–123). The titles of chapters in Robbe-Grillet's novel *La Jalousie* are incipits with variations*. The end of a text may also provide its title, as in Thomas Pynchon's novel *The Crying of Lot 49*.

R3: Titles in large capitals (see capital*, R1) at the top of the first page of a newspaper are *headlines*. *Half (or bastard) titles* are very short summaries of a book's title, printed in the centre of a blank page, before the complete title page. *Running titles* are summaries of up to a line, printed at the top of each page, with, on the left-hand page, the book's title, and on the right, that of the chapter (or of the entry in the case of a dictionary). In word processing, titles are called *headers*.

R4: Headlines, which are more often read than newspapers, come in various forms. An article's title, in the proper sense, appears in the largest capitals and is followed by a subtitle or sometimes preceded by a surtitle in smaller characters, which may, however, be underlined. There may also be *sub-subtitles*. See also paragraph*, R3.

R5: See also situational* signs, 1 and 2; pause*; echo* effect, R3; epanalepsis*, R3; interjection*, R2; final* word, R1; notation*; and schematization*, R1.

TMESIS 'The separation of the elements of a compound word by the interpolation of another word or words' (*OED*). See also Espy (1983), Lanham, Lausberg, Littré, Morier, Quinn, and Turco.

Exx: 'Oh so loverly sitting abso-blooming-lutely still' (A. Lerner and F. Loewe, *My Fair Lady*, a musical adaptation of G.B. Shaw's play,

Pygmalion); 'That man – *how dearly ever* parted' (Shakespeare, *Troilus and Cressida*, 3.3.96); 'See his wind – lilycocks – laced' (G.M. Hopkins, 'Harry Ploughman'); 'The most jammed-up boree I ever went to, and a houseful of chattering little boxes' (F. Packard, quoted in Espy, 1983, p. 142).

Other name: See hyperbaton*, R1.

R1: Normally interpolation is only possible between written words. Hyphens* serve to tie a word and its intercalation(s) together. See also embedding*, R1; and sentence* (types of), 4.

TRANSFERENCE A change of grammatical category, with or without a marker.

Ex: 'Five tallwhitehatted sandwichmen ... eeled themselves ... and plodded back ...' (Joyce, *Ulysses*, p. 188).

Addition of an article suffices to turn adjectives or verbs into nouns. Exx: 'in the pink'; 'The Naked and the Dead' (title); 'The Greening of America' (title); 'our goodbyes.' Nouns, even composites, once transformed into verbs, conjugate. Ex: 'He propositioned me.' Proper names used with the French prepositional form *à la* become adverbial phrases, possibly by analogy with phrases like 'à la mode' or 'à la carte.' Exx: 'fashion *à la* Princess Di'; ice cream *à la* mode.' See gallicism*.

When its foundation is not a lexical one, a possible transference is preceded by lexicalization* or by simple nominalization*. Syntagms* and even whole sentences may become adjectives. W.S. Gilbert, for instance, wrote of his 'aesthete' hero in *Patience*: 'A blue-and-white young man, / Francesca da Rimini, miminy, piminy, / Je-ne-sais-quoi young man!' ('When I go out of door,' act 2). Joyce writes: '... went Bloom, soft Bloom, I feel so lonely Bloom' (*Ulysses*, p. 235). Joyce also uses graphic juxtaposition*: 'Silent, each contemplating the other in both mirrors of the reciprocal flesh of theirhisnothis fellowfaces' (ibid., p. 577). In the expression 'a couldn't-care-less attitude,' there is transference derived from lexicalization*. See also hyphen*, R2.

Other names: hypostatization (Jacobs, p. 36); improper derivation (Robert). However, *transfer* [*transfert*], which Dubois's *Dictionnaire de linguistique* uses to describe the device, would complicate unnecessarily that word's usage in English, where it already means: 'the influence of a foreign speaker's mother tongue upon the target language' (Crystal, 1987, p. 432). See also Dumarsais, p. 227.

R1: In French, the credit goes to Lucien Tesnière (p. 361f.) for showing the importance of transference in the functioning of the language.

R2: Transference is a type of verbigeration* (see verbigeration, R5).

TRANSITION Specific turns of phrase used to link together different parts of a discourse*. '[They resemble] bridges between ideas and serve to unify a work' (Mestre, pp. 108–9).

Exx: See below, R1; reactualization*, R4; and squib*, R1.

Analogous: interlude (in broadcasting, a short transition, usually musical)

R1: Complete transitions repeat what has already been said and announce what is to follow. See plan*, R3. **Ex:** 'Those were my crimes. Here now is my reward' (Racine, *Britannicus*, 4.2). Mestre advises the disguising of transitions, both complete and incomplete, by the use of questions*, apostrophe*, concessions*, preterition*, *gradatio*, or corrections*.

R2: Transitions may be artificial; they may even disguise a *coq-à l'âne*. **Ex:**

> So you have two sponsors [for the Jockey-Club] who take you by the arm and 'relieve' you. 'Relieve' is the word. Let's talk about some other word.
> [New paragraph] The Count of Cambronne ... (Alfred Jarry, *La Chandelle verte*, p. 375)

TRANSLATION The introduction into the language of a work (called the target language) of a text or textual fragment in another language (called the source language).

Ex: 'Bentivenga urged others to touch a body's naked limbs; he declared this was the only way to freedom from the dominion of the senses, *homo nudus cum nuda iacebat*, "naked they lay together, man and woman" ... *Et non commiscebantur ad invicem*, "but there was no conjunction"' (U. Eco, *The Name of the Rose*, p. 57).

Other definitions: See isolexism*, other names. '[*Traductio*], that is the transference of the meaning of one word to another' (Quintilian, 9.3.71), from which Fabri derives his definition: 'repetition, except that the word must remain equivocal and is repeated at the beginning of successive clauses ... E.g. "Cures are achieved by doctors, cures are [ad]ministered by priests"' (*Pleine Rhétorique*, 2:161). (Note that '*pleine*' [or 'full'] rhetoric refers to the study of both prosodic and rhetorical figures.) See diaphora*.

R1: In *War and Peace* Tolstoy recounts that speaking French was one of the snobberies of Russian high society before Napoleon's Moscow campaign. The French translator resolved the problem of the two different languages used by aristocratic characters as opposed to speakers of Russian in the novel by italicizing dialogues* which were 'in French in the text.' Another constant danger is mistranslation (see mistake*, R1, and anglicism*, R1). But mistranslations aside, there remains the problem of connotation. Can one be content with word-by-word translation, as was the case with texts by Saint-Jean Perse, which their author refused to elucidate? Translators of texts must, in any case, most frequently produce *adaptations* that constitute equivalents in the *ethos* of the target language, or even in the new public's cultural world. Word-play* (see word-play, R1) falls victim to translation even more swiftly than does poetry. 'Humour is the first of the gifts to perish in a foreign tongue' (Virginia Woolf, *The Common Reader*, p. 57). However, translation may permit new word-play in the form of double translation. Ex:

PASQUIN. – ... the Conclave, proceeding in camera ...
MARFORIO. – Yes, in [the word] Conclave, we find *cave*.

Alfred Jarry, La Chandelle verte, p. 424

Translation may even inspire poets. Ex: 'Thou fill'st from the winged chalice of the soul / Thy lamp, O Memory, fire-winged to its goal' (Dante Gabriel Rossetti, 'Mnemosyne').

R2: *Juxtalinear* translations present the words in parallel columns with the translation of each one opposite (even if such a presentation entails subsequent repetition with greater clarity of style and syntax). Jarry parodies this scholarly method as follows: '*Omnis a Deo scientia*, which means: *omnis*, all; *a Deo*, science; *scientia*, comes from God' (*Ubu roi*, p. 163). The juxtaposition of syntagms* reduces these disadvantages. Ex:

| *quaedam animi incitatio*: | and what natural vivacity |
| *innata omnibus*: | innate in all men |

Claude Simon, Histoire, p. 119

R3: Translation may take the opposite form, starting from a definitional periphrasis* and arriving at the foreign term. Ex: 'That red, faintly murmuring liquid called *"blood,"* elsewhere *"blut,"* or *"sang,"* or even described proudly as *"sangre"* ' (H. Michaux, *Vigies sur les cibles*, p. 16). The recourse to definition* also permits intralingual translation: the name follows a description* of the thing defined. Onomasiology, the science which studies this procedure, remains largely undeveloped.

Intralingual translation becomes necessary when we coin neologisms*. Ex: '... what, in Proust's text, is not only *"readerly"* ([i.e.,] classical) but *"writerly"* (we translate that broadly as "modern")' (G. Genette, *Figures III*, p. 271). In the case of semantic neologisms 'translated' by means of a periphrasis*, what we have in reality is a purely rhetorical manipulation of the device: false translations intended to transmit explanations*. The latter may become interpretations. Desnos, for instance, makes of translation one of the surrealists' poetic devices. Ex: 'Louis means a throw of the dice / André means a reef' ('Rencontres').

Triangle

R4: For false translation, see quotation*, R2. See also celebration*, R4; flip-flop*; discourse*; and lapsus*, R1. Translation offers a new means of playing on the signifier. Allographic translations also exist, like the two volumes of nursery rhymes *N'Heures Souris Rames* and *Mots d'Heures: Gousses, Rames* [i.e., *Mother Goose Rhymes*], published by Ormonde de Kay (1983) and Luis d'Antin van Rooten (1967) respectively. **Exx:** 'Humpty Dumpty sat on a wall' / 'Un petit d'un petit s'étonne aux Halles'; 'There was a little man and he had a little gun' / 'Des rois élus dolmen, Hunyadi lit d'élégant' (Luis d'Antin van Rooten, nos. 1, 5).

R5: Are not quotations in a foreign language the opposite of translations? We might then call them counter-translations.

TRIANGLE The 'eternal triangle' is a ternary structure in dramas or comedies involving three characters: a husband, wife, and lover. Etienne Souriau made a particular study of it in *Les Deux cent mille situations dramatiques* (1950).

Ex: Tom Stoppard, *Another Moon Called Earth* (1967)

TRIPLICATION Threefold repetition*.

Ex: '... a strange, strange, strange hat ...' (R. Queneau, *Exercises in Style*, p. 35).

Other definitions: Greimas (*Du Sens*, p. 240) showed the importance of ternary narrative structure in folk-tales and short stories: the fearless hero must spend three successive nights in a place and undergo three trials. He adds that 'the device of triplication – with its paradigmatic meaning of totality and its syntax of achievement – clearly indicates that the final test will subsume the preceding two and will bring a decisive solution.' In his turn, Gerald Prince (*Dictionary of Narratology* [1987]) writes: 'Triplication. The double repetition, at the level of the *narrated*, of one or more (sequences of) events; *trebling*. A character may, for instance, violate three interdictions or perform three difficult tasks. Triplication is common in folk literature.' Triplication is also common in jokes involving implicit or explicit competitions between national stereotypes: 'An Englishman, Irishman, and Scotsman went to play golf ...'

R1: Besides triple lexical repetition*, syntactic and rhythmic triplications exist (see sentence*, R4; reprise*; and rhythmic echo*). **Ex:** 'I came, I saw, I conquered' (Julius Caesar).

TRUISM A proposition that states nothing not already implied in one of its terms. See Grambs, Littré, and Robert.

Exx: ' "I don't like my tea too hot" = "I don't like it hotter than I like it" ' (*Concise Oxford Dictionary*); 'If there were no Poland, there would be no Polish people' (Alfred Jarry, *Ubu roi*, p. 180).

Synonyms: self-evident truth, obvious remark. Common expression: 'That goes without saying.'

R1: Truisms differ from clichés*, which are figures of words, and from commonplaces, which express current, but not necessarily obvious, ideas. Like metabole*, the truism is a figure of thought, but it need not include repetition* because the cultural or real context makes it obvious. If this obviousness is due to the theme* of the assertion, we have a tautology*. Extenuation* (see extenuation, R3) is an even more pronounced expression of the self-evident.

R2: The truism is a mistake* caused by carelessness or attenuation* (see also litotes*, R4). **Ex:** 'Milton uses the word *thing* to refer to many things.' Truisms may serve to create both emphasis* and anticlimax* (see anticlimax, R3). They coexist quite happily with pseudo-simulation. **Ex:** 'Ah! My Lord the Russian Dragoon, be careful, don't fire in this direction, there are people here' (Alfred Jarry, *Ubu roi*, p. 147). Some truisms are, or are presented as being, poetic. **Ex:** 'There are days and still other days. There are mornings and evenings' (Gide, *Romans*, p. 205). They may take on the role of natural epithets, serving to show or 'paint' a scene. **Ex:** 'I cover my withered face with a piece of black velvet, like the soot *which fills chimneys*' (Lautréamont, *Les Chants de Maldoror*, 1.8).

Truisms appear frequently in scientific treatises, particularly in those parts presenting the most important line of reasoning*. **Ex:** 'CHARACTERISTICS OF FINGERPRINTS. The hands represented may be either right hands or left hands' (magazine article). The kind of humour* (see humour, R5) favoured by mathematicians frequently takes this form. **Ex** [concerning Gauss's Law]: 'for Gauss was only three years old when Laplace discovered the law (1780) ... Despite Gauss's well-known precocity, it is improbable that he too made the same discovery at that age' (Fréchet, quoted by H. Guitton, *Statistique*, p. 173). Comic use of truisms may be effective. **Ex:** 'Money can't buy friends, but you got a better class of enemy' (Spike Milligan, *Puckoon*, p. 71).

R3: Like tautologies*, truisms often permit the expression, in the form of some irrefutable utterance, of sentiments which one might not otherwise make known. **Exx:** 'He/she will never see seventeen again'; 'It is my view that the revolver was a long way off and that it did not get back on its own' (G. Bernanos, *Oeuvres romanesques*, p. 781).

R4: Banalities are semi-truisms. For inverted truisms, see paradox*, R5. Some truisms are truisms in appearance only (see image*, 2). **Ex:**

Variation

'... most of history's greatest transgressions and atrocities have been perpetrated by people acting with what they believed to be the best of intentions' (M. Baigent et al., *The Messianic Legacy*, p. 451). Others may be revived (see paralogism*, R2).

V

VARIATION A narrative* or description* starts over, presenting certain differences or even oppositions of detail. (See repetition*, R5).

Exx: 'In the beginning of the last chapter, I informed you exactly *when* I was born; – but I did not inform you *how*. No, that particular was reserved entirely for a chapter by itself' (L. Sterne, *Tristram Shandy*, vol. 1, ch. 6); 'They say they are not thirsty; they say that it's not a spring; they say it's not water; they say that it's not *their* idea of a spring or of water; they say water does not exist' (Paul Claudel, *Théâtre*, 2:524).

Other definitions: See reprise*, other def. 2; symploce*, epanalepsis*, R6; and intonation*, R1 and R5.

R1: The term is borrowed from music, in which variations operate upon a theme* (see theme, R2) and so cannot be a purely formal matter, as is the case with epanalepsis*.

R2: The French 'New Novelists' counted variation among their favourite techniques, and more recent novelists have parodied it. **Ex:**

> You have now read about thirty pages and you're becoming caught up in the story. At a certain point you remark: 'This sentence sounds somehow familiar. In fact, this whole passage reads like something I've read before.' Of course, there are themes that recur, the text is interwoven with these reprises, which serve to express the fluctuation of time ...
>   Wait a minute! Look at the page number. Damn! From page 32 you've gone back to page 17! What you thought was a stylistic subtlety on the author's part is simply a printer's mistake: they have inserted the same pages twice. (Italo Calvino, *If on a Winter's Night a Traveller*, trans. W. Weaver, p. 25)

See also title* (of work), R2.
   Variations have various causes: hesitation (see *dubitatio**); *gradatio**; foregrounding* the act of writing. In the latter case, the author seems to be saying to the reader: '*You* choose; it makes no difference to me!' **Exx:** the two endings of John Fowles's *The French Lieutenant's Woman* and

the two different endings in Harold Pinter's screenplay drawn from the novel.

VARIATION (TYPOGRAPHICAL) Changes in the form, place, or disposition of the typographical characters used.

Ex: In *Conversation-sinfonietta*, Jean Tardieu prints a 'cry in six voices' in the following type-faces:

> soprano: antique;
> tenor: *'didot'*;
> first contralto: *'plantin'*;
> second contralto: antique italic;
> first bass: cooper black;
> second bass: antique bold.

See also graphy*, R5.

R1: Among variations in the place of characters: *superposition* (characters placed above the line are more legible when different in size); the arrangement of characters in a *cross* (made easier if, as in crossword puzzles or printed games of *Scrabble*, the two words share a common letter); *inversion* (characters are turned upside down); the *turning around* of characters (from left to right, to be deciphered in a mirror); *irregular alignment* (the text is multi-columned with margins of different widths or with columns crossing each other); *insets* or *scroll-work* (characters have an ornate framework); *speech balloons* or *bubbles* (spaces in which the words spoken by cartoon characters are inscribed). **Exx** (of crossed characters):

$$
\begin{matrix}
\text{I} & & \text{B} & \text{I} & \text{R} \\
\text{GLACE} & & & & \\
\text{E} & & \text{ALOU} & & \text{TT}
\end{matrix}
$$

Modern typesetting techniques (Lumitype in particular) have made typographical variations a means of expression equal in some instances to images in publicity. The spatialists, an almost pictorial school of printers, use them in a wide range of applications (see graphic line* [of verse]). Contemporary poets are increasingly sensitive to the visual semiotics of texts (Ian Hamilton Finlay, Emmett Williams, bp Nichol, etc.).

R2: Other variations include the placing of characters closer together or spacing them out. Two characters are 'closer together' when their serifs (or 'feet') touch (the *set* is the distance between the face of a character and its 'beard'). In order to create a space between characters, we introduce a blank, of varying widths, but no wider than a single letter ('em quadrat' or 'em quad'). We may distinguish this type of variation from the type which consists in reducing or increasing characters' overrun, without changing their body. Letters are condensed or extended when their shape is made narrower or is dilated in width only, which produces bolding, semi-bold (in both of which thickening of the down-strokes and up-strokes usually accompanies dilation), thin-narrow, and thin-close-set (see Stanley Morison, *Tally of Types*, rev. ed. [1973]; and John N.C. Lewis, *Typography: Design and Practice* [1978]).

R3: We can draw analogies between some characteristics of sounds and type:

SOUND	TYPO
duration	spacing
timbre	typeset
intensity	thickness
pitch	body

We can justify the last of these, which may seem somewhat arbitrary, by pointing to its coherence with the others in the two series, in which it fills a vacant space. Making a larger-bodied character correspond to a melodic rise in the voice in a continuous text is perhaps as plausible, and more practical, than displacing the text into some imaginary range. These four correspondences, when used to transcribe speech, make possible reproduction of sounds of the kind most frequently found in the speech balloons of certain cartoon strips (see R.P. Nelson, *Comic Art and Caricature* [1978]; and W. Hewison, *Cartoon Connection: The Art of Pictorial Humour* [1977]). See also intonation*.

R4: A useful summary of the principal Western typesettings may be found in *Rookledge's International Type-Finder: The Essential Handbook of Typeface Recognition and Selection* (1983).

VERBIAGE 'Needless accumulation of words' (*Concise Oxford Dictionary*).

Ex:

> MR. SMITH: The heart is ageless. [*Silence.*]
> MR. MARTIN: That's true. [*Silence.*]
> MRS. SMITH: So they say. [*Silence.*]
> MRS. MARTIN: They also say the opposite. [*Silence.*]
> MR. SMITH: The truth lies somewhere between the two. [*Silence.*]
> Eugene Ionesco, *The Bald Soprano*, in *Four Plays*, pp. 20–1

Analogous terms: empty speeches; verbosity; garrulousness; 'Duckspeak' (Orwell, *Nineteen Eighty-Four*; cited by Grambs, p. 105)

R1: The *OED* defines verbiage as: 'wording of a superabundant or superfluous character; abundance of words without necessity or without much meaning; excessive wordiness.' We shall distinguish verbiage from verbigeration*, which the *OED* defines simply as a mental disease. In our view, verbigeration, or the production of a text without overall meaning*, presents greater difficulty than does mere talking for talking's sake, or producing a text with some vague meaning deriving from repetition* of commonplaces. What constitutes verbiage is the absence of a *denotatum* (an intended real object), which confines the subject to the realm of the undefined.

R2: Verbiage resembles battology* and redundancy*. Ex:

> Not to speak of hostels, leperyards, sweating chambers, plague-graves, their greatest doctors, the O'Shiels, the O'Hickeys, the O'Lees, have sedulously set down the divers methods by which the sick and the relapsed found again health whether the malady had been the trembling withering or loose boyconnell flux. Certainly in every public work which in it anything of gravity contains preparation should be with importance commensurate and therefore a plan was by them adopted (whether by having preconsidered or as the maturation of experience it is difficult in being said which the discrepant opinions of subsequent enquirers are not up to the present congrued to render manifest) whereby maternity was so far from all accident possibility removed that whatever care the patient in that allhardest of woman hour chiefly required and not solely for the copiously opulent but also for her who not being sufficiently moneyed scarcely and not even scarcely could subsist valiantly and for an inconsiderable emolument was provided. (Joyce, *Ulysses*, pp. 314–15)

R3: Semi-verbiage is called *prolixity, loquaciousness, glibness, facundity* (i.e., 'eloquence' or the 'gift of the gab,' depending on level* and connotation), or *volubility*. The number of non-pejorative terms in the list indicates that the phenomenon is fairly common. Exx: see accumulation* and oratorical amplification*.

R4: Verbosity 'achieved' by imitation* of so-called 'sublime' style soon turns into grandiloquence*.

R5: Another common type of verbomania is the digression*. Ex:

> ... and this leads me to the affair of *Whiskers* – but by what chain of ideas – I leave as a legacy in *mortmain* to Prudes and Tartuffes, to enjoy and make the most of.
>
> *Upon Whiskers*
> I'm sorry I made it – 'twas as inconsiderate a promise as ever entered a man's head – A chapter upon whiskers! alas! the world will not bear it – 'tis a delicate world – but I knew not of what

mettle it was made – nor had I ever seen the underwritten fragment; otherwise, as surely as noses are noses, and whiskers are whiskers still (let the world say what it will to the contrary), so surely would I have steered clear of this dangerous chapter.

The Fragment ... (Laurence Sterne, *Tristram Shandy*, vol. 5, ch. 1)

VERBIGERATION The production of a text without overall meaning*, notwithstanding that some of its syntagms*, if taken in isolation, may often be intelligible and may appear normally constructed. See Robert and Marchais. Like the *OED*, they emphasize the device's reliance on repetition*, which in our view, although common, is not essential. Both the *OED* and Grambs insist that in English the term designates a mental illness. We are using it as a device able to suggest such illness in a literary character.

Ex: 'LUCKY: Given the existence as uttered forth in the public works of Puncher and Wattman of a personal God quaquaquaqua with white beard quaquaquaqua outside time without extension who from the heights of divine apathia divine aphasia loves us dearly with some exceptions for reasons unknown but time will tell and suffers like the divine Miranda with those who for reasons unknown but time will tell are plunged in torment plunged in fire whose fire flames if that continues ...' (Samuel Beckett, *Waiting for Godot*, act 1).

Analogous terms: *logorrhoea* (pejorative); pure verbal fantasy (meliorative); *ectopy* (we might thus name a text without an isotopy*); verbal salad

R1: The word *verbigeration* is borrowed, as is *logorrhoea*, from psychiatry. We are therefore speaking of verbigeration chiefly as a psychological phenomenon rather than as a device. That does not mean, however, that the phenomenon is new to literature. On the contrary: 'A long tradition of irrational poetry has its source in the adynata* of late Latin poetry. From the *fatras* and *fatrasie* [medleys, hotchpotches, "irrational or obscure piece(s) of verse" (Preminger)], through *soties de menus-propos* [farcical farragoes of small talk], *coq-à-l'âne*, gibberish verses and nonsense rhymes, to eighteenth-century nonsense-verse, never did the tradition of *pure verbal fantasy* cease' (Marc Angenot, *Rhétorique du surréalisme*, p. 63).

R2: Verbigeration differs from *paragraphia, paraphasia,* and *paragrammatism*, which are language disorders (see mistake*, R2) characterized respectively by substitution* or deformation of letters, words, or constructions. Such disorders are due to cerebral lesions which interfere with the natural functioning of language but not with that of the intelligence. Although unable to express themselves, sufferers know what they want to say. Ex: see paragram*, R3. In literature, verbigeration is a device rather than a mental disorder. (See simulation*, R2.)

R3: Since the minimal syntagmatic linking device is accumulation*, this appears frequently in verbigerations. Ex: 'LUCKY: ... the practice of sports such as tennis football running cycling swimming flying floating riding gliding conating camogie skating ...' (Beckett, *Waiting for Godot*, act 1). Spitzer identified verbigeration in his discussion of 'chaotic enumeration'; and Garapon spotted it in inventories of incongruous elements. The *fatrasie* elevated dissociation* and *coq-à-l'âne** to the status of a literary genre (see Paul Zumthor, *Essai de poétique médiévale*, p. 141). We also find chaotic, but not absurd, enumeration* in verbiage*. See also the surrealist image, under image*, R1.

R4: Propositions may be linked together on the basis of sounds alone. Ex: see musication*, R4. In such a case, meaning* may drift about, changing direction on the basis of chance encounters between words. Ex: Margaret Schlausch (*The Gift of Language*, p. 237) collected, and provided the gloss of, the following examples of blends and distortions in Joyce's *Finnegans Wake*:

erigenating = originating; also Erigena-ting (from Duns Scotus Erigena, the 'Erin-born philosopher');
eroscope = horoscope; Eros-scope; hero-scope;
Champs de Mors = Champ de Mars; Field of Death (Mors);
herodotary = hereditary; hero-doter; Herodotus?;
pigmaid = made like a pig; pigmied.

And Umberto Eco (*The Aesthetics of Chaosmos*, trans. E. Esrock, pp. 64, 65–6) discovers in the same text the following examples in which sound dominates sense or plays with allusion*: '[Joyce's] language is primitive and barbaric because it is basically onomatopoeic ... it is [also] built upon linguistic fragments of previous languages by juxtaposing different foreign synonyms for the word "thunder": "bababababadalgharaghtakamminarronnkonnbronntonnerronntuonnthunntrovarrhounawnskawntoohoohoordenenthurnuk!' (*Finnegans Wake*, p. 1) ... In "Jungfraud's Messonge book" (*Ibid.*, p. 460) we detect, contemporaneously, Jung + Freud + young + fraud + *Jungfrau* + message + *songe* [i.e., dream] + *mensonge* [lie].' See also word-play*.

VERSET Although the word may be a diminutive form of *vers*, a line* of poetry or verse (i.e., Fr. *vers* + the diminutive suffix -*et*), it designates a line which is frequently longer, more irregular, and of a more subtle rhythm* than conventional verses.

Ex:

> The figs fall from the trees, they are good and sweet; and in falling
> the red skins of them break. A north wind am I to ripe figs.
> Thus, like figs, do these doctrines fall for you, my friends: imbibe
> now their juice and their sweet substance! It is autumn all around,
> and clear sky, and afternoon. (Friedrich Nietzsche, 'In the Happy
> Isles,' in *Thus Spake Zarathustra*, trans. T. Common, p. 90)

Analogous: *antiphon*, a liturgical term, 'a dialogue between choirs, one
choir singing the *versicle*, the other singing the response' (Turco, p. 171).
Ex:

> *'Canst Thou Draw?' (Job XLI: 1–7)*
>
> Canst thou draw out Leviathan with an hook, or his tongue with a
> cord which thou lettest down? Canst thou put an hook in his nose?
> or bore his jaw through with a thorn?
> *Vain attempt!*
> Will he make many supplications unto thee?
> *Terrible words!*
>
> Manoah Bodman, quoted by Turco, p. 171

R1: Turco (see 'Forensics,' pp. 154–5) links the French *verset* to the
katauta ('a Japanese form of question and answer') and also to lines of
'breath-length.' He quotes William Carlos Williams's concepts of the
'breath-pause' and of 'variable accentuals' in which 'two to four
stresses are approximately equal to an utterance, and six to twelve
accents are as many as can be uttered in a short breath.' **Ex:**

> The world of the spirits that comes afterward
> is the same as our own, just like you sitting
> there they come and talk to me, just the same.
>
> William Carlos Williams, 'The Horse Show'

Turco concludes: 'Thus, in Williams' prosody, each line is a phrase of
about two to four stresses, and three lines equal a clause of about six to
twelves stresses. Williams' system, however, does not necessarily have
anything to do with questions and answers.'

R2: See paragraph*, R1, and reactualization*, 6. The *versets* of Paul
Claudel also seem to imitate the rhythm of breathing: '... just as the
range of respiratory rhythms varies with the quality of emotion,
[Claudel's *versets*] swell and contract in turn' (Jacques Rivière, *Etudes*,
p. 69). Ex: 'Again! once again the sea returns to seek me out like a bark,
/ The sea again which returns to me like a spring tide and raises me
up and launches me like an unburdened galley' (Paul Claudel, 'Quatri-
ème Ode').

VULGARISM 'A word or form of expression which violates the purity of diction; a debased form of colloquialism' (Pei and Gaynor).

Ex [a description of epitaphs in a graveyard]: 'Glittery gilt lists the names and dates and the bullshit about them' (Peter Reading, *Ukelele Music*, p. 13).

Other names: coarseness, obscenity

R1: Vulgarisms belong with coarse expressions (see swear-word*). They may be distinguished from gauloiserie*, which adds a comic tone to an utterance, and from *scatological* texts, which are preoccupied with excremental and sexual matters. **Ex:** 'Markings on a shitter wall' (R. Fernandez in A. Chapman, *New Black Voices*, p. 380).

W

WELL-WISHING The attitude of an author or character who expresses an ardent desire that someone profit from something.

Ex:

CHORUS OF ISRAELITES:
Live, live for ever, pious David's son;
Live, live for ever, mighty Solomon.

G.F. Handel, *Solomon*, 2.1

Analogous: 'a wish exclaimed' (Lanham); *optatio* (Joseph, p. 249), an 'ardent wish or prayer.' **Ex:** 'A horse! a horse! my kingdom for a horse!' (Shakespeare, *Richard III*, 5.4.7). See also: *optation* (Fontanier, p. 438, Littré, Quillet, and Robert). In traditional rhetoric, *optatio* figures among arguments* appropriate for winning the jury's goodwill. It was customary to end one's plea by wishing for a happy outcome. A less official form is: 'best wishes,' 'warmest regards,' etc.; see letter*.

R1: Good wishes may be expressed by the subjunctive, as in the example quoted from Handel's *Solomon*, or by the use of exclamations* as in 'Happy Birthday!' and 'Happy New Year!' or by the use of a gallicism* such as 'Bon voyage!' **Ex:** 'MR. MARTIN (to the Fire Chief as he leaves): Good luck, and a good fire!' (Eugene Ionesco, *The Bald Soprano*, in *Four Plays*, p. 37). In indirect speech, the exclamation mark disappears, as does the emotion. Well-wishing has its own intonation*.

R2: Old expressions, like 'God grant that' and 'God forbid,' took into account our lack of control over our own destiny. When we address such wishes to the being we believe to be capable of answering them, we make a request (see supplication*), a prayer*, or exhortation*. But some accepted formulas lend themselves to hypocrisy. Ex: R.I.P., the abbreviation* found in epitaphs ('May he/she rest in peace'). It used to express forgiveness to both parties, both the quick and the dead, and urged the deceased to abandon any remorse or resentment which might have resulted in ghostly visitations. See notation*, R1.

R3: Supplications* addressed to no one in particular are merely a kind of wish. Ex: 'Ah! let it come then, the great crisis, I begged, illness, sharp pain!' (A. Gide, *Romans*, p. 159). On the other hand, strong wishes soon turn into supplications*. Ex:

> Yes there's the orderly. He'll change the sheets
> When I'm lugged out. Oh, couldn't I do that?
> ...
> I'd love to be a sweep's boy, black as Town;
> Yes, or a muck-man. Must I be his load?
> > Wilfred Owen, 'Wild with All Regrets'

R4: Ill-wishing is also called *malediction* or cursing. Ex:

> PANDULPH: Then, by the lawful power that I have,
> Thou shalt stand cursed and excommunicate.
> And blessed shall he be that doth revolt
> From his allegiance to an heretic
> ...
> That takes away by any secret course
> Thy hateful life.
> > Shakespeare, *King John*, 3.1.172–9

Ex: ' "I don't care whether he dies, damn the monster!" William cried' (U. Eco, *The Name of the Rose*, p. 482).

The formulas used recall ancient *imprecations*, a religious form of malediction, by which we call upon the Deity to punish someone.

WHISPER A noise* made by voices speaking quietly, without vibration of the vocal chords, so as to be heard as little as possible.

Ex: 'Confession ... Woman dying to. And I schschschschschsch. And did you chachachachacha?' (Joyce, *Ulysses*, p. 68).

Analogous: whispering ('*chuchotis*,' which is meliorative in Fr.)

WIT Being witty involves provoking others to use their wits by exercising one's own. In order to do this, one leaves aside, or refuses, the ordinary, the true, or at least the desirable structures of reality or language. Wit is an implicit means of recognizing such a refusal.

Witty devices may be classified into eight non-exclusive categories.

The witticism (see conceit*), a process of reasoning* whose logic is gratuitous or even false, makes a game of intelligence as it grapples with its object.

Nonsense* is an obscure form of witticism which replaces the reasoning process with feelings.

Simulation* leads into error, and pseudo-simulation* has a comic effect because it deceives no one.

Persiflage*, raillery or banter, consists of mocking or ridiculing someone as a joke.

Word-play* over-exploits language because of the different meanings* which attach to spoken syntagms*, whether modified or not.

Irony* and point* challenge the reader's shrewdness.

Humour* emphasizes the mind's limits and weaknesses and recognizes the supremacy of reality.

The burlesque* is a kind of vulgar, excessive comedy.

R1: Wit's aim is often simply to make people laugh, in which case it is called a *joke* or *jest*. But laughter may have various functions and may be triggered without funny remarks. One may wish to:

(a) show that one has seen the trick, the mistake*, the absurdity, play on words, or allusion*;

(b) defend oneself against a veiled attack without being led to counterattack. Such is the case when one is the butt of irony*, persiflage*, or even of insults* or threats* which one in such a case takes to be merely simulated, teasing, or made 'as a joke';

(c) repress one's 'true' reaction. Contradiction liberates the ego since it is not responsible for it. 'Laughter causes one to abandon positions which are too restricting' (H. Michaux, *Connaissance par les gouffres*, p. 24);

(d) have the pleasure or satisfaction of discovering that other people think as oneself does, that an idea or expression is correct, that a quip, oral or written, succeeded in 'settling someone's hash';

(e) show surprise;

(f) make a showing in society (see literary* games); etc.

R2: See gauloiserie* for Gallic humour. For other examples of wit, see lipogram*, R1, and metanalysis*, R2.

WORD-PLAY Written or spoken wit* or jokes based on certain elements of language: various forms of play on the signifier or signified.

Ex: a drug store, a source of orifice supplies

Here are two quite general forms not entirely covered by the previous definition*.

The rhyming lead-in plays on homophones to produce remotivation*
of a syntagm*. Ex:

So each one upwards in the air
His shot he did expend.
And may all other duels have
That upshot at the end.

Thomas Hood (1799–1845), quoted by Augarde, p. 208

See also Joyce's *Finnegans Wake* for examples like *dontelleries*, which,
constructed on the French word *dentelleries* (linen edged in lace),
suggests intimate garments that discreetly 'don't tell.' In such examples
discrete elements of a syntagm* combine to form a single word. Ex:
'Many people give punning names to their children or their homes (e.g.
"Kutyurbelyakin," which I took globally for a possibly Armenian
word, until I broke it down into its constituent sounds)' (W. Redfern,
Puns, p. 132). The opposite also occurs. Ex: Thomas Hood protested
against the unwelcome attentions of an officious undertaker by saying
that he wanted to 'urn a lively Hood' (Redfern, *Puns*, p. 125).

Lead-ins which employ diaphora* develop an utterance by introducing a second meaning for a term already used. Ex: '[Queen Elizabeth I
is said to have remarked]: "You may be burly, my Lord of Burleigh,
but ye shall make less stir in my realm than the Lord of Leicester" '
(quoted by Augarde, p. 205). But word-play in any form triumphs
when wit* manages to entrap language in its own contradictions. Ex:
'Assumed dongiovannism will not save him. No later undoing will
undo the first undoing' (Joyce, *Ulysses*, p. 161).

R1: Word-play rarely survives translation. Ex: 'He went off towards his
hometown as the master of the gods goes to heaven' comes from
'yayan puram svam svam ivamaresah' (*Ramayana*, 2.72.27), in which *sva*
means both 'his' (hometown understood) and 'heaven' (H.R. Diwekar,
Les Fleurs de rhétorique de l'Inde, p. 39). However, some translators, like
those who turned Joyce's *Ulysses* into French, for instance, can work
miracles.

R2: Rhyming lead-ins may serve as mnemonic devices. Ex (to remember the distinction between *stalactites* and *stalagmites*): 'The tights hang
down, the mites grow up.'

Z

ZEUGMA A figure of syntax which consists in uniting several parts of a sentence* by means of some common, non-repeated element. Zeugma includes both adjunction* and disjunction*. See Fabri (2:156), Fontanier (p. 313), Joseph, Lanham, Lausberg, Littré, and *OED*. However, all these definitions emphasize the ellipsis* rather than the syntactic union the device creates. See also brachylogia*.

Other definition: 'the word understood is not in grammatical agreement with the one expressed' (Morier). Fontanier and Littré call this *compound zeugma*. Ex: 'INSPECTOR: The head is warm, the hands cold, the legs icy' (Jean Giraudoux, *Intermezzo*, 3.5).

R1: Some examples of zeugma (like the previous one) entail anacoluthon*. Preminger speaks of faulty grammatical congruence. Such examples may also revive stereotyped expressions, and Cressot and Morier recall that *zeugos* in Greek means a 'yoke,' suggesting the example: 'To the sound of slaps and drums.'

R2: In English, zeugma frequently unites an abstract with a concrete term. Lausberg (sect. 707) calls this *semantic zeugma*, and Morier *yoking* (sense 2). The young Dickens seems particularly fond of this type of zeugma. **Exx:** 'Miss Bolo ... went straight home, in a flood of tears and a sedan-chair'; 'with this permission and the front-door key, Sam Weller issued forth'; 'to dinner they went with good digestion waiting on appetite, and health on both, and a waiter on all three' (Dickens, *Pickwick Papers*, chs. 35, 38, 51). This type seems particularly well suited to humour*. **Exx:** 'LIGHTHOUSE. A tall building on the seashore in which the government maintains a lamp and the friend of a politician' (Ambrose Bierce, *The Devil's Dictionary*); 'On the floor was broken glass and Mr. Weazeley' (Dylan Thomas, *Quite Early One Morning*, p. 34).
  Combined with irony*, zeugma may produce antithesis*: 'In which William and Adso enjoy the jolly hospitality of the abbot and the angry conversation of Jorge' (U. Eco, *The Name of the Rose*, p. 93). This trick is also particularly appropriate for presenting metaphors* involving a complex isotopy* which is 'in equilibrium' (see image*, 5). **Exx:** 'My long manuscript hair mingles with the aquatic plants and the invariable adverbs'; 'I had just missed my rendezvous and my entire life' (Hubert Aquin, *Prochain Episode*, trans. P. Williams, pp. 19, 121).

BIBLIOGRAPHY

INDEX

Bibliography

1. Criticism and Works of Reference

Abrams, M.H. *A Glossary of Literary Terms*. 4th ed. New York: Holt, Rinehart and Winston 1981

Académie Française. *Dictionnaire*. 83d ed. 2 vols. Paris: Hachette 1932

Adams, Valerie. *An Introduction to Modern English Word-Formation*. London: Longman 1973

Ad Herennium. Trans. Harry Caplan. Cambridge, Mass.: Loeb Classical Library 1947

Albalat, Antoine. *La Formation du style par l'assimilation des auteurs*. Paris: Colin 1921

Amar du Rivier, Jean-Augustin. *Cours complet de rhétorique*. Paris: Langlois 1811

Angenot, Marc. *Rhétorique du surréalisme*. 3 vols. Brussels: Université Libre de Bruxelles 1967

– *Glossaire de la critique littéraire contemporaine*. Montreal: Hurtubise HMH 1979

Antoine, G. *La Coordination en français*. 2 vols. Paris: d'Artey 1958–62

– *Les Cinq Grandes Odes de Claudel*. Abbeville: F. Paillart 1959

Aragon, Louis. *Traité du style*. Paris: Gallimard 1958

Aragon, Louis, et al. *Dictionnaire abrégé du surréalisme*. Paris: Corti 1969

Aristotle. *Rhetoric* and *Poetics*. New York: The Modern Library 1954

Arnauld, N. *Les Vies parallèlles de Boris Vian*. Paris: Union générale d'éditions 1970

Audet, J.-P. 'Esquisse historique du genre littéraire de la "Bénédiction" juive et de l' "Eucharistie" chrétienne.' *Revue biblique* 65 (1958), pp. 369–99

Auerbach, Erich. *Mimesis: The Representation of Reality in Western Literature*. Trans. Willard R. Trask. Princeton: Princeton University Press 1953

Augarde, Tony. *The Oxford Guide to Word Games*. Oxford: Oxford University Press 1984

Austin, John L. *How to Do Things with Words*. Cambridge: Harvard University Press 1962

Badiou, Alain. 'Marque et manque.' *Cahiers pour l'analyse*, no. 10 (1969)

Bagnall, N. *A Defence of Clichés*. London: Constable 1985

Baldick, Chris. *The Concise Oxford Dictionary of Literary Terms*. Oxford: Oxford University Press 1990

Bally, Charles. *Traité de stylistique française*. 3d ed. Paris: Klincksieck 1951

Banville, Théodore de. *Petit Traité de poésie française*. Paris: Charpentier 1888

Barthes, Roland. *Le Degré zéro de la littérature*. Paris: Seuil 1972
– *Mythologies*. London: Cape 1972
– *L'Aventure sémiologique*. Paris: Seuil 1985

Bartlett, John. *Familiar Quotations*. Boston: Little, Brown 1948

Bary, René. *La Rhétorique française*. Paris: Pierre le Petit 1665

Bauer, L. *English Word-Formation*. Cambridge: Cambridge University Press 1983

Beauzée, Nicolas. *Grammaire générale*. 1767. Paris: Barbon 1974

Beckson, Karl, and Arthur Ganz. *Literary Terms: A Dictionary*. New York: Farrar, Strauss and Giroux 1983

Beeching, Cyril L. *A Dictionary of Eponyms*. London: Clive Bingley 1979

Bélisle, Louis-Alexandre. *Dictionnaire Nord-Américain de la langue française*. Montreal: Beauchemin 1979

Bénac, Henri. *Vocabulaire de la dissertation*. Paris: Hachette 1959

Benayoun, Robert. *Le Ballon dans la bande dessinée: Vroom Tchac Zowie*. Paris: A. Balland 1968

Benét's Reader's Encyclopedia. 3d ed. New York: Harper and Row 1987

Ben-Porat, Z. 'The Poetics of Literary Allusion.' *PTL* 1 (1976), pp. 105–28

Benveniste, Emile. *Problèmes de linguistique générale*. 2 vols. Paris: Gallimard 1966

Berger, Pierre. *Robert Desnos*. Paris: Pierre Seghers 1953

Bergson, Henri. *Le Rire*. Paris: Presses Universitaires de France 1975

Bersani, Jacques, ed. *La Littérature en France depuis 1945*. Paris: Bordas 1974

Bertin, J. *Sémiologie graphique*. Paris: Mouton 1973

Birdwhistell, R.L. *Introduction to Kinesics*. Louisville: University of Louisville 1952

Blair, Hugh. *Lectures on Rhetoric and Belles Lettres*. 1783. Ed. H. Harding. Carbondale, Ill.: Southern Illinois University Press 1966

Blanche, Robert. *Introduction à la logique contemporaine*. Paris: Armand Colin 1968

Blinkenberg, A. *L'Ordre des mots en français moderne*. Copenhagen: Andr. Fred. 1928

Blois, C. Grégoire de. *Nouveau Dictionnaire de la correspondance*. Verdun, Quebec: Marcel Broquet 1979

Blumenfeld, Warren S. *Jumbo Shrimp and Other Almost Perfect Oxymorons*. New York: Putnam 1986

Boileau, Pierre, and Thomas Narcejac. *Le Roman policier*. Paris: Payot 1964

Boileau-Despréaux, Nicholas. *Art poétique* in *Oeuvres complètes*. Paris: Gallimard 1966

Bollinger, D.B. *Intonation and Its Parts*. Stanford: Stanford University Press 1986

Booth, Wayne C. *The Rhetoric of Fiction*. Chicago: University of Chicago Press 1961

- *A Rhetoric of Irony.* Chicago: University of Chicago Press 1974
Brahm, Alcanter de. *L'Ostensoir des ironies: essai de métacritique.* Paris: Bibliothèque d'art de la critique 1899
Bremond, Claude. *Logique du récit.* Paris: Seuil 1973
Brochu, A. *Amour, crime, révolution: essai sur 'Les Misérables.'* Montreal: Les Presses de l'Université de Montréal 1974
Brooke-Rose, Christine. *A Rhetoric of the Unreal.* Cambridge: Cambridge University Press 1981
Brooks, Cleanth. *The Well Wrought Urn.* New York: Harcourt 1947
Bureau, Conrad. *Linguistique fonctionnelle et stylistique objective.* Quebec: Presses de l'Université Laval 1976
Burke, Kenneth. *A Grammar of Motives.* New York: Prentice-Hall 1945
Cave, Terence. *Recognitions: A Study in Poetics.* Oxford: Clarendon Press 1988
Cellier, Léon. *De Sylvie à Aurélia.* Paris: Lettres Modernes 1971
Chabrol, Claude, ed. *Sémiotique narrative et textuelle.* Paris: Larousse 1973
Chaignet, Anselme-Edouard. *La Rhétorique et son histoire.* Paris: Wieveg 1888
Chatman, Seymour. *Story and Discourse.* Ithaca: Cornell University Press 1978
Cirlot, J.E. *A Dictionary of Symbols.* Trans. Jack Sage. New York: Philosophical Library 1962
Clarac, Pierre. *La Classe de français, le XIXe siècle.* Paris: Bélin 1960
Cohen, Jean. *Structure du langage poétique.* Paris: Flammarion 1966
Colletet, Guillaume. *Traitté de l'épigramme et traitté du sonnet.* Geneva: Droz 1965
Colpron, Gilles. *Les Anglicismes au Québec: répertoire classifié.* Montreal: Beauchemin 1970
Comeau, Marie. *La Rhétorique de Saint Augustin.* Paris, 1930
The Concise Oxford Dictionary. 6th ed. Ed. J.B. Sykes. Oxford: Clarendon Press 1966
Copi, Irving M. *Introduction to Logic.* New York: Macmillan 1961
Corbett, Edward P.J., ed. *Rhetorical Analyses of Literary Works.* New York: Oxford University Press 1969
- *Classical Rhetoric for the Modern Student.* 2d ed. New York: Oxford University Press 1971
Courault, Marcel. *Manuel pratique de l'art d'écrire.* Paris: Hachette 1956
Cressot, Marcel. *'La Liaison des phrases dans Salammbô.'* *Le Français moderne* 9 (1941), pp. 82–93
- *Le Style et ses techniques.* Paris: Presses Universitaires de France 1947
Croll, M.W. *Style, Rhetoric and Rhythm.* Princeton: Princeton University Press 1966
Crosbie, J. *Crosbie's Dictionary of Puns.* New York: Harmony 1977
Crystal, David. *Linguistics.* Harmondsworth: Penguin 1971
- *The Cambridge Encyclopaedia of Language.* Cambridge: Cambridge University Press 1987
- *The English Language.* London: Penguin 1988
Cuddon, J.A. *A Dictionary of Literary Terms.* London: André Deutsch 1977

Curtius, E.R. *European Literature and the Latin Middle Ages*. Trans. W.R. Trask. London: Routledge 1953
Dällenbach, Lucien. *Le Récit spéculaire*. Paris: Seuil 1977
Damourette, Jacques. *Traité moderne de ponctuation*. Paris: Larousse 1939
Davidson, M. *L=A=N=G=U=A=G=E Book*. Ed. B. Andrews and Ch. Bernstein. Carbondale, Ill.: Southern Illinois University Press 1984
Delas, Daniel. *Poétique-pratique*. Paris: Cedic 1977
Delas, Daniel, and Jacques Filliolet. *Linguistique et poétique*. Paris: Larousse 1973
Delattre, Pierre. 'Les Dix Intonations de base du français.' *French Review* 40 (1966), pp. 1–14
Deleuze, Gilles. *Logique du sens*. Paris: Editions de Minuit 1969
Deloffre, Frédéric. *Le Vers français*. Paris: Sedes 1969
Diwekar, H.-R. *Les Fleurs de rhétorique de l'Inde*. Paris: Maisonneuve 1930
Drabble, Margaret, ed. *The Oxford Companion to English Literature*. Oxford: Oxford University Press 1985
Du Bellay, Joachim. *La Défense et Illustration de la langue française (1549)*. Ed. H. Chamard. Paris: Société des Textes Français Modernes 1970
Dubois, Jean. *Etude sur la dérivation suffixale en français moderne et contemporain*. Paris: Larousse 1965
– *Grammaire structurale du français*. 3 vols. Paris: Larousse 1965
Dubois, Jean, et al. *Dictionnaire de linguistique*. Paris: Larousse 1972
– *Lexis*. Paris: Larousse 1975
Dubois, Philippe. 'La Métaphore filée.' *Le Français moderne* (July 1975), pp. 202–13
Ducrot, Oswald. *Dire et ne pas dire*. Paris: Hermann 1972
Ducrot, Oswald, and Tzvetan Todorov. *Encyclopedic Dictionary of the Sciences of Language*. Trans. Catherine Porter. Oxford: Blackwell 1981
Dumarsais, César Chesneau. *Des Tropes*. 1757. Paris: Flammarion 1988
Dupriez, Bernard. *L'Etude des styles ou la commutation en littérature*. 2d ed. Paris: Didier Erudition; Montreal: Didier Canada 1971
– 'Les Structures et l'inconscient dans le théâtre de Montherlant.' *Protée*, no. 6, pp. 47–64
Easthope, Antony. *Poetry as Discourse*. London: Methuen 1983
Eliot, T.S. *Selected Essays*. New York: Harcourt, Brace and World 1951
Elkhadem, Saad. *The York Dictionary of Literary Terms*. Fredericton, New Brunswick: York Press 1976
Empsom, William. *Seven Types of Ambiguity*. Harmondsworth: Penguin 1977
– *Using Biography*. London: Hogarth Press 1984
– *The Structure of Complex Words*. London: Hogarth Press 1987
Encyclopédie ou Dictionnaire raisonné des sciences, des arts et des métiers. Neuchâtel: Faulche 1765
Escarpit, R. *L'Humour*. 4th ed. Paris: Presses Universitaires de France 1967
Esnault, G. *Dictionnaire historique des argots français*. Paris: Larousse 1965
Espy, Willard R. *The Game of Words*. Newton Abbot, Devon: Readers Union 1971

- *The Garden of Eloquence: A Rhetorical Bestiary.* New York: E.P. Dutton 1983
Etiemble, René. *Parlez-vous franglais?* Paris: Gallimard 1964
Etiemble, René, and Jeannine Etiemble. *L'Art d'écrire.* Paris: Seghers 1970
Etienne, Luc. *L'Art du contrepet.* Paris: Pauvert 1972
Fabri, Pierre. *Le Grand et Vrai Art de pleine rhétorique.* 3 vols. Rouen: Eugiard 1889–90
Fage, Jean, and Christian Pagano, eds. *Dictionnaire des media.* Montreal: Hurtubise HMH 1989
Farb, Peter. *Word Play: What Happens When People Talk.* New York: Alfred A. Knopf 1974
Feldman, G., and G. Gartenberg, eds. *The Beat Generation and the Angry Young Men.* New York: Dell 1958
Ferguson, John. *Aristotle.* Boston: Twayne 1972
Fletcher, Angus. *Allegory: The Theory of a Symbolic Mode.* Ithaca: Cornell University Press 1964
Foclin [alt. sp. Fouquelin], Antoine. *La Rhétorique française d'Antoine Fouquelin.* Paris: A. Wechel 1555
Fontanier, Pierre. *Les Figures du discours.* 1821–30. Paris: Flammarion 1968
Foucault, Michel. *Les Mots et les choses.* Paris: Gallimard 1966
Fouché, P. *Traité de prononciation française.* Paris: Klincksieck 1959
Fournel, Paul. *Clefs pour la littérature potentielle.* Paris: Lettres Nouvelles 1972
Fowler, H.W. *A Dictionary of Modern English Usage.* 2d ed. Revised by Sir Ernest Gowers. New York: Oxford University Press 1978
Fowler, Roger, ed. *A Dictionary of Modern Critical Terms.* London: Routledge and Kegan Paul 1987
France, Peter. *Racine's Rhetoric.* Oxford: Clarendon Press 1965
Frye, Northrop. *The Great Code: The Bible and Literature.* Toronto: Academic Press 1982
Frye, Northrop, Sheridan Baker, and George Perkins, eds. *The Harper Handbook to Literature.* New York: Harper and Row 1985
Fussell, Paul. *The Great War and Modern Memory.* New York: Oxford University Press 1975
Garcin de Tassy, Joseph. *Rhétorique et prosodie des langues de l'Orient musulman.* 2d ed. Paris: Maisonneuve 1873
Garde, Paul. *L'Accent.* Paris: Presses Universitaires de France 1968
Geddes, Gary, ed. *Twentieth-Century Poetry and Poetics.* Toronto: Oxford University Press 1969
Genette, Gérard. *Figures I–III.* Paris: Seuil 1966–72
- *Narrative Discourse: An Essay in Method.* Trans. Jane E. Lewin. Ithaca: Cornell University Press 1980
Georgin, René. *Les Secrets du style.* Paris: Editions Sociales Françaises 1961
Gérold, Théodore. *La Musique au Moyen Age.* Paris: Champion 1932
Girard (L'Abbé). *Préceptes de rhétorique tirés des meilleurs auteurs anciens et modernes.* 9th ed. Rodez: Carrère 1828

Gleick, James. *Chaos: Making a New Science*. London: Cardinal 1988
Goldstein, Frantz. *Monogram Lexicon*. Berlin: de Gruyter 1964
Gourmont, Rémy de. *Esthétique de la langue française*. Paris: Mercure de France 1938
Grambs, David. *Literary Companion Dictionary: Words about Words*. London: Routledge and Kegan Paul 1985
Grammont, Maurice. *Traité de phonétique*. Paris: Delagrave 1933
– *Essai de psychologie linguistique*. Paris: Librairie Delagrave 1950
– *Le Vers français, ses moyens d'expression, son harmonie*. Paris: Delagrave 1954
Graves, Robert, and Alan Hodge. *The Reader over Your Shoulder*. 2d ed. New York: Vintage Books 1979
Gray, Martin. *A Dictionary of Literary Terms*. Harlow, Essex: Longman 1984
Greenstein, Carol H. *Dictionary of Logical Terms and Symbols*. New York: Van Nostrand Reinhold 1978
Greimas, Algirdas-Julien. *Sémantique structurale*. Paris: Larousse 1966. *Structural Semantics: An Attempt at a Method*. Trans. R. Scleifer and A. Velie. Lincoln: University of Nebraska Press 1983
– *Du Sens: essais sémiotiques*. Paris: Seuil 1970
– *Sémiotique: dictionnaire raisonné de la théorie du langage*. Paris: Hachette 1979
Grévisse, Maurice. *Le Bon Usage*. 7th ed. Gembloux: Duculot 1969
Group MU (J. Dubois, F. Edeline, J.-M. Klinkenberg, P. Minguet, F. Pire, H. Trinon). *Rhétorique générale*. Paris: Larousse 1970. *A General Rhetoric*. Trans. Paul B. Burrell and Edgar M. Slotkin. Baltimore: The Johns Hopkins University Press 1981
Guiraud, Pierre. *Essais de stylistique*. Paris: Klincksieck 1953
– *La Sémantique*. 6th ed. Paris: Presses Universitaires de France 1969
Guitton, Henri. *Statistique*. Paris: Dalloz 1967
Hamon, Philippe. *Le Personnel du roman*. Geneva: Droz 1983
Harrap's New Standard French and English Dictionary. 4 vols. London: George G. Harrap 1972
Harris, Z.S. *Structural Linguistics*. Chicago: University of Chicago Press 1951
Harvey, Sir Paul, comp. *The Oxford Companion to Classical Literature*. Oxford: Oxford University Press 1984
Hesbois, Laure. *Les Jeux de langage*. Ottawa: Editions de l'Université d'Ottawa 1986
Hewison, W. *Cartoon Connection: The Art of Pictorial Humour*. London: Elm Tree Books 1977
Hörmann, Hans. *Introduction à la psycholinguistique*. Paris: Larousse 1972
Hutcheon, Linda. *Narcissistic Narrative*. London: Methuen 1984
– *A Theory of Parody*. London: Methuen 1985
Hutchinson, Peter. *Games Authors Play*. London: Methuen 1983
Jacobs, Noah. *Naming Day in Eden*. London: Macmillan 1969
Jakobson, Roman. *Essais de linguistique générale*. Paris: Seuil 1970
Jankélévich, Vladimir. *Traité des vertus*. Paris: Bordas 1949
– *L'Ironie ou la bonne conscience*. Paris: Flammarion 1964
Jean, Raymond. *Paul Eluard par lui-même*. Paris: Seuil 1968

Jefferson, Anne. *The Nouveau Roman and the Poetics of Fiction.* Cambridge: Cambridge University Press 1980
Jespersen, Otto. *The Philosophy of Grammar.* London: Allen and Unwin 1924
– *Analytic Syntax.* New York: Holt 1969
Johnson, Samuel. *Lives of the English Poets.* 3 vols. Ed. G.B. Hill. Oxford: Clarendon Press 1905
Jolles, A. *Formes simples.* Paris: Seuil 1972
Joseph, Sister Miriam. *Shakespeare's Use of the Arts of Language.* New York: Harcourt, Brace and World 1947
Jump, John D. *The Ode.* London: Methuen 1974
Jung, John. *Verbal Learning.* New York: Holt Rinehart 1968
Kermode, Frank. *Essays on Fiction.* London: Routledge and Kegan Paul 1983
Kesteloot, Lilyan, ed. *L'Epopée traditionnelle: textes choisis.* Paris: Nathan 1971
Kibédi-Varga, A. *Rhétorique et littérature: études de structures classiques.* Paris: Didier 1970
Kristeva, Julia. *La Révolution du langage poétique.* Paris: Seuil 1974
– *Polylogue.* Paris: Seuil 1977
Lacan, Jacques. *Ecrits.* Paris: Seuil 1966
Lacroix, Jean. *L'Anagrammite.* Paris: Editions de la pensée moderne 1969
Ladrière, J. 'La Performativité du langage liturgique.' *Concilium: revue internationale de théologie* 82, nos. 7–8 (Feb. 1973), pp. 53–64
Lakatos, I., and A. Musgrove, eds. *Criticism and the Growth of Knowledge.* Cambridge: Cambridge University Press 1987
Lakoff, George, and Mark Johnson. *Metaphors We Live By.* Chicago: University of Chicago Press 1981
Lalande, André. *Vocabulaire technique et critique de la philosophie.* Paris: Presses Universitaires de France 1962
Lalo, Charles. 'Le Comique et le spirituel.' *La Revue d'esthétique* (1950), pp. 310–27
Lamy, Bernard. *La Rhétorique ou l'art de parler.* 3d ed. Paris: Pralard 1688
Lanham, Richard A. *A Handlist of Rhetorical Terms.* Berkeley and Los Angeles: University of California Press 1968
– *Style: An Anti-Textbook.* New Haven: Yale University Press 1974
Larousse du XXe siècle. 6 vols. Paris: Larousse 1931
Larousse (Grand Larousse encyclopédique en dix volumes). Paris: Larousse 1960
Lausberg, Heinrich. *Handbuch der literarischen rhetorik.* 2 vols. Munich: Max Hueber 1960
Le Bidois, Georges, and Robert Le Bidois. *Syntaxe du français moderne.* 2 vols. 2d ed. Paris: Picard 1967
Le Clerc, Jos Victor. *Nouvelle Rhétorique extraite des meilleurs auteurs anciens et modernes.* Paris: Delalaing 1855
Leech, Geoffrey N. *A Linguistic Guide to English Poetry.* Harlow, Essex: Longman 1969
– *Semantics.* Harmondsworth: Penguin 1976
Le Guern, Michel. *Sémantique de la métaphore et de la métonymie.* Paris: Larousse 1973

Bibliography

Le Hir, Yves. *Rhétorique et stylistique de la Pléiade au Parnasse.* Paris:
Presses Universitaires de France 1960
Lemon, L.T., and M.J. Reis, eds. *Russian Formalist Criticism: Four Essays.*
Lincoln: University of Nebraska Press 1965
Léon, Pierre. *Essais de phonostylistique.* Montreal: Marcel Didier 1971
Léon, Pierre, and Philippe Martin. *Prolégomènes à l'étude des structures
intonatives.* Montreal: Marcel Didier 1970
Lewis, John N.C. *Typography: Design and Practice.* London: Barrie 1978
Lieberman, P. *Intonation, Perception and Language.* Cambridge: MIT Press
1967
Littré, Emile. *Dictionnaire de la langue française.* 4 vols. Paris: Hachette
1877; Paris: Pauvert 1956
Longinus. *On the Sublime,* in *Classical Literary Criticism (Aristotle, Horace,
Longinus).* Trans. T.S. Dorsch. Harmondsworth: Penguin 1965
Longyear, Marie M., ed. *The McGraw-Hill Style Manual: A Concise Guide
for Writers and Editors.* New York: McGraw-Hill 1983
McCrum, Robert, William Cran, and Robert MacNeil. *The Story of
English.* New York: Viking Penguin 1986
Mahood, M.M. *Shakespeare's Wordplay.* London: Methuen 1979
Maloux, M. *Dictionnaire des proverbes, sentences et maximes.* Paris:
Larousse 1960
Marchais, Pierre. *Glossaire de psychiâtrie.* Paris: Masson 1970
Marouzeau, Jules. *Lexique de la terminologie linguistique.* 2d ed. Paris:
Geuthner 1943
Martinet, André. *Eléments de linguistique générale.* Paris: Colin 1960
– *La Linguistique: guide alphabétique.* Paris: Editions Denoel 1969
Martinon, Philippe. *Dictionnaire des rimes françaises précédé d'un traité de
versification.* Paris: Larousse 1962
Marx, Karl. *Critique of Hegel's 'Philosophy of Right.'* Cambridge: Cam-
bridge University Press 1970
Mazaleyrat, Jean. *Eléments de métrique française.* Paris: Colin 1974
Mélançon, Claude. *Légendes indiennes du Canada.* Montreal: Editions du
jour 1967
Merleau-Ponty, Maurice. *Phénoménologie de la perception.* Paris:
Gallimard 1945
– *Eloge de la philosophie et autres essais.* Paris: Gallimard 1960
Mestre (Le Père). *Préceptes de rhétorique.* 12th ed. Paris: Beauchesne
1922
Miller, Casey, and Kate Swift. *The Handbook of Non-Sexist Writing for
Writers, Editors and Speakers.* New York: Lippincott and Crowell
1982
Monaco, James. *How to Read a Film.* New York: Oxford University Press
1981
Monaghan, David. *Smiley's Circus: A Guide to the Secret World of John Le
Carré.* London: Collins 1986
Morel, Jacques. 'Glossaire.' *Le XVIIe siècle,* nos. 80–1 (1968), pp. 143–6
Morier, Henri. *Dictionnaire de poétique et de rhétorique.* 2d ed. Paris:
Presses Universitaires de France 1975
Morison, Stanley. *Tally of Types.* Cambridge: Cambridge University
Press 1973

486

Morreal, John, ed. *The Philosophy of Laughter and Humour*. Albany: State University of New York Press 1987

Morris, Desmond. *Manwatching: A Field Guide to Human Behaviour*. London: Triad/Granada 1980

Morris, William, and Mary Morris. *Harper Dictionary of Contemporary Usage*. 2d ed. New York: Harper and Row 1985

Muecke, D.C. *The Compass of Irony*. London: Methuen 1969

Murphy, James J. *Rhetoric in the Middle Ages*. Berkeley and Los Angeles: University of California Press 1974

Musique et poésie au XVIe siècle. Colloques internationaux du CNRS: sciences humaines, vol. 5. Paris: Centre national de la recherche scientifique 1954

Neaman, J.S., and C.G. Silver. *Kind Words: A Thesaurus of Euphemisms*. New York: Facts on File Publications 1983

Nelson, R.P. *Comic Art and Caricature*. Chicago: Contemporary Books 1978

Opie, Iona, and Peter Opie. *The Lore and Language of Schoolchildren*. Oxford: Clarendon Press 1959

– *Children's Games in Street and Playground*. Oxford: Clarendon Press 1969

Oster, Pierre, et al. *Nouveau Dictionnaire de citations françaises*. Paris: Hachette-Tchou 1970

Oulipo. *A Primer of Potential Literature*. Trans. Warren F. Motte, Jr. Lincoln: University of Nebraska Press 1986

The Oxford Dictionary of Quotations. 3d ed. Oxford: Oxford University Press 1980

The Oxford English Dictionary. Compact edition including *Supplement*. 3 vols. Oxford: Oxford University Press 1971, 1987

Pages, Max. *La Vie affective des groupes*. Paris: Dunod 1968

Palmier, J.-M. *Sur Marcuse*. Paris: Union générale d'éditions 1969

Parent, Monique, ed. *Le Vers français au XXe siècle*. Strasbourg: Université de Strasbourg 1967

Paul, Armand Laurent (L'Abbé). *Cours de rhétorique française à l'usage des jeunes rhétoriciens*. Paris: Delalaing 1810

Paulhan, Jean. *Les Fleurs de Tarbe ou la Terreur dans les lettres*. Paris: Gallimard 1941

– *Enigmes de Perse*. Paris: Gallimard 1963

Payen, Fernand. *Le Barreau et la langue française*. Paris: Grasset 1939

Peacham, Henry. *The Garden of Eloquence*. 1593. Facsimile reproduction. Gainesville, Florida: Scholar's Facsimiles and Reprints 1954

Pei, Mario, and Frank Gaynor. *Dictionary of Linguistics*. New York: Philosophical Library 1954

Peignot, J. *De l'écriture à la typographie*. Paris, 1967

Peirce, Charles Sanders. *Philosophical Writings of Peirce*. New York: Dover 1965

Perelman, Chaim. *Traité de l'argumentation*. Paris: Presses Universitaires de France 1958

Perrine, Laurence. *Sound and Sense: An Introduction to Poetry*. 4th ed. New York: Harcourt Brace Jovanovich 1973

Phillips, G.D. *Stanley Kubrick: A Film Odyssey*. New York: Popular Library 1975

Pleynet, Marcelin. 'La Poésie doit avoir pour but ...' In *Tel Quel: théorie d'ensemble*. Paris: Seuil 1968, pp. 97–129

Pons, Emile. Introduction to *Oeuvres*, by Jonathan Swift. Paris: Gallimard 1965

Porter, Lambert C. *La Fatrasie et la fatras*. Geneva: Droz 1960

Pouillon, Jean. *Temps et roman*. Paris: Gallimard 1946

Preminger, Alex, ed. *Princeton Encyclopedia of Poetry and Poetics*. Enlarged edition. London: Macmillan 1974

Prince, Gerald. *A Dictionary of Narratology*. Lincoln: University of Nebraska Press 1987

Probyn, C., ed. *The Art of Jonathan Swift*. London: Vision 1978

Puttenham, George. *The Arte of English Poesie (1589)*. Ed. Gladys D. Willcock and A. Walker. Cambridge, 1970

Quillet, Aristide. *Dictionnaire Quillet de la langue française*. 3 vols. Paris: Quillet 1946

Quinn, Arthur. *Figures of Speech*. Salt Lake City: Gibbs M. Smith 1982

Quintilian. *Institutes of Oratory*. Trans. H.E. Butler. 4 vols. London: Loeb Classical Library 1920–22

Rat, Maurice. *Dictionnaire des locutions françaises*. Paris: Larousse 1957

Redfern, Walter. *Puns*. Oxford: Blackwell 1984

Rey, Jean Michel. *L'Enjeu des signes*. Paris: Seuil 1971

Rheims, Maurice. *Dictionnaire des mots sauvages*. Paris: Larousse 1969

Richard, Jean-Pierre. *Onze Etudes sur la poésie moderne*. Paris: Seuil 1964

Rivière, Jacques. *Etudes*. Paris: La Nouvelle Revue Française 1924

Robert, Paul. *Dictionnaire alphabétique et analogique de la langue française*. 7 vols. Paris: Société du Nouveau Littré 1953–64

Roberts, Philip Davies. *How Poetry Works*. Harmondsworth: Penguin 1988

Rogers, James. *The Dictionary of Clichés*. New York: Facts on File 1985

Rookledge's International Type-Finder: The Essential Handbook of Typeface Recognition and Selection. London: Sarema Press 1983

Roure, Francine, and Alain Buttery. *Mathématiques pour les sciences sociales*. Paris: Presses Universitaires de France 1970

Russell, D.A., and M. Winterbottom, eds. *Ancient Literary Criticism*. Oxford: Clarendon Press 1972

Ruthven, K.K. *The Conceit*. London: Methuen 1969

Saint-Laurent, Cecil. *Paul et Jean-Paul*. Paris: Grasset 1951

Saussure, Ferdinand de. *Cours de linguistique générale*. Paris: Payot 1931

Scaliger, Jules-César. *Poetices libri septem*. 1561. Stuttgart: Frommann 1964

Schlausch, Margaret. *The Gift of Language*. New York: Dover 1955

Scholes, P.A. *The Oxford Companion to Music*. London: Oxford University Press 1972

Sebeok, Thomas A., ed. *Style in Language*. Cambridge: MIT Press 1960

– gen. ed. *Encyclopedic Dictionary of Semiotics*. 3 vols. Berlin: Mouton and Gruyter 1986

Seldes, George, comp. *The Great Thoughts*. New York: Ballantine Books 1985

Serres, J. *Le Protocole et les usages*. Paris: Presses Universitaires de France 1961

Smith, Christopher. *Alabaster, Bikinis and Calvados: An ABC of Toponymous Words*. London: Century 1985

Smyth, Herbert W. *Greek Grammar*. Cambridge: Harvard University Press 1956

Sommer, E., and M. Sommer. *The Similes Dictionary*. Detroit: Gale Research Co. 1988

Sonnino, Lee A. *A Handbook to Sixteenth-Century Rhetoric*. London: Routledge and Kegan Paul 1968

Souriau, Etienne. *Les Deux cent mille situations dramatiques*. Paris: Flammarion 1950

– *La Correspondance des arts*. 2d ed. Paris: Flammarion 1972

Spitzer, Léo. *Etudes de style*. Paris: Gallimard 1970

Starobinski, Jean. *Les Mots sous les mots: les Anagrammes de Ferdinand de Saussure*. Paris: Gallimard 1971

Stern, J.P. *Lichtenberg*. Bloomington: Indiana University Press 1959

Stillman, Frances. *The Poet's Manual and Rhyming Dictionary*. London: Thames and Hudson 1966

Straka, G. *Les Sons et les mots*. Paris: Klincksieck 1979

Suberville, Jean. *Théorie de l'art et des genres littéraires*. Paris: L'Ecole 1941

Taylor, Warren. *Tudor Figures of Rhetoric*. Whitewater, Wisconsin: The Language Press 1972

Tesnière, Lucien. *Eléments de syntaxe structurale*. Paris: Klincksieck 1959

Thierrin, Paul. *Toute la correspondance*. Paris: Panorama 1964

Todorov, Tzvetan, ed. *Théorie de la littérature*. Paris: Seuil 1965

– *The Fantastic: A Structural Approach to a Literary Genre*. Cleveland: Press of Case Western Reserve University 1973

Tomachevsky, B. 'Thématique.' In *Théorie de la littérature*. Ed. T. Todorov. Paris: Seuil 1965

Trésor de la langue française: dictionnaire de la langue du XIXe et du XXe siècle. 13 vols. Paris: Editions du Centre National de la Recherche Scientifique 1974

Trudgill, P. *Sociolinguistics: An Introduction*. Harmondsworth: Penguin 1978

Turco, Lewis. *The New Book of Forms: A Handbook of Poetics*. Hanover: University Press of New England 1986

Vanier, Antonin. *La Clarté française*. Paris: Nathan 1949

Verest, Jules. *Manuel de littérature: principes, faits généraux, lois*. Bruges: Desclée de Brouwer 1939

Vickers, Brian. *In Defence of Rhetoric*. Oxford: Clarendon Press 1988

– *Classical Rhetoric in English Poetry*. Carbondale, Ill.: Southern Illinois University Press 1989

Vié, Bernard, and Jean Chaumely. *La Composition automatique des textes*. Paris: Compagnie française d'éditions 1972

Vinay, Jean-Paul, and Jean Darbelnet. *Stylistique comparée du français et de l'anglais*. Paris: Didier 1958

Vuillaume, M.-J. *Cours de rhétorique*. Epinal: Saint-Michel 1938

Wagner, Robert, and J. Pinchon. *Grammaire du français classique et moderne*. Paris: Hachette 1962

Bibliography

Wartburg, Walter von, and Paul Zumthor. *Précis de syntaxe du français contemporain*. 2d ed. Berne: Francke 1947
Webster's New World Dictionary of American English. 3d college edition. New York: Simon and Schuster 1988
Willem, Albert. *Principes de rhétorique: aide-mémoire du rhétoricien*. Brussels: De Boeck 1954; Paris: Flammarion 1969
Williams, Miller. *Patterns of Poetry: An Encyclopedia of Forms*. Baton Rouge: Louisiana State University Press 1986
Wilmut, R. *From Fringe to Flying Circus*. London: Eyre Methuen 1980
Woodson, Linda. *A Handbook of Modern Rhetorical Terms*. Urbana, Ill.: National Council of Teachers of English 1979
Yee, Chiang. *L'Ecriture et la psychologie des peuples*. Paris: Centre International de Synthèse 1960
Zola, Emile. *Le Roman expérimental*. Paris: Garnier-Flammarion 1971
Zumthor, Paul. *Essai de poétique médiévale*. Paris: Seuil 1972

2. Literary and Other Non-Critical Works

Allais, Alphonse. *La Barbe et autres contes*. Paris: Union générale d'éditions 1968
– *Plaisir d'humour*. Paris: Livre de poche 1972
Amis, Kingsley. *One Fat Englishman*. New York: Harcourt, Brace and World 1963
– *The Old Devils*. Harmondsworth: Penguin 1987
Anderson, Maxwell. *Elizabeth the Queen*. New York: French's Standard Library Edition 1934
Anouilh, Jean. *Pièces brillantes*. Paris: La Table Ronde 1951
Apollinaire, Guillaume. *Oeuvres poétiques*. Paris: Gallimard 1965
Aquin, Hubert. *Trou de mémoire*. Montreal: Cercle du Livre de France 1968
– *Point de fuite*. Montreal: Cercle du Livre de France 1971
– *Prochain Episode*. Trans. P. Williams. Toronto: McClelland and Stewart 1972
– *The Antiphonary*. Trans. Allan Brown. Toronto: Anansi 1973
Aragon, Louis. *Le Crève-coeur*. Paris: Gallimard 1946
– *Les Yeux d'Elsa*. Paris: Seghers 1967
– *Le Paysan de Paris*. Paris: Gallimard 1978
Aron, R. *La Révolution introuvable*. Paris: Fayard 1958
Arp, Jean. *Jours effeuillés*. Paris: Gallimard 1966
Artaud, Antoine. *L'Ombilic des limbes*. Paris: Gallimard 1968
Ashton, John. *English Caricature and Satire of Napoleon I*. New York: Benjamin Blom 1968
Atwood, Margaret. *Lady Oracle*. Toronto: Seal Books 1982
– *Life before Man*. Toronto: Seal Books 1984
– *The Handmaid's Tale*. Toronto: Seal Books 1986
– *Cat's Eye*. Toronto: Seal Books 1989
Aubert de Gaspé, Philippe. *Les Anciens Canadiens*. Montreal: Fides 1975
Audiberti, Jacques. *Le Mal court suivi de l'Effet Glapion*. Paris: Gallimard 1968

Aveline, Claude. *Le Code des jeux*. Paris: Hachette 1961

Baigent, M., R. Leigh, and H. Lincoln. *The Messianic Legacy*. London: Corgi Books 1987

Bardèche, Maurice. *Le Procès de Nuremberg*. Paris: Les Sept Couleurs 1951

Barnes, Julian. *Flaubert's Parrot*. New York: Alfred A. Knopf 1985
- *Before She Met Me*. London: Picador 1987

Barrès, Maurice. *Les Déracinés*. Paris: Au club de l'Honnête Homme 1965

Barth, John. *Lost in the Funhouse*. Garden City, NY: Doubleday 1968

Barton, John. *Playing Shakespeare*. London: Methuen 1984

Baudelaire, Charles. *Oeuvres*. Paris: Gallimard 1951

Beckett, Samuel. *Waiting for Godot*. New York: Grove Press 1954
- *Molloy*. Paris: Club français du livre 1960
- *How It Is*. Trans. from French by the author. London: Calder 1966

Belloc, Hilaire. *Complete Verse*. London: Duckworth 1970

Benda, Julien. *Le Bergsonisme*. Paris: Grasset 1911

Bennett, A., P. Cook, J. Miller, and D. Moore. *The Complete Beyond the Fringe*. London: Methuen 1987

Berliner, Don. *Managing Your Hard Disk*. Carmel, Indiana: Que Corporation 1986

Bernanos, Georges. *Oeuvres romanesques*. Paris: Gallimard 1961

Berryman, John. *His Toy, His Dream, His Rest*. London: Faber 1969

Bessette, Gérard. *Le Libraire*. Paris: Julliard 1960
- *L'Incubation*. Montreal: Déom 1965
- *Le Cycle*. Montreal: Editions du Jour 1971

Bierce, Ambrose. *The Devil's Dictionary*, in *The Devil's Advocate: An Ambrose Bierce Reader*. Ed. Brian St. Pierre. San Francisco: Chronicle Books 1987

Blais, Marie-Claire. *Une Saison dans la vie d'Emmanuel*. Montreal: Editions du Jour 1965
- *Les Apparences* [1969]. Vol. 2 of *Manuscrits de Pauline Archange*. Montreal: Editions du Jour 1968–70. *Dürer's Angel* [*Les Apparences*, 1969]. Trans. David Lobdell. Vancouver: Talonbooks 1976

Bloy, Léon. *Belluaires et porchers*. Paris: Stock 1905

Bly, Robert. *Silence in the Snowy Fields*. Middleton, Conn.: Wesleyan University Press 1962

Borges, Jorge Luis. *Labyrinths*. New York: Modern Library 1983

Boyd, William. *The New Confessions*. London: Hamish Hamilton 1987

Bradley, Marion Zimmer. *The Firebrand*. New York: Simon and Schuster 1987

Bragg, Melvyn. *Rich: The Life of Richard Burton*. London: Hodder and Stoughton 1988

Brault, Jacques, ed. *Alain Grandbois*. Paris: Editions Pierre Seghers 1968

Breton, André. *Légitime Défense*. Paris: Editions surréalistes 1926
- *Nadja*. Paris: Gallimard 1928
- *Anthologie de l'humour noir*. Paris: Gallimard 1940

- *Clair de terre*. Paris: Plon 1947
- *Farouche à quatre feuilles*. Paris: Grasset 1954
- *Manifestes du surréalisme*. Paris: Gallimard 1963
- *L'Amour fou*. Paris: Gallimard 1966

Brett, Simon, ed. *The Faber Book of Parodies*. London: Faber 1984

Bright, Freda. *Decisions*. New York: St. Martin's Press 1984

Burgess, Anthony. *A Clockwork Orange*. Harmondsworth: Penguin 1972
- *But Do Blondes Prefer Gentlemen? Homage to* QWERT YUIOP *and Other Writings*. New York: McGraw-Hill 1986

Butor, Michel. *Intervalle*. Paris: Gallimard 1973

Calvino, Italo. *If on a Winter's Night a Traveller*. Trans. William Weaver. Toronto: Lester and Orpen Dennys 1983

Camus, Albert. *Les Justes*. Paris: Gallimard 1950
- *L'Etranger*. Paris: Gallimard 1957
- *The Plague*. Trans. Stuart Gilbert. Harmondsworth: Penguin 1960
- *Essais*. Paris: Gallimard 1965
- *La Chute*. Paris: Livre de poche 1968

Capote, Truman. *In Cold Blood*. New York: Signet Books 1965

Carroll, J., and T. Johnston, eds. *Northern California*. New York: Prentice-Hall 1984

Céline, L.F. *Guignol's Band, roman*. Paris: Livre de poche 1969

Cendrars, Blaise. *L'Homme foudroyé*. Paris: Denoel 1945

Cesbron, Gilbert. *Journal sans date*. Paris: Laffont 1963

Chapman, Abraham. *New Black Voices*. New York: New American Library 1972

Chapman, G., J. Cleese, T. Gilliam, E. Idle, T. Jones, and M. Palin. *Monty Python's Flying Circus: Just the Words*. 2 vols. London: Methuen 1989

Char, René. *Les Matinaux, poésie*. Paris: Gallimard 1950
- *Oeuvres complètes*. Paris: Gallimard 1985

Charlesworth, Roberta A., and Dennis Lee, eds. *An Anthology of Verse*. Toronto: Oxford University Press 1964

Cheyney, Peter. *Poison Ivy*. London: Fontana Books 1937

Christie, Agatha. *The Murder of Roger Ackroyd*. New York: Pocket Books 1939

Churchill, Winston S. *Lord Randolph Churchill*. 2 vols. London: Macmillan 1906
- *My Early Life, a Roving Commission*. Montreal: Reprint Society 1948
- *The Second World War*. Vol 1 of *The Gathering Storm*. Boston: Houghton Mifflin 1948

Clancy, Tom. *Patriot Games*. New York: Berkeley Books 1988

Claudel, Paul. *Oeuvres en prose*. Paris: Gallimard 1965
- *Théâtre*. 2 vols. Paris: Gallimard 1965
- *Journal*. 2 vols. Paris: Gallimard 1968

Cleese, John, and Charles Crighton. *A Fish Called Wanda: A Screenplay*. London: Methuen 1988

Cocteau, Jean. *Les Parents terribles*. Paris: Gallimard 1938
- *Opéra suivi de Plain-chant*. Paris: Livre de poche 1967

Colette. *Chéri*. Paris: Fayard 1920
Conan Doyle, Sir Arthur. *The Complete Sherlock Holmes*. 2 vols. Garden City, NY: Doubleday n.d.
Daninos, Pierre. *Les Carnets du Major Thompson*. Paris: Hachette 1968
Daudet, Alphonse. *Lettres de mon moulin*. Paris: Nelson 1910
- *Tartarin de Tarascon*. Paris: Flammarion 1927
Daumal, René. *Bharata*. Paris: Gallimard 1970
Davies, Robertson. *The Rebel Angels*. Markham, Ont.: Penguin 1983
- *High Spirits*. Markham, Ont.: Penguin 1984
- *What's Bred in the Bone*. Markham, Ont.: Penguin 1986
- *The Lyre of Orpheus*. Markham, Ont.: Penguin 1989
Davies, W.H. *Collected Poems*. London: Jonathan Cape 1963
Derême, Tristan. *La Verdure dorée*. Paris: Emile-Paul 1922
Desnos, Robert. *Domaine public*. Paris: Gallimard 1953
- *Corps et biens*. Paris: Gallimard 1968
- *Pénalités de l'enfer*. Paris: Maeght 1974
Didion, Joan. *A Book of Common Prayer*. New York: Simon 1977
Ducharme, Réjean. *L'Avalée des avalés*. Paris: Gallimard 1966
- *Le Nez qui voque*. Paris: Gallimard 1967
- *L'Océantume*. Paris: Gallimard 1968
- *La Fille de Christophe Colomb*. Paris: Gallimard 1969
Duguay, Raoul. *Ruts*. Montreal: Editions Esterel 1966
- *Lapokalipsô*. Montreal: Editions du Jour 1971
Durand, G. *Les Structures anthropologiques de l'imaginaire*. Paris: Bordas 1969
Duras, Marguerite. *Le Ravissement de Lol V. Stein*. Paris: Gallimard 1964
Ebert, Roger. *Two Weeks in the Midday Sun: A Cannes Notebook*. Kansas City: Andrews and McMeel 1987
Eco, Umberto. *The Aesthetics of Chaosmos: The Middle Ages of James Joyce*. Tulsa: The University of Tulsa 1982
- *The Name of the Rose*. New York: Harcourt Brace Jovanovich 1983
- *Postscript to 'The Name of the Rose.'* New York: Harcourt Brace Jovanovich 1984
- *Foucault's Pendulum*. New York: Harcourt Brace Jovanovich 1989
Edouard, Robert. *Dictionnaire des injures*. Paris: Tchou 1979
Ellmann, Richard, ed. *The Oxford Book of American Verse*. New York: Oxford University Press 1976
Eluard, Paul. *Oeuvres complètes*. 2 vols. Paris: Gallimard 1968
Ferron, Jacques. *La Barde de Fr. Hertel*. Montreal: VLB éditeur 1981
Folliet, Joseph. *Tu seras orateur*. Lyon: Editions de la chronique sociale de France 1961
Foster, Tony. *Rue du Bac*. Toronto: Methuen 1987
Fournier, J. *Mon Encrier*. Montreal: Fides 1965
Fowles, John. *The French Lieutenant's Woman*. London: Triad/Granada 1980
Fréchette, Louis. *Contes de Jos Violon*. Montreal: L'Aurore 1974
Freud, Sigmund. *Civilization and Its Discontents*. London: Hogarth Press 1963
- *The Basic Writings of Sigmund Freud*. Ed. A.A. Brill. New York: The Modern Library 1966

Fuentes, Carlos. *Old Gringo*. Trans. by the author and M. Sayers Peden. New York: Harper and Row 1989

Garcia Marquez, Gabriel. *One Hundred Years of Solitude*. New York: Avon Bard 1971

Gardner, Helen. *The Oxford Book of English Verse, 1250–1950*. New York: Oxford University Press 1972

Garvin, Fernande. *The Art of French Cooking*. New York: Bantam Books 1965

Gauvreau, Claude. *Oeuvres créatrices complètes*. Ottawa: Editions Parti pris 1971

Genet, Jean. *Les Bonnes*. Isère: Barbevezat 1958

Gibbons, Stella. *Cold Comfort Farm*. London: Folio Society 1977

Gide, André. *Journal 1889–1939*. Paris: Gallimard 1948

– *Romans, récits et soties: oeuvres lyriques*. Paris: Gallimard 1958

Giraudoux, Jean. *Intermezzo*. Paris: Grasset 1933

– *La Guerre de Troie n'aura pas lieu*. Paris: Grasset 1935

– *Electre*. Paris: Grasset 1937

Goethe, Johann Wolfgang von. *The Sorrows of Young Werther and Novella*. Trans. E. Mayer and L. Bogan. New York: Random House 1971

Gombrowicz, Witold. *Ferdydurke*. Paris: Union générale d'éditions 1967

Greenwood, L.B. *Sherlock Holmes and the Case of the Raleigh Legacy*. London: Macmillan 1986

Guèvremont, Germaine. *Le Survenant*. Montreal: Fides 1974

Hardie, Sean, and John Lloyd, eds. *Not! the Nine o'Clock News*. London: Treasure Press 1984

Hardwick, Michael. *Prisoner of the Devil*. London: Proteus 1979

Hartley, L.P. *The Go-Between*. Harmondsworth: Penguin 1971

Hawthorne, Nathaniel. *Stories*. Franklin Center, Pennsylvania: The Franklin Library 1978

Hébert, Anne. *Les Chambres de bois*. Paris: Seuil 1958

– *Kamouraska*. Paris: Seuil 1970

– *Le Torrent: nouvelles*. Montreal: L'Arbre HMH 1976

Hébert, J. *Le Temps sauvage*. Montreal: Editions HMH 1967

– *Blablabla du bout du monde*. Montreal: Editions du Jour 1971

Heller, Joseph. *Catch-22*. New York: Simon and Schuster 1961

Hemingway, Ernest. *For Whom the Bell Tolls*. New York: Charles Scribner's Sons 1940

Hémon, Louis. *Maria Chapdelaine*. Montreal: Fides 1970

Herodotus. *Histories*. Ed. F.R.B. Godolphin. New York: Random House 1942

Homer. *The Odyssey*. Trans. E.V. Rieu. Harmondsworth: Penguin 1946

Hughes, Robert. *The Fatal Shore: The Epic of Australia's Founding*. New York: Alfred Knopf 1987

Huysmans, J.K. *En ménage et A vau l'eau*. Paris: Union générale d'éditions 1975

Hyde, Christopher. *Whisperland*. Toronto: Totem 1987

Ingrams, Richard, ed. *The Life and Times of Private Eye, 1961–1971*. Harmondsworth: Penguin 1971

Ionesco, Eugène. *Four Plays*. Trans. Donald M. Allen. New York: Grove 1958

- *Théâtre.* 7 vols. Paris: Gallimard 1972–80
James, Henry. *The Golden Bowl.* Harmondsworth: Penguin 1973
James, John. *The Traveller's Key to Medieval France.* New York: Alfred Knopf 1986
Jarry, Alfred. *Ubu roi.* Paris: Le Club du meilleur livre 1958
- *La Chandelle verte.* Paris: Livre de poche 1969
- *Oeuvres complètes.* 2 vols. Paris: Gallimard 1972
Jean-Charles [Jean-Louis Charles]. *Les Perles du facteur.* Paris: Calmann-Lévy 1959
- *Hardi! les cancres.* 2d ed. Paris: Presses de la Cité 1968
Jefferson, Alan. *The Complete Gilbert and Sullivan Opera Guide.* Exeter: Webb and Bower 1984
Jouvenel, Robert de. *La République des camarades.* Paris: Grasset 1914
Joyce, James. *Stephen Hero.* New York: New Directions 1944
- *Finnegans Wake.* New York: Viking 1949
- *A Portrait of the Artist as a Young Man.* New York: Viking 1960
- *Dubliners.* Franklin Center, Pennsylvania: The Franklin Library 1979
- *Ulysses.* New York: Vintage Books 1986. *Ulysse.* Trans. Valéry Larbaud. Paris: Livre de poche 1965
Kafka, Franz. *The Complete Stories.* Trans. W. Muir and E. Muir. Ed. N. Glatzer. Franklin Center, Pennsylvania: The Franklin Library 1980
Kay, Ormonde de. *N'Heures Souris Rames.* London: Angus and Robertson 1983
King, Stephen. *The Shining.* New York: Signet Books 1978
- *The Dark Tower (I): The Gunslinger.* New York: Plume Books 1988
Kington, Miles. *Let's Parler Franglais.* Harmondsworth: Penguin 1981
- *Let's Parler Franglais Again.* Harmondsworth: Penguin 1982
La Bern, A. *Goodbye Piccadilly.* New York: Stein and Day 1966
Larbaud, Valéry. *Sous l'invocation de Saint Jérôme.* Paris: Gallimard 1946
Leacock, Stephen. *Literary Lapses.* Toronto: McClelland and Stewart 1957
Le Carré, John. *Tinker Tailor Soldier Spy.* London: Pan Books 1975
Leiris, Michel. *Aurora.* 5th ed. Paris: Gallimard 1946
Lennon, John. *In His Own Write.* London: Cape 1964
Lodge, David. *Changing Places.* Harmondsworth: Penguin 1985
- *Small World.* Harmondsworth: Penguin 1986
Lynn, J., and A. Jay. *The Complete 'Yes Minister.'* London: BBC Books 1984
- *Yes Prime Minister.* 2 vols. London: BBC Books 1987
McClure, Alexander. *Lincoln's Yarns and Stories.* Chicago: J.C. Winston 1911
Maillet, Antonine. *La Sagouine.* Montreal: Leméac 1973
Malraux, André. *Les Conquérants.* Paris: Gallimard 1960
- *Antimémoires.* Paris: Gallimard 1972
Marcuse, Herbert. *L'Homme unidimensionnel.* Paris: Editions de Minuit 1968
Marmontel, Jean-François. *Oeuvres complètes.* 18 vols. Paris: Verdière 1818–19
Mendel, G. *La Crise des générations.* Paris: Payot 1969
Michaux, Henri. *Ecuador.* Paris: Gallimard 1929
- *La Nuit remue.* Paris: Gallimard 1935

Bibliography

- *Lointain intérieur*. Paris: Gallimard 1938
- *Peintures*. Paris: Editions GLM 1939
- *Epreuves, exorcismes, 1940–1945*. Paris: Gallimard 1945
- *La Vie des plis*. Paris: Gallimard 1949
- *Mouvements*. Paris: Gallimard 1952
- *Vigies sur les cibles*. Paris: Editions du Dragon 1959
- *Face aux verrous*. Paris: Gallimard 1960
- *Passages*. Paris: Gallimard 1963
- *Les Grandes Epreuves de l'esprit*. Paris: Gallimard 1966
- *Plume*. Paris: Gallimard 1967
- *Un Barbare en Asie*. Paris: Gallimard 1967
- *L'Espace du dedans. Tranches de savoir*. Paris: Gallimard 1969
- *Connaissance par les gouffres*. Paris: Gallimard 1972
Milligan, Spike. *Puckoon*. Harmondsworth: Penguin 1973
Monsarrat, Nicholas. *The Cruel Sea*. Harmondsworth: Penguin 1956
Montherlant, Henri de. *Romans*. Paris: Gallimard 1959
- *Essais*. Paris: Gallimard 1963
- *Théâtre*. Paris: Gallimard 1968
Mortimer, John. *The Trials of Rumpole*. Harmondsworth: Penguin 1979
- *Clinging to the Wreckage*. Harmondsworth: Penguin 1983
Muir, Frank, and Denis Norden. *The 'My Word!' Stories*. London: Methuen 1976
Munro, Alice. *Who Do You Think You Are?* Scarborough, Ont.: Signet Books 1979
Nemerov, Howard. *Collected Poems of Howard Nemerov*. Chicago: University of Chicago Press 1977
Newman, P.C. *Company of Adventurers*. Markham, Ont.: Penguin 1986
Nietzsche, Friedrich. *Thus Spake Zarathustra*. Trans. Thomas Common. New York: The Modern Library 1980
Nims, John F. *The Iron Pastoral*. New York: W. Sloane 1947
Nizan, Paul. *Les Chiens de garde*. Paris: Maspero 1960
Norin, Luc, ed. *Anthologie de la littérature arabe contemporaine*. Paris: Seuil 1967
Olivier, Laurence. *On Acting*. New York: Simon and Schuster 1986
O'Neill, Eugene. *Long Day's Journey into Night*. New Haven: Yale University Press 1956
Orwell, George. *Nineteen Eighty-four*. New York: New American Library 1959
- *Inside the Whale and Other Essays*. Harmondsworth: Penguin 1962
- *Animal Farm*. Harmondsworth: Penguin 1963
- *Down and Out in Paris and London*. Harmondsworth: Penguin 1966
Owen, Wilfred. *The Poems*. Ed. John Silkin. Harmondsworth: Penguin 1985
Parker, Dorothy. 'But the One on the Right.' *New Yorker*, 19 Oct. 1929, pp. 25–7
Parkinson, C. Northcote. *The Law Complete*. New York: Ballantine Books 1983
Pepper, Frank S. *Twentieth-Century Quotations*. London: Sphere Books 1987

Perrault, P. *En Désespoir de cause.* Montreal: Pris 1971
Peter, Laurence J. *The Peter Principle.* New York: Morrow 1969
Pike, K.L. *The Intonation of American English.* Ann Arbor: University of Michigan Press 1945
Pirsig, Robert. *Zen and the Art of Motorcycle Maintenance.* New York: Bantam Books 1985
Plath, Sylvia. *Crossing the Water.* New York: Harper and Row 1960
Poe, E.A. *Selected Writings.* Harmondsworth: Penguin 1972
– *Collected Works.* Cambridge: Harvard University Press 1978
Ponge, Francis. *Le Parti pris des choses.* Paris: Gallimard 1942
– *Le Grand Recueil.* 3 vols. Paris: Gallimard 1961
Porter, Katherine Ann. *Ship of Fools.* Toronto: Signet Books 1963
Potter, Dennis. *Ticket to Ride.* London: Faber and Faber 1986
Poulet, Georges. *Aveux spontanés.* Paris: Plon 1963
Prévert, Jacques. *Paroles.* Paris: Point du jour 1949
– *La Pluie et le beau temps.* Paris: Gallimard 1955
Proust, Marcel. *A la recherche du temps perdu.* 3 vols. Paris: Gallimard 1954
– *Correspondance générale.* Vol. 6. Paris: Plon 1980
Pynchon, Thomas. *Gravity's Rainbow.* New York: Viking 1973
– *V.* New York: Bantam Books 1973
– *The Crying of Lot 49.* New York: Bantam Books 1978
Queneau, Raymond. *Pierrot mon ami.* 35th ed. Paris: Gallimard 1945
– *Exercises de style.* Paris: Gallimard 1947. *Exercises in Style.* Trans. Barbara Wright. New York: New Directions 1981
– *Histoire des littératures.* Paris: Gallimard 1955
– *Le Chiendent.* Paris: Gallimard 1956
– *Zazie dans le métro.* Paris: Gallimard 1959. *Zazie in the Metro.* Trans. Barbara Wright. London: John Calder 1982
– *Bâtons, chiffres et lettres.* Paris: Gallimard 1965
– *Saint-Glinglin.* Paris: Gallimard 1981
Racine, Jean. *Three Plays of Racine.* Trans. George Dillon. Chicago: University of Chicago Press 1961
Reading, Peter. *Ukelele Music.* London: Secker and Warburg 1985
Reed, Henry. *A Map of Verona and Other Poems.* London: Jonathan Cape 1946
Régnier, Henri de. *Vestigia Flammae.* Paris: Mercure de France 1921
Revel, Jean-François. *Pourquoi des philosophes?* Paris: Pauvert 1962
– *Contrecensures.* Paris: Payot 1969
Reverdy, Pierre. *Ferraille.* Paris: Gallimard 1981
Richler, Mordecai. *Shovelling Trouble.* London: Quartet Books 1974
Richler, Mordecai, ed. *The Best of Modern Humor.* New York: Alfred A. Knopf 1983
Robbe-Grillet, Alain. *Le Voyeur.* Paris: Editions de Minuit 1955
– *La Jalousie.* Paris: Editions de Minuit 1957
Roberts, Michael, ed. *The Faber Book of Comic Verse.* London: Faber and Faber 1978
Romains, Jules. *Théâtre.* Vol. 2. Paris: Nouvelle Revue française 1924
Rooten, Luis d'Antin van. *Mots d'Heures: Gousses, Rames.* Harmondsworth: Penguin 1980

Bibliography

Rossetti, Dante Gabriel. *Letters of D.G. Rossetti*. Ed. O. Doughty and J.R. Wahl. 4 vols. Oxford: Clarendon Press 1965
Rossiter, Leonard. *The Lowest Form of Wit*. London: Michael Joseph 1981
Rousseau, Jean-Jacques. *Correspondance générale*. Ed. Théophile Dufour. Paris: Colin 1934
Roy, Gabrielle. *Bonheur d'occasion*. Montreal: Stanké 1977
Saint-Exupéry, Antoine de. *The Little Prince*. Trans. Katherine Woods. New York: Harcourt, Brace and World 1943
Saint-Jean Perse [Alexis Saint-Léger]. *Amers*. Paris: Gallimard 1957
Salinger, J.D. *The Catcher in the Rye*. New York: Signet Books 1961
– *Nine Stories*. New York: The New American Library 1962
Sarraute, Nathalie. *Portrait d'un inconnu*. Paris: Union générale d'éditeurs 1956
Sarrazin, A. *L'Astragale*. Paris: Pauvert 1965
Sartre, Jean-Paul. *Huis-clos suivi de Les Mouches*. Paris: Gallimard 1972
– *L'Age de raison*. Paris: Gallimard 1976
– *Le Sursis*. Paris: Gallimard 1976
Sassoon, Siegfried. *The Complete Memoirs of George Sherston*. London: Faber 1941
Sauvageau, Y. *Wouf Wouf*. Montreal: Leméac 1970
Sharpe, Tom. *Porterhouse Blue*. London: Pan Books 1974
Shaw, G. Bernard. *Sixteen Self Sketches*. London: Constable 1949
Simon, Claude. *La Route des Flandres*. Paris: Editions de Minuit 1960
– *Histoire*. Paris: Editions de Minuit 1967
– 'Réponses de Claude Simon à quelques questions écrites de Ludovic Janvier.' *Entretiens*, no. 31 (1972)
Solzhenitsyn, Alexandr I. *The First Circle*. Trans. Thomas P. Whitney. New York: Bantam Books 1969
– *The Gulag Archipelago*. New York: Harper and Row 1973
– *August 1914*. Harmondsworth: Penguin 1974
Steinbeck, John. *Of Mice and Men*. New York: Bantam Books 1967
Stoppard, Tom. *Rosencrantz and Guildenstern Are Dead*. London: Faber and Faber 1967
– *Travesties*. London: Faber and Faber 1975
– *Lord Malquist and Mr. Moon*. London: Faber Paperbacks 1980
– *The Dog It Was That Died and Other Plays*. London: Faber and Faber 1983
Tailhade, Laurent. *Imbéciles et gredins*. Paris: Laffont 1969
Tard, L.-M. *Si vous saisissez l'astuce*. Montreal: Editions du Jour 1968
Tardieu, Jean. *Un Mot pour un autre*. Paris: Gallimard 1951
– *Conversation-sinfonietta*. Paris: Gallimard 1966
Teilhard de Chardin, Pierre. *Oeuvres*. 11 vols. Paris: Seuil 1955
Tempel, E. *Humor in the Headlines*. New York: Pocket Books 1969
Theatre Workshop [London]. *Oh What a Lovely War!* London: Methuen 1965
Thériault, Yves. *Agaguk*. Paris: Grasset 1958
– *Cul-de-sac*. Montreal: L'Actuelle 1970
Thomas, Dylan. *Portrait of the Artist as a Young Dog*. New York: New Directions 1955
– *Quite Early One Morning*. New York: New Directions 1960

Thompson, B. *The American Express Pocket Guide to California*. New York: Prentice Hall 1987

Thurber, James. *The Thurber Carnival*. Harmondsworth: Penguin 1972

Tolstoy, L.N. *War and Peace*. Trans. Rosemary Edmonds. Harmondsworth: Penguin 1978

Townsend, Sue. *The Secret Diary of Adrian Mole, Aged 13 3/4*. London: Methuen 1985

– *The Growing Pains of Adrian Mole*. London: Methuen 1985

Truffaut, François. *Hitchcock*. New York: Simon and Schuster 1967

Updike, John. *The Coup*. New York: Fawcett Crest 1978

Vac, Bertrand [Aimé Pelletier]. *Saint-Pépin P.Q*. Montreal: Cercle du Livre de France 1955

Valéry, P. *Poésies*. Paris: Gallimard 1930

– *Rhumbs*. Paris: Gallimard 1933

– *'Mon Faust' ébauches*. Paris: Gallimard 1946

– *Oeuvres complètes*. 2 vols. Paris: Gallimard 1960

Vian, Boris. *L'Ecume des jours*. Paris: Pauvert 1963

– *Théâtre*. Paris: Pauvert 1965

– *Les Fourmis*. Paris: Union générale d'éditions 1970

– *Le Loup-Garou*. Paris: Bourgeois 1970

Vidal, Gore. *Duluth*. London: Panther Books 1984

Villiers de l'Isle-Adam, Auguste. *Contes cruels*. Paris: Corti 1954

Villon, François. *Complete Poems of François Villon*. Trans. Beram Saklatvala. London: J.M. Dent 1968

Waterhouse, Keith. *Billy Liar*. Harmondsworth: Penguin 1963

Waugh, Evelyn. *The Essays, Articles and Reviews*. Ed. D. Gallagher. London: Methuen 1983

Weil, S. *La Pesanteur et la grâce*. Paris: Plon 1948

Wilbur, Richard. *Walking to Sleep: New Poems and Translations*. New York: Harcourt Brace Jovanovich 1968

Willans, G., and R. Searle. *Down with Skool!* London: Collins 1958

Williams, Tennessee. *Cat on a Hot Tin Roof*. New York: New Directions 1955

– *Summer and Smoke*. New York: New Directions 1971

Wolfe, Tom. *The Kandy-Kolored Tangerine-Flake Streamline Baby*. London: Mayflower Paperbacks 1968

Woolf, Virginia. *The Common Reader*. New York: Harcourt, Brace and World 1948

– *To the Lighthouse*. London: J.M. Dent 1955

– *The Waves*. New York: Harcourt, Brace and World 1959

Wright, Eric. *Death in the Old Country*. Don Mills, Ont.: Collins 1985

Wyndham, John. *Sometime, Never*. New York: Ballantine Books 1974

Yeats, W.B. *Collected Poems*. London: Macmillan 1971

Zumthor, Paul. *Anthologie des grands rhétoriqueurs*. Paris: 10/18 1978

Index

Terms in bold-face are the titles of the main entries in the dictionary. The page reference for each main entry is also in bold-face.

Index

adjuncts 10, 70
adjuration xv, 181
Adler, M. 439
admonition 67, 137, 455
adnominatio. See agnominatio
adverb 71, 104, 126, 140, 162, 191, 208, 237, 288; of place 295
adverbial phrase 440
adversary 12, 16, 17, 32, 43, 49, 68, 110, 292, 382, 385, 426, 455
advertising xviii, 159, 229, 241, 371, 440, 451
advice 30, 134, 137, 233
adynaton xv, **18–19**, 141, 186, 347
Aeneid 221, 455
aesthetic form 160
affective effect 458
affirmation 70, 162, 189, 302, 353, 386
affix 121, 275
affix-clipping 121, 275
affixation 125
afterword 272, 396
agglutination 276
aggressor 15, 16
agnominatio **19–20**, 26, 125, 174, 177, 329, 457
agrammatism xvi, 142, 150, 287, 290
agreement 399, 440, 475
alba 346
Albalat, A. 51
Alcanter de Brahm 244
Alexander, Sir William 446
alexandrine 55, 88, 90, 157, 256, 258, 403; romantic or ternary 257
Allais, A. 70, 187, 194, 315, 322, 354
allegation 64, 394
allegorism 21
allegory xv, xvii, **21–3**, 29, 53, 56, 134, 202, 220, 222, 276, 278, 340, 404, 417, 418, 454
Allen, W. 34, 163, 200, 221, 332, 352, 380, 391, 404
alliteration xv, xviii, 20, **23–4**, 26, 72, 85, 86, 87, 147, 208, 291, 306, 329, 390, 450
allocentric anchor 189, 191, 295, 297
allocentric discourse xvi
allocution 136
allograph 24, 26, 62, 82, 172, 308, 343

allusio 329
allusion xvi, 20, **24–6**, 38, 51, 85, 109, 117, 137, 138, 147, 170, 174, 205, 228, 245, 269, 275, 293, 300, 342, 349, 364, 408, 455, 469, 473
alluvion xvi, 175
alphabet 13, 14, 38, 120, 149, 204, 252, 253, 260, 283, 423
alphabet soup 13
alphabetism 12
alphametics 120
alteration 37, 271, 279, 316, 433
altercation 132
alternation 117, 259, 299, 400, 413
alternative xvi, **26–8**, 35, 66, 74, 398; false 27
Altman, R. 406
altruization 104
Alvarez, A. 373
amalgam xvi, 5, 28, 67
amalgam (syntagmatic) 28
amalgamation xx, 112, 304, 349, 386
amas 10
ambiguity xvi, **28–31**, 32, 44, 64, 123, 133, 172, 247, 270, 300, 301, 322, 329, 364, 365, 369, 385, 398, 408, 419, 427, 428, 449, 454; deliberate 28; involuntary 28
amelodia 287
Amis, K. 41, 195, 217, 263, 365, 411, 422, 452
amoebean verses 132
amphibol(og)y 28, **31–2**, 141, 144, 450
amphibrach 258
amphigouri 342
amplification xvi, xviii, 10, **32–3**, 60, 69, 99, 105, 112, 128, 153, 158, 201, 202, 287, 323, 345, 373, 379, 391, 403, 447, 467; oratorical 33, 323, 373, 467
anacephalaeosis 381
anachronism 33–4, 300, 433
anaclasis 43
anacoenosis 103, 145
anacoluthon xv, **34–6**, 336, 396, 454, 475
anacrusis 331, 403
anadiplosis xv, xvii, **36–7**, 43, 108, 164, 203, 318

Index

Index

Index

denotation 92, 106, 160, 205, 267, 269, 415, 458

denotatum 70, 467

dénouement 298, 343

density 171

denying the antecedent 320

deportmanteau word xvi, 349, 389

deprecation 434

Derême, T. 22

derision 339

derivation xvi, 38, 77, 100, **125–6**, 245, 246, 266, 304, 307, 333, 459

derivatives 13, 126, 248, 439

Derrida, J. 177, 309

Deschamps, E. 90

description x, 6, 33, 92, 97, 122, **126–9**, 134, 192, 193, 198, 219, 221, 223, 242, 247, 260, 273, 300, 304, 315, 318, 319, 332, 336, 337, 350, 355, 392, 423, 461, 464, 471; realistic 16; subjective 128

desideratum 206

designation 85, 98, 280, 336, 415, 445

Desnos, R. 13, 117, 188, 433, 461

Desportes, P. 55

detective fiction 190, 192, 404, 442

determinant 214

deviation xviii, 25, 186, 214, 239, 241, 274, 425; of meaning 25

device-mania 79

devocalization 4

diabole 356

diachrony 123, 389

diacope 383

diaeresis 63, 119, **129**, 153, 255, 279

diagram 127, 241, 409

dialectics 310, 372

dialects 333

dialelumenon 74

diallage 66

diallelon 321

diallelus 321

dialogism 130, 131, 296, 358

dialogismus 186

dialogue 34, 43, 44, 54, 58, 59, 83, 113, 114, **129–33**, 137, 138, 152, 160, 182, 183, 255, 288, 290, 296, 341, 347, 351, 352, 356, 358, 369, 370, 372, 375, 394, 422, 456, 470;

expositional 132, 182; expository 394; interior 131, 290, 370; of the deaf 132; of the illustrious dead 34; oratorical 132; tonal 132

dialogue-verbs 83

dialysis 325

dialyton 74

diaphora xvii, 28, 43, 44, 78, **133–4**, 143, 211, 451, 460, 474

diasyrmus 339

diatribe 137, 407

diatyposis 23, 126, **134–5**, 220, 222

Dickens, C. 3, 11, 39, 81, 98, 121, 125, 126, 138, 165, 191, 197, 198, 202, 205, 209, 282, 286, 325, 359, 384, 447, 475

dictation 239, 426

diction 83, 86, 94, 226, 286, 287, 401, 471

Dictionnaire de linguistique 62, 130, 160, 166, 208, 267, 280, 300, 310, 331, 343, 422, 444, 459

Dictionnaire des media 34, 128, 133, 209, 294, 305, 306

dictum 353, 360

Didion, J. 287

diegesis 299

diegetic universe 163

digest 381

digression 113, **135–6**, 314, 421, 438, 467

dilatation 403

dilation 466

dilemma 27, 192, 195, 385, 386, 441

diminutio 262

diminution 183

diminutive 439, 469

diorthosis 254, 351

diphthongization 119, 283

direct discourse 60, 151, 289, 296

direct utterance 295, 297, 299

dirge 250

dirheme 413

disappearing repetition 285

disappointment 46, 225

disarticulation 217

disavowal 303, 411

disclaimers 447

discontinuity 140, 209

Index

Index

Index

Hebraisms 332
Heidegger, M. 176
Heller, J. 153, 315
helper 15, 16
Hemingway, E. 127, 171, 298, 440
hemistich 88, 89, 90, 155, 156, 157, 400, 429
Hémon, L. 159, 164, 228
hendiadys 208–9, 214, 450
Henley, W.E. 76
Henry II 370
Heraclitus 51
Herbert, G. 27, 90, 338, 444
heresy of paraphrase 323
hermeticism 54, 225, 277, 342
hero 4, 5, 15, 16, 34, 37, 54, 58, 104, 118, 124, 168, 171, 182, 188, 190, 193, 194, 293, 298, 299, 305, 324, 359, 403, 405, 442, 459, 462, 469; false 15, 16
Herodotus 80, 327, 404, 469
heroic couplet 425, 431
Hesbois, L. 211, 261, 450
hesitation (rhetorical) 181
hesitation-form 166
heterometric verse 256, 400
heteronym 211
hiatus xvi, 87, 148, 209, 218, 256, 300
hieroglyphic writing 276
Hilts, P.J. 105
historical present 296
historical sayings 266
historiography 298
Hitchcock, A. 300, 437
hoarseness 287
hoax 419
Hobson-Jobson 333
Hodge, A. 274
hodonymy 123
Hoffnung, G. 251
Hollander, J. 90
holophrase 289, 290
holorhyme 173
Homer 61, 328, 356
Homeric or epic simile 417
homily 137
homiologia 382
homograph 211
homoioptoton 210, 246, 392

homoioteleuton 51, 72, 159, 206, 209–10, 246, 255, 336, 392, 400
homonym 62, 134, 211
homonymy 44, 78, 133, 177, 205, 211–12, 255, 364, 450
homophone 211
homophony 20, 44, 211, 212, 349
Hood, T. 329, 364, 474
hook 192, 358, 470
Hopkins, G.M. 23, 42, 94, 257, 329, 352, 459
Hörmann, H. 151, 305
Housman, A.E. 181
howler 81, 172, 242, 286
Hughes, R. 25, 61, 167, 336, 423
Hugo, V. 27, 51, 79, 122, 125, 156, 157, 256, 271, 291, 315, 365, 367
humour xii, 53, 96, 109, 153, 163, 180, 193, 197, 212–13, 225, 244, 265, 313, 315, 322, 363, 407, 432, 461, 463, 466, 473, 475
Hutcheon, L. 285, 327, 328
Hutchinson, P. 26, 84, 261, 322, 362
Huysmans, J.-K. 127, 182
hybridization 199
Hyde, C. 381, 408
hydrographia 127
hydronymy 123
hymn 346
hypallage 154, 193, 208, 213–14, 338, 439; double 154
hype 241, 424
hyperbaton xvii, 18, 40, 71, 154, 155, 170, 214–15, 325, 410, 459
hyperbole 18, 65, 67, 74, 91, 105, 116, 138, 183, 186, 187, 194, 202, 212, 215–16, 226, 244, 273, 337
hyperchleuasmos 96
hypercorrection 185, 232
hyperhypotaxis 216–17, 334, 336, 413, 445
hyperparataxis 139, 153, 217
hyphen 61, 217–18, 253, 421, 450, 459
hyphenation 218–19
hypobole 183
hypocoristic name 126, 439
hypogram 38
hypophora 371
hypostatization 459

520

Index

Index

Index

Index

notebook style 150
'Not! the Nine O'Clock News' 262, 307
notice ix, 42, 344, 351
noun complement 31, 417
noun phrase 140, 249, 306
nouveau roman 127, 129
numbering 344
numerology 442
nunegocentric present 295, 297

O'Neill, E. 289
oath 161, 181
Obaldia, R. de 23
objection 145, 161, 237, 356, 372, 386, 395
objective xix, 442
objective correlative 442
objurgation 137, 407
oblique stroke 4, 89, 144, 218, 256, **309–10**, 367, 399, 414, 423
obscenity 175, 438, 471
obscurity 50, 82, 83, 149, 216, 231, 288, 342, 452, 453
obsecration 435
observation 79, 128, 197, 378, 379
occultatio 353
occupatio 353, 356
octave 170, 426, 431
octet 431
octosyllable 256
ode 60, 93, 210, 250, 288, **310**, 346, 358, 364, 370, 402, 432, 470
Olivier, L. 150, 232, 377, 378
omission 190
onomasiology 461
onomastics 442
onomatopoeia 124, 147, 205, 208, 237, 304, 305, 306, 308, **310–11**, 333, 389
onzain 431
open letter 186, 359
opera 5, 13, 84, 85, 381, 384, 403, 453
operetta 193, 384, 403
Opie, I. 330
Opie, P. 330
opinion poll 394
opponent 68, 96, 162, 189, 242, 243, 279, 280, 321, 337, 339, 344, 356,

365, 371, 372, 374, 380, 382, 385, 386, 397, 455
opposition 9, 46
optatio 242, 471
optation 471
oracle 130, 356, 404
oral history 380
oral literature 56, 188, 293
oration 137
orator 58, 66, 111, 145, 148, 230, 331
oratorical questions 371
oratorical syllepsis 225, 260, 440
oratory 10, 33, 43, 47, 64, 65, 201, 217, 274; forensic 10
order of the day 137
ordinary language x, xviii, 148
orison 352
ornamentation 78, 226, 342
oronymy 123
Orwell, G. 21, 23, 78, 153, 314, 363, 424, 466
Osborne, J. 137
ostensive situation 273
Oster, P. 170, 373
ostranenie 420
Oulipo 166, 314, 445
outline 252, 276, 409
outs 131, 286
ovation 179
'overreacher' 215
overrun (of typographical character) 466
overstatement 116
Owen, W. 222, 250, 278, 398, 399, 472
Oxford Dictionary of English Proverbs 361
Oxford Dictionary of Quotations 373, 444
Oxford English Dictionary (OED) xiii, xiv, 4, 20, 27, 33, 35, 37, 46, 48, 63, 64, 68, 70, 75, 78, 80, 82, 83, 97, 107, 109, 110, 129, 130, 134, 135, 136, 158, 170, 172, 183, 196, 202, 206, 215, 219, 232, 242, 250, 252, 254, 264, 274, 275, 279, 280, 281, 284, 287, 289, 300, 304, 310, 314, 317, 318, 319, 321, 323, 325, 326, 328, 335, 337, 338, 339, 340, 345, 350, 353, 355, 356, 357, 359, 363, 366,

Index

Index

Index

133, 201, 214, 219, 266, 274, 282, 337, 338, 348, 404, 453, 460
quintilla 431
quip 347, 473
quotation 18, 49, 66, 69, 116, 131, 138, 154, 155, 162, 167, 227, 242, 260, 271, 309, 320, 327, 360, **372–5**, 386, 415, 419, 420, 421, 422, 423, 432, 462; oral 373; unconscious 374
quotation marks 131, 155, 162, 227, 373, 374, 421, 422, 423

Rabelais, F. 37, 90, 200, 271, 312, 427
Racine, J. 17, 23, 66, 83, 89, 132, 142, 145, 154, 201, 257, 312, 435, 441, 460
raillery 339, 473
rallying cry 424
Ramayana 174, 219, 474
rambling 324
rant 203
Rat, M. 418
ratiocination 377
reactualization 75, 127, 130, 190, 199, 271, 331, 358, **375–7**, 395, 450, 454, 456, 460, 470
reader xix, 3, 20, 26, 28, 29, 34, 38, 45, 54, 59, 74, 75, 79, 87, 102, 118, 128, 133, 144, 147, 150, 151, 156, 159, 160, 167, 170, 176, 180, 188, 189, 190, 191, 192, 194, 195, 199, 201, 220, 222, 224, 227, 228, 239, 244, 256, 262, 266, 267, 271, 272, 274, 291, 294, 297, 298, 299, 300, 314, 322, 341, 347, 348, 350, 351, 355, 366, 367, 375, 415, 418, 419, 437, 438, 442, 449, 461, 464, 473; intermediate 190
reader-response criticism 272
reality effect 129
reasoning 33, 46, 57, 64, 65, 69, 104, 105, 112, 183, 201, 319, 320, 321, 322, 347, 363, **377–81**, 385, 386, 390, 418, 425, 435, 436, 463, 473
rebound 23, 298
rebriche 384
rebus 24, 276, 330, 343, 405
recapitulation xvi, 33, 38, 64, 138,

159, 344, **381**; syntactic xvi
recasting 398, 415
receiver 16, 24, 30, 38, 50, 59, 71, 135, 160, 161, 186, 233, 294, 340, 347, 350, 363, 410
recipe 313, 366, **381–2**, 456
recognition scene 433
recovery xvi
recrimination xvii, 242, 280, **382**
recto tono 239
recursion 284
red herring (or *ignoratio elenchi*) 322
redditio causae 377
redefinition of the question 386
Redfern, W. 24, 51, 91, 172, 173, 176, 211, 250, 276, 304, 313, 315, 316, 328, 329, 339, 349, 364, 365, 399, 409, 440, 452, 474
redoublement 383
reduction 3, 12, 16, 47, 75, 205, 263, 357; graphic 3
reductionism 197, 415
redundancy 51, 80, 114, **382–3**, 467
reduplicatio 164
reduplication 36, 152, 164, 170, 246, **383–4**, 390, 411
Reed, H. 45, 158
reference x, xx, 18, 24, 25, 29, 34, 70, 165, 200, 440; in footnotes 323; to publishing information 308
referent 19, 25, 31, 44, 91, 160, 246, 267, 269, 364, 376, 423; homophonic 364
referential function x, 59, 70, 124, 141, 160, 201, 235, 236, 289, 307, 369
reflexio 44
refrain 40, 76, 164, 255, **384**, 432, 454
refusal 180
refutation 27, 48, 66, 67, 69, 70, 116, 161, 242, 318, 344, 356, 372, 380, **385–6**, 426, 435
regionalisms 333
register 241, 242
Régnier, H. de 20
regression 165, 381, **386–7**, 397, 450
regret 180; false 180
regrouped members 387–8
reincarnation 456
rejection 27, 280

536

Index

rhythmical accent 259
Ricci, F.M. 205
Richard, J.-P. 35, 47, 95, 96, 124, 134,
    140, 147, 221, 246, 247, 284, 362,
    448, 471
Richelieu (Cardinal) 44, 281
Richler, M. 152, 153, 196, 229, 409,
    432
riddle 5, 21, 23, 43, 46, 112, 153, 224,
    242, 262, 277, 300, 336, 342, 347,
    356, 360, **404–6**
Rimbaud, A. 72, 115, 180, 223, 272
rime brisée 429
rise in register 241
risqué stories 196
ritornello 384
Rivière, J. 470
roast 235
Robbe-Grillet, A. 4, 127, 145, 239, 248,
    429, 458
Robert, P. 17, 21, 24, 34, 37, 46, 49,
    50, 54, 58, 66, 70, 73, 76, 87, 90, 91,
    92, 95, 98, 101, 107, 110, 125, 132,
    135, 150, 154, 155, 158, 166, 168,
    177, 179, 196, 200, 203, 207, 215,
    219, 233, 249, 250, 265, 279, 280,
    281, 293, 310, 313, 316, 317, 318,
    319, 323, 337, 340, 350, 353, 359,
    364, 366, 372, 373, 377, 382, 383,
    396, 397, 407, 424, 427, 428, 437,
    445, 447, 451, 453, 459, 462, 468,
    471
Robinson, E.A. 129
Rochefort, H. 29
Rodin, A. 102, 110
rodomontade 342
Rogers, H. 27, 98
Roget, P.M. 32
Romains, J. 242
romance 63
rondeau 346
rondeau redoublé 346
rondelet 346
Ronsard, P. de 55, 110
Roosevelt, F.D. 43, 228, 245, 455
Rooten, L. d'Antin van 24, 462
rosary 352, 434, 457
Rose, R. 66
Rossetti, G. Dante 438, 461

Rossiter, L. 393, 408
Rostand, E. 134, 135, 137
round periods 335
roundel 346
Roure, F. 248
Rousseau, J.-J. 183, 358, 386
Roy, G. 81, 191
rubai 346
rubric 83, 91, 244, 308
rule of justice 65
run on 248, 395
Ruskin, J. 210
Ruthven, K.K. 109

Sabatier, R. 227
Safire, W. 345
Saint-Exupéry, A. de 320
Saint-Léger, Alexis [pseud. Saint-Jean
    Perse] 215, 226, 278, 461
Saklatvala, B. 15
Salinger, J. 82, 178, 298, 326
Samuel, Book of 392
Sandburg, C. 408
sapphic 346
sarcasm 26, 60, 77, 92, 94, 96, 125,
    167, 179, 186, 235, 242, 244, 339,
    407–8
Sarraute, N. 41, 62, 403
Sarrazin, A. 406
Sartre, J.-P. 27, 57, 73, 118, 122, 134,
    188, 244, 249, 284, 321, 416, 426
Sassoon, S. 4
Satan xix 187, 292
satire xii, 91, 328, 346, 391, 407
saupoudrage 166
Saussure, F. de xviii, 37, 38, 117, 316,
    388
Sauvageau, Y. 455
saying 372, 408
Scaliger, J.-C. 20, 66, 103, 110, 131,
    163, 183, 243, 324, 329, 356, 407
scansion 129, 259
Scarron, P. 85, 328
scatological texts 471
scene 187, 188, 220, 238, 251, 317, 402,
    463
scesis onomaton 408
schemata xviii
schematization xvi, 220, 409, 458

538

Index